WAR AT SEA

WAR AT SEA

A NAVAL ATLAS 1939–1945

MARCUS FAULKNER

Introduction
ANDREW LAMBERT

Cartography
PETER WILKINSON

NAVAL INSTITUTE PRESS
Annapolis, Maryland

TITLE PAGE: Capital ships bombard Salerno, by Richard Eurich
(© *National Maritime Museum, Greenwich, London, BHC1566*)

*This book was brought to publication with the generous assistance
of Marguerite and Gerry Lenfest*

Text Copyright © Marcus Faulkner 2012
Map copyright © Seaforth Publishing 2012

First published in Great Britain in 2012 by
Seaforth Publishing,
Pen & Sword Books Ltd,
47 Church Street,
Barnsley S70 2AS

Published and distributed in the
United States of America and Canada by the
Naval Institute Press,
291 Wood Road, Annapolis,
Maryland 21402-5034

www.nip.org

Library of Congress Control Number: 2012931089

ISBN 978 1 59114 560 8

Printed and bound in China

PREFACE

THE WAR AT SEA SPANNED the entire duration of the Second World War, from the outbreak of hostilities in Europe in September 1939 through to the formal Japanese surrender on board the American battleship USS *Missouri* on 2 September 1945. For seventy-two months naval operations were conducted on a hitherto unprecedented scale across all the world's oceans, from the Arctic to the shores of small, unheard of islands in the southern Pacific. Key naval engagements like the *Bismarck* hunt and the battle of Midway, or major campaigns such Leyte Gulf have always been central to any histories of the war, and each year countless new books are published that focus on individual operations, technical aspects, or personal memoirs; as a result, the broader view of the war at sea has sometimes become neglected and distorted. The magnitude of the conflict has often driven historians to divide up the history of the war in terms of theatres, themes, or other subjects, and as armies and air forces are inclined to think and operate in terms of theatres or campaigns, such compartmentalisation does not necessarily hinder an understanding the war on land and in the air.

Navies, however, tend to think and operate on a far wider and often global scale. They derive their strategic flexibility from their ability to withdraw into the vastness of the oceans, and they may strike from the depths, taking the enemy by surprise. Naval warfare is more fluid than its counterpart on land, with frontlines being permeable and lines of communications more pliable. By focusing on battles or ships, or the aircraft and men that were brought together into the largest fleets ever assembled, the scale, complexity and interdependence between the various theatres is easily lost. The ability of maps to convey both space and time in a concise manner makes an atlas the ideal medium with which to retell the history of the war at sea between 1939 and 1945.

This book can be used in two different ways. First, as the maps are organised along largely chronological lines, it may be read cover-to-cover as a naval history of the war. Secondly, as each individual spread has been designed to be self-contained, it can be used as a reference for those seeking to understand a particular campaign or type of operation. Maps are often used in books to support the narrative, but here they are at the centre. The aim is to provide an overview of the war at sea and, at the same time, a comprehensive treatment; so all levels of war are covered with strategic overviews, operational movements and small-scale tactical actions, and all major types of operations, surface engagements, aircraft carrier operations and amphibious assaults are included.

Although short texts accompany the majority of the maps to provide some context, the emphasis is always on the latter to convey the key details. Colour enables another layer of information to be added without affecting the clarity of the maps themselves. The use of colour and ship symbols is designed to be illustrative rather than dogmatic. For example, on some of the strategic overviews Vichy French territory is depicted as being under axis control insofar as it was neither neutral nor available for allied use, while on more detailed maps a distinction between Vichy and Italo-German controlled territory is made. Similarly, and depending on the context, at times allied territory is depicted in different shades of red when this matters. In the case of the small-scale tactical maps in the southwest Pacific, it is meaningless to attribute territorial control to one side or the other as many of the islands were largely unoccupied. Time poses another significant problem as the use of time zones differed between navies, but every effort has been made to be consistent within each map. Similarly, orders of battle have been checked against numerous sources, but it is not always possible to accurately determine which ship was with which force in large-scale, multi-day operations. Although a broad convention underpins the composition of the atlas, the level of detail differs from map to map. The ship symbols are employed to show types of vessels not individual classes. All vessels smaller than destroyers are collectively referred to as escorts.

Some maps will be familiar while others depict new material. The vast majority of naval maps in print today may be traced back to the maps and charts produced by the British Admiralty in the immediate aftermath of the events which formed the basis of those utilised in the British Official Histories, foremost in Stephen Roskill's *War at Sea*, but also in the various theatre histories. Similarly, Samuel Morrison's semi-official *History of the United States Naval Operations in World War II* contains a vast array of maps and charts. Both sources are invaluable, but need to be approached with a degree of caution as they suffer from inaccuracies, particularly regarding axis strengths and movements. All official maps need to be reinterpreted, and in the case of this atlas they have been modified and adapted in the light of more recent research.

I must thank a number of people who have assisted on this project. Gierr Haar, John Jordan, and David Hobbs deserve thanks for allowing some of their material – respectively on the battle of Norway, Mers el-Kebir, and aspects of the Indian Ocean – to be adapted for use here. My colleagues Alessio Patalano and Ben Jones came to the aid with materials when certain maps needed additional clarification. Jeffrey Michaels, Len Barnett, Quintin van Zyl, Carlos Alfaro-Zaforteza and Roger Arditti have kindly commented on drafts and made suggestions over the years. Andrew Lambert more generally has always provided encouragement where necessary. At Seaforth, Julian Mannering has provided invaluable guidance throughout and his dedication has seen this project through to it its conclusion. Special thanks must go to Peter Wilkinson who has persevered with my seemingly endless supply of sketches, notes and modifications, and translated these into what follows. Without him none of this would have been possible.

MARCUS FAULKNER
London, March 2012

CONTENTS

THE SECOND WORLD WAR AT SEA

FOR ALL THE FIGHTING ON LAND, the extensive bombing offensives, and even the use of atomic weapons in 1945, the outcome of the Second World War was settled by allied control of global oceanic communications. Control of communications served three critical functions. First, it secured key allied states against invasion, across the English Channel, the Atlantic and the Pacific. Secondly, it allowed the allies to pool resources, to shift ships, troops and aircraft between theatres as distinct and distant as the White Sea and the Sea of Japan, by way of the Mediterranean, the South Atlantic, or the Panama Canal. Finally, it enabled the allies to deliver land power by amphibious assault from Sicily and France to the distant islands of the Pacific. Sea power bound together the Grand Alliance of the United Nations, while at the same time keeping apart the axis powers. It gave the allies control over those parts of the world that were not engaged in the war, notably South America, and thus access to the key resources that they produced. This was not a question of winning battles, although they could be essential to maintain or exploit command, but of keeping open supply lines. The battles that mattered were fought to secure communications. As the great maritime strategist Sir Julian Corbett (1854–1922) wrote: 'Command of the sea, therefore, means nothing but the control of maritime communications, whether for commercial or military purposes. The object of naval warfare is the control of communications, and not, as in land warfare, the conquest of territory.' The maps in this innovative volume, while they cover the key actions and events, provide the ideal medium to visualise this movement of fleets, the interrelationship between theatres and the overall impact of sea power.

Corbett did not claim that sea power alone could win major wars; it had to be translated into land power. This process was most easily achieved in states far distant from the fighting, and the creation of the United States Army and Army Air Force between 1941 and 1945 is the most striking historical example of this process. Maritime strategists agree that the real measure of naval power is the impact it can generate on a conflict ashore. This much was obvious before 1914.

The First World War (1914–18) challenged some aspects of Corbett's strategic pattern, largely from the use of new air and subsurface weapons, but it did not alter the larger dynamics. The ability of Britain and France to control the world ocean gave them access to global sources of food, raw materials and industrial output, while effectively denying them to the Central Powers by blockade and linked economic warfare. For all the drama of the battle of Jutland on 31 May 1916, and the 1917–18 U-boat campaign against merchant shipping, Britain had working global sea control in August 1914 and retained it down to November 1918. Events like the failure of a major amphibious operation at Gallipoli did not threaten that maintenance of sea control. Not only did Imperial Germany fail to block British oceanic communications, but their attempt to do so through illegal and unrestricted submarine warfare played a major role in bringing the United States into the war as a co-belligerent alongside Britain and France. American troops, hardware and food began to flow into France in startling quantities in 1918, just as the German army lost momentum on the Western Front. As if to emphasise the uselessness of the High Seas Fleet, German sailors mutinied in October 1918 while the new German government scuttled most of the fleet at Scapa Flow the following year.

Limitations Between the Wars

While post-war British, Japanese, American and French tacticians re-fought the battle of Jutland, seeking a 'decisive' result, and more reflective men studied the U-boat campaign, the critical contribution of sea control to allied victory remained undervalued by nations that measured success in blood. The escalating cost of new warships – battleships were now three times bigger than the *Dreadnought* of 1906 – saw post-war reconstruction brought to a rapid conclusion with a disarmament treaty in 1922. American reluctance to fund the massive 1918 programme prompted the administration to sacrifice the projected 1918 ships, if other powers took similar action. The resulting Washington Treaty restricted the size of future warships, the numbers each power could own, and their replacement ages. It also imposed a capital ship building holiday that would ultimately last fifteen years. Several half-finished American and Japanese battleships were scrapped, along with an armada of older battleships, including the many British dreadnoughts. The Washington Treaty allotted Britain and the USA a ratio of 5 ships to 3 for Japan and 1.75 each for Italy and France. The tonnage limits translated this ratio into small battle fleets: by 1930 Britain and the United States had a mere fifteen capital ships, nine for Japan and five each for France and Italy. No one else mattered. Submarine campaigns against merchant shipping were declared illegal, but few can have been under any illusion about the effectiveness of such a stipulation. Washington saved money and defused tension but the process proved disastrous for the western democracies.

Avoiding a naval race suited the disinterested Americans and bankrupt Europeans, but the price of this short-term success was a massive asymmetric weakening of naval power in contemporary strategy. This mattered because armies and air forces had remained unlimited in size and power throughout the inter-war period. This severely disadvantaged the British who depended on the fleet to secure their global communications, trade and possessions, and deter continental military states. By contrast, it enhanced the relative power of continental military states, not least Nazi

Germany. When deepened and extended at the 1930 London Conference, the treaty process left Britain without the naval power needed to defend the oceanic communications of a global empire, gravely weakened the unique deterrent role of naval power in British strategy, and devastated the industrial infrastructure needed to rebuild the fleet.

Naval arms limitation was abandoned in 1936. The real cost of the Treaty policy became clear three years later. The Royal Navy was too weak to uphold vital British interests between 1939 and 1941 against resurgent German, Italian and Japanese fleets. As war approached, Britain and France recognised the need to exploit sea power, their only strategic advantage, to defeat Italy while relying on the Maginot line to hold, and economic warfare to defeat Nazi Germany. They could only hope that success in Europe would deter Japan. While the United States had begun a major naval reconstruction programme as part of Roosevelt's New Deal, this was primarily intended to drag the country out of recession, and Britain and France doubted that America would enter the war. They knew that in the long run sea power would win, but had good reason to fear the initial impulse of German aggression on land.

The key tool of aggressive land power would be the aeroplane. By 1939 aircraft had evolved from 100mph biplanes, with a tiny weapon loads, into 300mph all-metal monoplanes, flying long distances with heavy weapons. Mines and submarines had limited the offensive use of naval forces in the 1914–18 war; adding aircraft to land power assets further challenged the offensive role of sea power. However, the experience of the Great War had thrown up new ideas and weapons: purpose-built landing craft, aircraft carriers for overland strike missions, and improved gunnery systems and projectiles for shore bombardment. While these developments were important, their impact on the strategic balance between land and sea down to 1941–42 was limited by the Washington process, which restricted the size and numbers of platforms. New sensors also aided navies; British anti-submarine sonar was in operational service by 1939, and radar soon followed. Both would be critical to restoring the advantage of sea power.

Sea power produces its greatest strategic effect from a position of unchallenged control, something the allies would enjoy in the first six months of the war, and only recover in the middle of 1943. In the interval sea power functioned as a largely defensive asset.

The Global War

The Second World War witnessed the ultimate demonstration of sea power in global strategy. Allied sea control, contested but never broken, allowed them to concentrate their resources and overwhelm the essentially isolated axis powers.

In 1939 The Royal Navy was rapidly rebuilding but the fleet was still far too small, only a shadow of the mighty armada available in August 1914. Furthermore, it was hampered by obsolete, worn out ships, outdated machinery

and key weaknesses in air combat. However, other fleets were nowhere near as well prepared. None had the chain of global bases and support infrastructure needed to wage world war, let alone the number of skilled personnel, ships, or sonar. Recognising this weakness, Germany used its limited naval resources for diversionary attacks on oceanic trade, before throwing everything into a massive gamble to secure Denmark and Norway, using land-based air power to protect the invasion convoys and support troops ashore against the Anglo-French response. Crippled by a paucity of carrier-based fighters and ineffective anti-aircraft systems, the Royal Navy lost the Norwegian campaign. The first major contest between sea and land power had been won by land-based aircraft. The second blitzkrieg defeated France, and this time sea power was reduced to evacuating defeated troops from Dunkirk. But Germany lacked the warships and shipping to cross the Channel in the presence of the world's greatest navy, with or without air superiority. This time sea power won.

Unable to attempt an invasion, Germany used French Atlantic ports to open the 'battle of the Atlantic', around which all other campaigns revolved. With occasional surface and air support, U-boats attempted to interdict British supply lines, but allied losses were kept to manageable levels by the convoy system, intelligence breakthroughs, and improved weapons, sensors and training. Britain was aided by a massive addition of shipping provided by occupied European counties, especially Norway, which, along with increasingly effective American shipbuilding effort, denied the Germans any prospect of victory in an attritional battle.

British success in the Atlantic depended on maintaining a working command of the surface of the ocean. With the British Home Fleet based at Scapa Flow – the unseen, often unnoticed pivot point of the entire conflict, positioned to intercept German ships heading for the Atlantic – the defence of convoys could be left to anti-submarine forces. In June 1940 Italy entered the war and France surrendered, and this left Britain facing the dread prospect of being outnumbered at sea. Prime Minister Churchill moved quickly, despatching Home Fleet units to sink or demilitarise the French Fleet at Mers el-Kebir. This resolute action demonstrated that Britain would go to any lengths to secure sea control. Hitler, Stalin and Roosevelt realised Britain would fight on. When the Mediterranean Fleet crippled the Italian battlefleet at Taranto and sank three heavy cruisers at Matapan the British secured sea control, which they exploited to conquer Italian-held Ethiopia and Libya. An ill-fated British expedition to Greece and the arrival of German land and air units turned the strategic balance. The Luftwaffe sank or damaged many Royal Navy warships, effectively disabled the key base at Malta, and supported Rommel's ground offensive in North Africa. By the spring of 1942 the British Mediterranean Fleet had been reduced to a handful of cruisers and destroyers. Only the withdrawal of German air units for Operation *Barbarossa* and American entry into the war enabled the

British to rebuild, cut German supplies to North Africa, and build up the army in Egypt using supply lines around Africa, the famous WS convoys. This enabled the army to overwhelm Rommel at El Alamein.

In late 1942, American and British ground forces landed in Morocco and Algeria. Operation *Torch* linked up with the British army driving west. The American army had crossed the Atlantic direct to the North African beachheads, in what was the most impressive long-distance strategic movement of the war. After heavy fighting ashore, the German army, almost 250,000 men, was cut off by the Royal Navy and forced to surrender; this was a disaster on the same scale as Stalingrad. Further amphibious landings in Sicily and Italy defeated Fascist Italy, but did not secure the Italian peninsula.

By this stage, pre-war and wartime production had created a new Royal Navy; five battleships, six aircraft carriers and many more cruisers, destroyers, submarines and above all ocean escorts had entered service. These last were essential to winning the pivotal communications battle of the entire conflict. For much of the war, Britain, Canada and their allies were content simply to keep the Atlantic sea lanes open. The destruction of the *Bismarck* and the German surface logistics effort by the Home Fleet in May 1941 proved a critical turning point. Only the menace lingered. American entry into war gave the U-boats a brief period of success on the American coast, but Germany lacked the resources to mount a decisive threat to allied sea communications. The U-boats could only delay the inevitable. By early 1943 the main American army was ready to move to Europe. Unwilling to risk losing significant numbers of men and materiel on the Atlantic passage, Roosevelt and Churchill decided it was time to annihilate the U-boats. Allied naval, air and intelligence assets, with improved training, shattered the U-boat arm in April and May, sinking over fifty boats. This sudden shift from defence to attack was made possible by a surge of new ships, and ships temporarily released from other theatres.

Some ships came from the other great convoy route, the Arctic run to Murmansk and Archangel. Established soon after *Barbarossa*, the Arctic convoys were the shortest and most obvious link between Britain and her new Soviet ally. These convoys served several purposes. Initially, they provided vital hardware to hard-pressed Soviet forces. British Hurricanes helped defend the Russian ports, and stabilised the Norwegian frontier; British tanks, mainly Valentines, made up a large part of the Soviet tank fleet in the decisive battle for Moscow in December 1941. Once the Soviets could make enough tanks and guns, the convoys carried American trucks, boots, rations, machine tools and fuel. The convoys also helped stave off Stalin's demands for the early invasion of northwest Europe, but the Royal and Merchant navies paid a high price in lives and ships. The convoys faced determined German air, surface and submarine forces, which recognised their task as a defensive mission to support armies on the Eastern Front. Alongside the human enemy, the convoys faced a greater, more implacable foe – a bleak frozen hell of mountainous waves, pack ice, hurricane force winds and endless night or day. By any calculation these were the most difficult sustained naval operations of all time.

When Dönitz withdrew his submarines from the Atlantic in late May 1943 the British switched their efforts to the Arctic to keep up the unrelenting pressure that Admiral Horton knew would be the key to breaking the morale of the U-boat arm. Stalin no longer needed the supplies but the convoys continued, ostensibly to maintain allied solidarity, but in reality to draw out and destroy German forces. In December 1943 the battleship *Scharnhorst*, attempting to intercept a convoy, was caught and sunk by the Home Fleet.

In May 1944 the Arctic route was suspended, the escorting warships were withdrawn, and sent south for the last great maritime strategic task in the European theatre, the invasion of France. Operation *Overlord*, 6 June 1944, was an amphibious warfare master class that deployed American, British and Canadian armies into Normandy, demonstrating the offensive character of sea power despite powerful defences. Detailed and thorough planning, effective logistics, overwhelming firepower and complete air cover from British airfields saw the allied troops across four of the five beaches with relative success. Despite the losses at Omaha Beach, the experience of Gallipoli had been reversed. Operation *Dragoon* used much the same hardware to put another American army ashore in the south of France soon after.

With the European theatre safely in the hands of allied land and air forces, the main units of the modern Royal Navy began to prepare for another war, joining the United States Navy in the Pacific for the 1945 campaign. It was a far cry from the dark days of spring and early summer 1942.

The Pacific War had opened with a stunning strategic surprise attack carried out by a six-carrier task force, repeating a formula the Japanese had employed in previous wars, at Pearl Harbor on 7 December 1941. The Japanese then swept across South East Asia and the South Pacific, seizing the Philippines, Indonesia, Malaya and Burma. Off Malaya land-based Japanese bombers sank the British capital ships *Prince of Wales* and *Repulse*. Yet this startling Japanese success contained the seeds of disaster. Japan depended on massive imports of key strategic raw materials, notably oil, rubber, tin, iron, copper and food. The newly-won empire was so vast that it could not be effectively exploited by the existing Japanese merchant fleet, and very little extra tonnage was acquired in the early campaigns. From December 1941, the Japanese merchant fleet began to shrink as war losses and the stresses of the sea took a heavy toll, while both the navy and the army demanded ever more tonnage for military logistics. Many distant posts were effectively isolated. Nor should it be forgotten that Japan's main war effort from 1936 until 1945 was the conquest of China where vast armies were deployed. Every new possession only added to Japan's catastrophic overstretch, leaving it vulnerable to a major assault on maritime communications.

As their Asian Empire collapsed the British could only scrape together an extemporised Eastern Fleet of old battleships and new carriers, the latter with precious few modern aircraft and no operational training. There was nothing else available. The Home Fleet could not spare more ships; it had already sacrificed two capital ships to defend Singapore and needed every remaining ship to keep the German surface fleet locked up and to cover the Atlantic and Arctic convoys. The lowest point of the war for British sea power, and in consequence the closest the allies came to defeat, came when the Pearl Harbor task force surged into the Indian Ocean in March 1943. Fortunately, the Japanese did not stay long; after beating up Ceylon, raiding the Bay of Bengal and sinking some isolated warships, they went back to the Pacific.

No sooner had the Japanese departed than a British amphibious operation seized Vichy French Madagascar, blocking any attempt to either cut the vital convoy system that supplied and reinforced the British army in Egypt, or to reach the South Atlantic. Operation *Ironclad* kept the German and Japanese wars isolated. Having demonstrated the resilience of sea power the Eastern Fleet broke up; the old battleships provided fire support for amphibious operations: the carriers prepared for another ocean. Skilled men were key assets throughout the naval war, and there were never enough in any navy.

In June 1942, only a month after *Ironclad*, the Japanese set up a decisive battle off Midway Island, hoping to wipe out the last American carriers. The plan was unnecessarily complex, deploying several formations across vast ocean spaces, well beyond the possibility of mutual support, while relying on the carriers to conduct two key tasks. Initially, the carriers would soften up Midway for an invasion. This, it was assumed, would bring the American carriers scurrying out from Pearl Harbor, over a submarine ambush, before the Japanese carriers struck. Making bold use of partial intelligence insights, the Americans ambushed and sank all four Japanese carriers while they were still engaged in the first phase operation.

Despite Midway the Pacific war would hang in the balance for another year. The American invasion of the Solomon Islands set up a massive land/sea/air battle of attrition, slowly grinding down Japanese fighting power and effectively wiping out the elite cadre of pre-war carrier pilots. The Americans paid a heavy price for their victory, and it was not until mid 1943 when new ships, notably Essex class fast carriers, entered service that the next round of offensives could begin. After Midway the Americans built up irresistible naval and amphibious power, using overwhelming mobile logistics and armadas of fast carriers to cut off and capture key islands from New Guinea to the Philippines. The invasion of the Marianas and the Philippines forced the inferior Japanese force to risk fleet actions, where American

firepower and intelligent use of initiative at all command levels left the Imperial Japanese Navy a shattered remnant, without either the fuel to sail, or the trained pilots to fight. Resorting to Kamikaze suicide missions demonstrated that the Pacific war had become asymmetric. Japan could not win by conventional methods.

By late 1944 the Americans had secured island bases within heavy bomber range of the Japanese home islands. The bombing offensive culminated in fire-storm raids that devastated Tokyo. Meanwhile, the US submarine fleet annihilated largely unconvoyed Japanese merchant shipping. They succeeded because the Americans were dominant at sea and in the air. By 1945 American sea power had annihilated Japanese communications, dismantling the Empire, and paving the way for the amphibious conquest of Japan. Atomic bombs averted the need for invasion, or the slower sea power option of sustained blockade. The scale of the Pacific war forced the Americans to create new ways of using naval power, notably by adopting support forces to extend the operational range of fleets through refuelling and replenishing at sea.

The absolute ubiquity of allied sea power is eloquently exemplified by the wartime employment of two British capital ships. In 1939 the rebuilt Jutland veteran HMS *Warspite* was the flagship in the Mediterranean; in April 1940 she fought a major battle deep inside the Narvik Fjord in Northern Norway, before returning to sink an Italian cruiser at Matapan, and survive bomb damage off Crete. After a spell as flagship of the Eastern Fleet, *Warspite* supported the Salerno landings, only to be hit by a radio-guided bomb. Hastily patched up, with only three turrets working, she served at D-Day, and finally in the attack on Walcheren in November 1944. The new battleship HMS *King George V* entered service just in time to help sink the *Bismarck*, provided fire support in several European operations and then moved to the Pacific, where she was the last British capital ship to fire her guns in anger, on the very last day of the war.

The maps that follow offer a new and strikingly different approach to understanding the global naval war. They cover all the major events at sea, along with numerous smaller or largely unknown events. Critical battles are examined in detail, while the overviews set them in the wider strategic context, and illustrate where and how naval forces had an effect ashore. In a study that emphasises the maritime nature of allied grand strategy the maps cover air, submarine, and amphibious operations, as well as the critical convoys that linked the main theatres. Finally, this is a truly international perspective, covering the activities of all major and numerous minor navies. The scope, scale and cartographic nature of this volume offers a unique and rewarding new way of comprehending the sometimes unfathomable complexity of the naval war between 1939 and 1945.

ANDREW LAMBERT

GENERAL KEY AND ABBREVIATIONS

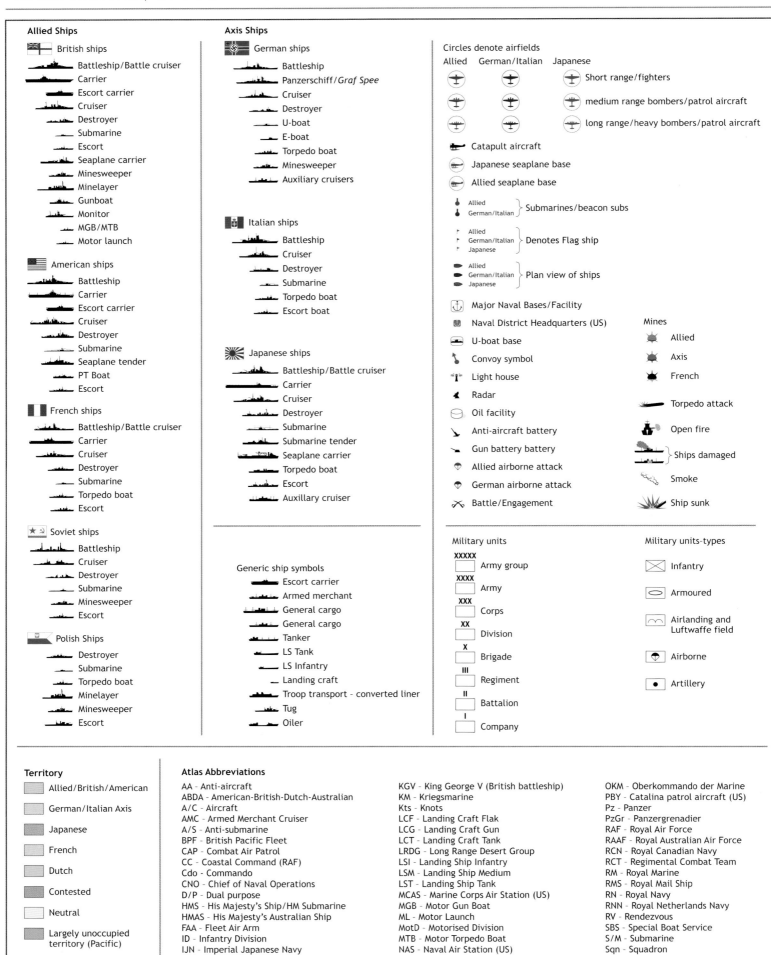

Allied Ships

British ships
- Battleship/Battle cruiser
- Carrier
- Escort carrier
- Cruiser
- Destroyer
- Submarine
- Escort
- Seaplane carrier
- Minesweeper
- Minelayer
- Gunboat
- Monitor
- MGB/MTB
- Motor launch

American ships
- Battleship
- Carrier
- Escort carrier
- Cruiser
- Destroyer
- Submarine
- Seaplane tender
- PT Boat
- Escort

French ships
- Battleship/Battle cruiser
- Carrier
- Cruiser
- Destroyer
- Submarine
- Torpedo boat
- Escort

Soviet ships
- Battleship
- Cruiser
- Destroyer
- Submarine
- Minesweeper
- Escort

Polish Ships
- Destroyer
- Submarine
- Torpedo boat
- Minelayer
- Minesweeper
- Escort

Axis Ships

German ships
- Battleship
- Panzerschiff/*Graf Spee*
- Cruiser
- Destroyer
- U-boat
- E-boat
- Torpedo boat
- Minesweeper
- Auxiliary cruisers

Italian ships
- Battleship
- Cruiser
- Destroyer
- Submarine
- Torpedo boat
- Escort boat

Japanese ships
- Battleship/Battle cruiser
- Carrier
- Cruiser
- Destroyer
- Submarine
- Submarine tender
- Seaplane carrier
- Torpedo boat
- Escort
- Auxillary cruiser

Generic ship symbols
- Escort carrier
- Armed merchant
- General cargo
- General cargo
- Tanker
- LS Tank
- LS Infantry
- Landing craft
- Troop transport – converted liner
- Tug
- Oiler

Circles denote airfields

Allied	German/Italian	Japanese	
			Short range/fighters
			medium range bombers/patrol aircraft
			long range/heavy bombers/patrol aircraft

- Catapult aircraft
- Japanese seaplane base
- Allied seaplane base

Allied
German/Italian } Submarines/beacon subs

Allied
German/Italian
Japanese } Denotes Flag ship

Allied
German/Italian
Japanese } Plan view of ships

- Major Naval Bases/Facility
- Naval District Headquarters (US)
- U-boat base
- Convoy symbol
- Light house
- Radar
- Oil facility
- Anti-aircraft battery
- Gun battery battery
- Allied airborne attack
- German airborne attack
- Battle/Engagement

Mines
- Allied
- Axis
- French

- Torpedo attack
- Open fire
- Ships damaged
- Smoke
- Ship sunk

Military units

- XXXXX — Army group
- XXXX — Army
- XXX — Corps
- XX — Division
- X — Brigade
- III — Regiment
- II — Battalion
- I — Company

Military units-types

- Infantry
- Armoured
- Airlanding and Luftwaffe field
- Airborne
- Artillery

Territory
- Allied/British/American
- German/Italian Axis
- Japanese
- French
- Dutch
- Contested
- Neutral
- Largely unoccupied territory (Pacific)

Atlas Abbreviations

AA – Anti-aircraft
ABDA – American-British-Dutch-Australian
A/C – Aircraft
AMC – Armed Merchant Cruiser
A/S – Anti-submarine
BPF – British Pacific Fleet
CAP – Combat Air Patrol
CC – Coastal Command (RAF)
Cdo – Commando
CNO – Chief of Naval Operations
D/P – Dual purpose
HMS – His Majesty's Ship/HM Submarine
HMAS – His Majesty's Australian Ship
FAA – Fleet Air Arm
ID – Infantry Division
IJN – Imperial Japanese Navy

KGV – King George V (British battleship)
KM – Kriegsmarine
Kts – Knots
LCF – Landing Craft Flak
LCG – Landing Craft Gun
LCT – Landing Craft Tank
LRDG – Long Range Desert Group
LSI – Landing Ship Infantry
LSM – Landing Ship Medium
LST – Landing Ship Tank
MCAS – Marine Corps Air Station (US)
MGB – Motor Gun Boat
ML – Motor Launch
MotD – Motorised Division
MTB – Motor Torpedo Boat
NAS – Naval Air Station (US)

OKM – Oberkommando der Marine
PBY – Catalina patrol aircraft (US)
Pz – Panzer
PzGr – Panzergrenadier
RAF – Royal Air Force
RAAF – Royal Australian Air Force
RCN – Royal Canadian Navy
RCT – Regimental Combat Team
RM – Royal Marine
RMS – Royal Mail Ship
RN – Royal Navy
RNN – Royal Netherlands Navy
RV – Rendezvous
SBS – Special Boat Service
S/M – Submarine
Sqn – Squadron

WAR AT SEA

A NAVAL ATLAS 1939–1945

BRITISH SEAPOWER, 1939

ON THE EVE of the Second World War Britain possessed the largest fleet and network of naval bases of any of the major powers. For Britain, as an island nation reliant on imports and at the centre of an imperial trading system, the maintenance of seapower was of fundamental importance. The traditional role of the Royal Navy was to secure maritime communications and trade protection. It was the only navy capable of operating worldwide and could also draw upon the resources of the small dominion navies.

Although financial and political factors had reduced the size of the Royal Navy since 1918 and limited its development throughout the inter-war years, the British remained at the forefront of naval innovation. In the 1920s British naval strategy focused on dealing with the Italian and Japanese navies, however, the re-emergence of the German naval threat after 1933 complicated planning and strained the available resources.

In response to the deteriorating international situation British naval rearmament increased considerably. First World War era battleships were modernised and new warships ordered. By 1937 Britain was already pulling ahead in the global naval arms race with five new battleships laid down that year along with four aircraft carriers having been ordered. More warships of all types were laid down before September 1939.

Operationally the Royal Navy was divided into two main fleets and a series of overseas stations. The Home Fleet, composed of the 2nd Battle Squadron, the Battle Cruiser Squadron and at least two carriers, was assigned to enforce a naval blockade of Germany. The 1st Battle Squadron served as the core of the Mediterranean Fleet assigned to deal with the Italians. The primary role of the overseas stations was local trade protection and around half the British cruiser strength was allocated to this role.

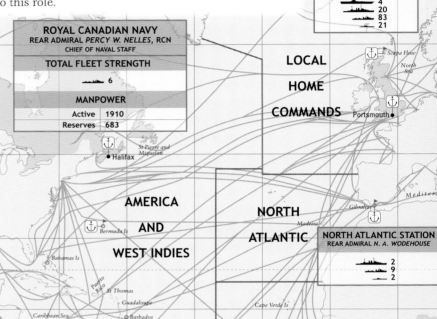

HOME WATERS
C-in-C HOME FLEET
ADMIRAL *SIR CHARLES FORBES*

	9
	4
	20
	83
	21

ROYAL CANADIAN NAVY
REAR ADMIRAL *PERCY W. NELLES*, RCN
CHIEF OF NAVAL STAFF

TOTAL FLEET STRENGTH

	6

MANPOWER

Active	1910
Reserves	683

NORTH ATLANTIC STATION
REAR ADMIRAL *N. A. WODEHOUSE*

	2
	9
	2

LOCAL
HOME
COMMANDS

AMERICA
AND
WEST INDIES

NORTH
ATLANTIC

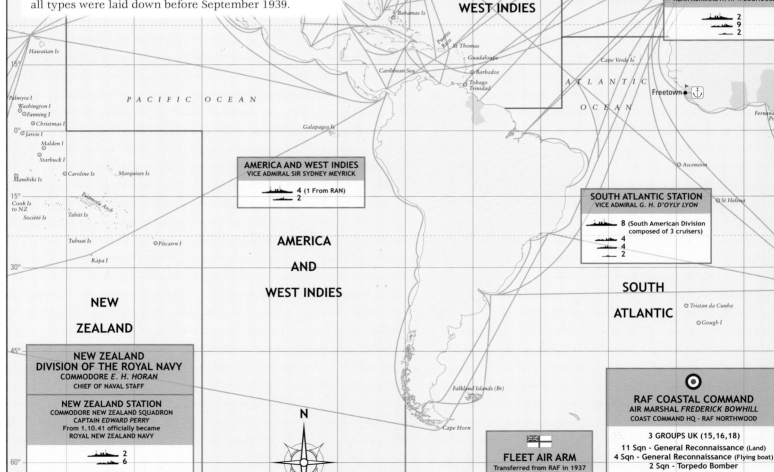

AMERICA AND WEST INDIES
VICE ADMIRAL SIR SYDNEY MEYRICK

	4 (1 From RAN)
	2

SOUTH ATLANTIC STATION
VICE ADMIRAL *G. H. D'OYLY LYON*

	8 (South American Division composed of 3 cruisers)
	4
	4
	2

AMERICA
AND
WEST INDIES

NEW
ZEALAND

SOUTH
ATLANTIC

**NEW ZEALAND
DIVISION OF THE ROYAL NAVY**
COMMODORE *E. H. HORAN*
CHIEF OF NAVAL STAFF

NEW ZEALAND STATION
COMMODORE NEW ZEALAND SQUADRON
CAPTAIN *EDWARD PERRY*
From 1.10.41 officially became
ROYAL NEW ZEALAND NAVY

	2
	6

MANPOWER

Active	1954
Reserves	670

FLEET AIR ARM
Transferred from RAF in 1937

	232 (Frontline)
	191 (Training)

RAF COASTAL COMMAND
AIR MARSHAL *FREDERICK BOWHILL*
COAST COMMAND HQ - RAF NORTHWOOD

3 GROUPS UK (15,16,18)
11 Sqn - General Reconnaissance (Land)
4 Sqn - General Reconnaissance (Flying boat)
2 Sqn - Torpedo Bomber

200 Aircraft in total.
2 Flying Squadrons short of planned establishment

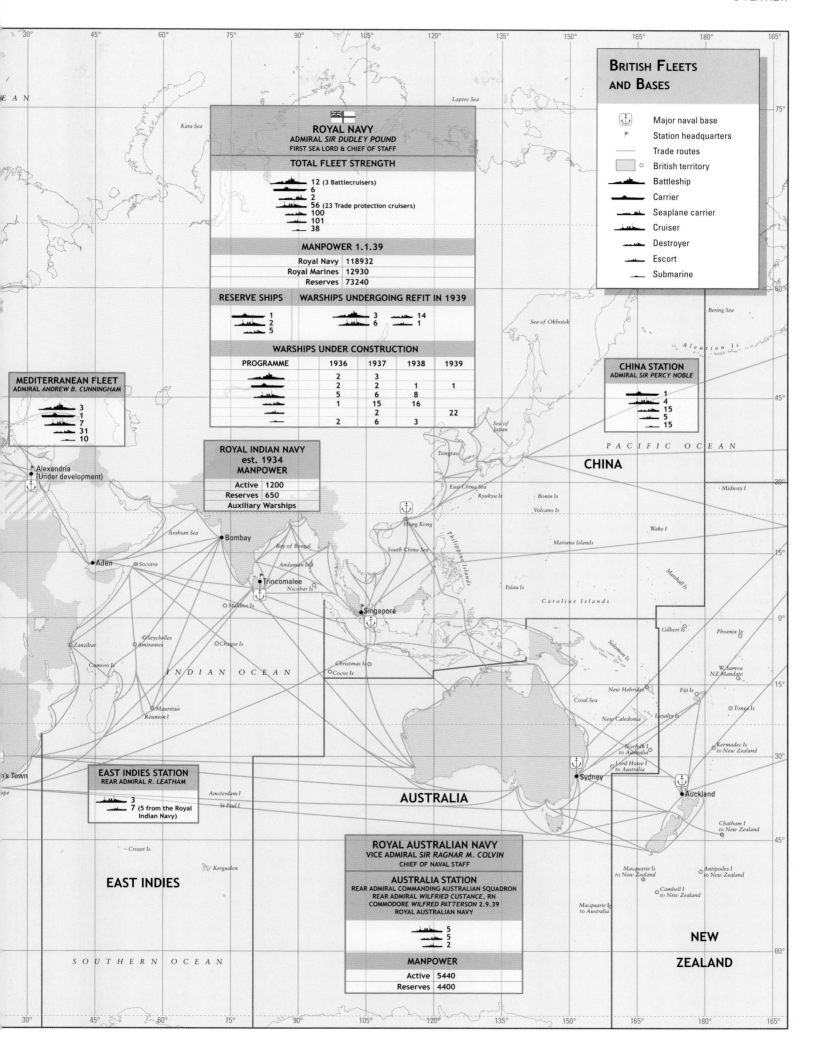

BRITISH FLEETS AND BASES

Legend:
- ⚓ Major naval base
- ⚑ Station headquarters
- — Trade routes
- British territory
- Battleship
- Carrier
- Seaplane carrier
- Cruiser
- Destroyer
- Escort
- Submarine

ROYAL NAVY
ADMIRAL *SIR DUDLEY POUND*
FIRST SEA LORD & CHIEF OF STAFF

TOTAL FLEET STRENGTH

- 12 (3 Battlecruisers)
- 6
- 2
- 56 (23 Trade protection cruisers)
- 100
- 101
- 38

MANPOWER 1.1.39

Royal Navy	118932
Royal Marines	12930
Reserves	73240

RESERVE SHIPS

- 1
- 2
- 5

WARSHIPS UNDERGOING REFIT IN 1939

- 3 — 14
- 6 — 1

WARSHIPS UNDER CONSTRUCTION

PROGRAMME	1936	1937	1938	1939
	2	3		
	2	2	1	1
	5	6	8	
	1	15	16	
		2		22
	2	6	3	

ROYAL INDIAN NAVY
est. 1934
MANPOWER

Active	1200
Reserves	650
Auxiliary Warships	

MEDITERRANEAN FLEET
ADMIRAL *ANDREW B. CUNNINGHAM*

- 3
- 1
- 7
- 31
- 10

Alexandria (Under development)

CHINA STATION
ADMIRAL *SIR PERCY NOBLE*

- 1
- 4
- 15
- 5
- 15

EAST INDIES STATION
REAR ADMIRAL *R. LEATHAM*

- 3
- 7 (5 from the Royal Indian Navy)

ROYAL AUSTRALIAN NAVY
VICE ADMIRAL *SIR RAGNAR M. COLVIN*
CHIEF OF NAVAL STAFF

AUSTRALIA STATION
REAR ADMIRAL COMMANDING AUSTRALIAN SQUADRON
REAR ADMIRAL *WILFRIED CUSTANCE*, RN
COMMODORE *WILFRED PATTERSON* 2.9.39
ROYAL AUSTRALIAN NAVY

- 5
- 5
- 2

MANPOWER

Active	5440
Reserves	4400

Map labels: Kara Sea, Laptev Sea, Sea of Okhotsk, Bering Sea, Aleutian Is, PACIFIC OCEAN, CHINA, Tsingtao, East China Sea, Ryukyu Is, Bonin Is, Volcano Is, Midway I, Wake I, Mariana Islands, Marshall Is, Hong Kong, South China Sea, Philippine Islands, Palau Is, Caroline Islands, Gilbert Is, Phoenix Is, Arabian Sea, Bombay, Bay of Bengal, Andaman Is, Trincomalee, Nicobar Is, Maldive Is, Singapore, Christmas Is, Cocos Is, Aden, Socotra, Seychelles, Amirantes, Chagos Is, Zanzibar, Comoro Is, INDIAN OCEAN, Mauritius, Réunion I, W. Samoa NZ Mandate, New Hebrides, Fiji Is, Tonga Is, Coral Sea, New Caledonia, Loyalty Is, Norfolk I to Australia, Kermadec Is to New Zealand, Lord Howe I to Australia, Sydney, AUSTRALIA, Auckland, NEW ZEALAND, Chatham I to New Zealand, EAST INDIES, Amsterdam I, St Paul I, Crozet Is, Kerguelen, SOUTHERN OCEAN, Macquarie Is to New Zealand, Antipodes I to New Zealand, Cambell I to New Zealand, Macquarie I to Australia

The Royal Navy in British Waters

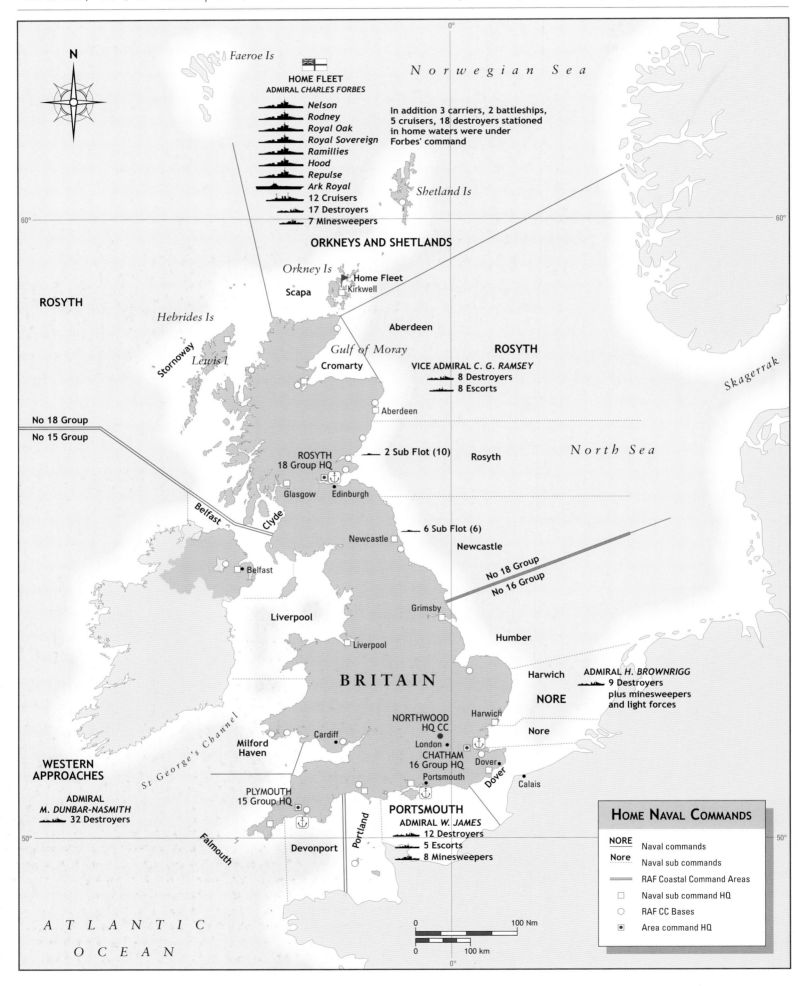

N

Faeroe Is

Norwegian Sea

HOME FLEET
ADMIRAL *CHARLES FORBES*

- *Nelson*
- *Rodney*
- *Royal Oak*
- *Royal Sovereign*
- *Ramillies*
- *Hood*
- *Repulse*
- *Ark Royal*
- 12 Cruisers
- 17 Destroyers
- 7 Minesweepers

In addition 3 carriers, 2 battleships,
5 cruisers, 18 destroyers stationed
in home waters were under
Forbes' command

Shetland Is

60°

ORKNEYS AND SHETLANDS

Orkney Is

► Home Fleet

Scapa ▪ Kirkwell

ROSYTH

Hebrides Is

Aberdeen

Stornoway

Lewis I.

Gulf of Moray

Cromarty

ROSYTH
VICE ADMIRAL *C. G. RAMSEY*

- 8 Destroyers
- 8 Escorts

Aberdeen

No 18 Group
No 15 Group

North Sea

Skagerrak

⊶ 2 Sub Flot (10)   Rosyth

ROSYTH
18 Group HQ

Glasgow   Edinburgh

⊶ 6 Sub Flot (6)

Newcastle

Newcastle

Belfast   Clyde

• Belfast

No 18 Group
No 16 Group

Liverpool

Grimsby

• Liverpool

Humber

BRITAIN

ADMIRAL *H. BROWNRIGG*
- 9 Destroyers
plus minesweepers
and light forces

Harwich

NORE

NORTHWOOD
HQ CC

Nore

Cardiff

Harwich

Milford
Haven

London •

**WESTERN
APPROACHES**

St George's Channel

CHATHAM
16 Group HQ

Portsmouth

Dover

Dover •

Calais

ADMIRAL
M. DUNBAR-NASMITH
- 32 Destroyers

PLYMOUTH
15 Group HQ

Portland

PORTSMOUTH
ADMIRAL *W. JAMES*
- 12 Destroyers
- 5 Escorts
- 8 Minesweepers

Falmouth

Devonport

50°

A T L A N T I C

O C E A N

0   100 Nm

0   100 km

HOME NAVAL COMMANDS

NORE   Naval commands
Nore   Naval sub commands
═══   RAF Coastal Command Areas
▫   Naval sub command HQ
○   RAF CC Bases
◉   Area command HQ

THE MARINE NATIONALE, 1939

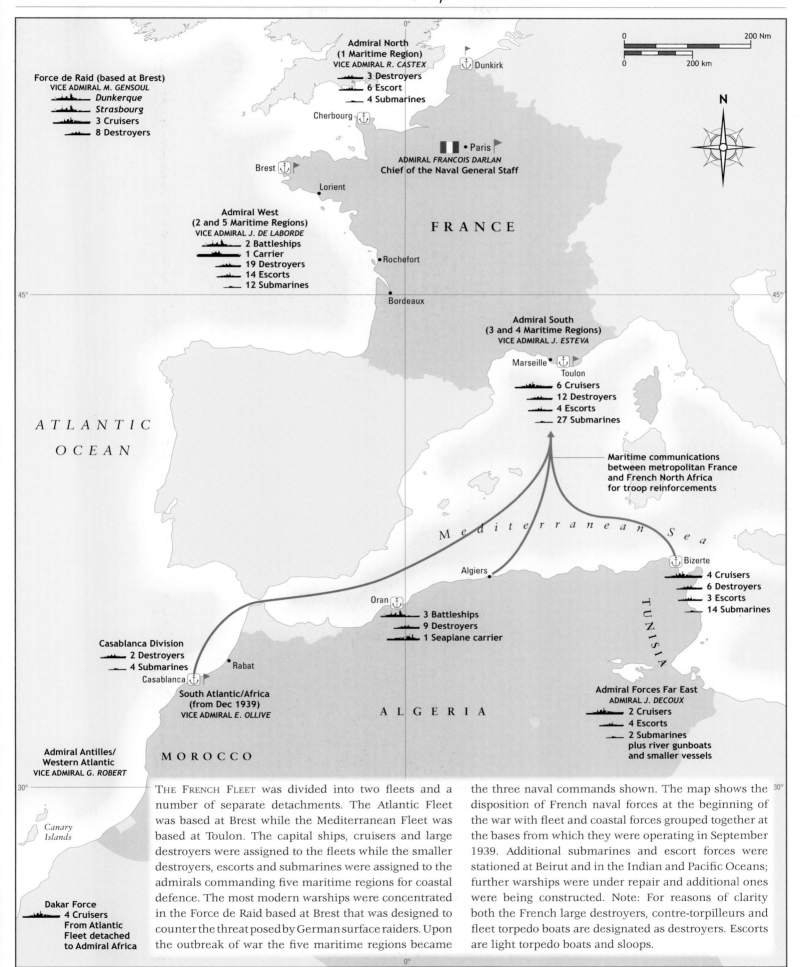

Force de Raid (based at Brest)
VICE ADMIRAL M. GENSOUL
Dunkerque
Strasbourg
3 Cruisers
8 Destroyers

Admiral North
(1 Maritime Region)
VICE ADMIRAL R. CASTEX
3 Destroyers
6 Escort
4 Submarines

Dunkirk

Cherbourg

• Paris
ADMIRAL FRANCOIS DARLAN
Chief of the Naval General Staff

Brest

Lorient

FRANCE

Admiral West
(2 and 5 Maritime Regions)
VICE ADMIRAL J. DE LABORDE
2 Battleships
1 Carrier
19 Destroyers
14 Escorts
12 Submarines

• Rochefort

Bordeaux

Admiral South
(3 and 4 Maritime Regions)
VICE ADMIRAL J. ESTEVA

Marseille
Toulon
6 Cruisers
12 Destroyers
4 Escorts
27 Submarines

ATLANTIC
OCEAN

Maritime communications
between metropolitan France
and French North Africa
for troop reinforcements

M e d i t e r r a n e a n   S e a

Bizerte
4 Cruisers
6 Destroyers
3 Escorts
14 Submarines

Algiers

Oran
3 Battleships
9 Destroyers
1 Seaplane carrier

TUNISIA

Casablanca Division
2 Destroyers
4 Submarines

Casablanca
• Rabat

South Atlantic/Africa
(from Dec 1939)
VICE ADMIRAL E. OLLIVE

ALGERIA

Admiral Forces Far East
ADMIRAL J. DECOUX
2 Cruisers
4 Escorts
2 Submarines
plus river gunboats
and smaller vessels

Admiral Antilles/
Western Atlantic
VICE ADMIRAL G. ROBERT

MOROCCO

Canary
Islands

Dakar Force
4 Cruisers
From Atlantic
Fleet detached
to Admiral Africa

THE FRENCH FLEET was divided into two fleets and a number of separate detachments. The Atlantic Fleet was based at Brest while the Mediterranean Fleet was based at Toulon. The capital ships, cruisers and large destroyers were assigned to the fleets while the smaller destroyers, escorts and submarines were assigned to the admirals commanding five maritime regions for coastal defence. The most modern warships were concentrated in the Force de Raid based at Brest that was designed to counter the threat posed by German surface raiders. Upon the outbreak of war the five maritime regions became the three naval commands shown. The map shows the disposition of French naval forces at the beginning of the war with fleet and coastal forces grouped together at the bases from which they were operating in September 1939. Additional submarines and escort forces were stationed at Beirut and in the Indian and Pacific Oceans; further warships were under repair and additional ones were being constructed. Note: For reasons of clarity both the French large destroyers, contre-torpilleurs and fleet torpedo boats are designated as destroyers. Escorts are light torpedo boats and sloops.

THE KRIEGSMARINE, 1939

THE GERMAN NAVY had been the second largest in the world during the First World War. However, Germany was only permitted a small and largely obsolete fleet under the Treaty of Versailles, and lack of funds meant that the navy was unable to maintain even the modest force it was entitled to. After 1933 the political and economic parameters changed, but competition with the army and newly created airforce, a small industrial base and a shortage of raw materials all delayed the pace and scale of naval rearmament. Germany, although a continental power, was dependent on access to the sea to import raw materials and export industrial products. High grade Swedish iron ore was the single most vital import and susceptible to interdiction by enemy naval forces.

The Kriegsmarine's organisation was complex and underwent a number of changes during the early phase of the war. The map shows a simplified structure and disposition of warships as assigned shortly before the outbreak of hostilities. More warships, like the battleships *Bismarck* and *Tirpitz* were still under construction. Territorial command was split between the two naval stations, the North Sea and Baltic, which were supplemented by Naval Group Commands, responsible for the conduct of operations. The fleet itself was organised by ship types rather than geographic allocations and reported to regional commanders as well as the naval staff in Berlin.

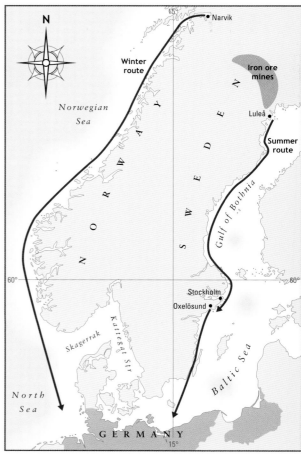

IRON ORE ROUTES

⟵ Trade routes to Germany

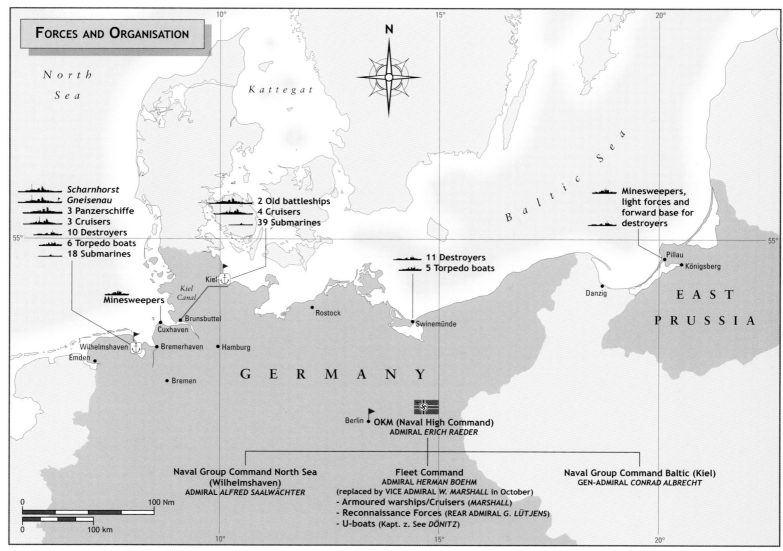

FORCES AND ORGANISATION

Scharnhorst
Gneisenau
3 Panzerschiffe
3 Cruisers
10 Destroyers
6 Torpedo boats
18 Submarines

Minesweepers

2 Old battleships
4 Cruisers
39 Submarines

11 Destroyers
5 Torpedo boats

Minesweepers, light forces and forward base for destroyers

Berlin • **OKM (Naval High Command)**
ADMIRAL *ERICH RAEDER*

**Naval Group Command North Sea
(Wilhelmshaven)**
ADMIRAL *ALFRED SAALWÄCHTER*

Fleet Command
ADMIRAL *HERMAN BOEHM*
(replaced by VICE ADMIRAL *W. MARSHALL* in October)
- Armoured warships/Cruisers (*MARSHALL*)
- Reconnaissance Forces (REAR ADMIRAL *G. LÜTJENS*)
- U-boats (Kapt. z. See *DÖNITZ*)

Naval Group Command Baltic (Kiel)
GEN-ADMIRAL *CONRAD ALBRECHT*

0 _____ 100 Nm
0 _____ 100 km

THE REGIA MARINA

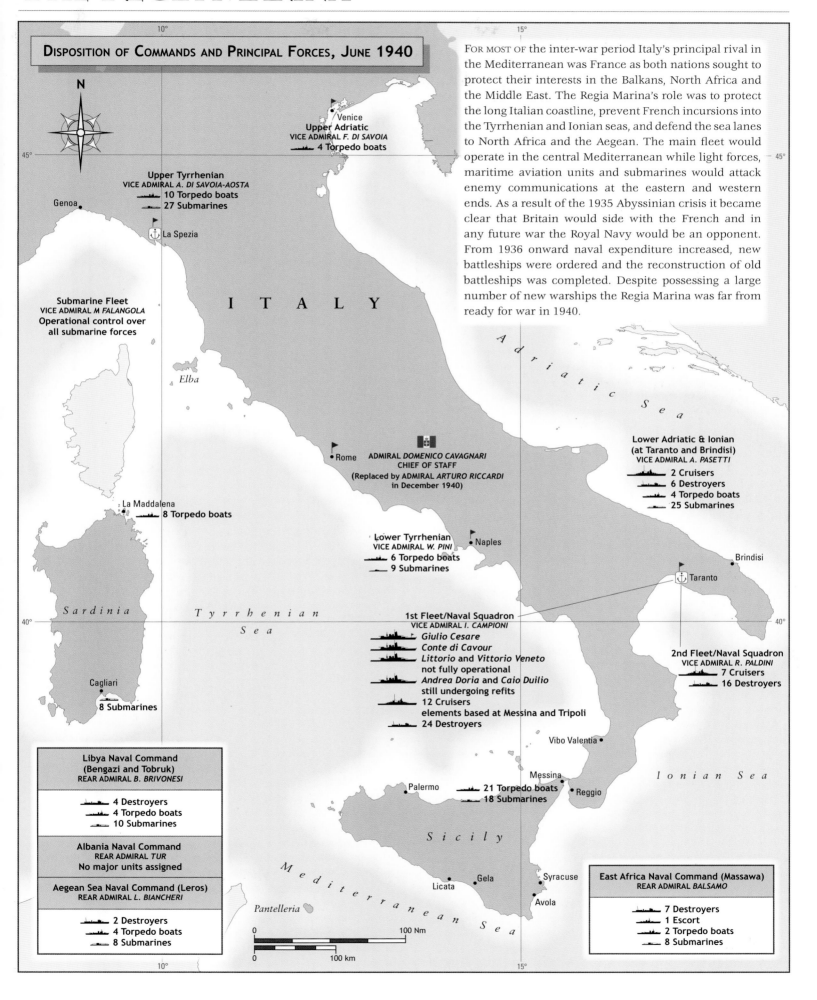

DISPOSITION OF COMMANDS AND PRINCIPAL FORCES, JUNE 1940

N

Upper Adriatic
VICE ADMIRAL *F. DI SAVOIA*
4 Torpedo boats
● Venice

Upper Tyrrhenian
VICE ADMIRAL *A. DI SAVOIA-AOSTA*
10 Torpedo boats
27 Submarines
Genoa ●
⚓ La Spezia

Submarine Fleet
VICE ADMIRAL *M FALANGOLA*
Operational control over
all submarine forces

Elba

I T A L Y

● Rome
ADMIRAL *DOMENICO CAVAGNARI*
CHIEF OF STAFF
(Replaced by ADMIRAL *ARTURO RICCARDI*
in December 1940)

A d r i a t i c   S e a

Lower Adriatic & Ionian
(at Taranto and Brindisi)
VICE ADMIRAL *A. PASETTI*
2 Cruisers
6 Destroyers
4 Torpedo boats
25 Submarines

La Maddalena
8 Torpedo boats

Lower Tyrrhenian
VICE ADMIRAL *W. PINI*
6 Torpedo boats
9 Submarines
▸ ● Naples

● Brindisi

⚓ Taranto

S a r d i n i a

*T y r r h e n i a n
S e a*

1st Fleet/Naval Squadron
VICE ADMIRAL *I. CAMPIONI*
Giulio Cesare
Conte di Cavour
Littorio and *Vittorio Veneto*
not fully operational
Andrea Doria and *Caio Duilio*
still undergoing refits
12 Cruisers
elements based at Messina and Tripoli
24 Destroyers

2nd Fleet/Naval Squadron
VICE ADMIRAL *R. PALDINI*
7 Cruisers
16 Destroyers

Cagliari ●
8 Submarines

Vibo Valentia ●

I o n i a n   S e a

Libya Naval Command
(Bengazi and Tobruk)
REAR ADMIRAL *B. BRIVONESI*

4 Destroyers
4 Torpedo boats
10 Submarines

Messina ●
Palermo ● 21 Torpedo boats ● Reggio
18 Submarines

Albania Naval Command
REAR ADMIRAL *TUR*
No major units assigned

S i c i l y

Aegean Sea Naval Command (Leros)
REAR ADMIRAL *L. BIANCHERI*

2 Destroyers
4 Torpedo boats
8 Submarines

M e d i t e r r a n e a n   S e a

● Gela
Licata ● ● Syracuse
Avola ●

Pantelleria 🏝

East Africa Naval Command (Massawa)
REAR ADMIRAL *BALSAMO*

7 Destroyers
1 Escort
2 Torpedo boats
8 Submarines

0 ————————————— 100 Nm
0 ————————————— 100 km

FOR MOST OF the inter-war period Italy's principal rival in the Mediterranean was France as both nations sought to protect their interests in the Balkans, North Africa and the Middle East. The Regia Marina's role was to protect the long Italian coastline, prevent French incursions into the Tyrrhenian and Ionian seas, and defend the sea lanes to North Africa and the Aegean. The main fleet would operate in the central Mediterranean while light forces, maritime aviation units and submarines would attack enemy communications at the eastern and western ends. As a result of the 1935 Abyssinian crisis it became clear that Britain would side with the French and in any future war the Royal Navy would be an opponent. From 1936 onward naval expenditure increased, new battleships were ordered and the reconstruction of old battleships was completed. Despite possessing a large number of new warships the Regia Marina was far from ready for war in 1940.

The War at Sea, 1939

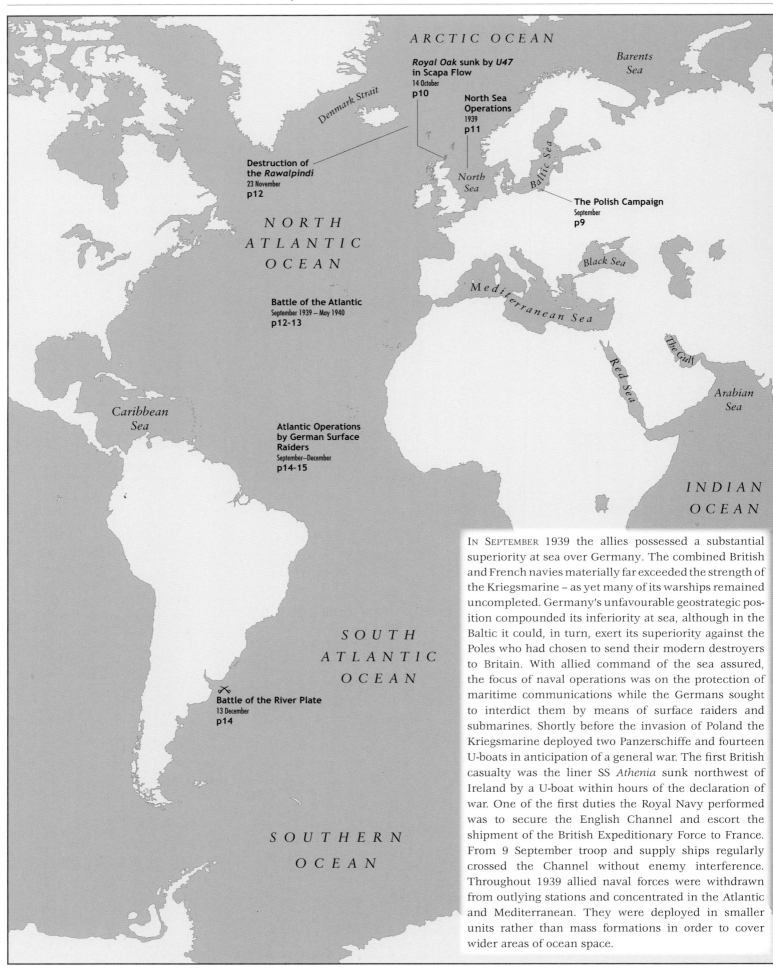

ARCTIC OCEAN

Barents Sea

Royal Oak sunk by U47 in Scapa Flow
14 October
p10

North Sea Operations
1939
p11

Denmark Strait

Destruction of the Rawalpindi
23 November
p12

North Sea

Baltic Sea

The Polish Campaign
September
p9

NORTH ATLANTIC OCEAN

Black Sea

Mediterranean Sea

Battle of the Atlantic
September 1939 – May 1940
p12-13

The Gulf

Red Sea

Arabian Sea

Caribbean Sea

Atlantic Operations by German Surface Raiders
September–December
p14-15

INDIAN OCEAN

SOUTH ATLANTIC OCEAN

Battle of the River Plate
13 December
p14

SOUTHERN OCEAN

IN SEPTEMBER 1939 the allies possessed a substantial superiority at sea over Germany. The combined British and French navies materially far exceeded the strength of the Kriegsmarine – as yet many of its warships remained uncompleted. Germany's unfavourable geostrategic position compounded its inferiority at sea, although in the Baltic it could, in turn, exert its superiority against the Poles who had chosen to send their modern destroyers to Britain. With allied command of the sea assured, the focus of naval operations was on the protection of maritime communications while the Germans sought to interdict them by means of surface raiders and submarines. Shortly before the invasion of Poland the Kriegsmarine deployed two Panzerschiffe and fourteen U-boats in anticipation of a general war. The first British casualty was the liner SS *Athenia* sunk northwest of Ireland by a U-boat within hours of the declaration of war. One of the first duties the Royal Navy performed was to secure the English Channel and escort the shipment of the British Expeditionary Force to France. From 9 September troop and supply ships regularly crossed the Channel without enemy interference. Throughout 1939 allied naval forces were withdrawn from outlying stations and concentrated in the Atlantic and Mediterranean. They were deployed in smaller units rather than mass formations in order to cover wider areas of ocean space.

THE POLISH CAMPAIGN, SEPTEMBER 1939

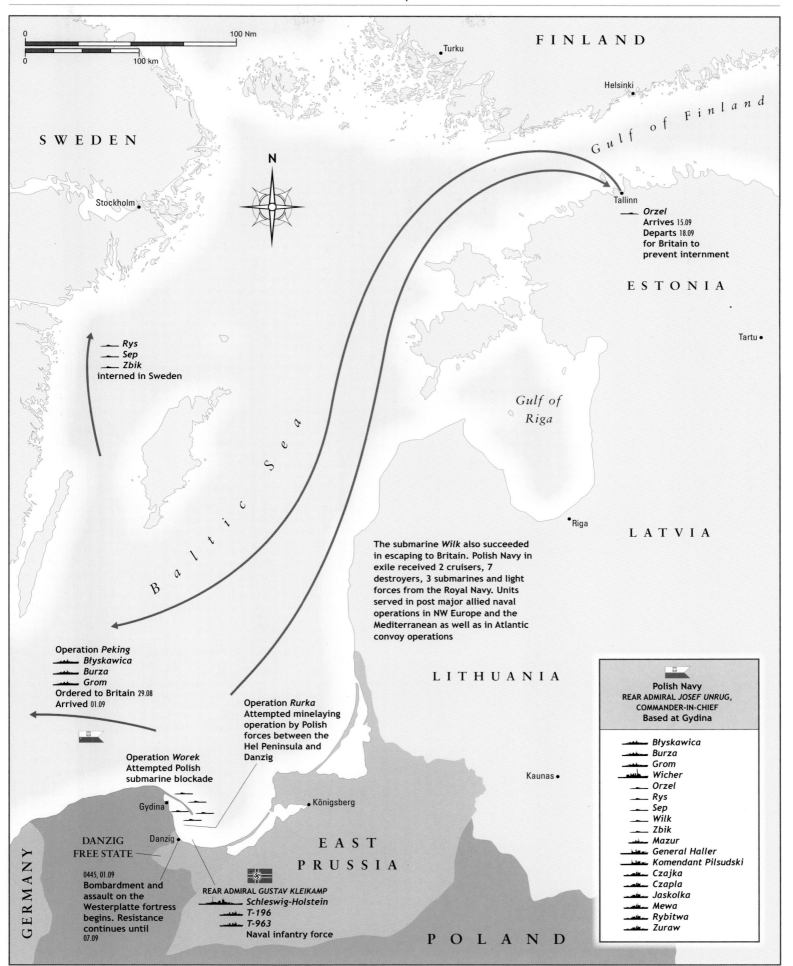

0   100 Nm

0   100 km

FINLAND

Turku

Helsinki

Gulf of Finland

SWEDEN

Stockholm

Tallinn

— *Orzel*
Arrives 15.09
Departs 18.09
for Britain to
prevent internment

ESTONIA

Tartu

— *Rys*
— *Sep*
— *Zbik*
interned in Sweden

*Gulf of
Riga*

Baltic Sea

Riga

LATVIA

The submarine *Wilk* also succeeded
in escaping to Britain. Polish Navy in
exile received 2 cruisers, 7
destroyers, 3 submarines and light
forces from the Royal Navy. Units
served in post major allied naval
operations in NW Europe and the
Mediterranean as well as in Atlantic
convoy operations

LITHUANIA

Operation *Peking*
— *Błyskawica*
— *Burza*
— *Grom*
Ordered to Britain 29.08
Arrived 01.09

Operation *Rurka*
Attempted minelaying
operation by Polish
forces between the
Hel Peninsula and
Danzig

Kaunas

Operation *Worek*
Attempted Polish
submarine blockade

Gydina

Königsberg

GERMANY

DANZIG
FREE STATE

Danzig

EAST
PRUSSIA

0445, 01.09
Bombardment and
assault on the
Westerplatte fortress
begins. Resistance
continues until
07.09

REAR ADMIRAL *GUSTAV KLEIKAMP*
— Schleswig-Holstein
— T-196
— T-963
Naval infantry force

POLAND

Polish Navy
REAR ADMIRAL *JOSEF UNRUG*,
COMMANDER-IN-CHIEF
Based at Gydina

— *Błyskawica*
— *Burza*
— *Grom*
— *Wicher*
— *Orzel*
— *Rys*
— *Sep*
— *Wilk*
— *Zbik*
— *Mazur*
— *General Haller*
— *Komendant Pilsudski*
— *Czajka*
— *Czapla*
— *Jaskolka*
— *Mewa*
— *Rybitwa*
— *Zuraw*

THE NORTH SEA, 1939–1940

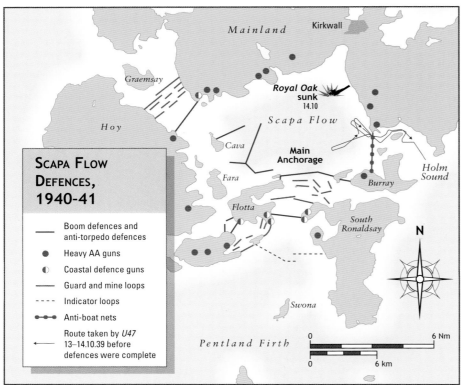

SCAPA FLOW DEFENCES, 1940-41

Boom defences and anti-torpedo defences
● Heavy AA guns
◐ Coastal defence guns
— Guard and mine loops
---- Indicator loops
●—●—● Anti-boat nets
←— Route taken by *U47* 13–14.10.39 before defences were complete

Mainland Kirkwall
Graemsay
Royal Oak sunk 14.10
Hoy
Scapa Flow
Cava
Main Anchorage
Fara
Holm Sound
Flotta
Burray
South Ronaldsay
N
Swona
Pentland Firth

0 —— 6 Nm
0 —— 6 km

U47 AND THE SINKING OF HMS *ROYAL OAK*, 13-14 OCTOBER 1939

◄···· *U47* Infiltration route
◄— *U47* attack run
◄·–·– *U47* escape route
······ Anti-boat net defence added 1940–41

Pegasus
Royal Oak
0058
0113
N
Orkney mainland
Kirk Sound
Lambs Holm
Skerry Sound
Glimps Holm
Holm Sound
Scapa Flow
Burray

0 —— 2 Nm
0 —— 2 km

U47
KPTLT. GÜNTHER PRIEN

ONE KEY ELEMENT of British strategy in a war with Germany was the implementation of a blockade designed to weaken the German economy and ability to sustain military operations. British operations in September 1939 followed the experience gathered during the First World War – a distant blockade that rested on the ability of the Home Fleet to seal off the North Sea exits from its wartime anchorage at Scapa Flow. Cruiser and auxiliary cruiser patrols would intercept German shipping. The Kriegsmarine would effectively be contained in the North Sea, as the Dover Straits would be secured with minefields and light forces.

Both sides declared the presence of defensive minefields to protect their coastlines upon the outbreak of war and began offensive mine laying. Although a British force initially patrolled off the Norwegian coast and a small number of high-speed surface patrols were undertaken into the eastern North Sea, operations were primarily undertaken by submarines. This was because of mines and aircraft and there was little operational need to take surface forces far south. Initially, eighteen submarines were available, but with redeployments this increased to nearly thirty by the spring of 1940. However, political and operational restrictions limited the effects of this campaign.

The Germans too relied primarily on the combination of U-boats and mines to attack British coastal shipping. An attempt by a Kriegsmarine cruiser and destroyer force to lay mines off the Tyne in December sustained heavy damage to submarine attacks on the homeward voyage. Both sides undertook a small number of costly, but otherwise ineffective, air raids on each other's principle anchorage sites. However, one important success was achieved with the sinking of the battleship *Royal Oak*, while at anchor in Scapa Flow, by *U47* in October. The work on the defences at Scapa Flow had progressed only slowly, something the Germans were aware of through aerial reconnaissance. Although the *Royal Oak* was old, 833 men were killed and, coming only shortly after the carrier *Courageous* had been sunk off Ireland, the propaganda effect was important.

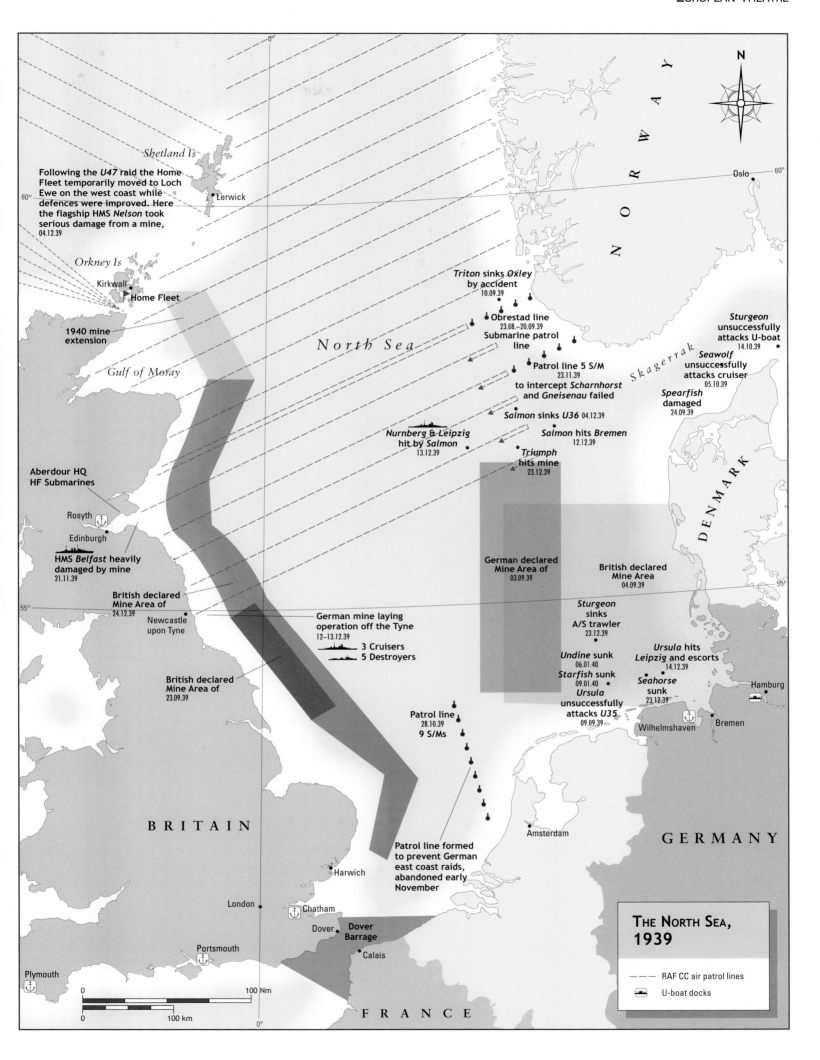

Shetland Is

Following the *U47* raid the Home Fleet temporarily moved to Loch Ewe on the west coast while defences were improved. Here the flagship HMS *Nelson* took serious damage from a mine, 04.12.39

Lerwick

Orkney Is

Kirkwall

Home Fleet

1940 mine extension

Gulf of Moray

North Sea

N O R W A Y

Oslo

Triton sinks *Oxley* by accident 10.09.39

Obrestad line 23.08.–20.09.39 Submarine patrol line

Sturgeon unsuccessfully attacks U-boat 14.10.39

Seawolf unsuccessfully attacks cruiser 05.10.39

Skagerrak

Patrol line 5 S/M 23.11.39 to intercept *Scharnhorst* and *Gneisenau* failed

Spearfish damaged 24.09.39

Salmon sinks *U36* 04.12.39

Nurnberg & Leipzig hit by *Salmon* 13.12.39

Salmon hits *Bremen* 12.12.39

Triumph hits mine 23.12.39

Aberdour HQ HF Submarines

Rosyth

Edinburgh

HMS *Belfast* heavily damaged by mine 21.11.39

British declared Mine Area of 24.12.39

Newcastle upon Tyne

German declared Mine Area of 03.09.39

British declared Mine Area 04.09.39

DENMARK

Sturgeon sinks A/S trawler 23.12.39

Ursula hits *Leipzig* and escorts 14.12.39

German mine laying operation off the Tyne 12–13.12.39

3 Cruisers
5 Destroyers

Undine sunk 06.01.40

Starfish sunk 09.01.40

Ursula unsuccessfully attacks *U35* 09.09.39

Seahorse sunk 23.12.39

Hamburg

Wilhelmshaven

Bremen

British declared Mine Area of 23.09.39

Patrol line 28.10.39 9 S/Ms

B R I T A I N

Patrol line formed to prevent German east coast raids, abandoned early November

Harwich

London

Chatham

Amsterdam

G E R M A N Y

Dover

Dover Barrage

Portsmouth

Calais

Plymouth

0   100 Nm
0   100 km

F R A N C E

THE NORTH SEA, 1939

- - - RAF CC air patrol lines

U-boat docks

BATTLE OF THE ATLANTIC, SEPTEMBER 1939 – MAY 1940

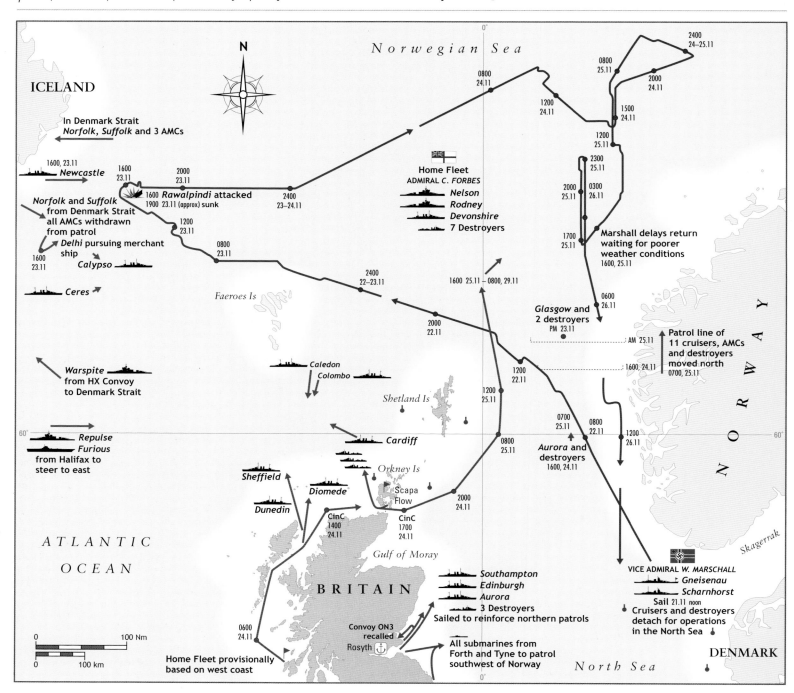

Norwegian Sea

N

ICELAND

In Denmark Strait
Norfolk, Suffolk and 3 AMCs

2400
24–25.11

0800
25.11

2000
24.11

1200
24.11

0800
24.11

1500
24.11

1200
25.11

1600, 23.11
Newcastle

1600
23.11

2000
23.11

2300
25.11

1600 *Rawalpindi* attacked
1900 23.11 (approx) sunk

2400
23–24.11

2000
25.11

0300
26.11

Norfolk and *Suffolk*
from Denmark Strait
all AMCs withdrawn
from patrol

1200
23.11

Home Fleet
ADMIRAL C. FORBES
  Nelson
  Rodney
  Devonshire
  7 Destroyers

1700
25.11

Marshall delays return
waiting for poorer
weather conditions
1600, 25.11

Delhi pursuing merchant
ship

0800
23.11

Calypso

1600
23.11

0600
26.11

Ceres

Faeroes Is

2400
22–23.11

1600 25.11 – 0800, 29.11

Glasgow and
2 destroyers
PM 23.11

Patrol line of
11 cruisers, AMCs
and destroyers
moved north
0700, 25.11

2000
22.11

AM 25.11

Warspite
from HX Convoy
to Denmark Strait

Caledon
Colombo

1200
22.11

1600, 24.11

1200
25.11

60°

Shetland Is

0700
25.11

0800
22.11

60°

Repulse

Furious
from Halifax to
steer to east

Cardiff

0800
25.11

1200
26.11

Aurora and
destroyers
1600, 24.11

Sheffield

Diomede

Orkney Is

**ATLANTIC
OCEAN**

Dunedin

Scapa
Flow

CinC
1400
24.11

CinC
1700
24.11

2000
24.11

Skagerrak

Gulf of Moray

VICE ADMIRAL W. MARSCHALL
  Gneisenau
  Scharnhorst

B R I T A I N

Southampton
Edinburgh
Aurora
3 Destroyers
Sailed to reinforce northern patrols

Sail 21.11 noon
Cruisers and destroyers
detach for operations
in the North Sea

0600
24.11

Convoy ON3
recalled

Rosyth ⚓

Home Fleet provisionally
based on west coast

All submarines from
Forth and Tyne to patrol
southwest of Norway

DENMARK

North Sea

0   100 Nm
0   100 km

0°

N   O   R   W   A   Y

THE DESTRUCTION OF THE *RAWALPINDI*

◄── Track of German
Task Force

◄── British movements

▮ Allied submarines

▮ German submarines

THE COMMERCE WAR in the Atlantic was one of the most complex, contested over the widest geographic area, and longest campaigns of the war. The Battle of the Atlantic, as it became known in 1940, began on 3 September with the sinking of the SS *Athenia* and continued until the last merchant ship and U-boat were sunk on the last day of the war, 8 May 1945. The British immediately introduced the convoy system upon the outbreak of hostilities as this provided the best means to reduce the chances of raiders finding ships in the vastness of the oceans, and allowed the limited escort forces to be used in the most efficient manner. Although U-boats sunk over 3,000 vessels by 1945, initially they were not considered the major threat owing to their limited numbers, allied anti-submarine defences and the long, dangerous approach routes they needed to take. The majority of allied merchant ships sunk in this first phase were not in convoys and the losses were sustainable. Indeed, by 1940 the initial U-boat campaign had begun to falter. By March eighteen out of the initially fifty-seven boats were lost, including crucially five out of eight of the original Type IX long-range boats. Of far greater concern to the British was the risk aircraft posed, particularly in the North Sea, and surface raiders. While convoys provided relatively good protection against submarines, their escorts could provide little defence against German heavy warships. This was demonstrated when the *Gneisenau* and *Scharnhorst* sunk the armed merchant cruiser *Rawalpindi* during their first Atlantic operation in November.

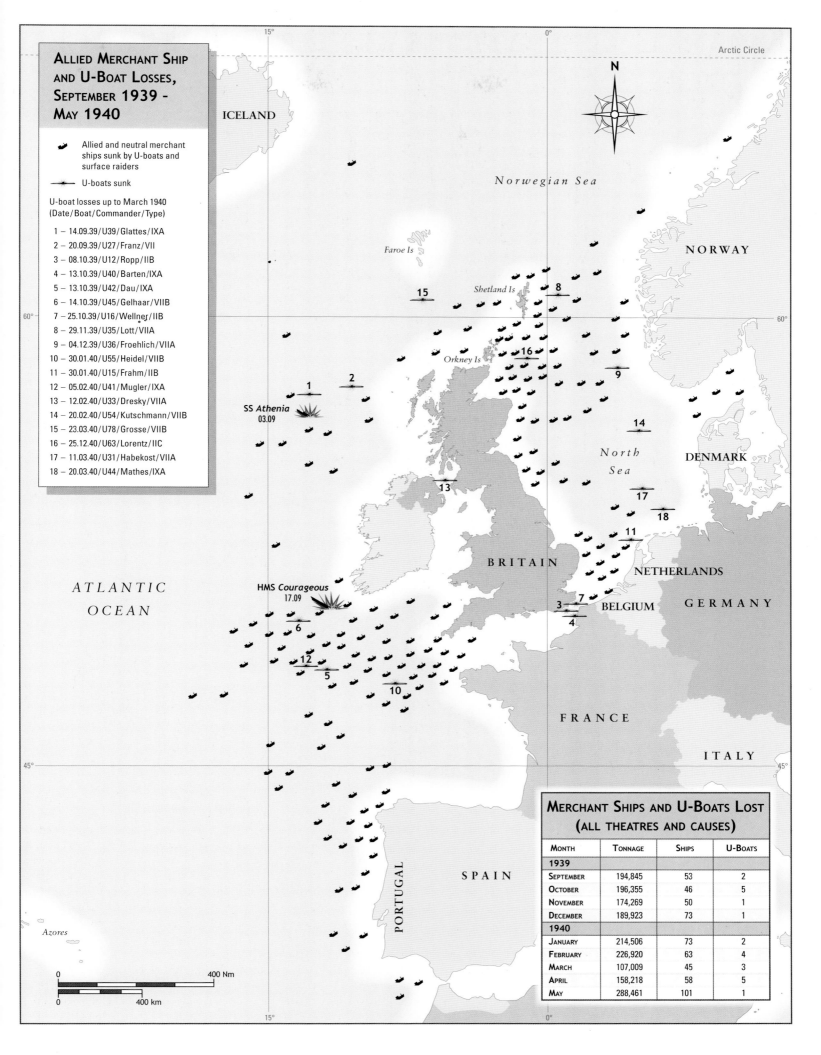

ALLIED MERCHANT SHIP
AND U-BOAT LOSSES,
SEPTEMBER 1939 –
MAY 1940

- Allied and neutral merchant ships sunk by U-boats and surface raiders
- U-boats sunk

U-boat losses up to March 1940
(Date / Boat / Commander / Type)

1 – 14.09.39 / U39 / Glattes / IXA
2 – 20.09.39 / U27 / Franz / VII
3 – 08.10.39 / U12 / Ropp / IIB
4 – 13.10.39 / U40 / Barten / IXA
5 – 13.10.39 / U42 / Dau / IXA
6 – 14.10.39 / U45 / Gelhaar / VIIB
7 – 25.10.39 / U16 / Wellner / IIB
8 – 29.11.39 / U35 / Lott / VIIA
9 – 04.12.39 / U36 / Froehlich / VIIA
10 – 30.01.40 / U55 / Heidel / VIIB
11 – 30.01.40 / U15 / Frahm / IIB
12 – 05.02.40 / U41 / Mugler / IXA
13 – 12.02.40 / U33 / Dresky / VIIA
14 – 20.02.40 / U54 / Kutschmann / VIIB
15 – 23.03.40 / U78 / Grosse / VIIB
16 – 25.12.40 / U63 / Lorentz / IIC
17 – 11.03.40 / U31 / Habekost / VIIA
18 – 20.03.40 / U44 / Mathes / IXA

MERCHANT SHIPS AND U-BOATS LOST (ALL THEATRES AND CAUSES)			
MONTH	TONNAGE	SHIPS	U-BOATS
1939			
SEPTEMBER	194,845	53	2
OCTOBER	196,355	46	5
NOVEMBER	174,269	50	1
DECEMBER	189,923	73	1
1940			
JANUARY	214,506	73	2
FEBRUARY	226,920	63	4
MARCH	107,009	45	3
APRIL	158,218	58	5
MAY	288,461	101	1

ATLANTIC OPERATIONS BY GERMAN SURFACE RAIDERS, 1939

IN LATE AUGUST two Panzerschiffe, the *Admiral Graf Spee* and *Deutschland*, left Germany to take up positions in the central and north Atlantic respectively. When these ships were designed and built in the early 1930s, oceanic commerce raiding had not been the primary requirement, but their long endurance, coupled with their ability to outfight cruisers and outrun most capital ships, made them ideal for this role. While U-boats would operate around Britain, the objective of the Panzerschiffe was to disrupt and destroy merchant shipping far out to sea. It was hoped that with the element of surprise allied shipping could be attacked before a proper convoy escort system was in place. However, Hitler did not authorise the ships to engage in commerce warfare until late September.

The British were only alerted to German surface raiders operating at sea when the survivors of the *Graf Spee*'s first victim were rescued off Brazil on 1 October.

The presence of the *Deutschland* was not known until later that month. The immediate response was to form eight anti-raider hunting groups as well as to order elements of the Home Fleet to escort Atlantic convoys to and from Halifax, Nova Scotia. The success of the surface raiders throughout the war cannot only be judged by the number of ships they sunk. In comparison to the U-boats' achievements the number was modest, but their disruptive effect on allied maritime communications and the allocation of naval forces was considerable.

Kapt.z.See Hans Langsdorff took the *Graf Spee* into the South Atlantic to hunt unprotected shipping, but after finding none off southern Africa moved towards the shipping lanes off South America in December. Here Commodore Henry Harwood engaged Langsdorff in the inconclusive Battle of the River Plate. The *Graf Spee* was eventually scuttled off Montevideo.

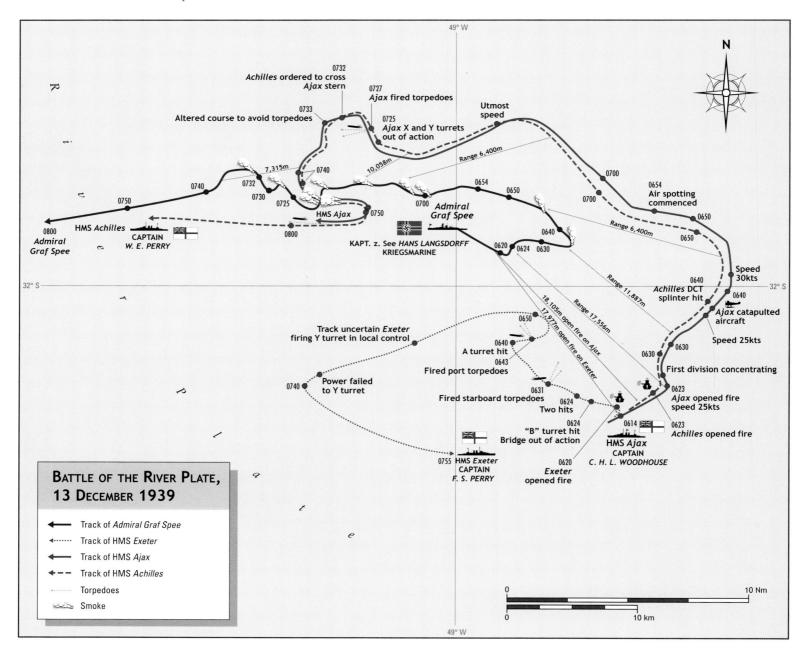

BATTLE OF THE RIVER PLATE, 13 DECEMBER 1939

- ← Track of *Admiral Graf Spee*
- ◄······ Track of HMS *Exeter*
- ← Track of HMS *Ajax*
- ◄ - - Track of HMS *Achilles*
- ······· Torpedoes
- Smoke

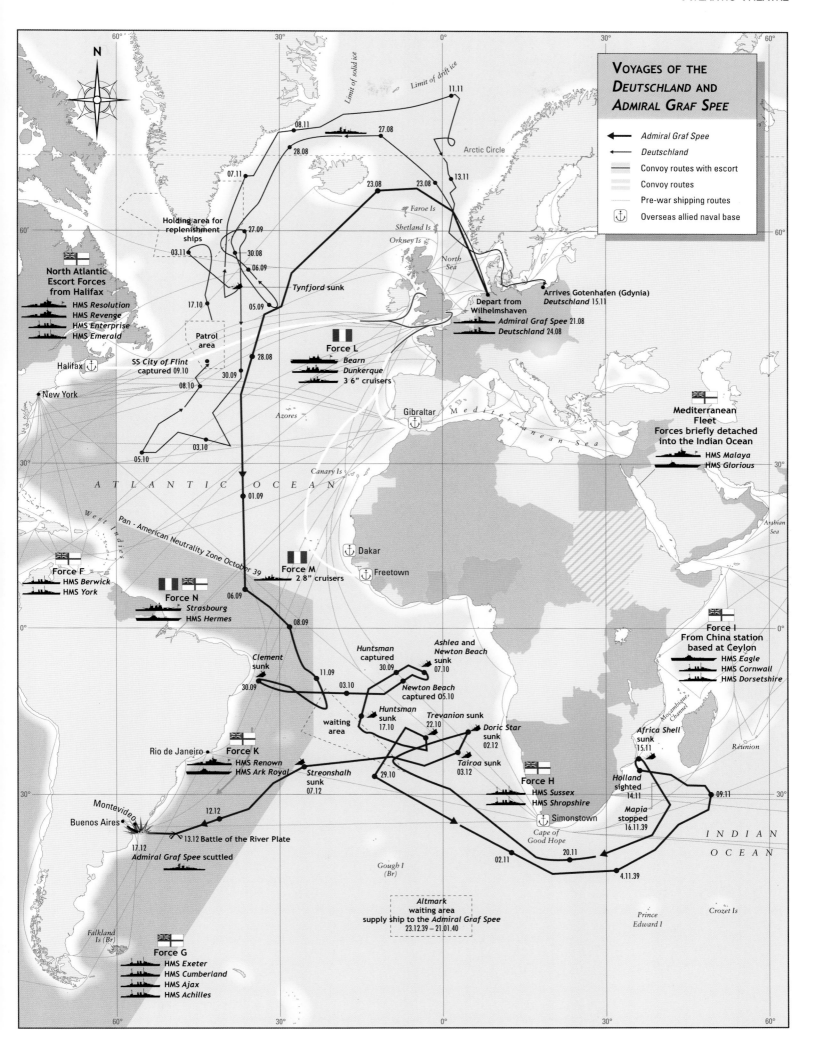

VOYAGES OF THE DEUTSCHLAND AND ADMIRAL GRAF SPEE

← Admiral Graf Spee
← Deutschland
  Convoy routes with escort
  Convoy routes
  Pre-war shipping routes
⚓ Overseas allied naval base

North Atlantic Escort Forces from Halifax
HMS *Resolution*
HMS *Revenge*
HMS *Enterprise*
HMS *Emerald*

Holding area for replenishment ships

Patrol area

SS City of Flint captured 09.10

Halifax ⚓

New York

Tynfjord sunk

Force L
Bearn
Dunkerque
3 6" cruisers

Depart from Wilhelmshaven
Admiral Graf Spee 21.08
Deutschland 24.08

Arrives Gotenhafen (Gdynia)
Deutschland 15.11

Gibraltar ⚓

Mediterranean Sea

Mediterranean Fleet Forces briefly detached into the Indian Ocean
HMS *Malaya*
HMS *Glorious*

Azores

Canary Is

ATLANTIC OCEAN

Pan-American Neutrality Zone October 39

West Indies

Force F
HMS *Berwick*
HMS *York*

Force N
Strasbourg
HMS *Hermes*

Force M
2 8" cruisers

Dakar ⚓
Freetown ⚓

Arabian Sea

Force I From China station based at Ceylon
HMS *Eagle*
HMS *Cornwall*
HMS *Dorsetshire*

Clement sunk

Huntsman captured 30.09

Ashlea and Newton Beach sunk 07.10

Newton Beach captured 05.10

waiting area

Huntsman sunk 17.10

Trevanion sunk 22.10

Doric Star sunk 02.12

Tairoa sunk 03.12

Africa Shell sunk 15.11

Réunion

Mozambique Channel

Rio de Janeiro

Force K
HMS *Renown*
HMS *Ark Royal*

Streonshalh sunk 07.12

Force H
HMS *Sussex*
HMS *Shropshire*

Simonstown ⚓

Holland sighted 14.11

Mapia stopped 16.11.39

Cape of Good Hope

Montevideo
Buenos Aires

13.12 Battle of the River Plate

17.12 *Admiral Graf Spee* scuttled

Gough I (Br)

Altmark waiting area supply ship to the *Admiral Graf Spee* 23.12.39 – 21.01.40

INDIAN OCEAN

Prince Edward I

Crozet Is

Falkland Is (Br)

Force G
HMS *Exeter*
HMS *Cumberland*
HMS *Ajax*
HMS *Achilles*

Faroe Is
Shetland Is
Orkney Is
North Sea
Arctic Circle
Limit of solid ice
Limit of drift ice

THE WAR AT SEA, 1940

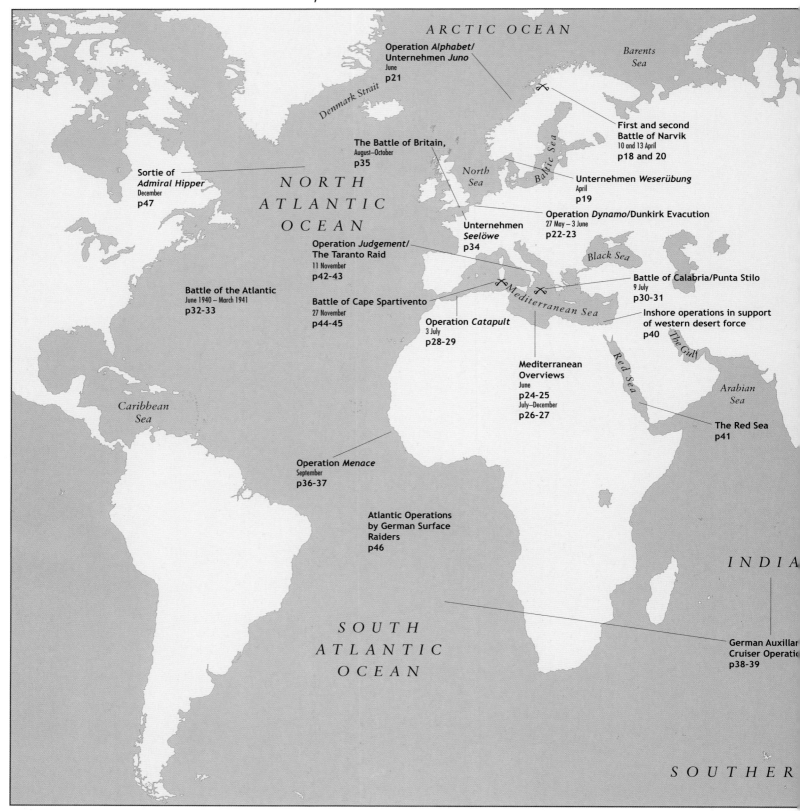

Operation *Alphabet*/
Unternehmen *Juno*
June
p21

First and second
Battle of Narvik
10 and 13 April
p18 and 20

Unternehmen *Weserübung*
April
p19

The Battle of Britain,
August–October
p35

Operation *Dynamo*/Dunkirk Evacution
27 May – 3 June
p22-23

Sortie of
Admiral Hipper
December
p47

Unternehmen
Seelöwe
p34

Operation *Judgement*/
The Taranto Raid
11 November
p42-43

Battle of Calabria/Punta Stilo
9 July
p30-31

Battle of the Atlantic
June 1940 – March 1941
p32-33

Battle of Cape Spartivento
27 November
p44-45

Inshore operations in support
of western desert force
p40

Operation *Catapult*
3 July
p28-29

Mediterranean
Overviews
June
p24-25
July–December
p26-27

The Red Sea
p41

Operation *Menace*
September
p36-37

Atlantic Operations
by German Surface
Raiders
p46

German Auxillar
Cruiser Operatic
p38-39

ARCTIC OCEAN

Barents Sea

Denmark Strait

NORTH
ATLANTIC
OCEAN

North Sea

Baltic Sea

Black Sea

Mediterranean Sea

Caribbean Sea

Red Sea

The Gulf

Arabian Sea

SOUTH
ATLANTIC
OCEAN

INDIA

SOUTHER

THE WAR AT SEA underwent a profound transformation in 1940. At the beginning of the year the allies held almost complete command of the sea and had effectively deflected the initial German attack on maritime communications. Merchant ship losses were at acceptable levels while the Germans had lost a significant number of their frontline U-boats. Operations were restricted to the waters around the British Isles and the North Sea, but by the early spring these had declined considerably as the German prepared for Unternehmen *Weserübung*.

The invasion of Norway and the defeat of the allied expeditionary force sent to assist the Norwegians,

coupled with the defeat of France in the early summer, altered Germany's geostrategic position considerably. It now possessed bases on the British flanks and could project naval forces far into the Atlantic. As British naval strategy throughout the inter-war years had focused on commerce protection in home waters, the Royal Navy now lacked the resources to adequately protect the oceanic sea-lanes.

The Italian declaration of war on 10 June opened up a new theatre of operations in the Mediterranean. The Royal Navy could deal with an Italo-German naval combination as the basis of pre-war planning had been a war against two opponents. However, the

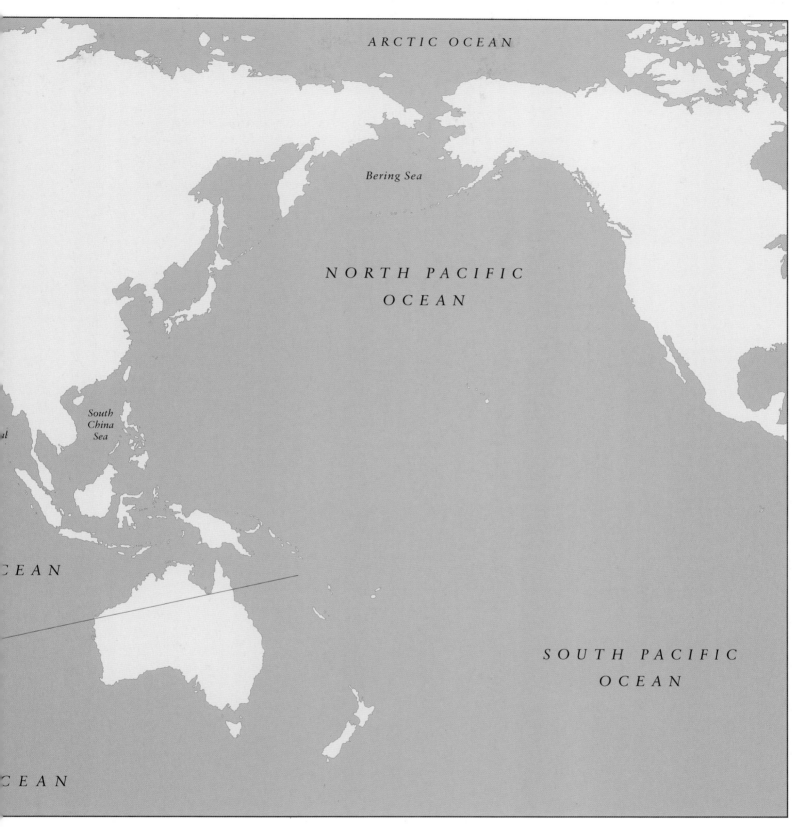

unexpected collapse of France opened the question about the fate of the relatively modern French fleet. To prevent its capture it had taken refuge in French African ports, but if it fell into German hands the axis would have sufficient naval forces to challenge British naval supremacy. French bases in North and West Africa would also give Axis forces greater access to the central and southern Atlantic. Consequently, neutralising the French fleet, particularly its capital ships, became the foremost British priority during the summer.

At the same time the threat of an invasion of Britain itself, Operation *Seelöwe*, was the highest it had been for nearly one and a half centuries. The outcome of the Battle

of Britain, the aerial battle over southeast Britain, and the concentration of cruisers, destroyers and light forces by the Royal Navy in southern ports led the Germans to postpone any invasion attempt. Instead, a maritime-air blockade of the British Isles was instituted in an attempt to starve Britain into submission. The intensity increased throughout the autumn with progressively more surface raiders, auxiliary cruisers and U-boats becoming available to attack convoy routes.

In the Mediterranean a number of fleet engagements and minor actions took place throughout the summer and autumn as both sides attempted to protect their supply lines while interdicting their opponents.

Unternehmen Weserübung, The German Invasion of Norway, 7–10 April 1940

In the first months of the war the British government struggled to find a way of cutting Germany's iron ore supply while maintaining Norwegian neutrality and not giving the Germans an excuse to occupy the country. Ultimately, this proved impossible as, when the winter shipments began, German vessels used the protection of the Norwegian Leads, the inner seas between the mainland and outer islands, making it nearly impossible to interdict the supply. Offensive action was needed.

The Kriegsmarine had long desired to break out of the North Sea, or 'wet triangle', and planning for an occupation of Norway and Denmark began in January 1940. Both sides' plans developed in parallel, though oblivious to the others' intentions. The British intended to lay mines, particularly in the approaches to Narvik. To deal with any German retaliation against Norway an expeditionary force was held ready to occupy the Narvik area and secure the key port of Stavanger in the south. The scale and audacious nature of Unternehmen Weserübung caught the British by surprise. Faced with overwhelming allied naval superiority the Germans opted to simultaneously take key Norwegian and Danish positions on a broad front involving eleven separate landings and numerous parachute drops.

Just as British destroyers and minelayers were undertaking Operation Wilfred, the mining operation on 7 April, intelligence suggested that a major German operation was underway. Assuming that this would be another Atlantic breakout R4, the landing operation, was abandoned and the Home Fleet sortied to cover the exits to the Atlantic, and by the time German intentions became clear it was too late to intercept the invasion forces. Although German forces succeeded in capturing most objectives in the opening phase, the naval losses were substantial, notably the sinking of the new heavy cruiser Blücher in Oslo Fjord. In two battles in the Ofotfjord, off Narvik, the entire German naval force was annihilated leaving the disembarked forces in a precarious position when allied reinforcements arrived on 14 April to assist the Norwegian defenders.

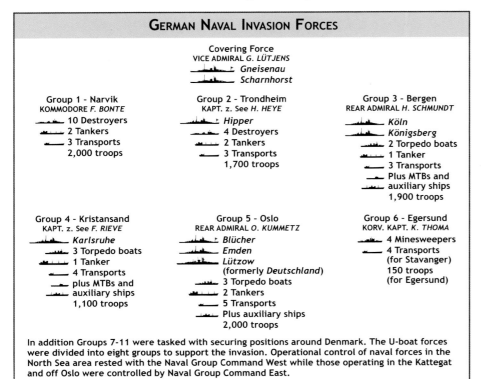

German Naval Invasion Forces

Covering Force
VICE ADMIRAL G. LÜTJENS
Gneisenau
Scharnhorst

Group 1 - Narvik
KOMMODORE F. BONTE
10 Destroyers
2 Tankers
3 Transports
2,000 troops

Group 2 - Trondheim
KAPT. z. See H. HEYE
Hipper
4 Destroyers
2 Tankers
3 Transports
1,700 troops

Group 3 - Bergen
REAR ADMIRAL H. SCHMUNDT
Köln
Königsberg
2 Torpedo boats
1 Tanker
3 Transports
Plus MTBs and
auxiliary ships
1,900 troops

Group 4 - Kristansand
KAPT. z. See F. RIEVE
Karlsruhe
3 Torpedo boats
1 Tanker
4 Transports
plus MTBs and
auxiliary ships
1,100 troops

Group 5 - Oslo
REAR ADMIRAL O. KUMMETZ
Blücher
Emden
Lützow
(formerly Deutschland)
3 Torpedo boats
2 Tankers
5 Transports
Plus auxiliary ships
2,000 troops

Group 6 - Egersund
KORV. KAPT. K. THOMA
4 Minesweepers
4 Transports
(for Stavanger)
150 troops
(for Egersund)

In addition Groups 7-11 were tasked with securing positions around Denmark. The U-boat forces were divided into eight groups to support the invasion. Operational control of naval forces in the North Sea area rested with the Naval Group Command West while those operating in the Kattegat and off Oslo were controlled by Naval Group Command East.

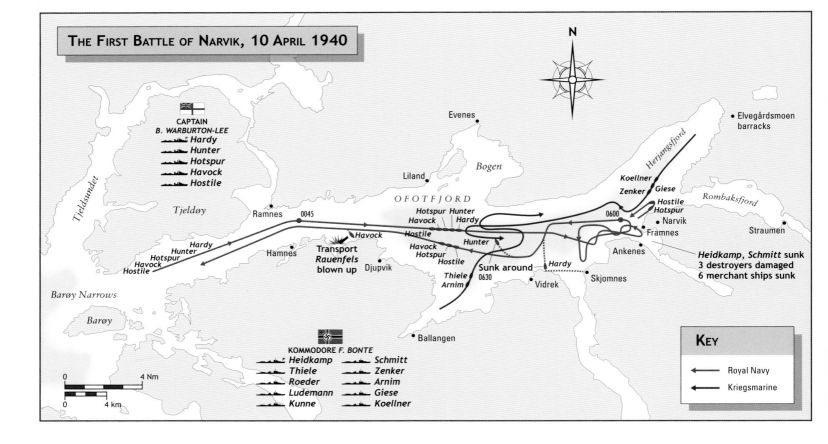

The First Battle of Narvik, 10 April 1940

N

CAPTAIN
B. WARBURTON-LEE
Hardy
Hunter
Hotspur
Havock
Hostile

Evenes

Elvegårdsmoen barracks

Herjangsfjord

Bogen

Liland

Koellner
Zenker · Giese

Rombaksfjord

Tjeldsundet

Tjeldøy

Ramnes   0045

OFOTFJORD

Hotspur Hunter
Havock   Hardy

Hostile
Hotspur

0600

Narvik

Straumen

Framnes

Hardy
Hunter
Hotspur
Havock
Hostile

Havock

Hamnes

Transport
Rauenfels
blown up   Djupvik

Hostile

Havock
Hotspur
Hostile

Thiele
Arnim

Hunter

Sunk around
0630

Hardy

Ankenes

Vidrek   Skjomnes

Heidkamp, Schmitt sunk
3 destroyers damaged
6 merchant ships sunk

Barøy Narrows

Barøy

Ballangen

KOMMODORE F. BONTE
Heidkamp   Schmitt
Thiele   Zenker
Roeder   Arnim
Ludemann   Giese
Kunne   Koellner

0   4 Nm

0   4 km

Key

Royal Navy

Kriegsmarine

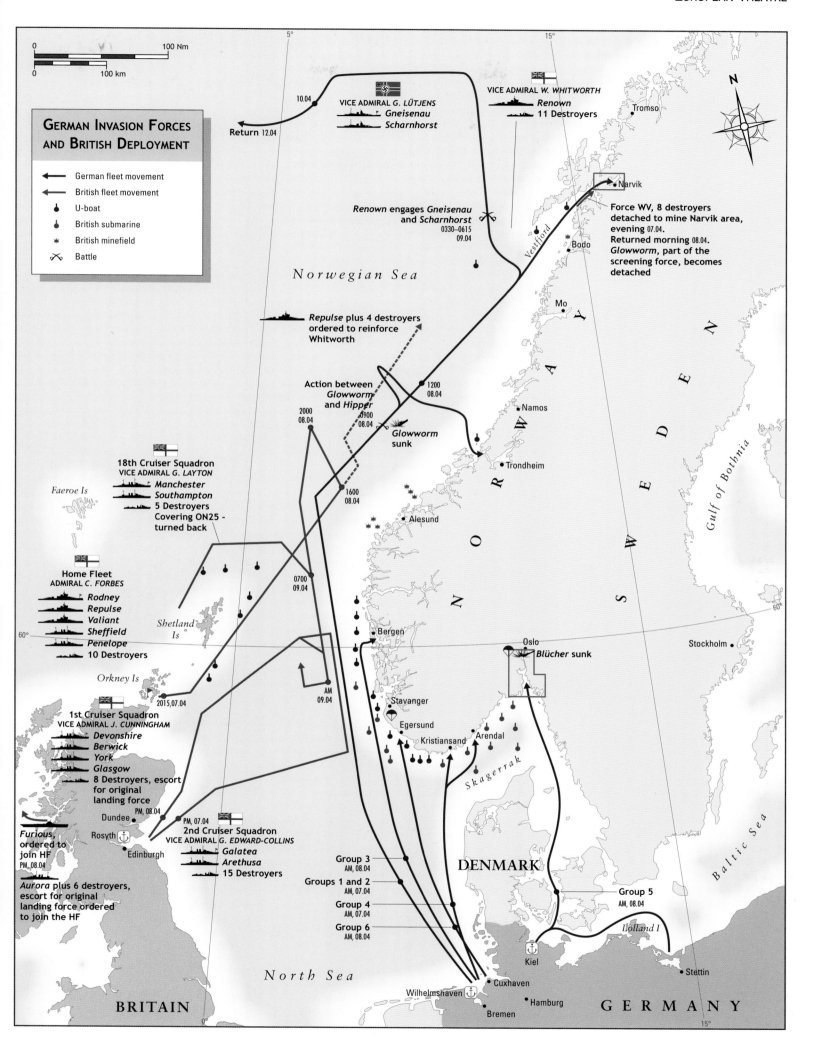

GERMAN INVASION FORCES
AND BRITISH DEPLOYMENT

0 ————— 100 Nm
0 ————— 100 km

German fleet movement
British fleet movement
U-boat
British submarine
British minefield
Battle

VICE ADMIRAL G. LÜTJENS
Gneisenau
Scharnhorst

VICE ADMIRAL W. WHITWORTH
Renown
11 Destroyers

10.04
Return 12.04

Renown engages *Gneisenau*
and *Scharnhorst*
0330–0615
09.04

Force WV, 8 destroyers
detached to mine Narvik area,
evening 07.04.
Returned morning 08.04.
Glowworm, part of the
screening force, becomes
detached

Narvik

Tromso

Bodo

Mo

Vestfiord

Norwegian Sea

Repulse plus 4 destroyers
ordered to reinforce
Whitworth

Namos

Action between
Glowworm and *Hipper*

2000
08.04
0900
08.04
0700
09.04

1200
08.04

Glowworm
sunk

Trondheim

18th Cruiser Squadron
VICE ADMIRAL G. LAYTON
Manchester
Southampton
5 Destroyers
Covering ON25 -
turned back

1600
08.04

Alesund

Faeroe Is

Home Fleet
ADMIRAL C. FORBES
Rodney
Repulse
Valiant
Sheffield
Penelope
10 Destroyers

Gulf of Bothnia

60°

Bergen

Stockholm

Shetland
Is

AM
09.04

Oslo

Blücher sunk

Orkney Is

2015,07.04

Stavanger

1st Cruiser Squadron
VICE ADMIRAL J. CUNNINGHAM
Devonshire
Berwick
York
Glasgow
8 Destroyers, escort
for original
landing force

Egersund

Kristiansand

Arendal

Skagerrak

Furious,
ordered to
join HF
PM,08.04

Dundee
PM, 08.04
Rosyth

Edinburgh

PM, 07.04
2nd Cruiser Squadron
VICE ADMIRAL G. EDWARD-COLLINS
Galatea
Arethusa
15 Destroyers

DENMARK

Baltic Sea

Aurora plus 6 destroyers,
escort for original
landing force ordered
to join the HF

Group 3
AM, 08.04

Groups 1 and 2
AM, 07.04

Group 4
AM, 07.04

Group 6
AM, 08.04

Group 5
AM, 08.04

Lolland I

Kiel

North Sea

Wilhelmshaven

Cuxhaven

Stettin

BRITAIN

Bremen

Hamburg

GERMANY

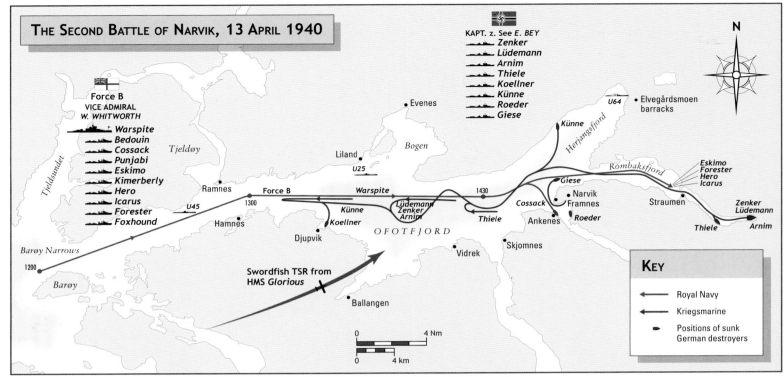

The Second Battle of Narvik, 13 April 1940

KAPT. z. See E. BEY
- Zenker
- Lüdemann
- Arnim
- Thiele
- Koellner
- Künne
- Roeder
- Giese

Force B
VICE ADMIRAL W. WHITWORTH
- Warspite
- Bedouin
- Cossack
- Punjabi
- Eskimo
- Kimerberly
- Hero
- Icarus
- Forester
- Foxhound

Tjeldøy · Tjeldsundet · Barøy Narrows · Barøy

Ramnes · Hamnes · Djupvik · Vidrek · Ballangen · Skjomnes

Evenes · Liland · Bogen · Herjangsfjord · Künne · Elvegårdsmoen barracks · U64

OFOTFJORD · Ankenes · Narvik · Framnes · Straumen · Rombaksfjord

Eskimo Forester Hero Icarus · Zenker Lüdemann · Thiele · Arnim

Giese · Cossack · Roeder · Thiele · Lüdemann Zenker Arnim · Künne · Koellner · Warspite · Force B

U45 · U25 · 1300 · 1430 · 1200

Swordfish TSR from HMS *Glorious*

0 — 4 Nm
0 — 4 km

Key
- Royal Navy
- Kriegsmarine
- Positions of sunk German destroyers

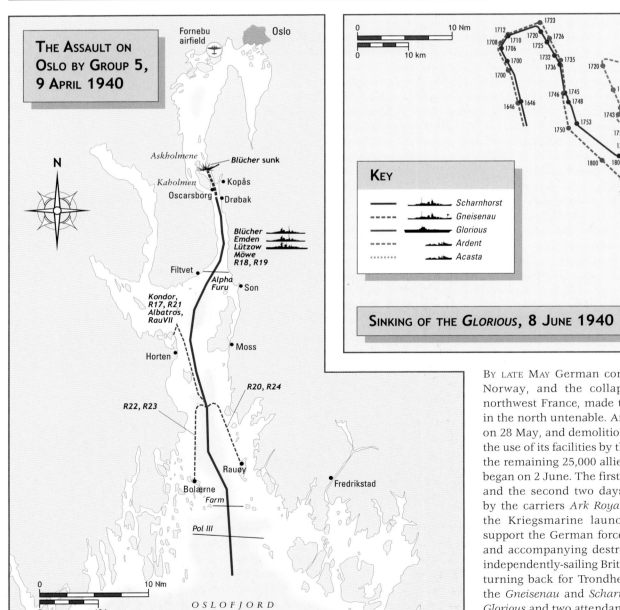

The Assault on Oslo by Group 5, 9 April 1940

Fornebu airfield · Oslo

Askholmene · *Blücher* sunk · Kopås · Kaholmen · Oscarsborg · Drøbak

Blücher Emden Lützow Möwe R18, R19

Filtvet · Alpha Furu · Son

Kondor, R17, R21 Albatros, RauVII

Horten · Moss · R20, R24 · R22, R23 · Rauøy · Bolærne Farm · Pol III · Fredrikstad

OSLOFJORD

0 — 10 Nm
0 — 10 km

Sinking of the *Glorious*, 8 June 1940

Key
- Scharnhorst
- Gneisenau
- Glorious
- Ardent
- Acasta

0 — 10 Nm
0 — 10 km

By late May German control of central and southern Norway, and the collapse of the allied armies in northwest France, made the remaining allied positions in the north untenable. After Narvik itself was captured on 28 May, and demolition work undertaken to prevent the use of its facilities by the Germans, the evacuation of the remaining 25,000 allied troops and their equipment began on 2 June. The first troop convoy sailed on 6 June and the second two days later under cover provided by the carriers *Ark Royal* and *Glorious*. Concurrently, the Kriegsmarine launched Unternehmen *Juno*, to support the German forces around Narvik. The *Hipper* and accompanying destroyers managed to sink some independently-sailing British transports on 8 June before turning back for Trondheim to refuel. That afternoon the *Gneisenau* and *Scharnhorst* encountered and sunk *Glorious* and two attendant destroyers, which had sailed ahead of the second evacuation convoy.

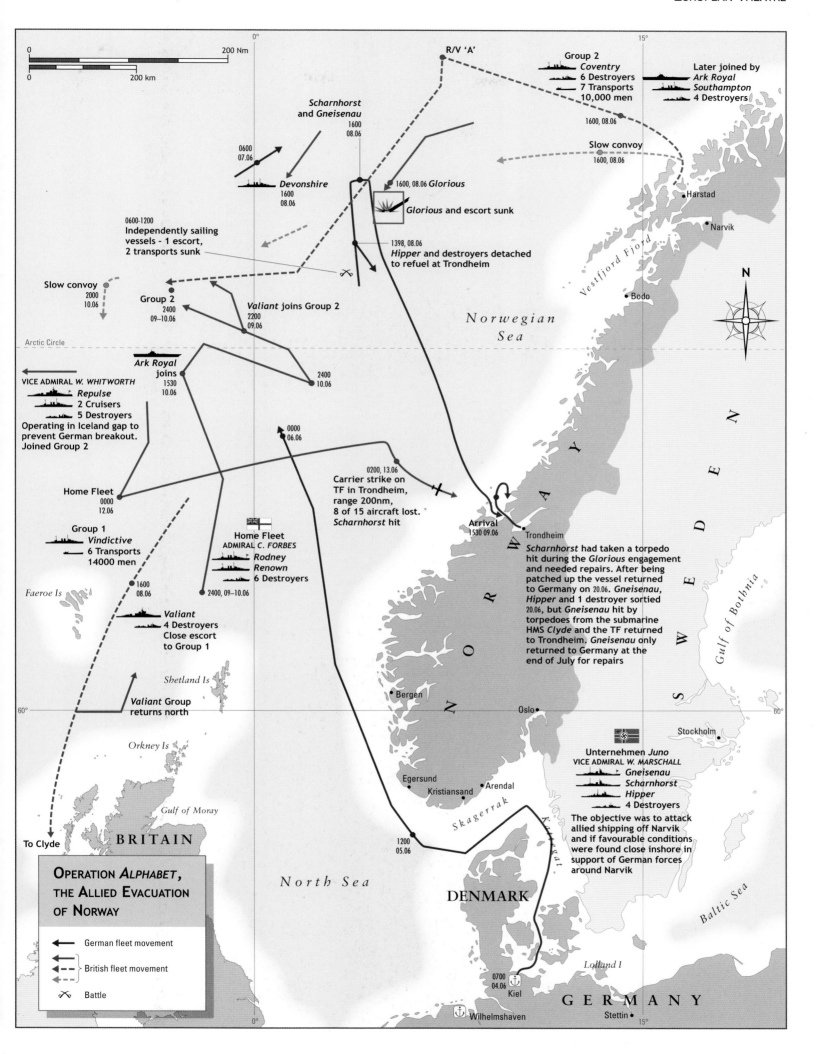

0 — 200 Nm
0 — 200 km

R/V 'A'

Group 2
Coventry
6 Destroyers
7 Transports
10,000 men

Later joined by
Ark Royal
Southampton
4 Destroyers

1600, 08.06

Harstad

Narvik

Scharnhorst
and Gneisenau
1600
08.06

0600
07.06

Slow convoy
1600, 08.06

Devonshire
1600
08.06

1600, 08.06 Glorious

Glorious and escort sunk

0600-1200
Independently sailing
vessels - 1 escort,
2 transports sunk

1398, 08.06
Hipper and destroyers detached
to refuel at Trondheim

Vestfjord Fjord

Bodo

Norwegian
Sea

Slow convoy
2000
10.06

Group 2
2400
09-10.06

Valiant joins Group 2
2200
09.06

2400
10.06

Arctic Circle

Ark Royal
joins
1530
10.06

VICE ADMIRAL W. WHITWORTH
Repulse
2 Cruisers
5 Destroyers
Operating in Iceland gap to
prevent German breakout.
Joined Group 2

0000
06.06

0200, 13.06
Carrier strike on
TF in Trondheim,
range 200nm,
8 of 15 aircraft lost.
Scharnhorst hit

Home Fleet
0000
12.06

Arrival
1530 09.06

Trondheim

Scharnhorst had taken a torpedo
hit during the Glorious engagement
and needed repairs. After being
patched up the vessel returned
to Germany on 20.06. Gneisenau,
Hipper and 1 destroyer sortied
20.06, but Gneisenau hit by
torpedoes from the submarine
HMS Clyde and the TF returned
to Trondheim. Gneisenau only
returned to Germany at the
end of July for repairs

Group 1
Vindictive
6 Transports
14000 men

Home Fleet
ADMIRAL C. FORBES
Rodney
Renown
6 Destroyers

N
O
R
W
A
Y

S
W
E
D
E
N

Gulf of Bothnia

Faeroe Is

1600
08.06

Valiant
4 Destroyers
Close escort
to Group 1

2400, 09-10.06

Shetland Is

Bergen

60°

Valiant Group
returns north

Oslo

Stockholm

Orkney Is

Unternehmen Juno
VICE ADMIRAL W. MARSCHALL
Gneisenau
Scharnhorst
Hipper
4 Destroyers

To Clyde

Gulf of Moray

BRITAIN

Egersund

Kristiansand

Arendal

The objective was to attack
allied shipping off Narvik
and if favourable conditions
were found close inshore in
support of German forces
around Narvik

Skagerrak

1200
05.06

Kattegat

North Sea

DENMARK

Baltic Sea

Lolland I

OPERATION ALPHABET,
THE ALLIED EVACUATION
OF NORWAY

0700
04.06
Kiel

G E R M A N Y

Stettin

Wilhelmshaven

German fleet movement
British fleet movement
Battle

OPERATION DYNAMO, THE DUNKIRK EVACUATION, 27 MAY – 3 JUNE 1940

EXTRACTING AN ARMY from an enemy held shoreline ranks amongst the most complex and dangerous of naval operations. Keeping the cohesion of the military forces, particularly in the aftermath of a defeat, in an ever-diminishing beachhead requires careful planning and sea and air control during the vulnerable embarkation phase. Amphibious withdrawals are rare yet within a year the Royal Navy conducted four such operations from Norway, France, Greece and Crete. Of these the Dunkirk evacuation stands out as one of the most spectacular and decisive feats of the war.

On 10 May *Fall Gelb*, the German attack on France and the Low Countries, commenced and by late 20 May lead elements had reached the English Channel near the port of Abbeville. This trapped the British Expeditionary Force, three French armies and the Belgian army in a pocket between Boulogne and the eastern tip of Belgian territory. The weakness of the allied position in northeastern France was obvious and on the same day British planning for a potential evacuation of the BEF began under the direction of Admiral Sir Bertram Ramsay in command at Dover. In the first weeks of the German offensive allied naval forces had provided support, demolished port facilities and undertaken some evacuations along the Dutch and Belgian coasts. Now the emphasis shifted to the French ports of Boulogne, Calais and the defensive perimeter around Dunkirk.

Destroyers brought in more forces to destroy the ports and evacuate allied personnel from the towns. However, the positions were untenable: Boulogne and Calais surrendered on the 25 and 27 May respectively.

The German offensive against the bulk of the allied forces around Dunkirk halted between the 24 and 27 allowing the perimeter defences to be reorganised. The evacuation plan, Operation *Dynamo*, was put into effect late on 26 May and the first troops were brought off the next day. Expectations were limited, it was assumed that at the most 45,000 troops could be evacuated in the face of heavy German air and ground attacks. Initially evacuations only took place from Dunkirk harbour with modest results. To increase the rate troops were embarked directly from the Mole and the arrival of many small vessels allowed troops to be taken off the beaches.

After Dunkirk further evacuations took place. Operation *Cycle* involved the destruction of part of Le Havre harbour and Operation *Aerial* encompassed further evacuations of allied forces and civilians from Channel and Atlantic ports. It was during one such evacuation that the liner *Lancastria* was sunk with the loss of around 4,000 people, the single largest loss in British maritime history.

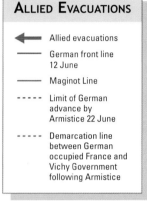

ALLIED EVACUATIONS

- Allied evacuations
- German front line 12 June
- Maginot Line
- Limit of German advance by Armistice 22 June
- Demarcation line between German occupied France and Vichy Government following Armistice

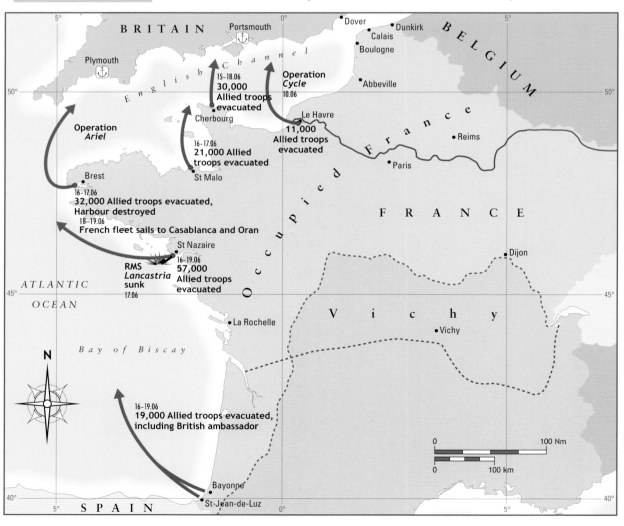

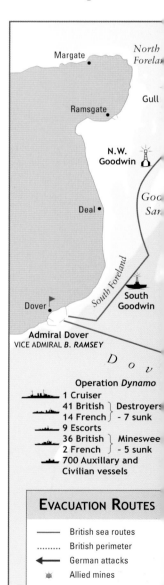

Admiral Dover
VICE ADMIRAL *B. RAMSEY*

Operation *Dynamo*

- 1 Cruiser
- 41 British } Destroyers
- 14 French } - 7 sunk
- 9 Escorts
- 36 British } Minesweepers
- 2 French } - 5 sunk
- 700 Auxillary and Civilian vessels

EVACUATION ROUTES

- British sea routes
- British perimeter
- German attacks
- Allied mines

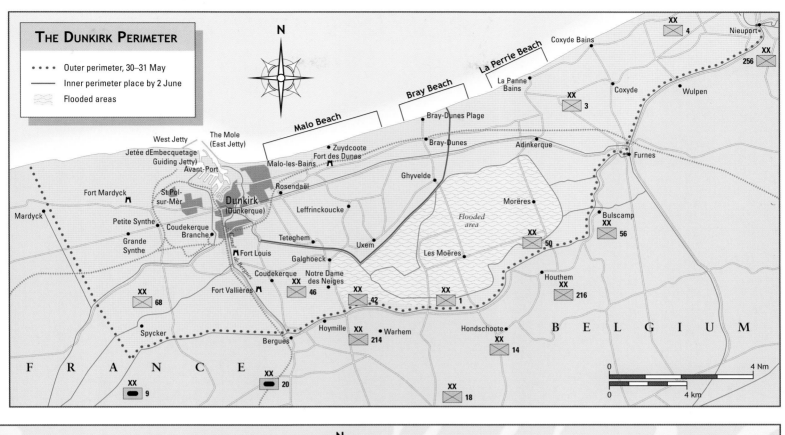

THE DUNKIRK PERIMETER

- •••• Outer perimeter, 30–31 May
- —— Inner perimeter place by 2 June
- 〰〰 Flooded areas

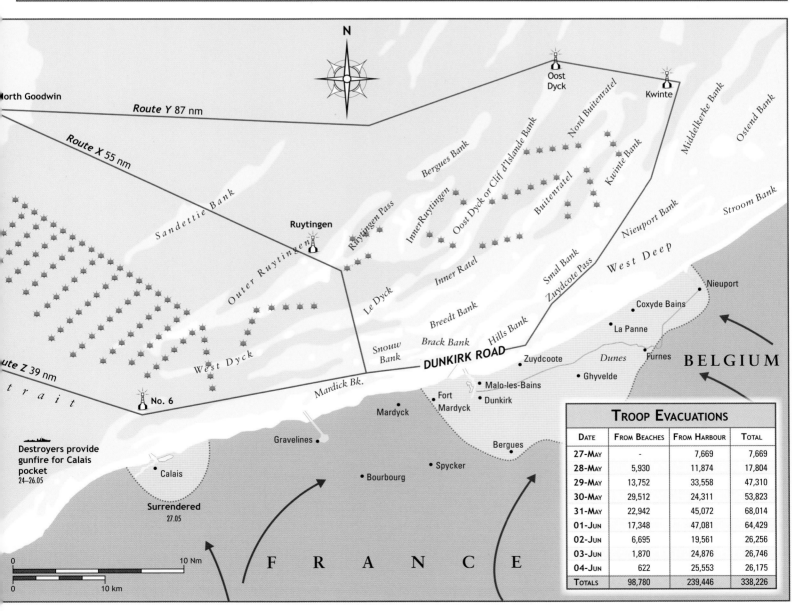

Route Y 87 nm

Route X 55 nm

Route Z 39 nm

Destroyers provide gunfire for Calais pocket 24–26.05

Surrendered 27.05

TROOP EVACUATIONS

DATE	FROM BEACHES	FROM HARBOUR	TOTAL
27-MAY	-	7,669	7,669
28-MAY	5,930	11,874	17,804
29-MAY	13,752	33,558	47,310
30-MAY	29,512	24,311	53,823
31-MAY	22,942	45,072	68,014
01-JUN	17,348	47,081	64,429
02-JUN	6,695	19,561	26,256
03-JUN	1,870	24,876	26,746
04-JUN	622	25,553	26,175
TOTALS	98,780	239,446	338,226

THE NAVAL SITUATION IN THE MEDITERRANEAN, JUNE 1940

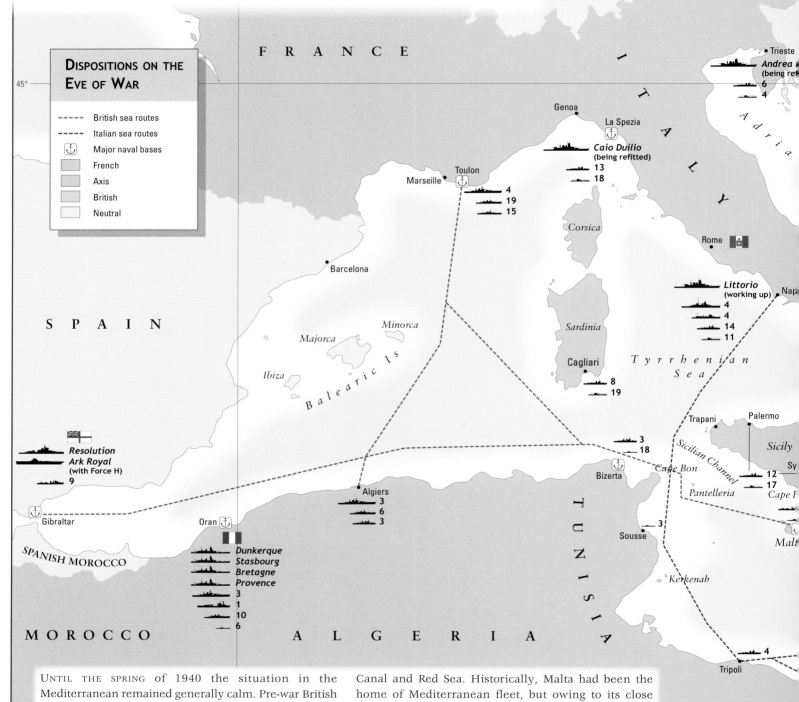

DISPOSITIONS ON THE EVE OF WAR

- - - - British sea routes
- - - - Italian sea routes
⚓ Major naval bases
▓ French
▓ Axis
▓ British
☐ Neutral

GERMAN

FRANCE

Trieste
Andrea
(being ref...)
6
4

Genoa

La Spezia ⚓
Caio Duilio
(being refitted)
13
18

Toulon ⚓
Marseille
4
19
15

Corsica

Rome 🏴

Littorio
(working up)
4
4
14
11
Nap...

Barcelona

SPAIN

Minorca

Majorca

Sardinia

T y r r h e n i a n   S e a

Ibiza

Cagliari
8
19

B a l e a r i c   I s

Trapani   Palermo

Sicilian Channel   *Sicily*

3
18

Sy...

⚓ Bizerta
Cape Bon
12
17
Cape...

Resolution
Ark Royal
(with Force H)
9

Pantelleria

Mal...

⚓ Gibraltar

Oran ⚓
Algiers
3
6
3

3

Sousse

SPANISH MOROCCO

Dunkerque
Stasbourg
Bretagne
Provence
3
1
10
6

T
U
N
I
S
I
A

Kerkenah

4

MOROCCO

A L G E R I A

Tripoli

UNTIL THE SPRING of 1940 the situation in the Mediterranean remained generally calm. Pre-war British and French plans had assumed that Italy would enter a European war on the side of Germany at the outset. In reality, Italy was not prepared for war in 1939 and from a naval perspective could not challenge Anglo-French supremacy. The Mediterranean Sea was a complex maritime theatre at the crossroads of competing interests. For the British it was a vital maritime artery as the majority of imperial trade with India and the Far East was transported through it rather than around the longer Cape route. Three strategically located bases, Gibraltar, Malta and Alexandria, secured the passage to and from the Atlantic and Indian Ocean via the Suez

Canal and Red Sea. Historically, Malta had been the home of Mediterranean fleet, but owing to its close proximity to Italian air bases and the poor state of its defences, the decision was taken to develop Alexandria as a naval base. However, work on the facilities only began in 1939 and was far from complete.

For the French, the Mediterranean was vital because it linked Metropolitan France to its most important colonial possession, French North Africa. In the event of war African troop reinforcements and supplies would play a significant role in overall French strategy. Although the actual sea-lanes between Metropolitan and African France were short, the proximity of Italian bases, the short-range but high-speed characteristics of many

Italian warships, and the large Italian submarine force constituted a serious threat. To the Italians, at the centre of the sea, the re-establishment of a Mediterranean empire was seen as the crucial step towards becoming a great power. Its north and east African possessions were linked by means of the sea and, more recently, in April 1939, Italian forces had also occupied Albania.

After the outbreak of hostilities in September 1939 allied naval forces in the Mediterranean were slightly reduced as reinforcements were sent to the North Sea and the anti-raider groups in the Atlantic. As the Mediterranean was quiet and could be considered reasonably safe owing to the control of its exits, it was also used as a training ground for newly-commissioned vessels and crews. The allies divided the Mediterranean into two sectors. The French would take responsibility for the western half while the British assumed responsibility for the eastern sector.

In March 1940 Italian troop convoys to Libya increased and in April, while allied attention was diverted by the German invasion of Norway, naval activity in the central Mediterranean expanded. The first defensive minefields were also laid off Albania. As tensions grew throughout the spring the allies gradually augmented their naval forces. The modernised battleship, *Warspite*, fresh from its success at Narvik, arrived at the end of April to become the flagship of the Mediterranean Fleet. As a sign of the progressively worsening situation, British shipping was ordered to halt passages through the Mediterranean on 27 April and instead sail around the Cape of Good Hope.

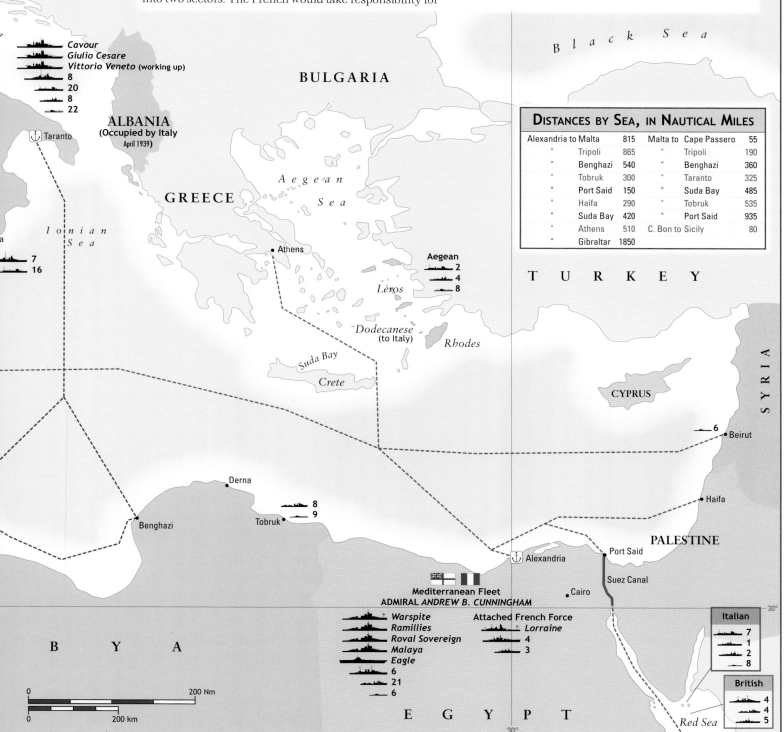

DISTANCES BY SEA, IN NAUTICAL MILES

Alexandria to	Malta	815	Malta to	Cape Passero	55
"	Tripoli	865	"	Tripoli	190
"	Benghazi	540	"	Benghazi	360
"	Tobruk	300	"	Taranto	325
"	Port Said	150	"	Suda Bay	485
"	Haifa	290	"	Tobruk	535
"	Suda Bay	420	"	Port Said	935
"	Athens	510	C. Bon to	Sicily	80
"	Gibraltar	1850			

Mediterranean Fleet
ADMIRAL *ANDREW B. CUNNINGHAM*

		Attached French Force	
Warspite		*Lorraine*	
Ramillies			4
Roval Sovereign			3
Malaya			
Eagle	6		
	21		
	6		

Italian

	7
	1
	2
	8

British

	4
	4
	5

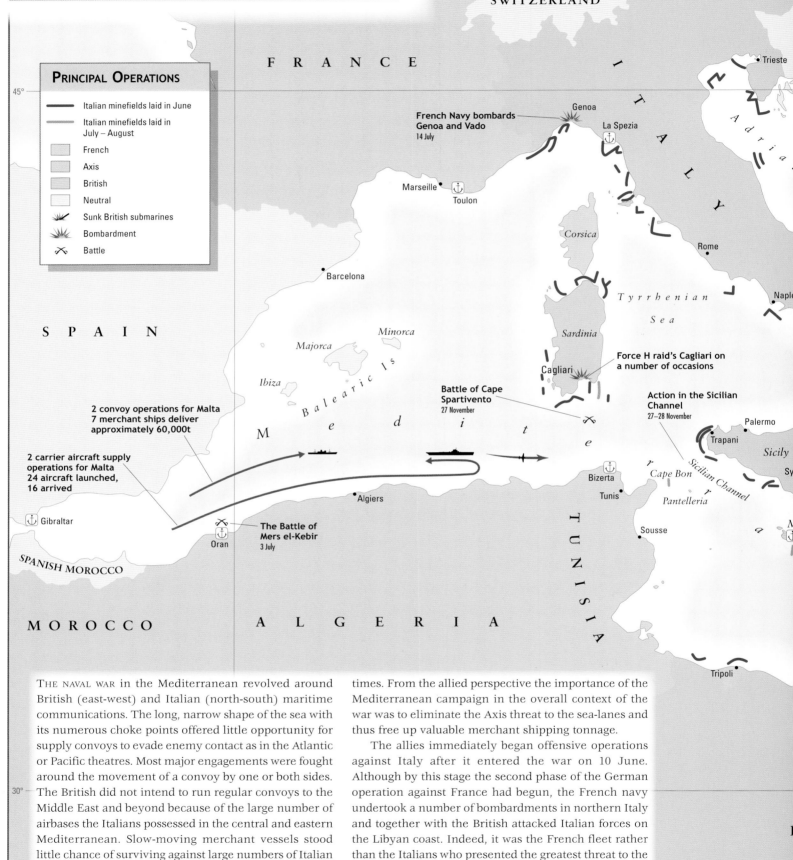

THE MEDITERRANEAN, JULY – DECEMBER 1940

GERMANY

SWITZERLAND

FRANCE

PRINCIPAL OPERATIONS

45° —

— Italian minefields laid in June

— Italian minefields laid in July – August

French

Axis

British

Neutral

Sunk British submarines

Bombardment

Battle

French Navy bombards Genoa and Vado
14 July

Genoa

La Spezia

Marseille

Toulon

Corsica

Rome

Trieste

Adriatic

Barcelona

SPAIN

Minorca

Majorca

Tyrrhenian Sea

Sardinia

Naples

Ibiza

Balearic Is

Cagliari

Force H raid's Cagliari on a number of occasions

2 convoy operations for Malta 7 merchant ships deliver approximately 60,000t

Battle of Cape Spartivento
27 November

Action in the Sicilian Channel
27–28 November

Palermo

Trapani

Sicily

2 carrier aircraft supply operations for Malta 24 aircraft launched, 16 arrived

M   e   d   i   t   e   r   r   a   n   e

Cape Bon

Bizerta

Tunis

Sicilian Channel

Pantelleria

Sy

Algiers

Gibraltar

Oran

The Battle of Mers el-Kebir
3 July

TUNISIA

Sousse

SPANISH MOROCCO

MOROCCO   A   L   G   E   R   I   A

Tripoli

30° —

0°

THE NAVAL WAR in the Mediterranean revolved around British (east-west) and Italian (north-south) maritime communications. The long, narrow shape of the sea with its numerous choke points offered little opportunity for supply convoys to evade enemy contact as in the Atlantic or Pacific theatres. Most major engagements were fought around the movement of a convoy by one or both sides. The British did not intend to run regular convoys to the Middle East and beyond because of the large number of airbases the Italians possessed in the central and eastern Mediterranean. Slow-moving merchant vessels stood little chance of surviving against large numbers of Italian aircraft and submarines. Allied shipping thus had to take the far longer Cape route adding weeks to the transit

times. From the allied perspective the importance of the Mediterranean campaign in the overall context of the war was to eliminate the Axis threat to the sea-lanes and thus free up valuable merchant shipping tonnage.

The allies immediately began offensive operations against Italy after it entered the war on 10 June. Although by this stage the second phase of the German operation against France had begun, the French navy undertook a number of bombardments in northern Italy and together with the British attacked Italian forces on the Libyan coast. Indeed, it was the French fleet rather than the Italians who presented the greatest threat to the British after France signed an armistice with Germany on 22 June. The French detachment at Alexandria,

HUNGARY

ROMANIA

YUGOSLAVIA

Operation *Judgement*, Taranto carrier strike
and cruiser sweep of the Strait of Otranto
11–12 November

Bombardment of
Valona by RN
19 December

BULGARIA

ALBANIA

Italian invasion of Greece
and Greek counter-attack
October – November

Regulus

Taranto

Triton

Odin

Rainbow

GREECE

*Aegean
Sea*

Battle of Calabria/
Punta Stilo
8 July

Oswald

rampus

enix

Athens

Léros

Dodecanese
(to Italy)

Rhodes

ttle of Cape Passero
ctober

Battle of Cape Spada
19 July

Suda Bay

Espero convoy action
28 June

Crete

Suda Bay developed as an
advanced base by the British
October – November

CYPRUS

LEBANON

e

a

n

S

e

a

Beirut

Haifa

Triad

Derna

Orpheus

RN bombardments and
inshore squadron operations

PALESTINE

Benghazi

Tobruk

Italian advance September

Port Said

Alexandria

British offensive
December–February 1941

Suez Canal

Cairo

L I B Y A

E G Y P T

0   200 Nm

0   200 km

Red Sea

Force X, was disarmed while the main body of the fleet
at Oran was attacked to prevent it from falling into
German hands.

Although Malta was no longer the main British
base for the Mediterranean Fleet it remained key to
interdicting Italian Africa-bound supplies with aircraft
and submarines. Maintaining Malta became the focus of
British operations, and every attempt at resupplying the
island involved a complex choreography between Force
H in the western basin, the Mediterranean Fleet in the
east and Malta's own air and naval forces. Throughout
1940 the British waged an offensive campaign and
Admiral Andrew Cunningham sought to engage the
Italian fleet at every opportunity. The object was to
defeat it and to implement an economic blockade
to which Italy, with its dependence on imports and
concentration of road and rail communications along
the coastlines, was particularly susceptible.

The Italians had anticipated such a strategy and laid
extensive defensive minefields and concentrated naval
forces in key areas. Partially owing to such measures,
and also because the conditions of the Mediterranean
were unfavourable for submarines, a number of British
boats were lost. The Italian invasion of Greece, which
began on 28 October, opened a new front and allowed
the British to use Greek bases. Within two weeks the
Italian offensive had stalled, the campaign becoming
a substantial burden on resources. In an attempt to
neutralise the Italian battle fleet the Royal Navy launched
an audacious, but highly successful, carrier strike on the
main Italian base at Taranto. By the end of the year the
British had regained mastery of the Mediterranean by
means of four major battles, and in conjunction with
General O'Connor's defeat of the Italian Tenth Army in
the Western Desert and the stalemate in Greece, Italy
was on the verge of defeat.

Operation Catapult, The Battle of Mers el-Kebir, 3 July 1940

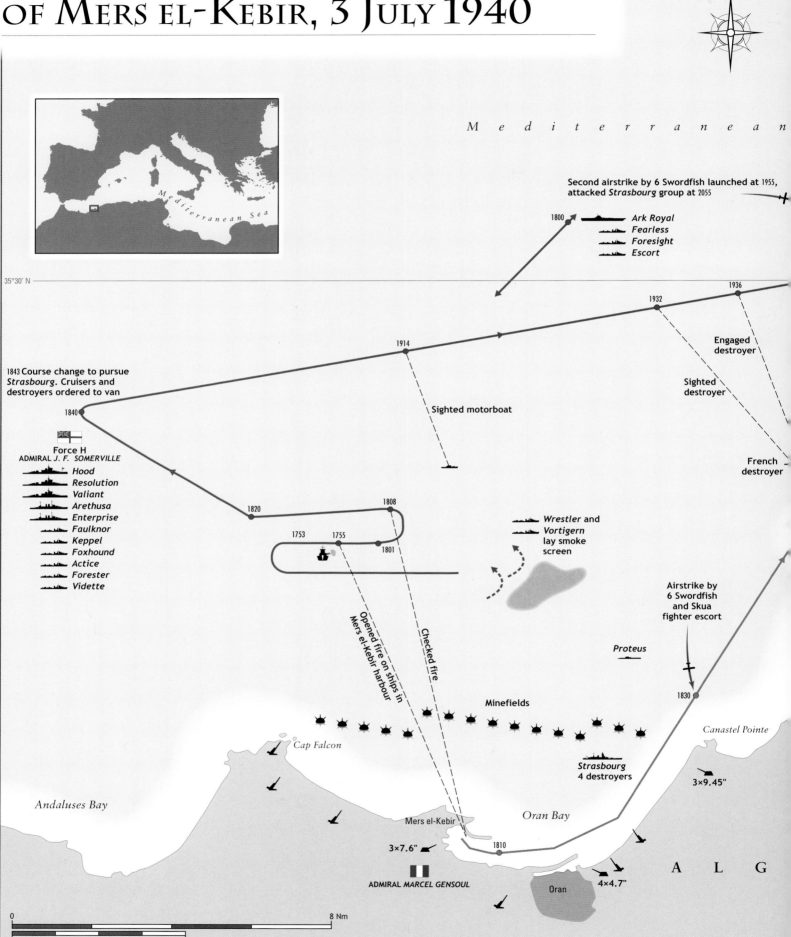

Mediterranean

Mediterranean Sea

Second airstrike by 6 Swordfish launched at 1955, attacked *Strasbourg* group at 2055

1800

Ark Royal
Fearless
Foresight
Escort

35°30′ N

1936

1932

Engaged destroyer

1914

Sighted destroyer

1843 Course change to pursue *Strasbourg*. Cruisers and destroyers ordered to van

Sighted motorboat

French destroyer

1840

Force H
ADMIRAL J. F. SOMERVILLE

Hood
Resolution
Valiant
Arethusa
Enterprise
Faulknor
Keppel
Foxhound
Actice
Forester
Vidette

1808

Wrestler and
Vortigern
lay smoke
screen

1820

1753   1755

1801

Airstrike by
6 Swordfish
and Skua
fighter escort

Proteus

Opened fire on ships in Mers el-Kebir harbour

Checked fire

1830

Minefields

Canastel Pointe

Cap Falcon

Strasbourg
4 destroyers

3×9.45″

Andaluses Bay

Oran Bay

Mers el-Kebir

3×7.6″

1810

A   L   G

ADMIRAL *MARCEL GENSOUL*

4×4.7″

Oran

0   8 Nm

0   8 km

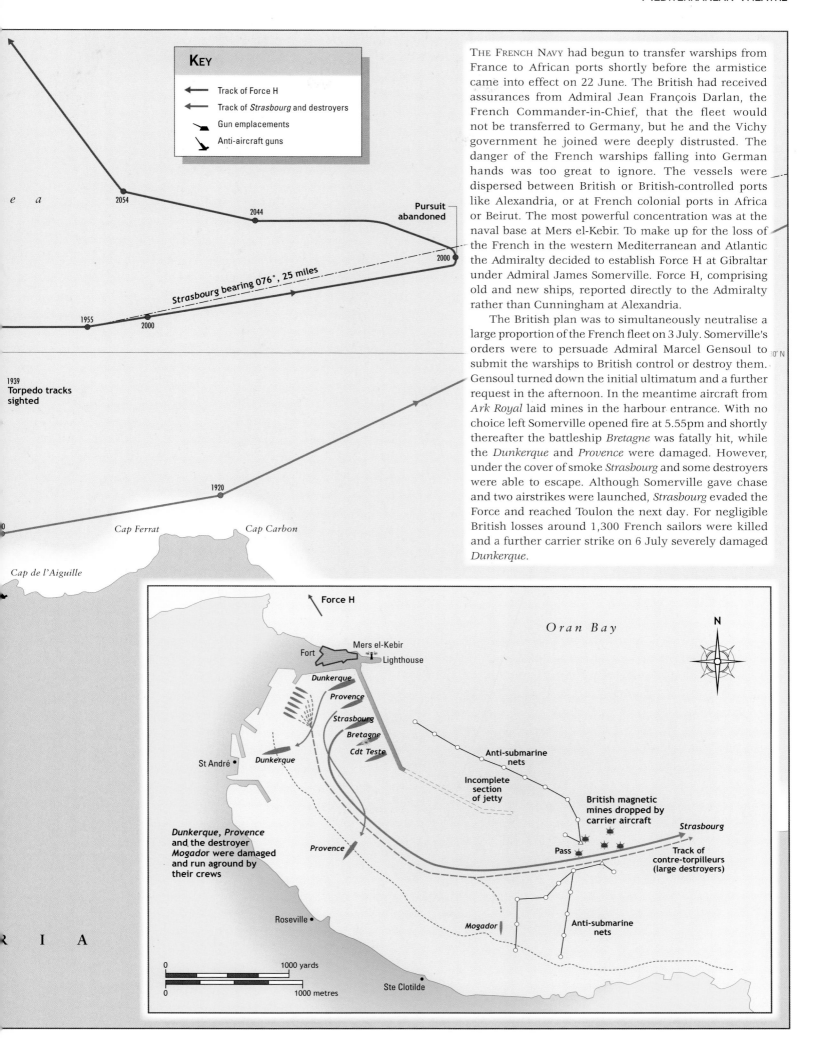

KEY

→ Track of Force H

→ Track of *Strasbourg* and destroyers

Gun emplacements

Anti-aircraft guns

2054

2044

2000

Pursuit
abandoned

Strasbourg bearing 076°, 25 miles

1955

2000

e   a

1939
**Torpedo tracks
sighted**

1920

Cap Ferrat

Cap Carbon

Cap de l'Aiguille

THE FRENCH NAVY had begun to transfer warships from France to African ports shortly before the armistice came into effect on 22 June. The British had received assurances from Admiral Jean François Darlan, the French Commander-in-Chief, that the fleet would not be transferred to Germany, but he and the Vichy government he joined were deeply distrusted. The danger of the French warships falling into German hands was too great to ignore. The vessels were dispersed between British or British-controlled ports like Alexandria, or at French colonial ports in Africa or Beirut. The most powerful concentration was at the naval base at Mers el-Kebir. To make up for the loss of the French in the western Mediterranean and Atlantic the Admiralty decided to establish Force H at Gibraltar under Admiral James Somerville. Force H, comprising old and new ships, reported directly to the Admiralty rather than Cunningham at Alexandria.

The British plan was to simultaneously neutralise a large proportion of the French fleet on 3 July. Somerville's orders were to persuade Admiral Marcel Gensoul to submit the warships to British control or destroy them. Gensoul turned down the initial ultimatum and a further request in the afternoon. In the meantime aircraft from *Ark Royal* laid mines in the harbour entrance. With no choice left Somerville opened fire at 5.55pm and shortly thereafter the battleship *Bretagne* was fatally hit, while the *Dunkerque* and *Provence* were damaged. However, under the cover of smoke *Strasbourg* and some destroyers were able to escape. Although Somerville gave chase and two airstrikes were launched, *Strasbourg* evaded the Force and reached Toulon the next day. For negligible British losses around 1,300 French sailors were killed and a further carrier strike on 6 July severely damaged *Dunkerque*.

30' N

R   I   A

Force H

Oran Bay

N

Mers el-Kebir

Fort

Lighthouse

Dunkerque

Provence

Strasbourg

Bretagne

Cdt Teste

St André

Dunkerque

Anti-submarine
nets

Incomplete
section
of jetty

**British magnetic
mines dropped by
carrier aircraft**

Strasbourg

Pass

**Track of
contre-torpilleurs
(large destroyers)**

***Dunkerque, Provence*
and the destroyer
Mogador were damaged
and run aground by
their crews**

Provence

Mogador

Anti-submarine
nets

Roseville

Ste Clotilde

0   1000 yards

0   1000 metres

The Battle of Calabria/Punta Stilo, 9 July 1940

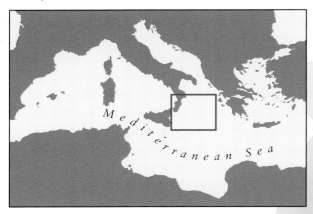

THE BATTLE OF Calabria, also referred to as the action off Calabria by the British and the battle of Punta Stilo by the Italians, was the first major fleet action in the Mediterranean between the Royal Navy and Regia Marina. In early July Admiral Andrew Cunningham drew up a plan (MA5) to use his fleet to sweep into the central Mediterranean to cover the passage of two small convoys from Malta to Alexandria. His aim was to use the evacuation of non-essential personnel and merchant ships to test the Italians and, if possible, engage in battle. Concurrently, the Italians planned to run a convoy carrying tanks and stores to North Africa and to ensure the arrival of these vital supplies Vice Admiral Campioni was tasked with using the battle fleet to provide cover. The Italian convoy left Naples on 6 July and was reinforced off Sicily the next day while Campioni brought the fleet south from Taranto. The British left Alexandria late that evening and by the 8 July both fleets were converging on the central Mediterranean.

Cunningham became aware of the Italian operation from a submarine report during the morning. Italian aircraft flying from Tobruk bombed the westward advancing British throughout the day, though Campioni only obtained an indication of British strength in the early afternoon. He turned east to meet the British in an attempt to protect the convoy, but then in the evening received orders not to engage in a night time action and return home to protect the Italian mainland from British strikes. Guided by signals intelligence and aerial reconnaissance Cunningham managed to edge around the Italian fleet. In the process the British force lost some of its cohesion, as the unmodernised *Malaya* and *Royal Sovereign* were unable to keep up. A British airstrike failed to inflict damage but did cause confusion as the various Italian forces began concentrating.

The main battleship action was fought at extreme range and began with *Giulio Cesare* firing a salvo at *Warspite* at 3.54pm at a range of over 24,000 yards. At 3.59pm *Warspite* hit *Cesare* inflicting heavy damage and prompting Campioni to order a retreat under smoke and destroyer attacks. Cunningham continued pursuit with the Italian mainland visible and under increasing, though ineffectual, land air attacks, until 7.30pm. On 10 July an airstrike was conducted against Augusta before the convoy was picked up from Malta and escorted to Alexandria from 11 to 15 July.

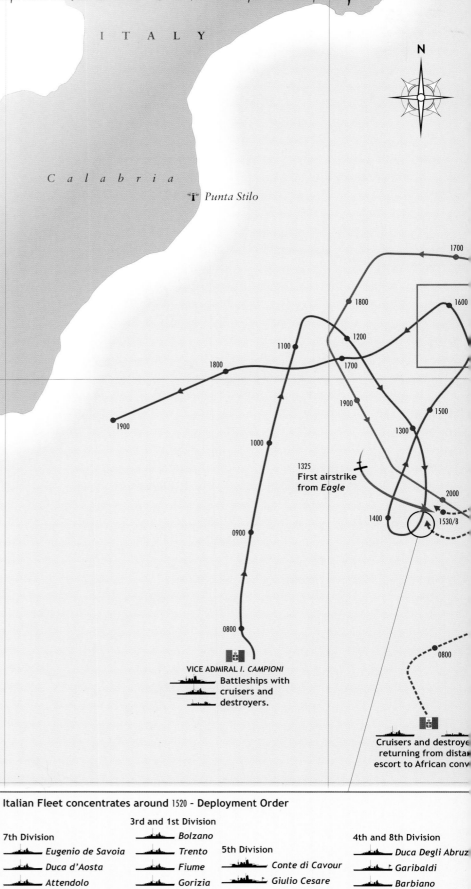

ITALY

Calabria

Punta Stilo

N

1700

1800

1600

1200

1100

1800

1700

1900

1500

1300

1900

1000

1325
First airstrike from *Eagle*

2000

1400

1530/8

0900

0800

0800

VICE ADMIRAL *I. CAMPIONI*
Battleships with cruisers and destroyers.

Cruisers and destroyer returning from distant escort to African conv

Mediterranean Sea

Italian Fleet concentrates around 1520 - Deployment Order

7th Division	3rd and 1st Division	5th Division	4th and 8th Division
Eugenio de Savoia	Bolzano	Conte di Cavour	Duca Degli Abruz
Duca d'Aosta	Trento	Giulio Cesare	Garibaldi
Attendolo	Fiume		Barbiano
Montecuccoli	Gorizia		Di Giussano
	Zara		
	Pola		

Accompanied by 16 destroyers from the 7th, 9th, 11th, 12th, 14th Destroyer Squadrons

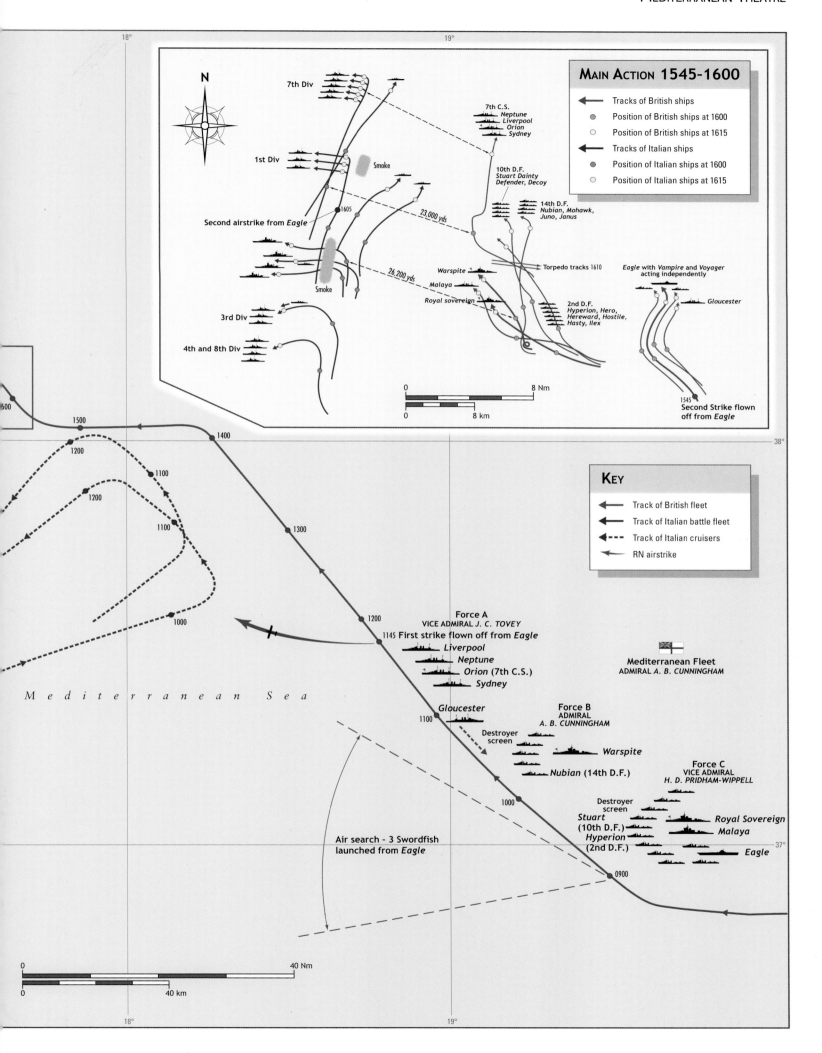

Main Action 1545–1600

← Tracks of British ships
● Position of British ships at 1600
○ Position of British ships at 1615
← Tracks of Italian ships
● Position of Italian ships at 1600
○ Position of Italian ships at 1615

N

7th Div

7th C.S.
Neptune
Liverpool
Orion
Sydney

1st Div

Smoke

10th D.F.
Stuart Dainty
Defender, Decoy

Second airstrike from *Eagle*

1605

23,000 yds

14th D.F.
Nubian, Mohawk,
Juno, Janus

26,200 yds

Smoke

Warspite

Malaya

Royal sovereign

Torpedo tracks 1610

Eagle with *Vampire* and *Voyager*
acting independently

Gloucester

2nd D.F.
Hyperion, Hero,
Hereward, Hostile,
Hasty, Ilex

3rd Div

4th and 8th Div

0   8 Nm
0   8 km

1545

Second Strike flown
off from *Eagle*

1600

1500

1400

1200

1100

1200

1300

1100

1000

1200

KEY

← Track of British fleet
← Track of Italian battle fleet
◄- - Track of Italian cruisers
← RN airstrike

Force A
VICE ADMIRAL J. C. TOVEY
1145 First strike flown off from *Eagle*
Liverpool
Neptune
Orion (7th C.S.)
Sydney

Mediterranean Sea

Gloucester

1100

Destroyer
screen

Mediterranean Fleet
ADMIRAL A. B. CUNNINGHAM

Force B
ADMIRAL
A. B. CUNNINGHAM

Warspite

Nubian (14th D.F.)

Force C
VICE ADMIRAL
H. D. PRIDHAM-WIPPELL

1000

Destroyer
screen

Stuart
(10th D.F.)
Hyperion
(2nd D.F.)

Royal Sovereign
Malaya

Eagle

Air search - 3 Swordfish
launched from *Eagle*

0900

0   40 Nm
0   40 km

BATTLE OF THE ATLANTIC, JUNE 1940 – MARCH 1941

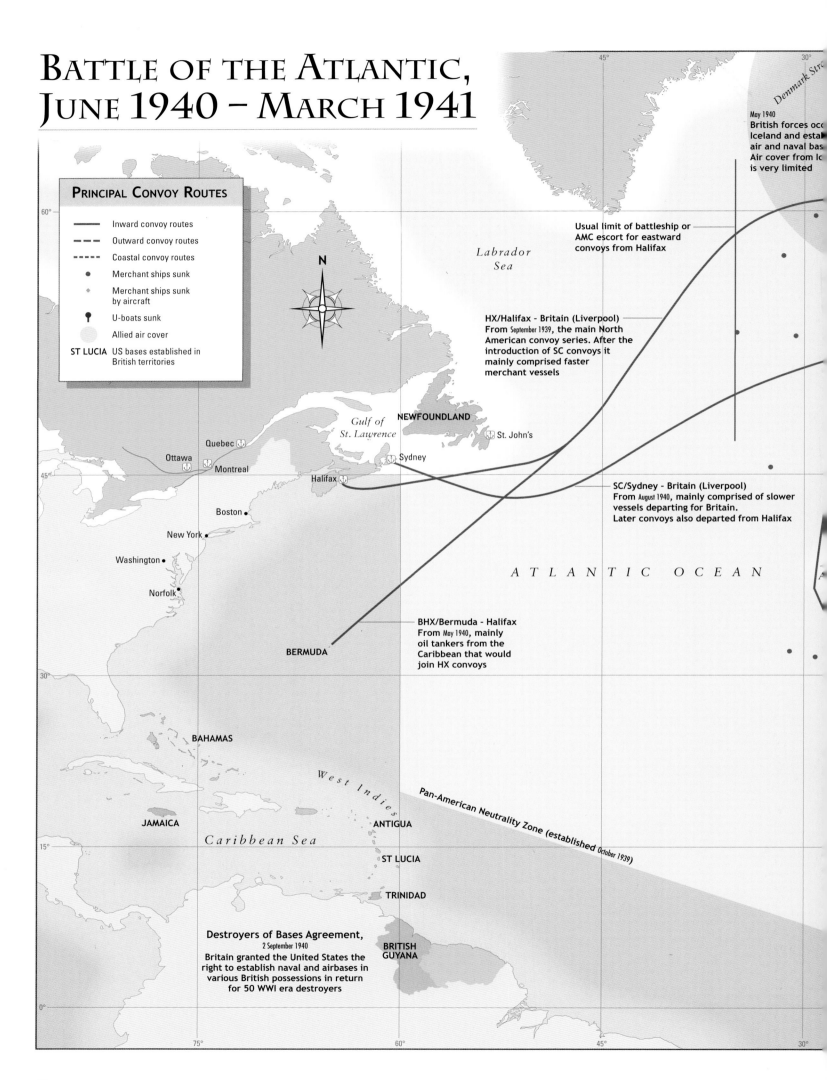

PRINCIPAL CONVOY ROUTES

— Inward convoy routes

- - - Outward convoy routes

----- Coastal convoy routes

● Merchant ships sunk

◆ Merchant ships sunk by aircraft

⚓ U-boats sunk

Allied air cover

ST LUCIA US bases established in British territories

Labrador Sea

May 1940
British forces occ
Iceland and esta
air and naval bas
Air cover from Ic
is very limited

Denmark Stra

Usual limit of battleship or AMC escort for eastward convoys from Halifax

HX/Halifax – Britain (Liverpool)
From September 1939, the main North American convoy series. After the introduction of SC convoys it mainly comprised faster merchant vessels

SC/Sydney – Britain (Liverpool)
From August 1940, mainly comprised of slower vessels departing for Britain. Later convoys also departed from Halifax

Gulf of St. Lawrence

NEWFOUNDLAND

⚓ St. John's

Quebec ⚓

Ottawa ⚓

Montreal

⚓ Sydney

Halifax ⚓

Boston ●

New York ●

Washington ●

Norfolk ●

ATLANTIC OCEAN

BHX/Bermuda – Halifax
From May 1940, mainly oil tankers from the Caribbean that would join HX convoys

BERMUDA

BAHAMAS

West Indies

Pan-American Neutrality Zone (established October 1939)

JAMAICA

Caribbean Sea

ANTIGUA

ST LUCIA

TRINIDAD

Destroyers of Bases Agreement,
2 September 1940
Britain granted the United States the right to establish naval and airbases in various British possessions in return for 50 WWI era destroyers

BRITISH GUYANA

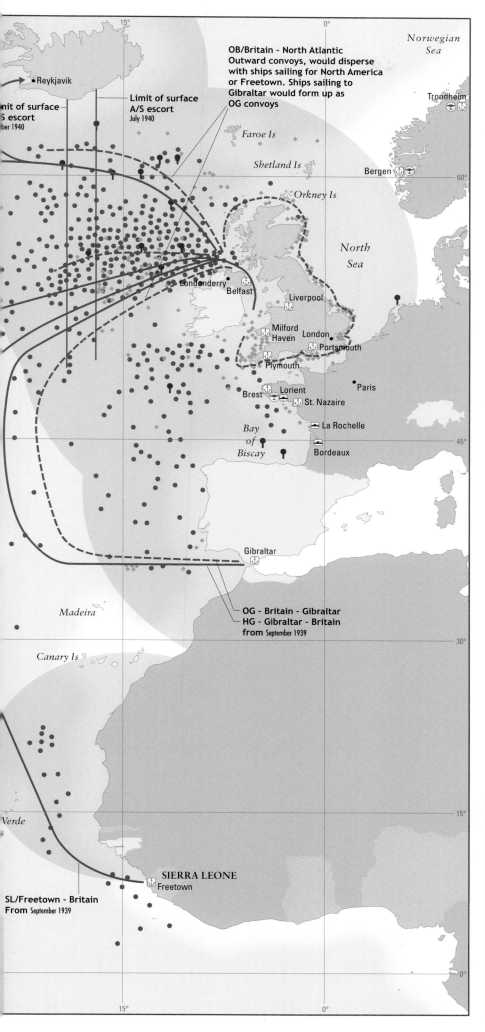

OB/Britain - North Atlantic
Outward convoys, would disperse
with ships sailing for North America
or Freetown. Ships sailing to
Gibraltar would form up as
OG convoys

Limit of surface
A/S escort
July 1940

OG - Britain - Gibraltar
HG - Gibraltar - Britain
from September 1939

SL/Freetown - Britain
From September 1939

THE DEFEAT OF France fundamentally changed the campaign in the Atlantic. While Norway provided the Kriegsmarine with access to the ocean, the French Atlantic coast provided the perfect position from which to attack Britain's maritime supply lines. From July, U-boats began to use French ports to resupply, effectively increasing their time on patrol by a fifth and enabling them to operate further out to sea. As the Royal Navy withdrew many of its escorts from the Atlantic to deal with a potential German invasion, the U-boats found plenty of unescorted ships, and the period from June to October became known as the first 'Happy Time' by the Germans. In four months U-boats sunk 274 ships while aircraft, mines and surface raiders accounted for another 266. Attacks by Luftwaffe FW200s, which flew patrols between French and Norwegian bases, accounted for a number of ships as they were able to range beyond British air cover and most vessels lacked adequate air defences. Indeed, this phase of the campaign into the spring was the most dangerous one precisely because the Germans employed different methods of attack and stretched British resources. German success, in the case of air and U-boat attacks, was achieved with modest resources. At any time there were only six to eight U-boats in the frontline and only around twenty to twenty-five patrols were conducted a month. Over time more U-boats were put into service, but their effectiveness continuously declined as experienced crews were lost and allied defences improved.

On the North American route convoys usually encompassed fifteen to thirty ships in the slow and fast series respectively. The numbers were similar for convoys from Sierra Leone, and the less frequent Gibraltar ones. Most convoys sailed unescorted for most of their journeys. At best, an armed merchant cruiser might provide some protection against German auxiliary cruisers, but they were vulnerable to warships. Anti-submarine escorts were only available in the waters around Britain and this cover was only slowly expanded westwards. While British and Canadian shipyards began to construct more escorts, fifty old American destroyers were obtained in return for basing rights. RAF Coastal Command also allocated more resources, but the number of aircraft and their range was limited in 1940. In February 1941, the British allocated more aircraft and ships, and air bases and refuelling facilities in Iceland were established. The Western Approaches Command, which was responsible for trade defence, was moved to Liverpool, to allow a better coordination of naval, air, intelligence and civilian resources involved in the campaign.

MERCHANT SHIPS AND U-BOATS LOST (ALL THEATRES AND CAUSES)			
MONTH	TONNAGE	SHIPS	U-BOATS
1940			
JUNE	585,496	140	0
JULY	386,913	105	2
AUGUST	397,229	92	3
SEPTEMBER	448,621	100	2
OCTOBER	442,985	103	1
NOVEMBER	385,715	97	2
DECEMBER	349,568	82	0
1941			
JANUARY	320,240	76	0
FEBRUARY	403,393	102	0
MARCH	529,706	139	6

UNTERNEHMEN SEELÖWE

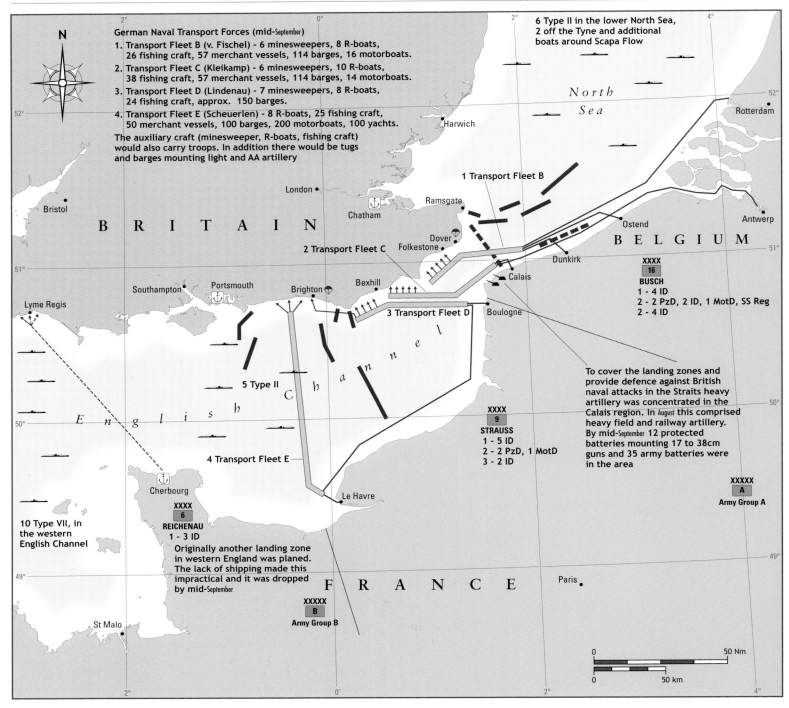

German Naval Transport Forces (mid-September)
1. Transport Fleet B (v. Fischel) - 6 minesweepers, 8 R-boats, 26 fishing craft, 57 merchant vessels, 114 barges, 16 motorboats.
2. Transport Fleet C (Kleikamp) - 6 minesweepers, 10 R-boats, 38 fishing craft, 57 merchant vessels, 114 barges, 14 motorboats.
3. Transport Fleet D (Lindenau) - 7 minesweepers, 8 R-boats, 24 fishing craft, approx. 150 barges.
4. Transport Fleet E (Scheuerlen) - 8 R-boats, 25 fishing craft, 50 merchant vessels, 100 barges, 200 motorboats, 100 yachts.

The auxiliary craft (minesweeper, R-boats, fishing craft) would also carry troops. In addition there would be tugs and barges mounting light and AA artillery

6 Type II in the lower North Sea, 2 off the Tyne and additional boats around Scapa Flow

North Sea

Rotterdam

Harwich

1 Transport Fleet B

London •

Ramsgate

Chatham

Dover

Ostend

Antwerp

BELGIUM

2 Transport Fleet C

Folkestone

Dunkirk

Bristol •

BRITAIN

Calais

XXXX
16
BUSCH
1 - 4 ID
2 - 2 PzD, 2 ID, 1 MotD, SS Reg
2 - 4 ID

Southampton •

Portsmouth

Brighton

Bexhill

3 Transport Fleet D

Boulogne

Lyme Regis

5 Type II

C h a n n e l

E n g l i s h

To cover the landing zones and provide defence against British naval attacks in the Straits heavy artillery was concentrated in the Calais region. In August this comprised heavy field and railway artillery. By mid-September 12 protected batteries mounting 17 to 38cm guns and 35 army batteries were in the area

XXXX
9
STRAUSS
1 - 5 ID
2 - 2 PzD, 1 MotD
3 - 2 ID

4 Transport Fleet E

XXXXX
A
Army Group A

Cherbourg

XXXX
6
REICHENAU
1 - 3 ID

Le Havre

10 Type VII, in the western English Channel

Originally another landing zone in western England was planed. The lack of shipping made this impractical and it was dropped by mid-September

FRANCE

Paris •

St Malo •

XXXXX
B
Army Group B

0   50 Nm
0   50 km

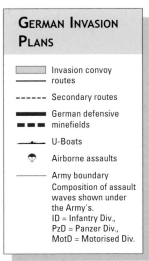

GERMAN INVASION PLANS

	Invasion convoy routes
——	Secondary routes
- - - -	German defensive minefields
▄ ▄ ▄	
⚓	U-Boats
⚓	Airborne assaults
——	Army boundary

Composition of assault waves shown under the Army's.
ID = Infantry Div.,
PzD = Panzer Div.,
MotD = Motorised Div.

THE GERMAN MILITARY had virtually no experience of amphibious operations and so, despite just having won a resounding victory in France, attacking Britain presented a considerable challenge. In the First World War only one operation had been conducted, and between the wars only a small number of battalion-sized landings were practiced. The invasion of Norway had been largely a seaborne one, but it had relied on surprise and was not comparable to an amphibious assault. Crossing the English Channel, even at its narrowest point in the Strait of Dover, presented almost insurmountable problems.

When in late July the army first examined an invasion of Britain, and began to train for the operation, it envisaged a landing on a broad front along the whole southern coast. The Kriegsmarine, which would be responsible for the crossing, objected. The transport requirements for the troops and their materiel, even with reductions in the heavy equipment, far outstripped the available shipping taken from across occupied northwest Europe and from German fishery and riverine fleets. Furthermore, the capacity of all the ports in France, Belgium and the Netherlands was insufficient to accommodate this invasion flotilla. The nature of the improvised force was far from ideal as the majority of craft were slow and never designed for military operations, and the troops would have been vulnerable to any air or naval attacks during the crossing. The time necessary to assemble the force was significant and it was estimated that mid September was the earliest possible date for a landing operation. In late August the army and navy agreed a new invasion plan focused on the southeast of England and involving smaller initial waves.

THE BATTLE OF BRITAIN

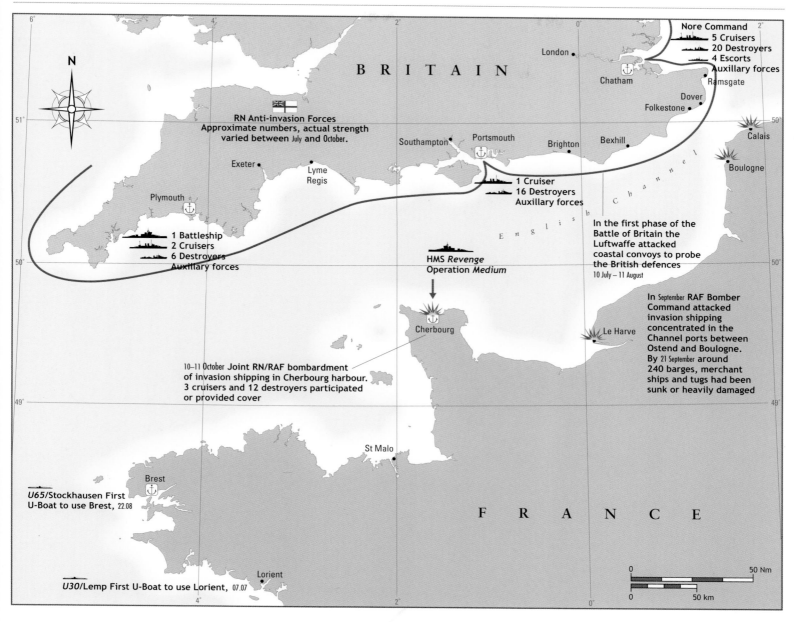

Nore Command
- 5 Cruisers
- 20 Destroyers
- 4 Escorts
- Auxillary forces

London

Chatham

Ramsgate

Dover

Folkestone

Calais

Boulogne

BRITAIN

RN Anti-invasion Forces
Approximate numbers, actual strength
varied between July and October.

Southampton   Portsmouth   Brighton   Bexhill

Exeter

Lyme
Regis

- 1 Cruiser
- 16 Destroyers
Auxillary forces

Plymouth

- 1 Battleship
- 2 Cruisers
- 6 Destroyers
Auxillary forces

English   *Channel*

In the first phase of the
Battle of Britain the
Luftwaffe attacked
coastal convoys to probe
the British defences
10 July – 11 August

HMS *Revenge*
Operation *Medium*

Le Harve

In September RAF Bomber
Command attacked
invasion shipping
concentrated in the
Channel ports between
Ostend and Boulogne.
By 21 September around
240 barges, merchant
ships and tugs had been
sunk or heavily damaged

Cherbourg

10–11 October Joint RN/RAF bombardment
of invasion shipping in Cherbourg harbour.
3 cruisers and 12 destroyers participated
or provided cover

St Malo

Brest

U65/Stockhausen First
U-Boat to use Brest, 22.08

FRANCE

U30/Lemp First U-Boat to use Lorient, 07.07

Lorient

KEY

— Coastal convoy

☆ Bombardment

⚓ Major Naval base

THE KRIEGSMARINE WAS in no position to support any invasion with its surface fleet as, after Norway, the majority of its remaining warships were undergoing repairs. It had only one operational heavy cruiser, *Admiral Hipper*, and three older light cruisers that were deemed unfit for high seas operations. During an invasion *Admiral Hipper* would be sent into the Atlantic in an attempt to distract the Royal Navy, and only U-boats and defensive minefields would protect the long streams of barges and other craft crossing the Channel. Under these circumstances the Germans needed absolute control of the eastern end of the Channel before undertaking any invasion.

From mid July the Luftwaffe increasingly attacked British Channel convoys in an attempt to deplete RAF fighter strength. The British were dependent on these coastal convoys as transferring this trade onto the railways for any length of time was simply not viable. These early attacks were not part of a coherent strategy and Hitler only directed the Luftwaffe to destroy the RAF at the beginning of August. The first phase of the intensified aerial campaign began on 12 August with

attacks on the British coastal airfields before spreading inland and eventually involved the bombing of cities from September.

British anti-invasion preparations after the defeat of the army at Dunkirk rested on maintaining working command of the air and sea. A surprise invasion was the greatest concern given what the Germans had achieved in Norway, and the Royal Navy organised hundreds of small craft into an Auxiliary Patrol to continuously watch likely invasion routes along with aerial reconnaissance. The British estimated that as long as they had twenty-four hours warning, elements of the Home Fleet could intervene. Concentrating capital ships in the Channel was not envisaged as this would allow German raiders to slip into the North Atlantic, but cruisers and destroyers were sent south. The British were not confined to only a defensive role during the height of the aerial battle over the southeast; Bomber and Coastal Commands, together with the Royal Navy, attacked shipping along the French coast and demonstrated that the Germans did not have the required control of the Channel to launch an invasion.

OPERATION MENACE, SEPTEMBER 1940

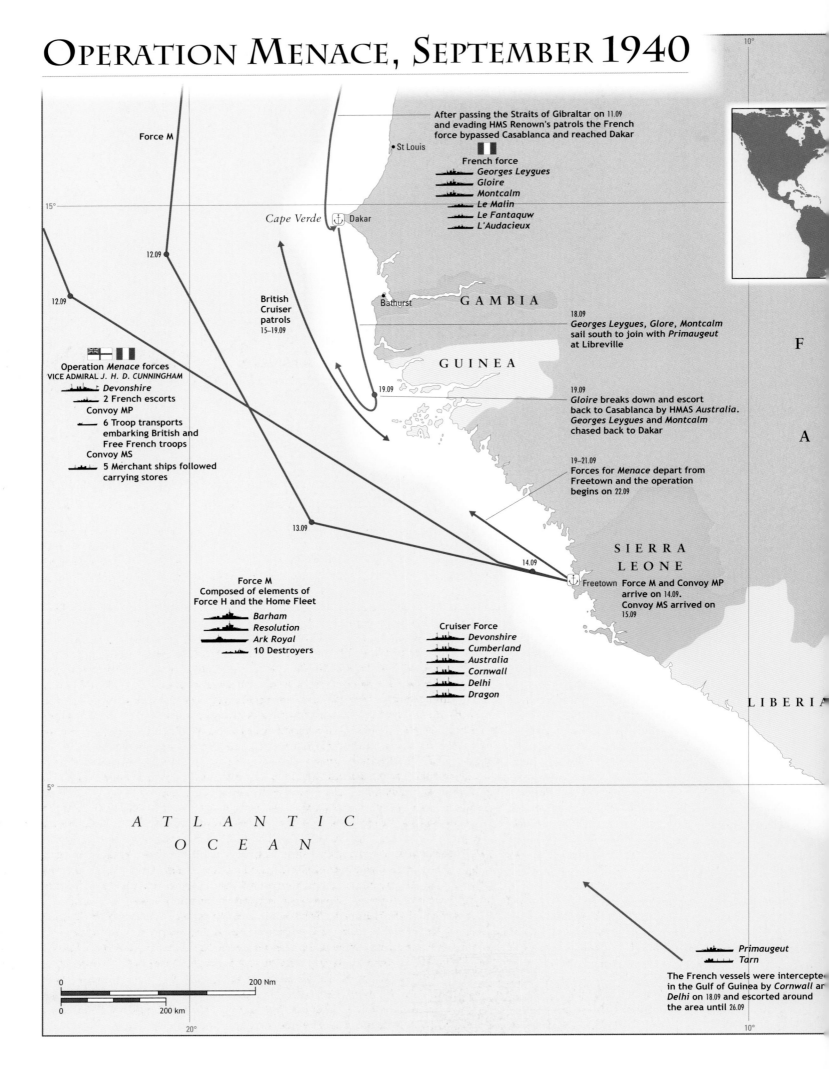

Force M

After passing the Straits of Gibraltar on 11.09 and evading HMS Renown's patrols the French force bypassed Casablanca and reached Dakar

St Louis

French force
Georges Leygues
Gloire
Montcalm
Le Malin
Le Fantaquw
L'Audacieux

Cape Verde · Dakar

British Cruiser patrols 15–19.09

Operation Menace forces
VICE ADMIRAL J. H. D. CUNNINGHAM
Devonshire
2 French escorts
Convoy MP
6 Troop transports embarking British and Free French troops
Convoy MS
5 Merchant ships followed carrying stores

Bathurst

GAMBIA

18.09
Georges Leygues, Glore, Montcalm sail south to join with Primaugeut at Libreville

GUINEA

19.09

19.09
Gloire breaks down and escort back to Casablanca by HMAS Australia. Georges Leygues and Montcalm chased back to Dakar

19–21.09
Forces for Menace depart from Freetown and the operation begins on 22.09

12.09

12.09

13.09

14.09

SIERRA LEONE

Freetown Force M and Convoy MP arrive on 14.09. Convoy MS arrived on 15.09

Force M
Composed of elements of Force H and the Home Fleet
Barham
Resolution
Ark Royal
10 Destroyers

Cruiser Force
Devonshire
Cumberland
Australia
Cornwall
Delhi
Dragon

LIBERIA

A T L A N T I C
O C E A N

Primaugeut
Tarn

The French vessels were intercepted in the Gulf of Guinea by Cornwall and Delhi on 18.09 and escorted around the area until 26.09

0   200 Nm

0   200 km

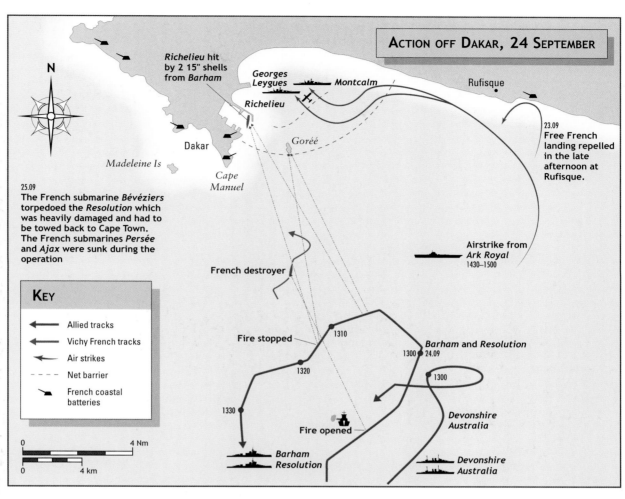

ACTION OFF DAKAR, 24 SEPTEMBER

Richelieu hit by 2 15" shells from *Barham*

Georges Leygues

Montcalm

Rufisque

Richelieu

Dakar

Gorée

23.09 Free French landing repelled in the late afternoon at Rufisque.

Madeleine Is

Cape Manuel

25.09 The French submarine *Bévéziers* torpedoed the *Resolution* which was heavily damaged and had to be towed back to Cape Town. The French submarines *Persée* and *Ajax* were sunk during the operation

Airstrike from *Ark Royal* 1430–1500

French destroyer

KEY

← Allied tracks

← Vichy French tracks

← Air strikes

- - - Net barrier

◣ French coastal batteries

Fire stopped

1310

Barham and *Resolution* 24.09

1300

1300

1320

Devonshire Australia

1330

Fire opened

Barham Resolution

Devonshire Australia

0   4 Nm

0   4 km

N C H
S   T
I C A

N

IN PARALLEL TO the events of *Catapult* at Mers el-Kebir the British also took steps to neutralise elements of the French fleet in British ports, Alexandria and at Dakar in French West Africa. As a naval base Dakar, which had a defended harbour capable of handling a dozen ships and further protected anchorage space, was well placed to interfere with shipping in the central Atlantic. In the aftermath of the armistice, Vichy French authorities took control of Dakar, but it was the arrival of the nearly complete French battleship *Richelieu* on 23 June from Brest that caused the greatest concern for the British. In early July a small squadron, including the carrier *Hermes* and a couple of cruisers, began to blockade Dakar and on 7 July the Vichy authorities were issued with an ultimatum to hand over or demilitarise *Richelieu* and other warships. When this was refused the British launched an attack that night on the battleship with a motorboat carrying depth charges, and an airstrike by six Swordfish torpedo-bombers early the next day. Beyond some light damage to *Richelieu* little was achieved and the British withdrew.

The matter remained unresolved and in early August General Charles de Gaulle of the Free French movement proposed an operation to eject the Vichy forces from Senegal. Churchill agreed and an expeditionary force of around 7,000 British and Free French troops left Britain on 31 August. However, the operation was based on little intelligence and the false assumption that the colony predominately favoured the Free French cause. Naval cover was provided by Force M, assembled from elements of the Home Fleet, Force H and ships from Atlantic trade protection force off West Africa. As the expedition sailed south a French squadron of three cruisers and three large destroyers from Toulon passed through the Strait of Gibraltar on 11 September and headed for Dakar. Confusion between the Admiralty and local British forces allowed this to occur, and in addition Force H was reduced to the battle cruiser *Renown* and a few destroyers as the other ships were making their way to Freetown.

The arrival of the French force constituted a threat to Operation *Menace* as it provided a boost to Vichy forces at Dakar. On 18 September the three French cruisers sailed south to proceed to Libreville in Gabon and rendezvous with a fourth cruiser and tanker. This operation failed as the *Gloire* broke down and was escorted to Casablanca by the cruiser *Australia* while *Cumberland* followed *Georges Leygues* and *Montcalm* back to Dakar. Meanwhile, the allied forces sailed from Freetown and arrived off Dakar early on 23 September. As the element of surprise had long been lost the plan was to first land Free French forces to attain a political settlement. If the Vichy forces resisted the British warships would bombard their positions and a joint Anglo-Free French force landed. In the event de Gaulle was not able to land and on 24 September British ships and aircraft bombarded the coastal batteries and warships at anchor. Poor visibility reduced the effect considerably and so it was decided to renew the attack the next day. During this next bombardment *Resolution* was hit at 9.02am by two torpedoes fired by the submarine *Bévéziers*, forcing her to retire. Two shells fired by coastal batteries lightly damaged *Barham*. In view of the heavy resistance it was decided to abandon the operation in the early afternoon and return to Freetown. Vichy forces lost a destroyer and two submarines.

GERMAN AUXILIARY CRUISERS, 1940

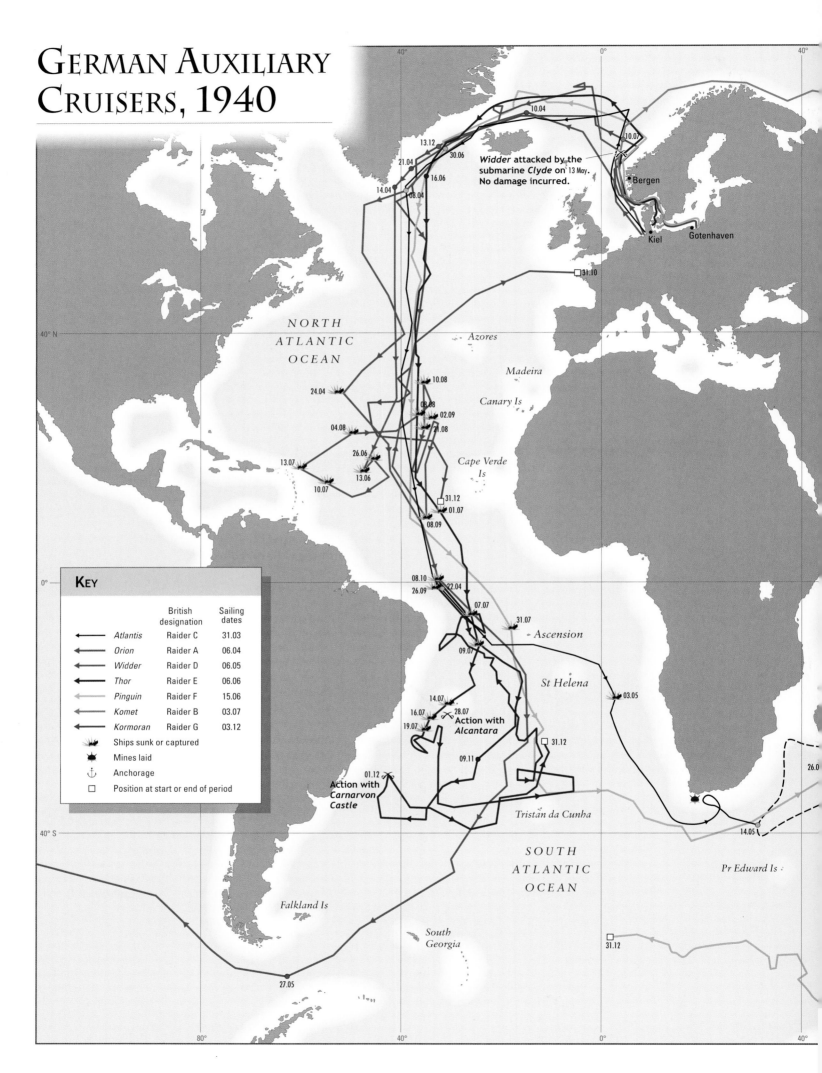

Widder attacked by the submarine *Clyde* on 13 May. No damage incurred.

Bergen

Kiel

Gotenhaven

NORTH
ATLANTIC
OCEAN

Azores

Madeira

Canary Is

Cape Verde
Is

Ascension

St Helena

Action with
Alcantara

Action with
*Carnarvon
Castle*

Tristan da Cunha

SOUTH
ATLANTIC
OCEAN

Falkland Is

South
Georgia

Pr Edward Is

KEY

	British designation	Sailing dates
Atlantis	Raider C	31.03
Orion	Raider A	06.04
Widder	Raider D	06.05
Thor	Raider E	06.06
Pinguin	Raider F	15.06
Komet	Raider B	03.07
Kormoran	Raider G	03.12
	Ships sunk or captured	
	Mines laid	
	Anchorage	
	Position at start or end of period	

Dates on map: 10.04, 13.12, 30.06, 10.07, 21.04, 16.06, 14.04, 08.04, 31.10, 24.04, 10.08, 08.08, 02.09, 04.08, 21.08, 26.06, 13.06, 13.07, 10.07, 31.12, 01.07, 08.09, 08.10, 26.09, 22.04, 07.07, 31.07, 09.07, 14.07, 28.07, 16.07, 19.07, 03.05, 31.12, 09.11, 01.12, 26.0, 14.05, 27.05, 31.12

THE KRIEGSMARINE DREW up the first plans for the use of auxiliary cruisers in the mid-1930s. The experience of the First World War had shown that large, fast liners were unsuited as commerce raiders as they consumed too much fuel and were easy to identify. Instead, inconspicuous moderately fast, long endurance freighters of around 7–8,000t displacement were selected for conversion into auxiliary cruisers. Upon the outbreak of war the first wave of six ships was requisitioned and converted in naval yards, three coming into service in 1939 and three in early 1940. They were equipped with six to eight 15cm guns, torpedo tubes, light guns, seaplanes and mines. The first ships left Germany around the time of the invasion of Norway and in order to maintain them at sea for long periods – the cruise of *Orion* lasted 510 days – an extensive network of supply vessels was necessary.

The objective of the auxiliary cruisers was to sink allied merchant ships and more generally cause confusion and uncertainty in the outer seas, spreading the limited allied forces even thinner. Only in May, when mines were discovered off South Africa, did the British become aware that at least one German auxiliary cruiser was operating at sea. Unlike 1939 there were insufficient forces to form hunting groups in the outer regions and all the British could do was to provide escorts for the most valuable oceanic convoys such as the troops transports. The German ships covered huge distances and operated in all the world's oceans; thus within less than a year the war had become a genuinely global conflict. By the end of 1940 the auxiliary cruisers had accounted for the loss of fifty-four merchant ships totalling 366,644 tons.

sage through ice
ed by Russian
breaker
anowitsch

14.05–14.12
Cruising area
of *Atlantis*

11.07

13.07

09.11   10.11

11.11

11.07

22.10

14.08

10.09

09.09

10.06

02.08   20.09

16.09

30.11

07.10

21.11

18.11

20.11

09.09

22.10

Maug

Lamotrek   30.09   14.10   *Ailinglap*

31.12   31.12

Nauru   08.12

06.12

PACIFIC
OCEAN

16.08

Fiji

19.06

18.06

27.11

20.08

INDIAN
OCEAN

40° N

0°

40° S

Kerguelen
14.12.40–11.01.41

SOUTHERN
OCEAN

Naval Operations in Support of the Western Desert Force, December 1940 – January 1941

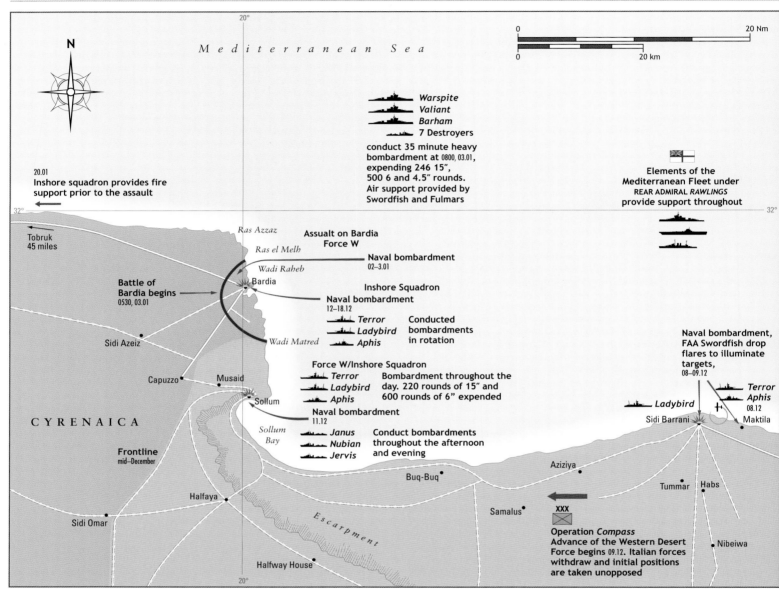

Mediterranean Sea

Warspite
Valiant
Barham
7 Destroyers

conduct 35 minute heavy bombardment at 0800, 03.01, expending 246 15", 500 6 and 4.5" rounds. Air support provided by Swordfish and Fulmars

Elements of the Mediterranean Fleet under REAR ADMIRAL *RAWLINGS* provide support throughout

20.01
Inshore squadron provides fire support prior to the assault

Tobruk 45 miles

Ras Azzaz
Ras el Melh
Wadi Raheb

Assualt on Bardia Force W

Naval bombardment 02–3.01

Bardia

Battle of Bardia begins 0530, 03.01

Inshore Squadron Naval bombardment 12–18.12

Terror
Ladybird
Aphis

Conducted bombardments in rotation

Sidi Azeiz

Wadi Matred

Force W/Inshore Squadron

Terror
Ladybird
Aphis

Bombardment throughout the day. 220 rounds of 15" and 600 rounds of 6" expended

Naval bombardment, FAA Swordfish drop flares to illuminate targets, 08–09.12

Capuzzo
Musaid

Sollum

C Y R E N A I C A

Sollum Bay

Naval bombardment 11.12

Janus
Nubian
Jervis

Conduct bombardments throughout the afternoon and evening

Ladybird

Sidi Barrani

Terror
Aphis
08.12

Maktila

Frontline mid–December

Aziziya

Buq-Buq

Tummar
Habs

Halfaya

Escarpment

Samalus

XXX

Tobruk

Nibeiwa

Sidi Omar

Operation *Compass*
Advance of the Western Desert Force begins 09.12. Italian forces withdraw and initial positions are taken unopposed

Halfway House

KEY

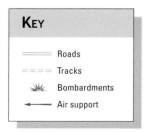

----- Roads
- - - - Tracks
🌿 Bombardments
◄— Air support

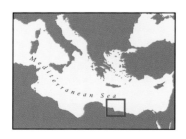

IN SEPTEMBER, THE Italian Tenth Army pushed across the Egyptian border and advanced to just east of Sidi Barrani before setting up defensive positions. British forces in Egypt were limited and amounted to around two divisions organised as the Western Desert Force. Over the next two years the nature of the desert war was very fluid with both sides regularly advancing and retreating over vast distances. The naval contribution on the British side was twofold. First, owing to the very limited infrastructure in the desert the ability to bring supplies nearer to the Italian front line by sea became increasingly important as more forces were deployed. Secondly, because of the military dependence on maritime supplies, attacking Italian ports like Bardia, Tobruk or Benghazi in western Cyrenaica had an impact on their operations in the desert. The first of many naval bombardments of Italian positions took place on 21 June when three British cruisers, a French battleship and four destroyers shelled Bardia. Two months later three battleships and a cruiser undertook a heavy bombardment of the port. RAF and FAA aircraft started to conduct operations against Italian shipping along the Libyan coast in July.

In September two gunboats, *Aphis* and *Ladybird*, operating with destroyers as Force W, operated against Italian coastal supply lines. In the first days of Operation *Compass* a number of bombardments were conducted, and once the first phase was completed on 18 December the navy brought supplies, particularly of water, into Sollum. When the second phase of the offensive began on 3 January 1941 part of the Mediterranean Fleet was brought up to provide support to the army which captured Bardia two days later. As the fighting rapidly moved east, a naval squadron too moved along the coast and eventually allied supplies were even brought in via Benghazi despite it being subjected to Italian air attacks.

THE RED SEA, JUNE 1940 – APRIL 1941

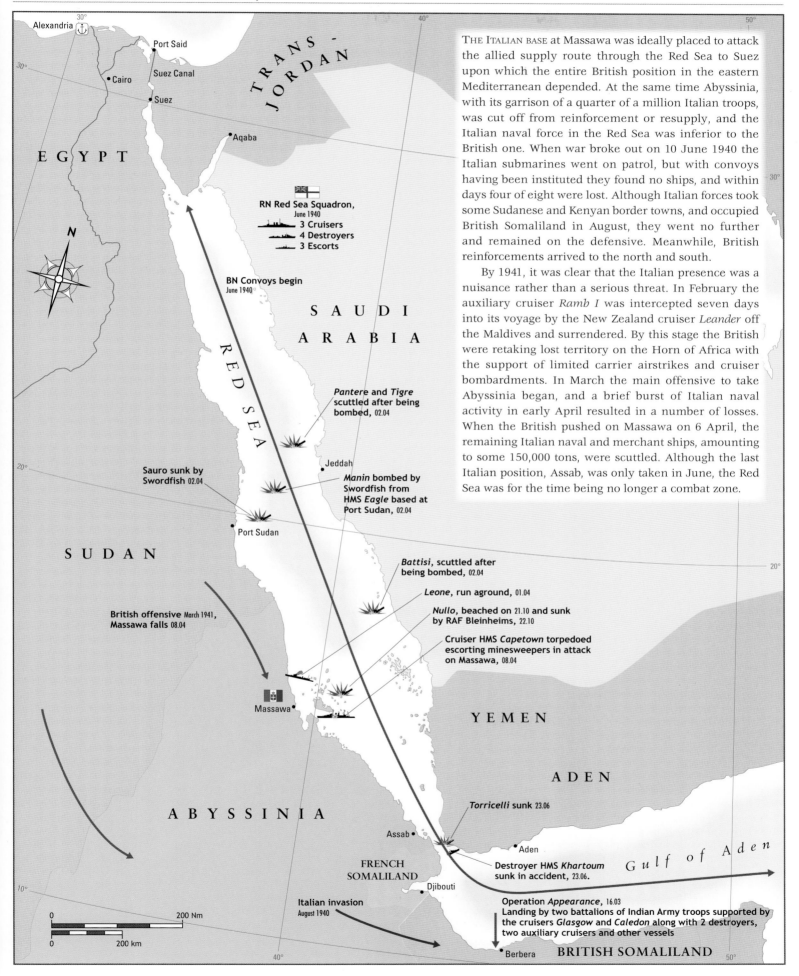

THE ITALIAN BASE at Massawa was ideally placed to attack the allied supply route through the Red Sea to Suez upon which the entire British position in the eastern Mediterranean depended. At the same time Abyssinia, with its garrison of a quarter of a million Italian troops, was cut off from reinforcement or resupply, and the Italian naval force in the Red Sea was inferior to the British one. When war broke out on 10 June 1940 the Italian submarines went on patrol, but with convoys having been instituted they found no ships, and within days four of eight were lost. Although Italian forces took some Sudanese and Kenyan border towns, and occupied British Somaliland in August, they went no further and remained on the defensive. Meanwhile, British reinforcements arrived to the north and south.

By 1941, it was clear that the Italian presence was a nuisance rather than a serious threat. In February the auxiliary cruiser *Ramb I* was intercepted seven days into its voyage by the New Zealand cruiser *Leander* off the Maldives and surrendered. By this stage the British were retaking lost territory on the Horn of Africa with the support of limited carrier airstrikes and cruiser bombardments. In March the main offensive to take Abyssinia began, and a brief burst of Italian naval activity in early April resulted in a number of losses. When the British pushed on Massawa on 6 April, the remaining Italian naval and merchant ships, amounting to some 150,000 tons, were scuttled. Although the last Italian position, Assab, was only taken in June, the Red Sea was for the time being no longer a combat zone.

Alexandria

Port Said

Suez Canal

Cairo

Suez

TRANS-JORDAN

Aqaba

EGYPT

RED SEA

RN Red Sea Squadron, June 1940
3 Cruisers
4 Destroyers
3 Escorts

BN Convoys begin June 1940

SAUDI ARABIA

Pantere and *Tigre* scuttled after being bombed, 02.04

Jeddah

Sauro sunk by Swordfish 02.04

Manin bombed by Swordfish from HMS *Eagle* based at Port Sudan, 02.04

Port Sudan

SUDAN

Battisi, scuttled after being bombed, 02.04

Leone, run aground, 01.04

Nullo, beached on 21.10 and sunk by RAF Bleinheims, 22.10

Cruiser HMS *Capetown* torpedoed escorting minesweepers in attack on Massawa, 08.04

British offensive March 1941, Massawa falls 08.04

Massawa

YEMEN

ADEN

ABYSSINIA

Torricelli sunk 23.06

Assab

Aden

Gulf of Aden

Destroyer HMS *Khartoum* sunk in accident, 23.06.

FRENCH SOMALILAND

Djibouti

Italian invasion August 1940

Operation *Appearance*, 16.03
Landing by two battalions of Indian Army troops supported by the cruisers *Glasgow* and *Caledon* along with 2 destroyers, two auxiliary cruisers and other vessels

Berbera

BRITISH SOMALILAND

0   200 Nm

0   200 km

OPERATION JUDGEMENT, THE TARANTO RAID, 11 NOVEMBER 1940

THE IDEA FOR a carrier airstrike on the Italian fleet in its home base at Taranto dated back to 1935. In the early stage of the war Admiral Cunningham lacked the means to conduct such an operation as *Eagle* only carried a small air group. The arrival of the modern armoured carrier *Illustrious* in August greatly increased the Mediterranean fleet's strike capability, while the deployment of long-range RAF reconnaissance aircraft to Malta provided the means with which to observe the Italian defences at Taranto. The operation was scheduled for 21 October, however, a small fire on *Illustrious* forced a delay and the Italian invasion of Greece on 28 October changed the situation in the Mediterranean.

The airstrike on Taranto (Operation *Judgement*) became part of a much larger sequence of convoy and reinforcement operations throughout the Mediterranean. Operation *MB8* encompassed four convoys, one each to and from the Aegean and Malta, the passage of a battleship, two cruisers and destroyers from Gibraltar to Alexandria and the passage of reinforcements to the newly established advanced base in Suda Bay, Crete. To cover these operations Cunningham was to take the bulk of the fleet into the central Mediterranean and then launch a simultaneous airstrike on Taranto and a raid on Italian shipping in the Strait on Otranto by a combined cruiser-destroyer force. Owing to a fuel leak *Eagle* did not participate and transferred its aircraft to *Illustrious*.

The operation began on 4 November with the passage of reinforcements to Greece while the main forces put to sea two days later. In the western Mediterranean Force H additionally bombarded Cagliari on Sardinia. By the morning of 11 November the various elements of the fleet concentrated off Malta for the key phase.

The northward passage proceeded as planned and in the final stage the carrier and escorts detached from the battle fleet for a high-speed run to the flying-off position. It was a calm night with a three-quarter moon and the strike was organised into two waves separated by an hour. Although the Italians had reinforced Taranto's air defences they succeeded in shooting down only two of the attacking Swordfish. A further strike for the following night was planned, but cancelled owing to bad weather, and the fleet was back in Alexandria on 14 November.

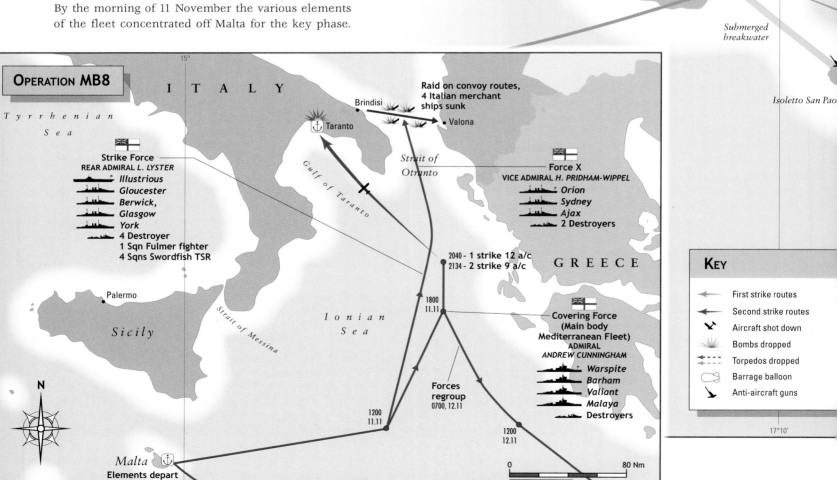

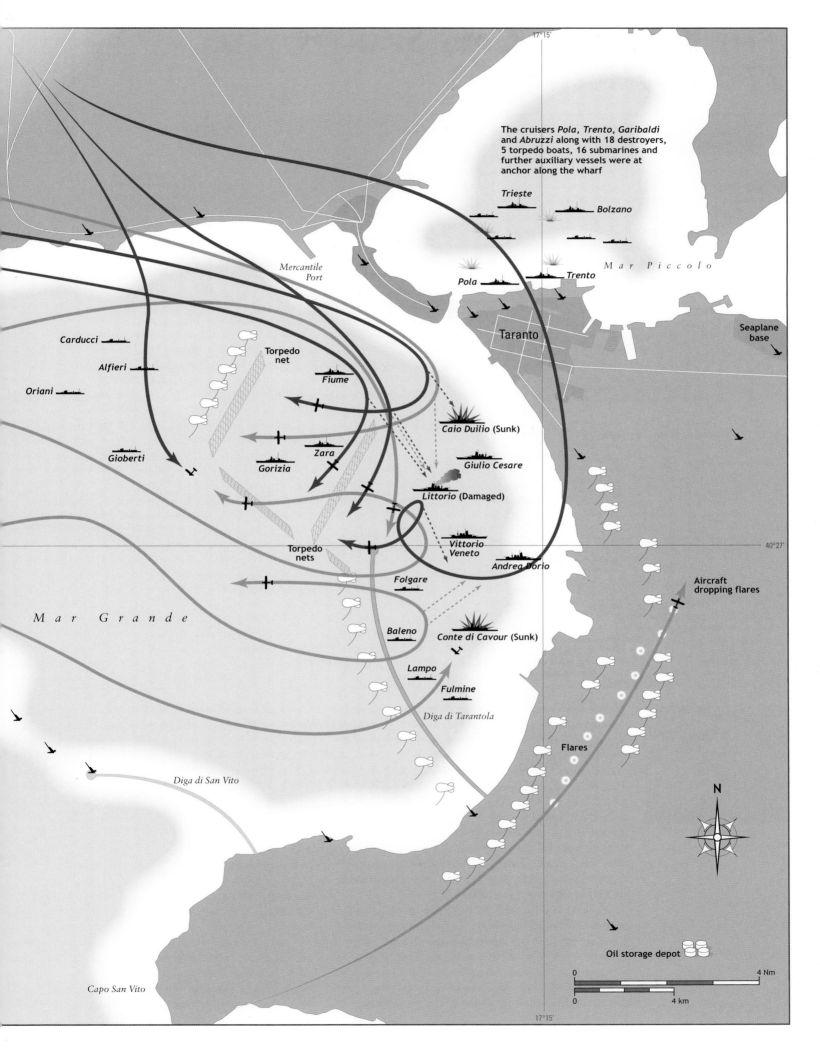

The cruisers *Pola*, *Trento*, *Garibaldi* and *Abruzzi* along with 18 destroyers, 5 torpedo boats, 16 submarines and further auxiliary vessels were at anchor along the wharf

Trieste

Bolzano

Mar Piccolo

Pola

Trento

Taranto

Seaplane base

Mercantile Port

Carducci

Alfieri

Oriani

Torpedo net

Fiume

Caio Duilio (Sunk)

Zara

Gioberti

Gorizia

Giulio Cesare

Littorio (Damaged)

Torpedo nets

Vittorio Veneto

Andrea Dorio

Mar Grande

Folgare

Aircraft dropping flares

Baleno

Conte di Cavour (Sunk)

Flares

Lampo

Fulmine

Diga di Tarantola

Diga di San Vito

N

Capo San Vito

Oil storage depot

0   4 Nm

0   4 km

17°15'

40°27'

17°15'

43

The Battle of Cape Spartivento, 27 November 1940

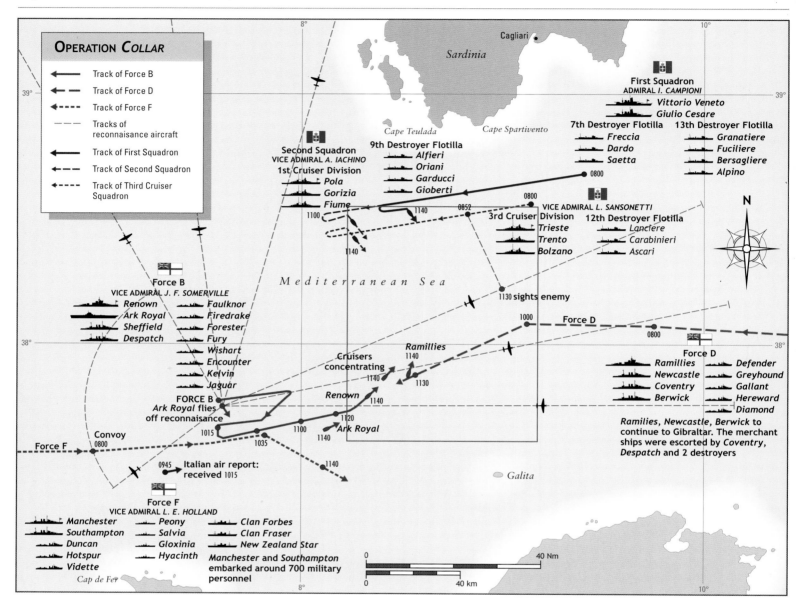

OPERATION COLLAR

- ← Track of Force B
- ←– – Track of Force D
- ←···· Track of Force F
- – – Tracks of reconnaisance aircraft
- ← Track of First Squadron
- ←– – Track of Second Squadron
- ←···· Track of Third Cruiser Squadron

Second Squadron
VICE ADMIRAL A. IACHINO
1st Cruiser Division
- Pola
- Gorizia
- Fiume

9th Destroyer Flotilla
- Alfieri
- Oriani
- Garducci
- Gioberti

First Squadron
ADMIRAL I. CAMPIONI
- Vittorio Veneto
- Giulio Cesare

7th Destroyer Flotilla
- Freccia
- Dardo
- Saetta

13th Destroyer Flotilla
- Granatiere
- Fuciliere
- Bersagliere
- Alpino

VICE ADMIRAL L. SANSONETTI
3rd Cruiser Division
- Trieste
- Trento
- Bolzano

12th Destroyer Flotilla
- Lanciere
- Carabinieri
- Ascari

Force B
VICE ADMIRAL J. F. SOMERVILLE
- Renown
- Ark Royal
- Sheffield
- Despatch
- Faulknor
- Firedrake
- Forester
- Fury
- Wishart
- Encounter
- Kelvin
- Jaguar

FORCE B
Ark Royal flies off reconnaisance

Cruisers concentrating

Renown

Ramillies

Ark Royal

1130 sights enemy

Force D

Force D
- Ramillies
- Newcastle
- Coventry
- Berwick
- Defender
- Greyhound
- Gallant
- Hereward
- Diamond

Ramillies, Newcastle, Berwick to continue to Gibraltar. The merchant ships were escorted by Coventry, Despatch and 2 destroyers

Convoy

Force F

0945 Italian air report: received 1015

Force F
VICE ADMIRAL L. E. HOLLAND
- Manchester
- Southampton
- Duncan
- Hotspur
- Vidette
- Peony
- Salvia
- Gloxinia
- Hyacinth
- Clan Forbes
- Clan Fraser
- New Zealand Star

Manchester and Southampton embarked around 700 military personnel

Cap de Fer

Sardinia
Cagliari
Cape Teulada
Cape Spartivento
Mediterranean Sea
Galita

40 Nm
40 km

FOLLOWING THE ATTACK on Taranto the British decided that conditions were right to attempt to run a fast convoy across the Mediterranean and in the process redistribute forces throughout the theatre. Operation *Collar* would encompass three merchant ships, two for Malta and one for Alexandria, while in addition the cruisers *Manchester* and *Southampton* would carry RAF personnel needed in Egypt. The old battleship *Ramillies* and the cruisers *Berwick* and *Newcastle* would also use the opportunity to come through from the east. At the same time, in the eastern basin, Admiral Cunningham would cover a supply convoy to Suda Bay in Crete and conduct carrier strikes on outlying Italian positions.

The Italians hoped to intercept a Malta-bound convoy and although they knew Force H had left Gibraltar they did not detect the convoy itself. Admiral Campioni sortied with two battleships from Naples and was joined by the other elements off southern Sardinia. At 10.15am *Bolzano*'s floatplane sighted Force H and Campioni decided to head south hoping to engage the British before the two forces had joined. The aim had

been to operate under air cover from Sardinia, but throughout the day this fared poorly. Vice Admiral Somerville was accurately informed of the strength and location of the Italian force, but until he could form up with Force D he was at a numerical disadvantage. In the event Force D was closer to Force H than to the Italians and once the British forces joined they turned north. Shortly before noon Campioni received reports of a large British formation with two or three capital ships and a carrier and ordered a retreat. A running battle developed mainly between the opposing cruiser forces. At 1.00pm the two Italian battleships entered the action prompting the British cruisers to withdraw on to the *Renown* and *Ramillies*. Campioni chose not to press home his advantage as *Ark Royal*'s aircraft dominated the air battle and subjected his forces to numerous airstrikes. He withdrew and Somerville in turn too chose not to give chase as his objective was to protect the convoy. Campioni was removed as a result of the battle that became known to the Italians as the Battle of Cape Teulada.

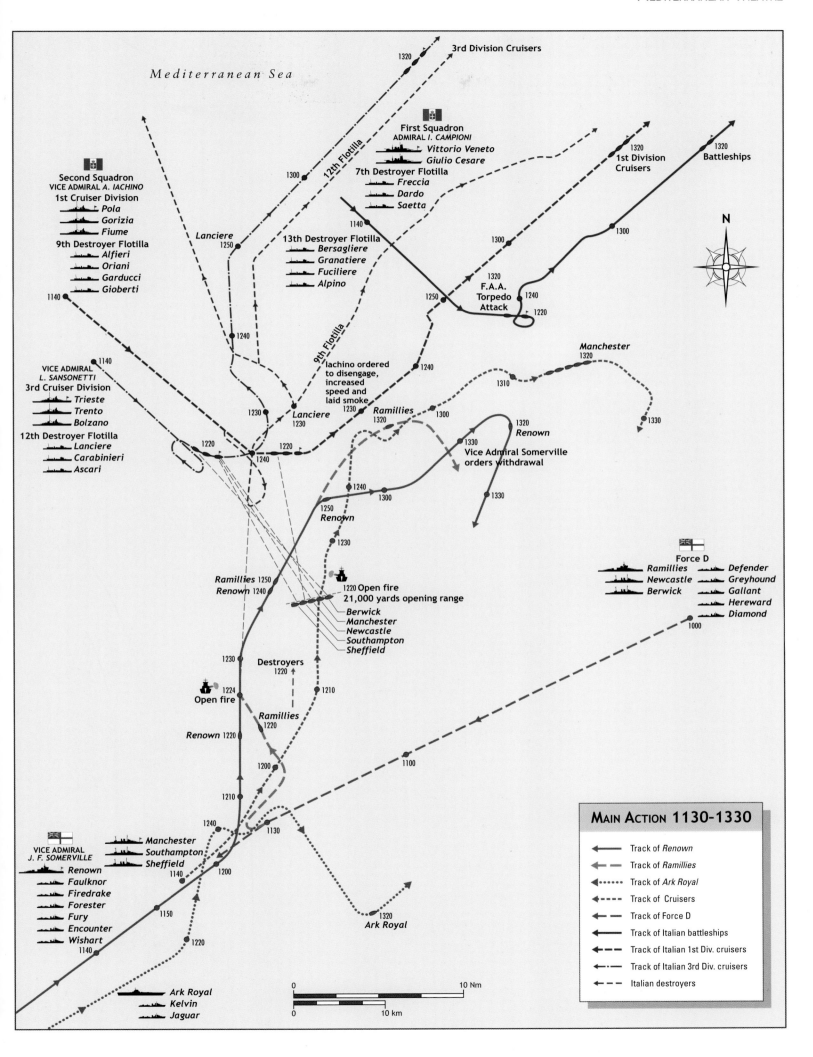

Mediterranean Sea

3rd Division Cruisers
1320

First Squadron
ADMIRAL I. CAMPIONI
Vittorio Veneto
Giulio Cesare
7th Destroyer Flotilla
Freccia
Dardo
Saetta

12th Flotilla
1300
1140

Second Squadron
VICE ADMIRAL A. IACHINO
1st Cruiser Division
Pola
Gorizia
Fiume
9th Destroyer Flotilla
Alfieri
Oriani
Garducci
Gioberti

Lanciere
1250
1140

13th Destroyer Flotilla
Bersagliere
Granatiere
Fuciliere
Alpino

1320
1st Division Cruisers
1320
Battleships
1320
1300

1300
1250

F.A.A.
Torpedo
Attack
1240
1220

VICE ADMIRAL
L. SANSONETTI
3rd Cruiser Division
Trieste
Trento
Bolzano
12th Destroyer Flotilla
Lanciere
Carabinieri
Ascari

1140

9th Flotilla

Iachino ordered
to disengage,
increased
speed and
laid smoke

1240
1230
1230
Lanciere
1230

1240

Manchester
1320
1310

Ramillies
1320
1300

1330
1320
Renown

Vice Admiral Somerville
orders withdrawal

1330

1240
1220
1240
1220

1240

1330

1240
1300
1250
Renown

1330

1230

Force D
Ramillies   Defender
Newcastle   Greyhound
Berwick   Gallant
             Hereward
             Diamond

Ramillies 1250
Renown 1240

1220 Open fire
21,000 yards opening range
Berwick
Manchester
Newcastle
Southampton
Sheffield

1230
Destroyers
1220

1224
Open fire

Ramillies
1220

Renown 1220

1210

1200

1210

1240

1230

1210

1100

1000

VICE ADMIRAL
J. F. SOMERVILLE
Renown
Faulknor
Firedrake
Forester
Fury
Encounter
Wishart

Manchester
Southampton
Sheffield

1130
1200
1140
1150
1220
1140

1320
Ark Royal

Ark Royal
Kelvin
Jaguar

0   10 Nm

0   10 km

Main Action 1130-1330

← Track of *Renown*
← Track of *Ramillies*
◀···· Track of *Ark Royal*
◀-- - Track of *Cruisers*
← Track of Force D
← Track of Italian battleships
←-- Track of Italian 1st Div. cruisers
←-·- Track of Italian 3rd Div. cruisers
←-- Italian destroyers

ATLANTIC OPERATIONS BY GERMAN SURFACE RAIDERS, 1940

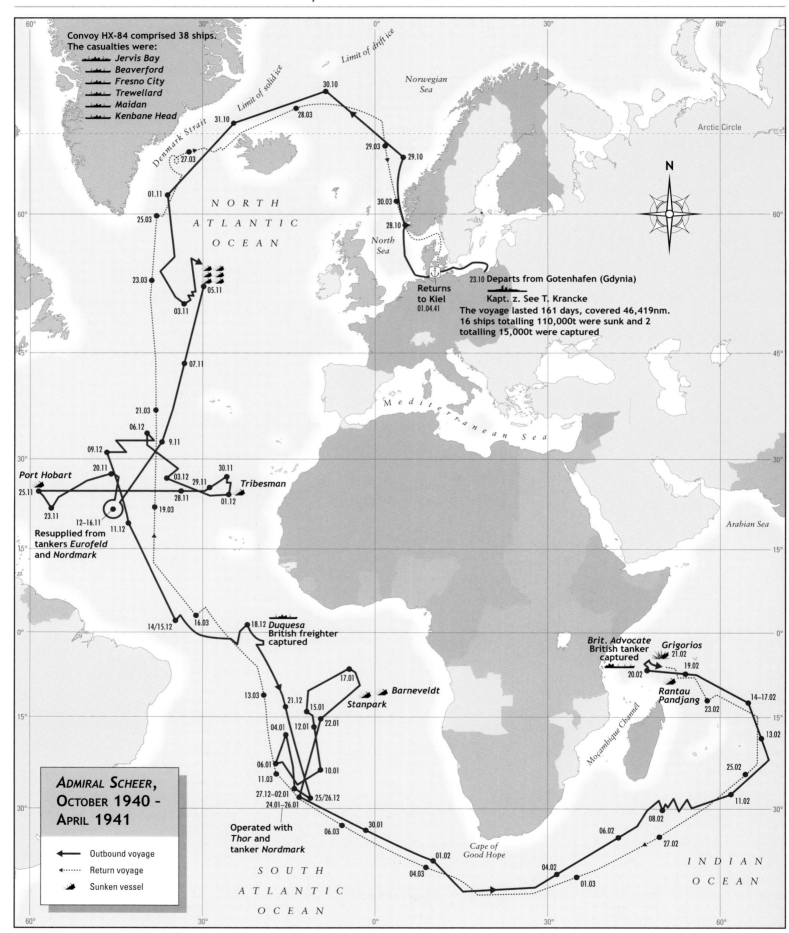

Convoy HX-84 comprised 38 ships.
The casualties were:
- Jervis Bay
- Beaverford
- Fresno City
- Trewellard
- Maidan
- Kenbane Head

Norwegian Sea

Arctic Circle

Limit of drift ice

Limit of solid ice

30.10

31.10   28.03

Denmark Strait   29.03   29.10

27.03

01.11   30.03

25.03   28.10

NORTH
ATLANTIC
OCEAN   *North Sea*

23.03

05.11   **23.10 Departs from Gotenhafen (Gdynia)**

03.11   **Returns
to Kiel
01.04.41**   **Kapt. z. See T. Krancke
The voyage lasted 161 days, covered 46,419nm.
16 ships totalling 110,000t were sunk and 2
totalling 15,000t were captured**

07.11

21.03   *Mediterranean Sea*

06.12   9.11

09.12

Port Hobart   20.11   03.12 29.11   30.11

25.11   28.11   01.12   *Tribesman*   *Arabian Sea*

23.11   19.03

12–16.11   11.12

**Resupplied from
tankers *Eurofeld*
and *Nordmark***

14/15.12   16.03   18.12 *Duquesa*
British freighter
captured   **Brit. Advocate**
British tanker
captured   *Grigorios*
21.02

13.03   17.01   20.02   19.02

21.12 15.01   *Barneveldt*   *Rantau
Pandjang*
04.01 12.01   *Stanpark*   23.02   14–17.02

22.01

06.01   10.01   13.02

11.03

27.12–02.01   25/26.12   25.02

24.01–26.01

11.02

Mozambique Channel

08.02

**ADMIRAL SCHEER,
OCTOBER 1940 –
APRIL 1941**   06.03   30.01   06.02

01.02   *Cape of
Good Hope*   04.02   27.02

→ Outbound voyage   06.03   *INDIAN
OCEAN*

◄···· Return voyage   04.03   01.03

🚢 Sunken vessel   **Operated with
Thor and
tanker *Nordmark***

SOUTH
ATLANTIC
OCEAN

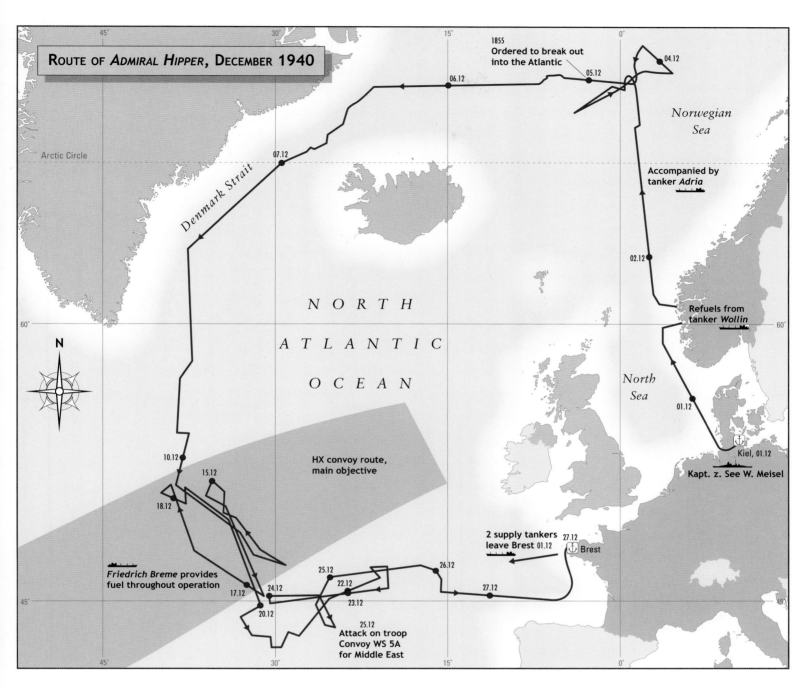

ROUTE OF *ADMIRAL HIPPER*, DECEMBER 1940

Norwegian Sea

1855
Ordered to break out into the Atlantic

04.12

05.12

06.12

07.12

Arctic Circle

Denmark Strait

Accompanied by tanker *Adria*

02.12

N O R T H

A T L A N T I C

O C E A N

Refuels from tanker *Wollin*

North Sea

01.12

Kiel, 01.12

Kapt. z. See W. Meisel

10.12

15.12

18.12

HX convoy route, main objective

Friedrich Breme provides fuel throughout operation

17.12   24.12

20.12

25.12   22.12

23.12

2 supply tankers leave Brest 01.12   27.12

Brest

26.12

27.12

25.12
Attack on troop Convoy WS 5A for Middle East

THE KRIEGSMARINE'S ABILTY to attack British supply lines in the Atlantic with its surface force was delayed until the autumn as many of the heavy units needed to undergo refits or extensive repairs after the Norwegian campaign. The first out was *Admiral Scheer*. She was to attempt to breakout into the Atlantic unnoticed and then use the element of surprise to attack convoys along the Halifax-Britain route. The object was to dislocate the North Atlantic convoy system before moving on to attack shipping in the southern Atlantic and the Indian oceans. The ship's light armour and moderate speed meant that it was only supposed to engage British warships if no alternative presented itself. It was known that a convoy had left Halifax on 27 October so Kapt.z.See Krancke aimed to intercept it around 3 November. Poor weather prevented a sighting until 5 November when in the late afternoon convoy HX-84 was attacked. The convoy scattered and the escorting armed merchant cruiser *Jervis Bay* and five ships (approx 55,000 tons) were sunk. Following this success *Scheer* immediately turned south to evade the inevitable British patrols that would be sent out. The Home Fleet did put to sea, but by

then *Scheer* had long moved on. For nearly two weeks, until 17 November, the entire North Atlantic convoy system was stopped. For the remainder of its voyage, the longest by a German warship during the war, *Scheer* operated in the southern seas drawing supplies from its replenishment ship *Nordmark* and on occasion joining with auxiliary cruisers. Here individually sailing ships rather than convoys were to be found.

The heavy cruiser *Admiral Hipper* was the next warship to operate in the Atlantic, but to very different parameters. *Admiral Hipper* was faster, more heavily armoured and thus could engage British cruisers. However, her high fuel consumption and much smaller radius of action meant she could not operate further than 600nm from a tanker. This was a severe limitation. Little was achieved against the main objective, the HX convoy route, in the harsh December weather. The shift to the southern route in late December was designed to draw British attention away from the north where the next surface raiders would arrive shortly. Apart from a skirmish with a heavily protected troop convoy little was achieved.

THE WAR AT SEA, 1941

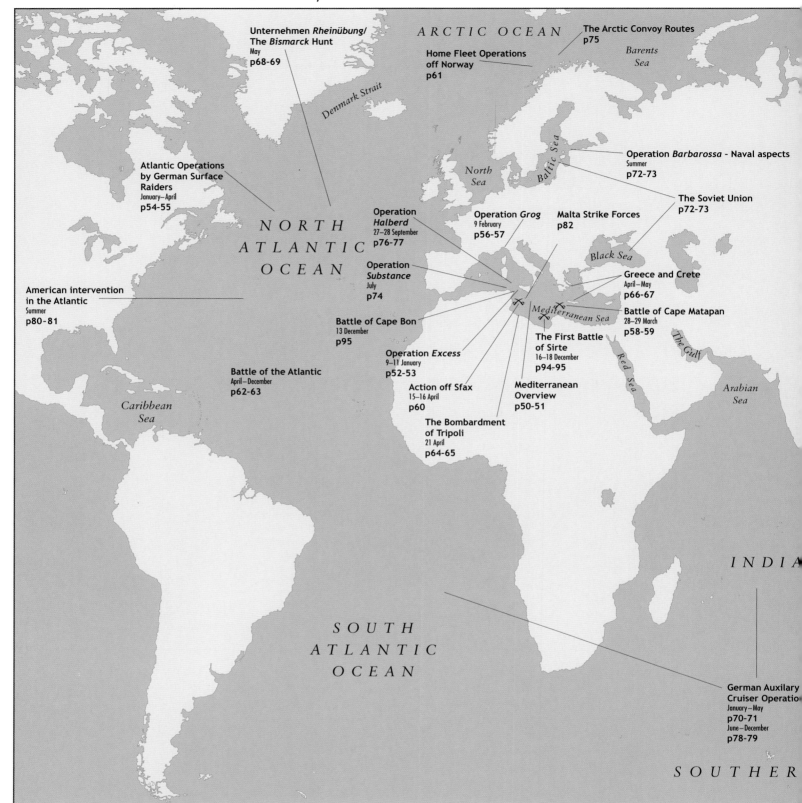

Unternehmen *Rheinübung*/
The *Bismarck* Hunt
May
p68-69

ARCTIC OCEAN

The Arctic Convoy Routes
p75

Home Fleet Operations
off Norway
p61

*Barents
Sea*

Denmark Strait

Atlantic Operations
by German Surface
Raiders
January–April
p54-55

*North
Sea*

Baltic Sea

Operation *Barbarossa* - Naval aspects
Summer
p72-73

The Soviet Union
p72-73

NORTH
ATLANTIC
OCEAN

Operation
Halberd
27–28 September
p76-77

Operation *Grog*
9 February
p56-57

Malta Strike Forces
p82

Black Sea

Operation
Substance
July
p74

Greece and Crete
April–May
p66-67

American intervention
in the Atlantic
Summer
p80-81

Mediterranean Sea

Battle of Cape Matapan
28–29 March
p58-59

The Gulf

Battle of Cape Bon
13 December
p95

The First Battle
of Sirte
16–18 December
p94-95

Red Sea

*Caribbean
Sea*

Operation *Excess*
9–11 January
p52-53

Action off Sfax
15–16 April
p60

Mediterranean
Overview
p50-51

*Arabian
Sea*

Battle of the Atlantic
April–December
p62-63

The Bombardment
of Tripoli
21 April
p64-65

INDIA

SOUTH
ATLANTIC
OCEAN

German Auxilary
Cruiser Operatio
January–May
p70-71
June–December
p78-79

SOUTHER

During the course of the year the war transformed from a European war, with some engagements on the periphery, into a global conflict, and Britain found herself in a vulnerable position despite having deterred a German invasion in the early autumn of 1940. Britain still possessed considerable industrial strength and was in the process of rebuilding and expanding its military forces. The Dominions, too, were expanding their armed forces, growing their industrial capacities and shifting the focus to wartime production, and, together with other imperial possessions, provided raw materials and agricultural products to keep Britain sustained. The long-term strength of the British Empire rested on its ability to keep its maritime communications open and supplies flowing. Securing the Atlantic theatre by building up the convoy escort forces and creating a network of air and naval bases along its periphery was the British priority. An oceanic trade defence campaign on this scale had not been anticipated, and the rapid expansion of Canadian naval power would ultimately also be crucial in this theatre. Gradual American involvement also shaped the campaign throughout the year.

The attempted German blockade of Britain came closest to having a severe impact at this stage of the war.

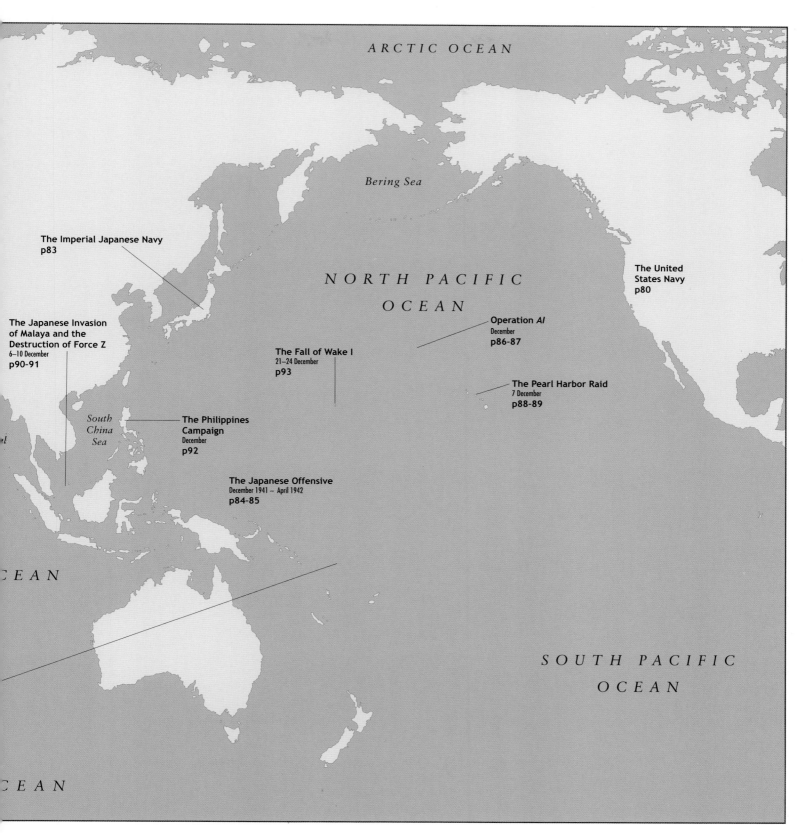

ARCTIC OCEAN

Bering Sea

NORTH PACIFIC
OCEAN

The Imperial Japanese Navy
p83

The United States Navy
p80

The Japanese Invasion of Malaya and the Destruction of Force Z
6–10 December
p90-91

Operation *AI*
December
p86-87

The Fall of Wake I
21–24 December
p93

South China Sea

The Pearl Harbor Raid
7 December
p88-89

The Philippines Campaign
December
p92

The Japanese Offensive
December 1941 – April 1942
p84-85

OCEAN

SOUTH PACIFIC
OCEAN

OCEAN

However, before the campaign could benefit from the mutually supporting efforts of surface raiders, U-boats and aircraft, the start of the campaign against the Soviet Union in the east began the process of drawing resources from other theatres. In the Mediterranean, a similar pattern emerged. The arrival of German forces to prevent an Italian collapse pushed the British back to the extreme ends of the sea, and, even more than in 1940, sustaining Malta became the focus of British activity. When the Luftwaffe moved some of its forces to the Eastern Front the British position marginally improved.

Overall, the British held on, but in the process the

Royal Navy sustained considerable losses. The British could deal with the German and Italian naval threats, but the removal of forces from the Far East, and the failure to reinforce the region, enabled the Japanese to prepare an offensive to take control of the British, Dutch and American possessions in the region. A force of two British capital ships sent to Singapore was hardly a deterrent and while American diplomatic and economic pressure on the Japanese intensified throughout the year, the military build-up progressed only slowly. When the Japanese then attacked in early December the allies were quickly pushed onto the defensive.

THE MEDITERRANEAN, 1941

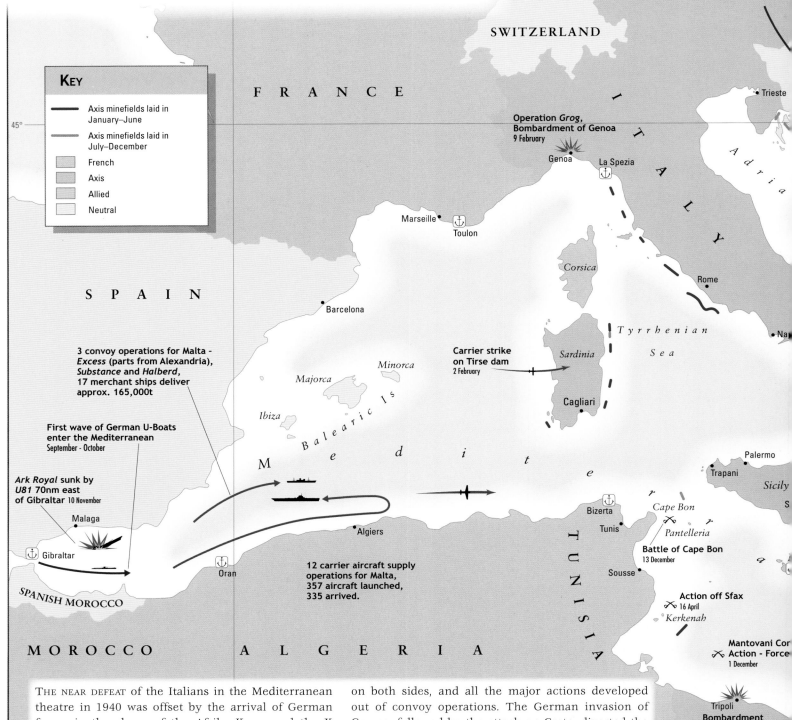

SWITZERLAND

FRANCE

KEY

— Axis minefields laid in January–June

— Axis minefields laid in July–December

◻ French

◻ Axis

◻ Allied

◻ Neutral

45°

Operation *Grog*, Bombardment of Genoa 9 February

Genoa • La Spezia

Marseille • ⚓ Toulon

S P A I N

Corsica

Barcelona •

ITALY

Trieste •

Adria

Rome •

Na•

Tyrrhenian Sea

3 convoy operations for Malta – *Excess* (parts from Alexandria), *Substance* and *Halberd*, 17 merchant ships deliver approx. 165,000t

Minorca

Majorca

Carrier strike on Tirse dam 2 February

Sardinia

Cagliari •

First wave of German U-Boats enter the Mediterranean September – October

Ibiza

Balearic Is

M

e   d   i   t   e   r

Palermo •

Trapani •

Sicily

Ark Royal sunk by U81 70nm east of Gibraltar 10 November

Malaga •

⚓ Bizerta

Cape Bon

Tunis •

Pantelleria

⚓ Gibraltar

Oran ⚓

• Algiers

T U N I S I A

Battle of Cape Bon 13 December

Sousse •

SPANISH MOROCCO

12 carrier aircraft supply operations for Malta, 357 aircraft launched, 335 arrived.

Action off Sfax 16 April
• Kerkenah

M O R O C C O   A L G E R I A

Mantovani Cor Action - Force 1 December

Tripoli •

Bombardment of Tripoli 21 April

THE NEAR DEFEAT of the Italians in the Mediterranean theatre in 1940 was offset by the arrival of German forces in the shape of the Afrika Korps and the X Fliegerkorps, a specialised Luftwaffe maritime strike wing; and the superiority of German air power over that of the Italians was shown in the first major action of the year, Operation *Excess*. However, the axis powers did not have the undisputed advantage in the air, as often Italo-German disagreements and inter-service rivalry prevented air power from exerting its full potential. Beyond the range of high-performance, single-engine, shore-based aircraft British naval aviation continued to be highly effective. This was one of the reasons for the Italian defeat at Cape Matapan in March.

Keeping maritime communications open and supplies flowing continued to be the focus of naval operations

on both sides, and all the major actions developed out of convoy operations. The German invasion of Greece, followed by the attack on Crete, diverted the focus away from the central Mediterranean to the Aegean. Despite suffering heavy losses, the Royal Navy managed to rescue a sizeable proportion of the allied expeditionary force. Axis control of the Aegean, and in particular airbases on Crete and on the North African shore, complicated the British position. To prevent axis forces from using Vichy-French controlled Lebanon and Syria, and so threatening the Suez Canal from another direction, allied forces invaded and defeated Vichy forces in June and July. Overall, however, from June to October the eastern Mediterranean was relatively quiet, mainly because of the German focus on the invasion of the Soviet Union that commenced on 22 June.

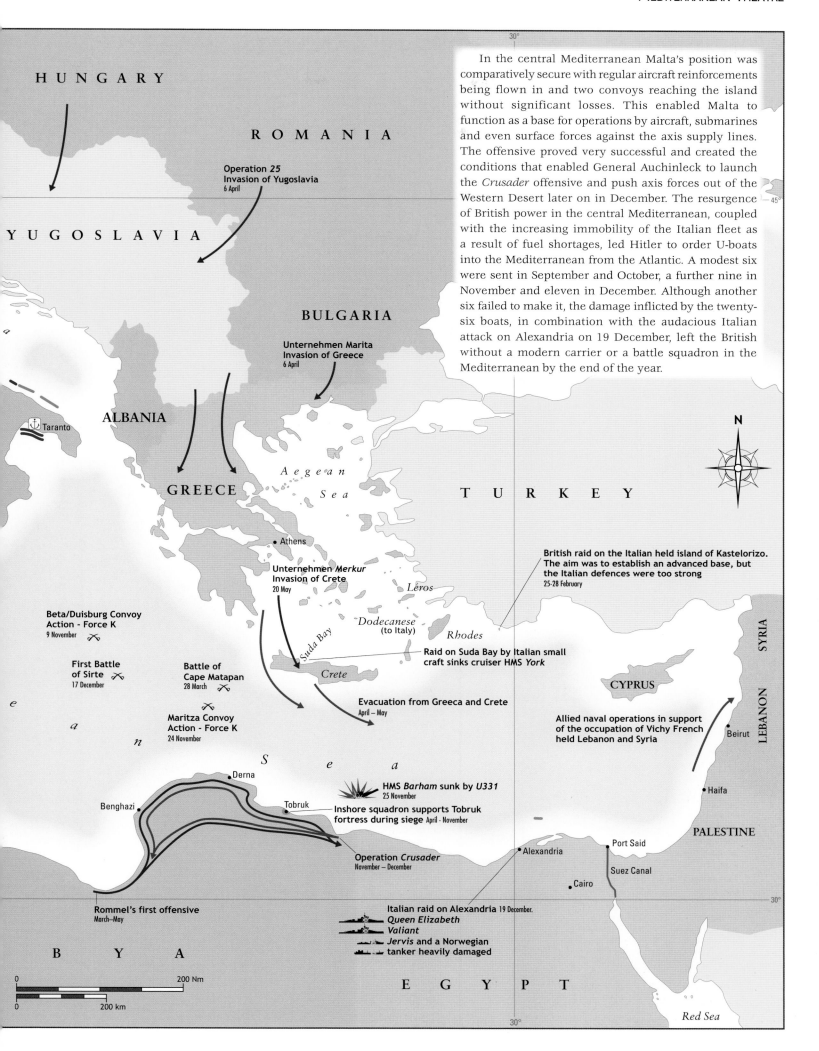

HUNGARY

ROMANIA

YUGOSLAVIA

Operation *25*
Invasion of Yugoslavia
6 April

BULGARIA

Unternehmen Marita
Invasion of Greece
6 April

ALBANIA

⚓ Taranto

Aegean Sea

GREECE

• Athens

TURKEY

N

Unternehmen *Merkur*
Invasion of Crete
20 May

British raid on the Italian held island of Kastelorizo.
The aim was to establish an advanced base, but
the Italian defences were too strong
25-28 February

Léros

Dodecanese
(to Italy)

Rhodes

Beta/Duisburg Convoy
Action - Force K
9 November

Suda Bay

Raid on Suda Bay by Italian small
craft sinks cruiser HMS *York*

SYRIA

First Battle
of Sirte
17 December

Battle of
Cape Matapan
28 March

Crete

CYPRUS

Maritza Convoy
Action - Force K
24 November

Evacuation from Greeca and Crete
April – May

Allied naval operations in support
of the occupation of Vichy French
held Lebanon and Syria

LEBANON

• Beirut

S

e

a

Derna

HMS *Barham* sunk by *U331*
25 November

• Haifa

Benghazi

Tobruk

Inshore squadron supports Tobruk
fortress during siege April - November

PALESTINE

Operation *Crusader*
November – December

• Alexandria

Port Said

Rommel's first offensive
March–May

Italian raid on Alexandria 19 December.

Suez Canal

Queen Elizabeth

Valiant

• Cairo

B   Y   A

Jervis and a Norwegian
tanker heavily damaged

0   200 Nm

0   200 km

E   G   Y   P   T

Red Sea

In the central Mediterranean Malta's position was comparatively secure with regular aircraft reinforcements being flown in and two convoys reaching the island without significant losses. This enabled Malta to function as a base for operations by aircraft, submarines and even surface forces against the axis supply lines. The offensive proved very successful and created the conditions that enabled General Auchinleck to launch the *Crusader* offensive and push axis forces out of the Western Desert later on in December. The resurgence of British power in the central Mediterranean, coupled with the increasing immobility of the Italian fleet as a result of fuel shortages, led Hitler to order U-boats into the Mediterranean from the Atlantic. A modest six were sent in September and October, a further nine in November and eleven in December. Although another six failed to make it, the damage inflicted by the twenty-six boats, in combination with the audacious Italian attack on Alexandria on 19 December, left the British without a modern carrier or a battle squadron in the Mediterranean by the end of the year.

OPERATION EXCESS, 9–11 JANUARY 1941

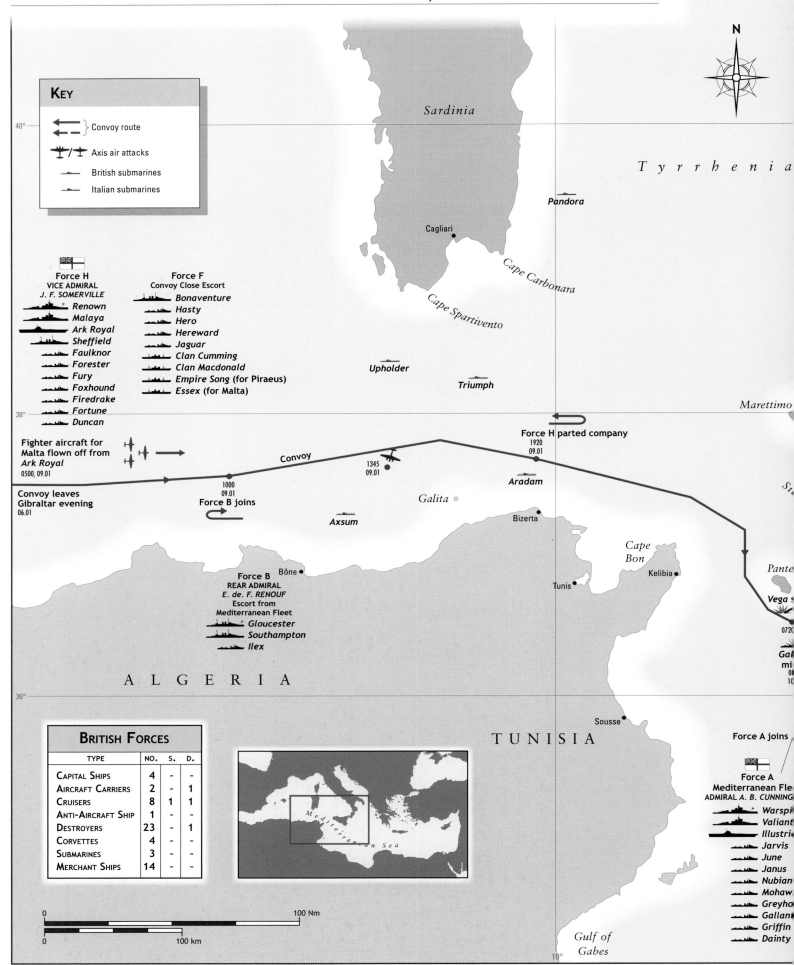

KEY

⇐ ⇐ } Convoy route

Axis air attacks

British submarines

Italian submarines

Sardinia

Pandora

Cagliari

Cape Carbonara

Cape Spartivento

Upholder

Triumph

Marettimo

Force H
VICE ADMIRAL
J. F. SOMERVILLE
Renown
Malaya
Ark Royal
Sheffield
Faulknor
Forester
Fury
Foxhound
Firedrake
Fortune
Duncan

Force F
Convoy Close Escort
Bonaventure
Hasty
Hero
Hereward
Jaguar
Clan Cumming
Clan Macdonald
Empire Song (for Piraeus)
Essex (for Malta)

Fighter aircraft for
Malta flown off from
Ark Royal
0500, 09.01

Convoy leaves
Gibraltar evening
06.01

Convoy

1000
09.01
Force B joins

1345
09.01

Force H parted company
1920
09.01

Aradam

Galita

Bizerta

Axsum

Bône

Force B
REAR ADMIRAL
E. de. F. RENOUF
Escort from
Mediterranean Fleet
Gloucester
Southampton
Ilex

Cape
Bon

Tunis

Kelibia

Pante

Vega s

072(

*Gal
mi*
0N
10

Sousse

A L G E R I A

T U N I S I A

Force A joins

Force A
Mediterranean Fle
ADMIRAL *A. B. CUNNING*
Warspi
Valiant
Illustri
Jarvis
June
Janus
Nubian
Mohaw
Greyho
Gallan
Griffin
Dainty

BRITISH FORCES			
TYPE	NO.	S.	D.
CAPITAL SHIPS	4	-	-
AIRCRAFT CARRIERS	2	-	1
CRUISERS	8	1	1
ANTI-AIRCRAFT SHIP	1	-	-
DESTROYERS	23	-	1
CORVETTES	4	-	-
SUBMARINES	3	-	-
MERCHANT SHIPS	14	-	-

Mediterranean Sea

0   100 Nm

0   100 km

*Gulf of
Gabes*

IN ORDER TO assist the Greek forces fighting the Italians on the Albanian front the British staged Operation *Excess* to pass supplies through the Mediterranean from the west. The convoy itself was composed of four ships, three for Piraeus with supplies for the Greek army and one carrying military equipment and supplies for Malta. Nearly the entire British strength in the Mediterranean was required to cover these ships and Admiral Cunningham took advantage of the movement to ensure the passage of three further small convoys to and from Malta from the east. The plan was for Force H to provide cover until the Sicilian Channel while a detachment from Cunningham, Force B, would provide additional cover through the narrows. Once through Cunningham and the Mediterranean Fleet would provide distant cover for the eastern leg of the voyage while other forces provided close escort to the various convoy elements. The operation also marked the first appearance of German forces in the Mediterranean. In December the first Luftwaffe units had arrived to stabilise the collapsing Italian war effort. Of these the most important was the X Fliegerkorps, a specialised maritime strike unit that transferred from Norway and was equipped with Me110 long-range fighters, Ju87 dive-bombers and Ju88 medium bombers capable of carrying torpedoes.

Somerville left Gibraltar late on 6 January while Cunningham left Alexandria the next day and until the early hours of 10 January the operation proceeded smoothly. An Italian torpedo boat attack south of Pantellaria was defeated and the *Vega* sunk. Shortly after noon, about 55nm west of Malta, the air attacks intensified and those by the Ju87s proved very effective. *Illustrious* was hit six times and had her flight deck wrecked; having sustained such damage it was decided to take her into Malta for repairs. Although all fourteen merchant ships got through unscathed Force B was heavily attacked the next day and the *Southampton* was lost. Thus in total the British lost one cruiser and sustained heavy damage to another and a destroyer. The arrival of the Luftwaffe ended British supremacy in the Mediterranean, while the loss of the *Illustrious* prevented the follow-on operation, a sweep against Italian shipping in the Aegean, from taking place.

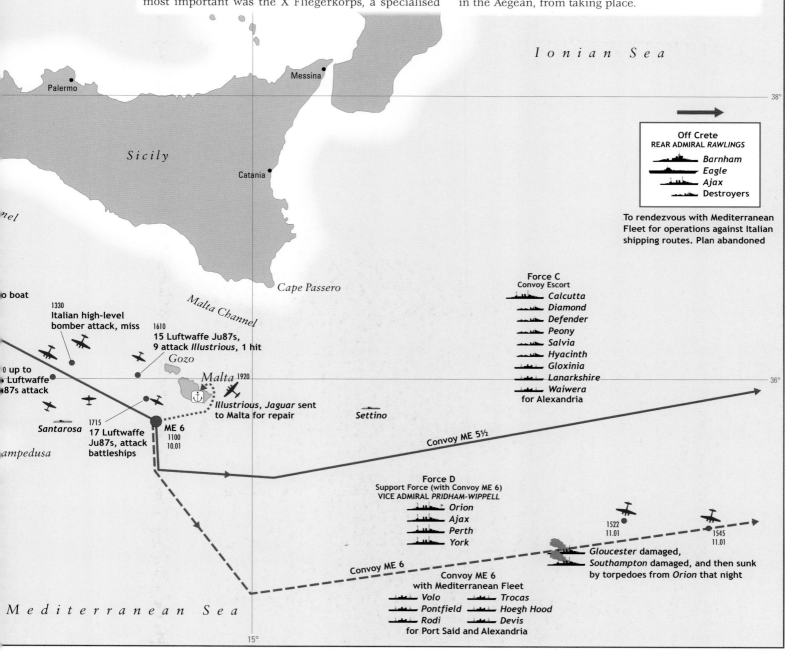

ATLANTIC OPERATIONS BY GERMAN SURFACE RAIDERS, JANUARY – MARCH 1941

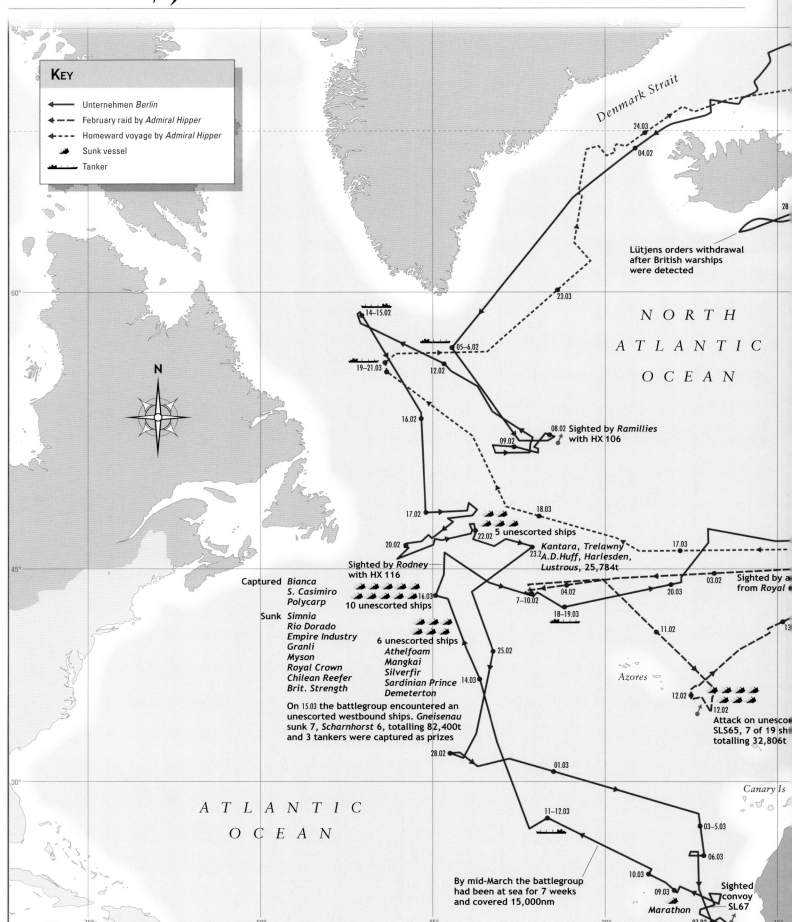

KEY

→ Unternehmen *Berlin*
◄- - Februrary raid by *Admiral Hipper*
◄····· Homeward voyage by *Admiral Hipper*
🚢 Sunk vessel
🚢 Tanker

Denmark Strait

24.03
04.02

Lütjens orders withdrawal after British warships were detected

23.03

NORTH ATLANTIC OCEAN

14–15.02
05–6.02
19–21.03
12.02

16.02

08.02 Sighted by *Ramillies* with HX 106
09.02

17.02
18.03

5 unescorted ships

20.02
22.02

Kantara, Trelawny
23.2 *A.D.Huff, Harlesden,*
Lustrous, 25,784t

17.03

03.02 Sighted by a from *Royal*

Sighted by *Rodney* with HX 116

04.02
7–10.02
20.03

Captured *Bianca*
S. Casimiro
Polycarp

16.03
10 unescorted ships

18–19.03
11.02

Sunk *Simnia*
Rio Dorado
Empire Industry
Granli
Myson
Royal Crown
Chilean Reefer
Brit. Strength

6 unescorted ships
Athelfoam
Mangkai
Silverfir
Sardinian Prince
Demeterton

25.02

14.03

Azores

12.02
12.02

Attack on unescor
SLS65, 7 of 19 shi
totalling 32,806t

On 15.03 the battlegroup encountered an unescorted westbound ships. *Gneisenau* sunk 7, *Scharnhorst* 6, totalling 82,400t and 3 tankers were captured as prizes

28.02
01.03

Canary Is

ATLANTIC
OCEAN

11–12.03
03–5.03

06.03

10.03

By mid-March the battlegroup had been at sea for 7 weeks and covered 15,000nm

09.03

Sighted convoy SL67

Marathon
07.03

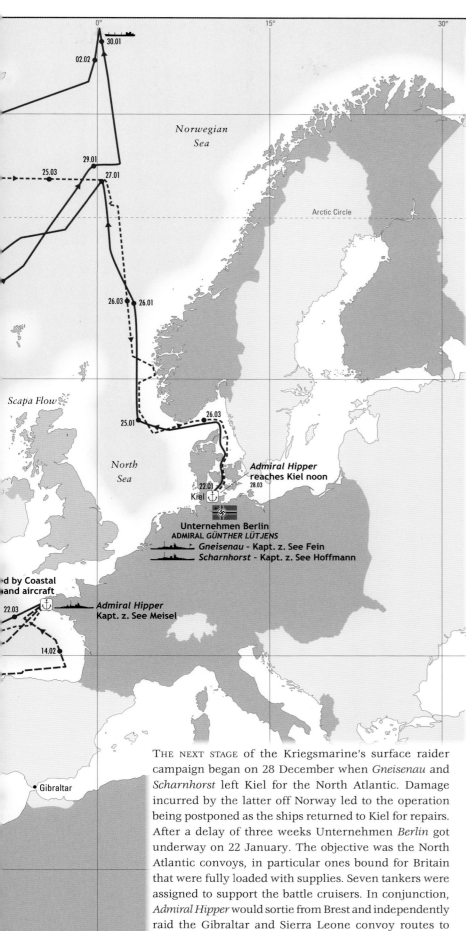

Norwegian Sea

Arctic Circle

Scapa Flow

North Sea

Admiral Hipper reaches Kiel noon
28.03

Kiel

Unternehmen Berlin
ADMIRAL *GÜNTHER LÜTJENS*
Gneisenau - Kapt. z. See Fein
Scharnhorst - Kapt. z. See Hoffmann

d by Coastal and aircraft

Admiral Hipper
Kapt. z. See Meisel

Gibraltar

little intelligence as to whether the Home Fleet was at Scapa Flow. Although Lütjens commanded the, to date, most powerful German squadron to enter the Atlantic an engagement with equal British forces was to be avoided. Even if both 12in battle cruisers encountered a 15in battleship, likely given that old British battleships escorted convoys, they were to turn away. This occurred when the Germans sighted HX106 on 8 February.

Meanwhile, *Hipper* was guided towards a convoy by signals intelligence and *U37*, and early on 12 February succeeded in making contact. Within two hours gunfire and torpedo attacks had sunk seven ships and the cruiser made for Brest. Lütjens continued to search along the HX route almost to Newfoundland where he hoped convoys would be easier to find. Yet no shipping was located and after four weeks at sea the results were disappointing. The first successes were some independently sailing ships. After having received the news that *Hipper* would not resume operations until the second week in March Lütjens decided to move his areas of operations to the south. This would perhaps yield some unprotected convoys and some diversionary cover for *Hipper*. U-boat reports guided him towards a SL convoy, but the presence of a British battleship and other forces prevented an attack.

After nearly two months at sea the ships not only required refitting, but also needed to be operational for the end of April to be able to operate in concert with the next wave of surface raiders coming from Germany. *Hipper*'s departure from Brest too was delayed so Lütjens decided to make one last attempt at the North Atlantic route. In order to increase the chances of making contact with allied merchant ships he used the two auxiliary ships he had just replenished from with his battle cruisers to form a loose line formation. This made it possible to sweep north covering a front of 120nm. Between 14 and 16 March a considerable number of merchant ships were destroyed and only the sighting of the battleship *Rodney* brought an end to this run. Having now attained some degree of success Lütjens decided to make for Brest.

In the event *Hipper* did not engage in any further commerce raiding. Around this time *Admiral Scheer* was nearing the end of her five-month operation and was due to return to Germany for a major refit. To do this it would be necessary to pass through one of the North Atlantic choke points. The original idea of *Hipper* and *Scheer* breaking through together was dismissed as impractical owing to the former's limited endurance and the latter's slower top speed. So as not to draw British attention to the North Atlantic, and into the path of the *Scheer*, Kapt.z.See Meisel did not intend to engage any allied vessels with the *Hipper*. During the passage through the Denmark Strait two British cruisers were detected and even though one could have been attacked with torpedoes Meisel refrained. The remainder of the journey was uneventful. Partly, this was also due to the British who, having been alerted by signals intelligence to the possibility of a German breakthrough, were focusing their efforts to the west. *Scheer* also detected some British cruisers, but evaded them and arrived in Kiel a few days later.

THE NEXT STAGE of the Kriegsmarine's surface raider campaign began on 28 December when *Gneisenau* and *Scharnhorst* left Kiel for the North Atlantic. Damage incurred by the latter off Norway led to the operation being postponed as the ships returned to Kiel for repairs. After a delay of three weeks Unternehmen *Berlin* got underway on 22 January. The objective was the North Atlantic convoys, in particular ones bound for Britain that were fully loaded with supplies. Seven tankers were assigned to support the battle cruisers. In conjunction, *Admiral Hipper* would sortie from Brest and independently raid the Gibraltar and Sierra Leone convoy routes to inflict damage and draw British attention away from the North Atlantic. Admiral Lütjens acted cautiously and abandoned his first breakout attempt as radar detected the presence of British warships and because there was

Operation Grog, The Bombardment of Genoa 9 February 1941

When in January intelligence suggested that a major Italian expeditionary force was being assembled at Genoa, the Admiralty tasked Admiral Somerville to use Force H to bombard the port. Somerville's plan was to first conduct a carrier airstrike on the hydroelectric dam on Lake Tirso in central Sardinia as a diversion to the actual bombardment. As Force H had raided Cagliari on numerous occasions the Italians would assume this to be a similar raid and not anticipate a northward thrust to Genoa. Operation *Picket* got underway on 31 January and in the early morning of 2 February eight Swordfish torpedo-bombers attacked the dam. Although carefully planned, the raid was unsuccessful and one aircraft was shot down. Force H then proceeded north for the second and main objective, but owing to the rapidly deteriorating weather Somerville decided to abandon the operation and return to Gibraltar.

On 6 February Force H sortied for a second attempt. The Italian navy knew that Force H had left Gibraltar but assumed it was undertaking another fly-off operation for Malta, a strike against Sardinia or perhaps a raid on the Ligurian coast. At 7pm on 8 February Admiral Iachino took the battle fleet out of La Spezia to rendezvous with a cruiser squadron sent north from Messina in anticipation of a British raid on Sardinia. Thus Force H's approach remained undetected and it achieved complete surprise. The attack was divided into two elements. *Ark Royal* was detached to carry out airstrikes against the oil refinery at Leghorn and lay mines in La Spezia harbour. At Genoa *Malaya* bombarded the docks while *Renown* and *Sheffield* hit the Ansaldo shipyards. Three Swordfish from *Ark Royal* provided the gunfire spotting. In total 273 15in, 782 6in and 400 4.5in shells were expended. Four merchant ships were sunk, eighteen damaged, but the battleship *Caio Duilio*, in dry-dock for repairs after the Taranto raid, remained undamaged. The city itself too was damaged. Iachino immediately turned north and although air searches were flown the British escaped without being detected. Two Italian reconnaissance planes were shot down while Iachino mistakenly chased a French convoy.

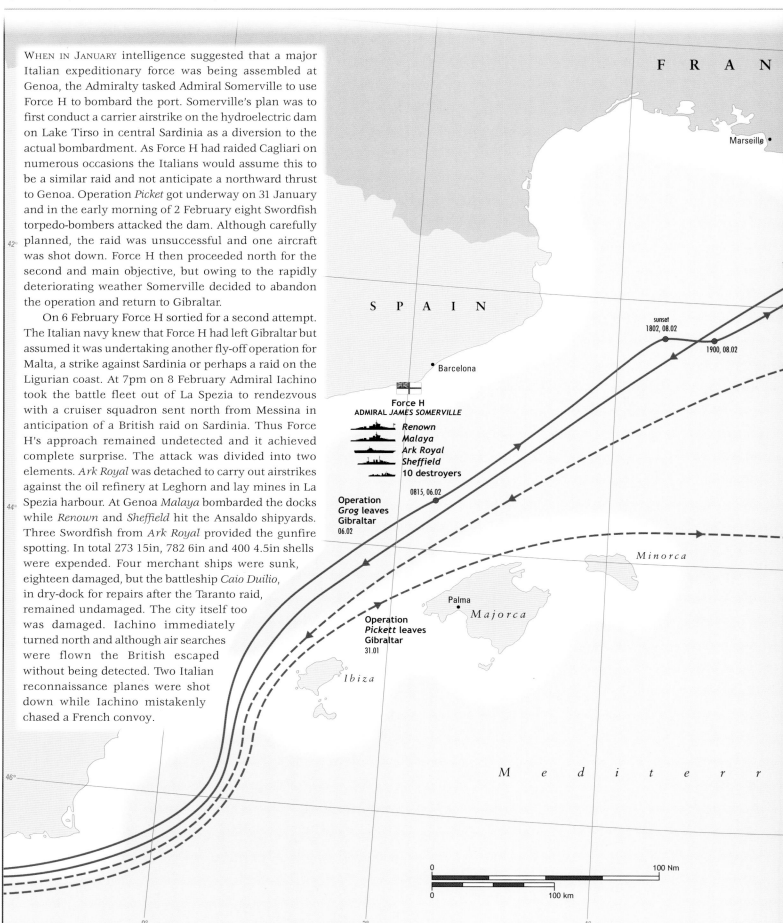

FRAN

Marseille •

SPAIN

sunset
1802, 08.02

1900, 08.02

• Barcelona

Force H
ADMIRAL *JAMES SOMERVILLE*

Renown
Malaya
Ark Royal
Sheffield
10 destroyers

0815, 06.02

Operation
***Grog* leaves**
Gibraltar
06.02

Minorca

Palma •
Majorca

Operation
***Pickett* leaves**
Gibraltar
31.01

Ibiza

M e d i t e r r

0   100 Nm

0   100 km

42°
44°
46°

0°   2°   4°

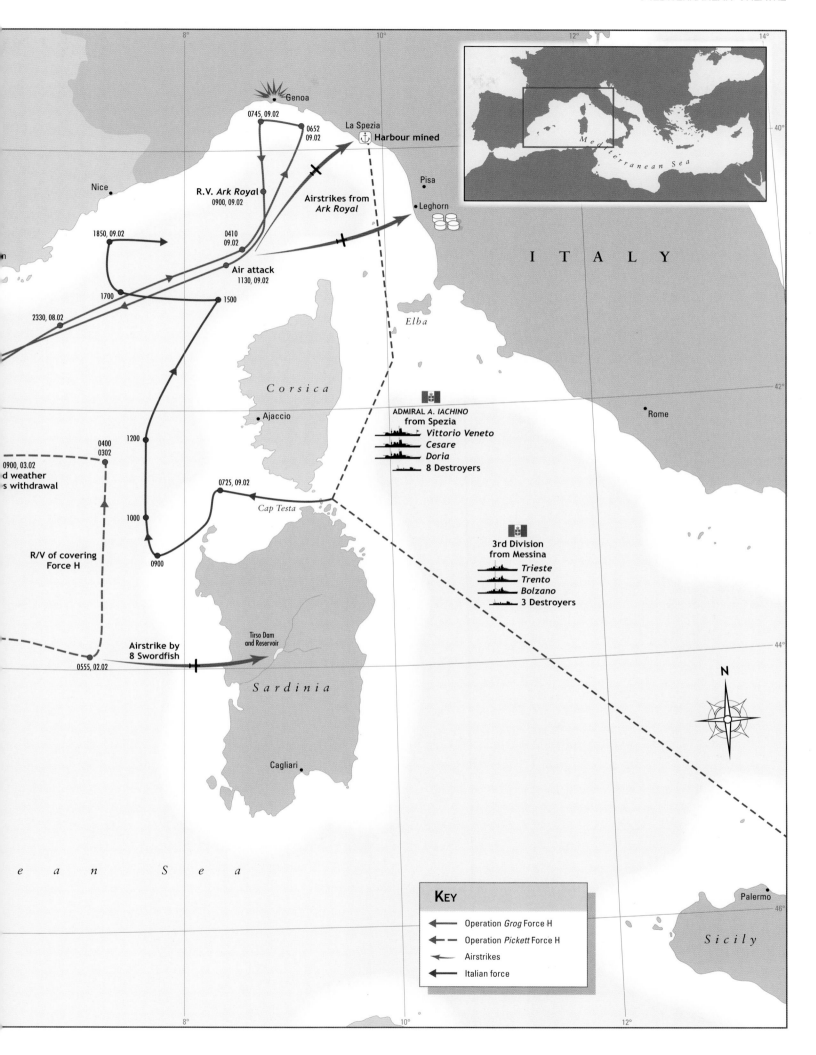

Genoa

0745, 09.02

0652
09.02

La Spezia

⚓ Harbour mined

Nice

R.V. *Ark Royal*
0900, 09.02

Airstrikes from
Ark Royal

Pisa

Leghorn

1850, 09.02

0410
09.02

1700

Air attack
1130, 09.02

2330, 08.02

1500

I T A L Y

Elba

Corsica

Ajaccio

🏴 ⚓
ADMIRAL A. IACHINO
from Spezia
Vittorio Veneto
Cesare
Doria
8 Destroyers

Rome

0400
0302

d weather
s withdrawal

0900, 03.02

1200

0725, 09.02

Cap Testa

🏴 ⚓
3rd Division
from Messina
Trieste
Trento
Bolzano
3 Destroyers

R/V of covering
Force H

1000

0900

Tirso Dam
and Reservoir

0555, 02.02

Airstrike by
8 Swordfish

S a r d i n i a

N

Cagliari

e a n   S e a

Palermo

S i c i l y

KEY

→ Operation *Grog* Force H
⇢ Operation *Pickett* Force H
← Airstrikes
← Italian force

57

THE BATTLE OF CAPE MATAPAN, 28–29 MARCH 1941

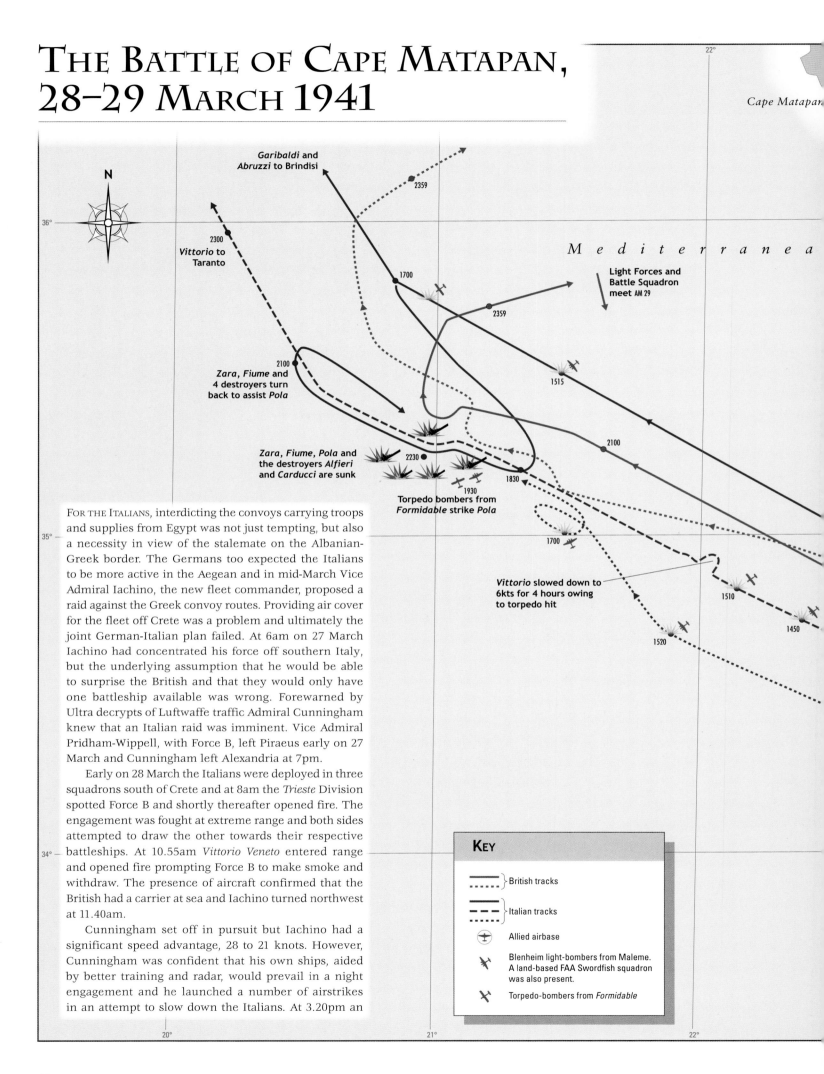

N

Garibaldi and
Abruzzi to Brindisi

2359

2300
Vittorio to
Taranto

1700

2359

M e d i t e r r a n e a

Light Forces and
Battle Squadron
meet AM 29

2100
Zara, Fiume and
4 destroyers turn
back to assist *Pola*

1515

2100

Zara, Fiume, Pola and
the destroyers *Alfieri*
and *Carducci* are sunk

2230

1830

1930
Torpedo bombers from
Formidable strike *Pola*

1700

Vittorio slowed down to
6kts for 4 hours owing
to torpedo hit

1510

1520

1450

FOR THE ITALIANS, interdicting the convoys carrying troops and supplies from Egypt was not just tempting, but also a necessity in view of the stalemate on the Albanian-Greek border. The Germans too expected the Italians to be more active in the Aegean and in mid-March Vice Admiral Iachino, the new fleet commander, proposed a raid against the Greek convoy routes. Providing air cover for the fleet off Crete was a problem and ultimately the joint German-Italian plan failed. At 6am on 27 March Iachino had concentrated his force off southern Italy, but the underlying assumption that he would be able to surprise the British and that they would only have one battleship available was wrong. Forewarned by Ultra decrypts of Luftwaffe traffic Admiral Cunningham knew that an Italian raid was imminent. Vice Admiral Pridham-Wippell, with Force B, left Piraeus early on 27 March and Cunningham left Alexandria at 7pm.

Early on 28 March the Italians were deployed in three squadrons south of Crete and at 8am the *Trieste* Division spotted Force B and shortly thereafter opened fire. The engagement was fought at extreme range and both sides attempted to draw the other towards their respective battleships. At 10.55am *Vittorio Veneto* entered range and opened fire prompting Force B to make smoke and withdraw. The presence of aircraft confirmed that the British had a carrier at sea and Iachino turned northwest at 11.40am.

Cunningham set off in pursuit but Iachino had a significant speed advantage, 28 to 21 knots. However, Cunningham was confident that his own ships, aided by better training and radar, would prevail in a night engagement and he launched a number of airstrikes in an attempt to slow down the Italians. At 3.20pm an

KEY

}British tracks

}Italian tracks

⊕ Allied airbase

✗ Blenheim light-bombers from Maleme.
A land-based FAA Swordfish squadron
was also present.

✗ Torpedo-bombers from *Formidable*

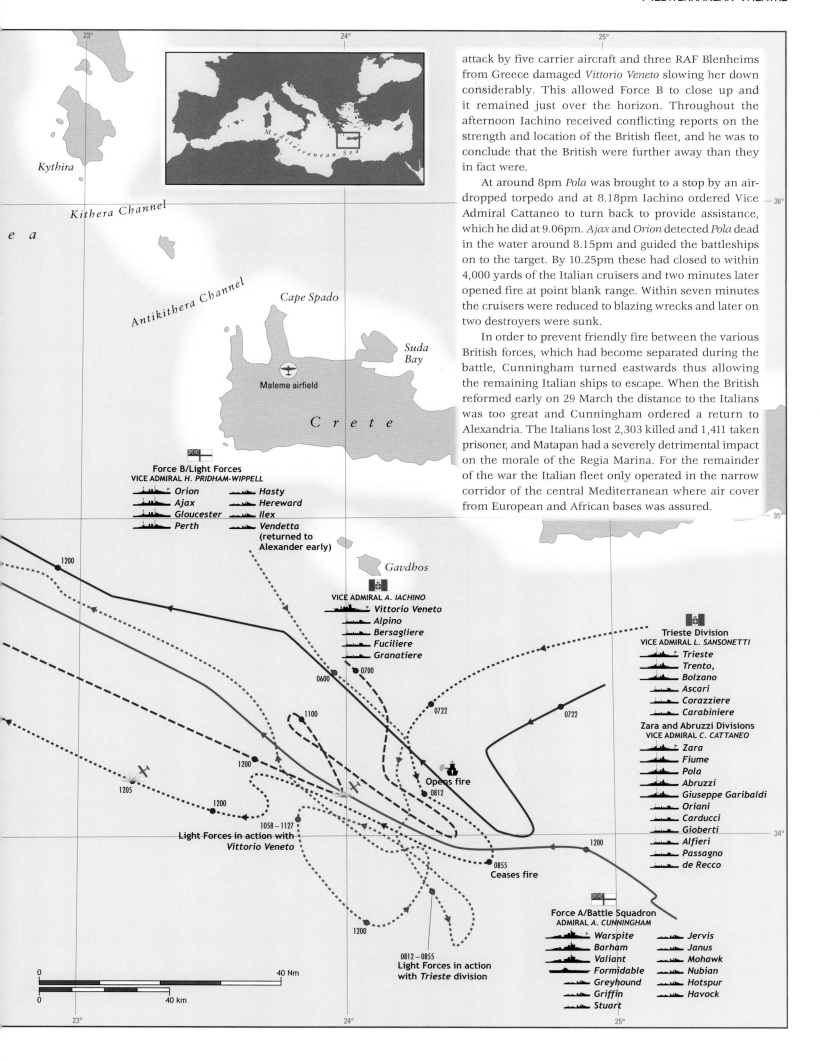

attack by five carrier aircraft and three RAF Blenheims from Greece damaged *Vittorio Veneto* slowing her down considerably. This allowed Force B to close up and it remained just over the horizon. Throughout the afternoon Iachino received conflicting reports on the strength and location of the British fleet, and he was to conclude that the British were further away than they in fact were.

At around 8pm *Pola* was brought to a stop by an air-dropped torpedo and at 8.18pm Iachino ordered Vice Admiral Cattaneo to turn back to provide assistance, which he did at 9.06pm. *Ajax* and *Orion* detected *Pola* dead in the water around 8.15pm and guided the battleships on to the target. By 10.25pm these had closed to within 4,000 yards of the Italian cruisers and two minutes later opened fire at point blank range. Within seven minutes the cruisers were reduced to blazing wrecks and later on two destroyers were sunk.

In order to prevent friendly fire between the various British forces, which had become separated during the battle, Cunningham turned eastwards thus allowing the remaining Italian ships to escape. When the British reformed early on 29 March the distance to the Italians was too great and Cunningham ordered a return to Alexandria. The Italians lost 2,303 killed and 1,411 taken prisoner, and Matapan had a severely detrimental impact on the morale of the Regia Marina. For the remainder of the war the Italian fleet only operated in the narrow corridor of the central Mediterranean where air cover from European and African bases was assured.

Force B/Light Forces
VICE ADMIRAL H. PRIDHAM-WIPPELL
- Orion
- Ajax
- Gloucester
- Perth
- Hasty
- Hereward
- Ilex
- Vendetta (returned to Alexander early)

VICE ADMIRAL A. IACHINO
- Vittorio Veneto
- Alpino
- Bersagliere
- Fuciliere
- Granatiere

Trieste Division
VICE ADMIRAL L. SANSONETTI
- Trieste
- Trento,
- Bolzano
- Ascari
- Corazziere
- Carabiniere

Zara and Abruzzi Divisions
VICE ADMIRAL C. CATTANEO
- Zara
- Fiume
- Pola
- Abruzzi
- Giuseppe Garibaldi
- Oriani
- Carducci
- Gioberti
- Alfieri
- Passagno
- de Recco

Force A/Battle Squadron
ADMIRAL A. CUNNINGHAM
- Warspite
- Barham
- Valiant
- Formidable
- Greyhound
- Griffin
- Stuart
- Jervis
- Janus
- Mohawk
- Nubian
- Hotspur
- Havock

Kythira

Kithera Channel

Antikithera Channel

Cape Spado

Suda Bay

Maleme airfield

C r e t e

Gavdhos

Light Forces in action with Vittorio Veneto 1058–1127

Opens fire 0812

Ceases fire 0855

0812–0855
Light Forces in action with Trieste division

1200

1205

1200

1200

1200

1100

0600

0700

0722

0722

1200

0 — 40 Nm
0 — 40 km

ACTION OFF SFAX, 15–16 APRIL 1941

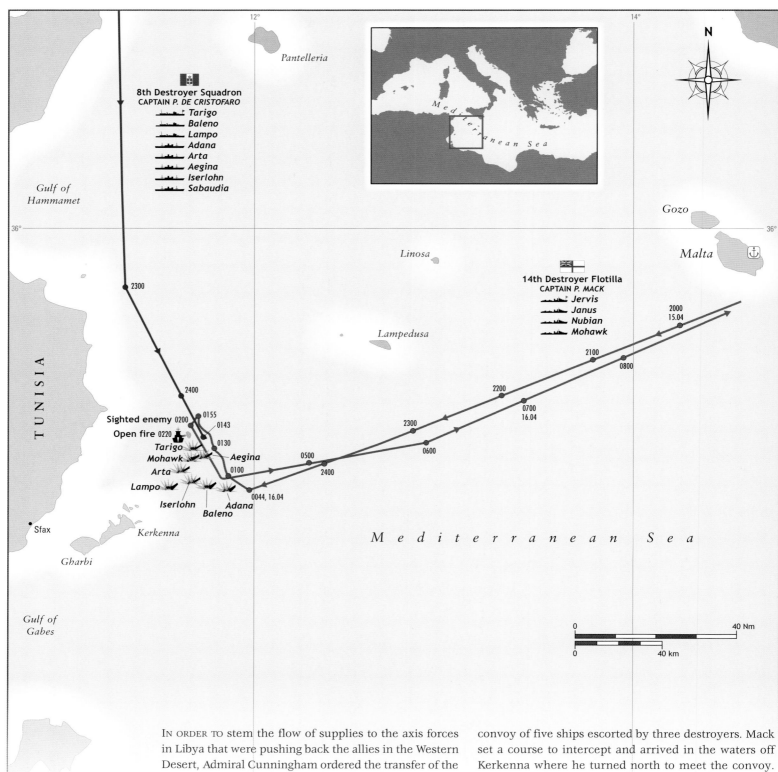

8th Destroyer Squadron
CAPTAIN P. DE CRISTOFARO
Tarigo
Baleno
Lampo
Adana
Arta
Aegina
Iserlohn
Sabaudia

14th Destroyer Flotilla
CAPTAIN P. MACK
Jervis
Janus
Nubian
Mohawk

Pantelleria

Gulf of
Hammamet

Gozo

Malta

Linosa

Lampedusa

2300

2400

Sighted enemy 0200
Open fire 0220

0155
0143
0130

Tarigo
Mohawk   Aegina
Arta   0100
Lampo
Iserlohn   Adana
Baleno   0044, 16.04

0500
2400

0600
0700
16.04

2300

2200

2100
0800

2000
15.04

TUNISIA

Sfax

Kerkenna

Gharbi

Gulf of
Gabes

Mediterranean   Sea

0   40 Nm

0   40 km

IN ORDER TO stem the flow of supplies to the axis forces in Libya that were pushing back the allies in the Western Desert, Admiral Cunningham ordered the transfer of the 14th Destroyer Flotilla, under Captain Philip Mack, from Crete to Malta on 10 April. It would operate with the Malta-based submarines to attack the axis supply convoys on the western route that crossed the Mediterranean at its narrowest point in the Sicilian Channel and then used the cover of the French Tunisian coastline. Mack's forces arrived at Malta on 11 April and immediately began to undertake offensive patrols. During the day they would operate under Malta's fighter cover and then during the darkness come out and operate along the convoy route. The first two patrols failed to yield any results. At 6pm on 15 April a Maryland light-bomber detected a convoy of five ships escorted by three destroyers. Mack set a course to intercept and arrived in the waters off Kerkenna where he turned north to meet the convoy. After an hour of fruitless searching Mack thought he had lost it and only on the return, southward, sweep was it located. The Italian commander knew that a British force was in the area, but did not expect it to approach from the astern. Shortly before 2pm the convoy was sighted and twenty minutes later the British destroyers opened fire from a range of 2,000 yards. In a short engagement, fought down to fifty yards, the entire convoy was sunk as was the British *Mohawk*. The exact axis losses remain unknown, but may have been as high as 1,800 while 1,217 men were rescued. Among the losses were 350 German troops, 300 vehicles and 3,500 tons of stores.

ROYAL NAVY HOME FLEET OPERATIONS IN NORWEGIAN WATERS, 1941

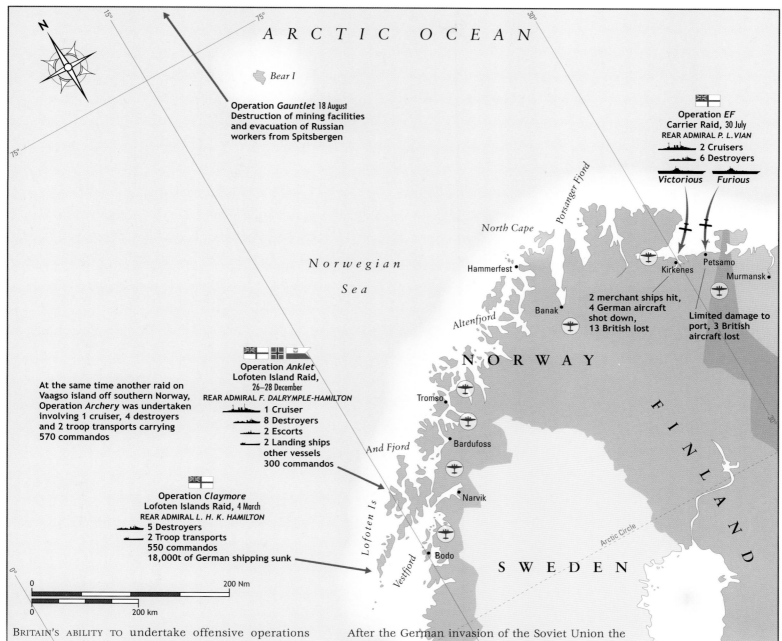

A R C T I C   O C E A N

Bear I

Operation *Gauntlet* 18 August
Destruction of mining facilities
and evacuation of Russian
workers from Spitsbergen

Operation *EF*
Carrier Raid, 30 July
REAR ADMIRAL *P. L. VIAN*
2 Cruisers
6 Destroyers
Victorious   *Furious*

Porsanger Fjord

North Cape

N o r w e g i a n

S e a

Hammerfest

Kirkenes   Petsamo
Murmansk

2 merchant ships hit,
4 German aircraft
shot down,
13 British lost

Banak

Altenfjord

Limited damage to
port, 3 British
aircraft lost

Operation *Anklet*
Lofoten Island Raid,
26–28 December
REAR ADMIRAL *F. DALRYMPLE-HAMILTON*
1 Cruiser
8 Destroyers
2 Escorts
2 Landing ships
other vessels
300 commandos

N O R W A Y

Tromso

At the same time another raid on
Vaagso island off southern Norway,
Operation *Archery* was undertaken
involving 1 cruiser, 4 destroyers
and 2 troop transports carrying
570 commandos

Bardufoss

F I N L A N D

And Fjord

Operation *Claymore*
Lofoten Islands Raid, 4 March
REAR ADMIRAL *L. H. K. HAMILTON*
5 Destroyers
2 Troop transports
550 commandos
18,000t of German shipping sunk

Narvik

Lofoten Is

Vestfjord

Bodo

Arctic Circle

S W E D E N

0 — 200 Nm
0 — 200 km

BRITAIN'S ABILITY TO undertake offensive operations in northwestern Europe after the defeats of 1940 was severely limited. Although Churchill wanted Europe to be set ablaze, through covert and commando actions, home defence, the Atlantic and Mediterranean all ranked higher in importance. By late 1940 it was clear that small-scale raids were needed to develop the experience needed for future amphibious operations. The Norwegian coastline, largely undefended with long hours of darkness in the winter months, was ideal. A raid on the Lofoten islands was undertaken on 4 March 1941 as they were sufficiently remote not to attract much German attention and the resident fish oil industry gave the plan some strategic purpose. At no cost an Anglo-Norwegian force destroyed the local industrial facilities and 19,350 tons of shipping. The military significance of Operation *Claymore* was minimal, but it was a success and it caused Hitler to become concerned about an allied invasion of Norway.

After the German invasion of the Soviet Union the latter asked the British to undertake operations to deflect German attention. The Admiralty ordered a reluctant Admiral Tovey to use the Home Fleet's carriers to strike German shipping and troops in Kirkenes and Petsamo to provide relief to Soviet forces on the Arctic front. Operation *EF* proved to be a failure as little damage was inflicted while a loss of surprise and heavy German defences resulted in heavy caualties to the air groups. There was some consideration to use Spitsbergen as a base for naval forces covering the Arctic convoys, but upon closer inspection the conditions were deemed too inhospitable. Instead, an expedition was mounted in August to land a Canadian force (Operation *Gauntlet*) to destroy the mining facilities and evacuate the resident Russian miners. A second raid on the Lofotens was mounted in December, but as long as the Germans held air superiority no more permanent results could be achieved.

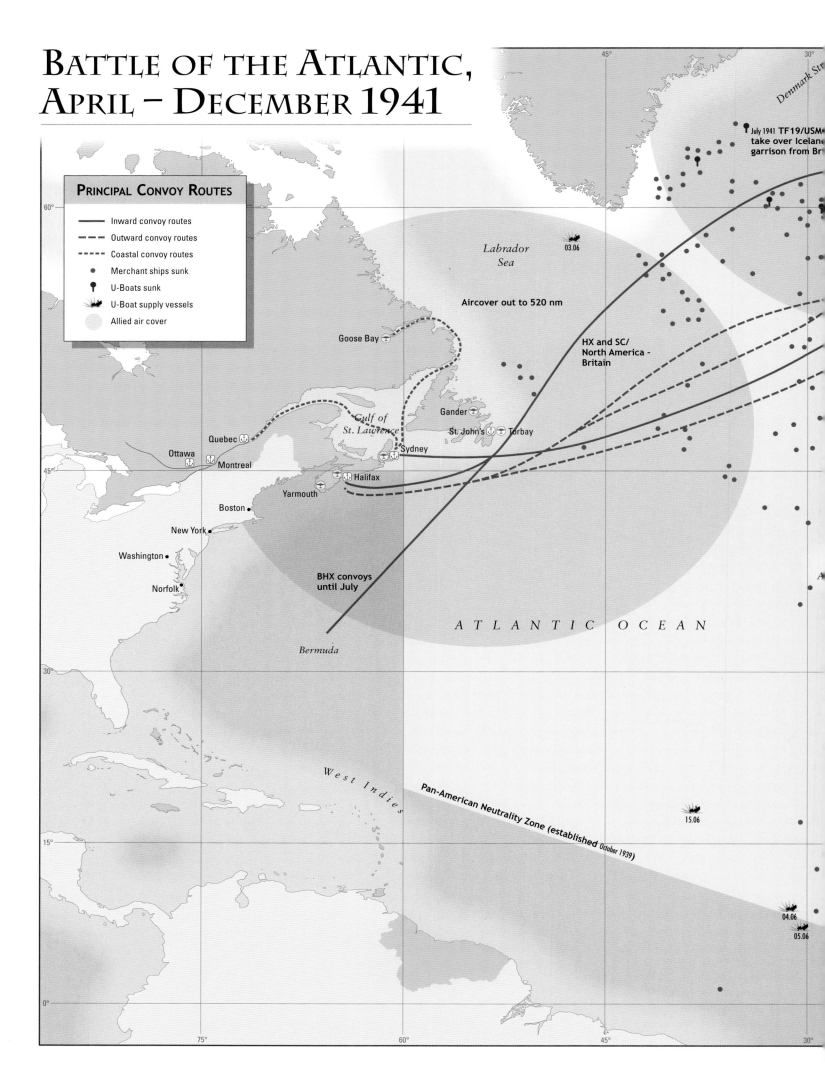

Battle of the Atlantic, April – December 1941

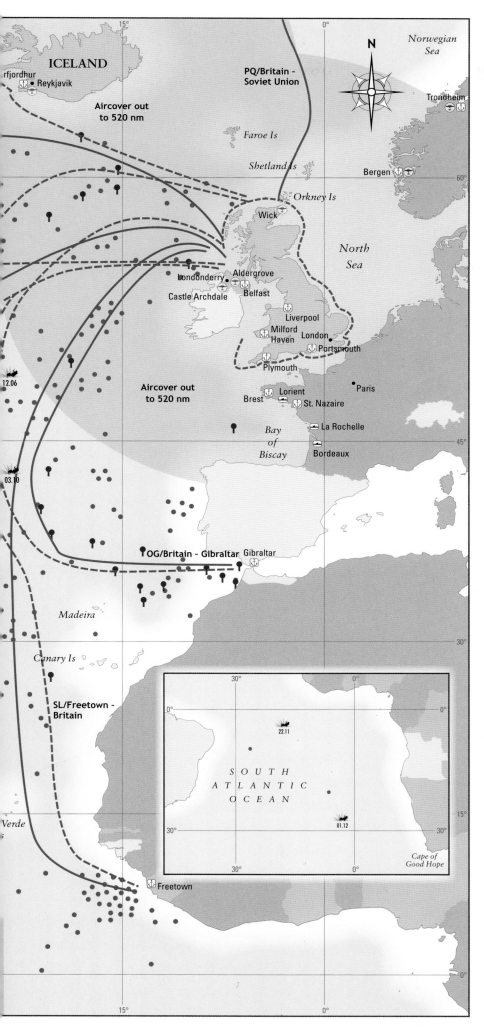

ALTHOUGH THE GERMANS were able to sink a record amount of allied shipping in April, the third phase of the battle saw their successes decline. Whereas previously the offensive relied on different methods of attack, throughout 1941 the U-boat became the dominant weapon. After the *Bismarck* was sunk, the Kriegsmarine's surface fleet no longer played an active role and the auxiliary cruiser operations shifted to the southern Atlantic and Indian Oceans. After the Russian campaign started, the Luftwaffe increasingly withdrew from the Atlantic campaign. Despite the number of operational U-boats the Kriegsmarine had at its disposal, increasing considerably from April onwards, their rewards decreased. While previously one U-boat was lost for every 150,000 tons of allied shipping sunk in the Atlantic, this dropped to one for every 75,000 tons.

There were numerous causes for the German decline, but the British reorganisation of the naval and air assets involved in trade protection was particularly crucial. Standing groups of escorts were formed and the area in which they escorted convoys was expanded westwards. By April, escorts were regularly refuelling in Iceland further extending their range. In May, the British asked the Canadians to operate beyond their coastal zone, and in June the first convoys were given transatlantic escorts. To do this larger, more capable escort vessels were needed, and these began to arrive having been ordered in late 1940. New equipment like radar, short-range voice radios and better anti-submarine weapons also enhanced the ability of escorts to coordinate their operations and destroy U-boats. The RCAF received some Catalina flying-boats that increased the range of air cover provided from Canadian airbases, although it still remained limited. Eastbound convoys were increased to between fifty and sixty ships to make more effective use of the still modest escort numbers, and these larger convoys also reduced the chances of running into U-boats that, too, were spread thinly. Signals intelligence allowed the re-routing of convoys around danger zones.

U-boats were unable to engage in surface attacks against the much better protected convoys in the eastern Atlantic and so had to operate in the central Atlantic and off Africa, but the increased transit times to these areas reduced the time on station. But successes could be achieved where the allies were weak, and of the fifty-eight ships sunk by U-boats in May, thirty-two were off Freetown where there were few anti-submarine forces. Increasing American intervention also had an impact, and then the diversion of U-boats to the Mediterranean and Arctic progressively brought the campaign to a standstill in the autumn.

MERCHANT SHIPS AND U-BOATS LOST (ALL THEATRES AND CAUSES)			
MONTH	TONNAGE	SHIPS	U-BOATS
1941			
APRIL	687,901	195	2
MAY	511,042	139	1
JUNE	432,025	109	4
JULY	120,975	43	1
AUGUST	130,699	41	3
SEPTEMBER	285,942	84	2
OCTOBER	218,289	51	2
NOVEMBER	104,640	35	5

THE BOMBARDMENT OF TRIPOLI, 21 APRIL 1941

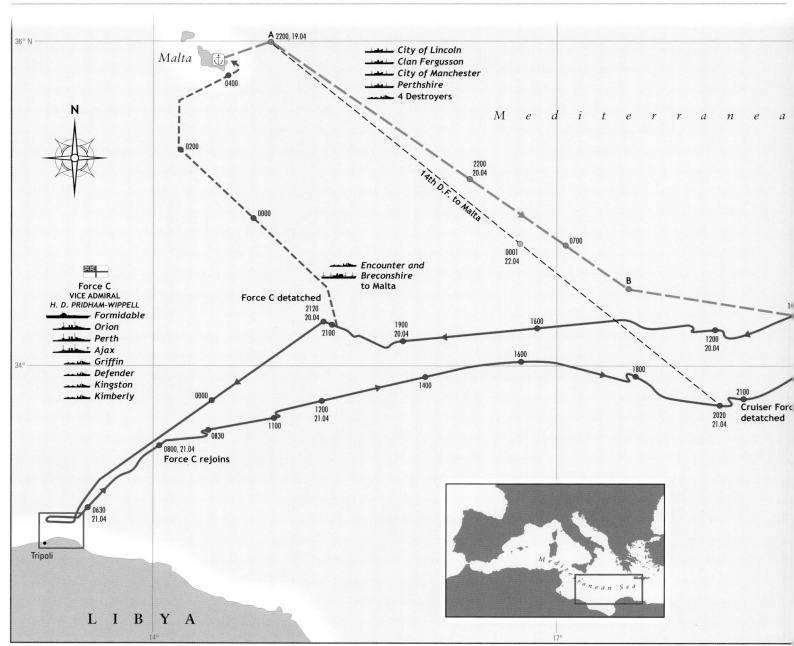

36° N

Malta

A 2200, 19.04

City of Lincoln
Clan Fergusson
City of Manchester
Perthshire
4 Destroyers

0400

M e d i t e r r a n e a

0200

2200
20.04

0000

14th D.F. to Malta

0700

0001
22.04

B

Encounter and
Breconshire
to Malta

Force C detached
2120
20.04

1900
20.04

1600

Force C
VICE ADMIRAL
H. D. PRIDHAM-WIPPELL
Formidable
Orion
Perth
Ajax
Griffin
Defender
Kingston
Kimberly

2100

1200
20.04

34°

1600

1800

0000

1400

2100

1200
21.04

2020
21.04

Cruiser For
detatched

1100

0830

0800, 21.04
Force C rejoins

0630
21.04

Tripoli

L I B Y A

14°

17°

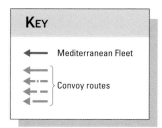

KEY

← Mediterranean Fleet

← Convoy routes

THE ALLIED POSITION in the Western Desert collapsed after General Erwin Rommel launched his offensive, on 24 March, to retake the ground lost by the Italians during the winter. By 14 April axis forces had crossed the Egyptian border and had also encircled a large allied force in Tobruk. Together with the German invasion of Greece the situation caused considerable concern in London and on 15 April Admiral Cunningham was instructed to take drastic action to prevent further deterioration. He had, in fact, already sent more destroyers to Malta, which were to demonstrate their value in interdicting axis supplies that very night off Sfax. The axis forces in North Africa were vulnerable as Tripoli was the only major port through which supplies could be sent. Up to twenty-four ships could be accommodated in the harbour and there were large oil and petrol depots. On the allied side, the loss of airfields in Cyrenaica reduced the British ability to interdict axis supplies but in any case a more immediate course of action was necessary.

Churchill wanted to sink a battleship, *Barham*, and a cruiser to block Tripoli harbour, but Cunningham was not willing to sacrifice valuable ships on such an operation. Instead, he proposed a bombardment of the port by the Mediterranean fleet on 21 April. This was to be a major operation involving most of the fleet and the opportunity was used to send supplies to Malta, bring out a number of ships from there and run convoys to Crete. The fleet sailed for Crete from Alexandria on 18 April to pick up further warships. Prior to the actual bombardment RAF Wellingtons and FAA Swordfish would bomb the port and aircraft from *Formidable* dropped flares and spotted for the ships' gunfire. The battleships and *Gloucester* shelled infrastructure targets while the destroyer attacked ships in port. The practical results were disappointing as smoke obscured the targets for most of the bombardment – around 500 15in and 1,500 lesser calibre shells were expended. However, the operation did take the Italians by surprise and encountered little enemy air opposition.

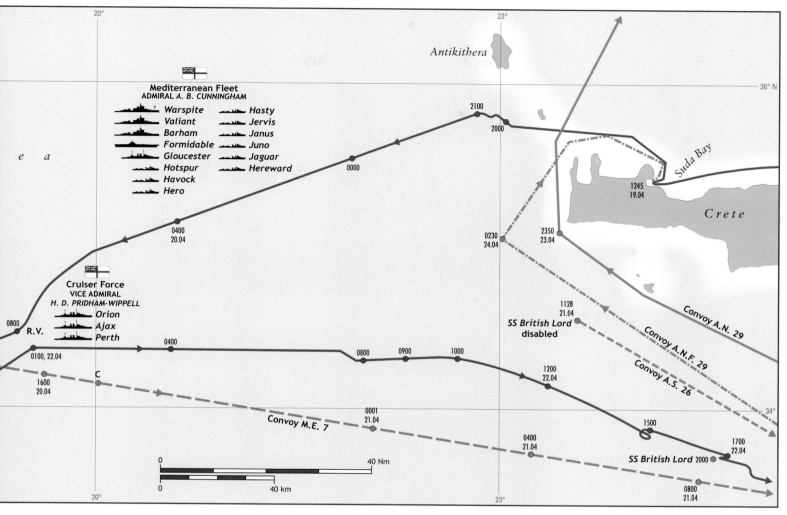

Mediterranean Fleet
ADMIRAL A. B. CUNNINGHAM

Warspite   Hasty
Valiant   Jervis
Barham   Janus
Formidable   Juno
Gloucester   Jaguar
Hotspur   Hereward
Havock
Hero

Cruiser Force
VICE ADMIRAL
H. D. PRIDHAM-WIPPELL
Orion
Ajax
Perth

Antikithera

Suda Bay

Crete

2100
2000
0000
0400
20.04
0800
R.V.
0400
0100, 22.04
1600
20.04
C
0800 0900 1000
0001
21.04
Convoy M.E. 7
0400
21.04
1200
22.04
1500
1700
22.04
SS British Lord 2000
0800
21.04

1245
19.04
2350
23.04
0230
24.04
1128
21.04
SS British Lord
disabled
Convoy A.N. 29
Convoy A.N.F. 29
Convoy A.S. 26

0   40 Nm
0   40 km

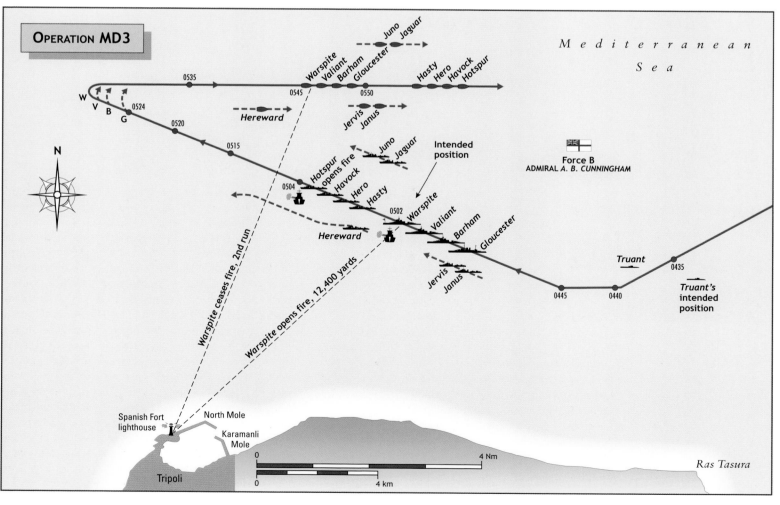

OPERATION MD3

Mediterranean Sea

Juno Jaguar
Warspite
Valiant
Barham
Gloucester   Hasty Hero Havock Hotspur
0535
0545   0550
W
V B 0524
G   0520
0515
Hereward   Jervis Janus

Hotspur
opens fire   Juno Jaguar
Havock   Intended
Hero   position
Hasty
0504
0502   Warspite
Valiant
Hereward   Barham
Gloucester

Force B
ADMIRAL A. B. CUNNINGHAM

Jervis
Janus   Truant   0435

Warspite ceases fire, 2nd run   0445   0440   Truant's
                                                    intended
Warspite opens fire, 12,400 yards   position

N

Spanish Fort
lighthouse   North Mole
              Karamanli
              Mole

Tripoli

Ras Tasura

0   4 Nm
0   4 km

65

THE EVACUATION OF GREECE AND CRETE, APRIL – MAY 1941

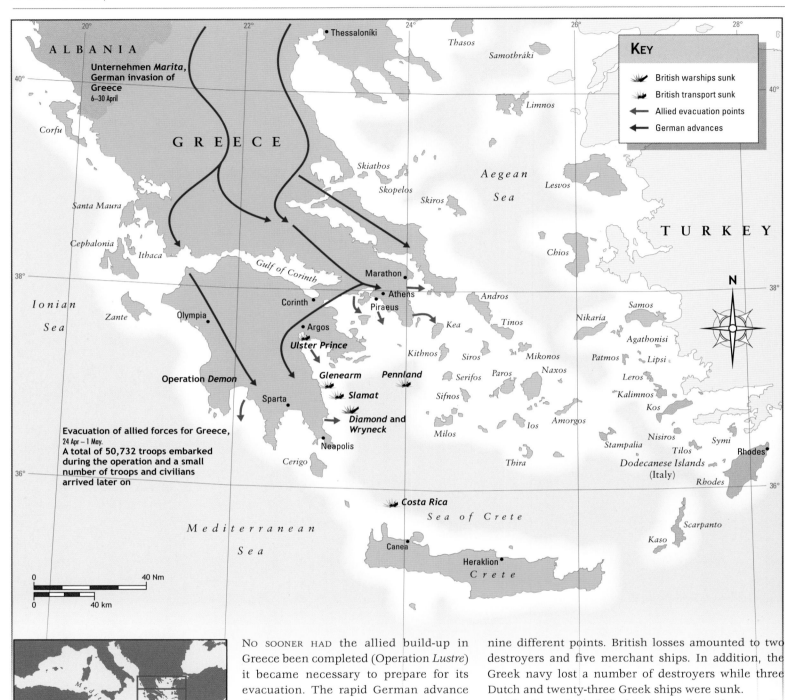

ALBANIA

Unternehmen *Marita*, German invasion of Greece 6–30 April

GREECE

Corfu

Santa Maura

Cephalonia

Ithaca

Ionian Sea

Zante

Olympia

Gulf of Corinth

Corinth

Marathon

Athens

Piraeus

Argos

Ulster Prince

Operation *Demon*

Sparta

Glenearm **Pennland**

Slamat

Diamond and Wryneck

Neapolis

Cerigo

Evacuation of allied forces for Greece, 24 Apr – 1 May.
A total of 50,732 troops embarked during the operation and a small number of troops and civilians arrived later on

Thessaloníki

Thasos

Samothráki

Limnos

Aegean Sea

Skiathos

Skopelos

Skiros

Lesvos

Chios

Andros

Kea

Tinos

Kithnos

Siros

Serifos

Paros

Sifnos

Milos

Ios

Amorgos

Mikonos

Naxos

Samos

Nikaría

Agathonisi

Patmos

Lipsi

Leros

Kalimnos

Kos

Nisiros

Stampalia

Tilos

Symi

Rhodes

Dodecanese Islands
(Italy)

Rhodes

Thira

Kaso

Scarpanto

TURKEY

N

Costa Rica

Sea of Crete

Mediterranean Sea

Canea

Heraklion

Crete

0   40 Nm
0   40 km

KEY

British warships sunk

British transport sunk

Allied evacuation points

German advances

Mediterranean Sea

NO SOONER HAD the allied build-up in Greece been completed (Operation *Lustre*) it became necessary to prepare for its evacuation. The rapid German advance through northern Greece meant that ten days into the campaign the British commanders in Alexandria initiated Operation *Demon*, and on 17 April Rear Admiral Baillie-Grohman arrived in Piraeus to organise the withdrawal. The problems were considerable as the Germans had air superiority and the British, Australian and New Zealand troops were spread across southern Greece. Piraeus harbour was largely unusable as a German airstrike on 6 April had hit the *Clan Fraser*, which was carrying explosives, causing a devastating explosion. *Demon* was supposed to start 28 April but the Greek surrender on 21 April accelerated the timetable. Between 24 April and 1 May troops were taken directly off the beaches during the night from nine different points. British losses amounted to two destroyers and five merchant ships. In addition, the Greek navy lost a number of destroyers while three Dutch and twenty-three Greek ships were sunk.

The focus then shifted to Crete where the majority of the evacuated troops had ended up. The Royal Navy's task was to prevent an axis seaborne invasion and keep allied troops on the island supplied. The Mediterranean Fleet was organised into four forces to conduct nightly sweeps of the approaches to Crete between 15 and 19 May (not all forces were on station all the time). The German attack began at 8am on 20 May with an airborne assault at key points on Crete, and German dominance in the air was a severe impediment to British naval operations. Although one of the German assault convoys was destroyed in the Lupo convoy action during the night 21–22 May the scale of the attack led to the evacuation being ordered on 26 May.

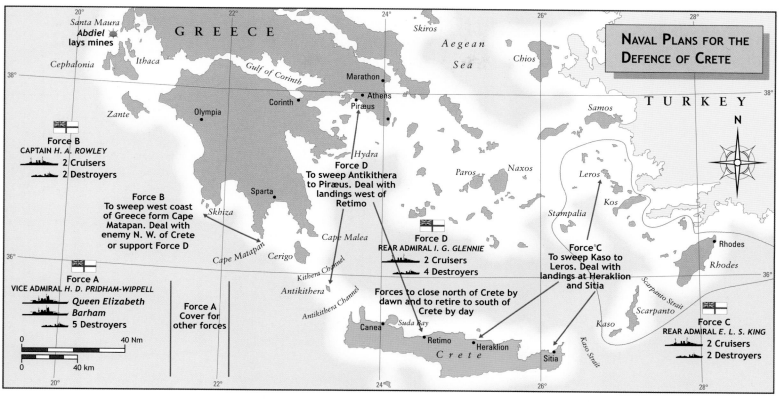

NAVAL PLANS FOR THE DEFENCE OF CRETE

Force B
CAPTAIN *H. A. ROWLEY*
2 Cruisers
2 Destroyers

Force B
To sweep west coast of Greece form Cape Matapan. Deal with enemy N. W. of Crete or support Force D

Force A
VICE ADMIRAL *H. D. PRIDHAM-WIPPELL*
Queen Elizabeth
Barham
5 Destroyers

Force A
Cover for other forces

Force D
To sweep Antikithera to Piræus. Deal with landings west of Retimo

Force D
REAR ADMIRAL *I. G. GLENNIE*
2 Cruisers
4 Destroyers

Forces to close north of Crete by dawn and to retire to south of Crete by day

Force C
To sweep Kaso to Leros. Deal with landings at Heraklion and Sitia

Force C
REAR ADMIRAL *E. L. S. KING*
2 Cruisers
2 Destroyers

Abdiel lays mines

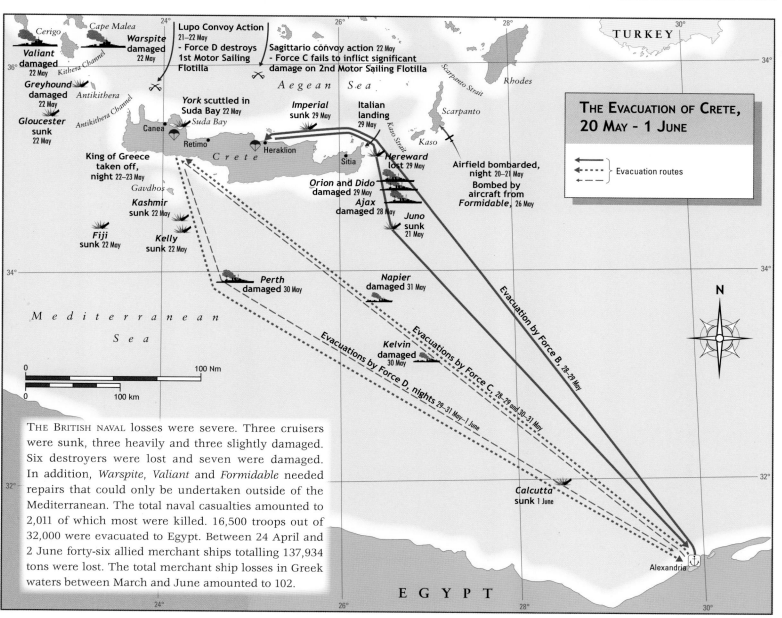

THE EVACUATION OF CRETE, 20 MAY - 1 JUNE

Evacuation routes

Valiant damaged 22 May

Warspite damaged 22 May

Lupo Convoy Action 21–22 May
- Force D destroys 1st Motor Sailing Flotilla

Sagittario convoy action 22 May
- Force C fails to inflict significant damage on 2nd Motor Sailing Flotilla

Greyhound damaged 22 May

Gloucester sunk 22 May

York scuttled in Suda Bay 22 May

Imperial sunk 29 May

Italian landing 29 May

Airfield bombarded, night 20–21 May
Bombed by aircraft from *Formidable*, 26 May

King of Greece taken off, night 22–23 May

Hereward lost 29 May

Orion and *Dido* damaged 29 May
Ajax damaged 28 May

Juno sunk 21 May

Kashmir sunk 22 May

Fiji sunk 22 May

Kelly sunk 22 May

Perth damaged 30 May

Napier damaged 31 May

Evacuation by Force B, 28–29 May

Evacuations by Force C, 28–29 and 30–31 May

Kelvin damaged 30 May

Evacuations by Force D, nights 29–31 May–1 June

Calcutta sunk 1 June

Alexandria

THE BRITISH NAVAL losses were severe. Three cruisers were sunk, three heavily and three slightly damaged. Six destroyers were lost and seven were damaged. In addition, *Warspite*, *Valiant* and *Formidable* needed repairs that could only be undertaken outside of the Mediterranean. The total naval casualties amounted to 2,011 of which most were killed. 16,500 troops out of 32,000 were evacuated to Egypt. Between 24 April and 2 June forty-six allied merchant ships totalling 137,934 tons were lost. The total merchant ship losses in Greek waters between March and June amounted to 102.

UNTERNEHMEN RHEINÜBUNG, 18–27 MAY 1941

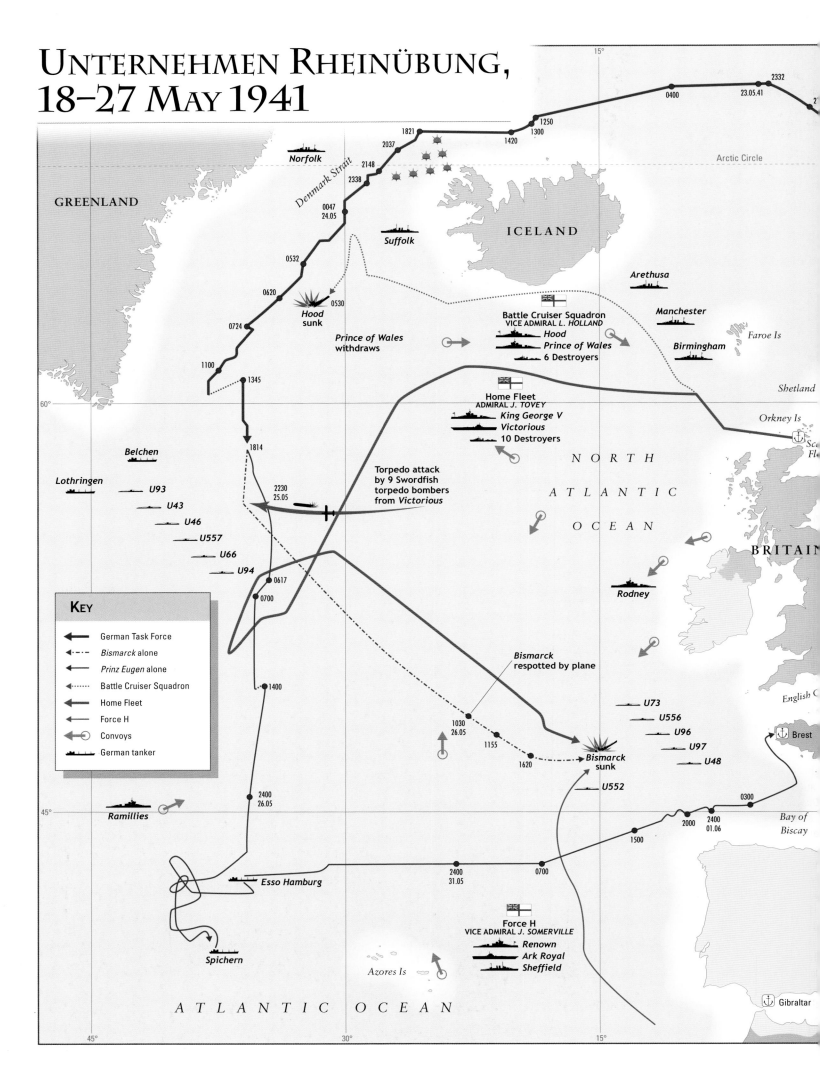

GREENLAND

Norfolk

Denmark Strait

ICELAND

Suffolk

Hood sunk

Prince of Wales withdraws

Arethusa

Manchester

Birmingham

Faroe Is

Arctic Circle

Battle Cruiser Squadron
VICE ADMIRAL L. HOLLAND
Hood
Prince of Wales
6 Destroyers

Shetland

Home Fleet
ADMIRAL J. TOVEY
King George V
Victorious
10 Destroyers

Orkney Is

Sc
Fl

Belchen

Lothringen
U93
U43
U46
U557
U66
U94

Torpedo attack
by 9 Swordfish
torpedo bombers
from *Victorious*

N O R T H

A T L A N T I C

O C E A N

BRITAIN

Rodney

Bismarck
respotted by plane

KEY

German Task Force
Bismarck alone
Prinz Eugen alone
Battle Cruiser Squadron
Home Fleet
Force H
Convoys
German tanker

U73
U556
U96
U97
U48

English C

Brest

Ramillies

Esso Hamburg

U552

Bismarck
sunk

Bay of
Biscay

Spichern

Azores Is

Force H
VICE ADMIRAL J. SOMERVILLE
Renown
Ark Royal
Sheffield

Gibraltar

A T L A N T I C   O C E A N

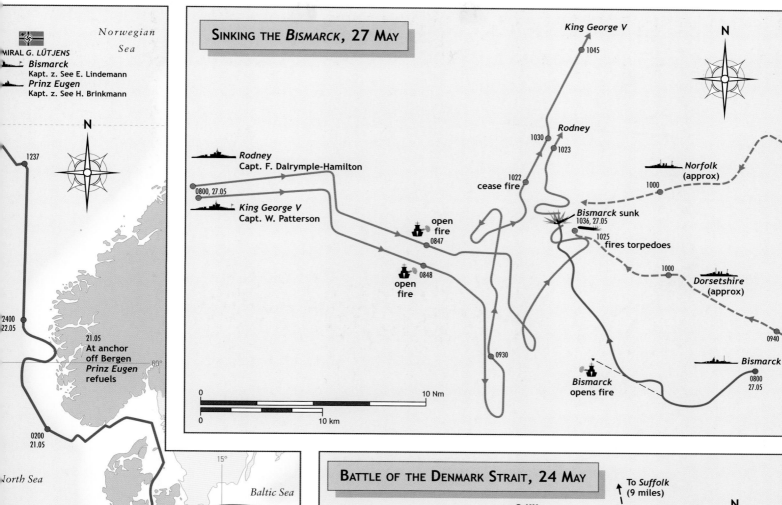

SINKING THE *BISMARCK*, 27 MAY

MIRAL G. LÜTJENS

Bismarck
Kapt. z. See E. Lindemann

Prinz Eugen
Kapt. z. See H. Brinkmann

Norwegian Sea

1237

2400
22.05

21.05
At anchor
off Bergen
Prinz Eugen
refuels

60°

0200
21.05

Rodney
Capt. F. Dalrymple-Hamilton

0800, 27.05

King George V
Capt. W. Patterson

King George V
1045

Rodney
1030
1023

1022
cease fire

Norfolk
(approx)
1000

open
fire
0847

Bismarck sunk
1036, 27.05

1025
fires torpedoes

open
fire
0848

1000

Dorsetshire
(approx)

0940

0930

Bismarck

0800
27.05

Bismarck
opens fire

0 — 10 Nm

0 — 10 km

North Sea

15°

Baltic Sea

Departs from
Gotenhafen (Gdynia)
2130
18.05

GERMANY

15°

15°

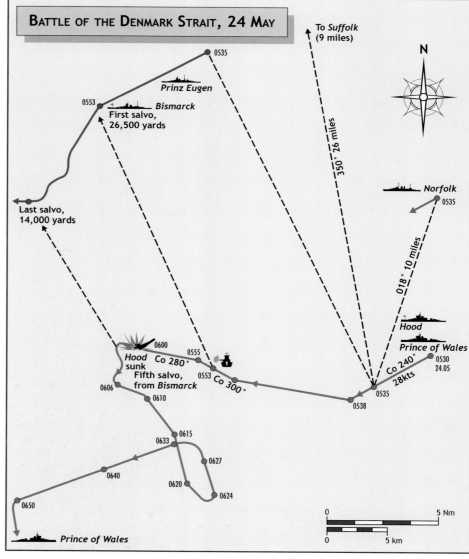

BATTLE OF THE DENMARK STRAIT, 24 MAY

To *Suffolk*
(9 miles)

0535

Prinz Eugen

0553

Bismarck
First salvo,
26,500 yards

350° 26 miles

Norfolk
0535

Last salvo,
14,000 yards

018° 10 miles

Hood

Prince of Wales
0530
24.05

Hood
sunk
Fifth salvo,
from *Bismarck*

0600
Co 280°
0555
0553 Co 300°
Co 240°
28kts

0535

0606
0610
0538

0615
0633
0627
0640
0620
0624

0650

0 — 5 Nm

0 — 5 km

Prince of Wales

E SURFACE RAIDER campaign reached its climax with battleship *Bismarck*'s raid into the Atlantic in May. sed on its analysis of the previous operations, the egsmarine believed that the British convoy system ld be brought to a breaking point if two battle groups erated in the Atlantic simultaneously. The British ald not have enough capital ships to deal with an ursion on this scale. A pair of modern German 15in tleships could also take on any protection a convoy ght have. However, the forces were simply not available such an operation. *Tirpitz* was not ready for action *Bismarck* had to sail with *Prinz Eugen* which, being of same design as *Admiral Hipper*, was unsuitable for antic operations. More importantly, the damage to *arnhorst* at Brest prevented the second group from ing part. The Kriegsmarine's decision to launch the eration nonetheless must be seen in the context of the asion of the Soviet Union which was less than four eks away. Unlike previous operations the Germans ld not count on surprise, as the British were aware of operation before the ships left the North Sea. Owing he threat *Bismarck* posed, all available British forces k part in the subsequent hunt – quite how dangerous s demonstrated when *Bismarck* sunk the most famous tish ship afloat, the battle cruiser *Hood*, in an eight- nute engagement.

GERMAN AUXILIARY CRUISERS, JANUARY – MAY 1941

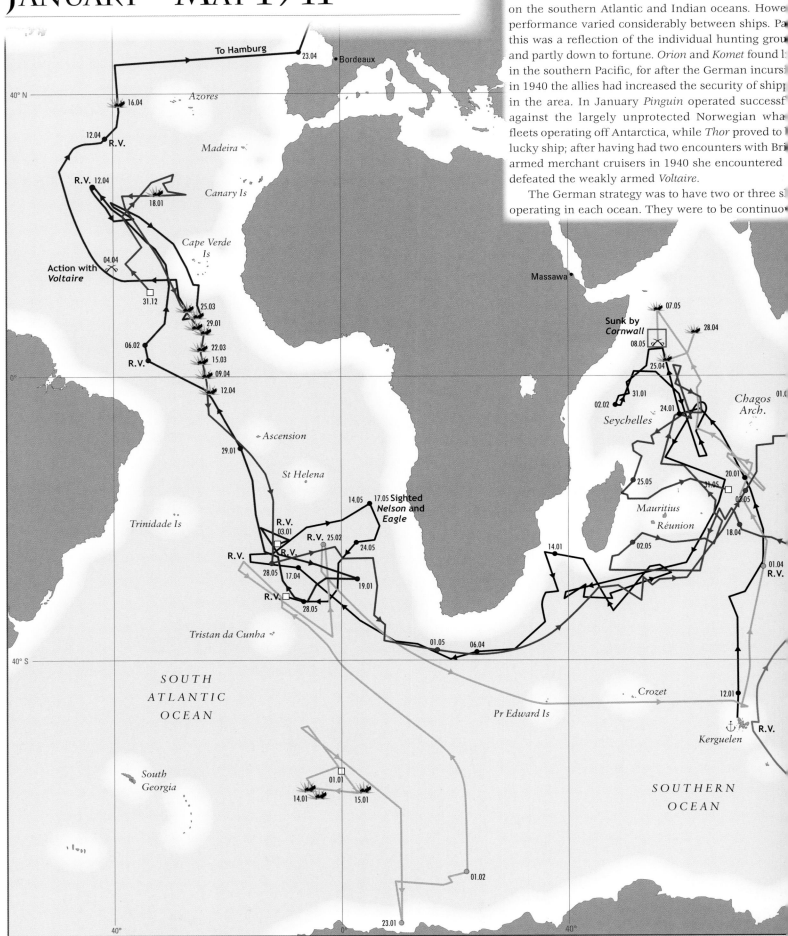

IN THE FIRST quarter of 1941 the German auxiliary cruis[ers]
reached the height of their success. While surface raid[ers]
operated in the north Atlantic, the auxiliaries focu[sed]
on the southern Atlantic and Indian oceans. Howe[ver]
performance varied considerably between ships. Pa[rtly]
this was a reflection of the individual hunting grou[nds]
and partly down to fortune. *Orion* and *Komet* found l[ittle]
in the southern Pacific, for after the German incurs[ions]
in 1940 the allies had increased the security of shipp[ing]
in the area. In January *Pinguin* operated successf[ully]
against the largely unprotected Norwegian wha[ling]
fleets operating off Antarctica, while *Thor* proved to [be a]
lucky ship; after having had two encounters with Bri[tish]
armed merchant cruisers in 1940 she encountered [and]
defeated the weakly armed *Voltaire*.

The German strategy was to have two or three s[hips]
operating in each ocean. They were to be continuo[usly]

the move and on occasion swap between oceans
spread confusion and have the greatest effect on
rupting allied shipping. The logistics effort necessary
eep the ships at sea continuously was considerable.
ween 1939 and 1941 thirty-nine merchant ships
tankers were used to resupply surface raiders and
iliary cruisers. In addition, twenty-two captured
ed ships were used as support vessels. On 8 May the
iser *Cornwall* caught up with the *Pinguin*, which had
tted the British warship on her radar and turned away
void an engagement. *Cornwall* followed and sunk her
r that afternoon. *Pinguin*'s voyage lasted around ten
nths during which she had captured or sank twenty-
t ships. One Italian auxiliary cruiser, *Ramb I*, sailed
n Massawa on 2 February, but was destroyed by the
v Zealand cruiser *Leander* on 27 February.

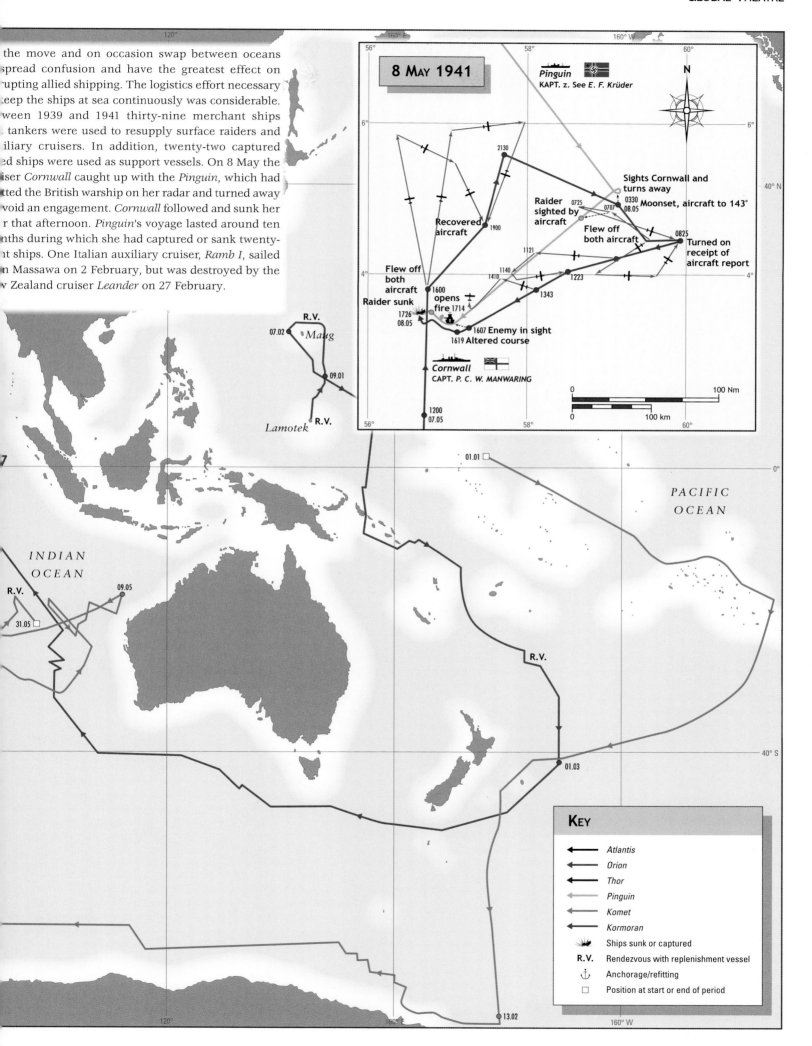

THE SOVIET UNION, 1941

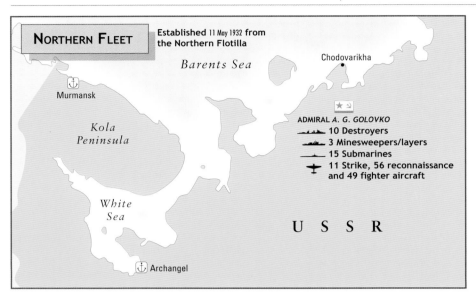

NORTHERN FLEET

Established 11 May 1932 from the Northern Flotilla

Barents Sea

Chodovarikha

Murmansk

Kola Peninsula

ADMIRAL A. G. GOLOVKO
- 10 Destroyers
- 3 Minesweepers/layers
- 15 Submarines
- 11 Strike, 56 reconnaissance and 49 fighter aircraft

White Sea

U S S R

Archangel

BLACK SEA FLEET

Odessa

Sea of Azov

U S S R

Crimea

Novorossijsk

VICE ADMIRAL F. S. OKTYABRSKY
- 1 Battleship (obsolete)
- 5 Cruisers
- 17 Destroyers
- 14 Minesweepers/layers
- 44 Submarines
- 143 Strike, 167 reconnaissance and 315 fighter aircraft

Sevastopol

B L A C K   S E A

Poti

Batumi

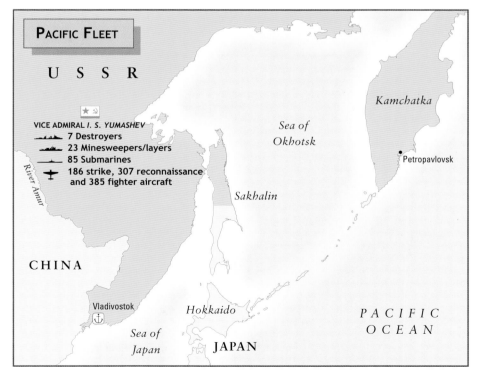

PACIFIC FLEET

U S S R

VICE ADMIRAL I. S. YUMASHEV
- 7 Destroyers
- 23 Minesweepers/layers
- 85 Submarines
- 186 strike, 307 reconnaissance and 385 fighter aircraft

River Amur

Kamchatka

Sea of Okhotsk

Petropavlovsk

Sakhalin

CHINA

Vladivostok

Hokkaido

Sea of Japan

JAPAN

P A C I F I C   O C E A N

HISTORICALLY, THE RUSSIAN navy had always suffered from the geographic separation of its three principle fleets that were based in the Baltic, the Black Sea and the Pacific. This was further compounded by the fact that in each case access to open waters was restricted. In the Baltic, ice and enemy control of the coastline in the Gulf of Finland could immobilise the Baltic Fleet. The Dardanelles controlled access to the Black Sea, while Japan guarded Russian access to the Pacific. During the inter-war years Soviet naval power diminished considerably, partly as a result of defeat in the First World War, partly due to the effects of the Revolution and ensuing civil wars, and as a result of the emphasis on modernising the Red Army. It was not until 1933 that more resources were put into the navy, but the emphasis was on light forces and on expanding the submarine arm. The role of the navy was defensive, and naval strategy focused on integrating surface forces, submarines, mine warfare, naval aviation and coastal artillery to protect the littoral regions. The Soviet maritime sector struggled to develop the naval forces required and much of the technology had to be imported. After 1937 Stalin shifted the emphasis towards constructing an oceanic fleet, but little progress was made by the time war broke out, and the navy's effectiveness was further reduced by the removal of much of the senior leadership during Stalin's purges. The occupation of the Baltic States improved the Soviet Union's geostrategic position as it obtained access to ice-free ports.

When German forces began their invasion of the Soviet Union on 22 June 1941 the naval dimension of *Barbarossa* in the Baltic was limited and of secondary importance. With the Kriegsmarine focused on the Atlantic, its role in the east was defensive. Nominally, the Soviets had a superior fleet, so before the invasion the Germans began to lay minefields to protect the maritime flank of the advance. The Soviets made no attempt to conduct offensive operations into the Baltic and by July German troops, advancing through the Baltic States, began to be resupplied by sea. In the second half of August the German army assaulted and took Tallinn, forcing the Soviet naval presence back to Kronstadt. The single most important activity of the Soviet Baltic Fleet was organising a number of seaborne evacuations, while clearing out Soviet forces from the West Estonian archipelago and other islands in the Gulf of Finland was the principal axis naval occupation in the Baltic that autumn. To cover the landings in mid September the Kriegsmarine brought in the battleship *Tirpitz*, the heavy cruiser *Admiral Scheer* and all available light cruisers and destroyers in case of a sortie by the Baltic Fleet.

After the islands were secured, German-Finnish naval forces focused on keeping the Soviet navy bottled up at the eastern end of the Gulf of Finland by means of extensive minefields and other barriers. The demands for light forces along the French coast, in the Aegean and, later, the Black Sea had stretched German naval resources thinly and allowed for little more. Until 1944 fighting was confined to the Gulf of Finland. With access through Finnish territory being important for the developing Arctic front and a German expeditionary force operating in the country, securing the maritime communications and escorting the shipping became the most important naval task.

As part of the Moscow Peace Treaty signed on 12 March 1940 Finland had to cede islands in the Gulf of Finland and lease Hanko Peninsula to the Soviet Union as a military base for 30 years

In October 1939 the Soviet Union forced the Baltic States to conclude Mutual Assistance Pacts. In Estonia the Soviets obtained the use of Tallinn and the small port of Paldiski that was to be developed as a major ice-free naval base. In August 1940 Estonia was annexed by the Soviet Union

VICE ADMIRAL *V. F. TRIBUTS*
2 Battleships (obsolete)
2 Cruisers
23 Destroyers
34 Minesweepers/layers
71 Submarines
183 Strike, 159 reconnaissance and 367 fighter aircraft

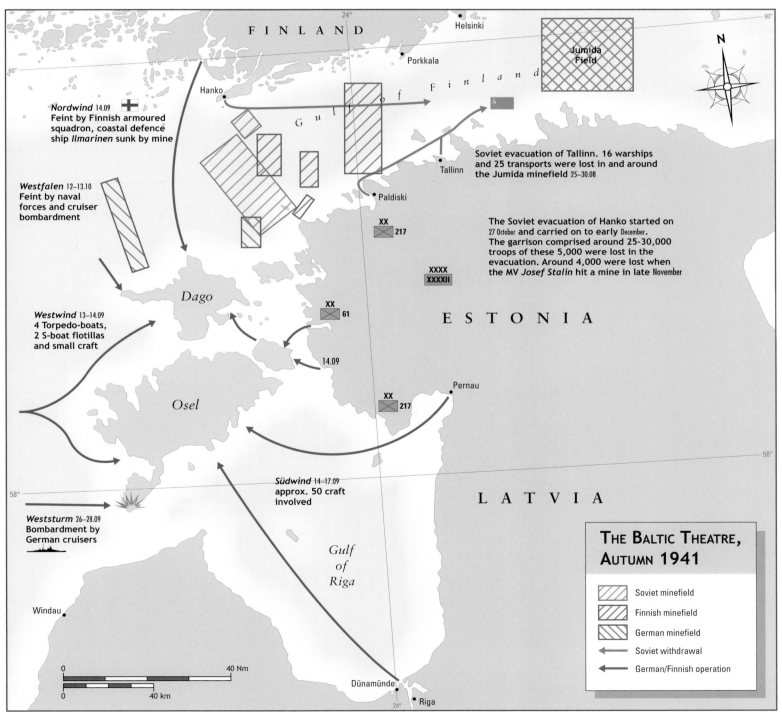

Nordwind 14.09
Feint by Finnish armoured squadron, coastal defence ship *Ilmarinen* sunk by mine

Westfalen 12–13.10
Feint by naval forces and cruiser bombardment

Westwind 13–14.09
4 Torpedo-boats, 2 S-boat flotillas and small craft

Weststurm 26–28.09
Bombardment by German cruisers

Südwind 14–17.09
approx. 50 craft involved

Soviet evacuation of Tallinn. 16 warships and 25 transports were lost in and around the Jumida minefield 25–30.08

The Soviet evacuation of Hanko started on 27 October and carried on to early December. The garrison comprised around 25-30,000 troops of these 5,000 were lost in the evacuation. Around 4,000 were lost when the MV *Josef Stalin* hit a mine in late November

THE BALTIC THEATRE, AUTUMN 1941

Soviet minefield
Finnish minefield
German minefield
Soviet withdrawal
German/Finnish operation

OPERATION SUBSTANCE, JULY 1941

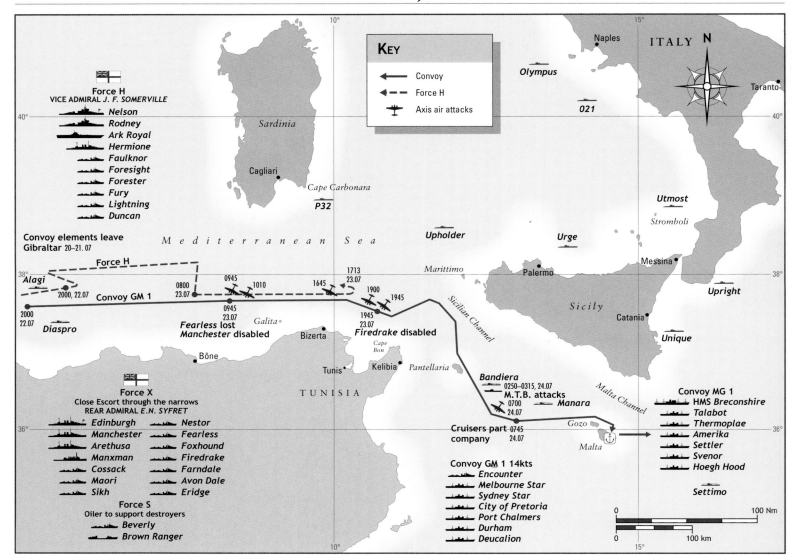

KEY

← Convoy
◄-- Force H
✈ Axis air attacks

Force H
VICE ADMIRAL J. F. SOMERVILLE
- Nelson
- Rodney
- Ark Royal
- Hermione
- Faulknor
- Foresight
- Forester
- Fury
- Lightning
- Duncan

Convoy elements leave
Gibraltar 20–21.07

Force H

Alagi
2000, 22.07
Convoy GM 1
2000 22.07
Diaspro

0800 23.07
0945
0945 23.07
Fearless lost
Manchester disabled

1010
Galita

1645

1713 23.07

1900
1945
1945 23.07
Firedrake disabled

Cape Bon

Force X
Close Escort through the narrows
REAR ADMIRAL E.N. SYFRET
- Edinburgh — Nestor
- Manchester — Fearless
- Arethusa — Foxhound
- Manxman — Firedrake
- Cossack — Farndale
- Maori — Avon Dale
- Sikh — Eridge

Force S
Oiler to support destroyers
- Beverly
- Brown Ranger

Bône
Bizerta
Tunis
Kelibia
Pantellaria

TUNISIA

Bandiera
0250–0315, 24.07
M.T.B. attacks
0700
24.07 Manara

Cruisers part 0745
company 24.07

Convoy GM 1 14kts
- Encounter
- Melbourne Star
- Sydney Star
- City of Pretoria
- Port Chalmers
- Durham
- Deucalion

Sardinia
Cagliari
Cape Carbonara
P32

Mediterranean Sea

Upholder
Urge

Marittimo
Palermo

Sicilian Channel

Gozo
Malta

Naples
Olympus
021

ITALY N
Taranto

Utmost
Stromboli

Messina

Sicily
Catania

Upright

Unique

Malta Channel

Convoy MG 1
- HMS Breconshire
- Talabot
- Thermoplae
- Amerika
- Settler
- Svenor
- Hoegh Hood

Settimo

0   100 Nm
0   100 km

BRITISH FORCES			
TYPE	NO.	S.	D.
CAPITAL SHIPS	2	-	-
AIRCRAFT CARRIERS	1	-	-
CRUISERS	4	-	1
MINELAYER	1	-	-
DESTROYERS	18	1	1
SUBMARINES	8	-	-
MERCHANT SHIPS	13	-	1

THE EVENTS IN the eastern Mediterranean basin throughout the spring of 1941 had profound implications for resupplying Malta. The axis air bases on Crete and on the North African coast, coupled with the depleted state of the Mediterranean fleet after the evacuations from Greece and Crete, ruled out the possibility of Malta being supplied from the east. Instead Admiral Somerville and Force H would cover the badly-needed supplies. The object was to run a convoy of six transports and a troopship to Malta (GM1) and at the same time cover a convoy of seven empty transports from Malta to Gibraltar (MG1). Around 5,000 troops were taken as reinforcements for the garrison on Malta, but of these around 1,000 remained in Gibraltar after the troopship *Leinster* ran ashore departing Algeciras Bay. The rest had been earlier distributed amongst the fleet. In comparison to *Excess* in January, the British could rely on a slightly greater degree of air support from Malta and Gibraltar. At the same time, the Luftwaffe had moved most of its units east while around 200 Italian aircraft were based on Sardinia and Sicily.

Force H would cover the convoy to the narrows before turning back and loitering southwest of Sardinia while Force X took the convoy to Malta and picked up the other one for the return voyage. In order to provide the convoy with a heavy escort in the Sicilian Channel,

most of Rear Admiral Syfret's ships had been sent from Britain. To avoid early detection by axis intelligence the warships, as usual, left Gibraltar incrementally, while the transports slipped through the straits during the night of 20–21 July. A new feature was the addition of an oiler from which Syfret's destroyers refuelled on 22 July to improve their endurance. The various forces joined around 8am on 23 July and it was about then that the Italians became aware of the operation. In the first attack at 9.45am by around fifteen Italian level and torpedo bombers the cruiser *Manchester* was disabled (and then ordered back to Gibraltar) and the destroyer *Fearless* sunk. This was despite *Ark Royal* having put aloft a combat air patrol of eleven Fulmar fighters, three of which were shot down.

Further air attacks followed in which numerous near misses were recorded; but *Firedrake* was disabled and towed back to Gibraltar by *Eridge*. During the night Italian motor torpedo boats attacked the convoy and succeeded in disabling the *Sydney Star* although she was eventually able to reach Malta with assistance of the Australian destroyer *Nestor*. In the early morning of 24 July the convoy broke up as the cruisers went ahead to disembark the troop contingents they were carrying. Convoy MG1 sailed from Malta early on 23 July with a single destroyer as escort. Despite numerous air attacks all its vessels had reached Gibraltar by 28 July.

THE ARCTIC CONVOY ROUTES

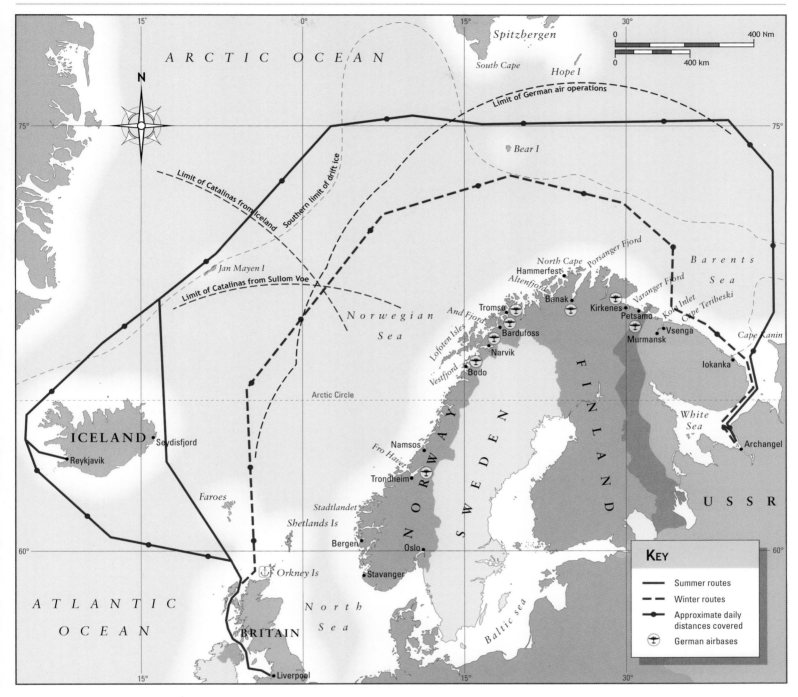

FOLLOWING THE GERMAN invasion on 22 June, Winston Churchill announced that Britain would supply weapons and material to the Soviet Union. Preventing a Soviet collapse and keeping the Red Army supplied was of vital importance in wearing down the German army. There were two supply routes from Britain (though once the US entered the war a third route via the Pacific came into use). The first was via the Arctic to either Murmansk or the port of Archangel on the White Sea. Although this direct route was shorter, the climatic conditions were harsh, particularly in winter, and it was well within range of numerous German airbases in Norway. The second route was far longer, rounding the Cape of Good Hope before heading to the Persian Gulf and then 1,000 miles across Iran and into the Caucasus. The Arctic route was the main conduit in the first critical phase of the war on the eastern front. The first convoy sailed in August and, because initially the supplies came from British stocks, they formed up at Liverpool. Later convoys carrying American supplies assembled in Iceland. During 1941 the convoys encountered very little resistance as German forces were concentrated in other theatres, and most of the 300,000 tons that were sent reached their destination. During the long winter the ice forced a more southerly route that was offset by a degree of protection that the almost continuous darkness afforded.

RUSSIAN CONVOYS, 1941				
DATE	NAME	SHIPS SAILED	SHIPS LOST	DESTINATION
AUGUST	DERVISH	7	–	ARCHANGEL
SEPT–OCT	PQ.1	10	–	ARCHANGEL
SEPT–OCT	QP.1	14	–	SCAPA
OCTOBER	PQ.2	6	–	ARCHANGEL
NOVEMBER	QP.2	12	–	SCAPA
NOVEMBER	PQ.3	8	–	ARCHANGEL
NOVEMBER	PQ.4	8	–	ARCHANGEL
NOV–DEC	PQ.5	7	–	ARCHANGEL
NOV–DEC	QP.3	8	–	SCAPA AND ICELAND
DECEMBER	PQ.6	7	–	MURMANSK
DEC–JAN	PQ.7	2	1	IOKANKA
DEC–JAN	PQ.7B	9	–	MURMANSK
DEC–JAN	QP.4	11	–	ICELAND

OPERATION HALBERD, 27–28 SEPTEMBER 1941

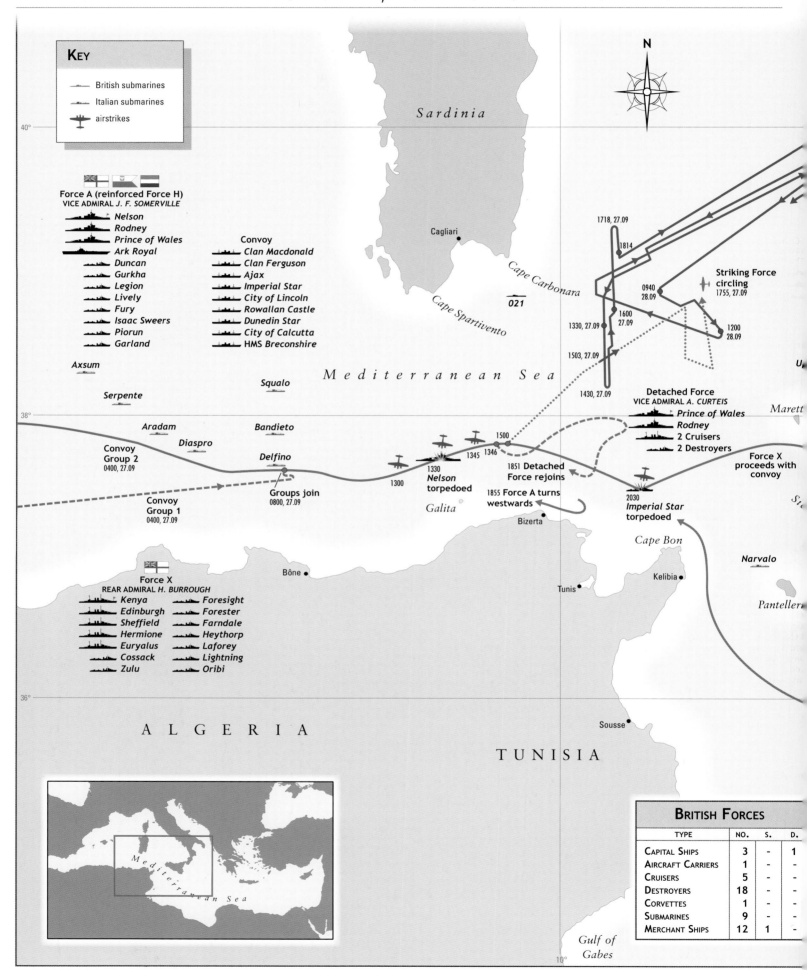

KEY

---- British submarines
---- Italian submarines
airstrikes

Force A (reinforced Force H)
VICE ADMIRAL J. F. SOMERVILLE
- *Nelson*
- *Rodney*
- *Prince of Wales*
- *Ark Royal*
- *Duncan*
- *Gurkha*
- *Legion*
- *Lively*
- *Fury*
- *Isaac Sweers*
- *Piorun*
- *Garland*

Convoy
- *Clan Macdonald*
- *Clan Ferguson*
- *Ajax*
- *Imperial Star*
- *City of Lincoln*
- *Rowallan Castle*
- *Dunedin Star*
- *City of Calcutta*
- *HMS Breconshire*

Axsum

Serpente

Squalo

Mediterranean Sea

Aradam
Bandieto

Diaspro

Convoy Group 2
0400, 27.09

Delfino

Convoy Group 1
0400, 27.09

Groups join
0800, 27.09

Galita

Bizerta

Bône

Tunis

Force X
REAR ADMIRAL H. BURROUGH
- *Kenya*
- *Edinburgh*
- *Sheffield*
- *Hermione*
- *Euryalus*
- *Cossack*
- *Zulu*
- *Foresight*
- *Forester*
- *Farndale*
- *Heythorp*
- *Laforey*
- *Lightning*
- *Oribi*

Sardinia

Cagliari

Cape Carbonara

Cape Spartivento

021

1718, 27.09

1814

0940 28.09

1600 27.09

1330, 27.09

1503, 27.09

1430, 27.09

Striking Force circling
1755, 27.09

1200 28.09

Detached Force
VICE ADMIRAL A. CURTEIS
- *Prince of Wales*
- *Rodney*
- 2 Cruisers
- 2 Destroyers

Marett

1500
1345 1346
1300

1330
Nelson torpedoed

1851 **Detached Force rejoins**

1855 **Force A turns westwards**

Force X proceeds with convoy

2030
Imperial Star torpedoed

Cape Bon

Narvalo

Kelibia

Sousse

Pantelle

St

ALGERIA

TUNISIA

Mediterranean Sea

Gulf of Gabes

10°

BRITISH FORCES			
TYPE	NO.	S.	D.
CAPITAL SHIPS	3	-	1
AIRCRAFT CARRIERS	1	-	-
CRUISERS	5	-	-
DESTROYERS	18	-	-
CORVETTES	1	-	-
SUBMARINES	9	-	-
MERCHANT SHIPS	12	1	-

40°

38°

36°

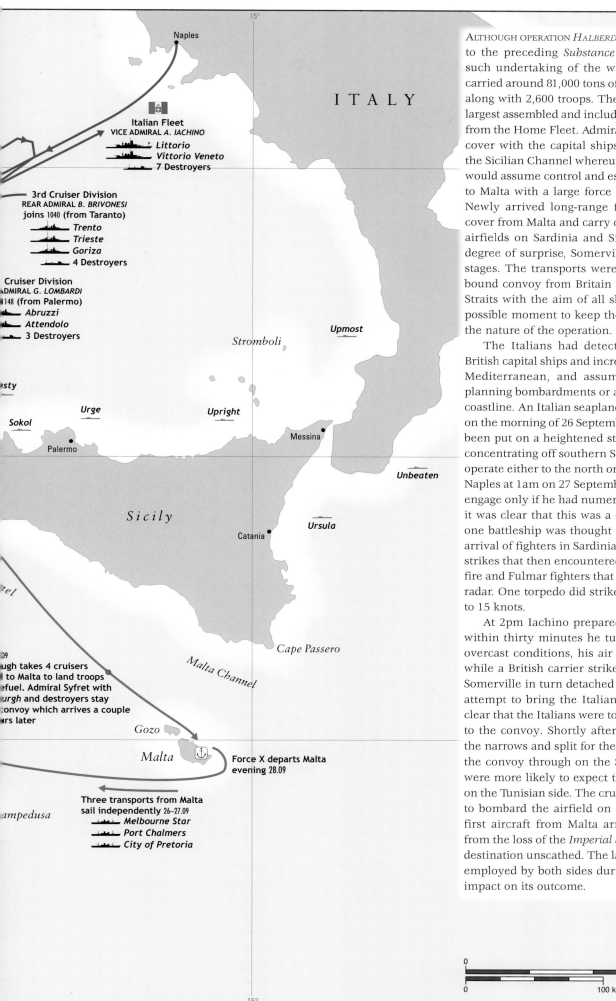

Naples

ITALY

Italian Fleet
VICE ADMIRAL A. IACHINO
Littorio
Vittorio Veneto
7 Destroyers

3rd Cruiser Division
REAR ADMIRAL B. BRIVONESI
joins 1040 (from Taranto)
Trento
Trieste
Goriza
4 Destroyers

Cruiser Division
ADMIRAL G. LOMBARDI
148 (from Palermo)
Abruzzi
Attendolo
3 Destroyers

Upmost

Stromboli

sty

Urge *Upright*

Sokol

Palermo Messina

Unbeaten

Ursula

Sicily

Catania

Cape Passero

Malta Channel

09
ugh takes 4 cruisers
to Malta to land troops
efuel. Admiral Syfret with
urgh and destroyers stay
onvoy which arrives a couple
rs later

Gozo

Malta ⚓

**Force X departs Malta
evening 28.09**

**Three transports from Malta
sail independently 26–27.09**
Melbourne Star
Port Chalmers
City of Pretoria

ampedusa

ALTHOUGH OPERATION *HALBERD* followed a similar approach to the preceding *Substance* convoy it was the largest such undertaking of the war and the nine freighters carried around 81,000 tons of military and civilian stores along with 2,600 troops. The escort was also one of the largest assembled and included two battleships detached from the Home Fleet. Admiral Somerville would provide cover with the capital ships until the convoy reached the Sicilian Channel whereupon Rear Admiral Burrough would assume control and escort the transports through to Malta with a large force of cruisers and destroyers. Newly arrived long-range fighters would provide air cover from Malta and carry out airstrikes against Italian airfields on Sardinia and Sicily. In order to ensure a degree of surprise, Somerville's forces left Gibraltar in stages. The transports were part of a larger Gibraltar-bound convoy from Britain and continued through the Straits with the aim of all ships forming up at the last possible moment to keep the Italians in the dark about the nature of the operation.

The Italians had detected the presence of more British capital ships and increased activity in the eastern Mediterranean, and assumed that the British were planning bombardments or airstrikes against the Italian coastline. An Italian seaplane spotted Somerville's ships on the morning of 26 September, and the Italian fleet had been put on a heightened state of alert with the aim of concentrating off southern Sardinia from where it could operate either to the north or south. Admiral Iachino left Naples at 1am on 27 September and was under orders to engage only if he had numerical superiority. By midday it was clear that this was a convoy for Malta, but only one battleship was thought to be escorting it. The late arrival of fighters in Sardinia delayed the first Italian air strikes that then encountered heavy British anti-aircraft fire and Fulmar fighters that were directed by shipborne radar. One torpedo did strike *Nelson*, slowing her down to 15 knots.

At 2pm Iachino prepared his forces for action, yet within thirty minutes he turned back north as, in the overcast conditions, his air cover failed to materialise while a British carrier strike seemed a real possibility. Somerville in turn detached Vice Admiral Curteis in an attempt to bring the Italians to battle. By 5pm it was clear that the Italians were too far north and he returned to the convoy. Shortly afterwards the convoy reached the narrows and split for the final phase. Burrough took the convoy through on the Sicilian side as the Italians were more likely to expect the British to come through on the Tunisian side. The cruiser *Hermione* was detached to bombard the airfield on Pantelleria. At 6.15am the first aircraft from Malta arrived overhead and, apart from the loss of the *Imperial Star*, the convoy reached its destination unscathed. The large number of submarines employed by both sides during the operation had little impact on its outcome.

GERMAN AUXILIARY CRUISERS, JUNE – DECEMBER 1941

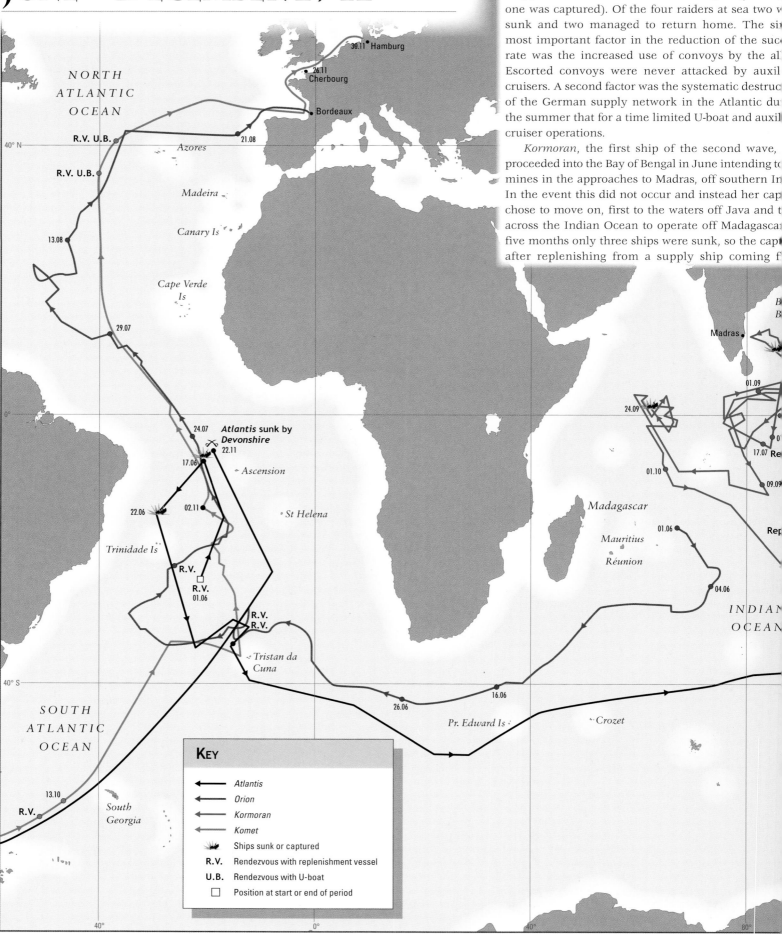

AFTER HAVING SUNK thirty-nine ships in the first ha[...]
1941 the number sunk by German auxiliary cru[...]
dropped to six in the second half of the year (in addi[...]
one was captured). Of the four raiders at sea two v[...]
sunk and two managed to return home. The si[...]
most important factor in the reduction of the suc[...]
rate was the increased use of convoys by the al[...]
Escorted convoys were never attacked by auxil[...]
cruisers. A second factor was the systematic destruc[...]
of the German supply network in the Atlantic du[...]
the summer that for a time limited U-boat and auxil[...]
cruiser operations.

Kormoran, the first ship of the second wave, [...]
proceeded into the Bay of Bengal in June intending to[...]
mines in the approaches to Madras, off southern In[...]
In the event this did not occur and instead her cap[...]
chose to move on, first to the waters off Java and t[...]
across the Indian Ocean to operate off Madagasca[...]
five months only three ships were sunk, so the cap[...]
after replenishing from a supply ship coming f[...]

NORTH ATLANTIC OCEAN

30.11 Hamburg

26.11 Cherbourg

Bordeaux

R.V. U.B.

R.V. U.B.

21.08

Azores

40° N

Madeira

13.08

Canary Is

Cape Verde Is

29.07

0°

24.07

Atlantis sunk by *Devonshire* 22.11

17.06

Ascension

22.06

02.11

St Helena

Trinidade Is

R.V.

R.V. 01.06

R.V. R.V.

Tristan da Cunha

40° S

26.06

Pr. Edward Is

Crozet

SOUTH ATLANTIC OCEAN

13.10

R.V.

South Georgia

Madras

01.09

24.09

01.10

09.09

Madagascar

01.06

Mauritius

Réunion

04.06

16.06

INDIAN OCEAN

17.07

KEY

⟵ *Atlantis*
⟵ *Orion*
⟵ *Kormoran*
⟵ *Komet*
☀ Ships sunk or captured
R.V. Rendezvous with replenishment vessel
U.B. Rendezvous with U-boat
☐ Position at start or end of period

...an, moved to Australian waters. On 19 November ...*Kormoran* encountered the Australian cruiser *Sydney* ...ut 150nm off the Australian coast. The *Sydney* made ...ight for the German ship, disguised as a Dutch ...ghter, asking it to identify itself and approached to ...hin less than a mile. The German captain knew that ...could not evade action and attempted to overwhelm ...cruiser with a surprise gun and torpedo attack. Within ...minutes both ships had inflicted mortal damage on ...h other and within thirty they were drifting apart out ...control. The *Sydney* disappeared over the horizon and ...645 of the crew perished while 317 of the *Kormoran*'s ...w survived and were taken prisoner. This, and the ...ee engagements *Thor* had previously been involved ...demonstrated that with the element of surprise ...d under the right circumstances an auxiliary cruiser ...ld inflict considerable damage. Three days later the ...*ntis*, one of the most successful raiders, was sunk in ...central Atlantic.

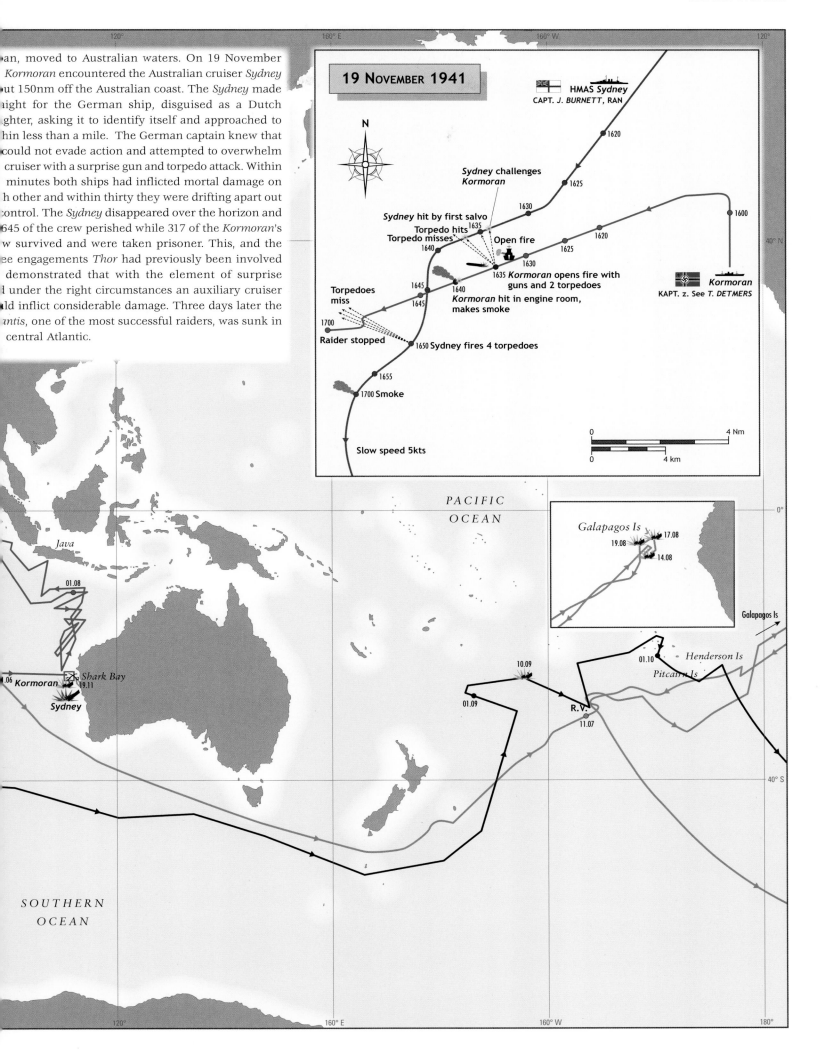

19 NOVEMBER 1941

HMAS *Sydney*
CAPT. J. BURNETT, RAN

N

Sydney challenges *Kormoran*

Sydney hit by first salvo
Torpedo hits 1635
Torpedo misses
1640
Open fire
1620
1625
1630
1625
1620
1600

1635 *Kormoran* opens fire with guns and 2 torpedoes

Kormoran
KAPT. z. See T. DETMERS

Torpedoes miss
1645
1640
1645

Kormoran hit in engine room, makes smoke

1700
Raider stopped

1650 *Sydney* fires 4 torpedoes

1655
1700 Smoke

Slow speed 5kts

0   4 Nm
0   4 km

PACIFIC OCEAN

Galapagos Is
17.08
19.08
14.08

Galapagos Is

Java

01.08

Henderson Is
01.10
Pitcairn Is

10.09

.06 *Kormoran*
Shark Bay
19.11
Sydney

01.09

R.V.
11.07

SOUTHERN OCEAN

THE UNITED STATES NAVY, 1941

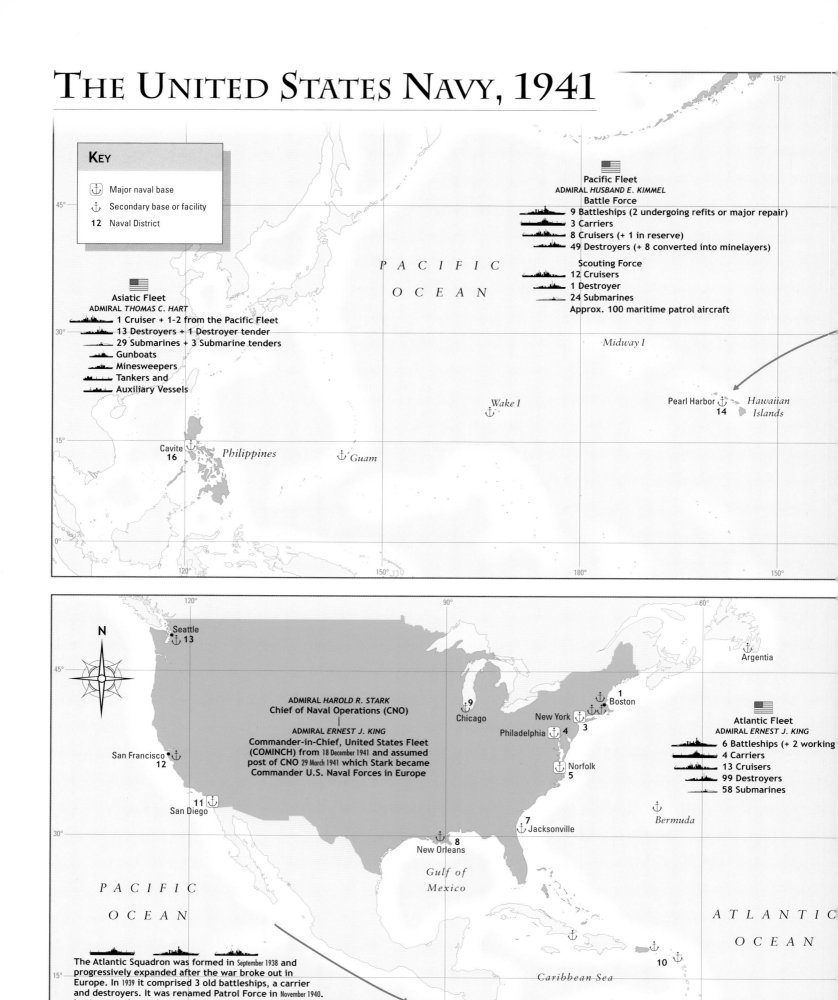

KEY

⚓ (open) Major naval base

⚓ Secondary base or facility

12 Naval District

Pacific Fleet
ADMIRAL *HUSBAND E. KIMMEL*
Battle Force
9 Battleships (2 undergoing refits or major repair)
3 Carriers
8 Cruisers (+ 1 in reserve)
49 Destroyers (+ 8 converted into minelayers)

Scouting Force
12 Cruisers
1 Destroyer
24 Submarines
Approx. 100 maritime patrol aircraft

Asiatic Fleet
ADMIRAL *THOMAS C. HART*
1 Cruiser + 1-2 from the Pacific Fleet
13 Destroyers + 1 Destroyer tender
29 Submarines + 3 Submarine tenders
Gunboats
Minesweepers
Tankers and
Auxiliary Vessels

PACIFIC OCEAN

Midway I

Wake I ⚓

Pearl Harbor ⚓ *Hawaiian*
14 *Islands*

Cavite ⚓ *Philippines*
16

⚓ *Guam*

N

Seattle ⚓ **13**

⚓ Argentia

San Francisco ⚓
12

Chicago ⚓ **9**

New York ⚓
Philadelphia ⚓ **4**

⚓ **1**
Boston

3

San Diego ⚓ **11**

⚓ Norfolk
5

ADMIRAL *HAROLD R. STARK*
Chief of Naval Operations (CNO)

ADMIRAL *ERNEST J. KING*
Commander-in-Chief, United States Fleet
(COMINCH) from 18 December 1941 **and assumed**
post of CNO 29 March 1941 **which Stark became**
Commander U.S. Naval Forces in Europe

Atlantic Fleet
ADMIRAL *ERNEST J. KING*
6 Battleships (+ 2 working)
4 Carriers
13 Cruisers
99 Destroyers
58 Submarines

⚓ **7**
Jacksonville

⚓ Bermuda

8
New Orleans

Gulf of Mexico

PACIFIC OCEAN

ATLANTIC OCEAN

⚓ **10** ⚓

Caribbean Sea

The Atlantic Squadron was formed in September 1938 and
progressively expanded after the war broke out in
Europe. In 1939 it comprised 3 old battleships, a carrier
and destroyers. It was renamed Patrol Force in November 1940.
In February 1941 the entire navy was reorganised and the Atlantic
and Pacific Fleets were established alongside the Asiatic Fleet.
A further carrier and 3 battleships were transferred. From the
Atlantic Fleet a Support Force was established initially comprising
3 destroyer squadrons and 4 maritime patrol squadrons

Panama Canal

Balboa
15

DURING THE COURSE of the war the US Navy became the world's largest navy, undergoing considerable expansion, and far exceeding any pre-war plans. The personnel strength grew from 157,986 officers and men in July 1940 to 3,334,454 in August 1945. American shipyards constructed nearly 1,000 warships, thousands of amphibious ships and craft, and some 56 million tons of merchant shipping. As a result of political and financial considerations, for most of the inter-war years the United States did not maintain the naval strength it was entitled to under the 1922 Washington and 1930 London treaties, and the core of the fleet was composed of battleships constructed in the First World War that underwent some modernisation to increase their effectiveness. The development of aircraft carriers was advanced methodically, albeit at a slightly slower pace than in the Royal Navy, but in terms of cruiser numbers, modern destroyers and submarines the Americans trailed. As the international climate deteriorated in the 1930s more resources were made available for naval rearmament and in 1938 the navy expanded by a quarter over the now expired treaty limitations.

The American focus was predominately on the Pacific with the Imperial Japanese Navy being seen as the most likely enemy, and the bulk of the fleet was stationed on the west coast at San Diego. In the event of a war with Japan the American War Plan Orange foresaw that the fleet would cross the Pacific to come to the relief of the Philippines and defeat the Japanese fleet. In the vast expanse of the Pacific Ocean, aerial reconnaissance and securing island bases were of vital importance. After the outbreak of war in Europe, the USN implemented the Neutrality Patrol that was designed to keep the war away from American waters and safeguard shipping in the western hemisphere. After the fall of France, the Two-Ocean Navy Act was passed to increase the size of the navy by over two-thirds to counter the threat that Germany now posed in the Atlantic. American intervention in the Atlantic campaign increased throughout 1941 as supplies provided by the Lend-Lease Agreement were progressively afforded a greater degree of protection by the USN.

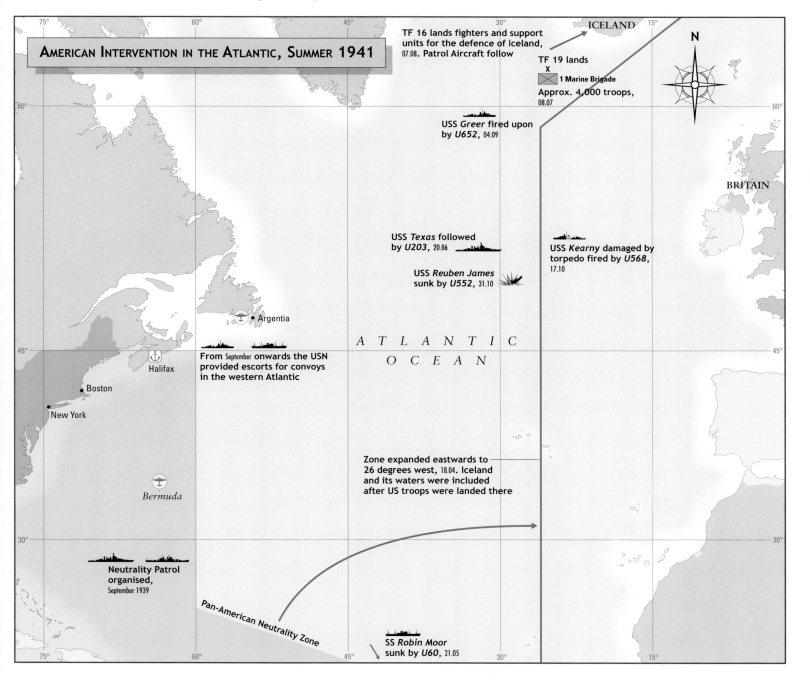

AMERICAN INTERVENTION IN THE ATLANTIC, SUMMER 1941

TF 16 lands fighters and support units for the defence of Iceland, 07.08. Patrol Aircraft follow

ICELAND

TF 19 lands
X
1 Marine Brigade
Approx. 4,000 troops, 08.07

USS *Greer* fired upon by *U652*, 04.09

BRITAIN

USS *Texas* followed by *U203*, 20.06

USS *Kearny* damaged by torpedo fired by *U568*, 17.10

USS *Reuben James* sunk by *U552*, 31.10

Argentia

ATLANTIC
OCEAN

Halifax

From September onwards the USN provided escorts for convoys in the western Atlantic

Boston

New York

Bermuda

Zone expanded eastwards to 26 degrees west, 18.04. Iceland and its waters were included after US troops were landed there

Neutrality Patrol organised, September 1939

Pan-American Neutrality Zone

SS *Robin Moor* sunk by *U60*, 21.05

MALTA STRIKE FORCES, 1941

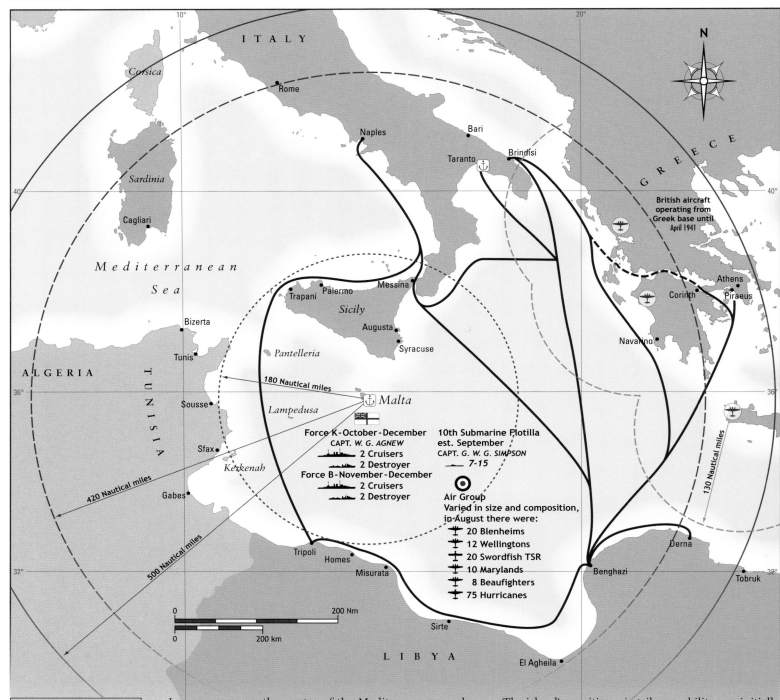

KEY

— Usual axis convoy routes

----- Radius of action of Swordfish TSR carrying a 1,500lb torpedo.

— — — Radius of action of a Wellington I carrying a 4,500lb bombload. When reduced to 1,000lb this increased to 900nm.

—— Radius of action of a Blenheim IV carrying a 1,500lb torpedo or 1,000lb bombload.

LOCATED RIGHT IN the centre of the Mediterranean, and on the two principle Italian convoy routes to North Africa, Malta was an ideal base from which to attack axis supplies bound for the desert war. The Italian air force began bombing the island upon Italy's entry into the war, which confirmed pre-war anxiety about Malta being too vulnerable for use by naval forces. Throughout 1940 warships only made brief visits while the Mediterranean Fleet submarines were divided between the 1st Flotilla at Alexandria and the smaller 8th Flotilla at Gibraltar. Alexandria's distance from the main operational areas reduced the efficacy of the allied submarines and throughout 1941 Malta increasingly came to be used as a forward base for attacking axis shipping and for the allied convoy operations. In September the Malta boats were organised as the 10th Flotilla and that month sunk over 65,000 tons of axis shipping.

The island's maritime airstrike capability was initially limited to a squadron of FAA Swordfish, RAF Maryland patrol aircraft and a few Wellington bombers. In April 1941 it was decided to increase the strike force with Blenheims redeployed from the North Sea. Generally, radar-equipped Swordfish (and later Albacores) and Blenheims used torpedoes and bombs respectively to attack shipping while the Wellingtons bombed axis ports (mainly Tripoli). After the redeployment of most of the Luftwaffe units in Sicily to the eastern Mediterranean in the early summer, the Italians failed to keep up the air attacks. By October the British thought the conditions favourable to base a surface strike force on Malta to augment the efforts of the aircraft and submarines. The impact of Force K, reinforced by the similarly-sized Force B, on axis supply flow's was immediate.

THE IMPERIAL JAPANESE NAVY, 1941

THE LARGER PART of Japanese naval strength was concentrated within the Combined Fleet, the navy's wartime fleet organisation. As a result of the Manchurian Incident in 1933, a permanent staff had been created, and in 1937, when the Sino-Japanese war broke out, the Combined Fleet was placed under the command of the Imperial General Headquarters. The fleet was divided and apportioned to different geographic areas, and these separate forces varied considerably in size and composition depending on their specific roles. The capital ships remained in home waters while the submarines of the 6th Fleet were assigned to provide a screen in the central Pacific against an advancing US fleet and reduce its strength prior to a decisive battle in the west. In support of the surface fleet the IJN possessed a large, well-equipped and trained air arm that by late 1941 operated around 3,000 aircraft, of which 1,800 were frontline. These were organised into air fleets; in April 1941 the First Air Fleet was formed by combining the aircraft carriers into a single unit, and this represented the greatest concentration of naval air power to date.

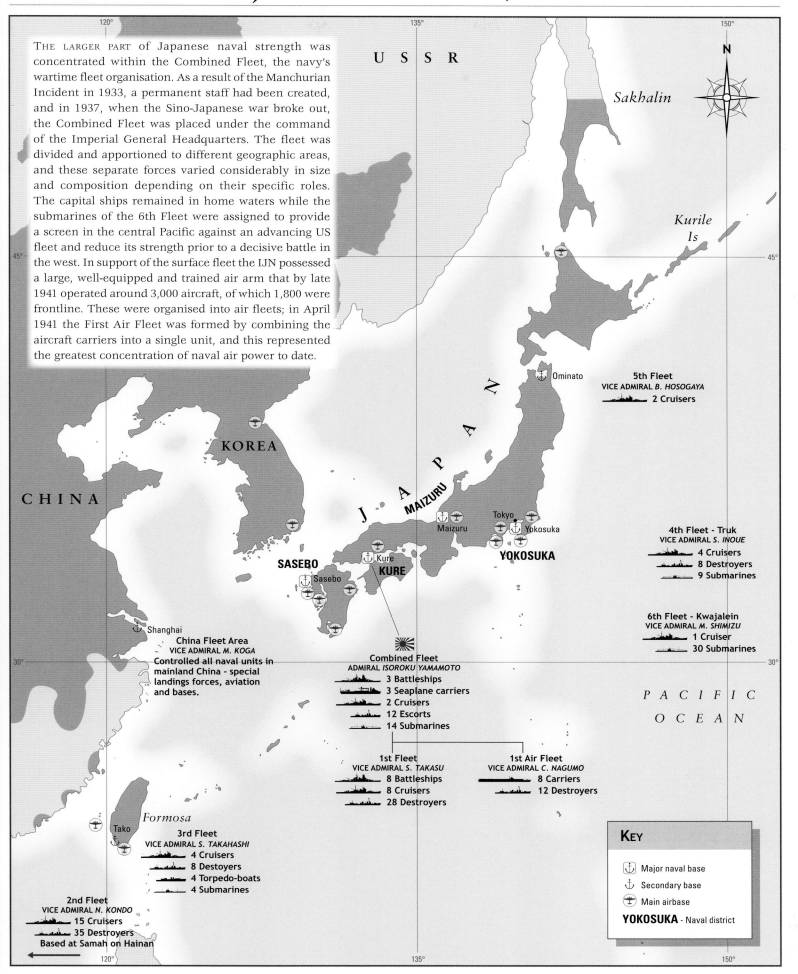

USSR

Sakhalin

Kurile Is

5th Fleet
VICE ADMIRAL *B. HOSOGAYA*
2 Cruisers

Ominato

KOREA

CHINA

J A P A N

Tokyo

Maizuru

MAIZURU

SASEBO
Sasebo

Kure
KURE

Yokosuka
YOKOSUKA

4th Fleet - Truk
VICE ADMIRAL *S. INOUE*
4 Cruisers
8 Destroyers
9 Submarines

6th Fleet - Kwajalein
VICE ADMIRAL *M. SHIMIZU*
1 Cruiser
30 Submarines

Shanghai

China Fleet Area
VICE ADMIRAL *M. KOGA*
Controlled all naval units in mainland China - special landings forces, aviation and bases.

Combined Fleet
ADMIRAL *ISOROKU YAMAMOTO*
3 Battleships
3 Seaplane carriers
2 Cruisers
12 Escorts
14 Submarines

*P A C I F I C
O C E A N*

1st Fleet
VICE ADMIRAL *S. TAKASU*
8 Battleships
8 Cruisers
28 Destroyers

1st Air Fleet
VICE ADMIRAL *C. NAGUMO*
8 Carriers
12 Destroyers

Formosa
Tako

3rd Fleet
VICE ADMIRAL *S. TAKAHASHI*
4 Cruisers
8 Destoyers
4 Torpedo-boats
4 Submarines

2nd Fleet
VICE ADMIRAL *N. KONDO*
15 Cruisers
35 Destroyers
Based at Samah on Hainan

KEY

⚓ Major naval base

⚓ Secondary base

⚓ Main airbase

YOKOSUKA - Naval district

THE JAPANESE OFFENSIVE, DECEMBER 1941 – MAY 1942

THOUGH RELATIONS BETWEEN Japan and the western powers had deteriorated in the late 1930s, as a result of the former's intervention in China, it was not until September 1941 that the Japanese decided to expand into southeast Asia. Strategically, Japan faced an intractable problem for, while the United States was long regarded as its principal opponent in the region, it had also become involved in a protracted continental war against the Chinese and, intermittently, the Soviet Union. Japan could not hope to compete with American

KOREA

Tokyo

JAPAN

Okinawa

Ryukyu Is

Bonin
Islands

Iwo Jima

Formosa

Hong Kong
Falls 25.12

Mariana
Is

Saipan

Guam

BURMA

**Invasion of
Burma**
April

FRENCH INDO-CHINA

Hainan
Second Fleet HQ

Luzon

Manila

PHILIPPINES

SIAM

Bangkok

South
China
Sea

**Andaman
Islands
occupied**

**Operation E,
Malay landings**

**Operation B,
invasion of
Sarawak and
Northern Borneo,**
December

Mindanao

Palau Is

1st Carrier
Division

MALAYA

Celebes
Sea

SARAWAK

**Operation H, invasion of Celebes,
Ambon and Timor,** February–March

2nd Carrier Division

Singapore
Falls
15.02

Borneo

Celebes

Moluccas

Sumatra

**Operation J, invasion of
Java,** February–March 1942

Celebes

**Operation L, invasion
of Sumatra,** February–March

Batavia

Java

Java Sea

**First Air Fleet/Kido Butai
Reassembled for the Indian Ocean Raid,
with 1st, 2nd and 5th Carrier Divisions**

D U T C H   E A S T   I N D I E S

NEW GUINEA

PAPUA

Port
Moresby

Timor

1st and 2nd Carrier Divisions,
February

Timor Sea

February

Darwin

Co
Se

Operation C, Indian Ocean Raid, March - April

INDIAN

OCEAN

Cairns

A U S T R A L I A

economic and military power in a long war and even less so against an Anglo-American alliance. However, German victories in 1940 enabled the Japanese to take control of French Indo-China while forcing the British to reduce their forces in the region.

The American response was to freeze Japanese assets and impose a series of embargoes that would have forced Japan to end the war in China and brought its economy to a standstill. Thus the Japanese sought to acquire the British and Dutch East Indies for their natural resources. First, the US Pacific Fleet at Pearl Harbor would be neutralised. Simultaneously, invasions of the Philippines and Malaya would begin, followed by operations to secure the East Indies. Finally, a network of bases across the south Pacific would be established as an outer perimeter.

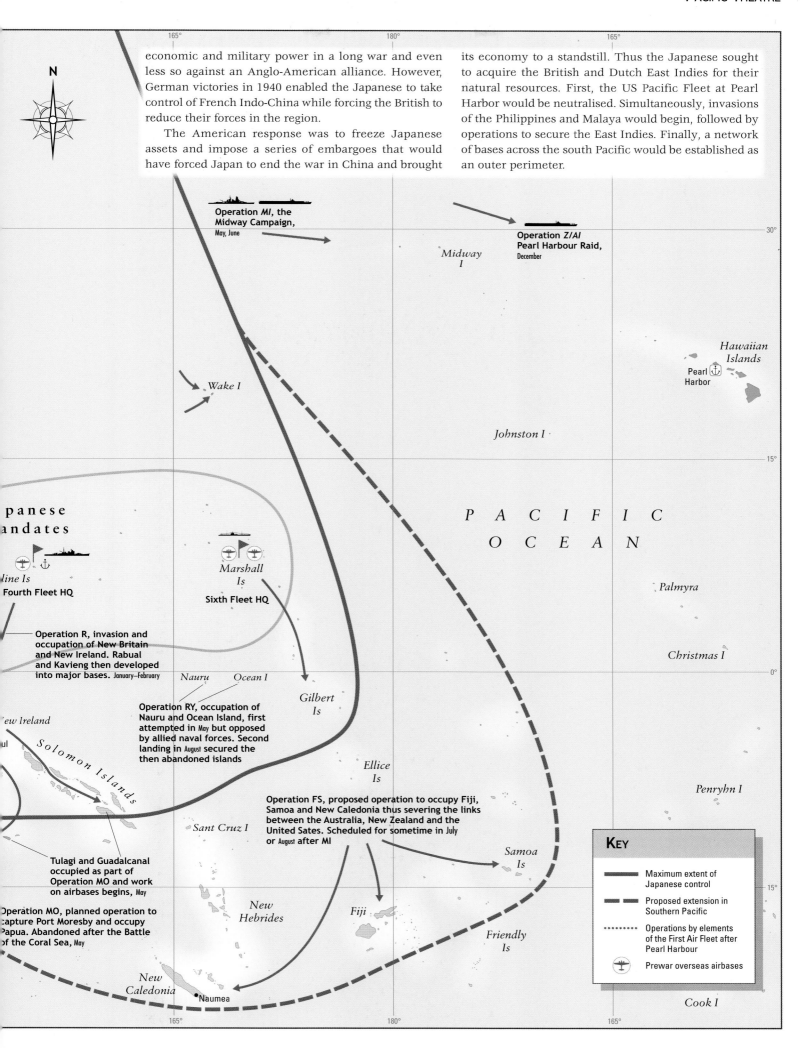

N

Operation MI, the Midway Campaign, May, June

Operation Z/AI Pearl Harbour Raid, December

Midway I

Hawaiian Islands

Pearl Harbor

Johnston I

P A C I F I C
O C E A N

Palmyra

Christmas I

Wake I

Japanese Mandates

Caroline Is
Fourth Fleet HQ

Operation R, invasion and occupation of New Britain and New Ireland. Rabual and Kavieng then developed into major bases. January–February

Marshall Is
Sixth Fleet HQ

Nauru   *Ocean I*

Gilbert Is

Operation RY, occupation of Nauru and Ocean Island, first attempted in May **but opposed by allied naval forces. Second landing in** August **secured the then abandoned islands**

New Ireland

Rabul

Solomon Islands

Ellice Is

Penryhn I

Operation FS, proposed operation to occupy Fiji, Samoa and New Caledonia thus severing the links between the Australia, New Zealand and the United Sates. Scheduled for sometime in July or August **after MI**

Sant Cruz I

Samoa Is

Tulagi and Guadalcanal occupied as part of Operation MO and work on airbases begins, May

Operation MO, planned operation to capture Port Moresby and occupy Papua. Abandoned after the Battle of the Coral Sea, May

New Hebrides

Fiji

Friendly Is

New Caledonia
•Naumea

Cook I

KEY

▬▬▬	Maximum extent of Japanese control
▬ ▬ ▬	Proposed extension in Southern Pacific
··········	Operations by elements of the First Air Fleet after Pearl Harbour
✈	Prewar overseas airbases

OPERATION AI, NOVEMBER–DECEMBER 1941

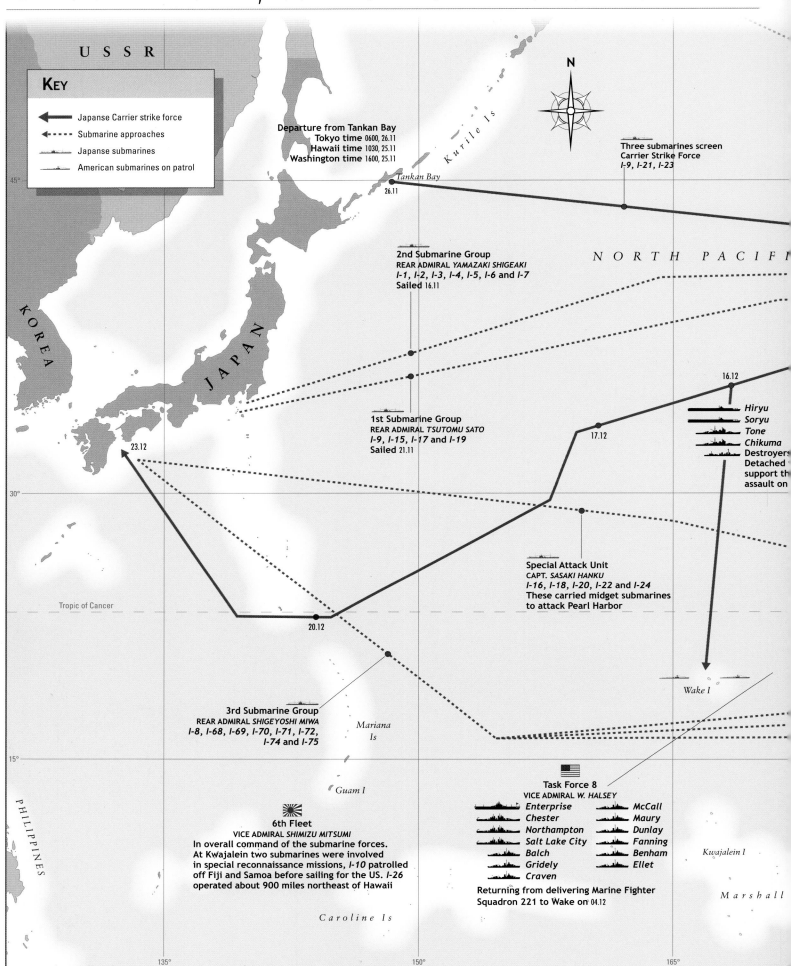

U S S R

KEY

← Japanse Carrier strike force
◄---- Submarine approaches
⚓ Japanese submarines
⚓ American submarines on patrol

Kurile Is

Departure from Tankan Bay
Tokyo time 0600, 26.11
Hawaii time 1030, 25.11
Washington time 1600, 25.11

Tankan Bay
26.11

Three submarines screen
Carrier Strike Force
I-9, I-21, I-23

N O R T H   P A C I F I

2nd Submarine Group
REAR ADMIRAL *YAMAZAKI SHIGEAKI*
I-1, I-2, I-3, I-4, I-5, I-6 and I-7
Sailed 16.11

KOREA

JAPAN

16.12

1st Submarine Group
REAR ADMIRAL *TSUTOMU SATO*
I-9, I-15, I-17 and I-19
Sailed 21.11

23.12

17.12

Hiryu
Soryu
Tone
Chikuma
Destroyers
Detached
support th
assault on

Special Attack Unit
CAPT. *SASAKI HANKU*
I-16, I-18, I-20, I-22 and I-24
These carried midget submarines
to attack Pearl Harbor

Tropic of Cancer

20.12

Wake I

3rd Submarine Group
REAR ADMIRAL *SHIGEYOSHI MIWA*
I-8, I-68, I-69, I-70, I-71, I-72,
I-74 and I-75

*Mariana
Is*

Guam I

Task Force 8
VICE ADMIRAL *W. HALSEY*

Enterprise   *McCall*
Chester   *Maury*
Northampton   *Dunlay*
Salt Lake City   *Fanning*
Balch   *Benham*
Gridely   *Ellet*
Craven

6th Fleet
VICE ADMIRAL *SHIMIZU MITSUMI*
In overall command of the submarine forces.
At Kwajalein two submarines were involved
in special reconnaissance missions, *I-10* patrolled
off Fiji and Samoa before sailing for the US. *I-26*
operated about 900 miles northeast of Hawaii

Kwajalein I

Marshall

Returning from delivering Marine Fighter
Squadron 221 to Wake on 04.12

PHILIPPINES

Caroline Is

135°   150°   165°

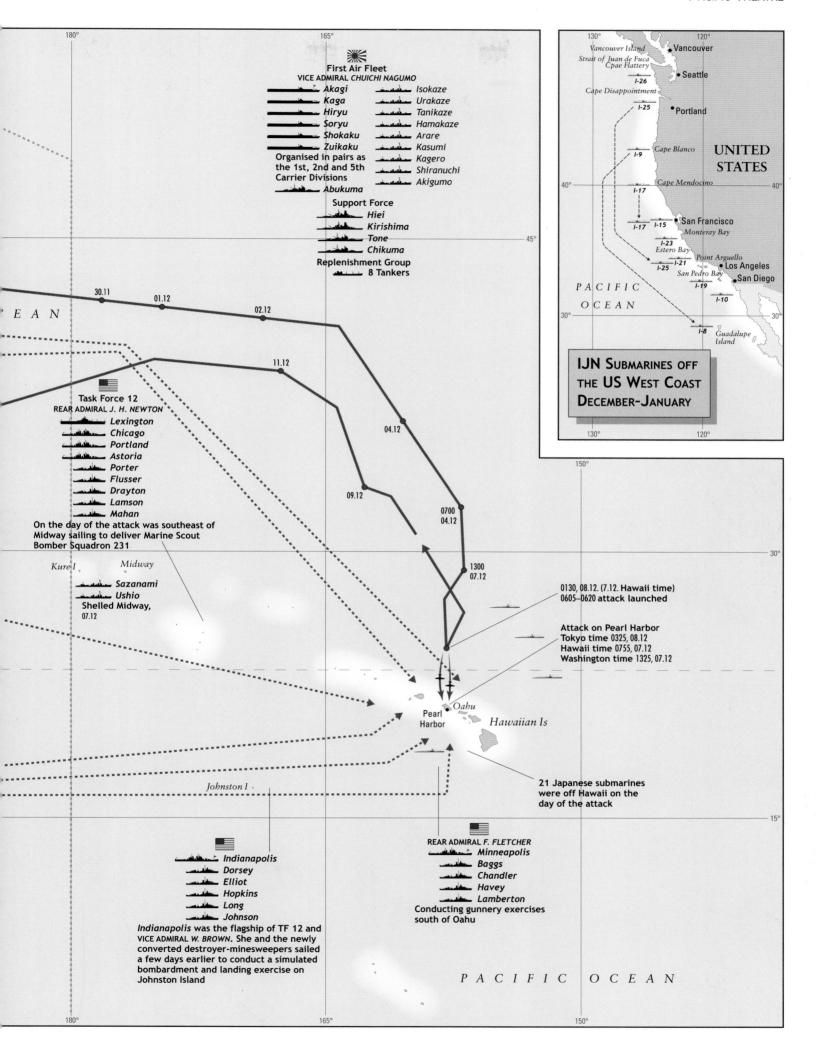

First Air Fleet
VICE ADMIRAL *CHUICHI NAGUMO*

Akagi   *Isokaze*
Kaga   *Urakaze*
Hiryu   *Tanikaze*
Soryu   *Hamakaze*
Shokaku   *Arare*
Zuikaku   *Kasumi*
Organised in pairs as   *Kagero*
the 1st, 2nd and 5th   *Shiranuchi*
Carrier Divisions   *Akigumo*
Abukuma

Support Force
Hiei
Kirishima
Tone
Chikuma
Replenishment Group
8 Tankers

30.11   01.12

02.12

11.12

Task Force 12
REAR ADMIRAL *J. H. NEWTON*

Lexington
Chicago
Portland
Astoria
Porter
Flusser
Drayton
Lamson
Mahan

On the day of the attack was southeast of
Midway sailing to deliver Marine Scout
Bomber Squadron 231

Kure I   *Midway*

Sazanami
Ushio
Shelled Midway,
07.12

04.12

09.12

0700
04.12

1300
07.12

0130, 08.12. (7.12. Hawaii time)
0605–0620 attack launched

Attack on Pearl Harbor
Tokyo time 0325, 08.12
Hawaii time 0755, 07.12
Washington time 1325, 07.12

Oahu
Pearl
Harbor   *Hawaiian Is*

21 Japanese submarines
were off Hawaii on the
day of the attack

Johnston I

REAR ADMIRAL *F. FLETCHER*
Minneapolis
Baggs
Chandler
Havey
Lamberton
Conducting gunnery exercises
south of Oahu

Indianapolis
Dorsey
Elliot
Hopkins
Long
Johnson

Indianapolis was the flagship of TF 12 and
VICE ADMIRAL *W. BROWN*. She and the newly
converted destroyer-minesweepers sailed
a few days earlier to conduct a simulated
bombardment and landing exercise on
Johnston Island

PACIFIC OCEAN

**IJN SUBMARINES OFF
THE US WEST COAST
DECEMBER–JANUARY**

Vancouver Island   • Vancouver
Strait of Juan de Fuca
Cpae Flattery
• Seattle

Cape Disappointment

I-26

I-25   • Portland

Cape Blanco

I-9   **UNITED
STATES**

Cape Mendocino

I-17

I-17   I-15   • San Francisco
Monteray Bay

I-23
Estero Bay
Point Arguello
I-25   I-21   • Los Angeles
San Pedro Bay
I-19   • San Diego

*PACIFIC
OCEAN*

I-8   *Guadalupe
Island*

THE PEARL HARBOR RAID, 7 DECEMBER 1941

THE FIRST WAVE of the Japanese raid on Pearl Harbor, comprising 183 aircraft under Commander Mitsuo Fuchida, was launched between 6am and 6.15am Hawaii time. Its objectives were an attack on the US battle fleet, and the destruction of as many fighter aircraft on the ground as possible to ensure air superiority over the target. The attack began at 7.48am against the Naval Air Station at Kaneohe, while Pearl Harbor itself was hit from 7.55am onwards. Ensuring surprise was crucial because the Kate torpedo-bombers, carrying specially modified torpedoes that were able to run in the shallow waters of the harbour, were slow and vulnerable to any counter attack. Capital ships were the priority: cruisers and destroyers generally left unmolested. Much of the damage on the American fleet was inflicted by this first wave. The second wave of 167 aircraft, launched around

7am, focused on Pearl Harbor and its two airfields. When the aircraft reached their targets around 9.15am the level and coordination of defensive fire had increased and by 10am the raid was over. Fearing that the remaining American aircraft might attack their carriers, Admiral Nagumo chose to abandon a third wave and instead withdrew westwards at high speed.

American casualties numbered 2,403 killed and 1,178 wounded, while 188 aircraft were destroyed and 159 badly damaged; only 43 remained operational. Proportionally, the PBY Catalina maritime patrol aircraft, based at Kaneohe, sustained the heaviest losses. Of the thirty-six aircraft, twenty-seven were destroyed, three damaged and only the three on patrol during the raid remained unscathed. The Japanese lost twenty-nine aircraft. The simultaneous attack by Japanese midget submarines failed to achieve any substantive results and four were sunk. Despite the considerable losses inflicted on the battle line of the US Pacific fleet, the Japanese gained only a partial victory as the base itself sustained limited damage; its repair facilities and workshops remained operative and immediately began repairing damaged warships. Crucially, the Pacific Fleet's fuel stocks, scattered around the base, remained untouched. Had these been destroyed the US fleet would have been immobilised. The submarine base and its boats also escaped unscathed and, together with the carriers, provided the first means of striking back at Japan.

KEY

⟵ A6M Zero fighter

⟵ D3A Val dive-bomber

⟵ B5N Kate torpedo-bomber and Kate high-level bomber

NAS Naval Air Station

MCAS Marine Corps Air Station

Other airbases maintained by the Army Air Force

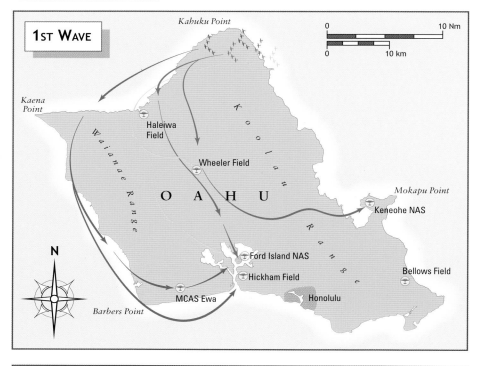

1ST WAVE

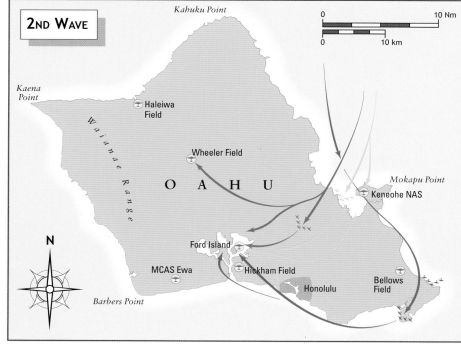

2ND WAVE

① Tender *Whitney* and destroyers *Tucker, Conyngham, Reid, Case* and *Selfridge*	㉖ Battleship *California*
	㉗ Seaplane tender *Avocet*
② Destroyer *Blue*	㉘ Destroyer *Shaw*
③ Light cruiser *Phoenix*	㉙ Destroyer *Downes*
④ Destroyers *Aylwin, Farragut, Dale* and *Monaghan*	㉚ Destroyer *Cassin*
	㉛ Battleship *Pennsylvania*
⑤ Destroyers *Patterson, Ralph, Talbot* and *Henry*	㉜ Submarine *Cachalot*
	㉝ Minelayer *Oglala*
⑥ Tender *Dobbin*, and destroyers *Worden, Hull, Dewey, Phelps* and *Macdonough*	㉞ Light cruiser *Helena*
	㉟ Auxiliary vessel *Argonne*
⑦ Hospital ship *Solace*	㊱ Gunboat *Sacramento*
⑧ Destroyer *Allen*	㊲ Destroyer *Jarvis*
⑨ Destroyer *Chew*	㊳ Destroyer *Mugford*
⑩ Destroyer-minesweepers *Gamble, Montgomery* and light-minelayer *Ramsey*	㊴ Auxiliary vessel *Argonne*
	㊵ Repair vessel *Rigel*
⑪ Destroyer-minesweepers *Trever, Breese, Zane, Perry* and *Wasmuth*	㊶ Oiler *Ramapo*
	㊷ Heavy cruiser *New Orleans*
⑫ Repair vessel *Medusa*	㊸ Destroyer *Cummings*, light-minelayers *Preble* and *Tracy*
⑬ Seaplane tender *Curtiss*	㊹ Heavy cruiser *San Francisco*
⑭ Light cruiser *Detroit*	㊺ Destroyer-minesweeper *Grebe*, destroyer *Schley*, light-minelayers *Pruitt* and *Sicard*
⑮ Light cruiser *Raleigh*	
⑯ Target battleship *Utah*	
⑰ Seaplane tender *Tangier*	㊻ Light cruiser *Honolulu*
⑱ Battleship *Nevada*	㊼ Light cruiser *St. Louis*
⑲ Battleship *Arizona*	㊽ Destroyer *Bagley*
⑳ Repair vessel *Vestal*	㊾ Submarines *Narwhal, Dolphin* and *Tautog*, tenders *Thornton* and *Hulbert*
㉑ Battleship *Tennessee*	
㉒ Battleship *West Virginia*	㊿ Submarine tender *Pelias*
㉓ Battleship *Maryland*	51 Auxiliary vessel *Sumner*
㉔ Battleship *Oklahoma*	52 Auxiliary vessel *Castor*
㉕ Oiler *Neosho*	

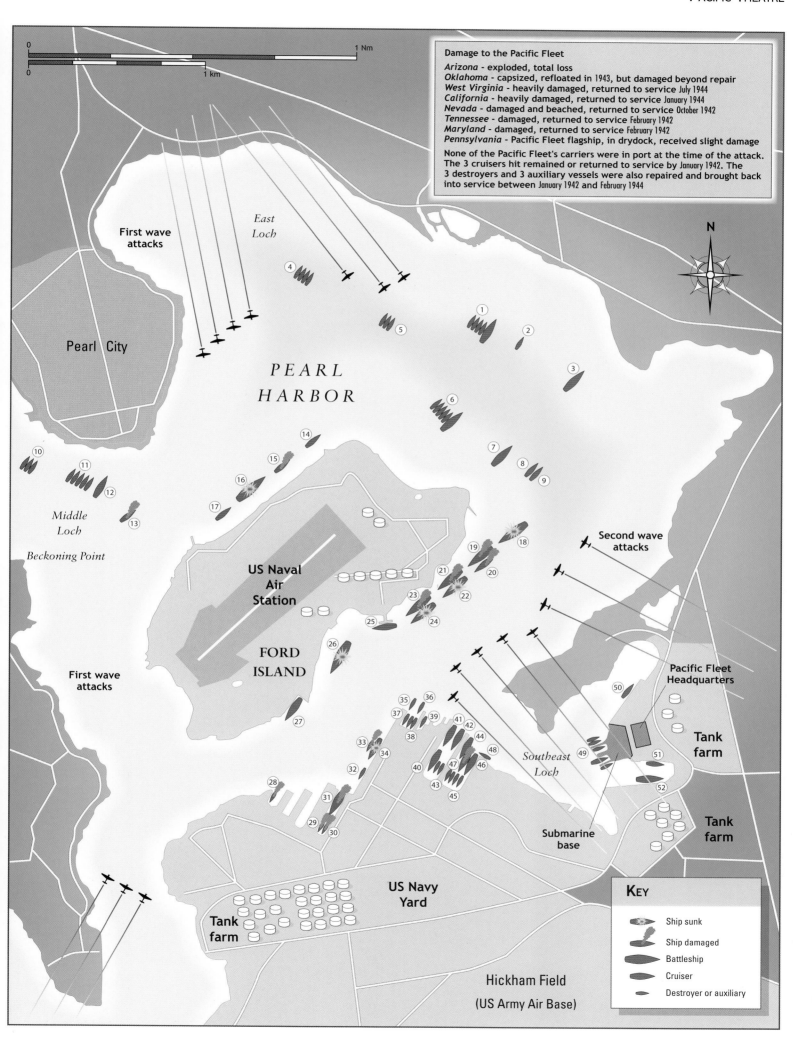

Damage to the Pacific Fleet

Arizona - exploded, total loss
Oklahoma - capsized, refloated in 1943, but damaged beyond repair
West Virginia - heavily damaged, returned to service July 1944
California - heavily damaged, returned to service January 1944
Nevada - damaged and beached, returned to service October 1942
Tennessee - damaged, returned to service February 1942
Maryland - damaged, returned to service February 1942
Pennsylvania - Pacific Fleet flagship, in drydock, received slight damage

None of the Pacific Fleet's carriers were in port at the time of the attack. The 3 cruisers hit remained or returned to service by January 1942. The 3 destroyers and 3 auxiliary vessels were also repaired and brought back into service between January 1942 and February 1944

First wave attacks

East Loch

N

Pearl City

PEARL HARBOR

Middle Loch

Beckoning Point

Second wave attacks

US Naval Air Station

Pacific Fleet Headquarters

First wave attacks

FORD ISLAND

Tank farm

Southeast Loch

Tank farm

Submarine base

US Navy Yard

Tank farm

Hickham Field

(US Army Air Base)

KEY

Ship sunk
Ship damaged
Battleship
Cruiser
Destroyer or auxiliary

The Japanese Invasion of Malaya, 6–10 December 1941

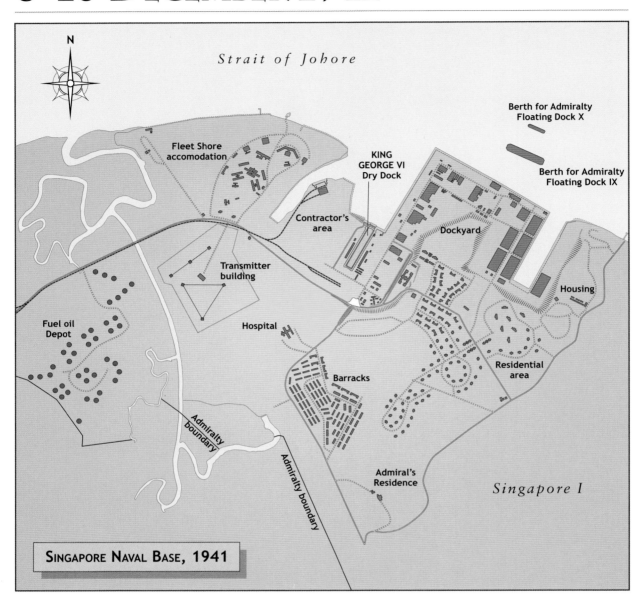

Singapore Naval Base, 1941

In October, Winston Churchill instructed the Admiralty to send a force of capital ships to Singapore to deter any Japanese attempts at expanding into Malaya and the Dutch East Indies. While the pre-war Singapore strategy had envisaged sending most of the battle fleet to the Far East, all that was available now was the battleship *Prince of Wales* and the battle cruiser *Repulse*, accompanied by four destroyers. It was originally intended that the aircraft carrier *Indomitable* would also be sent, but whilst working-up off Jamaica she ran aground and needed to be sent to Norfolk, Virginia, for repairs. By the time Admiral Phillips's force arrived in Singapore on 2 December the outbreak of war was imminent. *Repulse* was sent to Darwin, but recalled when air reconnaissance spotted Japanese transports and warships off Indo-China heading south. On 7 December an RAF reconnaissance plane again found the Japanese force but was shot down before it could relay its position. Phillips left Singapore during the afternoon of 8 December with the hope of intercepting the transports before the landings took place.

The Japanese first became aware of Force Z when the submarine *I-65* spotted them heading north at 1.45pm. Four hours later Japanese patrol aircraft also spotted the force; the element of surprise had been lost and Phillips turned south at 8.15pm. Around midnight, unconfirmed reports were received that that Japanese troops were landing at Kuantan, which was to the south of Force Z's position. Rather than making directly for Singapore, Phillips turned southwest and was off the Malay coast by 8am on 10 December. It was immediately clear that no Japanese forces were present, but Phillips remained in the area for two hours and at 10.15am a Japanese reconnaissance plane spotted the British. Even at this stage Phillips did not break radio silence to request air cover from Singapore. An hour later level- and torpedo-bombers from the Japanese 22nd Air Flotilla began a well-coordinated attack, and *Repulse* was sunk at 12.33pm followed by *Prince of Wales* at 1.30pm. With the destruction of the two capital ships the entire allied strategy for the defence of the Far East unravelled.

The Destruction of Force Z

- ← Japanese assault force
- ← British Force Z
- ← Route of Japanese aircraft
- ✈ Allied airbase
- ✈ Japanese airbase
- ⊢⊣ Japanese submarine
-   British possession
-   French possession
-   Dutch possession

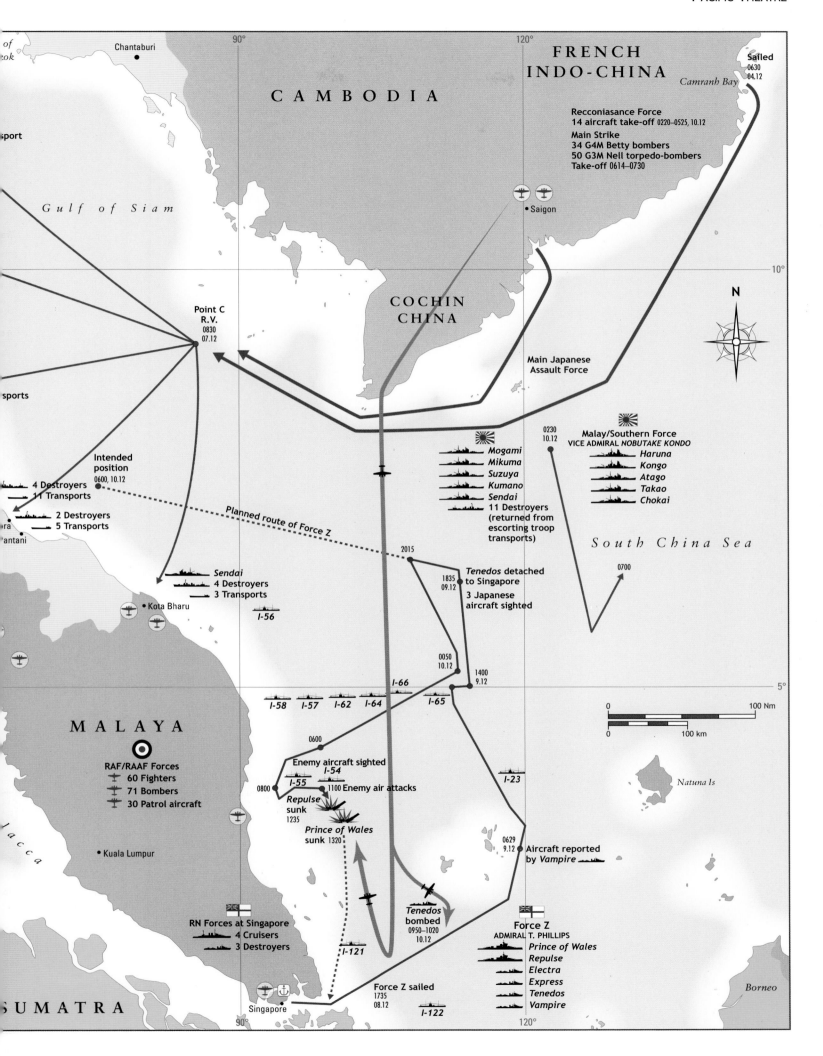

Chantaburi

FRENCH
INDO-CHINA

Sailed
0630
04.12

Camranh Bay

CAMBODIA

Gulf of Siam

Recconiasance Force
14 aircraft take-off 0220–0525, 10.12
Main Strike
34 G4M Betty bombers
50 G3M Nell torpedo-bombers
Take-off 0614–0730

Saigon

10°

COCHIN
CHINA

Point C
R.V.
0830
07.12

Main Japanese
Assault Force

sports

Mogami
Mikuma
Suzuya
Kumano
Sendai
11 Destroyers
(returned from
escorting troop
transports)

0230
10.12

Malay/Southern Force
VICE ADMIRAL *NOBUTAKE KONDO*

Haruna
Kongo
Atago
Takao
Chokai

Intended
position
0600, 10.12

4 Destroyers
11 Transports

2 Destroyers
5 Transports

South China Sea

Planned route of Force Z

0700

2015

Sendai
4 Destroyers
3 Transports

Tenedos detached
to Singapore
3 Japanese
aircraft sighted

1835
09.12

Kota Bharu

I-56

0050
10.12

1400
9.12

I-66

5°

MALAYA

I-58 *I-57* *I-62* *I-64*

I-65

RAF/RAAF Forces
60 Fighters
71 Bombers
30 Patrol aircraft

0600

Enemy aircraft sighted
I-54

I-23

0800

I-55 1100 Enemy air attacks

Natuna Is

Repulse
sunk
1235

Kuala Lumpur

Prince of Wales
sunk 1320

0629
9.12

Aircraft reported
by *Vampire*

RN Forces at Singapore
4 Cruisers
3 Destroyers

Tenedos
bombed
0950–1020
10.12

Force Z
ADMIRAL T. PHILLIPS
Prince of Wales
Repulse
Electra
Express
Tenedos
Vampire

I-121

Force Z sailed
1735
08.12

I-122

Singapore

SUMATRA

Borneo

100 Nm

100 km

THE PHILIPPINES CAMPAIGN, 1941–1942

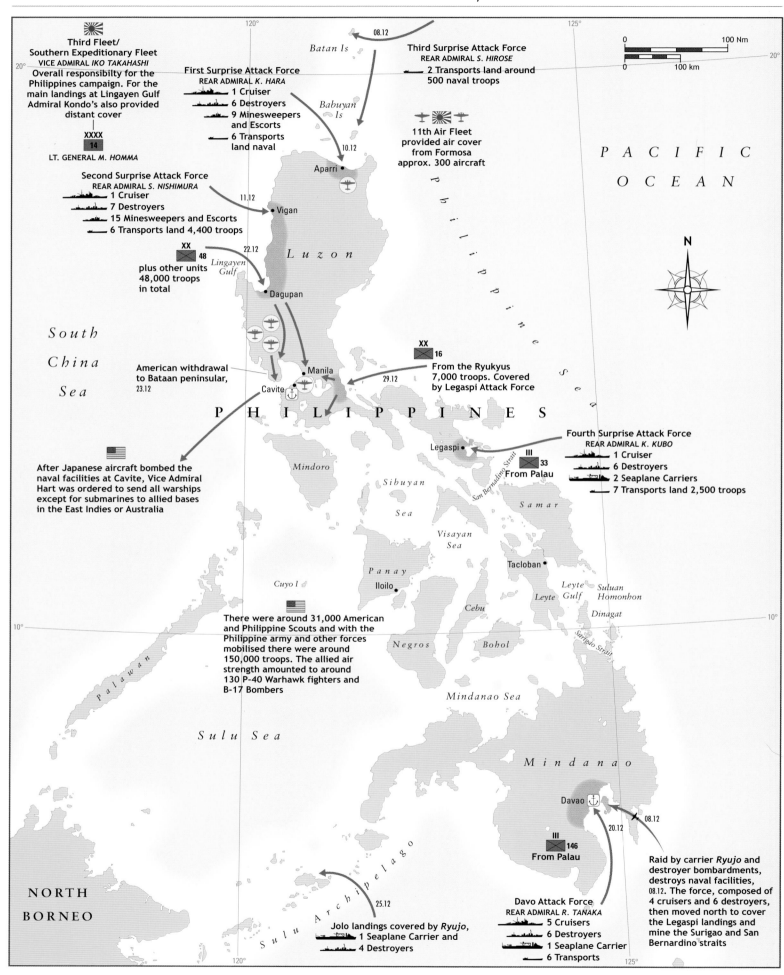

Third Fleet/ Southern Expeditionary Fleet
VICE ADMIRAL *IKO TAKAHASHI*
Overall responsibilty for the Philippines campaign. For the main landings at Lingayen Gulf Admiral Kondo's also provided distant cover

XXXX
14
LT. GENERAL M. HOMMA

First Surprise Attack Force
REAR ADMIRAL *K. HARA*
— 1 Cruiser
— 6 Destroyers
— 9 Minesweepers and Escorts
— 6 Transports land naval

Third Surprise Attack Force
REAR ADMIRAL *S. HIROSE*
— 2 Transports land around 500 naval troops

11th Air Fleet
provided air cover from Formosa approx. 300 aircraft

Second Surprise Attack Force
REAR ADMIRAL *S. NISHIMURA*
— 1 Cruiser
— 7 Destroyers
— 15 Minesweepers and Escorts
— 6 Transports land 4,400 troops

XX
48
plus other units 48,000 troops in total

American withdrawal to Bataan peninsular, 23.12

XX
16
From the Ryukyus 7,000 troops. Covered by Legaspi Attack Force

After Japanese aircraft bombed the naval facilities at Cavite, Vice Admiral Hart was ordered to send all warships except for submarines to allied bases in the East Indies or Australia

Fourth Surprise Attack Force
REAR ADMIRAL *K. KUBO*
— 1 Cruiser
— 6 Destroyers
— 2 Seaplane Carriers
— 7 Transports land 2,500 troops

III
33
From Palau

There were around 31,000 American and Philippine Scouts and with the Philippine army and other forces mobilised there were around 150,000 troops. The allied air strength amounted to around 130 P-40 Warhawk fighters and B-17 Bombers

III
146
From Palau

Raid by carrier *Ryujo* and destroyer bombardments, destroys naval facilities, 08.12. The force, composed of 4 cruisers and 6 destroyers, then moved north to cover the Legaspi landings and mine the Surigao and San Bernardino straits

Davo Attack Force
REAR ADMIRAL *R. TANAKA*
— 5 Cruisers
— 6 Destroyers
— 1 Seaplane Carrier
— 6 Transports

Jolo landings covered by *Ryujo*,
— 1 Seaplane Carrier and
— 4 Destroyers

0 / 100 Nm
0 / 100 km

PACIFIC OCEAN

Batan Is
Babuyan Is
Aparri
Vigan
Luzon
Lingayen Gulf
Dagupan
Manila
Cavite
PHILIPPINES
Legaspi
San Bernadino Strait
Samar
Tacloban
Leyte Gulf
Suluan
Homonhon
Dinagat
Mindoro
Sibuyan Sea
Visayan Sea
Panay
Iloilo
Cuyo I
Cebu
Negros
Bohol
Surigao Strait
Mindanao Sea
Sulu Sea
Mindanao
Davao
South China Sea
Palawan
Sulu Archipelago
NORTH BORNEO

N

08.12
10.12
11.12
22.12
29.12
23.12
25.12
20.12
08.12

THE FALL OF WAKE ISLAND, 21–24 DECEMBER 1941

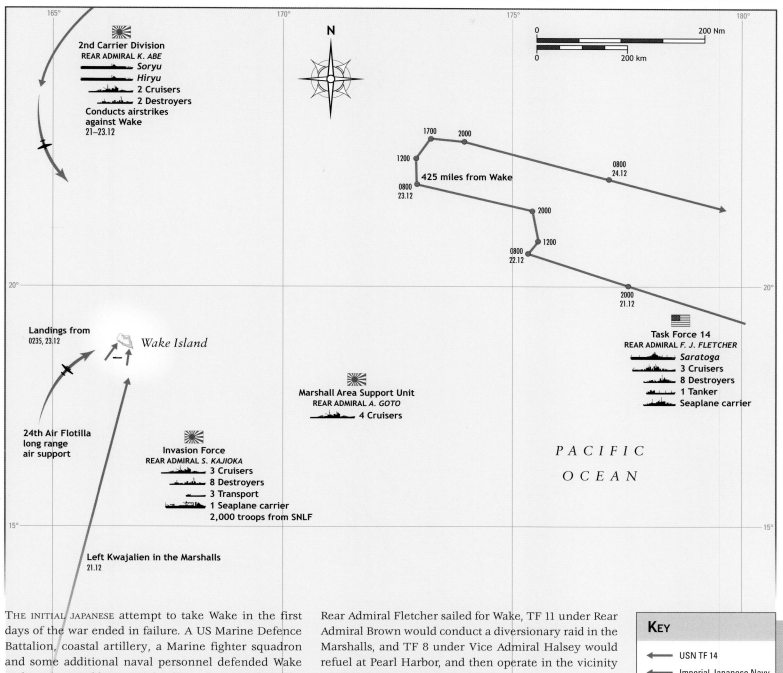

THE INITIAL JAPANESE attempt to take Wake in the first days of the war ended in failure. A US Marine Defence Battalion, coastal artillery, a Marine fighter squadron and some additional naval personnel defended Wake and its two neighbouring islands. A Japanese air strike on 8 December destroyed most of the fighters, but the landings on 11 December were beaten off. Two destroyers were sunk, a number of other ships were damaged and the Japanese suffered nearly 400 casualties, mostly dead. As a result, a second far larger assault force was prepared for a further assault two weeks later. The Truk-based 24th Air Flotilla conducted daily raids of Wake and a carrier division was detached from the returning First Air Fleet to add to the weight of the bombardment and cover the assault.

Within days of the Pearl Harbor attack, the Americans prepared a relief expedition for Wake as one of the first wartime operations undertaken. It was to make use of most of the Pacific Fleet's immediate frontline strength deployed in three carrier task forces. While TF 14 under

Rear Admiral Fletcher sailed for Wake, TF 11 under Rear Admiral Brown would conduct a diversionary raid in the Marshalls, and TF 8 under Vice Admiral Halsey would refuel at Pearl Harbor, and then operate in the vicinity of Midway as a covering force.

The various American forces departed Oahu between 14 and 16 December, but the lack of intelligence on current Japanese dispositions and movements handicapped the operation. In addition, Fletcher faced the problem that he only had one tanker from which to refuel and, given the distances involved, he could not make a high-speed run for Wake. On 21 December, Wake reported that carrier aircraft were conducting strikes that suggested that at least elements of the Japanese carrier force were operating in the vicinity. The landings took place early on 23 December and within hours Japanese forces had overrun the exhausted defenders. Although TF 11 had been diverted north on 20 December to join Fletcher, it was not yet in position and given that the Japanese had landed the relief operation was cancelled.

THE FIRST BATTLE OF SIRTE, 16–18 DECEMBER 194[

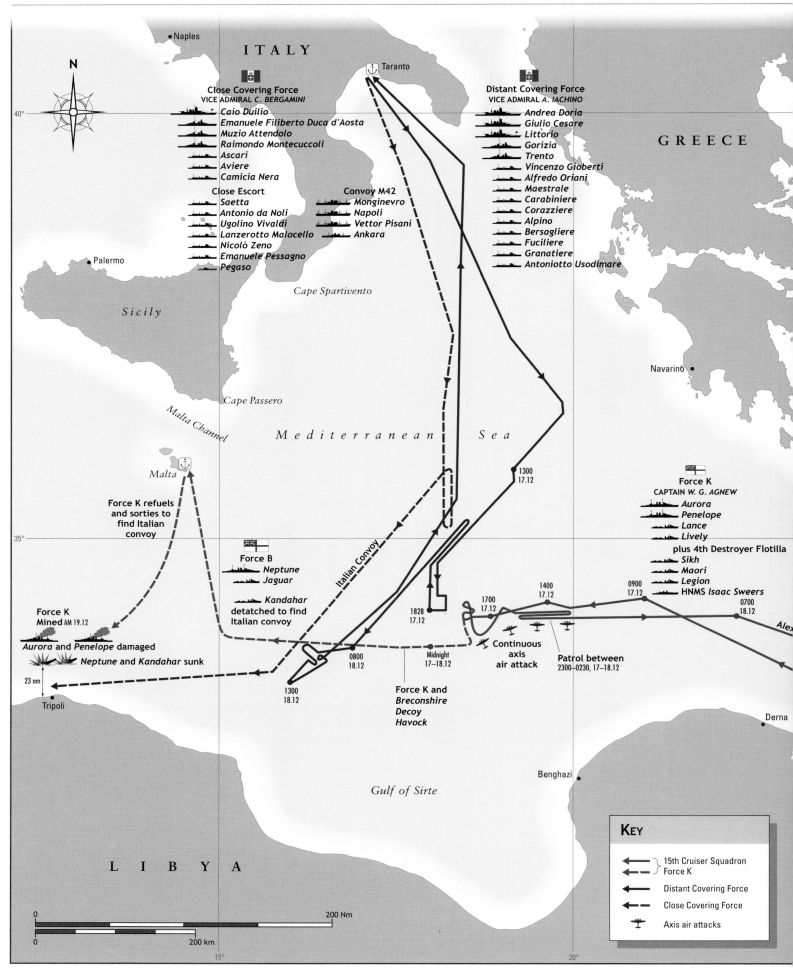

Close Covering Force
VICE ADMIRAL C. BERGAMINI
- Caio Duilio
- Emanuele Filiberto Duca d'Aosta
- Muzio Attendolo
- Raimondo Montecuccoli
- Ascari
- Aviere
- Camicia Nera

Close Escort
- Saetta
- Antonio da Noli
- Ugolino Vivaldi
- Lanzerotto Malocello
- Nicolò Zeno
- Emanuele Pessagno
- Pegaso

Convoy M42
- Monginevro
- Napoli
- Vettor Pisani
- Ankara

Distant Covering Force
VICE ADMIRAL A. IACHINO
- Andrea Doria
- Giulio Cesare
- Littorio
- Gorizia
- Trento
- Vincenzo Gioberti
- Alfredo Oriani
- Maestrale
- Carabiniere
- Corazziere
- Alpino
- Bersagliere
- Fuciliere
- Granatiere
- Antoniotto Usodimare

Force K
CAPTAIN W. G. AGNEW
- Aurora
- Penelope
- Lance
- Lively

plus 4th Destroyer Flotilla
- Sikh
- Maori
- Legion
- HNMS Isaac Sweers

Force B
- Neptune
- Jaguar

- Kandahar detached to find Italian convoy

Force K refuels and sorties to find Italian convoy

Force K Mined AM 19.12

Aurora and Penelope damaged
Neptune and Kandahar sunk

23 nm

Tripoli

1300
17.12

1828
17.12

0800
18.12

1300
18.12

Midnight
17–18.12

1700
17.12

1400
17.12

0900
17.12

0700
18.12

Continuous axis air attack

Patrol between 2300–0230, 17–18.12

Force K and Breconshire Decoy Havock

Italian Convoy

ITALY

GREECE

Sicily

Palermo

Naples

Taranto

Cape Spartivento

Cape Passero

Malta Channel

Malta

Mediterranean Sea

Navarino

Gulf of Sirte

LIBYA

Benghazi

Derna

Alex

KEY
- 15th Cruiser Squadron
- Force K
- Distant Covering Force
- Close Covering Force
- Axis air attacks

40°

35°

15°

20°

0   200 Nm
0   200 km

N

The events in the central Mediterranean throughout November and December were closely connected to the British offensive in the Western Desert, Operation *Crusader*, that, starting on 18 November, progressively pushed the axis forces west out of Cyrenaica. This was an intense phase in the naval war with both sides attaining victories and suffering considerable reverses. Malta's role in interdicting axis African traffic was crucial to the events in the desert war. In the *Duisburg* convoy action on the night of 8–9 November a heavily defended Italian convoy had all its seven freighters sunk by Force K. Malta-based submarines and aircraft in with Force K sunk more than sixty per cent of axis supplies going to Africa in November. However, the arrival of more German U-boats and aircraft from the Eastern Front had an impact. *U331* sank the battleship *Barham* off Bardia on 25 November. The Japanese entry into the war was immediately felt as the Australian destroyers with the Mediterranean fleet were sent to the Far East. To compensate for the loss, the 4th Destroyer Flotilla was transferred from the west and on its voyage to Malta ambushed an Italian cruiser force carrying supplies to Tripoli. Ultra intelligence had alerted the British to the Italian movement, but low fuel stocks on Malta prevented Force K from sortieing on this occasion.

To resupply Africa the Italians prepared convoy M41, of eight freighters, that was to be covered by the entire available fleet. While it was assembling on 13 December off Taranto two freighters were sunk by the submarine *Upright* and the next day *Vittorio Veneto* was heavily damaged by a torpedo from *Urge*. A smaller convoy, M42, was organised and set sail late on 16 December with a similarly large escort as the Italians erroneously believed the British had battleships based at Malta. This coincided with a British operation to move the 4th Destroyer Flotilla on to Alexandria and take badly needed supplies to Malta on *Breconshire* (disguised as a battleship). The two fleets briefly made contact but aggressive British destroyer tactics and the onset of darkness prevented Admiral Iachino pressing home his advantage. All ships reached their destinations. In the immediate aftermath Force K, sent out to find the convoy off Tripoli, ran into a minefield and was nearly completely destroyed while an attack by Italian frogmen on Alexandria disabled the battleships *Queen Elizabeth* and *Valiant*.

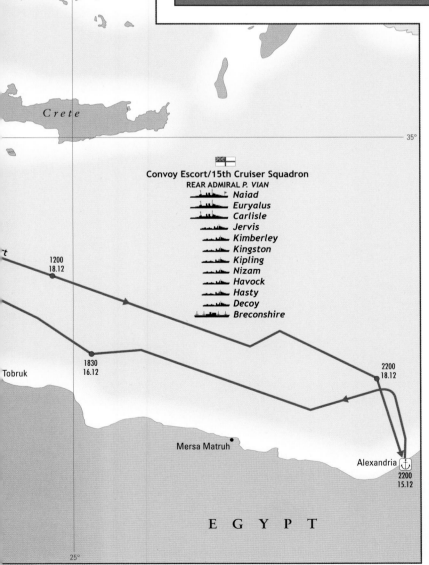

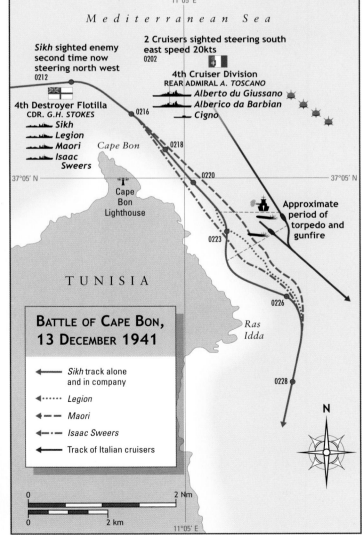

Battle of Cape Bon, 13 December 1941

Sikh track alone and in company

Legion

Maori

Isaac Sweers

Track of Italian cruisers

THE WAR AT SEA, 1942

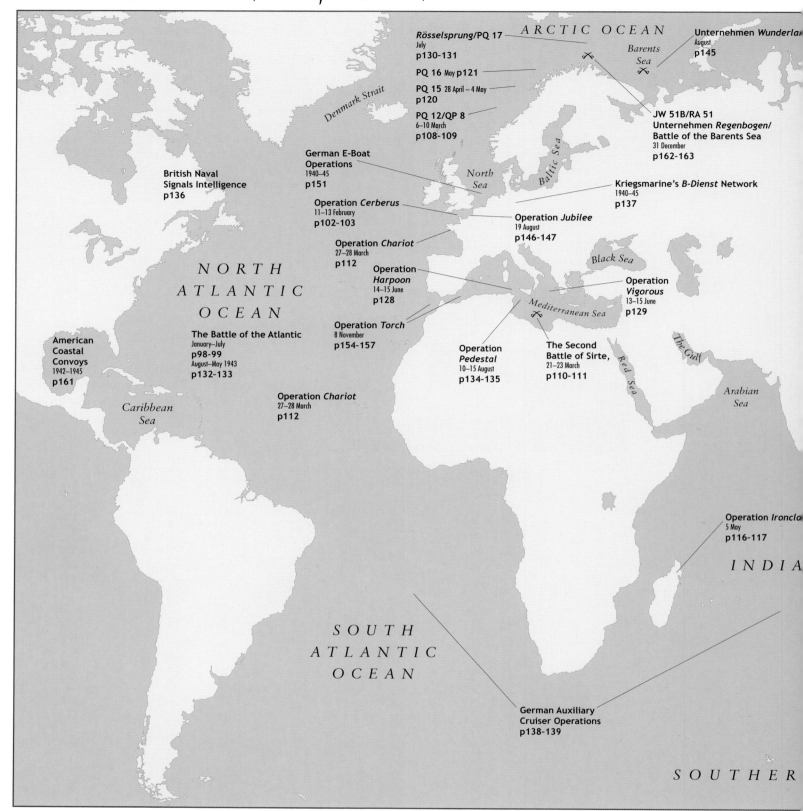

Rösselsprung/PQ 17
July
p130-131

PQ 16 May p121

PQ 15 28 April – 4 May
p120

PQ 12/QP 8
6–10 March
p108-109

**German E-Boat
Operations**
1940–45
p151

**British Naval
Signals Intelligence**
p136

Operation Cerberus
11–13 February
p102-103

Operation Chariot
27–28 March
p112

**Operation
Harpoon**
14–15 June
p128

**American
Coastal
Convoys**
1942–1945
p161

The Battle of the Atlantic
January–July
p98-99
August–May 1943
p132-133

Operation Chariot
27–28 March
p112

Operation Torch
8 November
p154-157

**Operation
Pedestal**
10–15 August
p134-135

**The Second
Battle of Sirte,**
21–23 March
p110-111

**Operation
Vigorous**
13–15 June
p129

Operation Jubilee
19 August
p146-147

Kriegsmarine's B-Dienst Network
1940–45
p137

**JW 51B/RA 51
Unternehmen Regenbogen/
Battle of the Barents Sea**
31 December
p162-163

Unternehmen Wunderlan
August
p145

Operation Ironcla
5 May
p116-117

**German Auxiliary
Cruiser Operations**
p138-139

ARCTIC OCEAN
Barents
Sea
Denmark Strait
North
Sea
Baltic Sea
Black Sea
Mediterranean Sea
The Gulf
Red Sea
Arabian
Sea
NORTH
ATLANTIC
OCEAN
Caribbean
Sea
SOUTH
ATLANTIC
OCEAN
INDIA
SOUTHER

BY THE SPRING of 1942 major naval operations were being conducted across all the oceans with the Arctic and the waters around the Solomon Islands seeing some of the most intense action. The six-month Japanese offensive, which had begun in the previous December, dominated the naval war and had implications for the allies in other theatres. Having largely immobilised the American Pacific Fleet at Pearl Harbor, the Japanese focussed on securing the East Indies, and this they achieved within months aided by their quantitative and qualitative superiority and a fractured allied command structure. The British were able to assemble a comparatively large fleet in a short time for service in the Indian Ocean to deal with an incursion, but the battleships were old and the carriers not as effective as those of the Japanese. When a Japanese fleet did arrive, the British avoided contact and abandoned the eastern portion of the ocean. To the Japanese, this British incursion was little more than a raid; the main threat emanated from the American carriers that were already raiding the periphery of the expanded empire. The contest for command of the Pacific was resolved by means of four great carrier battles – Coral Sea, Midway, Eastern Solomons and Santa Cruz –, which blunted the Japanese offensive and exhausted its pre-war carrier force as well as that of the United States Navy.

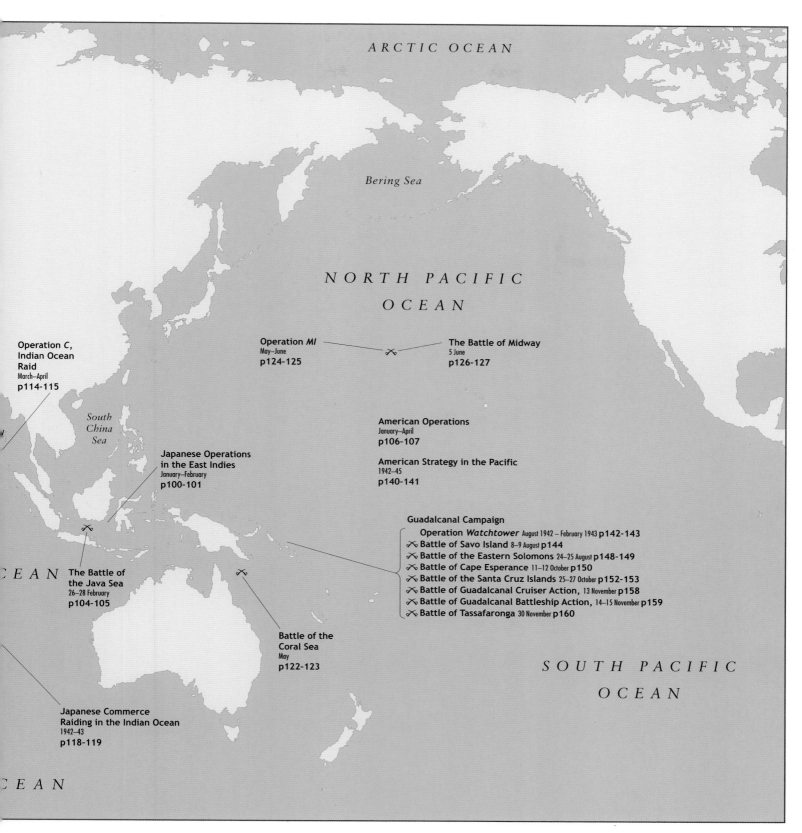

ARCTIC OCEAN

Bering Sea

NORTH PACIFIC
OCEAN

Operation *C*,
Indian Ocean
Raid
March–April
p114-115

South
China
Sea

Operation *MI*
May–June
p124-125

The Battle of Midway
5 June
p126-127

American Operations
January–April
p106-107

American Strategy in the Pacific
1942–45
p140-141

Japanese Operations
in the East Indies
January–February
p100-101

Guadalcanal Campaign
Operation *Watchtower* August 1942 – February 1943 p142-143
⚔ Battle of Savo Island 8–9 August p144
⚔ Battle of the Eastern Solomons 24–25 August p148-149
⚔ Battle of Cape Esperance 11–12 October p150
⚔ Battle of the Santa Cruz Islands 25–27 October p152-153
⚔ Battle of Guadalcanal Cruiser Action, 13 November p158
⚔ Battle of Guadalcanal Battleship Action, 14–15 November p159
⚔ Battle of Tassafaronga 30 November p160

CEAN

The Battle of
the Java Sea
26–28 February
p104-105

Battle of the
Coral Sea
May
p122-123

SOUTH PACIFIC
OCEAN

Japanese Commerce
Raiding in the Indian Ocean
1942–43
p118-119

CEAN

The British, concerned that the Japanese would return to the Indian Ocean and engage in commerce warfare in cooperation with the Germans, potentially bringing about a collapse of the entire eastern empire, sought to deny the use of Vichy-held Madagascar as a base and undertook a major expedition to recover it. Securing the Indian Ocean came at the expense of conceding the central Mediterranean as the Mediterranean Fleet was so depleted it could no longer resupply Malta. Instead, the Home Fleet had to do this from the west, in addition to covering the Arctic convoys; casualties, however, were considerable and supplying the island became unsustainable. Throughout the year

the Atlantic campaign intensified as the Germans, with an ever-increasing U-boat force, sought to overwhelm allied maritime communications before their defences became too strong.

The year also saw the first allied counter attacks against the axis. An Anglo-Canadian raid at Dieppe in France ended in a costly failure, while American landings on Guadalcanal developed into an attritional naval campaign in the Solomons. The landings in French North Africa in November were the first in a series of large-scale amphibious operations that would be needed to defeat the axis.

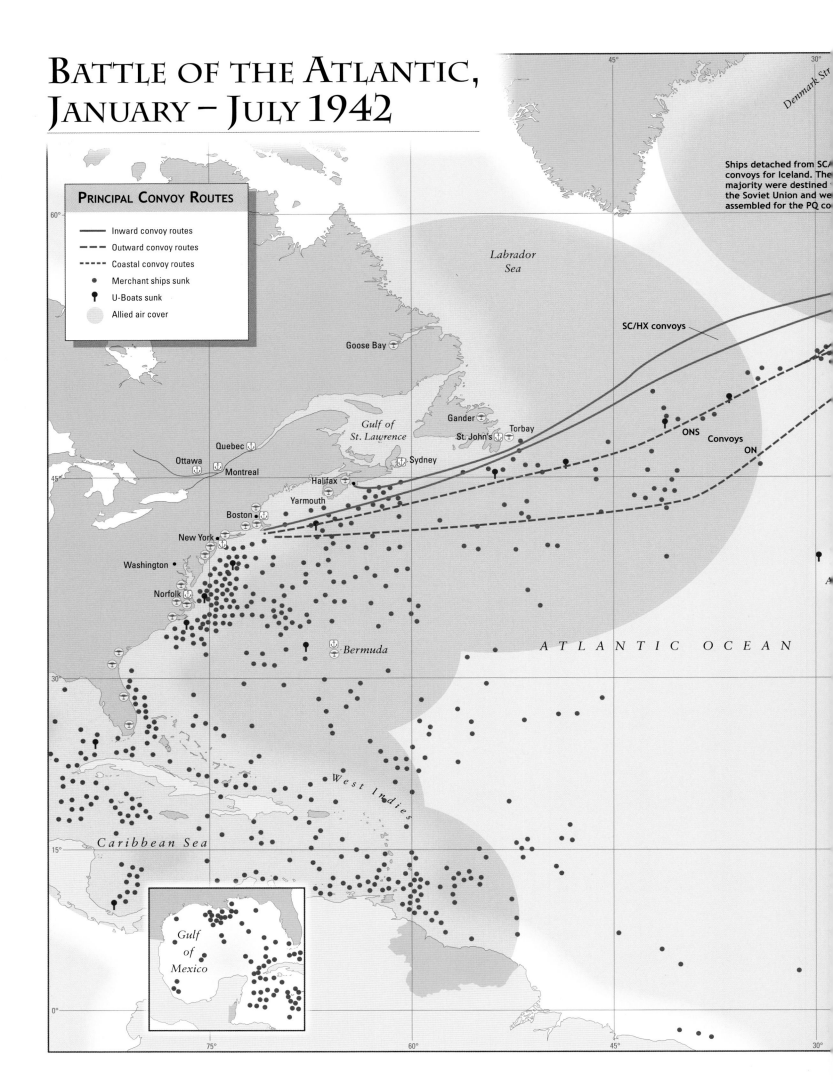

BATTLE OF THE ATLANTIC, JANUARY – JULY 1942

PRINCIPAL CONVOY ROUTES

——— Inward convoy routes
– – – Outward convoy routes
····· Coastal convoy routes
● Merchant ships sunk
⬤ U-Boats sunk
Allied air cover

Denmark Str

Ships detached from SC/
convoys for Iceland. The
majority were destined
the Soviet Union and wer
assembled for the PQ co

Labrador Sea

Goose Bay

SC/HX convoys

Gander
St. John's
Torbay

ONS

Convoys

ON

Gulf of St. Lawrence

Quebec
Ottawa
Montreal
Sydney
Halifax
Yarmouth
Boston
New York
Washington
Norfolk

Bermuda

ATLANTIC OCEAN

West Indies

Caribbean Sea

Gulf of Mexico

98

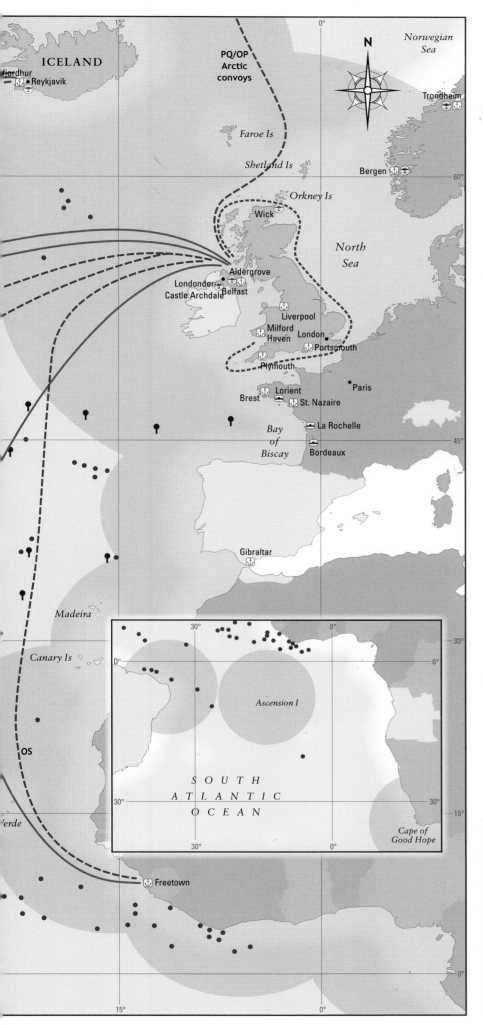

AMERICA'S ENTRY INTO the war provided Admiral Dönitz with an opportunity to once again sink significant enemy tonnage as American shipping along the East Coast was neither convoyed nor generally protected. Although an enticing target, the distance involved in crossing the Atlantic twice meant that only long-range Type IX boats could operate there, and Dönitz had twelve such boats available, six of which were operating off Gibraltar and Africa. This left only five with which to undertake Operation *Drumbeat*. On 2 January, the first wave left France to take up positions between the Gulf of St Lawrence and Cape Hatteras; however, poor weather conditions made it necessary to operate further south, and here shipping was even less protected and, with no convoys, relatively easy to find.

On 14 January the offensive began, and shipping losses rapidly increased, with U-boats often operating within sight of the shoreline. More concerning for the allies was the fact that more than half the tonnage sunk in the first months were valuable tankers. The depletion of the tanker fleet in turn had consequences for operations in other theatres, particularly in the southwest Pacific. The Americans did not institute convoys for a number of reasons. The USN lacked escort vessels with which to protect them and it was believed that poorly defended convoys were more vulnerable than lone vessels. Also, based on their intelligence assessment of the U-boat strength, they anticipated either a short, but intense U-boat campaign off the American seaboard, or a protracted but very limited campaign by a small number of boats. Neither case warranted the long-term disruption to shipping, port operations and the entire American transportation infrastructure that would result from convoying ships.

The Germans, however, overcame the endurance limitations of the medium-range Type VII boats, and were able to send out some of these as replacements in the second wave. In February, U-boats sank seventy-one ships in the Atlantic, the majority sailing independently in American waters. In total, the offensive encompassed five waves of U-boats operating along the East Coast. From April, new supply U-boats, the so-called 'Milk Cows', extended the endurance of the boats even further by providing them with fuel and supplies. That month saw the Americans begin to improvise escorts, and convoys were instigated in May. U-boats now began to suffer losses and moved into the Caribbean Sea, supported by the supply boats, and here, where as yet there were no convoys, they found plenty of vulnerable shipping.

MERCHANT SHIPS AND U-BOATS LOST (ALL THEATRES AND CAUSES)			
MONTH	**TONNAGE**	**SHIPS**	**U-BOATS**
1941			
DECEMBER	583,706	285	10
1942			
JANUARY	419,907	106	3
FEBRUARY	679,632	154	2
MARCH	834,164	273	6
APRIL	674,457	132	3
MAY	705,050	151	4
JUNE	834,196	172	3
JULY	618,113	128	11

JAPANESE OPERATIONS IN THE EAST INDIES, JANUARY – FEBRUARY 1942

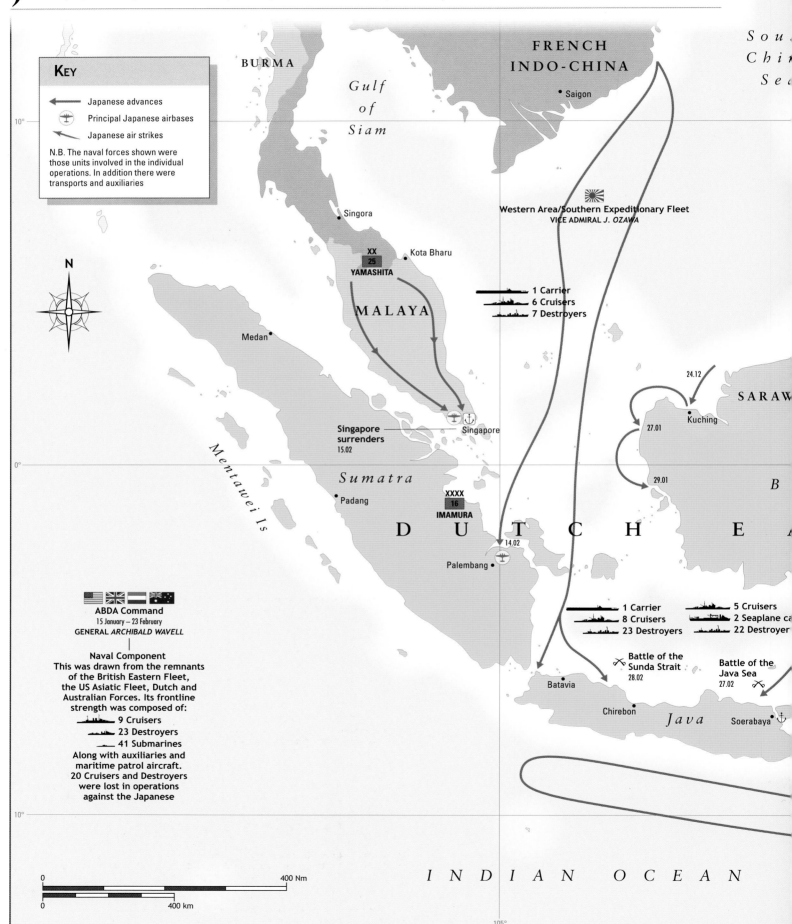

KEY

→ Japanese advances

⊕ Principal Japanese airbases

↖ Japanese air strikes

N.B. The naval forces shown were those units involved in the individual operations. In addition there were transports and auxiliaries

BURMA

Gulf of Siam

• Singora

FRENCH INDO-CHINA

• Saigon

Sou... Chi... Se...

✳ **Western Area/Southern Expeditionary Fleet**
VICE ADMIRAL *J. OZAWA*

▬ 1 Carrier
▬ 6 Cruisers
▬ 7 Destroyers

XX
25
YAMASHITA

• Kota Bharu

MALAYA

• Medan

N

Singapore surrenders
15.02

⊕⚓ Singapore

Mentawei Is

Sumatra

• Padang

XXXX
16
IMAMURA

D U T C H   E

⊕ 14.02

Palembang •

24.12

SARAW...

27.01
• Kuching

29.01

B...

▬ 1 Carrier   ▬ 5 Cruisers
▬ 8 Cruisers   ▬ 2 Seaplane ca...
▬ 23 Destroyers ▬ 22 Destroyer...

⚔ **Battle of the Sunda Strait**
28.02

⚔ **Battle of the Java Sea**
27.02

• Batavia

• Chirebon

Java

Soerabaya ⚓

ABDA Command
15 January – 23 February
GENERAL *ARCHIBALD WAVELL*

Naval Component
This was drawn from the remnants of the British Eastern Fleet, the US Asiatic Fleet, Dutch and Australian Forces. Its frontline strength was composed of:
▬ 9 Cruisers
▬ 23 Destroyers
▬ 41 Submarines
Along with auxiliaries and maritime patrol aircraft.
20 Cruisers and Destroyers were lost in operations against the Japanese

0 ——————————— 400 Nm
0 ——————————— 400 km

I N D I A N   O C E A N

105°

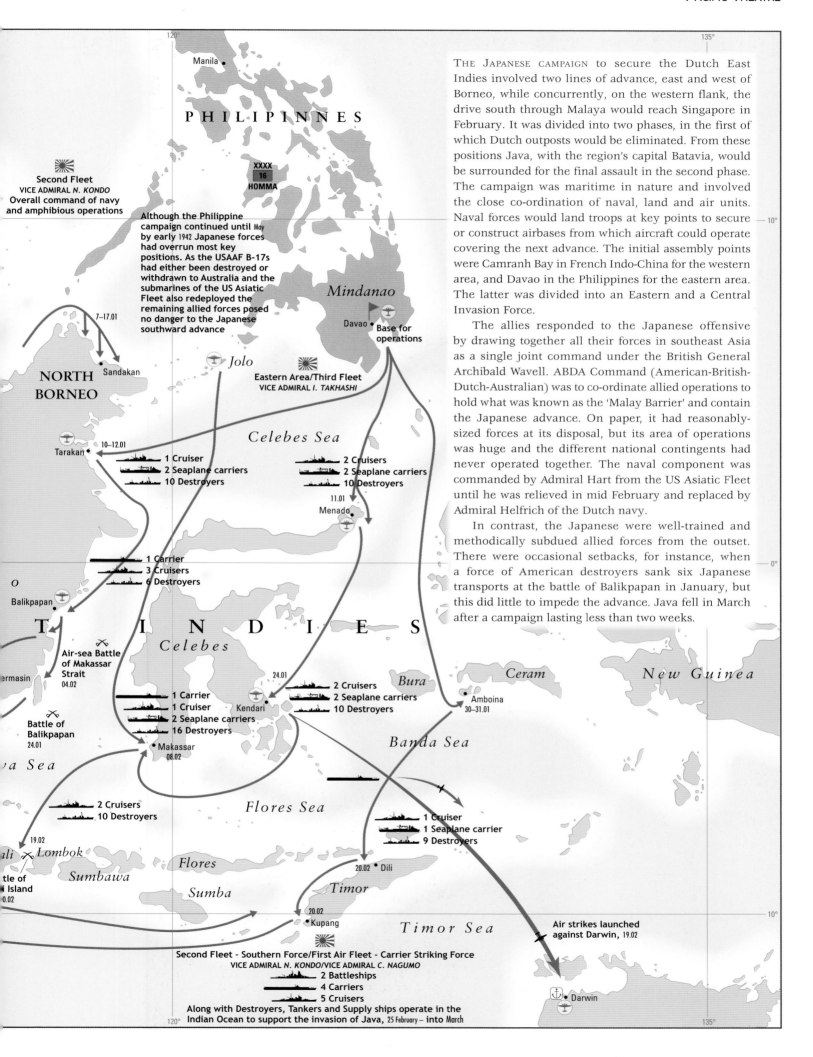

THE JAPANESE CAMPAIGN to secure the Dutch East Indies involved two lines of advance, east and west of Borneo, while concurrently, on the western flank, the drive south through Malaya would reach Singapore in February. It was divided into two phases, in the first of which Dutch outposts would be eliminated. From these positions Java, with the region's capital Batavia, would be surrounded for the final assault in the second phase. The campaign was maritime in nature and involved the close co-ordination of naval, land and air units. Naval forces would land troops at key points to secure or construct airbases from which aircraft could operate covering the next advance. The initial assembly points were Camranh Bay in French Indo-China for the western area, and Davao in the Philippines for the eastern area. The latter was divided into an Eastern and a Central Invasion Force.

The allies responded to the Japanese offensive by drawing together all their forces in southeast Asia as a single joint command under the British General Archibald Wavell. ABDA Command (American-British-Dutch-Australian) was to co-ordinate allied operations to hold what was known as the 'Malay Barrier' and contain the Japanese advance. On paper, it had reasonably-sized forces at its disposal, but its area of operations was huge and the different national contingents had never operated together. The naval component was commanded by Admiral Hart from the US Asiatic Fleet until he was relieved in mid February and replaced by Admiral Helfrich of the Dutch navy.

In contrast, the Japanese were well-trained and methodically subdued allied forces from the outset. There were occasional setbacks, for instance, when a force of American destroyers sank six Japanese transports at the battle of Balikpapan in January, but this did little to impede the advance. Java fell in March after a campaign lasting less than two weeks.

Map labels

Manila

PHILIPINNES

XXXX 16 HOMMA

Second Fleet
VICE ADMIRAL N. KONDO
Overall command of navy
and amphibious operations

Although the Philippine campaign continued until May by early 1942 Japanese forces had overrun most key positions. As the USAAF B-17s had either been destroyed or withdrawn to Australia and the submarines of the US Asiatic Fleet also redeployed the remaining allied forces posed no danger to the Japanese southward advance

Mindanao

Davao • Base for operations

7–17.01

NORTH BORNEO

Sandakan

Jolo

Eastern Area/Third Fleet
VICE ADMIRAL I. TAKHASHI

Celebes Sea

Tarakan • 10–12.01

1 Cruiser
2 Seaplane carriers
10 Destroyers

2 Cruisers
2 Seaplane carriers
10 Destroyers

11.01
Menado

1 Carrier
3 Cruisers
6 Destroyers

O
Balikpapan

T I N D I E S

Celebes

Air-sea Battle of Makassar Strait 04.02

ermasin

Battle of Balikpapan 24.01

24.01

Kendari

2 Cruisers
2 Seaplane carriers
10 Destroyers

1 Carrier
1 Cruiser
2 Seaplane carriers
16 Destroyers

Bura

Ceram

New Guinea

Amboina 30–31.01

Banda Sea

Makassar 08.02

a Sea

2 Cruisers
10 Destroyers

Flores Sea

1 Cruiser
1 Seaplane carrier
9 Destroyers

19.02

li Lombok

Flores

tle of Island

Sumbawa

Sumba

Dili 20.02

Timor

20.02 Kupang

Timor Sea

Air strikes launched against Darwin, 19.02

Second Fleet - Southern Force/First Air Fleet - Carrier Striking Force
VICE ADMIRAL N. KONDO/VICE ADMIRAL C. NAGUMO
2 Battleships
4 Carriers
5 Cruisers
Along with Destroyers, Tankers and Supply ships operate in the Indian Ocean to support the invasion of Java, 25 February – into March

⚓ Darwin

OPERATION CERBERUS, 11–13 FEBRUARY 1942

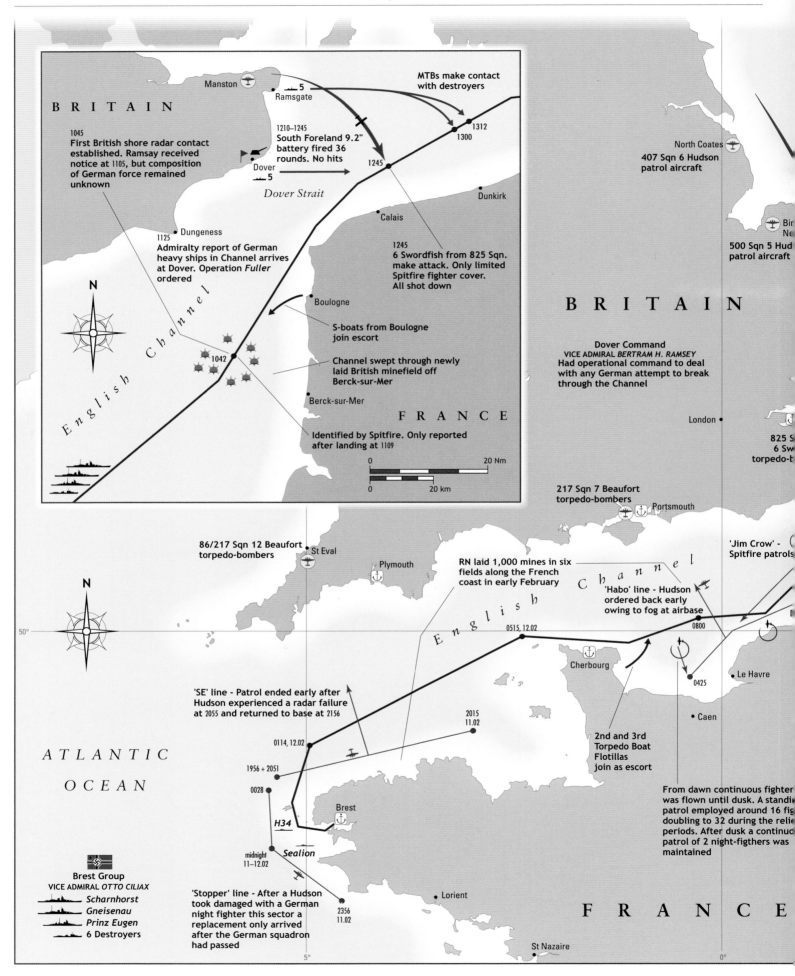

MTBs make contact with destroyers

1045
First British shore radar contact established. Ramsay received notice at 1105, but composition of German force remained unknown

BRITAIN

1210–1245
South Foreland 9.2" battery fired 36 rounds. No hits

Manston

Ramsgate

5

1312
1300

1245

Dover
5

Dover Strait

Calais

Dunkirk

North Coates
407 Sqn 6 Hudson patrol aircraft

1125
Admiralty report of German heavy ships in Channel arrives at Dover. Operation *Fuller* ordered

Dungeness

1245
6 Swordfish from 825 Sqn. make attack. Only limited Spitfire fighter cover. All shot down

500 Sqn 5 Hud
patrol aircraft

N

English Channel

Boulogne

S-boats from Boulogne join escort

Channel swept through newly laid British minefield off Berck-sur-Mer

1042

Berck-sur-Mer

FRANCE

BRITAIN

Dover Command
VICE ADMIRAL *BERTRAM H. RAMSEY*
Had operational command to deal with any German attempt to break through the Channel

London

825 S
6 Sw
torpedo-b

Identified by Spitfire. Only reported after landing at 1109

| 0 | 20 Nm |
| 0 | 20 km |

217 Sqn 7 Beaufort torpedo-bombers

Portsmouth

86/217 Sqn 12 Beaufort torpedo-bombers
St Eval

Plymouth

RN laid 1,000 mines in six fields along the French coast in early February

English   Channel

'Jim Crow' -
Spitfire patrols

'Habo' line - Hudson ordered back early owing to fog at airbase

0515, 12.02

0800

50°

Cherbourg

0425

Le Havre

'SE' line - Patrol ended early after Hudson experienced a radar failure at 2055 and returned to base at 2156

2015
11.02

Caen

0114, 12.02

1956 + 2051

ATLANTIC

OCEAN

0028

Brest

2nd and 3rd Torpedo Boat Flotillas join as escort

From dawn continuous fighter
was flown until dusk. A standi
patrol employed around 16 fig
doubling to 32 during the relie
periods. After dusk a continu
patrol of 2 night-fighters was
maintained

N

H34

Sealion

midnight
11–12.02

Brest Group
VICE ADMIRAL *OTTO CILIAX*

Scharnhorst
Gneisenau
Prinz Eugen
6 Destroyers

'Stopper' line - After a Hudson took damaged with a German night fighter this sector a replacement only arrived after the German squadron had passed

2356
11.02

Lorient

FRANCE

St Nazaire

5°

0°

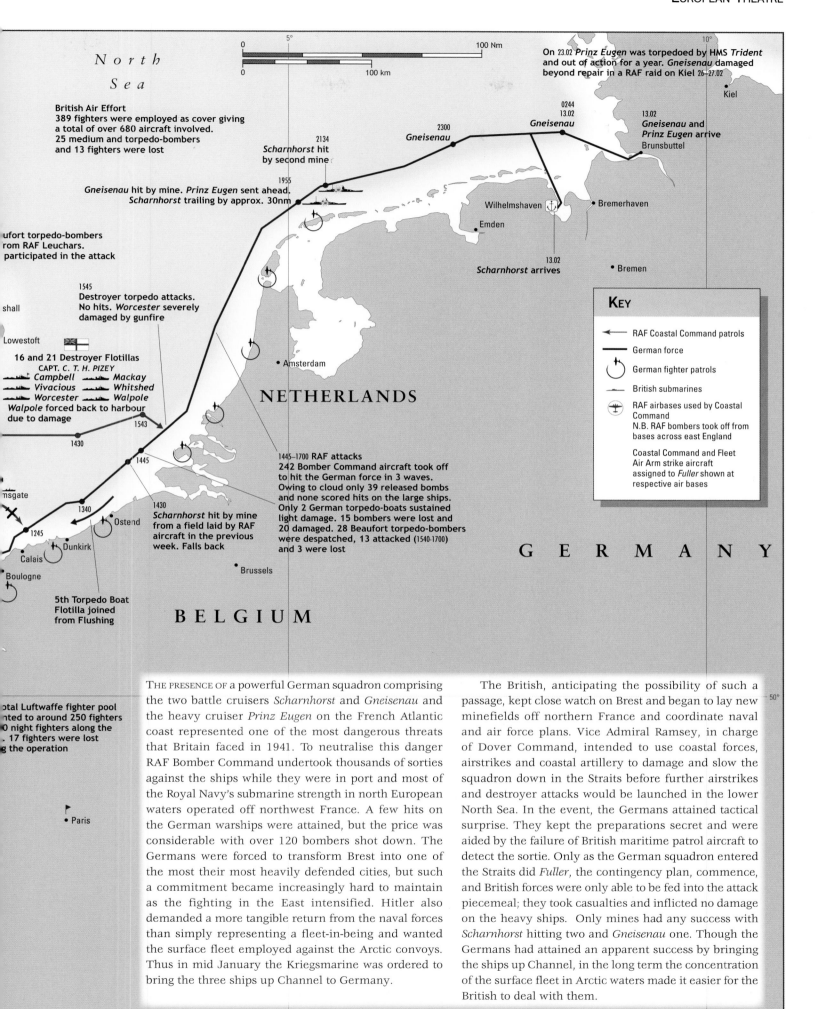

On 23.02 *Prinz Eugen* was torpedoed by HMS *Trident* and out of action for a year. *Gneisenau* damaged beyond repair in a RAF raid on Kiel 26–27.02

North
Sea

100 Nm

100 km

British Air Effort
389 fighters were employed as cover giving a total of over 680 aircraft involved.
25 medium and torpedo-bombers and 13 fighters were lost

Kiel

0244
13.02
Gneisenau

2300
Gneisenau

13.02
Gneisenau and
Prinz Eugen arrive
Brunsbuttel

2134
Scharnhorst hit
by second mine

1955
Gneisenau hit by mine. *Prinz Eugen* sent ahead.
Scharnhorst trailing by approx. 30nm

Wilhelmshaven

• Bremerhaven

• Emden

ufort torpedo-bombers
rom RAF Leuchars.
participated in the attack

13.02
Scharnhorst arrives

• Bremen

1545
Destroyer torpedo attacks.
No hits. *Worcester* severely
damaged by gunfire

shall

Lowestoft

16 and 21 Destroyer Flotillas
CAPT. *C. T. H. PIZEY*
Campbell   *Mackay*
Vivacious   *Whitshed*
Worcester   *Walpole*
Walpole forced back to harbour
due to damage

1543

1430

1445

• Amsterdam

NETHERLANDS

nsgate

1340

1245

Calais

Boulogne

1430
Scharnhorst hit by mine from a field laid by RAF aircraft in the previous week. Falls back

1445–1700 RAF attacks
242 Bomber Command aircraft took off to hit the German force in 3 waves. Owing to cloud only 39 released bombs and none scored hits on the large ships. Only 2 German torpedo-boats sustained light damage. 15 bombers were lost and 20 damaged. 28 Beaufort torpedo-bombers were despatched, 13 attacked (1540-1700) and 3 were lost

• Ostend

• Brussels

G E R M A N Y

Dunkirk

**5th Torpedo Boat
Flotilla joined
from Flushing**

B E L G I U M

otal Luftwaffe fighter pool
nted to around 250 fighters
0 night fighters along the
. 17 fighters were lost
g the operation

• Paris

THE PRESENCE OF a powerful German squadron comprising the two battle cruisers *Scharnhorst* and *Gneisenau* and the heavy cruiser *Prinz Eugen* on the French Atlantic coast represented one of the most dangerous threats that Britain faced in 1941. To neutralise this danger RAF Bomber Command undertook thousands of sorties against the ships while they were in port and most of the Royal Navy's submarine strength in north European waters operated off northwest France. A few hits on the German warships were attained, but the price was considerable with over 120 bombers shot down. The Germans were forced to transform Brest into one of the most their most heavily defended cities, but such a commitment became increasingly hard to maintain as the fighting in the East intensified. Hitler also demanded a more tangible return from the naval forces than simply representing a fleet-in-being and wanted the surface fleet employed against the Arctic convoys. Thus in mid January the Kriegsmarine was ordered to bring the three ships up Channel to Germany.

The British, anticipating the possibility of such a passage, kept close watch on Brest and began to lay new minefields off northern France and coordinate naval and air force plans. Vice Admiral Ramsey, in charge of Dover Command, intended to use coastal forces, airstrikes and coastal artillery to damage and slow the squadron down in the Straits before further airstrikes and destroyer attacks would be launched in the lower North Sea. In the event, the Germans attained tactical surprise. They kept the preparations secret and were aided by the failure of British maritime patrol aircraft to detect the sortie. Only as the German squadron entered the Straits did *Fuller*, the contingency plan, commence, and British forces were only able to be fed into the attack piecemeal; they took casualties and inflicted no damage on the heavy ships. Only mines had any success with *Scharnhorst* hitting two and *Gneisenau* one. Though the Germans had attained an apparent success by bringing the ships up Channel, in the long term the concentration of the surface fleet in Arctic waters made it easier for the British to deal with them.

BATTLE OF THE JAVA SEA, 27 FEBRUARY 1942

IN THE SECOND half of February the allied position along the 'Malay Barrier' deteriorated markedly with the Japanese passing through to strike at Australia and taking Bali and Timor. ABDA Command was dissolved on 25 February, leaving the Dutch to organise the defence of Java. The naval forces, still amounting to eight cruisers and twenty destroyers, were split between Batavia and Surabaya, with an Anglo-Australian force at the former and an American-Dutch based at the latter. On 25 February British ships were sent to Surabaya to reinforce Admiral Doorman as an invasion was expected first from the east. In was known that concentrations of Japanese shipping were moving south from Jolo in the Philippines, but patrols on 26 February found nothing. Doorman returned to port the next day but just as his ships were refuelling the Japanese assault convoys were sighted and he put back to sea.

Both sides were roughly equal, with five allied cruisers and ten destroyers facing four Japanese cruisers and fourteen destroyers. However, the Japanese ships operated more cohesively as a unit and launched devastating torpedo attacks. Once the British *Exeter* was hit the allied line became confused and never fully recovered. Eventually, both sides retired, but Doorman, who was determined to find the convoy, turned north again and in a night battle two allied cruisers were lost. In the following days, and in a number of engagements, most of the remaining allied naval forces were destroyed.

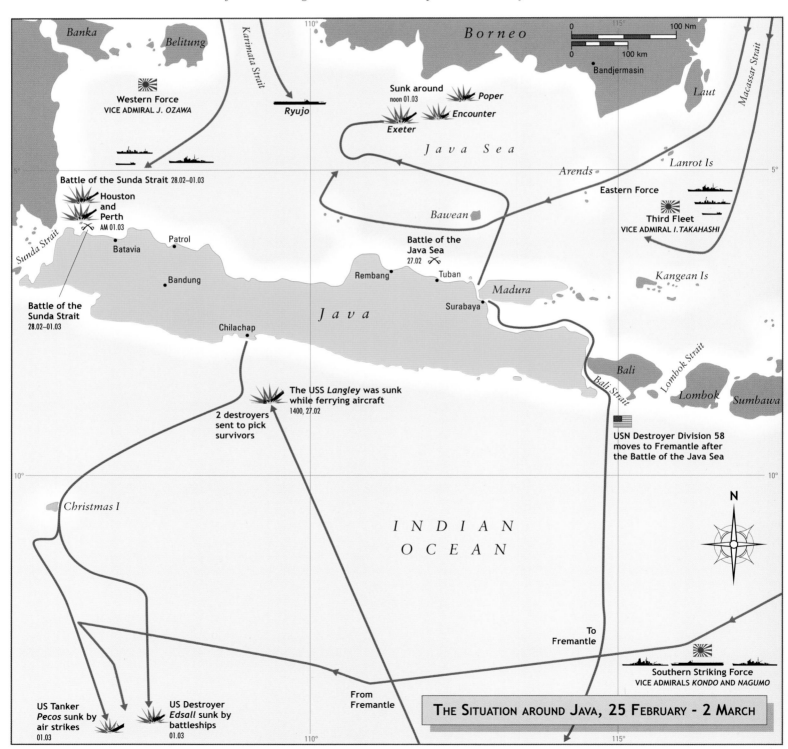

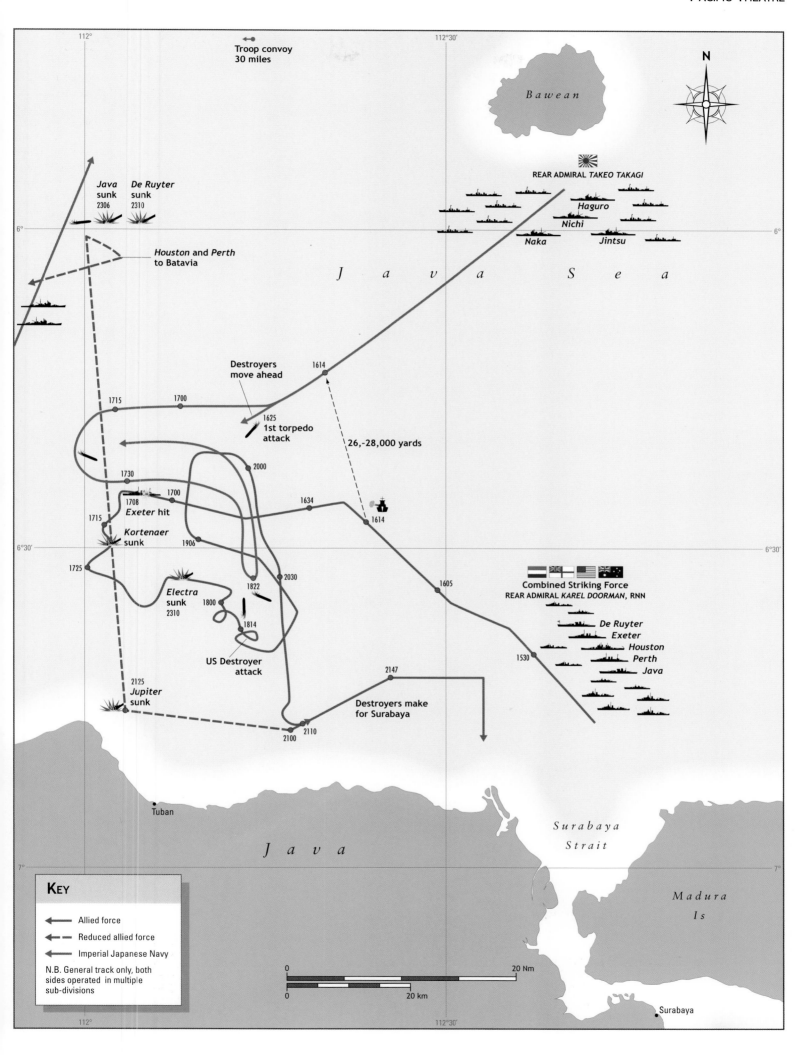

Troop convoy
30 miles

Bawean

N

REAR ADMIRAL *TAKEO TAKAGI*

Haguro
Nichi
Naka   *Jintsu*

Java sunk 2306   *De Ruyter* sunk 2310

Houston and *Perth* to Batavia

J   a   v   a   S   e   a

Destroyers move ahead

1614

1715   1700

1625
1st torpedo attack

26,-28,000 yards

2000

1730

1634
1708   1700
Exeter hit
1614

1715
Kortenaer sunk

1906

1725

1822   2030

Combined Striking Force
REAR ADMIRAL *KAREL DOORMAN*, RNN

De Ruyter
Exeter
Houston
Perth
Java

1605

Electra sunk 2310
1800
1814

US Destroyer attack

2125
Jupiter sunk

2147

Destroyers make for Surabaya

1530

2100   2110

Tuban

Surabaya Strait

J a v a

Madura Is

KEY

Allied force

Reduced allied force

Imperial Japanese Navy

N.B. General track only, both sides operated in multiple sub-divisions

0   20 Nm

0   20 km

Surabaya

AMERICAN PACIFIC OPERATIONS, JANUARY – APRIL 1942

CHINA

TEN DAYS AFTER the raid on Pearl Harbor, Admiral Kimmel was relieved of his post and President Roosevelt chose Rear Admiral Chester W Nimitz as the new Commander in Chief Pacific Fleet. Nimitz arrived at Pearl Harbor on 25 December, was promoted to Admiral, and would remain in charge of the Pacific Fleet for the duration of the war. In the immediate aftermath of the attack, the American priority was to repair the damage on Oahu and secure the outposts on Wake, Johnston, Midway and Palmyra islands. While Wake eventually fell on 23 December, the others all received reinforcements in December. The first four convoys for Hawaii also left San Francisco and had arrived by the beginning of January.

Apart from safeguarding Hawaii, the Pacific Fleet also needed to secure the maritime communications between America, Australia and New Zealand. Admiral King instructed Nimitz to hold a line from Midway through Samoa and Fiji to Brisbane in Australia. A network of airbases and anchorages on British-held islands would be developed to protect the supply lines. The first 4,800 Marines left San Diego for Samoa on 6 January, followed by another six more convoys that month with troops for the south Pacific. The largest came from New York and embarked the 26th Infantry Division for New Caledonia. The first convoys carrying troops and equipment for Australia left the West Coast in February.

The Pacific remained relatively quiet with only a few dispersed Japanese submarine attacks and long-range airstrikes. However, in early January, Japanese forces overran the small Australian garrison at Rabaul and thus controlled the Bismarck Archipelago, and threatened the allied supply lines. Only once Samoa had been secured could Nimitz strike back, utilising his carrier task forces. These had the speed and range to operate against the Japanese periphery. Even though the Pacific Fleet's battle line was restored through repairs and transfers from the Atlantic, there were not enough tankers to keep the battleships at sea for long periods. Consequently, now organised as Task Force 1, they remained on the West Coast.

The first carrier raids on the Marshall Is in February inflicted little damage, but were important to gain experience and improve morale. They were followed by a strike against Rabaul by the *Lexington*, and *Enterprise*, operating deep in nominally Japanese-held territory, raided Wake and Marcus islands. Each operation became more complex and daring than the last. In March, *Yorktown* and *Lexington* operated together against Japanese transports landing troops on New Guinea with the strike aircraft having to fly over the Owen-Stanley mountain range to reach their targets. This was followed in April with *Enterprise* and *Hornet* closing to within 620 miles of the Japanese coast to launch a small bomber force to strike Tokyo, the Doolittle Raid. The raid had little material impact, but did in part contribute to the Japanese decision to launch the Midway campaign.

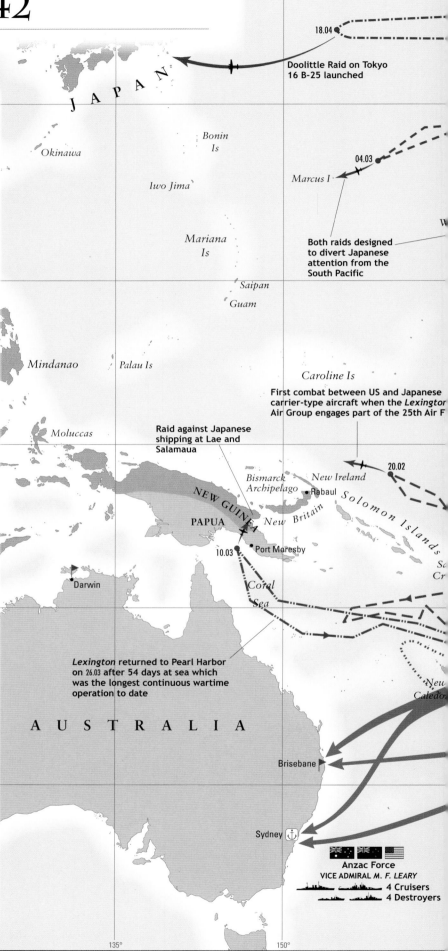

Doolittle Raid on Tokyo
16 B-25 launched

Both raids designed to divert Japanese attention from the South Pacific

First combat between US and Japanese carrier-type aircraft when the *Lexington* Air Group engages part of the 25th Air F

Raid against Japanese shipping at Lae and Salamaua

Lexington returned to Pearl Harbor on 26.03 after 54 days at sea which was the longest continuous wartime operation to date

Anzac Force
VICE ADMIRAL M. F. LEARY
4 Cruisers
4 Destroyers

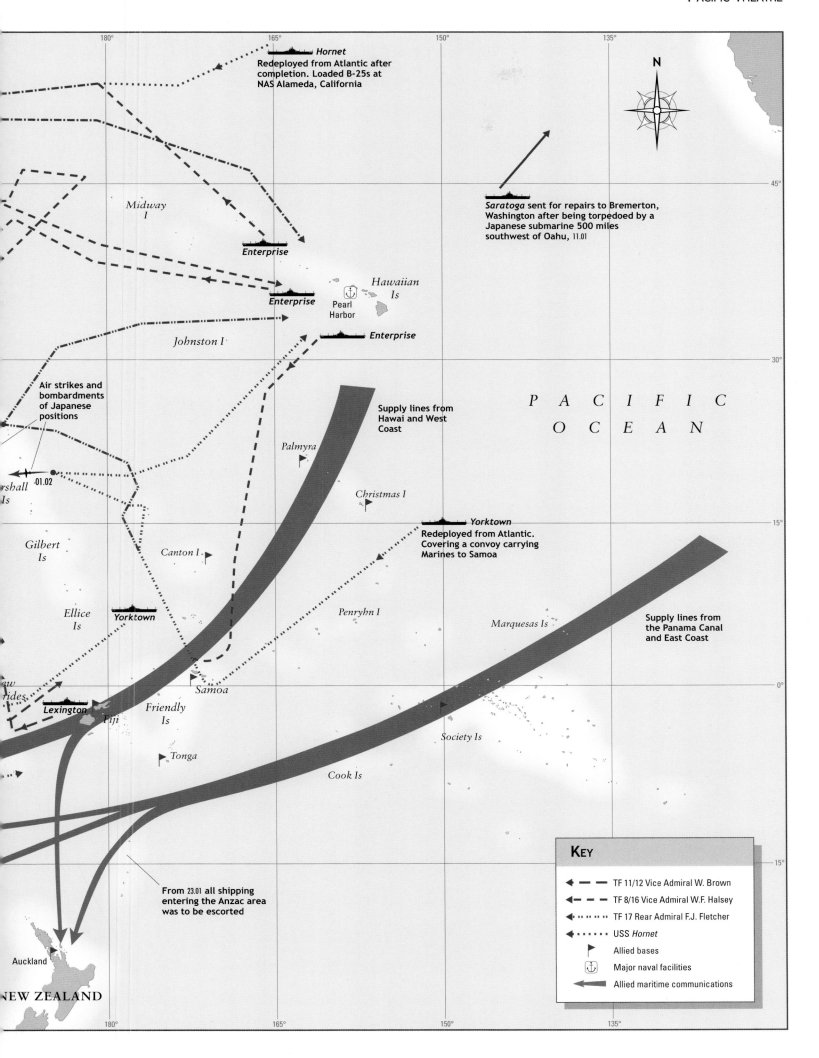

Hornet
Redeployed from Atlantic after completion. Loaded B-25s at NAS Alameda, California

Saratoga sent for repairs to Bremerton, Washington after being torpedoed by a Japanese submarine 500 miles southwest of Oahu, 11.01

Midway I

Enterprise

Enterprise
Pearl Harbor

Hawaiian Is

Johnston I
Enterprise

Air strikes and bombardments of Japanese positions

P A C I F I C

O C E A N

Supply lines from Hawai and West Coast

Palmyra

-01.02

Christmas I

Marshall Is

Yorktown
Redeployed from Atlantic. Covering a convoy carrying Marines to Samoa

Gilbert Is

Canton I

Penrhyn I

Marquesas Is

Supply lines from the Panama Canal and East Coast

Ellice Is
Yorktown

Samoa

ew rides

Lexington
Fiji

Friendly Is

Society Is

Tonga

Cook Is

From 23.01 all shipping entering the Anzac area was to be escorted

Auckland

NEW ZEALAND

KEY

— ◄— ·— TF 11/12 Vice Admiral W. Brown

— ◄— — TF 8/16 Vice Admiral W.F. Halsey

◄···· TF 17 Rear Admiral F.J. Fletcher

◄······ USS *Hornet*

▶ Allied bases

⚓ Major naval facilities

◄— Allied maritime communications

107

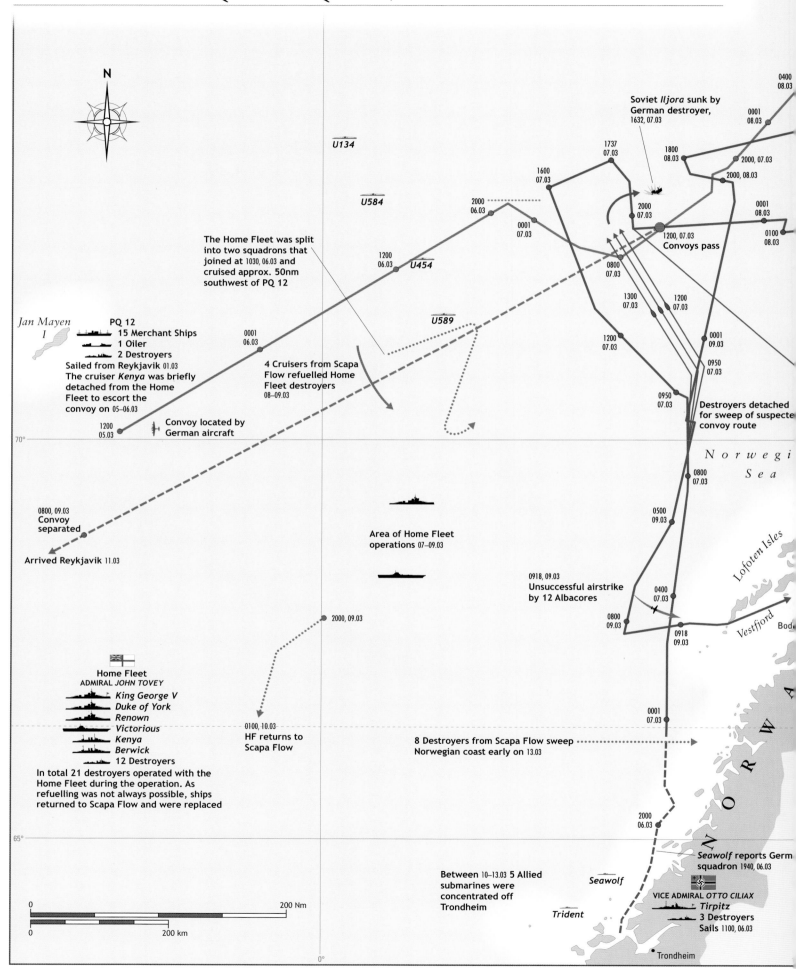

Convoy PQ 12/QP 8, 6–10 March 1942

N

U134

Soviet *Iljora* sunk by
German destroyer,
1632, 07.03

0400
08.03

0001
08.03

1737
07.03

1800
08.03

2000, 07.03

1600
07.03

2000, 08.03

U584

2000
06.03

2000
07.03

0001
08.03

0001
07.03

The Home Fleet was split
into two squadrons that
joined at 1030, 06.03 and
cruised approx. 50nm
southwest of PQ 12

1200, 07.03
Convoys pass

0100
08.03

1200
06.03

U454

0800
07.03

1300
07.03

1200
07.03

Jan Mayen
I

PQ 12

15 Merchant Ships
1 Oiler
2 Destroyers

0001
06.03

U589

1200
07.03

0001
09.03

Sailed from Reykjavik 01.03
The cruiser *Kenya* was briefly
detached from the Home
Fleet to escort the
convoy on 05–06.03

4 Cruisers from Scapa
Flow refuelled Home
Fleet destroyers
08–09.03

0950
07.03

0950
07.03

Destroyers detached
for sweep of suspected
convoy route

1200
05.03

Convoy located by
German aircraft

N o r w e g i
S e a

70°

0800
07.03

0800, 09.03
Convoy
separated

0500
09.03

L o f o t e n   I s l e s

Arrived Reykjavik 11.03

Area of Home Fleet
operations 07–09.03

0918, 09.03
Unsuccessful airstrike
by 12 Albacores

0400
07.03

0800
09.03

V e s t f j o r d   Bod

0918
09.03

2000, 09.03

Home Fleet
ADMIRAL *JOHN TOVEY*

King George V
Duke of York
Renown
Victorious
Kenya
Berwick
12 Destroyers

0001
07.03

0100, 10.03
HF returns to
Scapa Flow

8 Destroyers from Scapa Flow sweep
Norwegian coast early on 13.03

N O R W A

In total 21 destroyers operated with the
Home Fleet during the operation. As
refuelling was not always possible, ships
returned to Scapa Flow and were replaced

2000
06.03

65°

Seawolf reports Germ
squadron 1940, 06.03

0   200 Nm

0   200 km

Between 10–13.03 5 Allied
submarines were
concentrated off
Trondheim

Seawolf

VICE ADMIRAL *OTTO CILIAX*
Tirpitz
3 Destroyers
Sails 1100, 06.03

Trident

0°

• Trondheim

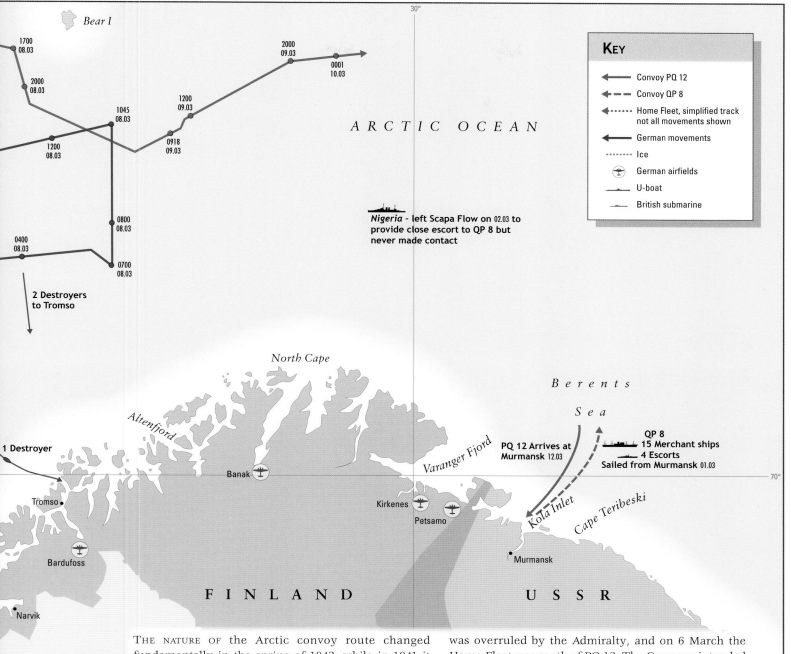

Key

- → Convoy PQ 12
- ⤐ Convoy QP 8
- ◁┈┈ Home Fleet, simplified track not all movements shown
- ← German movements
- ┄┄┄ Ice
- ✈ German airfields
- ⌁ U-boat
- ⌁ British submarine

Nigeria - left Scapa Flow on 02.03 to provide close escort to QP 8 but never made contact

ARCTIC OCEAN

Bear I

1700
08.03

2000
09.03

0001
10.03

2000
08.03

1045
08.03

1200
09.03

1200
08.03

0918
09.03

0800
08.03

0400
08.03

0700
08.03

2 Destroyers
to Tromso

North Cape

B e r e n t s

S e a

Altenfjord

Varanger Fjord

PQ 12 Arrives at
Murmansk 12.03

QP 8
15 Merchant ships
4 Escorts
Sailed from Murmansk 01.03

1 Destroyer

Banak

Kirkenes

Petsamo

Kola Inlet

Cape Teribeski

Tromso

Bardufoss

Murmansk

Narvik

F I N L A N D

U S S R

S W E D E N

c Circle

THE NATURE OF the Arctic convoy route changed fundamentally in the spring of 1942; while in 1941 it had been a comparatively safe passage it now became increasingly difficult for the British to resupply the Soviet Union via the North. The theatre took on a greater importance for the Germans after the failure to defeat the Soviets in a single campaigning season in 1941. Consequently, the Kriegsmarine concentrated its surface fleet strength in Norway and diverted submarines from the Atlantic, while the Luftwaffe assembled a potent maritime strike force for operations in the Arctic. In January, the battleship *Tirpitz* arrived in Norwegian waters after completing its work-up in the Baltic.

The convoy pair PQ 12/QP 8 was the first to be exposed to the increased threat of German attack. Admiral Tovey only intended to provide distant cover with half the Home Fleet's strength, as he did not expect the *Tirpitz* to put to sea. Using the entire Home Fleet for every convoy would risk exhausting the men and material, leading to a decline in its efficiency by the summer when he expected a much larger German fleet to be stationed in Norwegian waters. However, he

was overruled by the Admiralty, and on 6 March the Home Fleet was south of PQ 12. The Germans intended to attack, and after a FW200 located PQ 12 a U-boat patrol line was established in its path and *Tirpitz*'s squadron put to sea. The weather conditions between 6 and 8 March were appalling so though a considerable number of ships were operating in relatively close proximity the only contact made was the sinking of a Soviet merchant ship *Iljora* by a German destroyer. Both sides were unable to undertake air reconnaissance and destroyers ran low on fuel. By the evening of 8 March the convoys were out of danger and Tovey attempted to intercept *Tirpitz* but was handicapped by a lack of destroyers to screen his capital ships. A carrier strike on 9 March failed to damage *Tirpitz* and she reached Narvik around 4pm. In the aftermath, the British unsuccessfully attempted to ambush the battleship when she returned to Trondheim with submarines and destroyers. Although the allies suffered no material damaged, the presence of the *Tirpitz* necessitated a large fleet be retained in northern waters when the ships were urgently needed elsewhere.

THE SECOND BATTLE OF SIRTE, 21–23 MARCH 1942

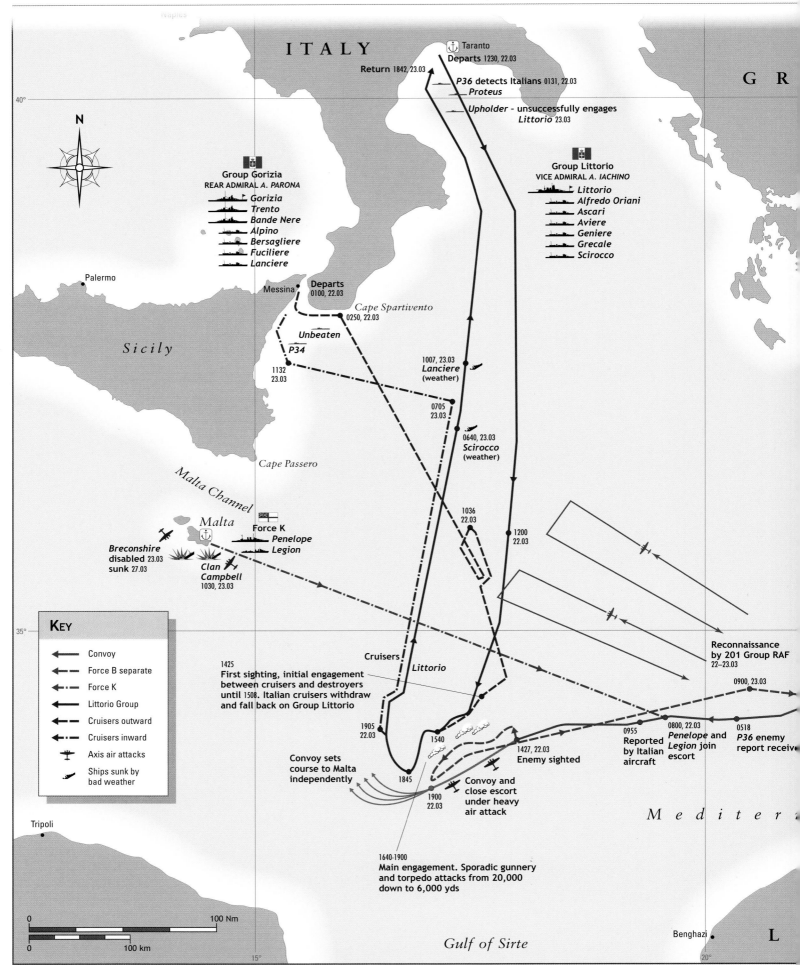

ITALY

Taranto
Departs 1230, 22.03

Return 1842, 23.03

P36 detects Italians 0131, 22.03
Proteus

Upholder – unsuccessfully engages
Littorio 23.03

G R

Group Gorizia
REAR ADMIRAL *A. PARONA*
Gorizia
Trento
Bande Nere
Alpino
Bersagliere
Fuciliere
Lanciere

Group Littorio
VICE ADMIRAL *A. IACHINO*
Littorio
Alfredo Oriani
Ascari
Aviere
Geniere
Grecale
Scirocco

Palermo

Messina

Departs
0100, 22.03

Cape Spartivento
0250, 22.03

Unbeaten
P34

Sicily

1132
23.03

1007, 23.03
Lanciere
(weather)

0705
23.03

0640, 23.03
Scirocco
(weather)

Cape Passero

Malta Channel

1036
22.03

1200
22.03

Malta
Force K
Penelope
Legion

Breconshire
disabled 23.03
sunk 27.03

**Clan
Campbell**
1030, 23.03

Reconnaissance
by 201 Group RAF
22–23.03

0900, 23.03

KEY

←	Convoy
←	Force B separate
←	Force K
←	Littorio Group
←	Cruisers outward
←	Cruisers inward
✈	Axis air attacks
⚓	Ships sunk by bad weather

Cruisers

Littorio

1425
First sighting, initial engagement
between cruisers and destroyers
until 1508. Italian cruisers withdraw
and fall back on Group Littorio

1905
22.03

1540

**Convoy sets
course to Malta
independently**

1845

1900
22.03

**Convoy and
close escort
under heavy
air attack**

1427, 22.03
Enemy sighted

0955
**Reported
by Italian
aircraft**

0800, 22.03
Penelope and
Legion join
escort

0518
P36 enemy
report receive

M e d i t e r r a

1640-1900
**Main engagement. Sporadic gunnery
and torpedo attacks from 20,000
down to 6,000 yds**

Tripoli

0

100 Nm

0

100 km

Benghazi

L

Gulf of Sirte

By March, Malta's supply situation had once again become critical as the British ability to sustain the island reached a low point. The events of late 1941 had left the Mediterranean Fleet without capital ships and now the Japanese threat in the Indian Ocean meant that none of the Eastern Fleet's ships could be spared. Force H too was depleted owing to the preparations for the Madagascar campaign, Operation *Ironclad*. Its main strength consisted of an old battleship and the two small, old carriers, *Argus* and *Eagle*. With such limited strength it could do little more than undertake fly-off operations for Malta-bound fighter reinforcements. Thus any convoy would have to come from the east. After an attempt in February ended with all three freighters being sunk or disabled Admiral Cunningham planned *M.G.1* which was to employ all his available cruiser and destroyer forces. A fly-off operation from Gibraltar and RAF attacks on axis airfields would provide some diversionary effect.

The Italians suspected a supply operation was underway and this time Admiral Iachino had the advantage. He had a more powerful and faster force, reasonably good intelligence and air cover. Rear Admiral Vian, warned by a submarine report that the Italians had sortied, knew that the speed advantage they possessed would place them between the convoy and Malta. A first brief action was fought between the British escorts and Italian cruisers from 2.27 to 3.15pm when the latter withdrew to fall back on the *Littorio*. In the main engagement, from 4.37 to 6.56pm, the British used smoke and torpedo attacks to keep the Italians at a distance. In the confused fighting both sides suffered damage, but despite closing range considerably, Iachino ordered a withdrawal at 6.45pm as he was under instructions not to engage in a night action. On the return two Italian destroyers were lost in a storm.

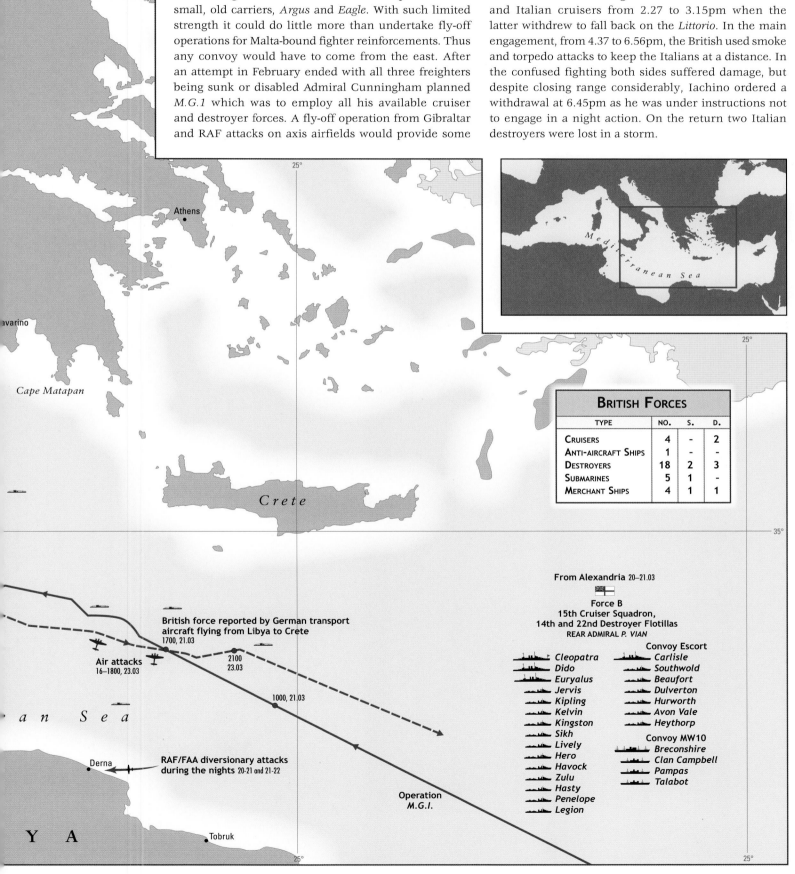

BRITISH FORCES			
TYPE	NO.	S.	D.
CRUISERS	4	-	2
ANTI-AIRCRAFT SHIPS	1	-	-
DESTROYERS	18	2	3
SUBMARINES	5	1	-
MERCHANT SHIPS	4	1	1

British force reported by German transport aircraft flying from Libya to Crete
1700, 21.03

Air attacks 16–1800, 23.03

2100 23.03

1000, 21.03

RAF/FAA diversionary attacks during the nights 20-21 and 21-22

Operation M.G.I.

From Alexandria 20–21.03

Force B
15th Cruiser Squadron,
14th and 22nd Destroyer Flotillas
REAR ADMIRAL P. VIAN

Convoy Escort

Cleopatra
Dido
Euryalus
Jervis
Kipling
Kelvin
Kingston
Sikh
Lively
Hero
Havock
Zulu
Hasty
Penelope
Legion

Carlisle
Southwold
Beaufort
Dulverton
Hurworth
Avon Vale
Heythorp

Convoy MW10

Breconshire
Clan Campbell
Pampas
Talabot

Athens

Cape Matapan

Crete

avarino

Derna

Tobruk

C E

Y A

a n S e a

Mediterranean Sea

OPERATION CHARIOT, 27–28 MARCH 1942

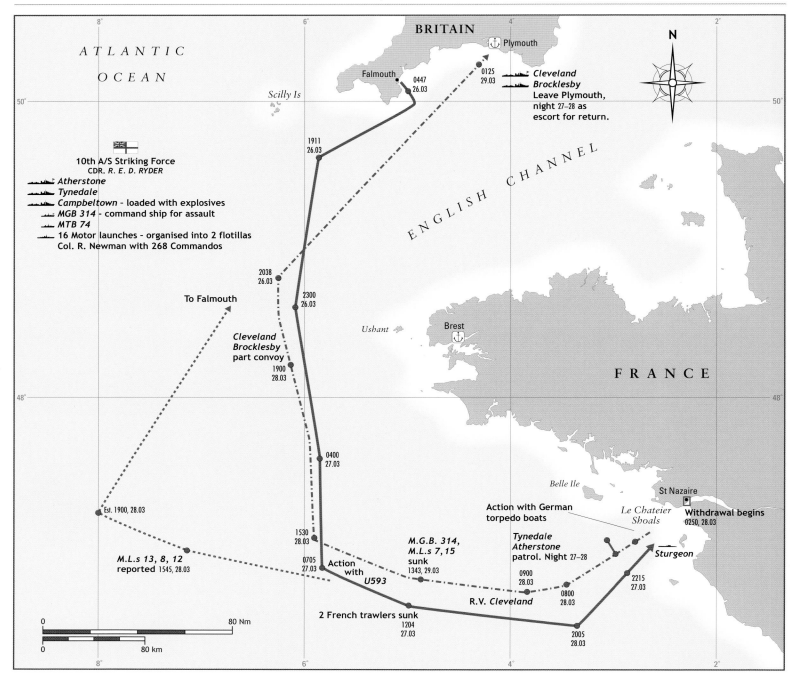

ATLANTIC

OCEAN

BRITAIN

⚓ Plymouth

Falmouth

0447
26.03

0125
29.03

Cleveland
Brocklesby
Leave Plymouth,
night 27–28 as
escort for return.

N

Scilly Is

🏴 10th A/S Striking Force
CDR. R. E. D. RYDER
Atherstone
Tynedale
Campbeltown – loaded with explosives
MGB 314 – command ship for assault
MTB 74
16 Motor launches – organised into 2 flotillas
Col. R. Newman with 268 Commandos

1911
26.03

ENGLISH CHANNEL

To Falmouth

2038
26.03

2300
26.03

Ushant

Brest
⚓

FRANCE

Cleveland
Brocklesby
part convoy

1900
28.03

0400
27.03

Est. 1900, 28.03

Belle Ile

St Nazaire

Action with German
torpedo boats

Le Chateier
Shoals

Withdrawal begins
0250, 28.03

1530
28.03

M.G.B. 314,
M.L.s 7,15
sunk
1343, 29.03

Tynedale
Atherstone
patrol. Night 27–28

Sturgeon

M.L.s 13, 8, 12
reported 1545, 28.03

0705
27.03

Action
with

U593

0900
28.03

2215
27.03

R.V. Cleveland

0800
28.03

2 French trawlers sunk
1204
27.03

2005
28.03

0   80 Nm

0   80 km

ST NAZAIRE RAID

← Outward passage

←·— Homeward passage

←--- M.L.s 13, 8, 12 homeward

THE COMMANDO RAID on the port of St Nazaire ranks as one of the most daring operations of the entire war. The port housed the Normandie dry dock, then the largest in the world, and the only one on the French Atlantic coast capable of handling German capital ships. The object was to put the dock out of action, thus removing the necessary support infrastructure for future German surface raiders, principally the battleship *Tirpitz*. To achieve this the destroyer *Campbeltown* would be rammed into the southern lock gate and scuttled. On board, set to explode two and a half hours later, were three tons of high explosives. Commandos would be landed from motor launches and the destroyer at the Old Entrance and onto the Old Mole to destroy other facilities and act as a distraction to the main operation. St Nazaire, also a major U-boat base, was heavily defended and thus surprise would be crucial.

The force, designated the 10th A/S Striking Force as cover, was assembled in mid-March and trained at Falmouth. On 26 March the order came to execute *Chariot* and at 2pm the force sailed, taking a route that Luftwaffe reconnaissance flights did not cover. Apart from encountering a U-boat the voyage was uneventful and the assault force managed to get to within a mile of the dock early on 28 March undetected. At 1.28am German batteries opened fire and as the commandos landed fighting erupted across the port. *Campbeltown* rammed the dock gates at 1.34am; when she exploded at noon the entrance and a number of ships were destroyed putting the dock out of use. At 2.50am the remaining naval forces retreated. At sea there was a brief skirmish between the waiting British destroyers and a flotilla of German torpedo boats. During the operation fourteen craft were lost, 169 men were killed, 215 captured and 227 returned to Britain.

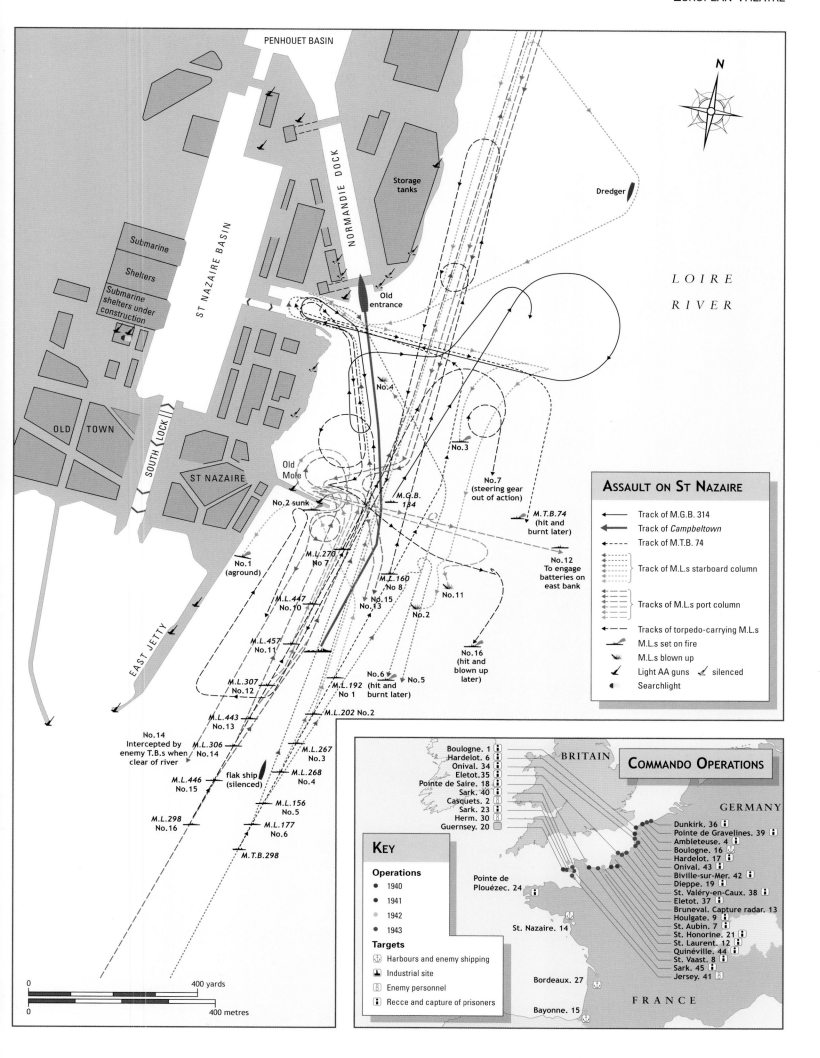

PENHOUET BASIN

NORMANDIE DOCK

Storage
tanks

Dredger

L O I R E

R I V E R

ST NAZAIRE BASIN

Submarine

Shelters

Submarine
shelters under
construction

Old
entrance

No.4

OLD TOWN

SOUTH LOCK

No.3

ST NAZAIRE

No.7
(steering gear
out of action)

Old
Mole

M.G.B.
184

M.T.B.74
(hit and
burnt later)

No.2 sunk

No.12
To engage
batteries on
east bank

No.1
(aground)

M.L.270
No 7

No.11

M.L.160
No 8

No.15
No.13

M.L.447
No.10

No.2

M.L.457
No.11

No.16
(hit and
blown up
later)

M.L.307
No.12

M.L.192
No 1

No.6
(hit and
burnt later)

No.5

M.L.202 No.2

EAST JETTY

M.L.443
No.13

No.14
Intercepted by
enemy T.B.s when
clear of river

M.L.306
No.14

M.L.267
No.3

M.L.446
No.15

flak ship
(silenced)

M.L.268
No.4

M.L.156
No.5

M.L.298
No.16

M.L.177
No.6

M.T.B.298

0   400 yards

0   400 metres

Assault on St Nazaire

— Track of M.G.B. 314

▬ Track of *Campbeltown*

- - - Track of M.T.B. 74

Track of M.L.s starboard column

Tracks of M.L.s port column

Tracks of torpedo-carrying M.L.s

M.L.s set on fire

M.L.s blown up

Light AA guns   silenced

Searchlight

Commando Operations

KEY

Operations

● 1940
● 1941
● 1942
● 1943

Targets

⌂ Harbours and enemy shipping

▣ Industrial site

▣ Enemy personnel

▣ Recce and capture of prisoners

BRITAIN

GERMANY

Boulogne. 1
Hardelot. 6
Onival. 34
Eletot. 35
Pointe de Saire. 18
Sark. 40
Casquets. 2
Sark. 23
Herm. 30
Guernsey. 20

Dunkirk. 36
Pointe de Gravelines. 39
Ambleteuse. 4
Boulogne. 16
Hardelot. 17
Onival. 43
Biville-sur-Mer. 42
Dieppe. 19
St. Valéry-en-Caux. 38
Eletot. 37
Bruneval. Capture radar. 13
Houlgate. 9
St. Aubin. 7
St. Honorine. 21
St. Laurent. 12
Quinéville. 44
St. Vaast. 8
Sark. 45
Jersey. 41

Pointe de
Plouézec. 24

St. Nazaire. 14

Bordeaux. 27

Bayonne. 15

F R A N C E

C Operation, Japanese Indian Ocean Raid, March – April 1942

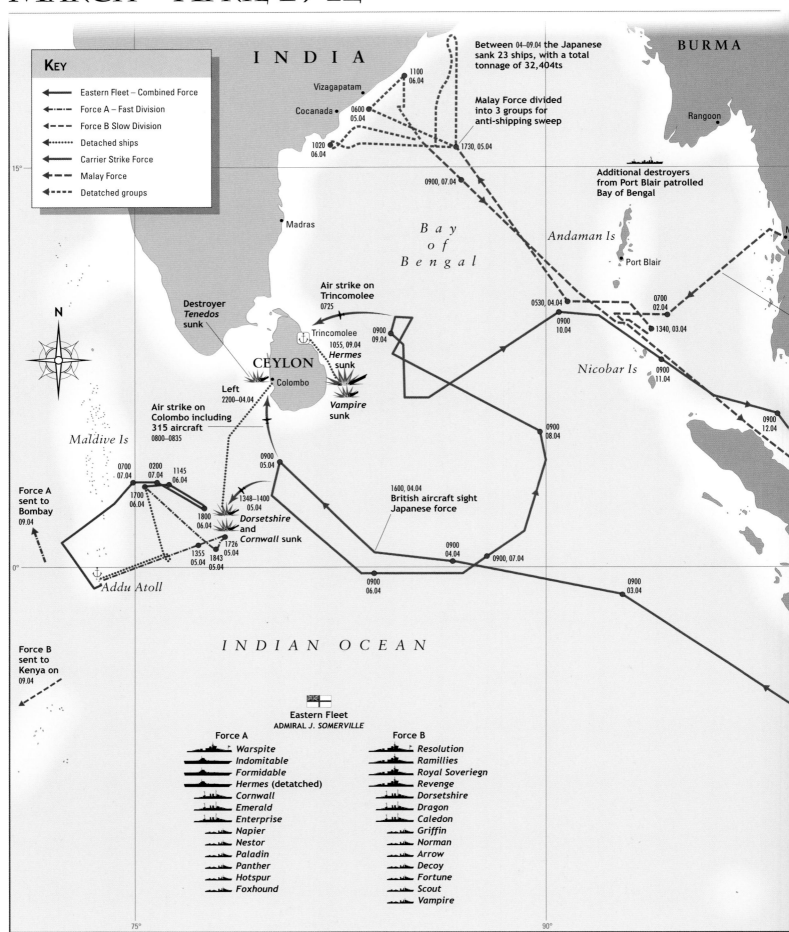

KEY

- ⟵ Eastern Fleet – Combined Force
- ⟵ Force A – Fast Division
- ⟵ Force B Slow Division
- ⟵ Detached ships
- ⟵ Carrier Strike Force
- ⟵ Malay Force
- ⟵ Detatched groups

INDIA

BURMA

Between 04–09.04 the Japanese sank 23 ships, with a total tonnage of 32,404ts

Vizagapatam
1100 06.04

Cocanada
0600 05.04

Rangoon

Malay Force divided into 3 groups for anti-shipping sweep

1730, 05.04

1020 06.04

0900, 07.04

Additional destroyers from Port Blair patrolled Bay of Bengal

Madras

Bay of Bengal

Andaman Is

Port Blair

0700 02.04

Air strike on Trincomolee 0725

Destroyer *Tenedos* sunk

Trincomolee
1055, 09.04
Hermes sunk

0900 09.04

0530, 04.04

0900 10.04

1340, 03.04

CEYLON   Colombo

Vampire sunk

Nicobar Is

0900 11.04

Left 2200–04.04

Air strike on Colombo including 315 aircraft 0800–0835

Maldive Is

0900 08.04

0900 12.04

0900 05.04

1600, 04.04 British aircraft sight Japanese force

Force A sent to Bombay 09.04

0700 07.04

0200 07.04

1145 06.04

1700 06.04

1800 06.04

1348–1400 05.04

Dorsetshire and *Cornwall* sunk

1726 05.04

1355 05.04

1843 05.04

0900 04.04

0900, 07.04

0900 03.04

⚓ *Addu Atoll*

0900 06.04

INDIAN OCEAN

Force B sent to Kenya on 09.04

Eastern Fleet
ADMIRAL *J. SOMERVILLE*

Force A	Force B
Warspite	*Resolution*
Indomitable	*Ramillies*
Formidable	*Royal Soveriegn*
Hermes (detatched)	*Revenge*
Cornwall	*Dorsetshire*
Emerald	*Dragon*
Enterprise	*Caledon*
Napier	*Griffin*
Nestor	*Norman*
Paladin	*Arrow*
Panther	*Decoy*
Hotspur	*Fortune*
Foxhound	*Scout*
	Vampire

CHINA

WITH THE CAMPAIGN in the East Indies completed, and little American activity in the Pacific, the Japanese sought to eliminate the last significant threat with a massive raid into the Indian Ocean to destroy the remainder of the British fleet and its bases on Ceylon. Three separate operations were planned. First, a small force would capture Christmas Island off Java and establish a base on it. In the event it was considered unsuitable for development and abandoned. Secondly, Admiral Nagumo would take a large force to attack Ceylon, while a third force would cross the Bay of Bengal to raid shipping along the Indian coast.

In a short time the British had assembled a large force with which to defend the Indian Ocean. Three carriers and five battleships, along with thirty cruisers, destroyers and submarines including the remnants of the Dutch navy, were concentrated off Ceylon. Admiral Somerville, who took command of the Eastern Fleet on 26 March, was, however, fully aware that his old units were qualitatively inferior and that his new carriers not fully worked up or sufficient in number to deal with the Japanese. Thus he split his force in two with the intention of keeping the old battleships of the *Revenge*-class out of harm's way. He planned to operate away from the Japanese during daylight and close for a night attack.

The British anticipated a Japanese strike on Ceylon on 1 April, thus Somerville concentrated his force at the British anchorage on Addu Atoll. In fact, the Japanese attack came a few days later, by which time Somerville had sent some of his ships back to Ceylon to replenish. On 4 April, a reconnaissance aircraft spotted the Japanese approaching. Somerville was too far west to be able to intervene. The cruisers *Dorsetshire* and *Cornwall* left Columbo that night. Early on 5 April the Japanese launched a larger strike against Colombo and that afternoon eighty-eight planes were sent to sink the two cruisers after they were spotted.

Somerville then expected the Japanese to make for Addu Atoll, but they knew nothing of the base and instead Nagumo took a circuitous route around Ceylon to strike Trincomalee on 9 April. At the same time, Vice Admiral Ozawa's forces were creating havoc along the Indian coast. By the time Trincomalee was hit the British had decided to abandon the eastern Indian Ocean. In a final act, Japanese aircraft sank the carrier *Hermes* and destroyer *Vampire*. Having achieved his aim Nagumo turned east and headed for Japan to enable the carriers and their air groups, which had been on operations since late November, to rest and refit.

Second Expedition Fleet - Malay Force
VICE ADMIRA J. OZAWA
Ryujo
6 Cruisers
4 Destroyers

Return to Japan

MALAYA

Strait of Malacca

⚓ Singapore

atra

BRUNEI

NORTH BORNEO

SARAWAK

Borneo

Celebes

Carrier Strike Force
ADMIRAL *CHUICHI NAGUMO*

Akagi		*Tanikaze*
Hiryu		*Urakaze*
Soryu		*Isokaze*
Shokaku		*Hamakaze*
Zuikaku		*Arare*
Haruna		*Shiranuhi*
Kirishima		*Kasumi*
Hiei		*Kagero*
Kongo		*Maikaze*
Tone		*Hagikaze*
Chikuma		*Akigumo*
Abukuma		

D U T C H E A S T I N D I E S

Java Sea

Depart
26.03

Java

Ombaya Strait

Operation X - Occupation of Christmas Island
REAR ADMIRAL *K. KUBO*
3 Cruisers
2 Destroyers
Transports
31.03

Christmas I

0		400 Nm
0		400 km

Operation Ironclad, The Invasion of Madagascar, May 1942

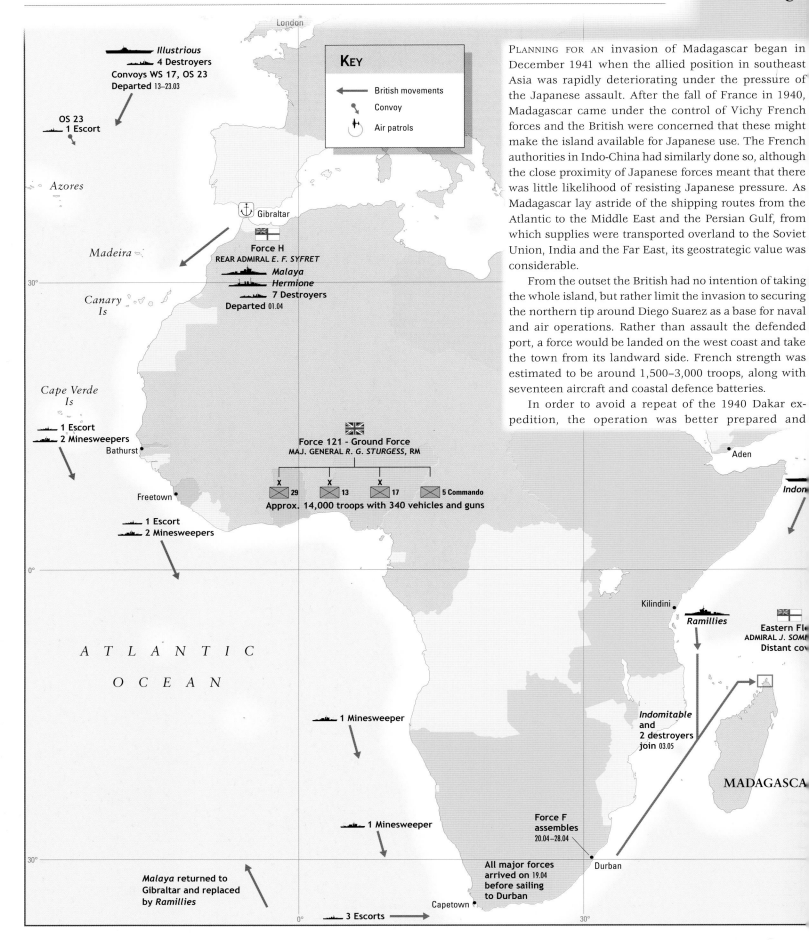

KEY

← British movements

Convoy

Air patrols

Illustrious
4 Destroyers
Convoys WS 17, OS 23
Departed 13–23.03

OS 23
1 Escort

Azores

Madeira

⚓ Gibraltar

Force H
REAR ADMIRAL *E. F. SYFRET*
Malaya
Hermione
7 Destroyers
Departed 01.04

Canary Is

30°

Cape Verde Is

1 Escort
2 Minesweepers
Bathurst

Freetown

1 Escort
2 Minesweepers

Force 121 - Ground Force
MAJ. GENERAL *R. G. STURGESS*, RM

X 29   X 13   X 17   5 Commando

Approx. 14,000 troops with 340 vehicles and guns

Aden

Indon

0°

A T L A N T I C

O C E A N

Kilindini

Ramillies

Eastern Fle
ADMIRAL *J. SOM*
Distant co

Indomitable and 2 destroyers join 03.05

1 Minesweeper

MADAGASCA

Malaya returned to Gibraltar and replaced by *Ramillies*

1 Minesweeper

Force F assembles 20.04–28.04

All major forces arrived on 19.04 before sailing to Durban

Durban

30°

Capetown

3 Escorts →

0°   30°

PLANNING FOR AN invasion of Madagascar began in December 1941 when the allied position in southeast Asia was rapidly deteriorating under the pressure of the Japanese assault. After the fall of France in 1940, Madagascar came under the control of Vichy French forces and the British were concerned that these might make the island available for Japanese use. The French authorities in Indo-China had similarly done so, although the close proximity of Japanese forces meant that there was little likelihood of resisting Japanese pressure. As Madagascar lay astride of the shipping routes from the Atlantic to the Middle East and the Persian Gulf, from which supplies were transported overland to the Soviet Union, India and the Far East, its geostrategic value was considerable.

From the outset the British had no intention of taking the whole island, but rather limit the invasion to securing the northern tip around Diego Suarez as a base for naval and air operations. Rather than assault the defended port, a force would be landed on the west coast and take the town from its landward side. French strength was estimated to be around 1,500–3,000 troops, along with seventeen aircraft and coastal defence batteries.

In order to avoid a repeat of the 1940 Dakar expedition, the operation was better prepared and

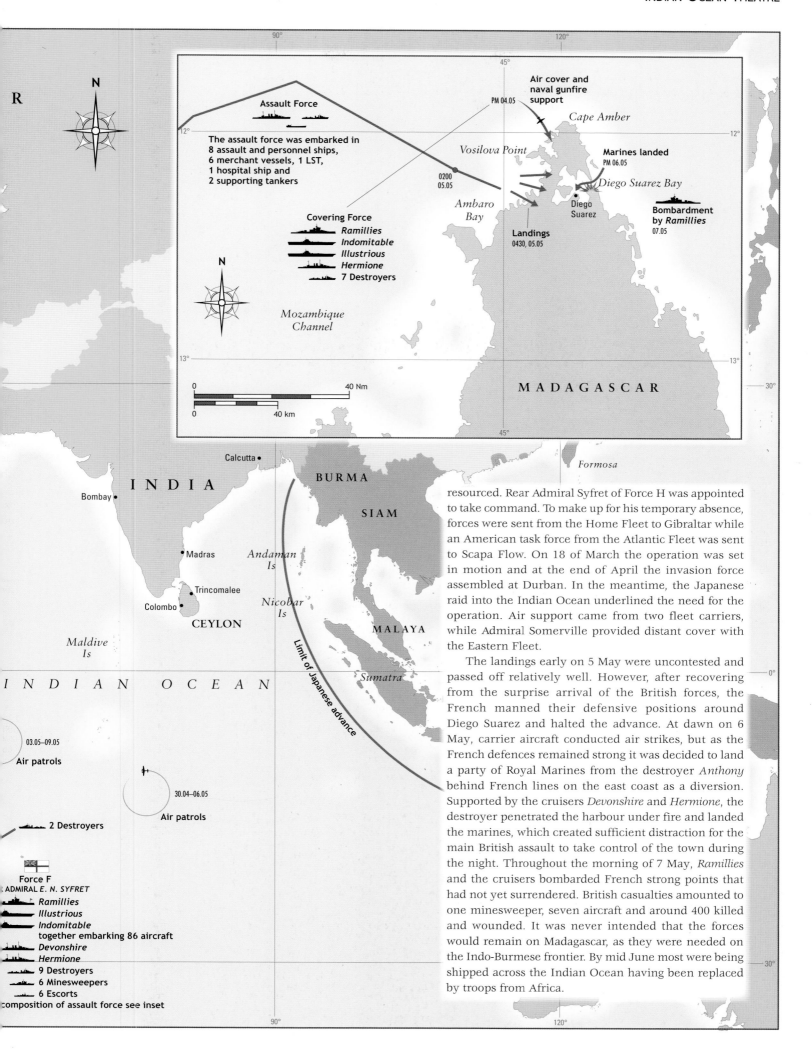

Assault Force

The assault force was embarked in
8 assault and personnel ships,
6 merchant vessels, 1 LST,
1 hospital ship and
2 supporting tankers

Covering Force

Ramillies
Indomitable
Illustrious
Hermione
7 Destroyers

Mozambique
Channel

0   40 Nm
0   40 km

PM 04.05

Air cover and
naval gunfire
support

Cape Amber

Vosilova Point

Marines landed
PM 06.05

Diego Suarez Bay

0200
05.05

*Ambaro
Bay*

Diego
Suarez

**Bombardment
by** *Ramillies*
07.05

Landings
0430, 05.05

M A D A G A S C A R

Calcutta •

Formosa

I N D I A

BURMA

Bombay •

SIAM

• Madras

*Andaman
Is*

• Trincomalee

*Nicobar
Is*

Colombo •

CEYLON

MALAYA

*Maldive
Is*

I N D I A N   O C E A N

Sumatra

03.05–09.05

Air patrols

30.04–06.05

Air patrols

2 Destroyers

Force F
ADMIRAL E. N. SYFRET

Ramillies
Illustrious
Indomitable
together embarking 86 aircraft
Devonshire
Hermione
9 Destroyers
6 Minesweepers
6 Escorts
composition of assault force see inset

resourced. Rear Admiral Syfret of Force H was appointed to take command. To make up for his temporary absence, forces were sent from the Home Fleet to Gibraltar while an American task force from the Atlantic Fleet was sent to Scapa Flow. On 18 of March the operation was set in motion and at the end of April the invasion force assembled at Durban. In the meantime, the Japanese raid into the Indian Ocean underlined the need for the operation. Air support came from two fleet carriers, while Admiral Somerville provided distant cover with the Eastern Fleet.

The landings early on 5 May were uncontested and passed off relatively well. However, after recovering from the surprise arrival of the British forces, the French manned their defensive positions around Diego Suarez and halted the advance. At dawn on 6 May, carrier aircraft conducted air strikes, but as the French defences remained strong it was decided to land a party of Royal Marines from the destroyer *Anthony* behind French lines on the east coast as a diversion. Supported by the cruisers *Devonshire* and *Hermione*, the destroyer penetrated the harbour under fire and landed the marines, which created sufficient distraction for the main British assault to take control of the town during the night. Throughout the morning of 7 May, *Ramillies* and the cruisers bombarded French strong points that had not yet surrendered. British casualties amounted to one minesweeper, seven aircraft and around 400 killed and wounded. It was never intended that the forces would remain on Madagascar, as they were needed on the Indo-Burmese frontier. By mid June most were being shipped across the Indian Ocean having been replaced by troops from Africa.

Japanese Commerce Raiding in the Indian Ocean, 1942–43

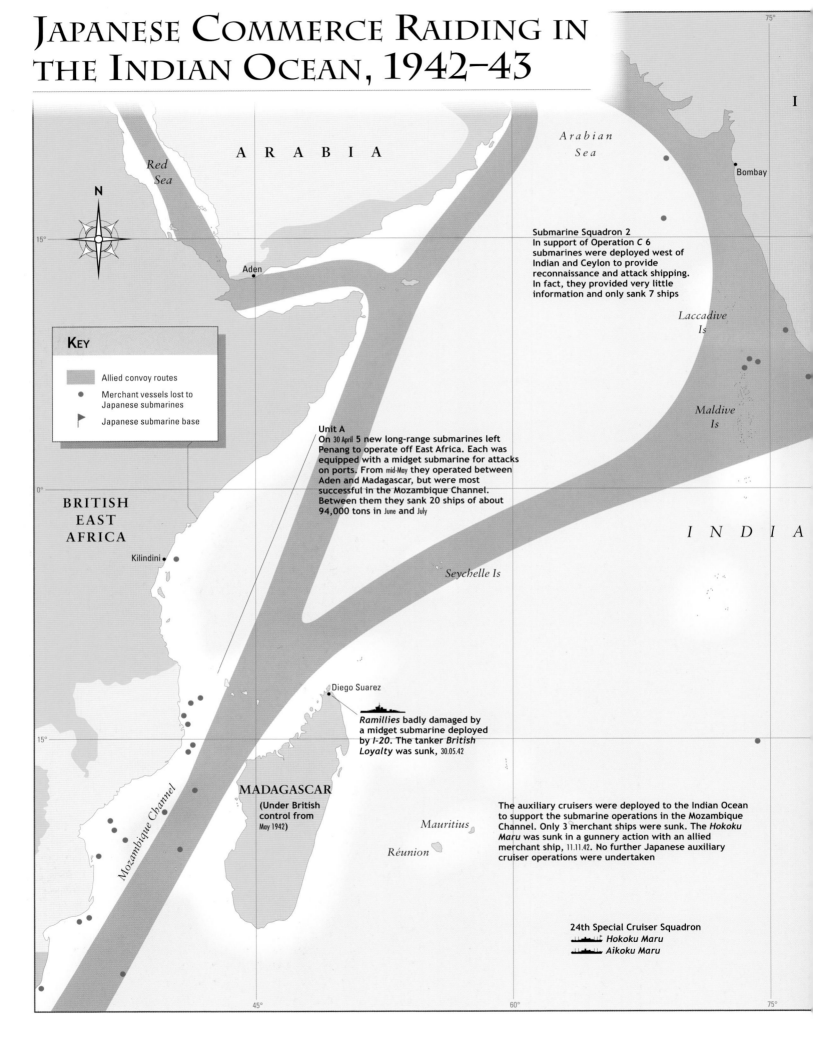

I

N

Key

Allied convoy routes

• Merchant vessels lost to Japanese submarines

▶ Japanese submarine base

Submarine Squadron 2
In support of Operation C 6 submarines were deployed west of Indian and Ceylon to provide reconnaissance and attack shipping. In fact, they provided very little information and only sank 7 ships

Unit A
On 30 April 5 new long-range submarines left Penang to operate off East Africa. Each was equipped with a midget submarine for attacks on ports. From mid-May they operated between Aden and Madagascar, but were most successful in the Mozambique Channel. Between them they sank 20 ships of about 94,000 tons in June and July

Ramillies badly damaged by a midget submarine deployed by *I-20*. The tanker *British Loyalty* was sunk, 30.05.42

MADAGASCAR
(Under British control from May 1942)

The auxiliary cruisers were deployed to the Indian Ocean to support the submarine operations in the Mozambique Channel. Only 3 merchant ships were sunk. The *Hokoku Maru* was sunk in a gunnery action with an allied merchant ship, 11.11.42. No further Japanese auxiliary cruiser operations were undertaken

24th Special Cruiser Squadron
Hokoku Maru
Aikoku Maru

Arabian Sea

Bombay

Red Sea

ARABIA

Aden

Laccadive Is

Maldive Is

BRITISH EAST AFRICA

Kilindini •

INDIA

Seychelle Is

Diego Suarez

Mauritius

Réunion

Mozambique Channel

15°

0°

15°

45°

60°

75°

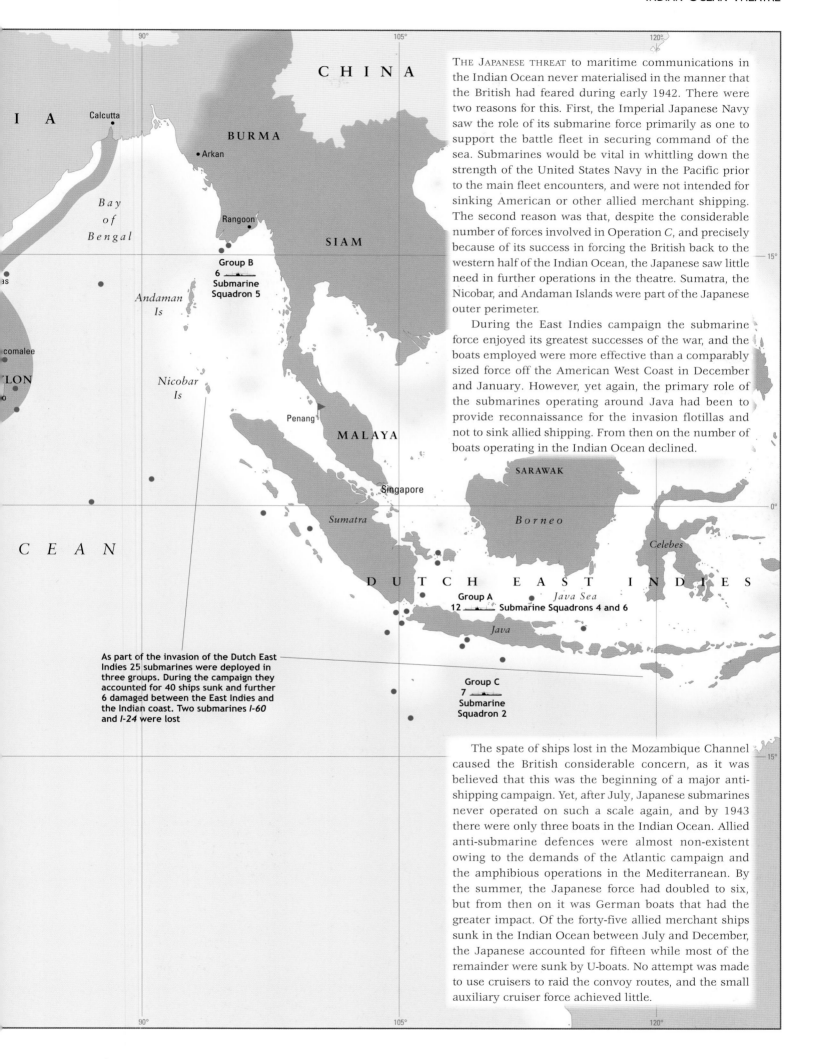

CHINA

BURMA

• Arkan

Bay
of
Bengal

Rangoon

SIAM

Calcutta

Andaman
Is

Nicobar
Is

Penang

MALAYA

Singapore

Sumatra

SARAWAK

Borneo

Celebes

DUTCH   EAST   INDIES

Java Sea

Java

Group B
6 ▲ **Submarine**
Squadron 5

Group A
12 ▲ **Submarine Squadrons 4 and 6**

Group C
7 ▲
Submarine
Squadron 2

As part of the invasion of the Dutch East Indies 25 submarines were deployed in three groups. During the campaign they accounted for 40 ships sunk and further 6 damaged between the East Indies and the Indian coast. Two submarines *I-60* and *I-24* were lost

THE JAPANESE THREAT to maritime communications in the Indian Ocean never materialised in the manner that the British had feared during early 1942. There were two reasons for this. First, the Imperial Japanese Navy saw the role of its submarine force primarily as one to support the battle fleet in securing command of the sea. Submarines would be vital in whittling down the strength of the United States Navy in the Pacific prior to the main fleet encounters, and were not intended for sinking American or other allied merchant shipping. The second reason was that, despite the considerable number of forces involved in Operation *C*, and precisely because of its success in forcing the British back to the western half of the Indian Ocean, the Japanese saw little need in further operations in the theatre. Sumatra, the Nicobar, and Andaman Islands were part of the Japanese outer perimeter.

During the East Indies campaign the submarine force enjoyed its greatest successes of the war, and the boats employed were more effective than a comparably sized force off the American West Coast in December and January. However, yet again, the primary role of the submarines operating around Java had been to provide reconnaissance for the invasion flotillas and not to sink allied shipping. From then on the number of boats operating in the Indian Ocean declined.

The spate of ships lost in the Mozambique Channel caused the British considerable concern, as it was believed that this was the beginning of a major anti-shipping campaign. Yet, after July, Japanese submarines never operated on such a scale again, and by 1943 there were only three boats in the Indian Ocean. Allied anti-submarine defences were almost non-existent owing to the demands of the Atlantic campaign and the amphibious operations in the Mediterranean. By the summer, the Japanese force had doubled to six, but from then on it was German boats that had the greater impact. Of the forty-five allied merchant ships sunk in the Indian Ocean between July and December, the Japanese accounted for fifteen while most of the remainder were sunk by U-boats. No attempt was made to use cruisers to raid the convoy routes, and the small auxiliary cruiser force achieved little.

119

PQ 15 AND QP 11, 28 APRIL – 4 MAY 1942

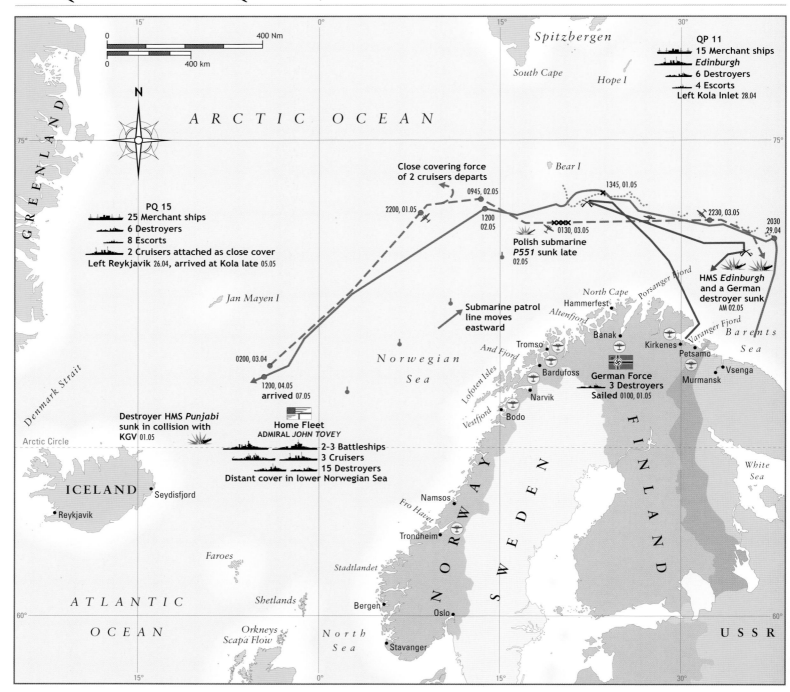

QP 11
15 Merchant ships
Edinburgh
6 Destroyers
4 Escorts
Left Kola Inlet 28.04

Close covering force
of 2 cruisers departs

0945, 02.05

2200, 01.05

1345, 01.05

1200
02.05

2230, 03.05

2030
29.04

0130, 03.05

Polish submarine
P551 sunk late
02.05

HMS *Edinburgh*
and a German
destroyer sunk
AM 02.05

PQ 15
25 Merchant ships
6 Destroyers
8 Escorts
2 Cruisers attached as close cover
Left Reykjavik 26.04, arrived at Kola late 05.05

Submarine patrol
line moves
eastward

0200, 03.04

1200, 04.05
arrived 07.05

Destroyer HMS *Punjabi*
sunk in collision with
KGV 01.05

Home Fleet
ADMIRAL *JOHN TOVEY*
2-3 Battleships
3 Cruisers
15 Destroyers
Distant cover in lower Norwegian Sea

German Force
3 Destroyers
Sailed 0100, 01.05

Spitzbergen

South Cape

Hope I

Bear I

ARCTIC OCEAN

GREENLAND

Jan Mayen I

Norwegian Sea

North Cape
Porsanger Fjord
Hammerfest
Altenfjord
And Fjord
Tromso
Banak
Kirkenes
Varanger Fjord
Petsamo
Barents Sea
Vsenga
Murmansk

Lofoten Isles
Bardufoss
Narvik
Vestfjord
Bodo

Denmark Strait

Arctic Circle

ICELAND
• Seydisfjord

• Reykjavik

Faroes

ATLANTIC
OCEAN

Shetlands

Orkneys
Scapa Flow

Fro Havet
Namsos

Trondheim

Stadtlandet

Bergen

Oslo

North Sea

Stavanger

NORWAY

SWEDEN

FINLAND

White Sea

USSR

WITH EVERY ARCTIC convoy operation the intensity of the German attacks increased, and although each passage followed a broadly similar scheme both sides continuously innovated at the operational and tactical levels to achieve greater success. The introduction of a moving submarine patrol line stemmed from the longer summer days that made a continuous close presence off Trondheim increasingly difficult. This was also the first operation in which American naval forces operated with the Home Fleet in the Arctic; in April TF 39, composed of a battleship, a carrier, two cruisers and six destroyers had arrived at Scapa Flow.

Initially, the German focus was on the westbound QP 11 and they were able to achieve an early success when a U-boat succeeded in hitting the stern of the cruiser *Edinburgh* on 29 April, forcing her back towards Murmansk. The next day the convoy fought off five German destroyer attacks before the latter withdrew. They turned east to find the *Edinburgh* and early on 2 May the cruiser and a German destroyer were sunk after an hour long gun and torpedo engagement. Just as QP 11 left the danger zone, PQ 15 entered the crucial phase of its passage. Late on 2 May its escorts damaged the Polish submarine *P551* that had drifted out of its designated patrol area forcing the boat to be scuttled. Then early on 3 May six German aircraft attacked the convoy with torpedoes, and although three were shot down, three ships were sunk. Throughout this phase U-boats also shadowed the convoy, but could not close in to attack. Another airstrike later in the evening caused no damage and a further German aircraft was shot down. During the last two days at sea, in the final run to Murmansk, bad weather provided protection from further attacks.

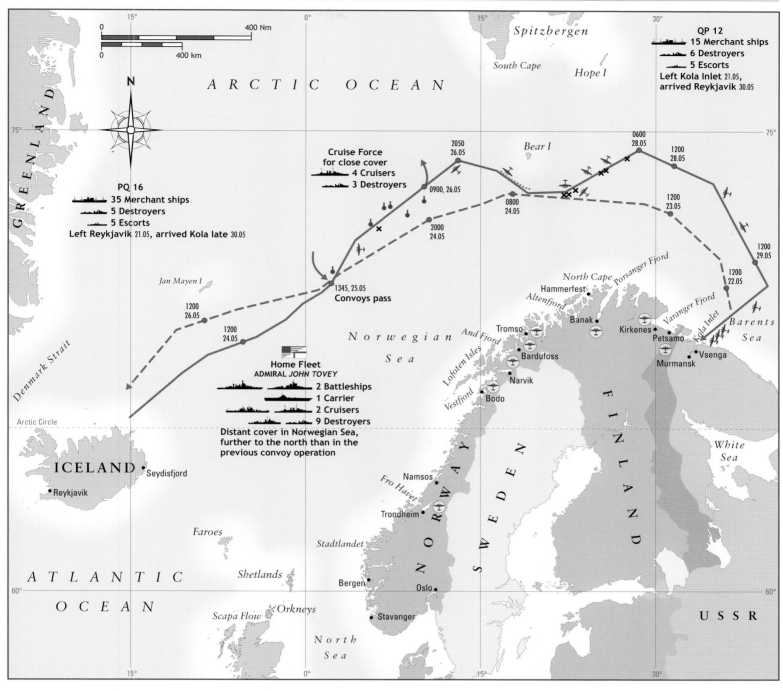

PQ 16 AND QP 12, 24–30 MAY 1942

KEY

⬅	Convoy PQ 16
⬅	Convoy QP 12
⋯	Ice
✈	German airbases
⚔	German airstrike
✕	Merchant ship sunk
⬤	German U-boat

THE NEXT CONVOYS were given a greater degree of protection and the Home Fleet sent out more ships in anticipation that the Germans would attempt to intercept the convoys with a surface force. As insurance these later PQ convoys included submarines as part of their escort force. The focus of the action rested entirely on the eastbound PQ 16, and QP 12 took no losses and encountered little German activity. One shadowing aircraft was shot down by a Hurricane launched from the convoy's CAM (Catapult Aircraft Merchantman) vessel. The Germans had no intention of sending out warships and instead intended to rely on the growing force of maritime strike aircraft being assembled in northern Norway. From about 6.30am on 25 May until late on 29 May PQ 16 was almost continuously shadowed from the air.

The first attacks occurred late that evening, while the first loss was inflicted by a U-boat the next day. It was, however, the air strikes on the 27 May that inflicted the heaviest toll. Throughout the day well over 100 sorties were flown against the convoy, and in addition to six vessels being sunk a further three were damaged. More attacks followed, but no further ships were lost. The loss of seven out of thirty-five ships was substantial. The need to increase the anti-aircraft defences afforded to convoys was clear. In the short term more escorts and CAMs needed to be found, but the solution really lay in providing convoys with escort carriers. At this stage in the war there were virtually no such vessels in operation. However, the long daylight hours did at least reduce the chances of U-boat attacks.

BATTLE OF THE CORAL SEA, 4–8 MAY 1942

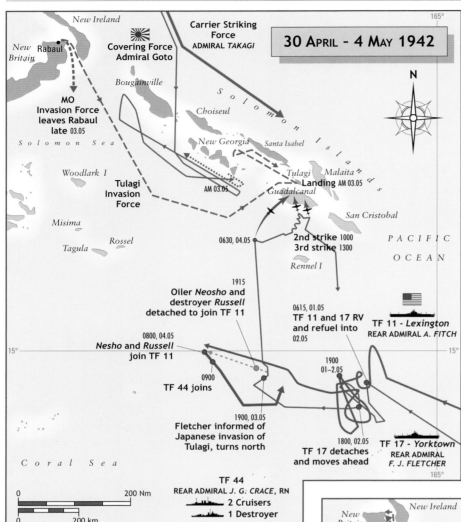

30 APRIL – 4 MAY 1942

New Ireland

New Britain

Rabaul

Covering Force Admiral Goto

Carrier Striking Force ADMIRAL *TAKAGI*

MO Invasion Force leaves Rabaul late 03.05

Bougainville

Solomon Sea

Choiseul

New Georgia

Santa Isabel

Woodlark I

AM 03.05

Tulagi Invasion Force

Tulagi Malaita

Landing AM 03.05

Guadalcanal

Misima

Rossel

0630, 04.05

San Cristobal

2nd strike 1000 3rd strike 1300

PACIFIC OCEAN

Tagula

Rennel I

1915

Oiler *Neosho* and destroyer *Russell* detached to join TF 11

0615, 01.05

TF 11 and 17 RV and refuel into 02.05

TF 11 - *Lexington*
REAR ADMIRAL A. *FITCH*

0800, 04.05

***Nesho* and *Russell* join TF 11**

0900

TF 44 joins

1900 01–2.05

1900, 03.05

Fletcher informed of Japanese invasion of Tulagi, turns north

1800, 02.05

TF 17 detaches and moves ahead

TF 17 - *Yorktown*
REAR ADMIRAL F. J. FLETCHER

Coral Sea

0 — 200 Nm
0 — 200 km

TF 44
REAR ADMIRAL J. G. *CRACE*, RN
2 Cruisers
1 Destroyer

delayed the process and Fletcher went ahead. When reports of the Japanese landing on Tulagi reached him late on the 3 May he turned north, while Rear Admiral Fitch, unaware, proceeded west to meet with the cruisers. *Yorktown*'s strikes on 4 May sunk some shipping and caused the Japanese support forces to move northwestwards to cover the convoy for Port Moresby. The allied force regrouped, and Takagi's carriers also entered the Coral Sea from the east. On 5 and 6 May, neither side knew the whereabouts of the other, but early on 7 May contact was made. The Americans got in the first strike, overwhelming the carrier *Shoho*, while the two large Japanese carriers wasted their efforts on an oiler and a destroyer. The presence of Crace's cruisers induced the Japanese to pull the convoy back. Now in close proximity, both carrier forces exchanged air strikes on 8 May in which one American carrier was lost and another heavily damaged, as was one Japanese carrier.

THE BATTLE OF the Coral Sea was critical: it was the first major fleet engagement in the Pacific war; it was also the first battle fought between aircraft carriers, and the first battle in which the two opposing fleets made no visual contact. It resulted from the Japanese attempt to take Port Moresby as the central element in a wider operation to secure the Solomons. The outer perimeter was to be extended beyond the pre-war plan in order to sever the link between Australia, New Zealand and the United States. A force would first be sent out to a capture Tulagi, to establish a seaplane base, and a small expedition sent into the Pacific to take the islands of Nauru and Ocean. Three separate forces would provide cover. One of these, Vice Admiral Takagi's Carrier Strike Force, had been detached from the First Air Fleet and would deal w ith any intervention by the American carriers. Originally, it was envisaged that these would proceed southwest and strike at Australia.

From signals intelligence, the Americans knew by mid April that a significant operation was being planned against Port Moresby. Admiral Nimitz sent the *Lexington* from Pearl Harbor, while General MacArthur dispatched a small cruiser force. Both were to rendezvous with Rear Admiral Fletcher's *Yorktown* task force south of the Solomons. The two carrier forces joined on 1 May and started to refuel, but the poor weather conditions

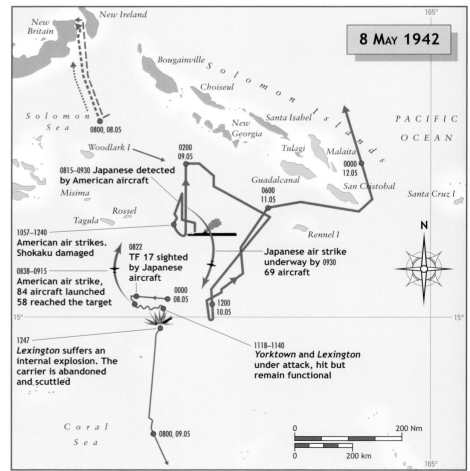

8 MAY 1942

New Ireland

New Britain

Bougainville

Solomon Islands

Choiseul

Solomon Sea

0800, 08.05

New Georgia

Santa Isabel

PACIFIC OCEAN

Woodlark I

0200 09.05

0815–0930 Japanese detected by American aircraft

Tulagi Malaita

0000 12.05

Misima

Guadalcanal

0600 11.05

San Cristobal

Santa Cruz I

Rossel

Tagula

Rennel I

1057–1240 American air strikes. Shokaku damaged

0822 **TF 17 sighted by Japanese aircraft**

Japanese air strike underway by 0930 69 aircraft

0838–0915 American air strike, 84 aircraft launched 58 reached the target

0000 08.05

1200 10.05

1247 *Lexington* suffers an internal explosion. The carrier is abandoned and scuttled

1118–1140 *Yorktown* and *Lexington* under attack, hit but remain functional

Coral Sea

0800, 09.05

0 — 200 Nm
0 — 200 km

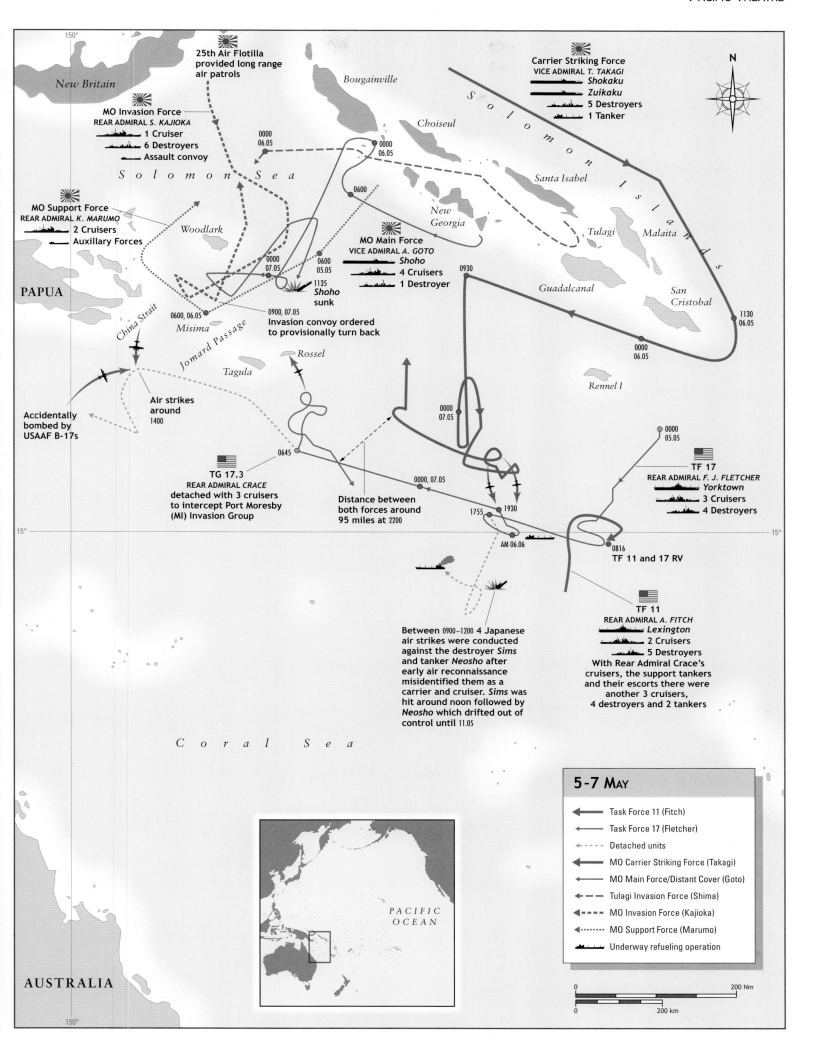

25th Air Flotilla provided long range air patrols

MO Invasion Force
REAR ADMIRAL S. KAJIOKA
- 1 Cruiser
- 6 Destroyers
- Assault convoy

MO Support Force
REAR ADMIRAL K. MARUMO
- 2 Cruisers
- Auxillary Forces

Carrier Striking Force
VICE ADMIRAL T. TAKAGI
- Shokaku
- Zuikaku
- 5 Destroyers
- 1 Tanker

MO Main Force
VICE ADMIRAL A. GOTO
- Shoho
- 4 Cruisers
- 1 Destroyer

New Britain

Bougainville

Choiseul

Santa Isabel

New Georgia

Solomon Sea

Solomon Islands

Tulagi

Malaita

PAPUA

Woodlark

0000 06.05

0000 06.05

0600

0000 05.05

0600 05.05

0000 07.05

1135 Shoho sunk

0930

Guadalcanal

San Cristobal

1130 06.05

0000 06.05

0900, 07.05 Invasion convoy ordered to provisionally turn back

China Strait

0600, 06.05

Misima

Jomard Passage

Tagula

Rossel

Accidentally bombed by USAAF B-17s

Air strikes around 1400

0645

TG 17.3
REAR ADMIRAL CRACE
detached with 3 cruisers to intercept Port Moresby (MI) Invasion Group

Distance between both forces around 95 miles at 2200

0000, 07.05

0000 07.05

Rennel I

0000 05.05

TF 17
REAR ADMIRAL F. J. FLETCHER
- Yorktown
- 3 Cruisers
- 4 Destroyers

1755

1930

AM 06.06

0816 TF 11 and 17 RV

TF 11
REAR ADMIRAL A. FITCH
- Lexington
- 2 Cruisers
- 5 Destroyers

With Rear Admiral Crace's cruisers, the support tankers and their escorts there were another 3 cruisers, 4 destroyers and 2 tankers

Between 0900–1200 4 Japanese air strikes were conducted against the destroyer *Sims* and tanker *Neosho* after early air reconnaissance misidentified them as a carrier and cruiser. *Sims* was hit around noon followed by *Neosho* which drifted out of control until 11.05

Coral Sea

PACIFIC OCEAN

AUSTRALIA

5-7 MAY
- Task Force 11 (Fitch)
- Task Force 17 (Fletcher)
- Detached units
- MO Carrier Striking Force (Takagi)
- MO Main Force/Distant Cover (Goto)
- Tulagi Invasion Force (Shima)
- MO Invasion Force (Kajioka)
- MO Support Force (Marumo)
- Underway refueling operation

0   200 Nm

0   200 km

OPERATION MI, THE MIDWAY CAMPAIGN

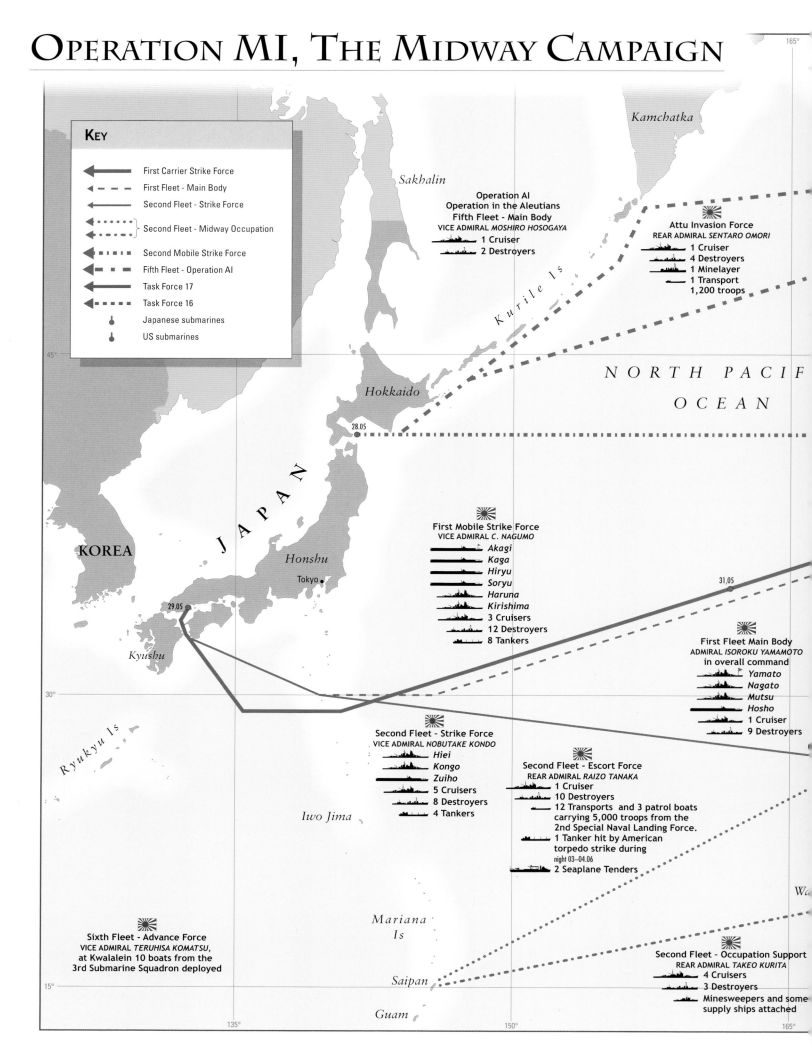

KEY

- First Carrier Strike Force
- First Fleet - Main Body
- Second Fleet - Strike Force
- Second Fleet - Midway Occupation
- Second Mobile Strike Force
- Fifth Fleet - Operation AI
- Task Force 17
- Task Force 16
- Japanese submarines
- US submarines

Kamchatka

Sakhalin

Operation AI
Operation in the Aleutians
Fifth Fleet - Main Body
VICE ADMIRAL *MOSHIRO HOSOGAYA*
- 1 Cruiser
- 2 Destroyers

Attu Invasion Force
REAR ADMIRAL *SENTARO OMORI*
- 1 Cruiser
- 4 Destroyers
- 1 Minelayer
- 1 Transport
- 1,200 troops

Kurile Is

Hokkaido

28.05

NORTH PACIFIC OCEAN

Honshu

Tokyo

First Mobile Strike Force
VICE ADMIRAL *C. NAGUMO*
- Akagi
- Kaga
- Hiryu
- Soryu
- Haruna
- Kirishima
- 3 Cruisers
- 12 Destroyers
- 8 Tankers

J A P A N

KOREA

29.05

31,05

First Fleet Main Body
ADMIRAL *ISOROKU YAMAMOTO*
in overall command
- Yamato
- Nagato
- Mutsu
- Hosho
- 1 Cruiser
- 9 Destroyers

Kyushu

30°

Ryukyu Is

Second Fleet - Strike Force
VICE ADMIRAL *NOBUTAKE KONDO*
- Hiei
- Kongo
- Zuiho
- 5 Cruisers
- 8 Destroyers
- 4 Tankers

Second Fleet - Escort Force
REAR ADMIRAL *RAIZO TANAKA*
- 1 Cruiser
- 10 Destroyers
- 12 Transports and 3 patrol boats carrying 5,000 troops from the 2nd Special Naval Landing Force.
- 1 Tanker hit by American torpedo strike during night 03–04.06
- 2 Seaplane Tenders

Iwo Jima

Mariana Is

Sixth Fleet - Advance Force
VICE ADMIRAL *TERUHISA KOMATSU*,
at Kwalalein 10 boats from the
3rd Submarine Squadron deployed

Saipan

Guam

Second Fleet - Occupation Support
REAR ADMIRAL *TAKEO KURITA*
- 4 Cruisers
- 3 Destroyers
- Minesweepers and some supply ships attached

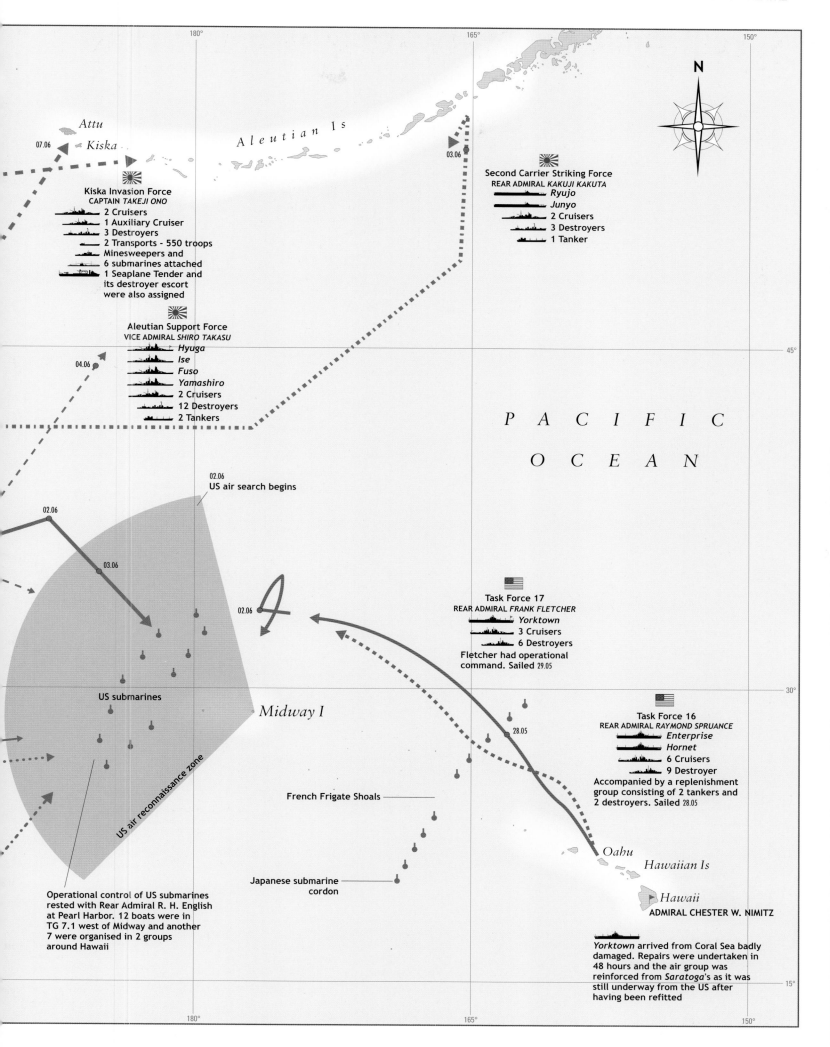

N

Attu

07.06 *Kiska*

A l e u t i a n   I s

03.06

Kiska Invasion Force
CAPTAIN *TAKEJI ONO*
2 Cruisers
1 Auxiliary Cruiser
3 Destroyers
2 Transports - 550 troops
Minesweepers and
6 submarines attached
1 Seaplane Tender and
its destroyer escort
were also assigned

Second Carrier Striking Force
REAR ADMIRAL *KAKUJI KAKUTA*
Ryujo
Junyo
2 Cruisers
3 Destroyers
1 Tanker

Aleutian Support Force
VICE ADMIRAL *SHIRO TAKASU*
Hyuga
Ise
Fuso
Yamashiro
2 Cruisers
12 Destroyers
2 Tankers

04.06

45°

P A C I F I C

O C E A N

02.06
US air search begins

02.06

03.06

02.06

Task Force 17
REAR ADMIRAL *FRANK FLETCHER*
Yorktown
3 Cruisers
6 Destroyers
Fletcher had operational
command. Sailed 29.05

30°

US submarines

Midway I

28.05

Task Force 16
REAR ADMIRAL *RAYMOND SPRUANCE*
Enterprise
Hornet
6 Cruisers
9 Destroyer
Accompanied by a replenishment
group consisting of 2 tankers and
2 destroyers. Sailed 28.05

US air reconnaissance zone

French Frigate Shoals

Oahu

Hawaiian Is

Operational control of US submarines
rested with Rear Admiral R. H. English
at Pearl Harbor. 12 boats were in
TG 7.1 west of Midway and another
7 were organised in 2 groups
around Hawaii

Japanese submarine
cordon

Hawaii
ADMIRAL CHESTER W. NIMITZ

Yorktown arrived from Coral Sea badly
damaged. Repairs were undertaken in
48 hours and the air group was
reinforced from *Saratoga*'s as it was
still underway from the US after
having been refitted

15°

180°   165°   150°

The Battle of Midway, 4 June 1942

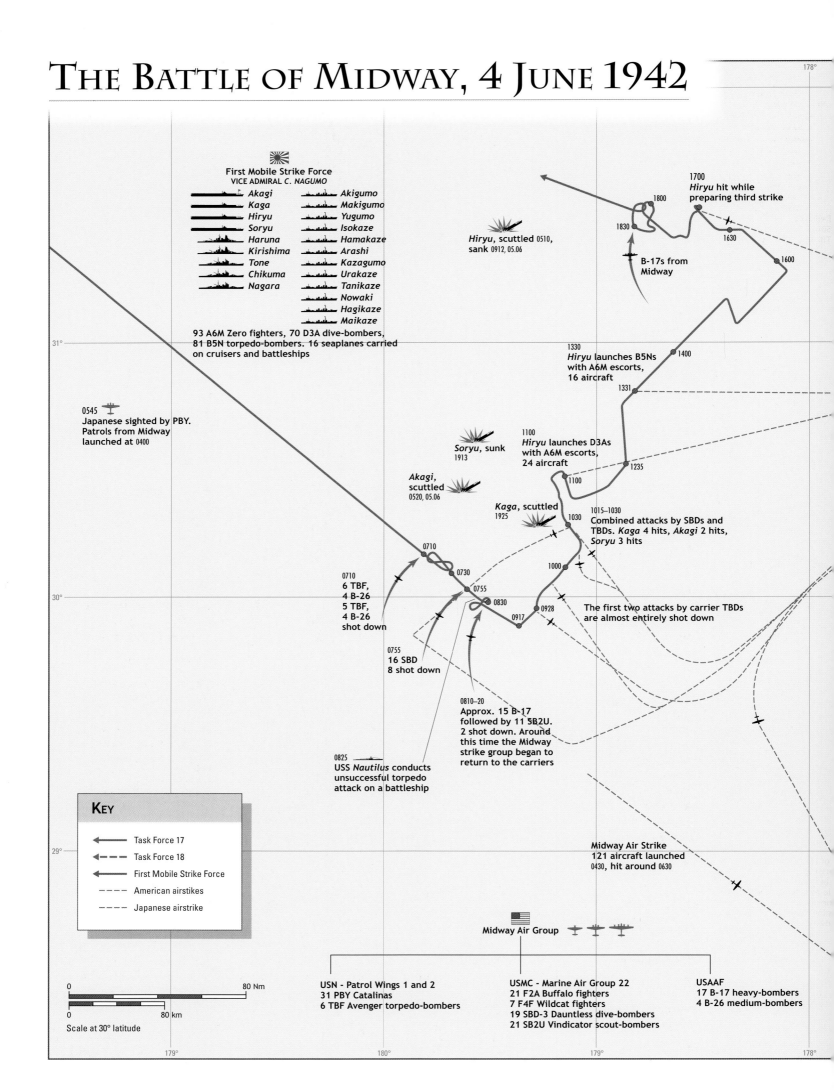

First Mobile Strike Force
VICE ADMIRAL *C. NAGUMO*

Akagi		*Akigumo*
Kaga		*Makigumo*
Hiryu		*Yugumo*
Soryu		*Isokaze*
Haruna		*Hamakaze*
Kirishima		*Arashi*
Tone		*Kazagumo*
Chikuma		*Urakaze*
Nagara		*Tanikaze*
		Nowaki
		Hagikaze
		Maikaze

93 A6M Zero fighters, 70 D3A dive-bombers, 81 B5N torpedo-bombers. 16 seaplanes carried on cruisers and battleships

1700
Hiryu hit while preparing third strike

1800

1830

1630

1600

B-17s from Midway

Hiryu, scuttled 0510, sank 0912, 05.06

1330
Hiryu launches B5Ns with A6M escorts, 16 aircraft

1400

1331

0545
Japanese sighted by PBY. Patrols from Midway launched at 0400

Soryu, sunk 1913

1100
Hiryu launches D3As with A6M escorts, 24 aircraft

Akagi, scuttled 0520, 05.06

1235

1100

Kaga, scuttled 1925

1030

1015–1030
Combined attacks by SBDs and TBDs. *Kaga* 4 hits, *Akagi* 2 hits, *Soryu* 3 hits

0710

0710
6 TBF, 4 B-26 5 TBF, 4 B-26 shot down

0730

0755

0830

1000

0928

0917

The first two attacks by carrier TBDs are almost entirely shot down

0755
16 SBD 8 shot down

0810–20
Approx. 15 B-17 followed by 11 SB2U. 2 shot down. Around this time the Midway strike group began to return to the carriers

0825
USS *Nautilus* conducts unsuccessful torpedo attack on a battleship

Midway Air Strike
121 aircraft launched 0430, hit around 0630

Key

←	Task Force 17
◄---	Task Force 18
←	First Mobile Strike Force
- - -	American airstikes
- - -	Japanese airstrike

Midway Air Group

USN – Patrol Wings 1 and 2	USMC – Marine Air Group 22	USAAF
31 PBY Catalinas	21 F2A Buffalo fighters	17 B-17 heavy-bombers
6 TBF Avenger torpedo-bombers	7 F4F Wildcat fighters	4 B-26 medium-bombers
	19 SBD-3 Dauntless dive-bombers	
	21 SB2U Vindicator scout-bombers	

0   80 Nm
0   80 km
Scale at 30° latitude

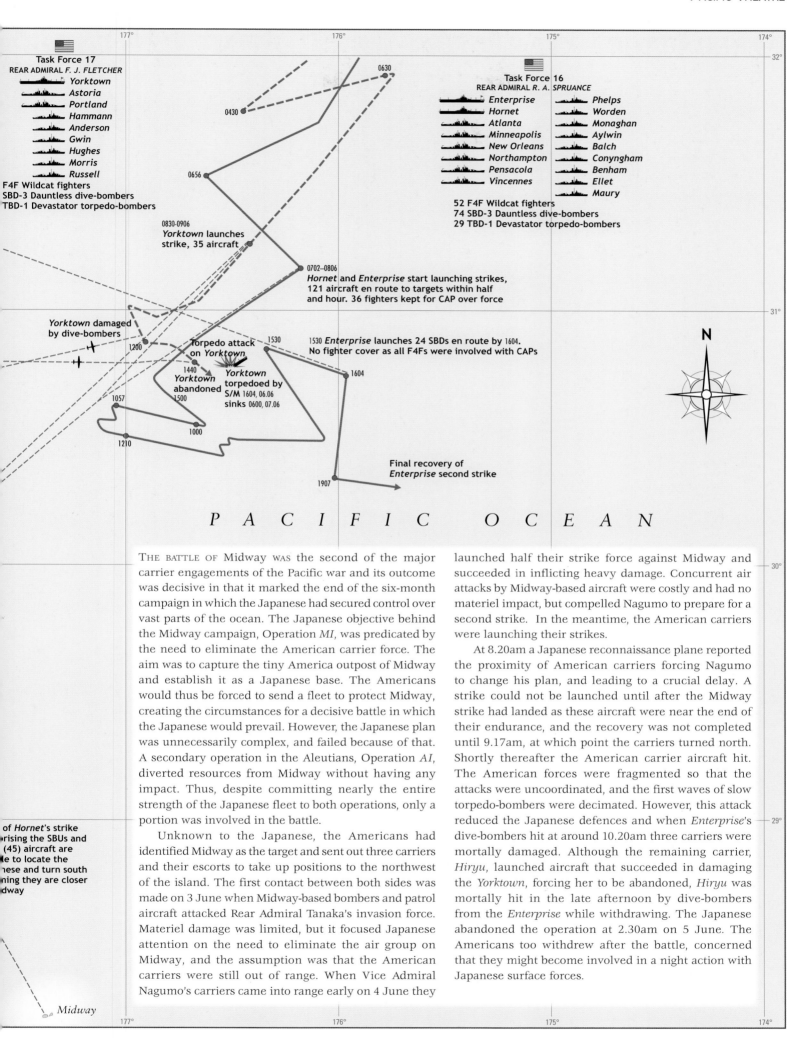

Task Force 17
REAR ADMIRAL *F. J. FLETCHER*
- Yorktown
- Astoria
- Portland
- Hammann
- Anderson
- Gwin
- Hughes
- Morris
- Russell

F4F Wildcat fighters
SBD-3 Dauntless dive-bombers
TBD-1 Devastator torpedo-bombers

Task Force 16
REAR ADMIRAL *R. A. SPRUANCE*
- Enterprise
- Hornet
- Atlanta
- Minneapolis
- New Orleans
- Northampton
- Pensacola
- Vincennes
- Phelps
- Worden
- Monaghan
- Aylwin
- Balch
- Conyngham
- Benham
- Ellet
- Maury

52 F4F Wildcat fighters
74 SBD-3 Dauntless dive-bombers
29 TBD-1 Devastator torpedo-bombers

0630

0430

0656

0830-0906
Yorktown launches
strike, 35 aircraft

0702–0806
Hornet and *Enterprise* start launching strikes,
121 aircraft en route to targets within half
and hour. 36 fighters kept for CAP over force

Yorktown damaged
by dive-bombers

1200

Torpedo attack
on *Yorktown*

1530

1530 *Enterprise* launches 24 SBDs en route by 1604.
No fighter cover as all F4Fs were involved with CAPs

1440
Yorktown
abandoned
1500

Yorktown
torpedoed by
S/M 1604, 06.06
sinks 0600, 07.06

1604

1057

1000

1210

1907

Final recovery of
Enterprise second strike

N

P A C I F I C   O C E A N

THE BATTLE OF Midway WAS the second of the major carrier engagements of the Pacific war and its outcome was decisive in that it marked the end of the six-month campaign in which the Japanese had secured control over vast parts of the ocean. The Japanese objective behind the Midway campaign, Operation *MI*, was predicated by the need to eliminate the American carrier force. The aim was to capture the tiny America outpost of Midway and establish it as a Japanese base. The Americans would thus be forced to send a fleet to protect Midway, creating the circumstances for a decisive battle in which the Japanese would prevail. However, the Japanese plan was unnecessarily complex, and failed because of that. A secondary operation in the Aleutians, Operation *AI*, diverted resources from Midway without having any impact. Thus, despite committing nearly the entire strength of the Japanese fleet to both operations, only a portion was involved in the battle.

Unknown to the Japanese, the Americans had identified Midway as the target and sent out three carriers and their escorts to take up positions to the northwest of the island. The first contact between both sides was made on 3 June when Midway-based bombers and patrol aircraft attacked Rear Admiral Tanaka's invasion force. Materiel damage was limited, but it focused Japanese attention on the need to eliminate the air group on Midway, and the assumption was that the American carriers were still out of range. When Vice Admiral Nagumo's carriers came into range early on 4 June they launched half their strike force against Midway and succeeded in inflicting heavy damage. Concurrent air attacks by Midway-based aircraft were costly and had no materiel impact, but compelled Nagumo to prepare for a second strike. In the meantime, the American carriers were launching their strikes.

At 8.20am a Japanese reconnaissance plane reported the proximity of American carriers forcing Nagumo to change his plan, and leading to a crucial delay. A strike could not be launched until after the Midway strike had landed as these aircraft were near the end of their endurance, and the recovery was not completed until 9.17am, at which point the carriers turned north. Shortly thereafter the American carrier aircraft hit. The American forces were fragmented so that the attacks were uncoordinated, and the first waves of slow torpedo-bombers were decimated. However, this attack reduced the Japanese defences and when *Enterprise*'s dive-bombers hit at around 10.20am three carriers were mortally damaged. Although the remaining carrier, *Hiryu*, launched aircraft that succeeded in damaging the *Yorktown*, forcing her to be abandoned, *Hiryu* was mortally hit in the late afternoon by dive-bombers from the *Enterprise* while withdrawing. The Japanese abandoned the operation at 2.30am on 5 June. The Americans too withdrew after the battle, concerned that they might become involved in a night action with Japanese surface forces.

of *Hornet*'s strike
rising the SBUs and
(45) aircraft are
e to locate the
nese and turn south
ning they are closer
dway

Midway

OPERATION HARPOON, 14–15 JUNE 1942

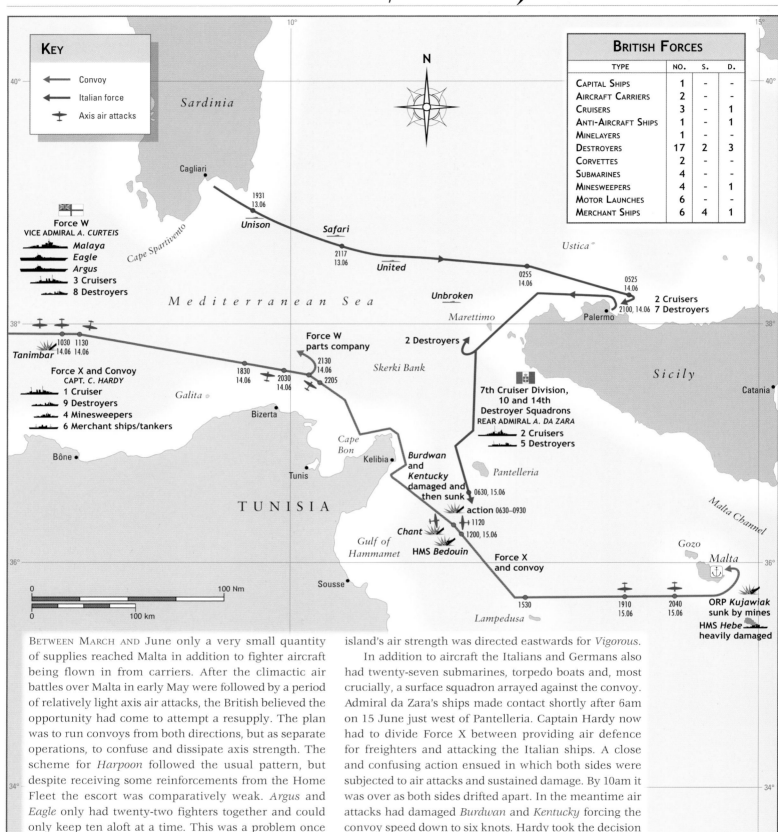

KEY

← Convoy

← Italian force

✈ Axis air attacks

BRITISH FORCES			
TYPE	NO.	S.	D.
CAPITAL SHIPS	1	–	–
AIRCRAFT CARRIERS	2	–	–
CRUISERS	3	–	1
ANTI-AIRCRAFT SHIPS	1	–	1
MINELAYERS	1	–	–
DESTROYERS	17	2	3
CORVETTES	2	–	–
SUBMARINES	4	–	–
MINESWEEPERS	4	–	1
MOTOR LAUNCHES	6	–	–
MERCHANT SHIPS	6	4	1

Sardinia

Cagliari

1931 13.06

Unison   Safari

United

2117 13.06

0255 14.06

0525 14.06

Ustica

2 Cruisers
7 Destroyers

2100, 14.06

Palermo

Unbroken

Marettimo

Force W
VICE ADMIRAL A. CURTEIS

Malaya
Eagle
Argus
3 Cruisers
8 Destroyers

Mediterranean Sea

Cape Spartivento

1030 1130
14.06 14.06
Tanimbar

Force X and Convoy
CAPT. C. HARDY

1 Cruiser
9 Destroyers
4 Minesweepers
6 Merchant ships/tankers

Galita

Bizerta

1830 14.06

2030 14.06

2130 14.06

2205

Force W
parts company

Skerki Bank

2 Destroyers

Sicily

Catania

7th Cruiser Division,
10 and 14th
Destroyer Squadrons
REAR ADMIRAL A. DA ZARA

2 Cruisers
5 Destroyers

Bône

Cape Bon

Kelibia

Tunis

TUNISIA

Burdwan
and
Kentucky
damaged and
then sunk

0630, 15.06

action 0630–0930

1120

1200, 15.06

Chant

HMS *Bedouin*

Pantelleria

Force X
and convoy

Gulf of
Hammamet

Sousse

1530

Lampedusa

1910 15.06

2040 15.06

Malta Channel

Gozo

Malta

ORP *Kujawiak*
sunk by mines

HMS *Hebe*
heavily damaged

0   100 Nm

0   100 km

BETWEEN MARCH AND June only a very small quantity of supplies reached Malta in addition to fighter aircraft being flown in from carriers. After the climactic air battles over Malta in early May were followed by a period of relatively light axis air attacks, the British believed the opportunity had come to attempt a resupply. The plan was to run convoys from both directions, but as separate operations, to confuse and dissipate axis strength. The scheme for *Harpoon* followed the usual pattern, but despite receiving some reinforcements from the Home Fleet the escort was comparatively weak. *Argus* and *Eagle* only had twenty-two fighters together and could only keep ten aloft at a time. This was a problem once the convoy entered the danger zone on 14 June and was subjected to numerous air attacks. In the first the cruiser *Liverpool* was badly damaged, needing to be towed back to Gibraltar, and the Dutch freighter *Tanimbar* sunk. Once the convoy reached the narrows, late on 14 June, Beaufighters from Malta were able to provide a small degree of protection and reconnaissance, but most of the island's air strength was directed eastwards for *Vigorous*.

In addition to aircraft the Italians and Germans also had twenty-seven submarines, torpedo boats and, most crucially, a surface squadron arrayed against the convoy. Admiral da Zara's ships made contact shortly after 6am on 15 June just west of Pantelleria. Captain Hardy now had to divide Force X between providing air defence for freighters and attacking the Italian ships. A close and confusing action ensued in which both sides were subjected to air attacks and sustained damage. By 10am it was over as both sides drifted apart. In the meantime air attacks had damaged *Burdwan* and *Kentucky* forcing the convoy speed down to six knots. Hardy took the decision to scuttle them. The Italian squadron reappeared and in another hour long engagement the British destroyer *Bedouin* was damaged and then sunk by an Italian air-dropped torpedo. The convoy suffered further air attacks, ran into an Italian minefield off Malta and reached Valletta that night exhausted and considerably depleted.

Gulf of Sirte

OPERATION VIGOROUS, 13–15 JUNE 1942

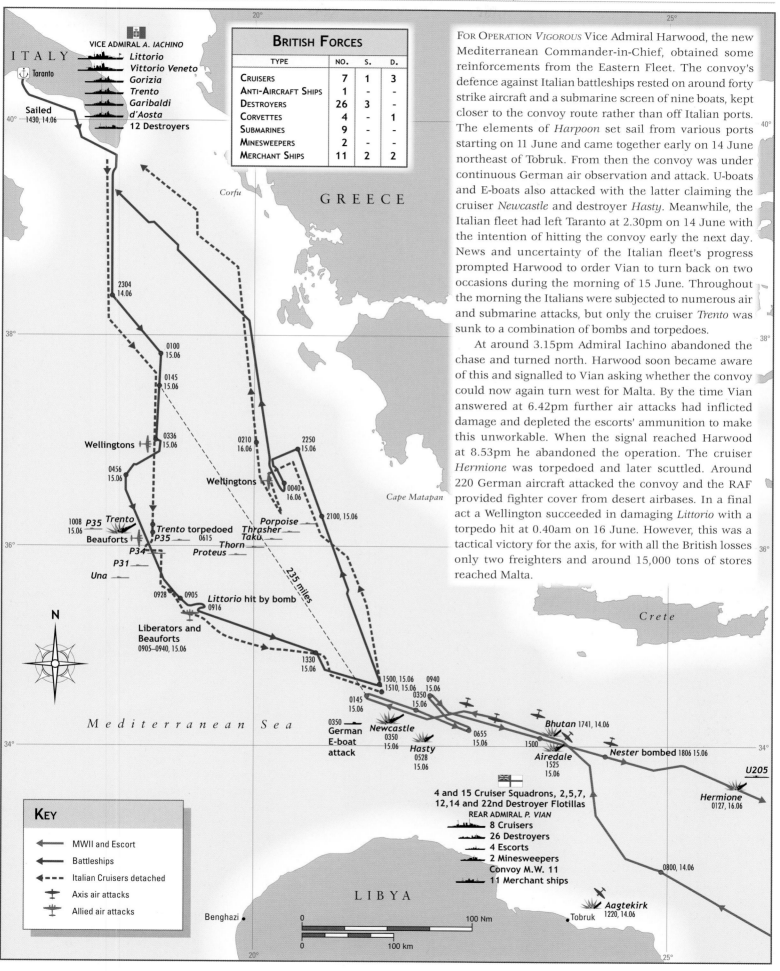

VICE ADMIRAL A. IACHINO
- Littorio
- Vittorio Veneto
- Gorizia
- Trento
- Garibaldi
- d'Aosta
- 12 Destroyers

ITALY

Taranto

Sailed 1430, 14.06

Corfu

GREECE

BRITISH FORCES			
TYPE	NO.	S.	D.
CRUISERS	7	1	3
ANTI-AIRCRAFT SHIPS	1	-	-
DESTROYERS	26	3	-
CORVETTES	4	-	1
SUBMARINES	9	-	-
MINESWEEPERS	2	-	-
MERCHANT SHIPS	11	2	2

For Operation *Vigorous* Vice Admiral Harwood, the new Mediterranean Commander-in-Chief, obtained some reinforcements from the Eastern Fleet. The convoy's defence against Italian battleships rested on around forty strike aircraft and a submarine screen of nine boats, kept closer to the convoy route rather than off Italian ports. The elements of *Harpoon* set sail from various ports starting on 11 June and came together early on 14 June northeast of Tobruk. From then the convoy was under continuous German air observation and attack. U-boats and E-boats also attacked with the latter claiming the cruiser *Newcastle* and destroyer *Hasty*. Meanwhile, the Italian fleet had left Taranto at 2.30pm on 14 June with the intention of hitting the convoy early the next day. News and uncertainty of the Italian fleet's progress prompted Harwood to order Vian to turn back on two occasions during the morning of 15 June. Throughout the morning the Italians were subjected to numerous air and submarine attacks, but only the cruiser *Trento* was sunk to a combination of bombs and torpedoes.

At around 3.15pm Admiral Iachino abandoned the chase and turned north. Harwood soon became aware of this and signalled to Vian asking whether the convoy could now again turn west for Malta. By the time Vian answered at 6.42pm further air attacks had inflicted damage and depleted the escorts' ammunition to make this unworkable. When the signal reached Harwood at 8.53pm he abandoned the operation. The cruiser *Hermione* was torpedoed and later scuttled. Around 220 German aircraft attacked the convoy and the RAF provided fighter cover from desert airbases. In a final act a Wellington succeeded in damaging *Littorio* with a torpedo hit at 0.40am on 16 June. However, this was a tactical victory for the axis, for with all the British losses only two freighters and around 15,000 tons of stores reached Malta.

2304 14.06

0100 15.06

0145 15.06

0336 15.06

Wellingtons

0456 15.06

0210 16.06

2250 15.06

Wellingtons

0040 16.06

Cape Matapan

2100, 15.06

1008 15.06 P35 Trento

Beauforts

Trento torpedoed P35 0615

Porpoise Thrasher Taku

P34

Thorn

P31

Proteus

Una

0928 0905

Littorio hit by bomb 0916

Liberators and Beauforts 0905–0940, 15.06

235 miles

Crete

N

1330 15.06

1500, 15.06 1510, 15.06

0940 15.06

0145 15.06

0350 15.06

Mediterranean Sea

0350 German E-boat attack

Newcastle 0350 15.06

Hasty 0528 15.06

0655 15.06

1500

Bhutan 1741, 14.06

Airedale 1525 15.06

Nester bombed 1806 15.06

U205

Hermione 0127, 16.06

4 and 15 Cruiser Squadrons, 2,5,7, 12,14 and 22nd Destroyer Flotillas

REAR ADMIRAL P. VIAN
- 8 Cruisers
- 26 Destroyers
- 4 Escorts
- 2 Minesweepers
- Convoy M.W. 11
- 11 Merchant ships

0800, 14.06

LIBYA

Benghazi

Tobruk

Aagtekirk 1220, 14.06

KEY

- → MWII and Escort
- → Battleships
- ◄-- Italian Cruisers detached
- ✈ Axis air attacks
- ✈ Allied air attacks

0 100 Nm

0 100 km

129

The Destruction of Convoy PQ 17, July 1942

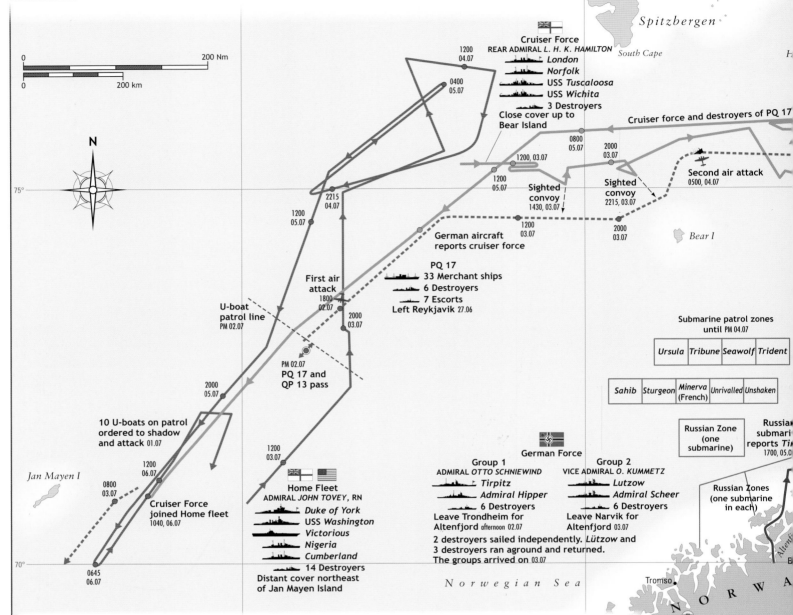

Cruiser Force
REAR ADMIRAL *L. H. K. HAMILTON*
- *London*
- *Norfolk*
- USS *Tuscaloosa*
- USS *Wichita*
- 3 Destroyers
Close cover up to
Bear Island

1200 04.07

0400 05.07

Spitzbergen

South Cape

Cruiser force and destroyers of PQ 17

0800 05.07

2000 03.07

Second air attack 0500, 04.07

1200, 03.07

1200 05.07

Sighted convoy 1430, 03.07

Sighted convoy 2215, 03.07

1200 03.07

2000 03.07

Bear I

German aircraft reports cruiser force

2215 04.07

1200 05.07

PQ 17
- 33 Merchant ships
- 6 Destroyers
- 7 Escorts
Left Reykjavik 27.06

First air attack 1800 02.07

2000 03.07

Submarine patrol zones
until PM 04.07

Ursula	Tribune	Seawolf	Trident

Sahib	Sturgeon	Minerva (French)	Unrivalled	Unshaken

U-boat patrol line PM 02.07

PM 02.07
PQ 17 and QP 13 pass

2000 05.07

Russian Zone (one submarine)

Russian submari reports *Ti*

1700, 05.0

10 U-boats on patrol ordered to shadow and attack 01.07

1200 06.07

1200 03.07

Russian Zones (one submarine in each)

0800 03.07

Jan Mayen I

Cruiser Force joined Home fleet 1040, 06.07

Home Fleet
ADMIRAL *JOHN TOVEY*, RN
- *Duke of York*
- USS *Washington*
- *Victorious*
- *Nigeria*
- *Cumberland*
- 14 Destroyers
Distant cover northeast of Jan Mayen Island

German Force

Group 1
ADMIRAL *OTTO SCHNIEWIND*
- *Tirpitz*
- *Admiral Hipper*
- 6 Destroyers
Leave Trondheim for Altenfjord afternoon 02.07

Group 2
VICE ADMIRAL *O. KUMMETZ*
- *Lutzow*
- *Admiral Scheer*
- 6 Destroyers
Leave Narvik for Altenfjord 03.07

2 destroyers sailed independently. *Lützow* and 3 destroyers ran aground and returned. The groups arrived on 03.07

Altenf

Norwegian Sea

Tromso

N O R W A

Bardufoss

Narvik

0645 06.07

THE DESTRUCTION OF convoy PQ 17 was one of the most significant British defeats in the war. It also demonstrated how dangerous a combination of surface, air and sub-surface attacks was to maritime communications. By July the Germans had assembled a significant force of warships, U-boats and aircraft in northern Norway and intended to attack a convoy in strength. PQ 17 sailed on 27 June and was destined for Archangel, as Murmansk had recently suffered heavy bombing. The receding ice in the summer months allowed a more northerly course around Bear Island to be taken. Its counterpart, QP 13, had lost five ships in its passage and was out of the danger zone by the time PQ 17 entered the most dangerous part of its voyage. On 1 July, German signals intelligence and U-boats had located the convoy and set in motion *Rösselsprung*, the plan for a surface strike, prompting two groups of warships to move up from Trondheim and Narvik to Altenfjord over the next two days.

The Germans were, however, unclear about the exact movements of the various components of the Home Fleet, and so did not attack immediately. On the British side, concern about the German surface force prompted the First Sea Lord, Admiral Pound, just after 9pm on 4 July, to order the convoy's cruiser cover and escorting force to turn back and the merchant ships to scatter. By early 5 July the Germans were aware of this development and sent out the surface force, but an unsuccessful Soviet submarine attack and further indications of a strong allied submarine presence, as well as uncertainty about the Home Fleet's location, prompted the operation to be abandoned. Instead, aircraft and submarines hunted down the individual merchant ships. Twenty-three ships totaling 142,000 tons were sunk against a loss of five German aircraft. The last survivor made it to port on 28 July.

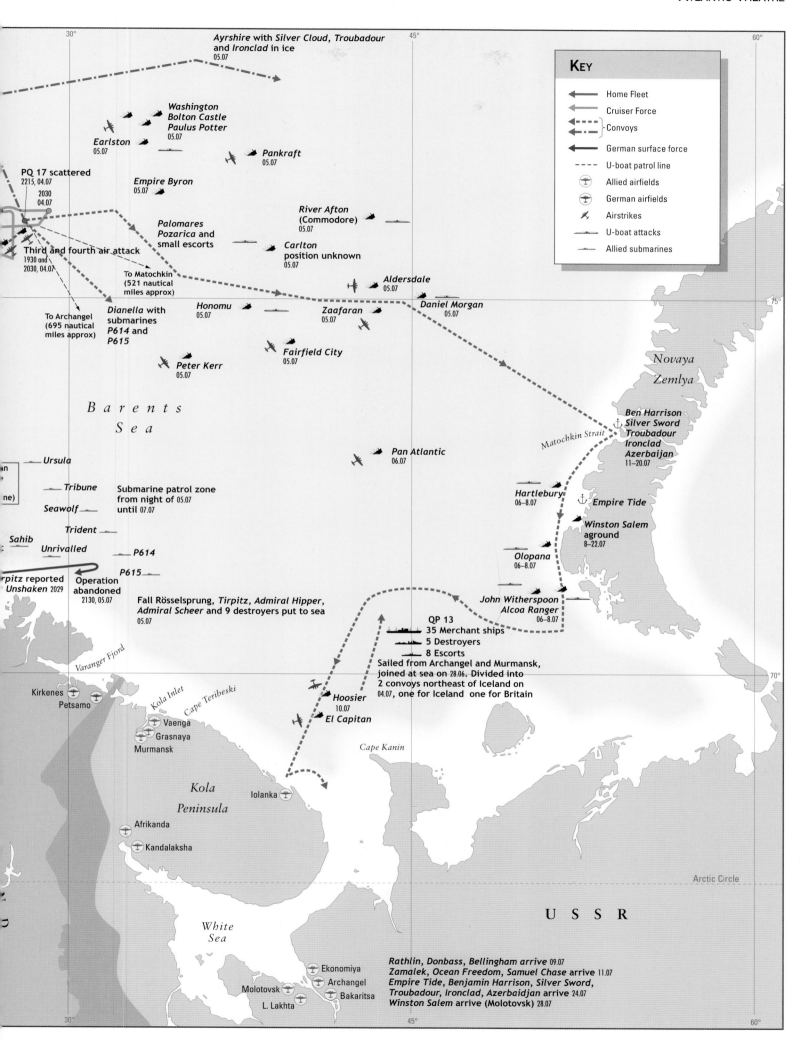

Ayrshire with *Silver Cloud*, *Troubadour* and *Ironclad* in ice
05.07

Washington
Bolton Castle
Paulus Potter
05.07

Earlston
05.07

Pankraft
05.07

Empire Byron
05.07

PQ 17 scattered
2215, 04.07
2030
04.07

River Afton
(Commodore)
05.07

Carlton
position unknown
05.07

Palomares
Pozarica and
small escorts

Third and fourth air attack
1930 and
2030, 04.07

To Matochkin
(521 nautical
miles approx)

To Archangel
(695 nautical
miles approx)

Aldersdale
05.07

Dianella with
submarines
P614 and
P615

Honomu
05.07

Zaafaran
05.07

Daniel Morgan
05.07

Fairfield City
05.07

Peter Kerr
05.07

*Novaya
Zemlya*

*B a r e n t s
S e a*

Pan Atlantic
06.07

*Ben Harrison
Silver Sword
Troubadour
Ironclad
Azerbaijan*
11–20.07

Ursula

Tribune

Submarine patrol zone
from night of 05.07
until 07.07

Seawolf

Trident

Sahib

Unrivalled

P614

P615

Matochkin Strait

Hartlebury
06–8.07

Empire Tide

Winston Salem
aground
8–22.07

Olopana
06–8.07

*John Witherspoon
Alcoa Ranger*
06–8.07

Tirpitz reported
Unshaken 2029

Operation
abandoned
2130, 05.07

Fall Rösselsprung, *Tirpitz*, *Admiral Hipper*,
Admiral Scheer and 9 destroyers put to sea
05.07

QP 13
35 Merchant ships
5 Destroyers
8 Escorts
Sailed from Archangel and Murmansk,
joined at sea on 28.06. Divided into
2 convoys northeast of Iceland on
04.07, one for Iceland one for Britain

Varanger Fjord

Kirkenes
Petsamo

Kola Inlet

Cape Teribeski

Hoosier
10.07

El Capitan

Vaenga
Grasnaya
Murmansk

Cape Kanin

*Kola
Peninsula*

Iolanka

Afrikanda

Kandalaksha

Arctic Circle

U S S R

*White
Sea*

Ekonomiya

Archangel

Molotovsk

Bakaritsa

L. Lakhta

Rathlin, *Donbass*, *Bellingham* arrive 09.07
Zamalek, *Ocean Freedom*, *Samuel Chase* arrive 11.07
Empire Tide, *Benjamin Harrison*, *Silver Sword*,
Troubadour, *Ironclad*, *Azerbaijan* arrive 24.07
Winston Salem arrive (Molotovsk) 28.07

KEY

Home Fleet
Cruiser Force
Convoys
German surface force
U-boat patrol line
Allied airfields
German airfields
Airstrikes
U-boat attacks
Allied submarines

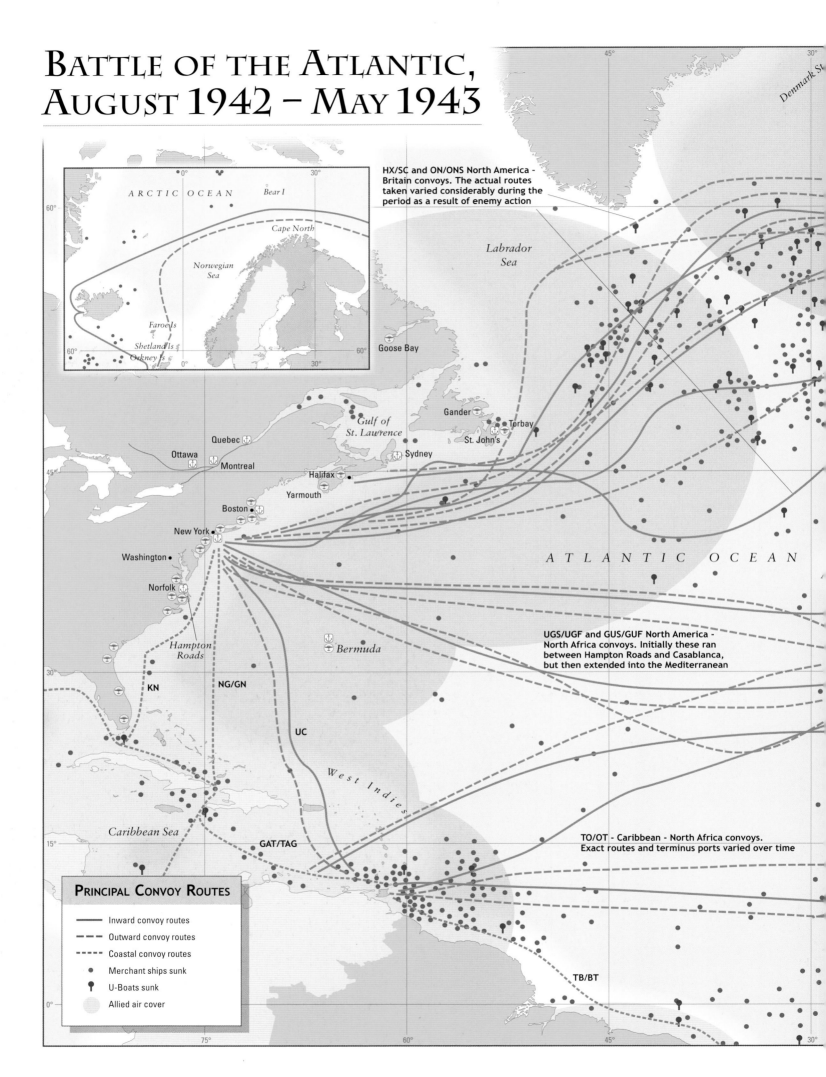

Battle of the Atlantic, August 1942 – May 1943

HX/SC and ON/ONS North America - Britain convoys. The actual routes taken varied considerably during the period as a result of enemy action

UGS/UGF and GUS/GUF North America - North Africa convoys. Initially these ran between Hampton Roads and Casablanca, but then extended into the Mediterranean

TO/OT - Caribbean - North Africa convoys. Exact routes and terminus ports varied over time

ARCTIC OCEAN

Bear I

Cape North

Norwegian Sea

Faroe Is

Shetland Is

Orkney Is

Denmark St

Labrador Sea

Goose Bay

Gander

Torbay

St. John's

Sydney

Quebec

Ottawa

Montreal

Halifax

Yarmouth

Gulf of St. Lawrence

Boston

New York

Washington

Norfolk

Hampton Roads

KN

NG/GN

UC

Bermuda

ATLANTIC OCEAN

West Indies

Caribbean Sea

GAT/TAG

TB/BT

Principal Convoy Routes

— Inward convoy routes

- - - Outward convoy routes

···· Coastal convoy routes

● Merchant ships sunk

⚓ U-Boats sunk

　 Allied air cover

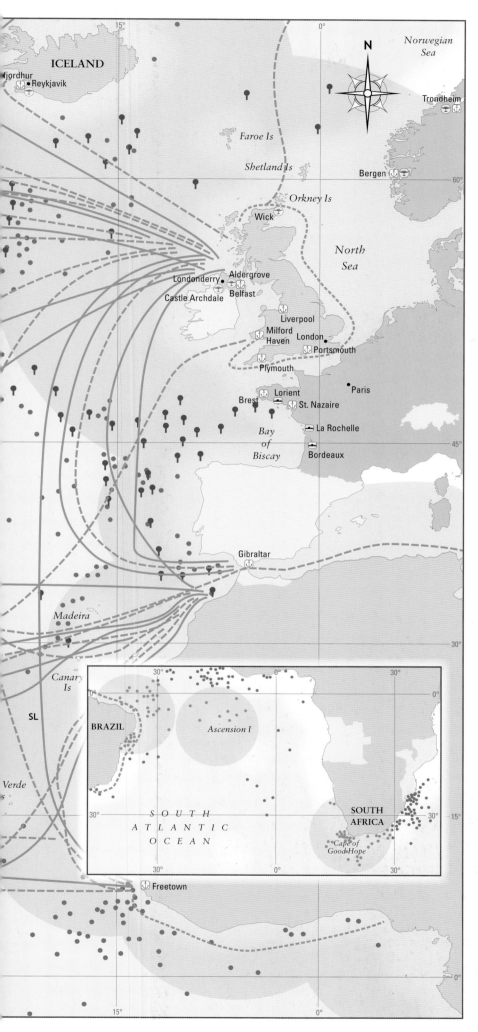

THREE YEARS INTO the war the Atlantic campaign entered its most decisive phase. In June, the U-boats sank 136 ships, the highest monthly score, and in July Admiral Dönitz again focused on the central Atlantic, opening what is sometimes described as the Second Atlantic Campaign. Despite the inflicted losses, two factors had restricted the impact of the German offensive. First, the modest size and slow initial expansion of the U-boat force affected its ability to find and engage convoys. Secondly, throughout 1941 signals intelligence allowed the British to re-route many convoys around U-boat concentrations. By late 1942, U-boat numbers had increased sufficiently to enable the employment of multiple wolfpacks, each consisting of between ten and fifteen boats, to overwhelm convoy defences. For most of the year the allies also had no access to high-grade Enigma traffic.

Despite the heavy allied losses, the Germans too were taking greater casualties and while the ratio of merchant ships to U-boats sunk had been in the region of sixty to one in 1940, by 1942 this dropped to ten to one. There were sufficient escorts to form specialised Support Groups that could reinforce convoys under attack, while better weapons and more Very Long Range aircraft increased the danger to U-boats. Operation *Torch*, and the protracted campaign in French North Africa, placed considerable demands on the allied escort forces and depleted the numbers available on the North Atlantic routes. Consequently, these suffered in early 1943 and the shipping losses reached a crisis point in March. Success and failure were closely linked as, within two months, the German offensive had collapsed.

As the threat of German auxiliary cruisers operating in distant waters receded so that of the U-boats increased. Previous German attempts at operating U-boats in the South Atlantic had been foiled by the destruction of their supply ships. From October, a small number of large, long-range boats operated in the Cape area and were able to sink a number of ships including liners used as troop transports, and freighters carrying military cargoes. Pressed in the North Atlantic, the allies could only send limited reinforcements and were spared greater losses only because of the limited German boats committed. In early 1943, only seven U-boats operated between the Caribbean and the Cape. In February, four boats and a tanker were sent out to operate off South Africa and into the Indian Ocean. While the allies had improved convoy defences around the Cape, the U-boats found ample shipping off East Africa to sink.

MERCHANT SHIPS AND U-BOATS LOST (ALL THEATRES AND CAUSES)			
	TONNAGE	SHIPS	U-BOATS
1942			
AUGUST	661,133	123	11
SEPTEMBER	567,327	114	12
OCTOBER	637,833	101	16
NOVEMBER	807,754	134	14
DECEMBER	348,902	73	5
1943			
JANUARY	261,359	50	6
FEBRUARY	403,062	73	20
MARCH	693,389	120	18
APRIL	344,680	64	15
MAY	299,428	58	41

OPERATION PEDESTAL, 10–15 AUGUST 1942

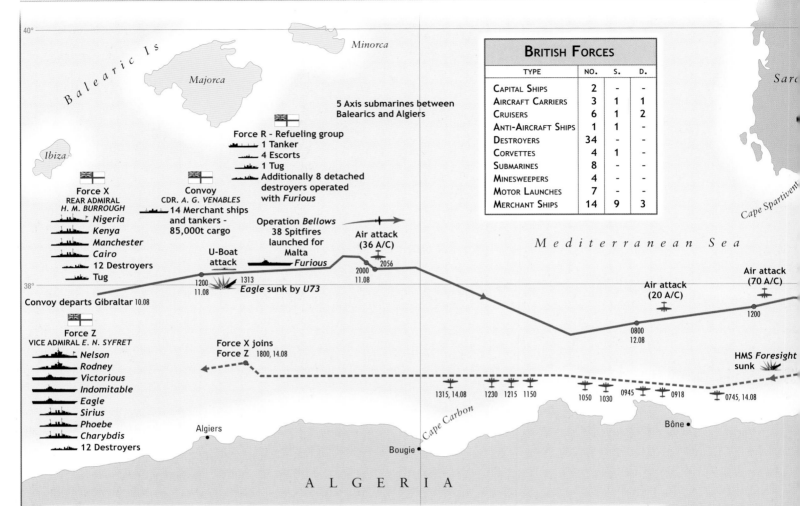

Balearic Is

Minorca

Majorca

Ibiza

5 Axis submarines between Balearics and Algiers

Force R - Refueling group
- 1 Tanker
- 4 Escorts
- 1 Tug
- Additionally 8 detached destroyers operated with *Furious*

Force X
REAR ADMIRAL
H. M. BURROUGH
- *Nigeria*
- *Kenya*
- *Manchester*
- *Cairo*
- 12 Destroyers
- Tug

Convoy
CDR. A. G. VENABLES
- 14 Merchant ships and tankers - 85,000t cargo

U-Boat attack

Operation *Bellows*
38 Spitfires launched for Malta

Furious

Air attack (36 A/C)

2056

2000
11.08

1200
11.08

1313
11.08

Eagle sunk by *U73*

Convoy departs Gibraltar 10.08

Force Z
VICE ADMIRAL *E. N. SYFRET*
- *Nelson*
- *Rodney*
- *Victorious*
- *Indomitable*
- *Eagle*
- *Sirius*
- *Phoebe*
- *Charybdis*
- 12 Destroyers

Force X joins Force Z 1800, 14.08

Algiers

Mediterranean Sea

Air attack (20 A/C)

Air attack (70 A/C)

0800
12.08

1200

HMS *Foresight* sunk

1315, 14.08   1230 1215 1150   1050 1030   0945   0918   0745, 14.08

Cape Carbon

Bougie •

Bône •

ALGERIA

Cape Spartivent

Sar

BRITISH FORCES			
TYPE	NO.	S.	D.
CAPITAL SHIPS	2	-	-
AIRCRAFT CARRIERS	3	1	1
CRUISERS	6	1	2
ANTI-AIRCRAFT SHIPS	1	1	-
DESTROYERS	34	-	-
CORVETTES	4	1	-
SUBMARINES	8	-	-
MINESWEEPERS	4	-	-
MOTOR LAUNCHES	7	-	-
MERCHANT SHIPS	14	9	3

AFTER THE *HARPOON/VIGOROUS* operations another convoy for Malta was urgently required. The experience of *Vigorous* in 'bomb alley' between Crete and Africa precluded a further convoy from the east and instead *Pedestal* would be a heavily escorted one from the west. A dummy convoy from Alexandria and bombardment of Rhodes was planned as a diversion. An unprecedented four carriers were involved, three to provide air cover while the fourth, *Glorious*, carried Spitfires for Malta. Between them the *Victorious*, *Indomitable* and *Eagle* embarked seventy-two fighters and twenty-eight strike aircraft. In fact, a fifth carrier, *Argus*, was also at Gibraltar. This concentration was only possible because the arctic convoys were suspended after PQ17, freeing up Home Fleet ships, while the Japanese defeat at Midway allowed a reduction in the Indian Ocean. Most of the convoy forces assembled at Scapa Flow on 27 July sailed south on 2 August and passed through the Straits of Gibraltar on 10 August. Other ships joined from Freetown and Gibraltar.

The main operation got off to a bad start when in the middle of *Furious*'s fly-off operation, on 11 August, *Eagle* was sunk by a salvo of four torpedoes fired by *U73* from within the destroyer screen. The very large German air attacks on 12 August inflicted some damage, but the operation proceeded reasonably well until Force Z turned back at 7pm. Then very quickly the situation deteriorated under axis air and submarine attack. The

Italian submarine *Axum* succeeded in blowing the stern off the cruiser *Cairo* requiring her to be scuttled, and damaged *Nigeria*, forcing her to return to Gibraltar, and Burrough to move to the destroyer *Ashanti*. Then an air attack by twenty Ju88 cost two merchant ships and another submarine, and the *Alagi* torpedoed and damaged the cruiser *Nigeria*. Had the Italian warships entered the action that night further heavy losses would have ensued. Fortuitously for the British, Italo-German disagreements over air cover delayed this part of the operation and Italian concerns about the diversionary British raids then deflected attention to the east.

Just after midnight the convoy passed Cape Bon and into the area in which German and Italian torpedo boats were waiting. The first ship hit was the cruiser *Manchester* that later had to be abandoned. Five freighters were also lost. Throughout the morning of 13 August what remained of the convoy endured further air attacks, although the air cover from Malta increasingly improved. At 2.30pm a force of minesweepers and launches came out from Malta to cover the three merchant ships and tow the tanker *Ohio* to Valetta. A fifth ship arrived later, and in total 15,000 tons of fuel and 32,000 tons of stores were discharged. Force X turned west and used the night to pass back through the narrows, but was again attacked by Sardinian-based aircraft before joining up with Force Z and arriving at Gibraltar at 6pm on 15 August.

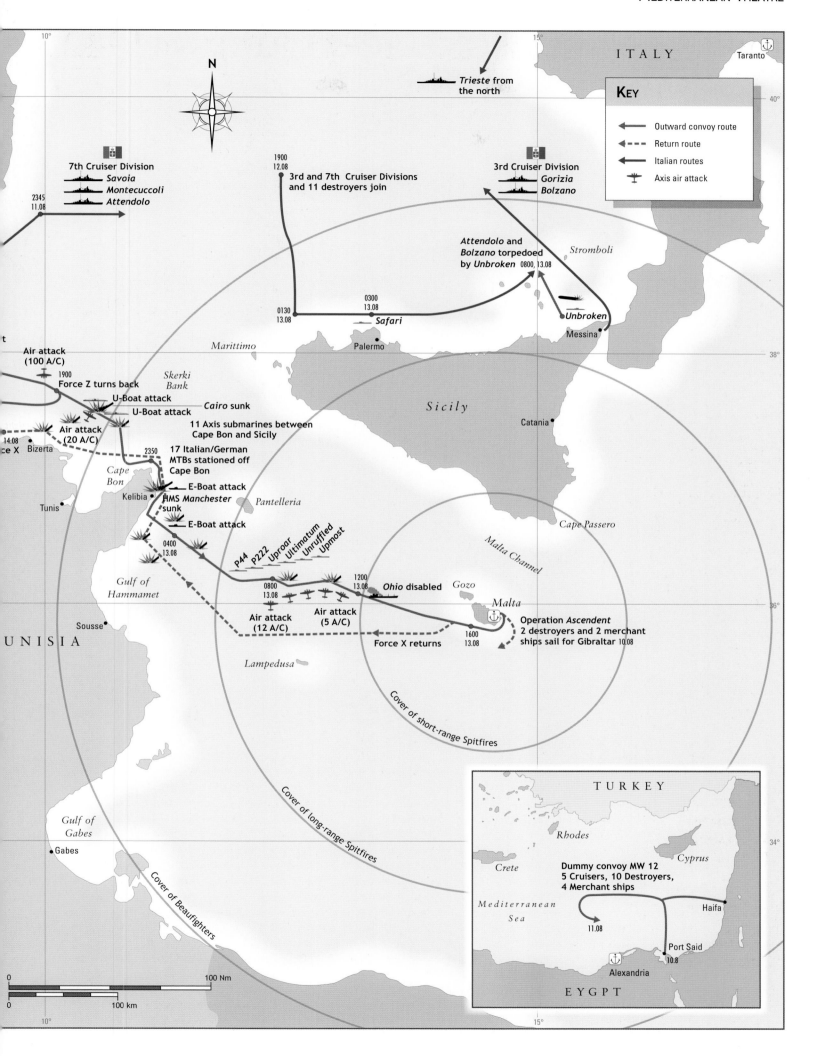

ITALY

Taranto

Trieste from the north

7th Cruiser Division
Savoia
Montecuccoli
Attendolo

2345
11.08

N

1900
12.08

3rd and 7th Cruiser Divisions and 11 destroyers join

3rd Cruiser Division
Gorizia
Bolzano

KEY

← Outward convoy route
◀--- Return route
◀ Italian routes
✈ Axis air attack

Stromboli

Attendolo and *Bolzano* torpedoed by *Unbroken* 0800, 13.08

0130
13.08

0300
13.08

Safari

Unbroken

Messina

Marittimo

Palermo

Air attack
(100 A/C)

1900
Force Z turns back

Skerki Bank

U-Boat attack

Sicily

Catania

Cairo sunk

U-Boat attack

Air attack
(20 A/C)

14.08

ce X

Bizerta

2350

11 Axis submarines between Cape Bon and Sicily

17 Italian/German MTBs stationed off Cape Bon

Cape Bon

Kelibia

E-Boat attack

HMS *Manchester* sunk

Pantelleria

Tunis

E-Boat attack

Cape Passero

0400
13.08

P44 P222 *Uproar Ultimatum Unruffled Upmost*

Malta Channel

1200
13.08

Ohio disabled

Gozo

Malta

Operation *Ascendent* 2 destroyers and 2 merchant ships sail for Gibraltar 10.08

Gulf of Hammamet

0800
13.08

Air attack
(12 A/C)

Air attack
(5 A/C)

Force X returns

1600
13.08

Cover of short-range Spitfires

Sousse

TUNISIA

Lampedusa

Gulf of Gabes

Gabes

Cover of long-range Spitfires

Cover of Beaufighters

TURKEY

Rhodes

Crete

Cyprus

Dummy convoy MW 12 5 Cruisers, 10 Destroyers, 4 Merchant ships

Mediterranean Sea

Haifa

11.08

Port Said
10.8

Alexandria

EYGPT

0   100 Nm

0   100 km

British Naval Signals Intelligence

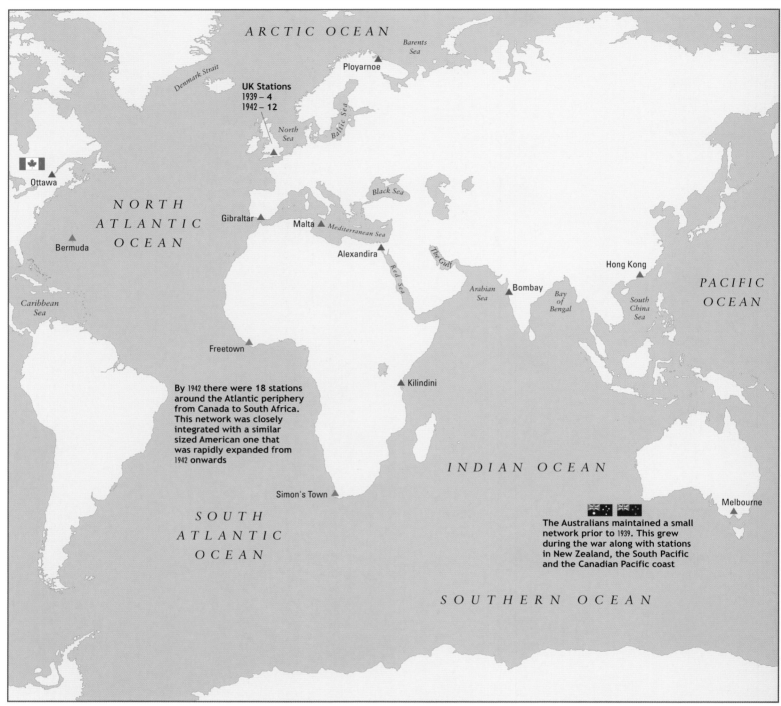

UK Stations
1939 – 4
1942 – 12

Ployarnoe

By 1942 there were 18 stations around the Atlantic periphery from Canada to South Africa. This network was closely integrated with a similar sized American one that was rapidly expanded from 1942 onwards

The Australians maintained a small network prior to 1939. This grew during the war along with stations in New Zealand, the South Pacific and the Canadian Pacific coast

MAIN LISTENING POSTS/HIGH-FREQUENCY/DIRECTION

▲ Original prewar stations

▲ Atlantic network extension, 1939/40

▲ Wartime extension, main stations only

THROUGHOUT THE WAR signals intelligence increasingly played a central role in the planning and execution of naval operations. Although this source of intelligence gathering had been developed in the First World War, and all major powers employed it during peacetime to gather information on foreign operations and developments, it was widely assumed that its utility in the coming war would be negligible as naval forces at sea would simply stop using radio communication, or at least curtail its use. In fact, the opposite occurred and from September 1939 the volume of radio communications grew rapidly in all navies. The advantages radio communications offered for the command and control of forces exceeded the dangers that its use could bring to compromise the location of forces. Effective air and submarine operations were indeed completely dependent on its use.

The two main types of information derived from signals intelligence were, first, the reading of encrypted enemy signals by means of cryptanalysis (Ultra) and, secondly, locating the position of enemy units by means of radio direction-finding. Throughout the war High-Frequency Direction Finding (HF/DF), both from land and sea, was significantly enhanced and was one of the key components in the defeat of the U-boats. The British began the war with a fairly small network and initially focused its expansion on the Atlantic theatre as this was the most likely area in which German commerce raiders would operate. As the war became global, the network was increased and was operated by around 2,100 personnel alongside the thousands who worked in cryptanalysis at Bletchley Park and elsewhere.

THE KRIEGSMARINE'S B-DIENST NETWORK

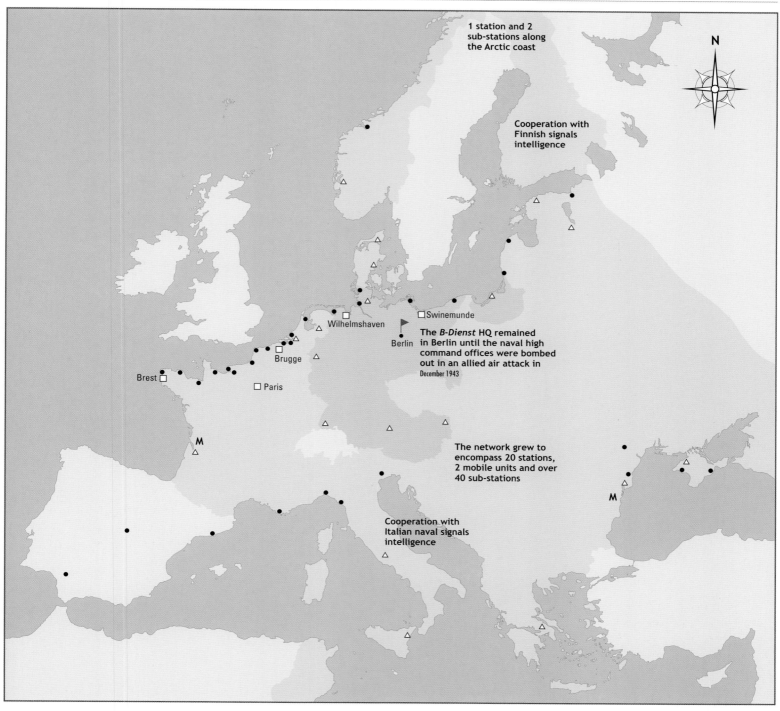

1 station and 2
sub-stations along
the Arctic coast

Cooperation with
Finnish signals
intelligence

□Swinemunde

▶ Berlin

The *B-Dienst* HQ remained
in Berlin until the naval high
command offices were bombed
out in an allied air attack in
December 1943

□ Wilhelmshaven

Brugge

Brest □

□ Paris

The network grew to
encompass 20 stations,
2 mobile units and over
40 sub-stations

Cooperation with
Italian naval signals
intelligence

ALONGSIDE THE BRITISH, the Germans were pioneers in the development of signals intelligence. Between the wars the navy continued to invest in the *B-Dienst* (Beobachtungs-Dienst or Observation Service). Most of the work was devoted to deciphering and reading British naval traffic and at the beginning of the war all existing British, French and Soviet code systems could be read. In January 1940, a copy of the British Merchant Navy Code was obtained, enabling a better observation of allied shipping movements. Throughout the invasions of Norway and France the *B-Dienst* was instrumental in shaping German naval operations with a third to a half of all Royal Navy signals being read.

It was in the battle of the Atlantic that signals intelligence proved most valuable and until 1943 the Germans had the advantage. In the first phases of the

campaign it enabled Admiral Dönitz to make the most of his comparatively small U-boat force. An extensive network of listening posts was established from the Arctic to the Mediterranean and from the Atlantic to the Black Sea. At its height, the *B-Dienst* employed around 8,000 personnel. By 1941 nearly all British naval and shipping traffic was being read and providing advanced warning of convoy movements. This continued, with small variations, until 1943. The situation changed that June with the introduction of Naval Cypher 5 and the increased use of Typex electro-mechanical encryption machines by the allies. These were similar to the German Enigma, but unlike the allies the Germans did not have the resources available to decipher Typex traffic and their overall ability to observe allied movements declined.

KEY

□   Regional sigint HQ

△   HF/DF station

●   Sub-station

M   Mobile unit

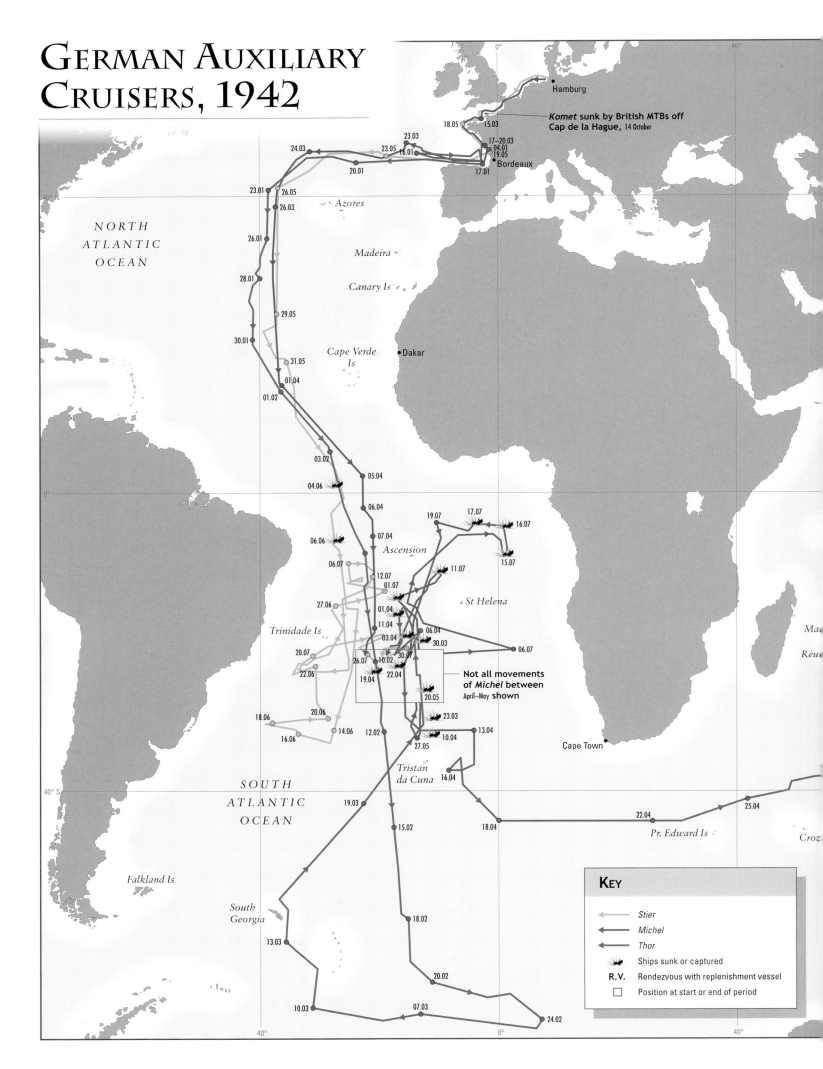

GERMAN AUXILIARY CRUISERS, 1942

Hamburg

Komet sunk by British MTBs off
Cap de la Hague, 14 October

18.05   15.03

17–20.03
04.01
19.05

17.01   Bordeaux

23.03
24.03   23.05   16.01
20.01

23.01   26.05

Azores

NORTH
ATLANTIC
OCEAN

26.03

26.01

Madeira

28.01

Canary Is

29.05

30.01

*Cape Verde
Is*   Dakar

31.05

01.04

01.02

03.02

05.04

04.06

06.04

06.06   07.04

Ascension

19.07   17.07   16.07

15.07

06.07   11.07

12.07
01.07

27.06   01.04   *St Helena*

11.04

06.04
03.04   30.03

20.07   26.07   10.02   30.07   06.07

22.06   19.04   22.04   **Not all movements
of *Michel* between
April–May shown**

Trinidade Is   20.05

18.06   20.06   23.03

16.06   14.06   12.02   13.04

10.04
27.05

*Tristan
da Cuna*   16.04

SOUTH
ATLANTIC   19.03

OCEAN   15.02   18.04   22.04   25.04

Pr. Edward Is   Croz

Cape Town

Ma

Réu

Falkland Is

*South
Georgia*   18.02

13.03   20.02

10.03   07.03   24.02

KEY

→	*Stier*
→	*Michel*
→	*Thor*
💥	Ships sunk or captured
R.V.	Rendezvous with replenishment vessel
☐	Position at start or end of period

0°   40°

40° N

0°

40° S

40°   0°   40°

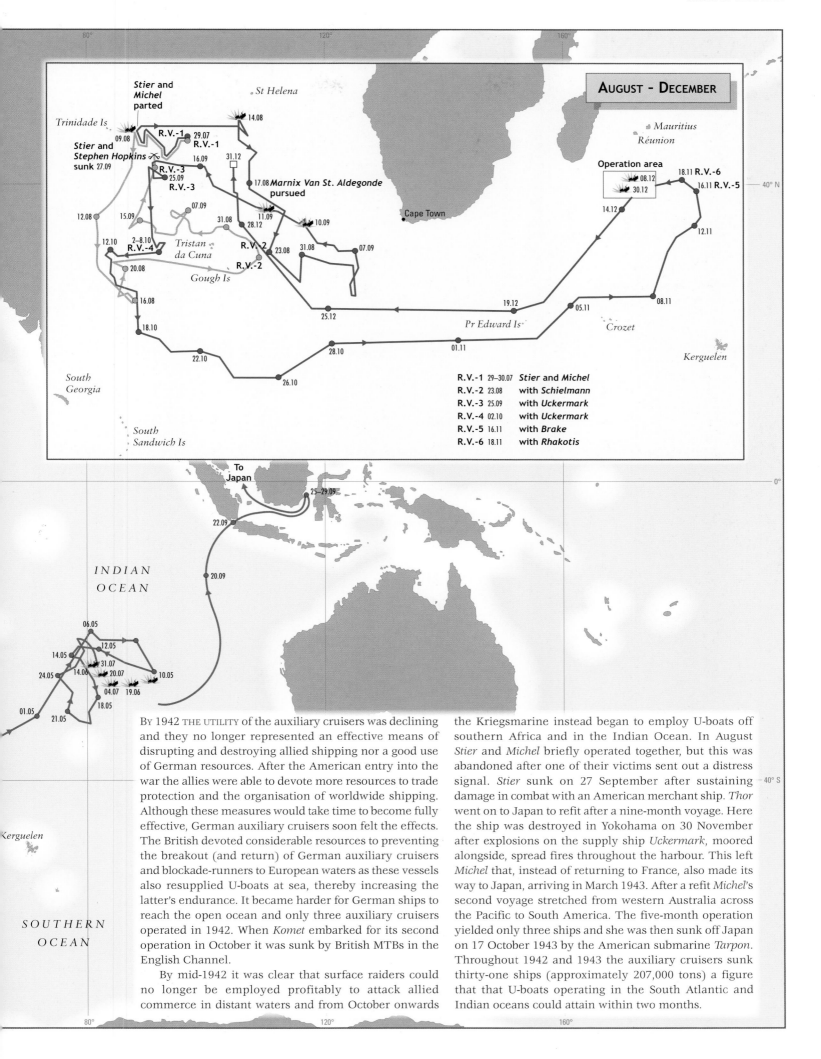

AUGUST - DECEMBER

Stier and Michel parted

Trinidade Is

Stier and Stephen Hopkins sunk 27.09

09.08

R.V.-1 29.07
R.V.-1

14.08

St Helena

Mauritius
Réunion

16.09

31.12

Operation area

08.12
30.12

18.11 R.V.-6
16.11 R.V.-5

40° N

R.V.-3 25.09
R.V.-3

17.08 Marnix Van St. Aldegonde pursued

14.12

12.11

12.08   15.09

07.09

31.08

11.09
28.12

10.09

Cape Town

2–8.10
R.V.-4

Tristan da Cuna

R.V.-2
R.V.-2

23.08   31.08

07.09

31.08

12.10

20.08

Gough Is

19.12

05.11

08.11

16.08

25.12

Pr Edward Is

Crozet

18.10

01.11

Kerguelen

South Georgia

22.10

28.10

26.10

R.V.-1 29–30.07 *Stier* and *Michel*
R.V.-2 23.08   with *Schielmann*
R.V.-3 25.09   with *Uckermark*
R.V.-4 02.10   with *Uckermark*
R.V.-5 16.11   with *Brake*
R.V.-6 18.11   with *Rhakotis*

South Sandwich Is

To Japan

25–29.09

22.09

INDIAN OCEAN

20.09

06.05

12.05

14.05   31.07

24.05   14.08   20.07

04.07   19.06   10.05

18.05

01.05   21.05

Kerguelen

SOUTHERN OCEAN

BY 1942 THE UTILITY of the auxiliary cruisers was declining and they no longer represented an effective means of disrupting and destroying allied shipping nor a good use of German resources. After the American entry into the war the allies were able to devote more resources to trade protection and the organisation of worldwide shipping. Although these measures would take time to become fully effective, German auxiliary cruisers soon felt the effects. The British devoted considerable resources to preventing the breakout (and return) of German auxiliary cruisers and blockade-runners to European waters as these vessels also resupplied U-boats at sea, thereby increasing the latter's endurance. It became harder for German ships to reach the open ocean and only three auxiliary cruisers operated in 1942. When *Komet* embarked for its second operation in October it was sunk by British MTBs in the English Channel.

By mid-1942 it was clear that surface raiders could no longer be employed profitably to attack allied commerce in distant waters and from October onwards

the Kriegsmarine instead began to employ U-boats off southern Africa and in the Indian Ocean. In August *Stier* and *Michel* briefly operated together, but this was abandoned after one of their victims sent out a distress signal. *Stier* sunk on 27 September after sustaining damage in combat with an American merchant ship. *Thor* went on to Japan to refit after a nine-month voyage. Here the ship was destroyed in Yokohama on 30 November after explosions on the supply ship *Uckermark*, moored alongside, spread fires throughout the harbour. This left *Michel* that, instead of returning to France, also made its way to Japan, arriving in March 1943. After a refit *Michel*'s second voyage stretched from western Australia across the Pacific to South America. The five-month operation yielded only three ships and she was then sunk off Japan on 17 October 1943 by the American submarine *Tarpon*. Throughout 1942 and 1943 the auxiliary cruisers sunk thirty-one ships (approximately 207,000 tons) a figure that that U-boats operating in the South Atlantic and Indian oceans could attain within two months.

AMERICAN STRATEGY IN THE PACIFIC, 1942–45

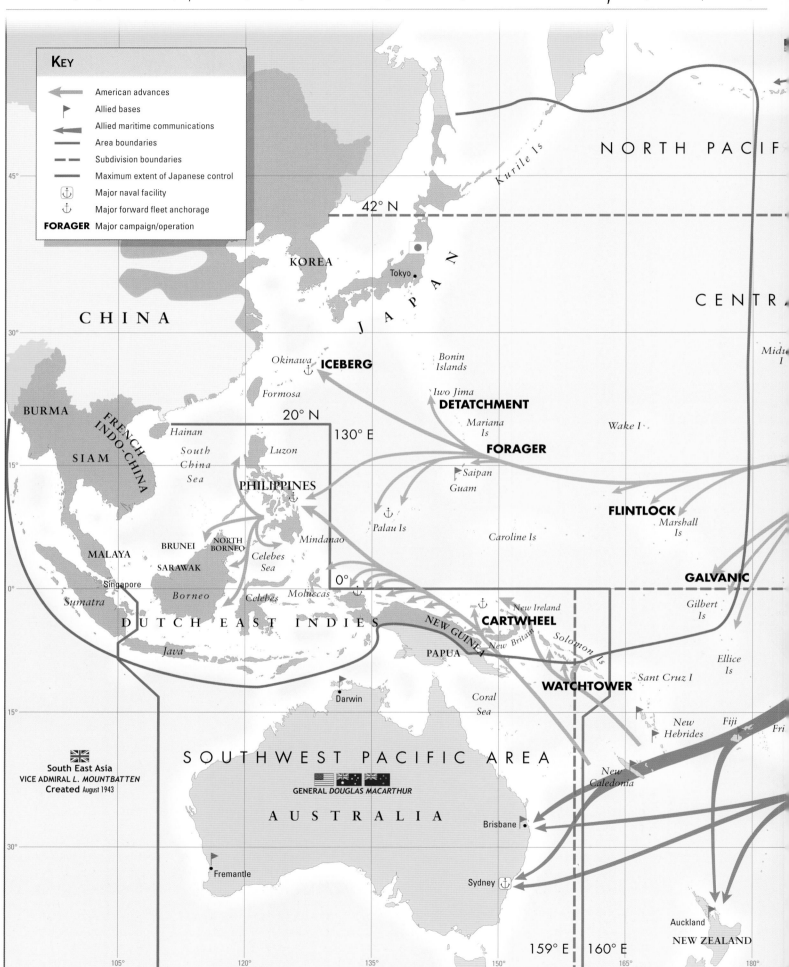

KEY

←	American advances
▷	Allied bases
←	Allied maritime communications
—	Area boundaries
– –	Subdivision boundaries
—	Maximum extent of Japanese control
⚓	Major naval facility
⚓	Major forward fleet anchorage
FORAGER	Major campaign/operation

NORTH PACIFIC

CENTR

Kurile Is

45°

42° N

KOREA

JAPAN

Tokyo

30°

CHINA

Midu
I

Okinawa **ICEBERG**

*Bonin
Islands*

Formosa

Iwo Jima **DETACHMENT**

20° N

BURMA

FRENCH INDO-CHINA

*Mariana
Is*

Wake I

Hainan

130° E

SIAM

*South
China
Sea*

Luzon

FORAGER

15°

Saipan
Guam

PHILIPPINES

FLINTLOCK
*Marshall
Is*

MALAYA

BRUNEI

NORTH BORNEO

Mindanao

Palau Is

Caroline Is

SARAWAK

*Celebes
Sea*

Singapore

0°

GALVANIC

Sumatra

Borneo

Celebes

Moluccas

NEW GUINEA

CARTWHEEL

New Ireland

*Gilbert
Is*

DUTCH EAST INDIES

New Britain

Solomon Is

*Ellice
Is*

Java

PAPUA

WATCHTOWER

Sant Cruz I

15°

Darwin

*Coral
Sea*

*New
Hebrides*

Fiji

Fri

SOUTHWEST PACIFIC AREA

🇬🇧
South East Asia
VICE ADMIRAL *L. MOUNTBATTEN*
Created August 1943

🇺🇸🇦🇺🇦🇺
GENERAL *DOUGLAS MACARTHUR*

*New
Caledonia*

AUSTRALIA

Brisbane

30°

Fremantle

Sydney

Auckland

159° E 160° E

NEW ZEALAND

105° 120° 135° 150° 165° 180°

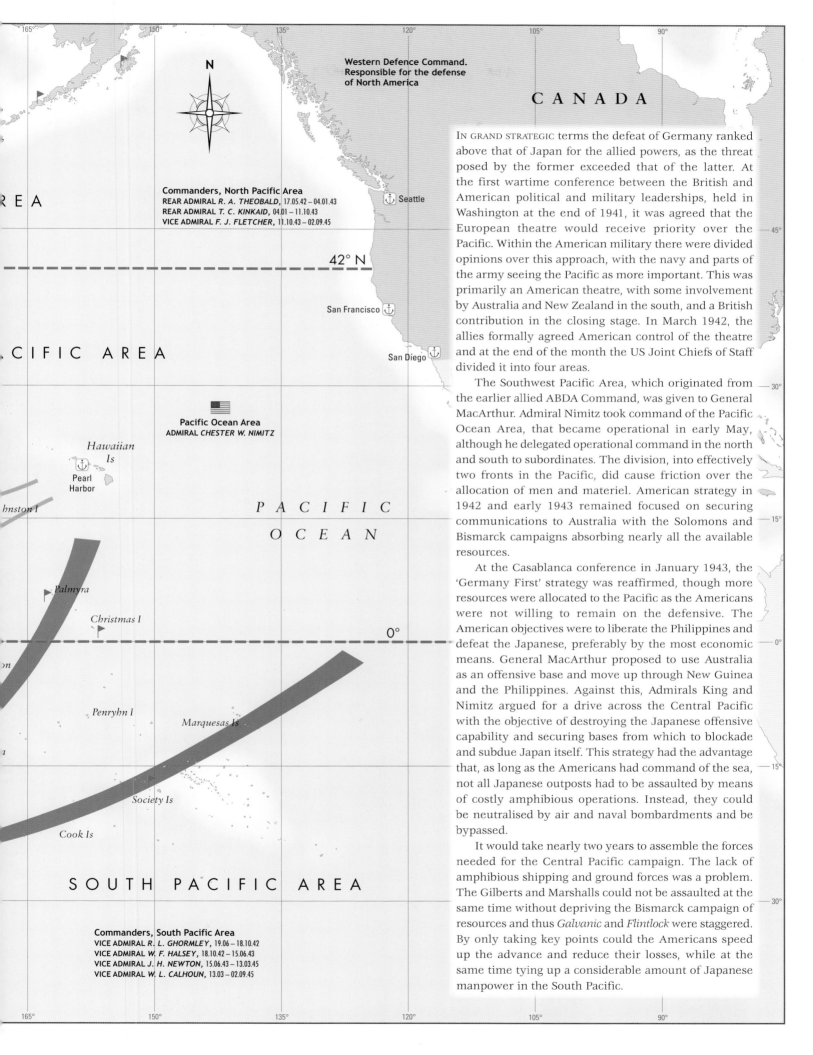

Western Defence Command.
Responsible for the defense
of North America

CANADA

Commanders, North Pacific Area
REAR ADMIRAL *R. A. THEOBALD*, 17.05.42 – 04.01.43
REAR ADMIRAL *T. C. KINKAID*, 04.01 – 11.10.43
VICE ADMIRAL *F. J. FLETCHER*, 11.10.43 – 02.09.45

Seattle

42° N

San Francisco

San Diego

Pacific Ocean Area
ADMIRAL *CHESTER W. NIMITZ*

Hawaiian Is
Pearl Harbor

Johnston I

P A C I F I C

O C E A N

Palmyra

Christmas I

0°

Penryhn I

Marquesas Is

Society Is

Cook Is

S O U T H   P A C I F I C   A R E A

Commanders, South Pacific Area
VICE ADMIRAL *R. L. GHORMLEY*, 19.06 – 18.10.42
VICE ADMIRAL *W. F. HALSEY*, 18.10.42 – 15.06.43
VICE ADMIRAL *J. H. NEWTON*, 15.06.43 – 13.03.45
VICE ADMIRAL *W. L. CALHOUN*, 13.03 – 02.09.45

IN GRAND STRATEGIC terms the defeat of Germany ranked above that of Japan for the allied powers, as the threat posed by the former exceeded that of the latter. At the first wartime conference between the British and American political and military leaderships, held in Washington at the end of 1941, it was agreed that the European theatre would receive priority over the Pacific. Within the American military there were divided opinions over this approach, with the navy and parts of the army seeing the Pacific as more important. This was primarily an American theatre, with some involvement by Australia and New Zealand in the south, and a British contribution in the closing stage. In March 1942, the allies formally agreed American control of the theatre and at the end of the month the US Joint Chiefs of Staff divided it into four areas.

The Southwest Pacific Area, which originated from the earlier allied ABDA Command, was given to General MacArthur. Admiral Nimitz took command of the Pacific Ocean Area, that became operational in early May, although he delegated operational command in the north and south to subordinates. The division, into effectively two fronts in the Pacific, did cause friction over the allocation of men and materiel. American strategy in 1942 and early 1943 remained focused on securing communications to Australia with the Solomons and Bismarck campaigns absorbing nearly all the available resources.

At the Casablanca conference in January 1943, the 'Germany First' strategy was reaffirmed, though more resources were allocated to the Pacific as the Americans were not willing to remain on the defensive. The American objectives were to liberate the Philippines and defeat the Japanese, preferably by the most economic means. General MacArthur proposed to use Australia as an offensive base and move up through New Guinea and the Philippines. Against this, Admirals King and Nimitz argued for a drive across the Central Pacific with the objective of destroying the Japanese offensive capability and securing bases from which to blockade and subdue Japan itself. This strategy had the advantage that, as long as the Americans had command of the sea, not all Japanese outposts had to be assaulted by means of costly amphibious operations. Instead, they could be neutralised by air and naval bombardments and be bypassed.

It would take nearly two years to assemble the forces needed for the Central Pacific campaign. The lack of amphibious shipping and ground forces was a problem. The Gilberts and Marshalls could not be assaulted at the same time without depriving the Bismarck campaign of resources and thus *Galvanic* and *Flintlock* were staggered. By only taking key points could the Americans speed up the advance and reduce their losses, while at the same time tying up a considerable amount of Japanese manpower in the South Pacific.

THE GUADALCANAL CAMPAIGN, AUGUST 1942 – FEBRUARY 1943

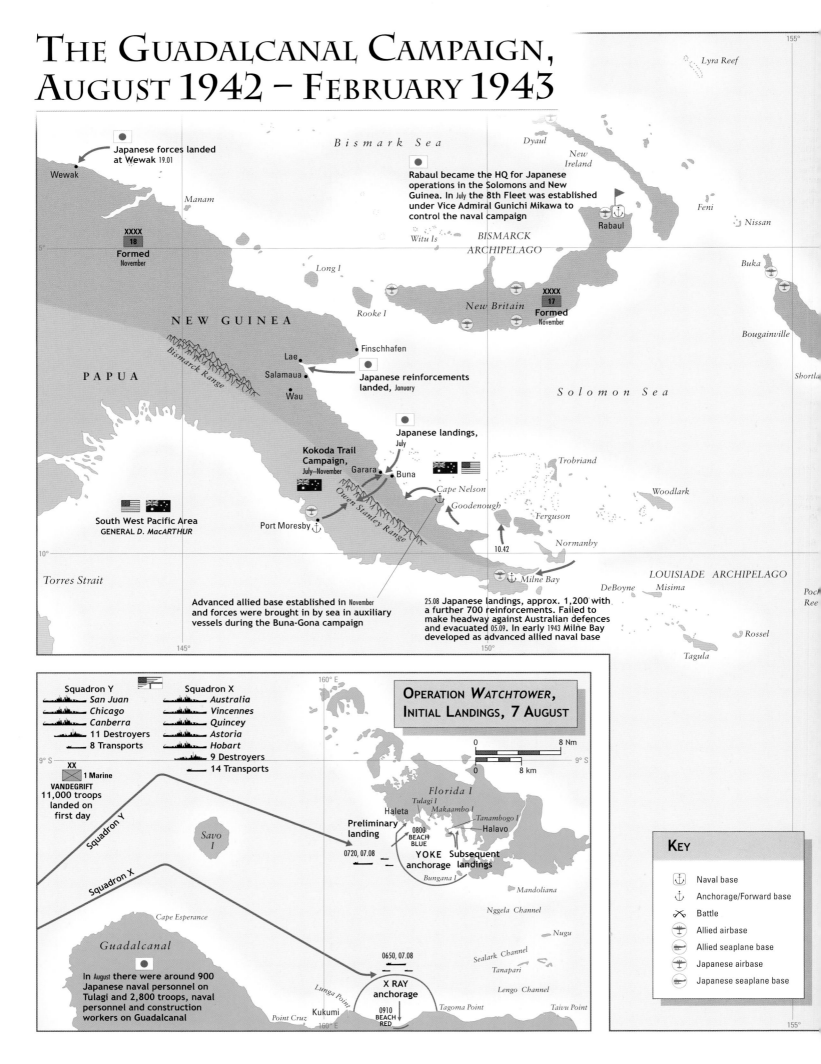

Bismarck Sea

Japanese forces landed at Wewak 19.01

Wewak

Dyaul

New Ireland

Manam

Feni

Nissan

Rabaul became the HQ for Japanese operations in the Solomons and New Guinea. In July the 8th Fleet was established under Vice Admiral Gunichi Mikawa to control the naval campaign

Rabaul

Witu Is

BISMARCK ARCHIPELAGO

Buka

XXXX 18 Formed November

Long I

Rooke I

NEW GUINEA

Bismarck Range

New Britain

XXXX 17 Formed November

Bougainville

Finschhafen

Lae

Salamaua

Japanese reinforcements landed, January

Wau

Solomon Sea

Shortla

PAPUA

Kokoda Trail Campaign, July–November

Garara

Japanese landings, July

Buna

Trobriand

Woodlark

Cape Nelson

Owen Stanley Range

Goodenough

Ferguson

Port Moresby

South West Pacific Area GENERAL D. MacARTHUR

Normanby

10.42

Torres Strait

Milne Bay

LOUISIADE ARCHIPELAGO

DeBoyne

Misima

Poc Ree

Advanced allied base established in November **and forces were brought in by sea in auxiliary vessels during the Buna-Gona campaign**

25.08 **Japanese landings, approx. 1,200 with a further 700 reinforcements. Failed to make headway against Australian defences and evacuated 05.09. In early 1943 Milne Bay developed as advanced allied naval base**

Rossel

Tagula

Squadron Y
— San Juan
— Chicago
— Canberra
— 11 Destroyers
— 8 Transports

Squadron X
— Australia
— Vincennes
— Quincey
— Astoria
— Hobart
— 9 Destroyers
— 14 Transports

160° E

OPERATION WATCHTOWER, INITIAL LANDINGS, 7 AUGUST

0 ___ 8 Nm
0 ___ 8 km

9° S

9° S

XX 1 Marine VANDEGRIFT 11,000 troops landed on first day

Squadron Y

Squadron X

Savo I

Florida I

Tulagi I

Makaambo I

Haleta

Halavo

Tanambogo I

Preliminary landing

0800 BEACH BLUE

0720, 07.08

YOKE anchorage

Subsequent landings

Bungana I

Mandoliana

Nggela Channel

Cape Esperance

Nugu

Guadalcanal

0650, 07.08

X RAY anchorage

Sealark Channel

Tanapari

In August there were around 900 Japanese naval personnel on Tulagi and 2,800 troops, naval personnel and construction workers on Guadalcanal

Lunga Point

Kukumi

Point Cruz

0910 BEACH RED

Lengo Channel

Tagoma Point

Taivu Point

160° E

KEY

⚓ Naval base

⚓ Anchorage/Forward base

✕ Battle

✈ Allied airbase

✈ Allied seaplane base

✈ Japanese airbase

✈ Japanese seaplane base

155°

155°

Lyra Reef

Lyra Reef

160°

165°

IN MAY, JAPANESE naval forces landed on Tulagi to establish a seaplane base, and in the following month more troops and construction workers landed on the neighbouring island of Guadalcanal and began the construction of a large airbase. The southern Solomon Islands were sparsely populated and on the fringes of Japanese controlled territory, but from these bases the Japanese could threaten American maritime communications with Australia and New Zealand. In addition, they provided forward defence to the extensive base facilities being constructed around Rabaul on New Britain. In response, Admiral King, with the support of General Marshall, proposed that American forces undertake a major operation to eject the Japanese from the South Pacific. In the first phase the Santa Cruz Islands, Tulagi and Guadalcanal would be secured. General MacArthur had wanted the thrust against Rabaul to come from his Southwest Pacific command, but President Roosevelt approved the former plan.

The 1st Marine Division set sail from Fiji on 31 July and landed a week later on 7 August, commencing the six-month campaign. The Japanese brought in the first reinforcements on 19 August and both sides were operating at the end of their supply lines. The key to the campaign was control of the air, and once the Americans brought Henderson Field into use the Japanese were forced to bring in supplies by night down the New Georgia Sound. In an attempt to dislodge the Americans they flew long-range bombing missions from Rabaul and conducted naval bombardments. Numerous naval engagements were fought around Guadalcanal and although both sides incurred significant losses, by February 1943 the Americans had achieved such a degree of naval and air superiority that the Japanese position became untenable.

Air Fleet
arge of naval air
rations, subordinated
ombined Fleet at Truk
December when it
ame part of the South-
Area fleet along
the 8th Fleet

Tokyo Express -
maritime supply route
from Rabaul

Lord Howe
Is

Battle of the Eastern
Solomons 23–25.08

Choiseul

SOLOMON

ISLANDS

avella

Kolombangara

New Georgia Sound / The Slot

Santa Isabel

Ndai

Battle of Santa
Cruz 25–27.10

New Georgia

ga

Rendova

Vangunu

San
Jorge

Tetipari

Gatura

ration Ke, Japanese
cuation 19.01–07.02
0 troops

Russell

Savo

Florida

Malaita

Battle of Tassafaronga
30.11

Maramasike

Battle of Cape Esperance 11–12.10

Henderson
Field

Guadalcanal

Battle of Savo Island 09.08

Action in Sealark
Channel 25.10

PACIFIC

OCEAN

SANTA

Naval Battle of
Guadalcanal 12–15.11

San
Cristobal

CRUZ

ISLANDS

Destroyer action in Savo Sound 23.08
Action off Lunga Point 05.09

Ndeni

Bellona

Rennell

Utapua

Vanikoro

Indispensable
Reefs

South Pacific Area
VICE ADMIRAL R. L. GHORMLEY June–October
VICE ADMIRAL W. F. HALSEY October →

Torres Is

N

TF63/Air South Pacific
VICE ADMIRAL J. S. McCAIN
All land based aircraft in the
South Pacific including the
units at Henderson Field

Vanua
Levu

Banks Is

Coral Sea

Espiritu
Santo

Maewo

Pentacost

LOSSES DURING THE GUADALCANAL CAMPAIGN		
TYPE	ALLIED	JAPANESE
BATTLESHIPS	0	2
AIRCRAFT CARRIERS	2	1
CRUISERS	8	4
DESTROYERS	15	11
SUBMARINES	0	6
TRANSPORTS AND DESTROYER-TRANSPORTS	4	14
AIRCRAFT:		
01.08-15.11	480	507
16.11-09.02	134	117

Malekula

Ambrim

Around 36,200 Japanese army and naval personnel were deployed on Guadalcanal of which 9,860 were eventually evacuated. At least 3,500 naval personnel were lost at sea along with 1,200 airmen. Japanese casualties were around 30,300. The Americans landed around 60,000 troops on Guadalcanal of which around 1.769 were lost along with 4,911 sailors and 343 airmen giving a total of 7,100

Efate

Vila

0   100 Nm

0   100 km

160°

165°

BATTLE OF SAVO ISLAND, 8–9 AUGUST 1942

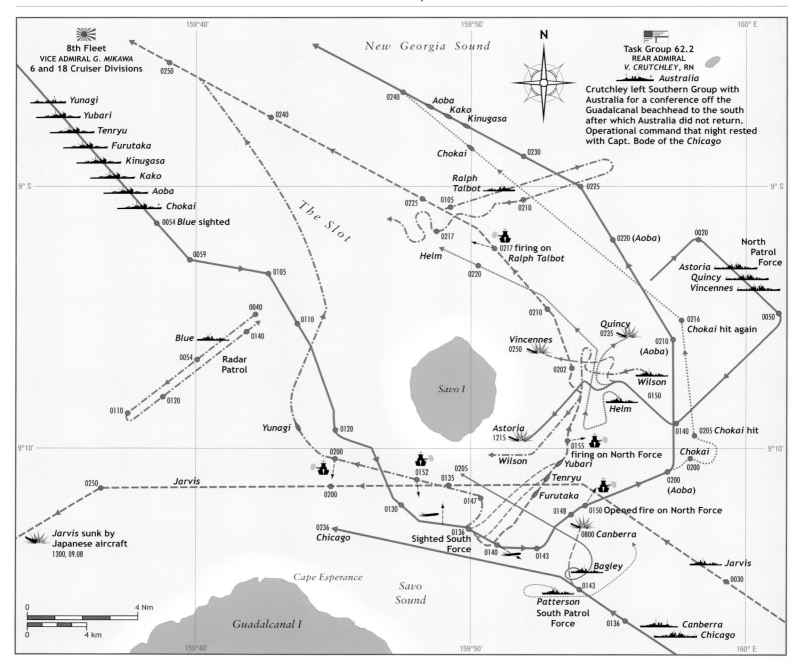

8th Fleet
VICE ADMIRAL *G. MIKAWA*
6 and 18 Cruiser Divisions

Yunagi
Yubari
Tenryu
Furutaka
Kinugasa
Kako
Aoba
Chokai

0054 *Blue* sighted

New Georgia Sound

Task Group 62.2
REAR ADMIRAL
V. CRUTCHLEY, RN
Australia
Crutchley left Southern Group with
Australia for a conference off the
Guadalcanal beachhead to the south
after which Australia did not return.
Operational command that night rested
with Capt. Bode of the *Chicago*

The Slot

Aoba
Kako
Kinugasa
Chokai

Ralph Talbot

0217 firing on
Ralph Talbot

Helm

North
Patrol
Force
Astoria
Quincy
Vincennes

0216
Chokai hit again

Blue
Radar Patrol

Quincy
Vincennes

Wilson

Helm

Savo I

Astoria
1215

firing on North Force

Chokai hit

Yunagi

Wilson

Yubari
Tenryu
Furutaka

Chokai

0150 Opened fire on North Force

Jarvis

0800 *Canberra*

*Jarvis sunk by
Japanese aircraft*
1300, 09.08

0236
Chicago

0136
Sighted South
Force

Bagley

Jarvis

Cape Esperance

*Savo
Sound*

**Patterson
South Patrol
Force**

Canberra
Chicago

0   4 Nm
0   4 km

Guadalcanal I

PACIFIC
OCEAN

NEW
GUINEA

Solomon Islands

Coral
Sea

AUSTRALIA

KEY

Task Force 62
movements

IJN movements

ALTHOUGH SURPRISED BY the American
landings on Guadalcanal, the Japanese
quickly responded with airstrikes
from Rabaul. In addition, Vice Admiral
Mikawa, commander of the 8th Fleet
at Rabaul, intended to take his cruisers
south and attack the transports off
Guadalcanal in a night engagement for
which his forces were both trained and
equipped. His ships sailed in groups in
order to confuse allied reconnaissance
regarding the size and composition of the force, and
although they were spotted early this information did
not reach allied forces off Guadalcanal until the evening.
Thus Mikawa was able to make his final approach
undetected.

On the allied side, Vice Admiral Fletcher, in overall
command, intended to pull his carriers, providing
distant cover, eastwards and out of Japanese air range.

Alarmed by this, Rear Admiral Turner, commanding the
landing forces, called a conference with Rear Admiral
Crutchley and Major General Vandegrift that evening.
To protect the transports in Savo Sound Crutchley had
split his force in three: two around Savo Island and
one to the east. When Mikawa attacked the allied force
found itself fragmented and with no flag officer in
command. Mikawa manoeuvred to avoid the destroyer
pickets and used low clouds to cover his approach,
and at 1.38am the first torpedoes were fired. Although
the allied South Force detected the Japanese shortly
thereafter, it sustained heavy damage in the confusion.
The Japanese force in turn slowly lost cohesion, but
nonetheless managed to surprise the North Force. None
of the three American cruisers were ready for action and
soon started taking heavy damage. Mikawa decided not
to turn back to attack the transports as his formation was
now in disarray and the time needed to regroup would
leave him exposed to American airstrikes at dawn.

UNTERNEHMEN WUNDERLAND, 16–31 AUGUST 1942

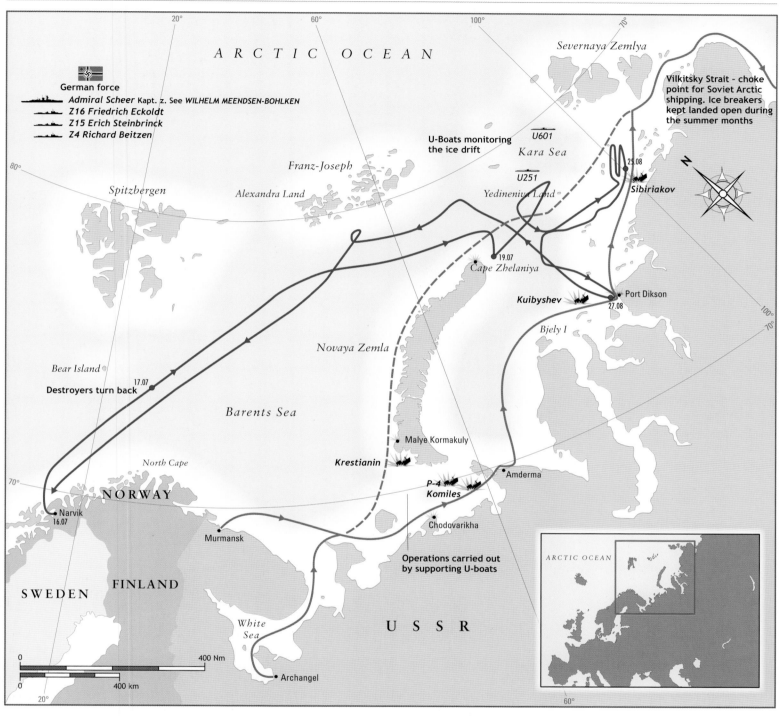

German force
Admiral Scheer Kapt. z. See WILHELM MEENDSEN-BOHLKEN
Z16 Friedrich Eckoldt
Z15 Erich Steinbrinck
Z4 Richard Beitzen

ARCTIC OCEAN

Severnaya Zemlya

Vilkitsky Strait – choke point for Soviet Arctic shipping. Ice breakers kept landed open during the summer months

U-Boats monitoring the ice drift

U601
Kara Sea
U251

Franz-Joseph
Spitzbergen
Alexandra Land
Yedineniya Land

Sibiriakov
25.08

19.07
Cape Zhelaniya

Kuibyshev
Port Dikson
27.08

Bear Island
17.07
Destroyers turn back

Novaya Zemla

Bjely I

Barents Sea

North Cape

Malye Kormakuly

Krestianin

Amderma

P-4
Komiles

Chodovarikha

Narvik
16.07

NORWAY

Murmansk

Operations carried out by supporting U-boats

ARCTIC OCEAN

SWEDEN   FINLAND

White Sea

U S S R

0   400 Nm
0   400 km

Archangel

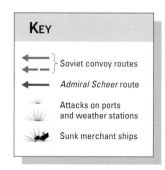

KEY

Soviet convoy routes

Admiral Scheer route

Attacks on ports and weather stations

Sunk merchant ships

THE SEALANES AROUND northern Siberia, though only really free of ice for around three months a year, were considered by the Germans to be favourable for attack. Not only was shipping in the area lightly protected, but also the destruction of icebreakers would have a severe impact on the Soviet's ability to keep the lanes open. Intelligence from the Japanese in mid July suggested that a major allied westbound convoy had passed the Bering Straits. The Germans now planned to send *Admiral Scheer* on a raid into the Arctic Ocean as far east as the Vilkitsky Strait. Preceding the operation, U-boats conducted reconnaissance off Spitsbergen and in particular pushed into the Kara Sea to monitor the

extent of the ice formation. This was important as *Scheer* was not designed for operations under such conditions and could not risk becoming caught in the ice.

Once *Scheer* left Narvik, it conducted two reconnaissance flights a day with its seaplane in an attempt to find the convoy or other concentrations of Soviet shipping. Although some were sighted, the ice made closing with these impossible, and the only success *Scheer* had was sinking the icebreaker *Sibiriakov* and bombarding Port Dikson. A small number of merchant ships were sunk by U-boats supporting the operation and a minelayer laid mines off Cape Zhelaniya.

Operation Jubilee, 19 August 1942

The object of the raid against Dieppe was to gain experience in amphibious operations by landing a divisional-sized force at a port on the French coastline and holding it for a day. Apart from any material damage caused, the practical lessons would be invaluable for the future landing operations in northwestern Europe and the Mediterranean. Dieppe was chosen because it had worthwhile military targets and was within the range of shore-based fighter cover. Admiral Mountbatten's Combined Operations Headquarters originally conceived of the idea for such a raid in April, although it was not until July that Churchill authorised its execution. The plan involved conducting a frontal attack on the port and relying on surprise rather than heavy preliminary naval or air bombardments to overcome the German defences.

The forces sailed in the evening of 18 August in thirteen separate groups. The voyage was uneventful, but shortly before 4am a group of landing craft on the eastern flank ran into a German coastal convoy and the ensuing chaos derailed the timetable so that the commandos failed to neutralise their allocated battery. In the centre and west the landings proceeded exactly on time. However, without neutralising bombardments the plan was fundamentally flawed. The German defences decimated the first wave of infantry and the tanks were unable to penetrate beyond the beaches. The second wave, landed around 7am, could do little to change the situation and by 9am it was clear that the operation had failed. What was left of the force was evacuated around noon, but of the 6,000 allied troops 1,179 were killed and 2,190 taken prisoner. Thirty-three landing craft and a destroyer were lost and there were 500 naval casualties.

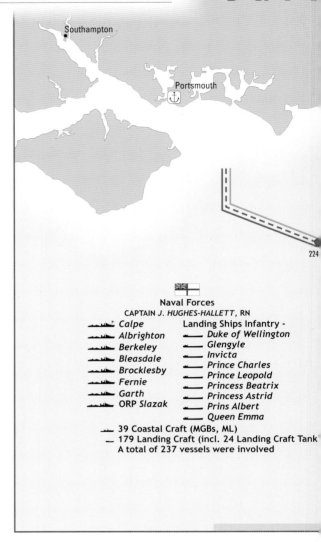

Naval Forces
CAPTAIN J. HUGHES-HALLETT, RN

	Landing Ships Infantry -
Calpe	Duke of Wellington
Albrighton	Glengyle
Berkeley	Invicta
Bleasdale	Prince Charles
Brocklesby	Prince Leopold
Fernie	Princess Beatrix
Garth	Princess Astrid
ORP Slazak	Prins Albert
	Queen Emma

39 Coastal Craft (MGBs, ML)
179 Landing Craft (incl. 24 Landing Craft Tank
A total of 237 vessels were involved

Key

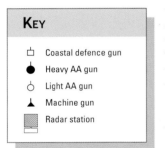

- ⌂ Coastal defence gun
- ● Heavy AA gun
- ○ Light AA gun
- ⚒ Machine gun
- ▦ Radar station

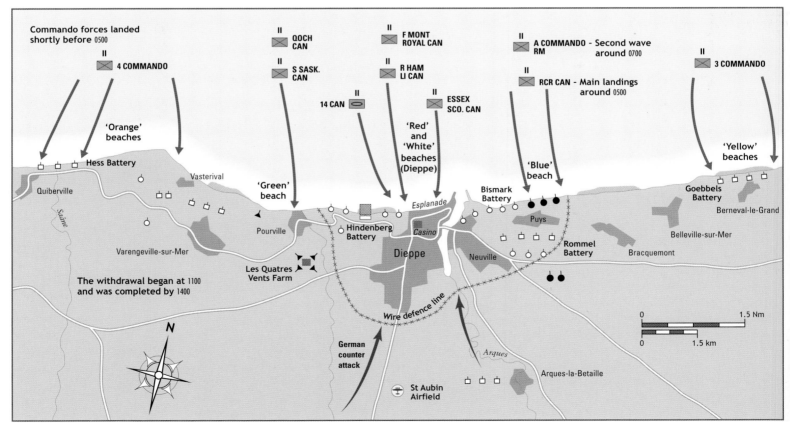

Commando forces landed shortly before 0500

4 COMMANDO

QOCH CAN

S SASK. CAN

14 CAN

F MONT ROYAL CAN

R HAM LI CAN

ESSEX SCO. CAN

A COMMANDO – Second wave RM around 0700

RCR CAN – Main landings around 0500

3 COMMANDO

'Orange' beaches

Hess Battery

Vasterival

Quiberville

Saâne

Varengeville-sur-Mer

'Green' beach

Pourville

'Red' and 'White' beaches (Dieppe)

Esplanade

Hindenberg Battery

Casino

Dieppe

Neuville

Bismark Battery

Puys

'Blue' beach

Rommel Battery

'Yellow' beaches

Goebbels Battery

Berneval-le-Grand

Belleville-sur-Mer

Bracquemont

The withdrawal began at 1100 and was completed by 1400

Les Quatres Vents Farm

Wire defence line

German counter attack

Arques

St Aubin Airfield

Arques-la-Betaille

N

0   1.5 Nm
0   1.5 km

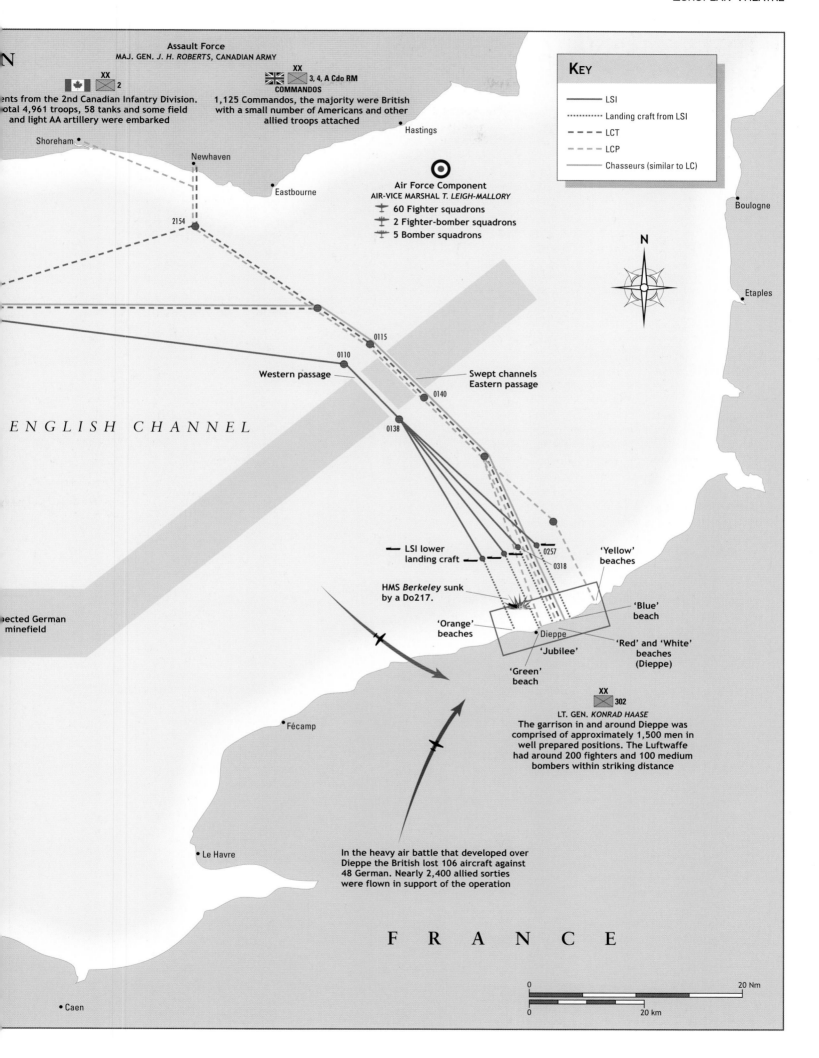

Assault Force
MAJ. GEN. *J. H. ROBERTS*, CANADIAN ARMY

XX 2

ents from the 2nd Canadian Infantry Division.
otal 4,961 troops, 58 tanks and some field
and light AA artillery were embarked

XX 3, 4, A Cdo RM
COMMANDOS

1,125 Commandos, the majority were British
with a small number of Americans and other
allied troops attached

Hastings

Shoreham

Newhaven

Eastbourne

2154

Air Force Component
AIR-VICE MARSHAL *T. LEIGH-MALLORY*
60 Fighter squadrons
2 Fighter-bomber squadrons
5 Bomber squadrons

KEY
———— LSI
·········· Landing craft from LSI
– – – LCT
– – – LCP
———— Chasseurs (similar to LC)

Boulogne

N

Etaples

0115

0110

Western passage

Swept channels
Eastern passage

0140

E N G L I S H   C H A N N E L

0138

LSI lower
landing craft

0257

0318

'Yellow'
beaches

HMS *Berkeley* sunk
by a Do217.

'Orange'
beaches

'Blue'
beach

'Red' and 'White'
beaches
(Dieppe)

Dieppe

ected German
minefield

'Jubilee'

'Green'
beach

XX 302

LT. GEN. *KONRAD HAASE*
The garrison in and around Dieppe was
comprised of approximately 1,500 men in
well prepared positions. The Luftwaffe
had around 200 fighters and 100 medium
bombers within striking distance

Fécamp

Le Havre

In the heavy air battle that developed over
Dieppe the British lost 106 aircraft against
48 German. Nearly 2,400 allied sorties
were flown in support of the operation

F R A N C E

Caen

0 ——————— 20 Nm
0 ——————— 20 km

BATTLE OF THE EASTERN SOLOMONS, 23–25 AUGUST 1942

Despite having attained a victory at the battle of Savo Island, the Japanese still needed to reinforce their forces on Guadalcanal. Admiral Yamamoto intended to use part of the Combined Fleet, and on 16 August two forces left Truk. A small one under Rear Admiral Tanaka would land troops on Guadalcanal, while the main force would provide distant cover and engage any American carriers in the vicinity. The execution of the Operation *KA* was considerably more complex than its conception as a number of different subsidiary operations were envisaged depending on the American reaction. A naval bombardment of American positions on Guadalcanal was planned, and if no American carriers were present the carriers would also launch strikes against Guadalcanal. Warships and aircraft from Rabaul would also operate in the area, but there was little coordination between the various forces. Crucially, Tanaka's force was not assigned any specific air cover. Rather than concentrating the main body, the carriers operated behind two surface groups as it was hoped that air strikes would slow down any American force that could then be finished off by the battleships and cruisers.

A sudden drop in Japanese radio traffic in the second half of August alerted the Americans that some major operation was underway. At 9.50am on 23 August a PBY Catalina spotted Tanaka's convoy around 250nm north of Guadalcanal and in the mid-afternoon aircraft from Henderson Field and *Saratoga* were sent to strike the ships. Realising the danger, Tanaka had reversed course and the American's found nothing. Vice Admiral Fletcher, operating with the carriers to the southeast, decided to detach the *Wasp* group to refuel as there was no intelligence indicating that the Japanese carriers were at sea. The Japanese too had no information on the whereabouts of the American carriers and kept the surface group closer than planned and also detached *Ryujo* to strike Guadalcanal. The Americans had 154 aircraft on two carriers against the 171 that the three Japanese carriers had embarked.

Early morning searches by both sides on 24 August brought no results, but at around 2pm Admiral Fletcher launched a strike against *Ryujo* after its strike on Guadalcanal was detected by *Saratoga*'s radar. Shortly thereafter, a Japanese floatplane spotted the American

carriers and Admiral *Nagumo* sent his heavy ships ahead and launched aircraft just before 3pm. At about the same time American search planes detected the main Japanese force, but Fletcher could do little about this now. *Ryujo* was hit and fatally damaged around 4pm, and thirty minutes later the Japanese aircraft hit TF 61. *Enterprise* was badly damaged, but underway within an hour and the Americans headed south. The Japanese gave chase until midnight before turning north.

Meanwhile, Tanaka was ordered north at 8.07pm and south again three hours later when reports erroneously suggested the American carriers had been sunk. Early on 25 August American aircraft took off from Henderson Field to search for the *Ryujo*, but instead found Tanaka's convoy and during the morning sunk a cruiser, a destroyer and a transport. In addition to the ships, the Japanese lost seventy-five aircraft against twenty-five American. Although the *Enterprise* needed to return to Pearl Harbor, the Americans attained an important victory, and the Japanese realised they could not resupply Guadalcanal with slow transports; instead, they resorted to using destroyers in high-speed runs down the New Georgia Sound.

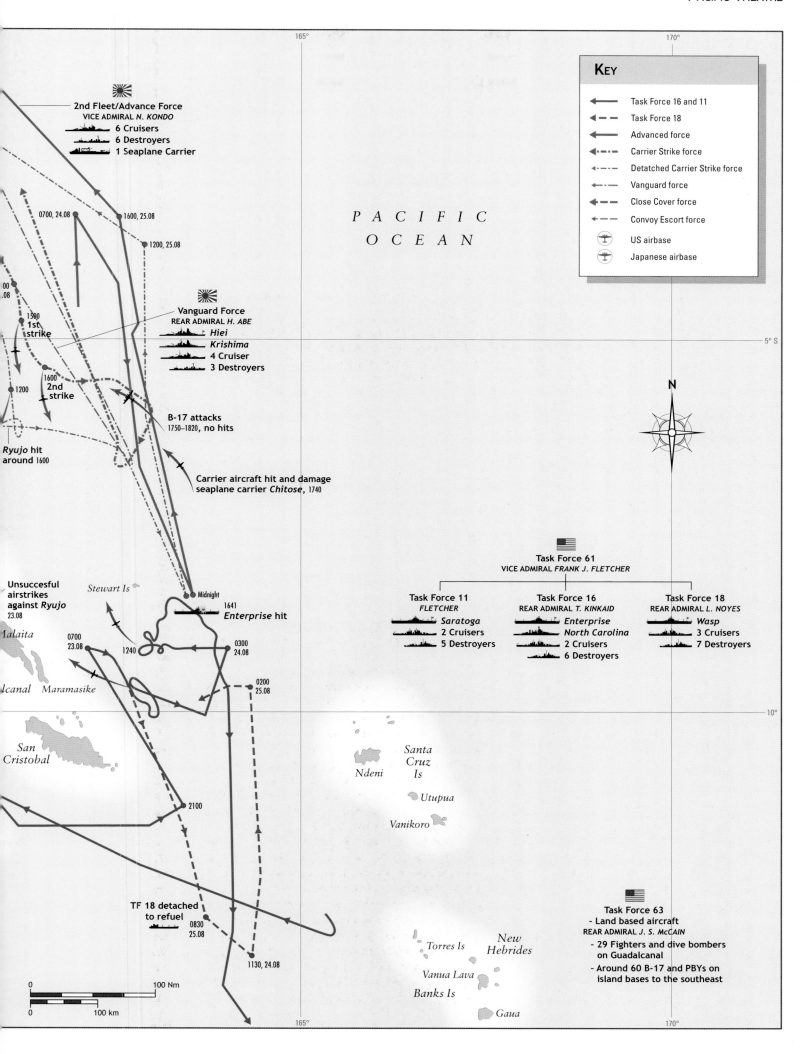

PACIFIC
OCEAN

KEY

←	Task Force 16 and 11
◄---	Task Force 18
←	Advanced force
◄-·-·	Carrier Strike force
◄-·-·	Detached Carrier Strike force
←-·-·	Vanguard force
◄---	Close Cover force
←---	Convoy Escort force
✈	US airbase
✈	Japanese airbase

2nd Fleet/Advance Force
VICE ADMIRAL *N. KONDO*
6 Cruisers
6 Destroyers
1 Seaplane Carrier

0700, 24.08   1600, 25.08
1200, 25.08

1500
1st
strike

1600
2nd
strike

1200

Ryujo hit
around 1600

Vanguard Force
REAR ADMIRAL *H. ABE*
Hiei
Krishima
4 Cruiser
3 Destroyers

B-17 attacks
1750–1820, no hits

Carrier aircraft hit and damage
seaplane carrier *Chitose*, 1740

5° S

N

Unsuccesful
airstrikes
against *Ryujo*
23.08

Stewart Is

Midnight
1641
Enterprise hit

Malaita

0700
23.08

1240

0300
24.08

0200
25.08

lcanal *Maramasike*

*San
Cristobal*

Task Force 61
VICE ADMIRAL *FRANK J. FLETCHER*

Task Force 11
FLETCHER
Saratoga
2 Cruisers
5 Destroyers

Task Force 16
REAR ADMIRAL *T. KINKAID*
Enterprise
North Carolina
2 Cruisers
6 Destroyers

Task Force 18
REAR ADMIRAL *L. NOYES*
Wasp
3 Cruisers
7 Destroyers

10°

*Santa
Cruz
Is*

Ndeni

Utupua

Vanikoro

2100

TF 18 detached
to refuel

0830
25.08

1130, 24.08

Torres Is   *New
Hebrides*

Vanua Lava

Banks Is

Gaua

Task Force 63
- Land based aircraft
REAR ADMIRAL *J. S. McCAIN*

- 29 Fighters and dive bombers
  on Guadalcanal
- Around 60 B-17 and PBYs on
  island bases to the southeast

0		100 Nm

0		100 km

BATTLE OF CAPE ESPERANCE, 11–12 OCTOBER 1942

THIS WAS THE SECOND major surface engagement off Guadalcanal and is also known as the second battle of Savo Island. In early October the Japanese planned a substantial reinforcement to dislodge the Americans from Guadalcanal. On the night of 11 October two naval operations were planned; one resupply run followed shortly thereafter by a bombardment of Henderson airfield. Meanwhile, the Americans too had reinforced Guadalcanal with an infantry regiment and TF 64, covering its landing, continued to loiter to the south. Its commander, Rear Admiral Scott, intended to intercept the next Japanese supply run and on 11 October an opportunity arose when a B-17 spotted a Japanese force coming down the New Georgia Sound at 2.15pm. The two Japanese forces had left the Shortland Islands at 8am and 2pm respectively, and Scott made for Savo around 4pm. The battle was marked by a considerable degree of confusion. The Japanese were surprised by the presence of an American force while the Americans were surprised by the presence of a second Japanese force. TF 64 was effectively crossing the T of the Japanese force when the cruiser *Helena* made radar contact at 11.25pm but did not pass on the information; shortly thereafter Scott reversed course. When *Helena* opened fire at 11.46pm, followed by the others, the range was down to 3,600 yards. The action only lasted minutes. The Americans briefly gave chase to the retreating Japanese, but soon disengaged having lost cohesion.

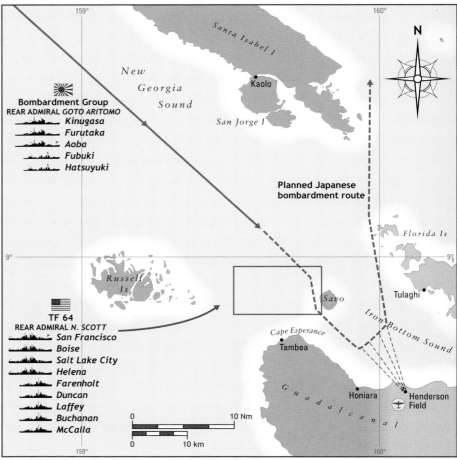

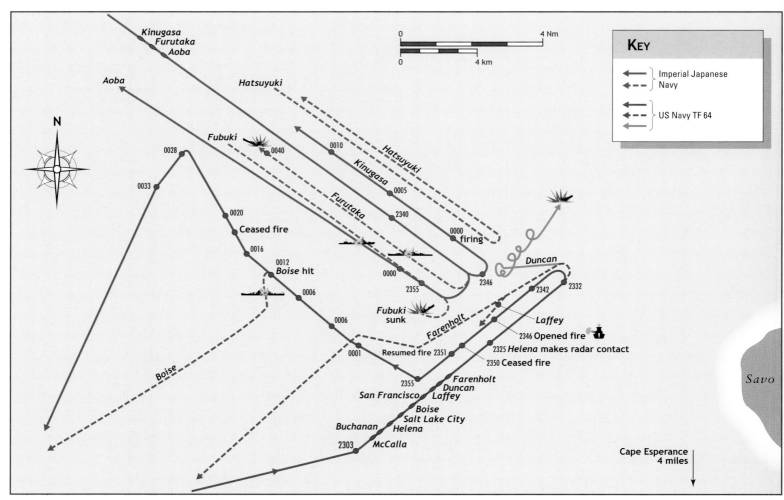

GERMAN E-BOAT ATTACKS, 1940–45

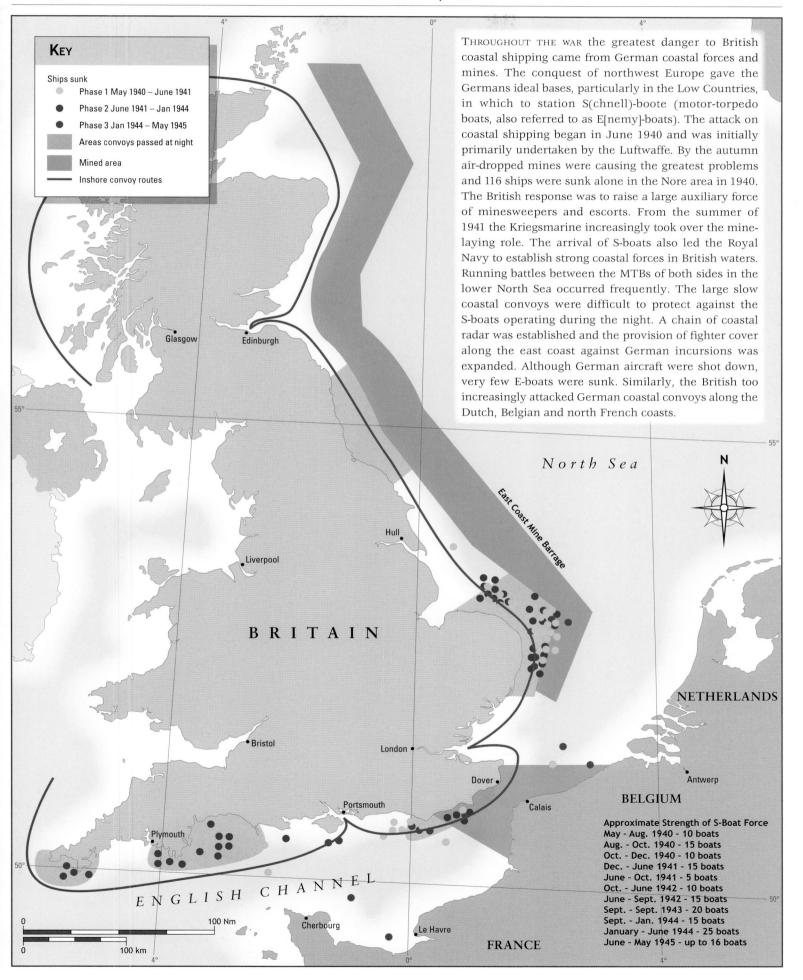

KEY

Ships sunk

● Phase 1 May 1940 – June 1941
● Phase 2 June 1941 – Jan 1944
● Phase 3 Jan 1944 – May 1945
▨ Areas convoys passed at night
▨ Mined area
— Inshore convoy routes

THROUGHOUT THE WAR the greatest danger to British coastal shipping came from German coastal forces and mines. The conquest of northwest Europe gave the Germans ideal bases, particularly in the Low Countries, in which to station S(chnell)-boote (motor-torpedo boats, also referred to as E[nemy]-boats). The attack on coastal shipping began in June 1940 and was initially primarily undertaken by the Luftwaffe. By the autumn air-dropped mines were causing the greatest problems and 116 ships were sunk alone in the Nore area in 1940. The British response was to raise a large auxiliary force of minesweepers and escorts. From the summer of 1941 the Kriegsmarine increasingly took over the mine-laying role. The arrival of S-boats also led the Royal Navy to establish strong coastal forces in British waters. Running battles between the MTBs of both sides in the lower North Sea occurred frequently. The large slow coastal convoys were difficult to protect against the S-boats operating during the night. A chain of coastal radar was established and the provision of fighter cover along the east coast against German incursions was expanded. Although German aircraft were shot down, very few E-boats were sunk. Similarly, the British too increasingly attacked German coastal convoys along the Dutch, Belgian and north French coasts.

Glasgow

Edinburgh

North Sea

N

Hull

Liverpool

East Coast Mine Barrage

BRITAIN

NETHERLANDS

Bristol

London

Dover

Antwerp

Portsmouth

Calais

BELGIUM

Plymouth

ENGLISH CHANNEL

Cherbourg

Le Havre

FRANCE

Approximate Strength of S-Boat Force
May - Aug. 1940 - 10 boats
Aug. - Oct. 1940 - 15 boats
Oct. - Dec. 1940 - 10 boats
Dec. - June 1941 - 15 boats
June - Oct. 1941 - 5 boats
Oct. - June 1942 - 10 boats
June - Sept. 1942 - 15 boats
Sept. - Sept. 1943 - 20 boats
Sept. - Jan. 1944 - 15 boats
January - June 1944 - 25 boats
June - May 1945 - up to 16 boats

0   100 Nm
0   100 km

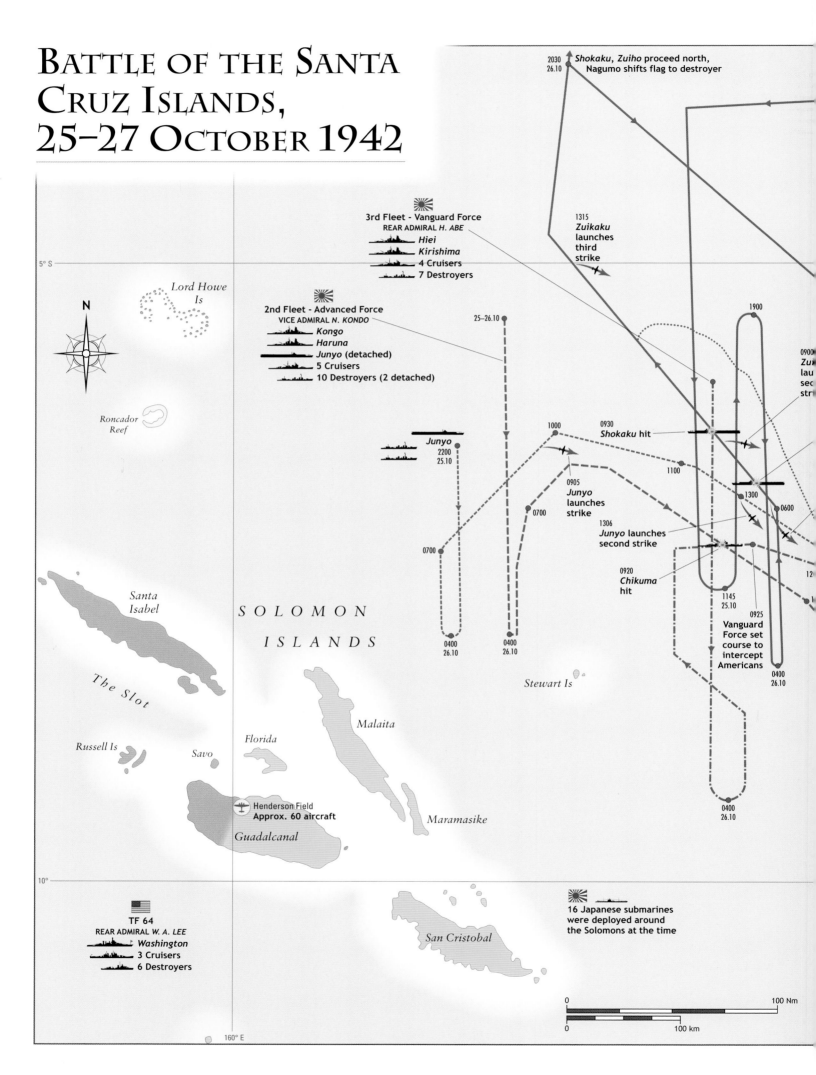

BATTLE OF THE SANTA CRUZ ISLANDS, 25–27 OCTOBER 1942

3rd Fleet - Vanguard Force
REAR ADMIRAL *H. ABE*
- *Hiei*
- *Kirishima*
- 4 Cruisers
- 7 Destroyers

2nd Fleet - Advanced Force
VICE ADMIRAL *N. KONDO*
- *Kongo*
- *Haruna*
- *Junyo* (detached)
- 5 Cruisers
- 10 Destroyers (2 detached)

Junyo
2200
25.10

Lord Howe
Is

Roncador
Reef

Santa
Isabel

The Slot

S O L O M O N
I S L A N D S

Russell Is

Savo

Florida

Malaita

Stewart Is

Maramasike

Henderson Field
Approx. 60 aircraft

Guadalcanal

San Cristobal

TF 64
REAR ADMIRAL *W. A. LEE*
- *Washington*
- 3 Cruisers
- 6 Destroyers

16 Japanese submarines were deployed around the Solomons at the time

2030
26.10
Shokaku, Zuiho proceed north, Nagumo shifts flag to destroyer

1315
Zuikaku launches third strike

1900

0900
Zu
lau
sec
str

0930
Shokaku hit

1000

1100

0905
Junyo launches strike

0700

1300

0600

1306
Junyo launches second strike

0920
Chikuma hit

1145
25.10

0925

Vanguard Force set course to intercept Americans

0700

0400
26.10

0400
26.10

0700

0400
26.10

0400
26.10

25–26.10

0400
26.10

0
100 Nm

0
100 km

5° S

10°

160° E

152

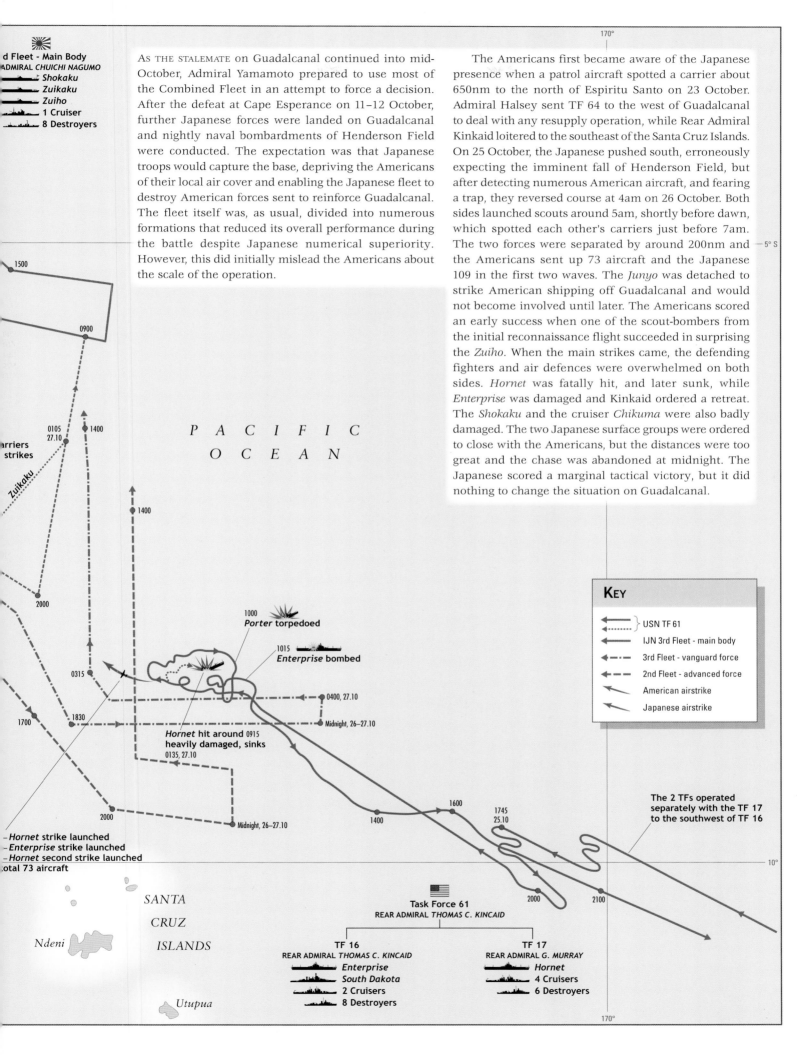

d Fleet - Main Body
ADMIRAL *CHUICHI NAGUMO*
— *Shokaku*
— *Zuikaku*
— *Zuiho*
1 Cruiser
8 Destroyers

AS THE STALEMATE on Guadalcanal continued into mid-October, Admiral Yamamoto prepared to use most of the Combined Fleet in an attempt to force a decision. After the defeat at Cape Esperance on 11–12 October, further Japanese forces were landed on Guadalcanal and nightly naval bombardments of Henderson Field were conducted. The expectation was that Japanese troops would capture the base, depriving the Americans of their local air cover and enabling the Japanese fleet to destroy American forces sent to reinforce Guadalcanal. The fleet itself was, as usual, divided into numerous formations that reduced its overall performance during the battle despite Japanese numerical superiority. However, this did initially mislead the Americans about the scale of the operation.

The Americans first became aware of the Japanese presence when a patrol aircraft spotted a carrier about 650nm to the north of Espiritu Santo on 23 October. Admiral Halsey sent TF 64 to the west of Guadalcanal to deal with any resupply operation, while Rear Admiral Kinkaid loitered to the southeast of the Santa Cruz Islands. On 25 October, the Japanese pushed south, erroneously expecting the imminent fall of Henderson Field, but after detecting numerous American aircraft, and fearing a trap, they reversed course at 4am on 26 October. Both sides launched scouts around 5am, shortly before dawn, which spotted each other's carriers just before 7am. The two forces were separated by around 200nm and the Americans sent up 73 aircraft and the Japanese 109 in the first two waves. The *Junyo* was detached to strike American shipping off Guadalcanal and would not become involved until later. The Americans scored an early success when one of the scout-bombers from the initial reconnaissance flight succeeded in surprising the *Zuiho*. When the main strikes came, the defending fighters and air defences were overwhelmed on both sides. *Hornet* was fatally hit, and later sunk, while *Enterprise* was damaged and Kinkaid ordered a retreat. The *Shokaku* and the cruiser *Chikuma* were also badly damaged. The two Japanese surface groups were ordered to close with the Americans, but the distances were too great and the chase was abandoned at midnight. The Japanese scored a marginal tactical victory, but it did nothing to change the situation on Guadalcanal.

170°

—5° S

1500

0900

0105
27.10

1400

arriers
strikes

Zuikaku

P A C I F I C
O C E A N

1400

2000

1000
Porter torpedoed

1015
Enterprise bombed

0315

0400, 27.10

1700

1830

Midnight, 26–27.10

Hornet hit around 0915
heavily damaged, sinks
0135, 27.10

2000

Midnight, 26–27.10

1600

1745
25.10

2000   2100

The 2 TFs operated
separately with the TF 17
to the southwest of TF 16

—10°

– *Hornet* strike launched
– *Enterprise* strike launched
– *Hornet* second strike launched
otal 73 aircraft

SANTA

CRUZ

Ndeni

ISLANDS

Utupua

Task Force 61
REAR ADMIRAL *THOMAS C. KINCAID*

TF 16
REAR ADMIRAL *THOMAS C. KINCAID*
Enterprise
South Dakota
2 Cruisers
8 Destroyers

TF 17
REAR ADMIRAL *G. MURRAY*
Hornet
4 Cruisers
6 Destroyers

KEY

USN TF 61

IJN 3rd Fleet - main body

3rd Fleet - vanguard force

2nd Fleet - advanced force

American airstrike

Japanese airstrike

170°

OPERATION TORCH, 8 NOVEMBER 1942

THE ANGLO-AMERICAN decision to land in French North Africa was reached in July and the objective was, together with an advance by the British Eight Army from Egypt, to clear out axis forces from Africa as a prelude to removing Italy from the war. There were, however, differences between the two sides. The British wanted landings on a broad front in order to prevent a German occupation of Tunisia, which would prolong the campaign, and to secure the remainder of the French fleet. The Americans were concerned about the U-boat threat and believed that concentrating the assault forces would allow them to be better protected. A compromise was reached with the British taking responsibility of the landings in the Mediterranean and the Americans on the Atlantic coast. The plans were approved at the end of September and the orders issued on 8 October.

In terms of scale and complexity *Torch* marked a turning point in the conduct of amphibious operations.

In order to assemble the forces necessary for this trans-oceanic assault other theatres had their naval forces reduced, and British warships alone were to number some 160. The logistics requirements of the British First Army and air force units that would be built up in the French territories were substantial, and merchant shipping was diverted from Atlantic routes and even South Atlantic convoys temporarily suspended. Although Gibraltar was an important staging post, and the operation was commanded from there, its limited facilities meant that most of the support and replenishment for the assaulting forces had to come from ships. In addition to the fire support provided by warships, aircraft carriers would furnish much of the initial fighter cover. The first advance convoys comprising slower supply vessels and auxiliaries sailed in mid October followed by the large assault convoys at the end of the month.

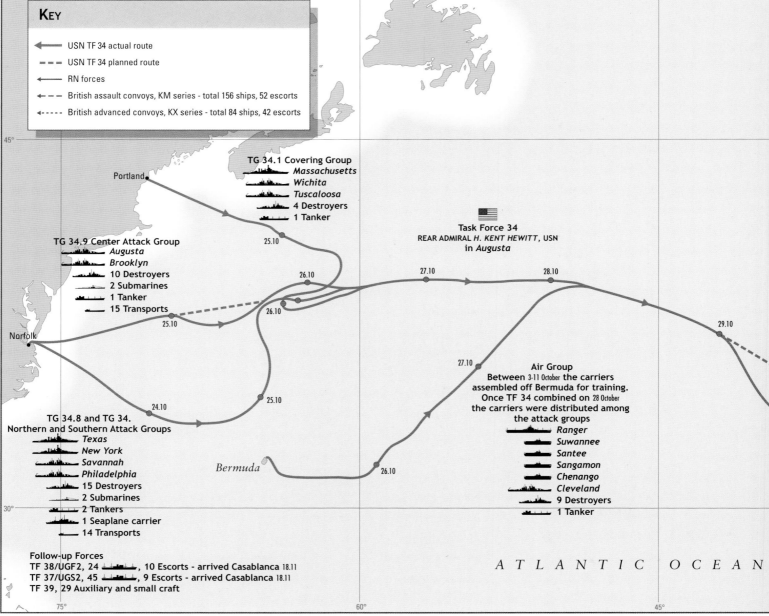

KEY

- USN TF 34 actual route
- USN TF 34 planned route
- RN forces
- British assault convoys, KM series - total 156 ships, 52 escorts
- British advanced convoys, KX series - total 84 ships, 42 escorts

TG 34.1 Covering Group
- *Massachusetts*
- *Wichita*
- *Tuscaloosa*
- 4 Destroyers
- 1 Tanker

Portland

25.10

TG 34.9 Center Attack Group
- *Augusta*
- *Brooklyn*
- 10 Destroyers
- 2 Submarines
- 1 Tanker
- 15 Transports

25.10

26.10

26.10

Norfolk

24.10

25.10

Task Force 34
REAR ADMIRAL *H. KENT HEWITT*, USN
in *Augusta*

27.10   28.10

27.10

Air Group
Between 3-11 October the carriers assembled off Bermuda for training. Once TF 34 combined on 28 October the carriers were distributed among the attack groups
- *Ranger*
- *Suwannee*
- *Santee*
- *Sangamon*
- *Chenango*
- *Cleveland*
- 9 Destroyers
- 1 Tanker

29.10

TG 34.8 and TG 34.
Northern and Southern Attack Groups
- *Texas*
- *New York*
- *Savannah*
- *Philadelphia*
- 15 Destroyers
- 2 Submarines
- 2 Tankers
- 1 Seaplane carrier
- 14 Transports

Bermuda

26.10

Follow-up Forces
TF 38/UGF2, 24 ⊢⊣, 10 Escorts - arrived Casablanca 18.11
TF 37/UGS2, 45 ⊢⊣, 9 Escorts - arrived Casablanca 18.11
TF 39, 29 Auxiliary and small craft

ATLANTIC OCEAN

75°   60°   45°

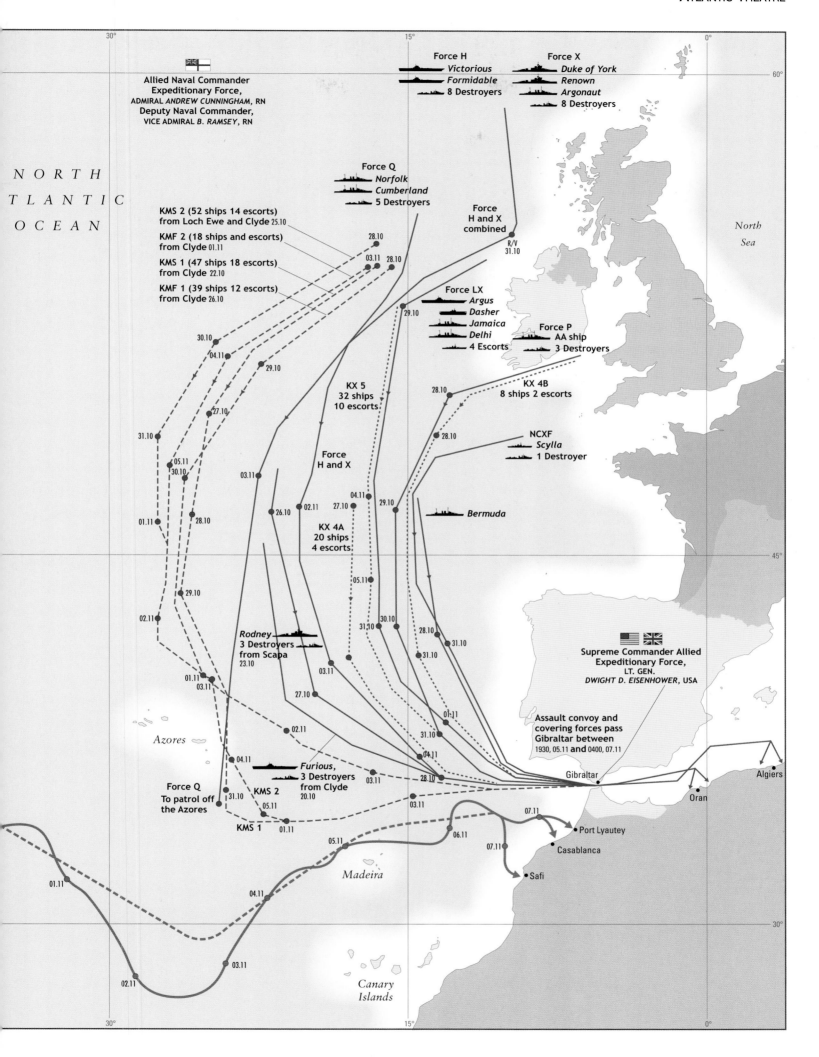

NORTH
ATLANTIC
OCEAN

North
Sea

Allied Naval Commander Expeditionary Force,
ADMIRAL *ANDREW CUNNINGHAM*, RN
Deputy Naval Commander,
VICE ADMIRAL *B. RAMSEY*, RN

Force H
Victorious
Formidable
8 Destroyers

Force X
Duke of York
Renown
Argonaut
8 Destroyers

Force Q
Norfolk
Cumberland
5 Destroyers

Force H and X combined
R/V
31.10

KMS 2 (52 ships 14 escorts)
from Loch Ewe and Clyde 25.10

KMF 2 (18 ships and escorts)
from Clyde 01.11

KMS 1 (47 ships 18 escorts)
from Clyde 22.10

KMF 1 (39 ships 12 escorts)
from Clyde 26.10

Force LX
Argus
Dasher
Jamaica
Delhi
4 Escorts

Force P
AA ship
3 Destroyers

28.10
03.11   28.10

29.10

KX 5
32 ships
10 escorts

KX 4B
8 ships 2 escorts

28.10

28.10

NCXF
Scylla
1 Destroyer

30.10

04.11

29.10

27.10

31.10

05.11
30.10

28.10

01.11

03.11

26.10   02.11

27.10

04.11   29.10

Bermuda

KX 4A
20 ships
4 escorts

29.10

05.11

31.10   30.10

28.10

31.10

Rodney
3 Destroyers
from Scapa
23.10

02.11

31.10

Supreme Commander Allied Expeditionary Force,
LT. GEN.
DWIGHT D. EISENHOWER, USA

Assault convoy and covering forces pass Gibraltar between
1930, 05.11 **and** 0400, 07.11

01.11
03.11

03.11

27.10

Azores

02.11

04.11

Furious,
3 Destroyers
from Clyde
20.10

03.11

28.10

Gibraltar

Algiers

Oran

**Force Q
To patrol off the Azores**

31.10   KMS 2
05.11

KMS 1   01.11

03.11

07.11

06.11   Port Lyautey

07.11
Casablanca

05.11

04.11

Madeira

Safi

01.11

02.11

03.11

*Canary
Islands*

OPERATION TORCH, LANDING ZONES

N

Carrier Air Support

WNTF
Ranger - 54 Wildcat, 18 Dauntless
Suwannee - 29 Wildcat, 9 Avenger
Sangamon - 12 Wildcat, 9 Avenger, 9 Dauntless
Chenango - 76 Warhawk (for land basing)
Santee - 14 Wildcat, 8 Avenger, 9 Dauntless

Force H
Victorious - 6 Fulmar, 11 Martlet, 9 Seafire, 21 Albacore
Formidable - 24 Martlet, 6 Seafire, 6 Albacore

CNTF
Furious - 24 Seafire, 8 Albacore, 1 Fulmar
Biter - 15 Sea Hurricane, 3 Swordfish
Dasher - 12 Sea Hurricane

ENTF
Argus - 12 Seafire
Avenger - 12 Sea Hurricane, 3 Swordfish

Lisbon

PORTUGAL

S P A I N

Force H
VICE ADMIRAL *E. N. SYFRET*, RN
Duke of York
Renown
Rodney (to CNTF)
Victorious
Formidable
Furious (to CNTF)
Bermuda (to ENTF)
Argonaut
Sirius
17 Destroyers

HQ
Gibraltar

Ceuta

Central Naval Task Force
COMMODORE *T. TROUTBRIDGE*, RN
Largs
Bitter
Dasher
Aurora
Jamaica
13 Destroyers

Melilla

SPANISH MOROCCO

Western Naval Task Force/TF 34
REAR ADMIRAL *H. K. HEWITT*, USN

Massachusetts	*Wichata*
Texas	*Tuscalasa*
New York	*Philadelphia*
Ranger	*Savannah*
Santee	*Augusta*
Sangamon	*Brooklyn*
Chenango	*Cleveland*
Suwannee	38 Destroyers

Ursu

Unshaken

Oran

X

XX 1

1 Parachute Infantry Regiment
in from Britain was also droppe
the first wave the 1st Infantry
Division and an Armored Comba
Team from the 1st Armored Div
was landed, approx. 18,500 me

Port Lyautey

Rabat

MAJOR GENERAL *G. PATTON*, USA
**Overall command of
WTF landforces**

Casablanca
Fedala

XX 3

Under the terms of the armistice with Germany the
Vichy government was limited to a force of 120,000
troops in North Africa. Around 55,000 were in
Morocco, 50,000 in Algeria and 15,000 Tunisia.
The air component amounted to around 500
mostly obsolete types.

M O R O C C O

Safi

XX 9   XX 2

Elements of both divisions landed in the north and south.
Tanks from the 2nd Armored also landed in the centre.
In total 5 Regimental Combat and 1 Armored Combat
Team landed in the first wave. With support troops
this amounted to approx. 34,000 men.

0   100 Nm

0   100 km

Agadir

Barcelona

Balearic Islands

Menorca

Majorca

Ibiza

COMPOSITION OF ASSAULT FORCES

	FORCE H AND FUELLING FORCE (ADMIRAL SYFRET)	CENTRE TASK FORCES (COMMODORE TROUTBRIDGE)	EASTERN TASK FORCES (ADMIRAL BURROUGH)	WESTERN TASK FORCES (ADMIRAL HEWITT, USN)
H.Q. SHIPS	–	1	1	–
BATTLESHIPS AND BATTLECRUISERS	3	–	–	3
AIRCRAFT CARRIERS	3	–	1	1
ESCORT CARRIERS	–	2	1	4
CRUISERS	3	2	3	7
MONITORS	–	–	1	–
A.A. SHIPS	–	2	3	–
DESTROYERS	17	13	13	38
CUTTERS	–	2	–	–
FLEET MINESWEEPERS	–	8	7	8
SLOOPS	–	2	3	–
CORVETTES	1	6	6	–
TRAWLERS (A/S-M/S)	4	8	8	–
MINELAYERS	–	–	–	3
SEAPLANE TENDERS	–	–	–	1
MOTOR LAUNCHES	–	10	8	–
SUBMARINES	–	2	3	4
LANDING SHIPS INFANTRY	–	15	11	–
COMBAT LOADERS/ATTACK TRANSPORT	–	–	4	23
LANDING SHIPS TANK	–	3	–	–
LANDING SHIPS GANTRY	–	1	2	–
TRANSPORT AND MERCHANT SHIPS	–	28	16	8
TANKERS	2	–	–	5

Eastern Naval Task Force
VICE ADMIRAL *H. BURROUGH*, RN
- *Bulolo*
- *Argus*
- *Avenger*
- *Sheffield*
- *Scylla*
- *Bermuda*
- *Charybdis*
- 1 Monitor
- 13 Destroyers

Mediterranean Sea

Unrivalled

Shakespeare — P48

Algiers

Tunis

XXXX
1
LT. GEN. *K. ANDERSON*
**1st Army became active on
9 November**

XX 78 **XX 34** **X Commandos**

Each division landed the equivalent of 2 brigades
on the first day and together with around 2,000
British and American commandos this amounted
to approx. 20,000 men.

T U N I S I A

A L G E R I A

WITH THE LANDINGS along the French North African coast which started on 8 November, the allies succeeded in taking the Germans by surprise. The level of French resistance varied between the different landings, but in general the objectives were attained and the sectors firmly under allied control within days. At Casablanca, which not only had extensive coastal defences but also contained the harboured battleship *Jean Bart*, the Americans chose to land near Fedala and take the port from the landward side. A 'naval battle of Casablanca' developed in which American air and surface units succeeded in sinking or damaging a French cruiser, six destroyers and eight submarines. The *Massachusetts* was tasked with putting the *Jean Bart* out of action with its 16in guns. The port was important as supplies could be directly brought in there from America.

In an attempt to persuade the Vichy French authorities not to resist, most of the forces landed in the initial wave were American. At Algiers three landings were made, and while those on the flanks went well, in the centre there was some confusion. In order to assist the assault forces each beach was allocated a submarine to act as a guiding beacon. A frontal assault by destroyers to take the harbour and so prevent the French from wrecking it failed, but by the end of the day the town and its surroundings had been secured. The landings at Oran were very similar to those at Algiers. Some landing craft went ashore on the wrong beaches and a similar attempt to force the harbour defences also ended in failure. Tactical reverses were inevitable given how much was still to be learnt about conducting large-scale, contested amphibious assaults, but the allies were able to put their experiences at *Torch* to good use in the Italian campaign. Although the landings were a success, the campaign was only partially so because the Germans were able to take Tunisia and hold on to it for nearly six months.

THE NAVAL BATTLE OF GUADALCANAL, 12–15 NOVEMBER 1942

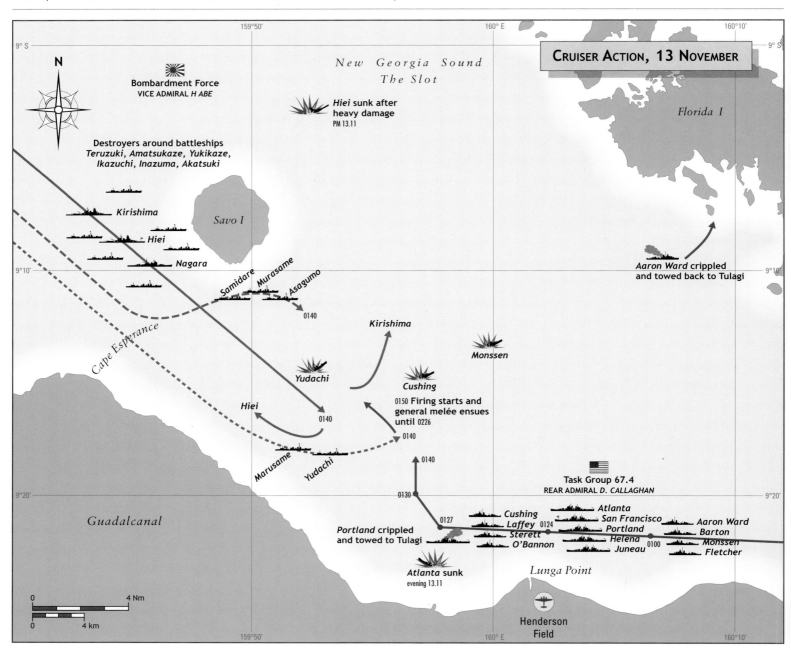

CRUISER ACTION, 13 NOVEMBER

New Georgia Sound
The Slot

Bombardment Force
VICE ADMIRAL H ABE

Hiei sunk after heavy damage
PM 13.11

Florida I

Destroyers around battleships
Teruzuki, Amatsukaze, Yukikaze, Ikazuchi, Inazuma, Akatsuki

Kirishima

Savo I

Hiei

Nagara

Aaron Ward crippled and towed back to Tulagi

Samidare Murasame Asagumo

0140

Kirishima

Cape Esperance

Monssen

Yudachi

Cushing

0150 Firing starts and general melée ensues until 0226

Hiei

0140

0140

Marusame Yudachi

0140

0130

Task Group 67.4
REAR ADMIRAL D. CALLAGHAN

Guadalcanal

0127

Cushing   Atlanta
Laffey 0124 San Francisco   Aaron Ward
Sterett   Portland   Barton
Portland crippled and towed to Tulagi
O'Bannon   Helena   Monssen
Juneau 0100   Fletcher

Atlanta sunk evening 13.11

Lunga Point

0   4 Nm
0   4 km

Henderson Field

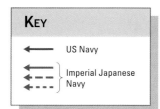

PACIFIC OCEAN

AUSTRALIA

IN ORDER TO shift the balance on Guadalcanal, the Japanese planned a major resupply operation for mid-November that would bring in food and ammunition for nearly a month along with 7,000 fresh troops. The escort for this valuable convoy, loaded onto eleven transports, would be nearly the entire available strength of the Eighth and Combined Fleets. The latter was reduced to only one carrier after the losses incurred by the air groups in late October resulted in three carriers having to return to Japan. Instead, battleships would provide the core strength and, as part of the plan, along with their escorting destroyers they would conduct a bombardment of Henderson Field in an attempt to destroy American air power on the island. At the same time as the Japanese convoy was getting underway to move down the Slot, six American transports unloaded troops and supplies at Lunga Point on 12 November.

American reconnaissance aircraft spotted Rear Admiral Abe's bombardment force approaching from the north as well as the convoy. It was reasonable to assume that the Japanese battleships were either going to conduct a bombardment or attempt to sink the transports. Thus all available cruisers and destroyers were assembled for a night-time engagement where it was hoped torpedo attacks would negate the broadside advantage that the Japanese force enjoyed. The Americans had the advantage of radar and were preparing to attack when the surprised Japanese spotted them. The battle was a confused affair. Rear Admiral Callaghan was killed when a Japanese shell hit *San Francisco*'s bridge and his deputy, Rear Admiral Scott, was killed when *Atlanta* was mistakenly hit by American gunfire in addition to the Japanese torpedoes. *Hiei* was badly damaged and subjected to numerous American air strikes throughout the day before being sunk.

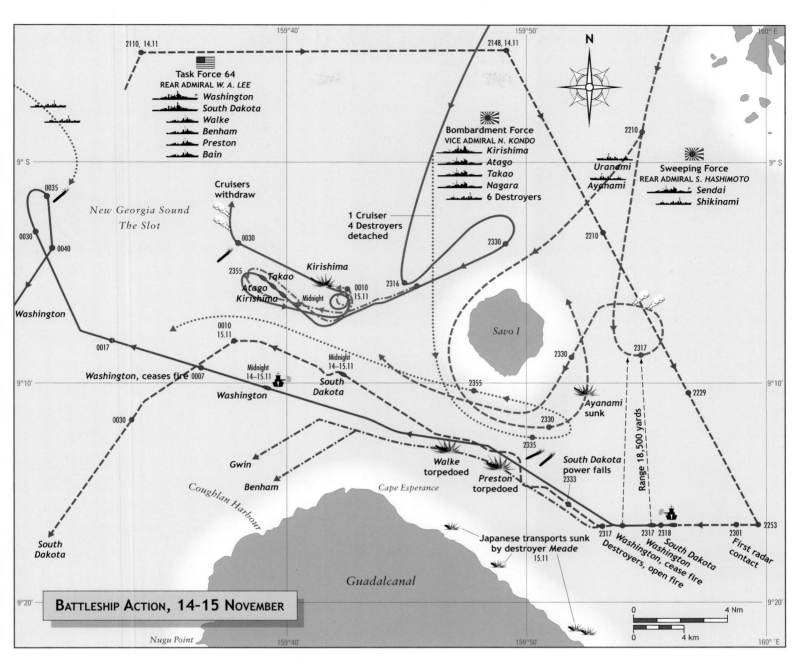

Task Force 64
REAR ADMIRAL *W. A. LEE*
- *Washington*
- *South Dakota*
- *Walke*
- *Benham*
- *Preston*
- *Bain*

Bombardment Force
VICE ADMIRAL *N. KONDO*
- *Kirishima*
- *Atago*
- *Takao*
- *Nagara*
- 6 Destroyers

Sweeping Force
REAR ADMIRAL *S. HASHIMOTO*
- *Sendai*
- *Shikinami*

Uranami
Ayanami

New Georgia Sound
The Slot

Cruisers withdraw

1 Cruiser 4 Destroyers detached

Kirishima

Takao
Atago
Kirishima

Midnight

0010 15.11

2355
2316
2330

2210

2210

2148, 14.11

2110, 14.11

0035
0030
0040

Washington

0017
0010 15.11

Washington, ceases fire 0007

0030

Washington

Midnight
14–15.11

Midnight
14–15.11

South Dakota

Gwin

Benham

Coughlan Harbour

Cape Esperance

South Dakota

2355

2330

2335

Ayanami sunk

2229

2317

Range 18,500 yards

2330

Savo I

Walke torpedoed

Preston torpedoed

South Dakota power fails
2333

2317 2317 2318

Washington, cease fire
Washington
Destroyers, open fire

South Dakota

2301

2253

First radar contact

Japanese transports sunk by destroyer *Meade*
15.11

Guadalcanal

BATTLESHIP ACTION, 14-15 NOVEMBER

Nugu Point

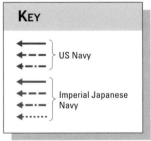

0   4 Nm
0   4 km

KEY

US Navy

Imperial Japanese Navy

THE ENGAGEMENT ON 13 November delayed the Japanese convoy from Shortland to Guadalcanal. Instead, Vice Admiral Kondo would first take the *Kirishima*, the cruisers and destroyers, and bombard Henderson Field late on 14 November. Two more battleships and the sole carrier available would remain north of Guadalcanal in case a large American force arrived. As the remaining naval forces were no longer capable of any action, Vice Admiral Halsey ordered the battleships *Washington* and *South Dakota*, then with TF 16 well over 300 miles to the south, to patrol off Savo. TF 64 under Rear Admiral Lee also had four destroyers.

Vice Admiral Mikawa bombarded Henderson Field during the night of 13–14 November with his cruisers. Meanwhile, the convoy under Rear Admiral Tanaka also left Shortland at dusk on 13 November. Both these forces were subjected to American airstrikes from Henderson Field and *Enterprise*, throughout 14 November. Tanaka's force took heavy casualties, with some ships turning back, and only nightfall protected the remaining ships that arrived off Guadalcanal. At around 9pm, Rear Admiral Lee began to patrol off Savo. Kondo, who was around an hour away, split his force and sent Rear Admiral Hashimoto ahead to scout. His ships identified

the American battleships as cruisers leading Kondo to underestimate the force he faced. This time the Americans had the broadside advantage, although Lee assumed that he would be facing a superior force as he did not anticipate the Japanese deploying only a fraction of their strength.

The Americans made radar contact with Hashimoto's force at 11pm and fifteen minutes later opened fire, but soon ceased as the approach of a second force from the west caused confusion. The American destroyers were subjected to torpedo attacks and two were sunk; the others were ordered to turn southwest. Despite receiving numerous warnings, Kondo failed to believe he was facing two battleships when *South Dakota* was illuminated at midnight. The Japanese then focused their fire on her but remained unaware of *Washington*'s presence, which in turn poured fire into *Kirishima*. *South Dakota* turned southwest and *Washington* continued to fight before also withdrawing. Kondo abandoned the operation, and this was the second Japanese defeat in two days as, in addition to a second battleship, a number of transports were sunk in the morning; the resupply operation had failed.

BATTLE OF TASSAFARONGA, 30 NOVEMBER 1942

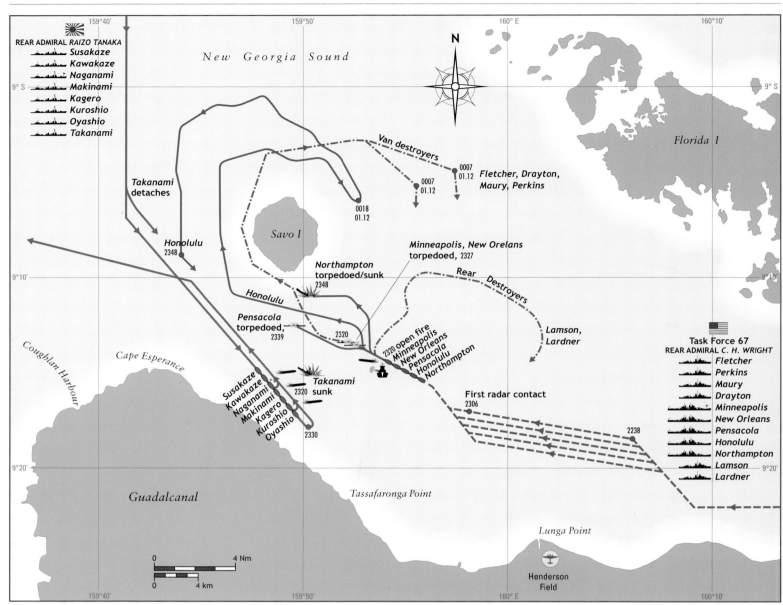

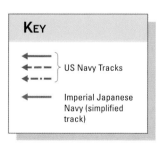

AS THE SITUATION on Guadalcanal deteriorated throughout November, the Japanese attempted to bring in supplies using submarines and small craft operating down the Slot in stages at night. Neither proved effective, so Rear Admiral Tanaka was tasked with employing a new method that involved dropping supplies packed in fuel drums linked together by means of rope. These could be pushed overboard near the coastline and pulled ashore, and the destroyers would spend little time exposed off Guadalcanal. Tanaka sailed on 29 November with six destroyers carrying between 200 and 240 drums each and two destroyers as a screen. His force was spotted off southern Bougainville by an allied coastal watcher, and the Americans were able to attempt an interception. In the aftermath of the Guadalcanal naval battles the American forces were reorganised to compensate for the losses incurred. A new force, TF 67, had been formed to operate around Guadalcanal, but Rear Admiral Wright had only assumed command hours before being ordered to intercept the Japanese.

Late on 30 November both forces were heading straight towards each other south of Savo. At 11.06pm

Minneapolis made first radar contact, prompting Wright to bring his ships back into column. Tanaka ordered his ships to prepare to attack at 11.16pm. At 11.20pm the American ships started to fire but focused on the *Takanami*, allowing the other Japanese destroyers to launch their torpedoes and then slip past the American line before turning north at 11.30pm. *Minneapolis* and *New Orleans* were hit, the latter having her entire bow to the second turret blown off. Twenty minutes later the *Pensacola* and *Northampton* were hit, the latter so badly that she eventually sunk at 3.04am. In the confusion the American ships failed to find further targets. At 11.45pm Tanaka ordered his forces to retreat, although he detached two destroyers to locate the *Takanami*. For the Americans the heavy losses were embarrassing, particularly so as their superior force was effectively put out of action in forty minutes. In the future they relied on PT boats to intercept Japanese supply convoys, and the IJN in turn felt that the losses it was incurring were unsustainable; by mid-December the American blockade of Guadalcanal was near absolute.

CONVOY ROUTES AND ANTI-SUBMARINE DEFENCES IN US WATERS, 1942–45

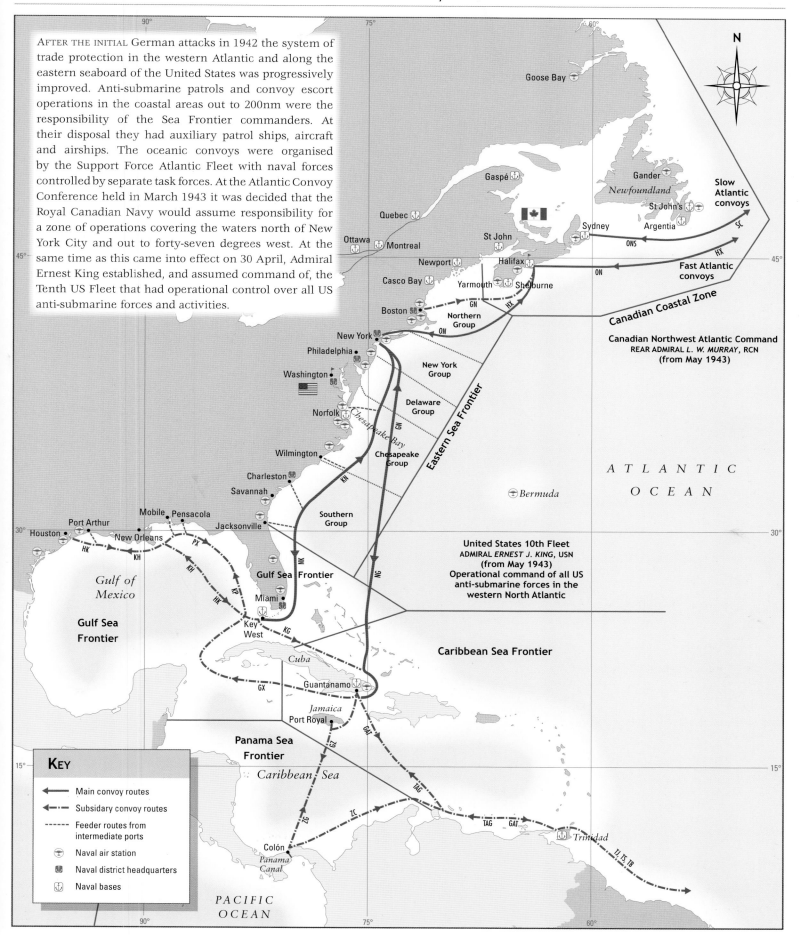

AFTER THE INITIAL German attacks in 1942 the system of trade protection in the western Atlantic and along the eastern seaboard of the United States was progressively improved. Anti-submarine patrols and convoy escort operations in the coastal areas out to 200nm were the responsibility of the Sea Frontier commanders. At their disposal they had auxiliary patrol ships, aircraft and airships. The oceanic convoys were organised by the Support Force Atlantic Fleet with naval forces controlled by separate task forces. At the Atlantic Convoy Conference held in March 1943 it was decided that the Royal Canadian Navy would assume responsibility for a zone of operations covering the waters north of New York City and out to forty-seven degrees west. At the same time as this came into effect on 30 April, Admiral Ernest King established, and assumed command of, the Tenth US Fleet that had operational control over all US anti-submarine forces and activities.

Slow Atlantic convoys

Fast Atlantic convoys

Canadian Coastal Zone

Canadian Northwest Atlantic Command
REAR ADMIRAL *L. W. MURRAY*, RCN
(from May 1943)

ATLANTIC OCEAN

⊕ Bermuda

United States 10th Fleet
ADMIRAL *ERNEST J. KING*, USN
(from May 1943)
Operational command of all US anti-submarine forces in the western North Atlantic

Caribbean Sea Frontier

Gulf Sea Frontier

Panama Sea Frontier

Caribbean Sea

Gulf of Mexico

Goose Bay

Gaspé
Gander
Newfoundland
St John's
Argentia
Quebec
St John
Sydney
ONS
HX
Ottawa
Montreal
Newport
Halifax
ON
Casco Bay
Yarmouth
Shelburne
Boston
GN
HX
Northern Group
ON
New York
Philadelphia
New York Group
Washington
Delaware Group
Norfolk
Chesapeake Bay
Chesapeake Group
Eastern Sea Frontier
Wilmington
KM
Charleston
Savannah
Mobile Pensacola
Port Arthur
Houston
New Orleans
Jacksonville
Southern Group
HK
KH
PX
KP
Gulf Sea Frontier
KH
HK
Miami
Key West
KG
Cuba
GX
Guantánamo
Jamaica
Port Royal
GZ
GAT
TAG
ZG
ZC
TAG GAT
TAG GAT
Trinidad
TJ TS TB
Colón
Panama Canal

PACIFIC OCEAN

KEY

⟶ Main convoy routes

⟵- - - Subsidary convoy routes

- - - - - Feeder routes from intermediate ports

⊕ Naval air station

🏛 Naval district headquarters

⊕ Naval bases

CONVOYS JW 51B AND RA 51, 28 DECEMBER 1942 – 4 JANUARY 1943

THE DEMANDS PLACED on the Home Fleet by Operation *Torch* led to a suspension of the Arctic convoys in the autumn. The heavy losses incurred by PQ 17 and PQ 18 showed that unless convoys were heavily protected they would suffer considerably. It was also debated whether it was more advantageous to concentrate merchant ships into one convoy, where defensive firepower could be maximised, or whether the diversionary effect of two convoys could assist in confusing the Germans. When the convoys were restarted in December they were also given new designations. Three convoys were organised: two from the west staggered by a week, and one from the east. A cruiser close escort force was to pass through to the Barents Sea and in turn cover each of the convoys. In the event, incorrect information sent to Rear Admiral Burnett about the position of JW 51B placed him further away from the convoy than planned during the crucial two days of the operation, 30–31 December.

On 30 December, a U-boat reported a convoy to the south of Bear Island prompting Vice Admiral Kummetz

to put to sea immediately. The Germans were, however, unaware of the presence of Force R, and had Kummetz known he would not have sailed as his orders were to avoid combat with equal or superior forces, or risk a night battle where his ships might be subject to destroyer torpedo attacks. He intended to attack the convoy from two directions simultaneously to confuse the defenders. First contact was made around 8.30am on 31 December, and around an hour later the fighting commenced. The battle developed into a confused running skirmish with neither side having an overview of the situation. Smoke and snow added to the problem and Burnett, in particular, initially found it difficult to distinguish between allied and German ships, but the escorts were able to keep the German ships away from the convoy until the cruisers arrived. Around noon the cruisers on both sides briefly exchanged fire before the German force withdrew. No merchant ships were lost and the battle of the Barents Sea was an important success for the British.

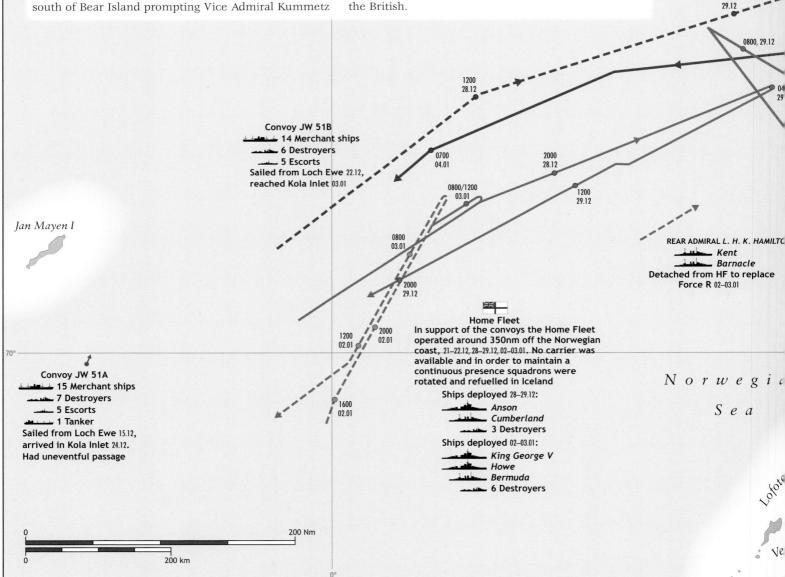

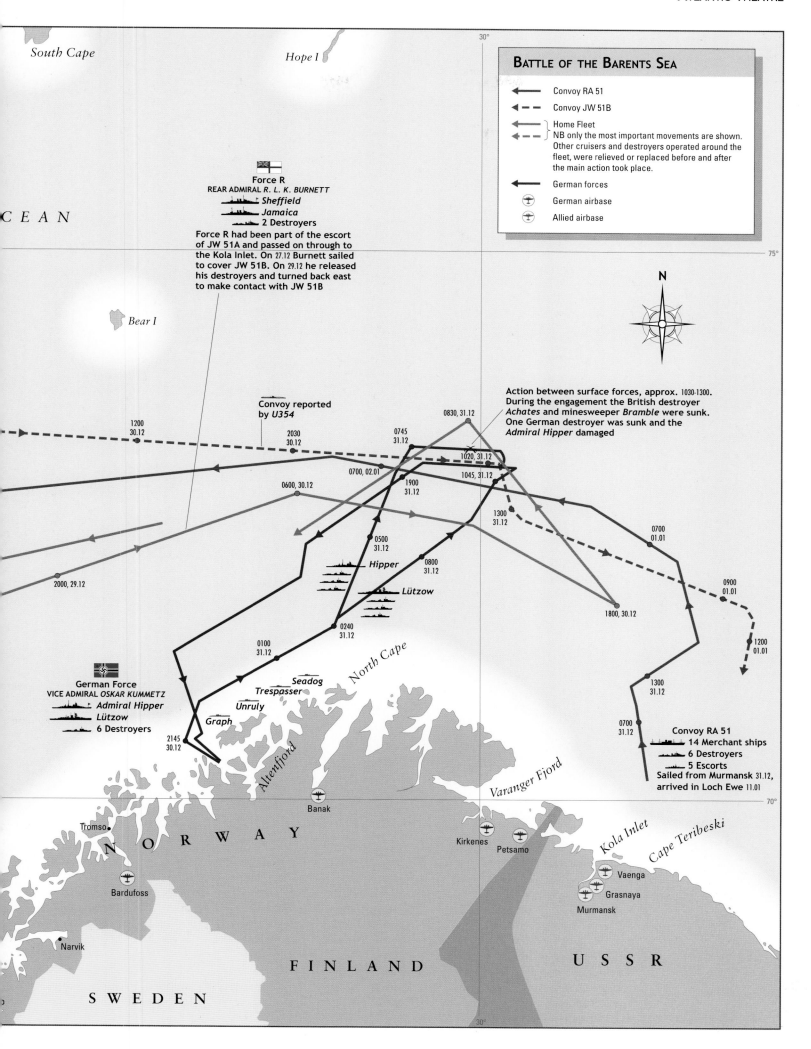

South Cape

Hope I

30°

BATTLE OF THE BARENTS SEA

Convoy RA 51
Convoy JW 51B
} Home Fleet
NB only the most important movements are shown. Other cruisers and destroyers operated around the fleet, were relieved or replaced before and after the main action took place.
German forces
German airbase
Allied airbase

OCEAN

Force R
REAR ADMIRAL *R. L. K. BURNETT*
Sheffield
Jamaica
2 Destroyers
Force R had been part of the escort of JW 51A and passed on through to the Kola Inlet. On 27.12 Burnett sailed to cover JW 51B. On 29.12 he released his destroyers and turned back east to make contact with JW 51B

75°

N

Bear I

Action between surface forces, approx. 1030-1300. During the engagement the British destroyer *Achates* and minesweeper *Bramble* were sunk. One German destroyer was sunk and the *Admiral Hipper* damaged

Convoy reported by *U354*

0830, 31.12

0745
31.12

1200
30.12

2030
30.12

0700, 02.01

1020, 31.12

1045, 31.12

0600, 30.12

1900
31.12

0700
01.01

1300
31.12

0500
31.12

2000, 29.12

Hipper

0800
31.12

0900
01.01

Lützow

1800, 30.12

1200
01.01

0240
31.12

0100
31.12

North Cape

1300
31.12

Seadog

0700
01.01

Trespasser

German Force
VICE ADMIRAL *OSKAR KUMMETZ*
Admiral Hipper
Lützow
6 Destroyers

Unruly

Graph

0700
31.12

Convoy RA 51
14 Merchant ships
6 Destroyers
5 Escorts
Sailed from Murmansk 31.12, arrived in Loch Ewe 11.01

2145
30.12

Altenfjord

Varanger Fjord

Kola Inlet

Cape Teribeski

70°

Banak

Tromso

N O R W A Y

Kirkenes

Petsamo

Vaenga

Bardufoss

Grasnaya

Murmansk

Narvik

F I N L A N D

U S S R

SWEDEN

30°

THE WAR AT SEA, 1943

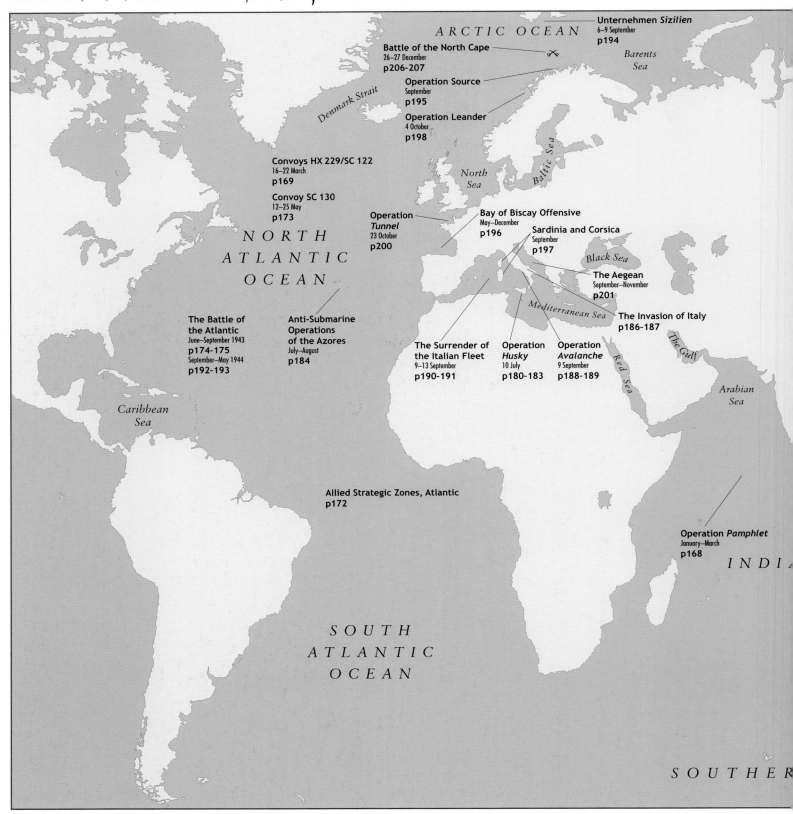

ARCTIC OCEAN

Unternehmen *Sizilien*
6–9 September
p194

Battle of the North Cape
26–27 December
p206-207

Barents Sea

Operation Source
September
p195

Denmark Strait

Operation Leander
4 October
p198

Convoys HX 229/SC 122
16–22 March
p169

Baltic Sea

Convoy SC 130
12–25 May
p173

North Sea

Operation
Tunnel
23 October
p200

Bay of Biscay Offensive
May–December
p196

Sardinia and Corsica
September
p197

NORTH
ATLANTIC
OCEAN

Black Sea

The Aegean
September–November
p201

Mediterranean Sea

The Battle of
the Atlantic
June–September 1943
p174-175
September–May 1944
p192-193

Anti-Submarine
Operations
of the Azores
July–August
p184

The Invasion of Italy
p186-187

The Gulf

The Surrender of
the Italian Fleet
9–13 September
p190-191

Operation
Husky
10 July
p180-183

Operation
Avalanche
9 September
p188-189

Red Sea

*Arabian
Sea*

*Caribbean
Sea*

Allied Strategic Zones, Atlantic
p172

Operation *Pamphlet*
January–March
p168

INDIA

SOUTH
ATLANTIC
OCEAN

SOUTHER

For the allies, 1943 was a transitional year and by its close they were on the offensive in all the major theatres. Attaining command of the oceans enabled the allies to move men, materiel and resources in preparation for opening a second front in Europe to force Germany's unconditional surrender. Keeping the maritime supply routes to the Soviet Union, via the Arctic, the Persian Gulf and the North Pacific, open was also vital, for by delivering raw materials, food and transportation the western allies enabled the Soviets to focus on raising and equipping a large mechanised force for the invasion of Germany from the East.

In the Atlantic, defeating the U-boat threat became the allied priority. Previously, it had been sufficient to restrict shipping losses within acceptable limits, and commitments in other theatres never allowed the allies to focus on one campaign. The American build-up of forces in Britain, Operation *Bolero*, had slowed down considerably in the second half of 1942, mainly as a result of the campaigns in the South Pacific and North Africa. In 1943, with preparations for an invasion of northwestern Europe advancing, thousands of American personnel would cross the Atlantic every week. This made eliminating the U-boat threat imperative.

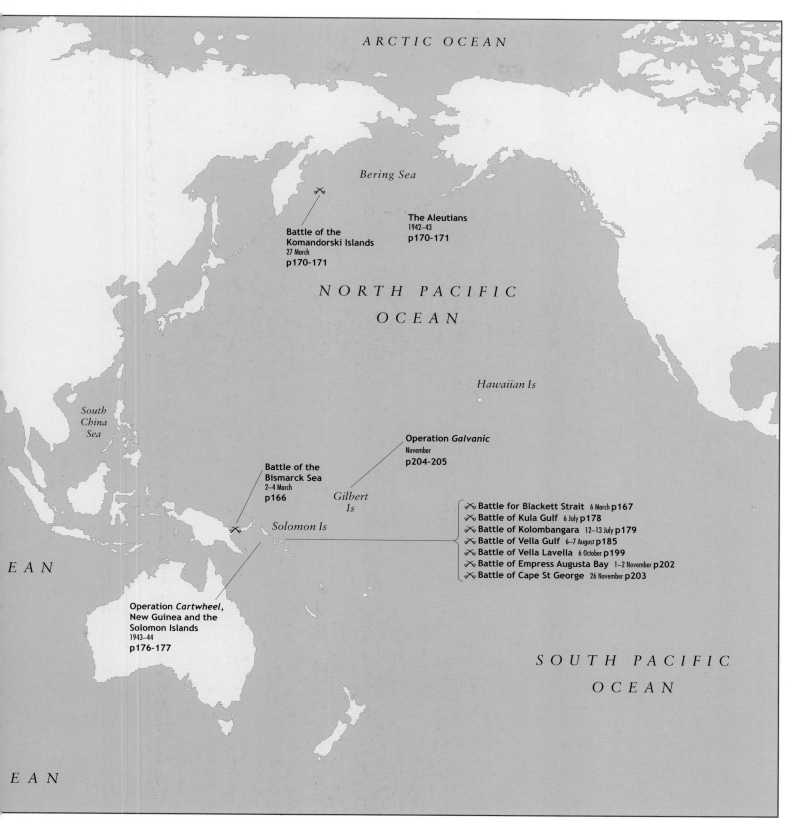

ARCTIC OCEAN

Bering Sea

Battle of the
Komandorski Islands
27 March
p170-171

The Aleutians
1942–43
p170-171

NORTH PACIFIC
OCEAN

Hawaiian Is

Operation *Galvanic*
November
p204-205

*South
China
Sea*

Battle of the
Bismarck Sea
2–4 March
p166

*Gilbert
Is*

⚔ Battle for Blackett Strait 6 March **p167**
⚔ Battle of Kula Gulf 6 July **p178**
⚔ Battle of Kolombangara 12–13 July **p179**
⚔ Battle of Vella Gulf 6–7 August **p185**
⚔ Battle of Vella Lavella 6 October **p199**
⚔ Battle of Empress Augusta Bay 1–2 November **p202**
⚔ Battle of Cape St George 26 November **p203**

Solomon Is

EAN

Operation *Cartwheel*,
New Guinea and the
Solomon Islands
1943–44
p176-177

SOUTH PACIFIC
OCEAN

EAN

The allied objective in the Mediterranean was to reopen the sea for maritime traffic, and to secure this an invasion of Sicily was launched in July. The lack of naval power in the Mediterranean cost the axis the entire Army Group Africa that surrendered in Tunisia in May, comprising more men than were lost at Stalingrad. Keeping supplies moving across waters controlled by allied naval and air forces was impossible, something that the Japanese were experiencing at the same time in the Solomons. For the allies, knocking Italy out of the war then proved too tempting and in September landings took place on the mainland. The campaign quickly became bogged down and allied naval power could only marginally influence the outcome on land.

After the exhausting battles in 1942, the Pacific remained quiet in the first half of the year as both sides recovered. In the long term the Americans had the advantage as huge, well-equipped fleets were being assembled. For most of the year fighting took place on the periphery. The Japanese presence in the Aleutians was short lived and a second campaign in the Solomons sapped more Japanese resources than it did American in the long run. By the autumn the Americans were ready to take to the offensive in the Central Pacific and launched the westward advance with amphibious landings on the Gilbert Islands.

BATTLE OF THE BISMARCK SEA, 2–4 MARCH 1943

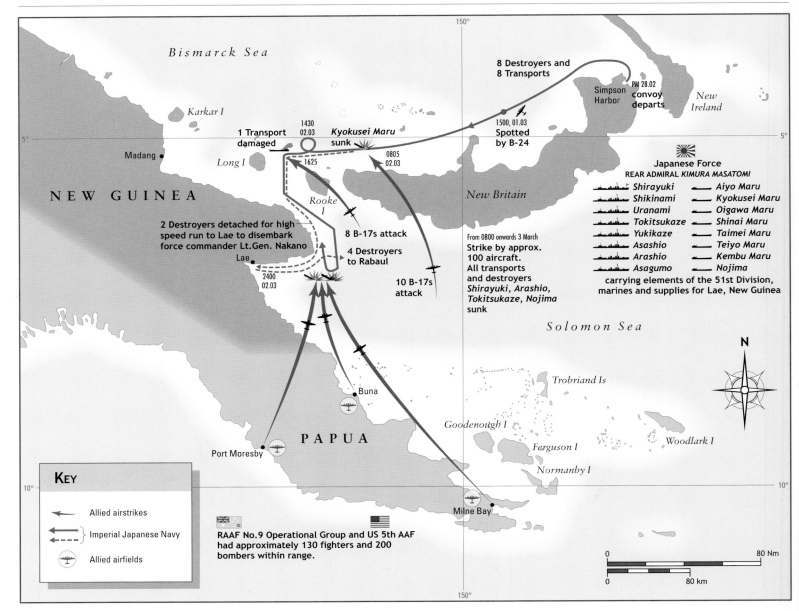

Bismarck Sea

Karkar I

Madang

Long I

NEW GUINEA

1430 02.03
1 Transport damaged

Kyokusei Maru sunk

8 Destroyers and 8 Transports

Simpson Harbor

PM 28.02 convoy departs

New Ireland

1500, 01.03 **Spotted by B-24**

1625

0805 02.03

Rooke I

New Britain

2 Destroyers detached for high speed run to Lae to disembark force commander Lt.Gen. Nakano

Lae

2400 02.03

8 B-17s attack

4 Destroyers to Rabaul

10 B-17s attack

From 0800 onwards 3 March **Strike by approx. 100 aircraft.** All transports and destroyers *Shirayuki, Arashio, Tokitsukaze, Nojima* sunk

Japanese Force
REAR ADMIRAL *KIMURA MASATOMI*

Shirayuki	*Aiyo Maru*
Shikinami	*Kyokusei Maru*
Uranami	*Oigawa Maru*
Tokitsukaze	*Shinai Maru*
Yukikaze	*Taimei Maru*
Asashio	*Teiyo Maru*
Arashio	*Kembu Maru*
Asagumo	*Nojima*

carrying elements of the 51st Division, marines and supplies for Lae, New Guinea

Solomon Sea

Buna

N

Trobriand Is

Goodenough I

PAPUA

Port Moresby

Ferguson I

Normanby I

Woodlark I

KEY

→ Allied airstrikes

← Imperial Japanese Navy

✈ Allied airfields

Milne Bay

RAAF No.9 Operational Group and US 5th AAF had approximately 130 fighters and 200 bombers within range.

0 — 80 Nm
0 — 80 km

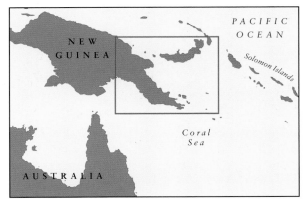

PACIFIC OCEAN

NEW GUINEA

Solomon Islands

Coral Sea

AUSTRALIA

IN EARLY 1943 the Japanese decided to reinforce and reorganise their forces in the southwest Pacific. As allied forces had been able to push north on New Guinea, the Japanese prepared to send two further divisions to the island. In the first wave a convoy would land 6,900 troops and supplies at Lae, but owing to allied air power in the region this would be a risky operation. Another and safer option, landing further north at Madang, would commit the troops to a 200km march over inhospitable terrain. On 25 February allied signals intelligence revealed that a Japanese resupply operation for New Guinea was imminent and so air patrols were increased. The convoy was spotted by a B-24 on 1 March,

a day after it left Rabaul. The next day it was attacked by small groups of B-17s that succeeded in sinking a transport.

On 3 March the convoy passed between New Guinea and New Britain and into the range of allied fighters and medium bombers that began their attacks around 10am. The Japanese fighter cover tended to target the B-17s operating higher up, thus leaving the ships vulnerable to low and medium altitude attacks. It was at these heights that the majority of allied strikes were flown and consequently the convoy was decimated. The American B-25s and Australian Beaufighters proved to be particularly effective. All seven remaining transports and four destroyers were sunk against an allied loss of a few aircraft. During the night American PT boats interfered with Japanese rescue attempts, and though Japanese destroyers and submarines picked up 2,734 men, around 5,000 were lost. From then on only small vessels sailing at night were employed, but this was insufficient to cover the garrison's requirements.

THE BATTLE FOR BLACKETT STRAIT, 6 MARCH 1943

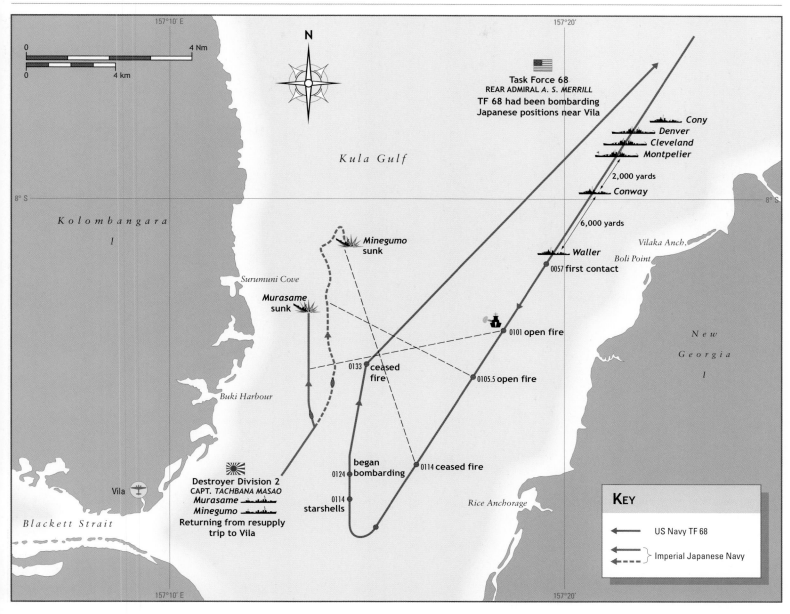

AFTER THE AMERICAN victory in the Guadalcanal campaign, the Japanese continued to hold onto a number of bases in the central Solomons. American naval power had steadily been growing in the region and by the spring of 1943 two carrier and two battleship groups were operating in the open waters to the east, while two cruiser-destroyer task forces operated in amongst the islands. In January TF 67 had conducted a bombardment of the Japanese air bases at Vila and Munda, an exercise that was perceived as highly successful by the Americans. In the immediate aftermath of the Japanese evacuation of Guadalcanal the Solomons remained quiet, but by March the Americans were looking to attack the outlying Japanese bases.

Another bombardment of Munda and Vila was planned for early on 6 March. While four destroyers hit the former, the bulk of TF 68, under Rear Admiral Merrill, hit Vila. This operation coincided with a routine Japanese destroyer resupply mission for Kolombangara. At 5pm two Japanese destroyers left Shortland Island for Vila and at around 11.30pm an American PBY Black

Cat night maritime patrol plane, acting as scout for TF 68, detected them. By then the Japanese had unloaded their cargo and were making for home using the shorter route through the Kula Gulf. This put them right in the path of TF 68. Just before 1am they appeared on the radar of the destroyer *Waller*. At 1.01am the American ships opened fire on the

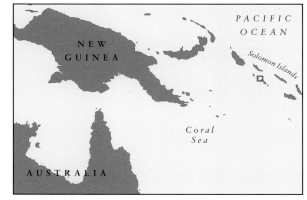

unsuspecting Japanese and quickly overwhelmed them with shells and torpedoes. Then TF 68 undertook its planned bombardment of Vila airfield. Officially, the engagement was not named and is sometimes referred to as the first battle of Kula Gulf or the battle of Vila-Stanmore.

OPERATION PAMPHLET, JANUARY–MARCH 1943

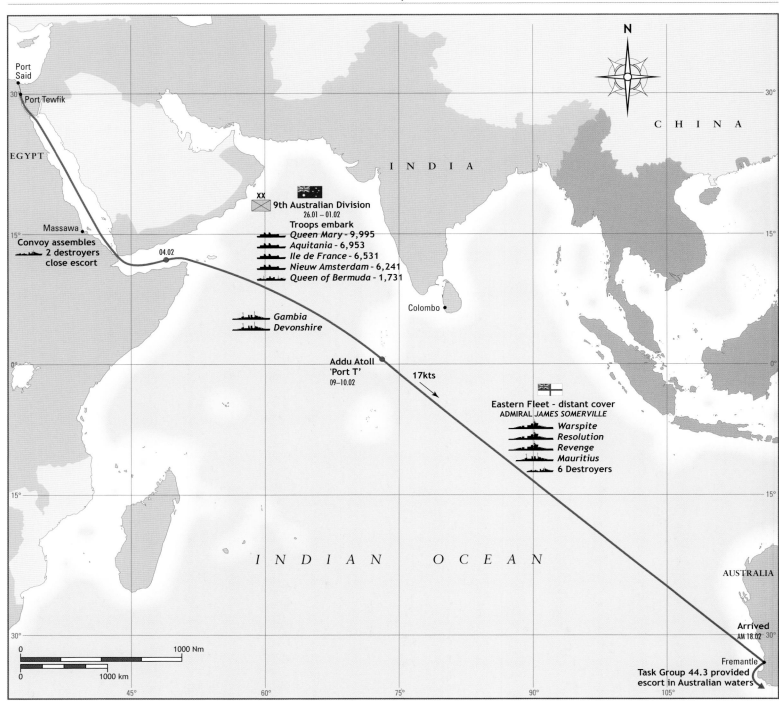

N

Port Said
Port Tewfik
30°

EGYPT

Massawa
15°
Convoy assembles
2 destroyers
close escort

04.02

XX
9th Australian Division
26.01 – 01.02
Troops embark
Queen Mary - 9,995
Aquitania - 6,953
Ile de France - 6,531
Nieuw Amsterdam - 6,241
Queen of Bermuda - 1,731

Gambia
Devonshire

Colombo

CHINA

INDIA

Addu Atoll
'Port T'
09–10.02

17kts

Eastern Fleet - distant cover
ADMIRAL JAMES SOMERVILLE
Warspite
Resolution
Revenge
Mauritius
6 Destroyers

INDIAN   OCEAN

AUSTRALIA

Arrived
AM 18.02

0   1000 Nm

0   1000 km

Fremantle
Task Group 44.3 provided
escort in Australian waters

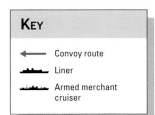

KEY

⟵ Convoy route

⚓ Liner

⚓ Armed merchant
cruiser

IN 1940 AND 1941 the Australians sent a force of four infantry divisions to the Middle East, but following the Japanese entry into the war the government was anxious that its troops should return as soon as possible. By the spring of 1942 the 9th Division was the last to remain with the 8th Army in Egypt and both the British and Americans were reluctant to see it withdrawn owing to the German successes in the Western Desert. However, by October the victory at El Alamein and the forthcoming *Torch* landings enabled the division to be withdrawn. To transport the 31,000 troops only four liners, including the huge *Queen Mary*, and an armed merchant cruiser were available. Even by wartime standards the *Pamphlet* convoy was very cramped. As only a single large liner could take on troops at Port Tewfik at a time the whole embarkation process was staggered and the individual

liners then proceeded to Massawa where the convoy formed up.

Normally the liners used their speed as protection against enemy submarines, but in this case the greatest threat was considered to be from Japanese warships. Thus the convoy was kept together and two cruisers joined as escorts. However, this meant that the convoy was limited to 17 knots, the top speed of the *Queen of Bermuda*, and the duration of the voyage was nearly doubled from eighteen to thirty-three days. The first leg of the journey was to the secret British base at Addu Atoll. During the second, more dangerous leg, distant cover was provided by a substantial part of Admiral Somerville's Eastern Fleet. After a brief stop in Fremantle the majority of the convoy proceeded to Sydney where it arrived on 27 February.

CONVOYS HX 229 AND SC 122, 16–22 MARCH 1943

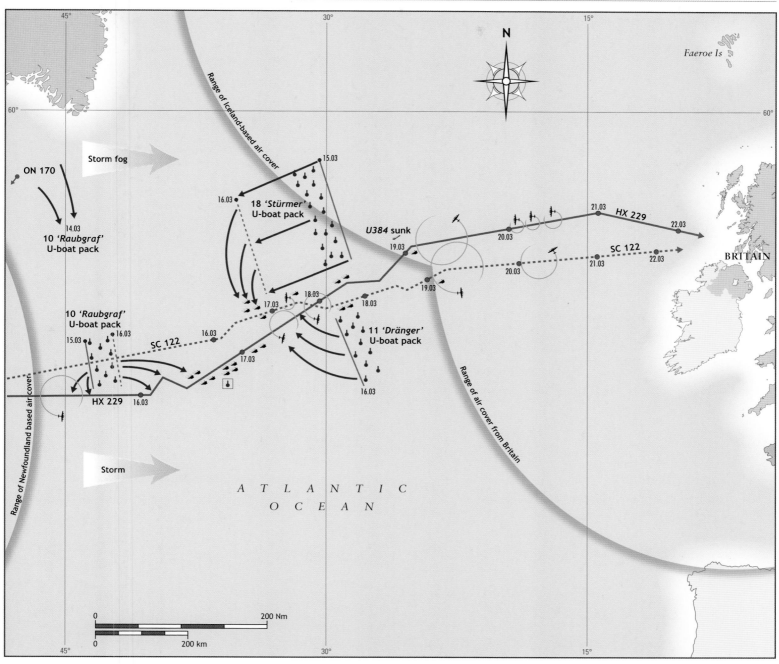

THE BATTLE FOR convoys HX 229 and SC 122 is often seen as the climax of the German Atlantic offensive and the greatest convoy battle of all time involving nearly 40 U-boats and over 100 merchant ships. Throughout February and March the conditions suited Admiral Dönitz's plan to operate against convoys in the air gap. The poor weather conditions scattered ships and made the work of the escorts exceedingly difficult. In the signals intelligence contest the Germans held the upper hand, the allies being unable, for instance, to read the latest *Triton* cipher. The convoys SC 122 and HX 229 left New York on 5 and 8 March respectively, but from the outset the weather impeded progress and by 9 March a number of ships had run into Halifax. The battle for HX 229/SC1 22 developed out of the battle for the preceding convoys. Late on 13 March the *B-Dienst*

alerted Dönitz to the presence of HX 229 southeast of Newfoundland and that it was being re-routed south of the *Raubgraf* group then engaging a west-bound convoy. In response he ordered *Raubgraf* south and formed two new groups, *Stürmer* and *Dränger*, in the path of the convoys. Although *Raubgraf* boats failed to find HX 229 on the night 15/16 March owing to the bad weather, the first merchant ships were sunk a day later. A running battle developed over the next four days in which the two individual battles effectively became one larger engagement. A small number of Liberator patrols from Iceland did manage to find the convoys on 17–18 March and a few additional escorts reinforced the screen. By the 19 March twenty-two ships had been sunk in return for only one U-boat lost, *U384*, which was sunk by depth charges dropped by a B-17.

THE ALEUTIANS, 1942–43

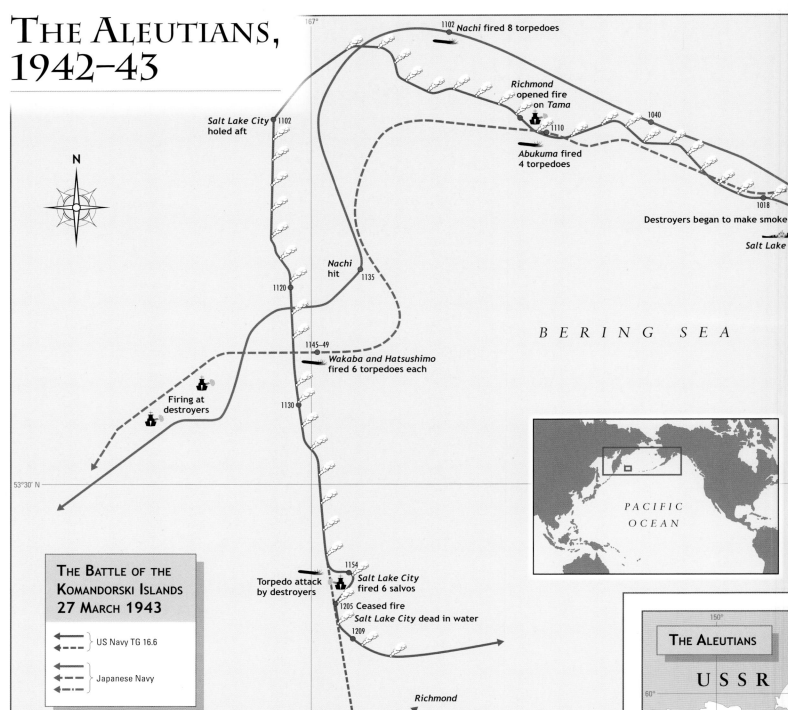

1102 *Nachi* fired 8 torpedoes

Richmond
opened fire
on *Tama*

1040

1110

Abukuma fired
4 torpedoes

1018

Destroyers began to make smoke

Salt Lake City 1102
holed aft

Salt Lake C

N

Nachi
hit

1135

1120

B E R I N G   S E A

1145–49
Wakaba and *Hatsushimo*
fired 6 torpedoes each

Firing at
destroyers

1130

PACIFIC
OCEAN

53°30′ N

1154

Torpedo attack
by destroyers

Salt Lake City
fired 6 salvos

1205 Ceased fire
Salt Lake City dead in water

1209

THE BATTLE OF THE KOMANDORSKI ISLANDS 27 MARCH 1943

US Navy TG 16.6

Japanese Navy

Richmond

167°

150°

THE ALEUTIANS

U S S R

N

60°

50°

150°

THE JAPANESE ATTACK on the Aleutians was executed in parallel to the Midway operation. Strategically, the islands were a dead-end and after establishing two garrisons as outposts on the northern flank of the Japanese empire no further action was taken. On the allied side the Americans increased the size of the Alaskan forces with a view to ejecting the Japanese as soon as possible. In early 1943 the Americans began to patrol the waters west of Attu to intercept Japanese supplies for the island outposts. After a small American cruiser-destroyer group succeeded in sinking a Japanese merchant ship in February, the latter responded by employing nearly the entire strength of the Fifth Fleet to cover the next resupply mission. In anticipation, the Americans sent out a task group, but underestimated the size of the Japanese force.

The ensuing battle of the Komandorski Islands,

fought on the morning of 27 March, was the only major engagement in the region. It was also one of the few engagements fought only between surface forces during the Pacific war. The American force located the Japanese by means of signals intelligence and was attempting to pursue the convoy when it became clear the latter had a numerical advantage. The Americans turned away and were in turn pursued so that a running battle developed in which both sides sustained damage, but the Japanese gradually gained the advantage. Ultimately, the engagement ended inconclusively as the Japanese commander turned for home, concerned about his ammunition expenditure. Strategically, the battle marked a turning point as the Japanese now abandoned any attempt to keep the Aleutians resupplied by ship. The American landings on Attu in May prompted the Japanese to evacuate Kiska at the end of July.

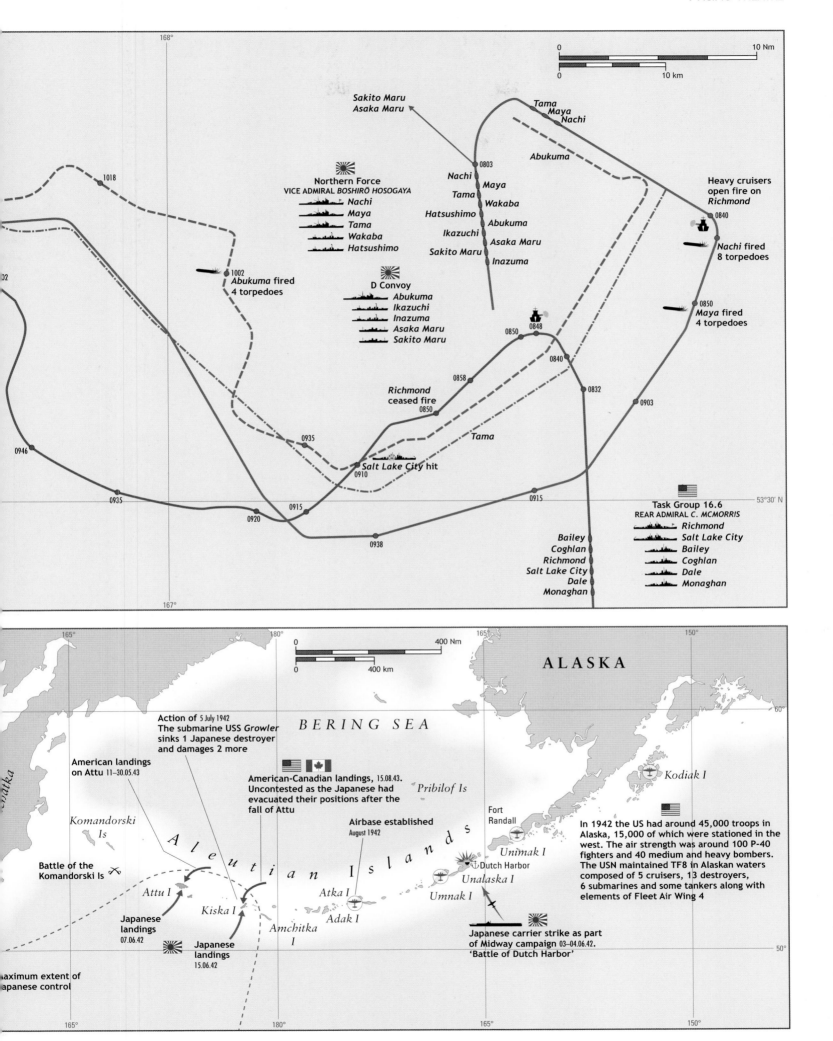

0 ⟶ 10 Nm
0 ⟶ 10 km

Sakito Maru
Asaka Maru

Tama
Maya
Nachi

Northern Force
VICE ADMIRAL *BOSHIRŌ HOSOGAYA*

Nachi
Maya
Tama
Wakaba
Hatsushimo

0803

Nachi
Maya
Tama
Wakaba
Hatsushimo
Abukuma
Ikazuchi
Asaka Maru
Sakito Maru
Inazuma

Abukuma

Heavy cruisers
open fire on
Richmond

0840

Nachi fired
8 torpedoes

1018

1002 *Abukuma* fired
4 torpedoes

D Convoy

Abukuma
Ikazuchi
Inazuma
Asaka Maru
Sakito Maru

02

0850 0848

0850

Maya fired
4 torpedoes

0840

0832

0903

Richmond
ceased fire
0850

0858

Tama

0946

0935

Salt Lake City hit
0910

0935

0915

0920

0915

Task Group 16.6
REAR ADMIRAL *C. McMORRIS*

Richmond
Salt Lake City
Bailey
Coghlan
Dale
Monaghan

53°30' N

0938

Bailey
Coghlan
Richmond
Salt Lake City
Dale
Monaghan

ALASKA

BERING SEA

0 ⟶ 400 Nm
0 ⟶ 400 km

Action of 5 July 1942
The submarine USS *Growler*
sinks 1 Japanese destroyer
and damages 2 more

American-Canadian landings, 15.08.43.
Uncontested as the Japanese had
evacuated their positions after the
fall of Attu

American landings
on Attu 11–30.05.43

*Komandorski
Is*

Battle of the
Komandorski Is

Battle of the
Komandorski Is

Attu I

Japanese
landings
07.06.42

Kiska I

Japanese
landings
15.06.42

*Amchitka
I*

Maximum extent of
Japanese control

Pribilof Is

Airbase established
August 1942

Atka I

Adak I

Fort
Randall

Unimak I

Dutch Harbor

Unalaska I

Umnak I

Japanese carrier strike as part
of Midway campaign 03–04.06.42.
'Battle of Dutch Harbor'

Kodiak I

In 1942 the US had around 45,000 troops in
Alaska, 15,000 of which were stationed in the
west. The air strength was around 100 P-40
fighters and 40 medium and heavy bombers.
The USN maintained TF8 in Alaskan waters
composed of 5 cruisers, 13 destroyers,
6 submarines and some tankers along with
elements of Fleet Air Wing 4

Aleutian Islands

171

ALLIED STRATEGIC ZONES, ATLANTIC

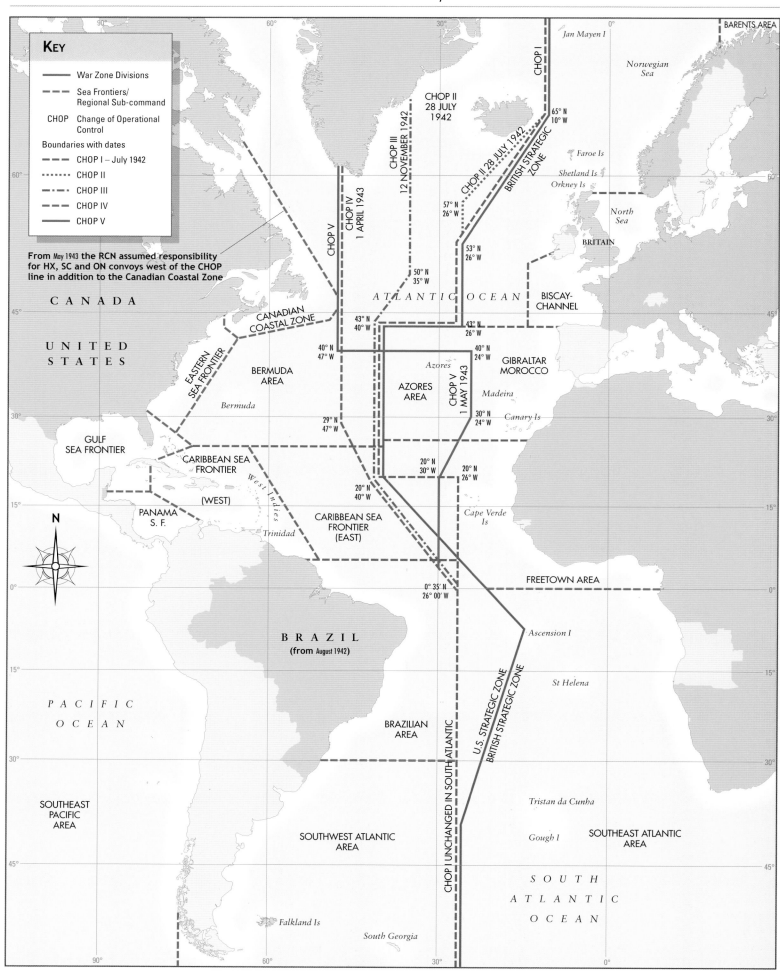

KEY

——	War Zone Divisions
- - -	Sea Frontiers/ Regional Sub-command
CHOP	Change of Operational Control

Boundaries with dates

– – –	CHOP I – July 1942
··········	CHOP II
–·–·–	CHOP III
– – –	CHOP IV
——	CHOP V

From May 1943 the RCN assumed responsibility for HX, SC and ON convoys west of the CHOP line in addition to the Canadian Coastal Zone

BARENTS AREA

Jan Mayen I

Norwegian Sea

CHOP I

CHOP II 28 JULY 1942

CHOP III 12 NOVEMBER 1942

65° N 10° W

Faroe Is

CHOP II 28 JULY 1942

BRITISH STRATEGIC ZONE

Shetland Is

Orkney Is

North Sea

57° N 26° W

CHOP V

CHOP IV 1 APRIL 1943

BRITAIN

53° N 26° W

CANADA

50° N 35° W

ATLANTIC OCEAN

BISCAY-CHANNEL

UNITED STATES

CANADIAN COASTAL ZONE

43° N 40° W

43° N 26° W

EASTERN SEA FRONTIER

40° N 47° W

Azores

40° N 24° W

GIBRALTAR MOROCCO

BERMUDA AREA

AZORES AREA

CHOP V 1 MAY 1943

Madeira

Bermuda

29° N 47° W

30° N 24° W

Canary Is

GULF SEA FRONTIER

CARIBBEAN SEA FRONTIER

20° N 30° W

20° N 26° W

(WEST)

West Indies

20° N 40° W

PANAMA S. F.

Cape Verde Is

Trinidad

CARIBBEAN SEA FRONTIER (EAST)

N

FREETOWN AREA

0° 35′ N 26° 00′ W

Ascension I

BRAZIL (from August 1942)

St Helena

PACIFIC OCEAN

BRAZILIAN AREA

U.S. STRATEGIC ZONE

BRITISH STRATEGIC ZONE

SOUTHEAST PACIFIC AREA

Tristan da Cunha

SOUTHEAST ATLANTIC AREA

Gough I

SOUTHWEST ATLANTIC AREA

CHOP I UNCHANGED IN SOUTH ATLANTIC

SOUTH ATLANTIC OCEAN

Falkland Is

South Georgia

CONVOY SC 130, 12–25 MAY 1943

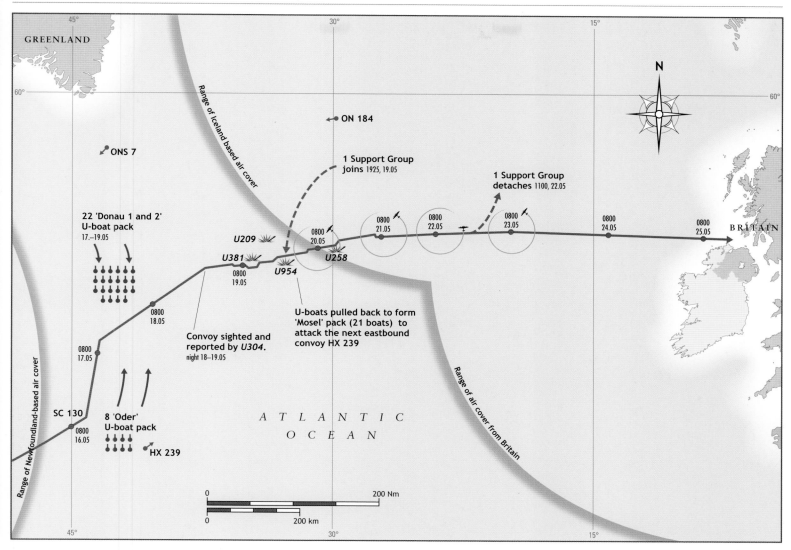

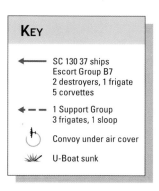

THE ALLIED ORGANISATION of the Atlantic theatre underwent numerous changes as the war progressed, and the better coordination of forces and resources was one of the key factors in defeating the U-boats. Until early 1942 the British had operational control of the Atlantic campaign. Although the Royal Canadian Navy was rapidly expanding, the Canadians only exercised direct control in their coastal waters with vessels coming under British control when they operated in the Atlantic. After the American entry into the war, a clear division of responsibility in the Atlantic became a necessity and the entire ocean from the Arctic to the Antarctic was divided into two zones, American and British.

The so-called 'Chop' line regulated which navy was responsible for which area and had operational control of all naval and air assets involved in the anti-submarine campaign. Initially, the operational division of the theatre mirrored the strategic one. However, in July and August 1942 the line in the North Atlantic was moved westward, and again in April 1943, as a result of the Washington Atlantic Conference that March. The reason for these shifts was to enable a better Anglo-Canadian coordination in, and control of, the North Atlantic. A final reorganisation came in effect in May whereby the Americans assumed a much greater responsibility in the central Atlantic to cover their convoys to the

Mediterranean. The Canadians also took responsibility of their own oceanic zone. The command arrangements in the South Atlantic remained the same for the duration of the war.

After the successes of the spring, the U-boat offensive collapsed in May with forty-one U-boats being sunk. Of these, fourteen were sunk by surface escorts and eleven by aircraft while attempting to attack convoys. The action fought around convoy SC 130 is representative of the decisive shift in the Atlantic. The convoy left Halifax on 11 May and met with its oceanic escort, Escort Group B7, on 15 May. Through signals intelligence the Germans were aware that three convoys, SC 130, HX 239 and ON S7 were entering the Air Gap, but it was only on 18 May that contact with SC 130 was made by *U304*. Throughout 19 May the escorts kept the U-boats from attacking the convoy and towards the end of the day a Support Group reinforced it. VLR aircraft from Iceland also arrived and covered the convoy for three days and two nights, during which time they made twenty-eight sightings and ten attacks, two of which were successful. By 20 May, four U-boats had been sunk and one badly damaged, prompting Admiral Dönitz to abandon the operation. One of his sons was killed in the sinking of *U954*. During the second half of May no allied merchant ships were lost from convoys in the North Atlantic.

173

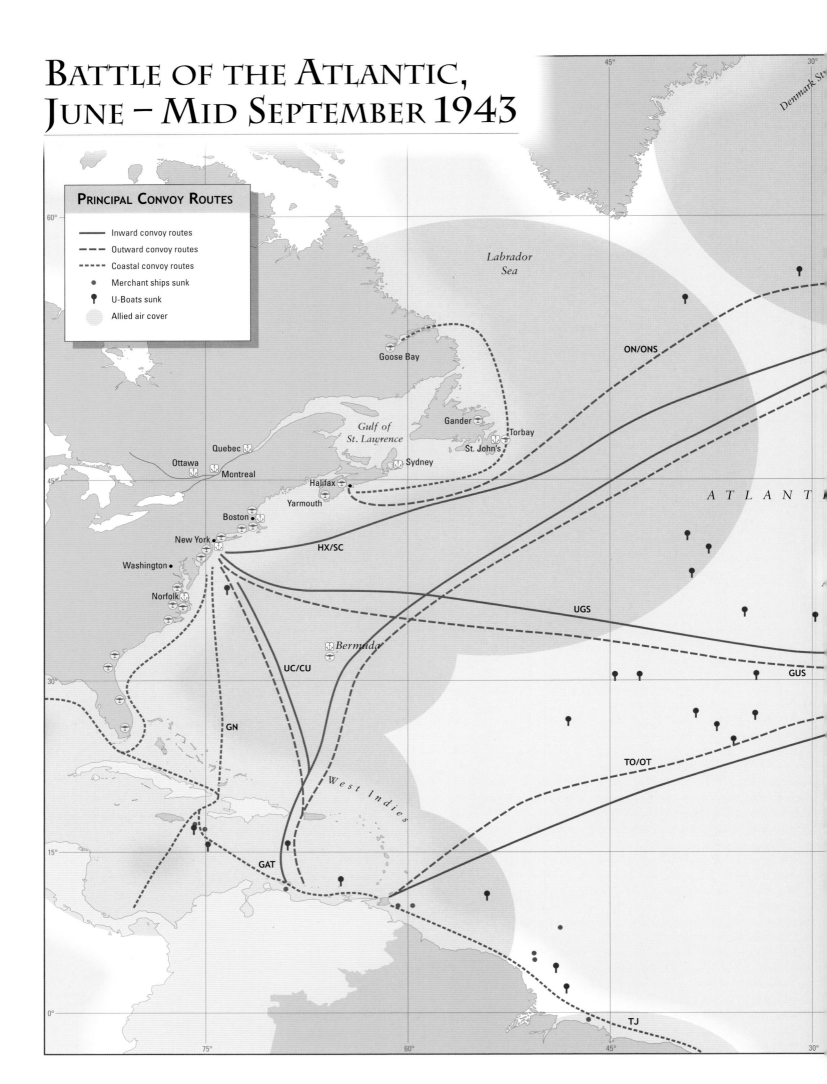

BATTLE OF THE ATLANTIC, JUNE – MID SEPTEMBER 1943

PRINCIPAL CONVOY ROUTES

— Inward convoy routes
--- Outward convoy routes
···· Coastal convoy routes
● Merchant ships sunk
⚓ U-Boats sunk
Allied air cover

Denmark Str

Labrador Sea

ON/ONS

Goose Bay

Gander
Torbay
St. John's

Gulf of St. Lawrence

Quebec
Ottawa
Montreal
Sydney
Halifax
Yarmouth
Boston
New York
Washington
Norfolk

HX/SC

ATLANT

UGS

Bermuda

UC/CU

GUS

GN

TO/OT

West Indies

GAT

TJ

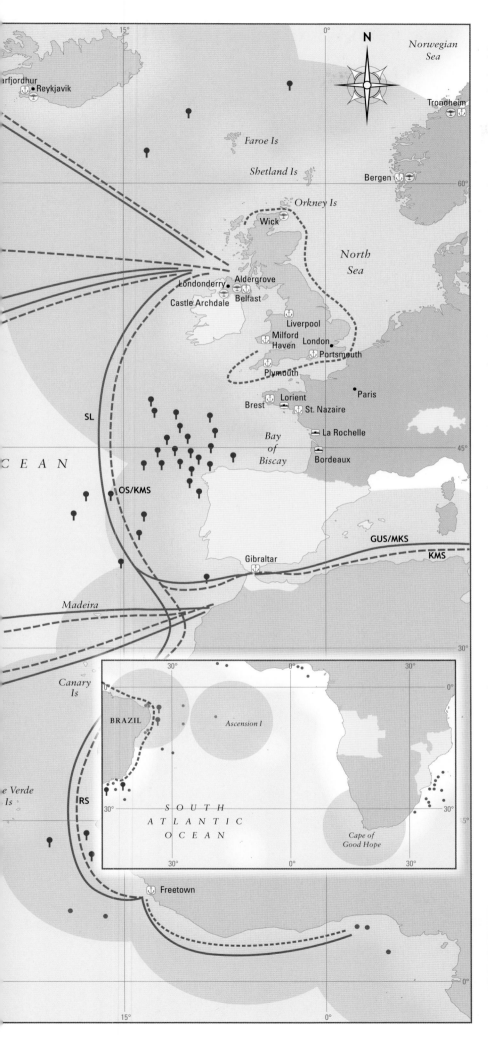

BY 1943, ABOUT fifteen convoys a month were crossing the Atlantic each containing, on average, fifty ships escorted by seven escorts and covered by aircraft for most of the way. On 24 May Admiral Dönitz pulled the U-boats off the North Atlantic convoy route and throughout the summer the shift in the German campaign was clear. Between June and mid-September U-boats sank fifteen ships, only one of which was travelling in convoy. Dönitz turned his attention on the central Atlantic, around the Azores, and the more distant waters of the South Atlantic and Indian Ocean, but it would take until mid-July before this redeployment had any noticeable effect. While minor local successes might be obtained, the Germans could not stem the build-up of American forces in Britain in this way, but Dönitz intended to use this break in the North Atlantic campaign to train new crews and await the arrival of new equipment, particularly homing torpedoes.

By the summer, the allies had sufficient strength to take to the offensive to the U-boats, although there were some differences in approach. The Americans wanted to wipe out the U-boat threat in distant waters by eliminating the tanker boats, and they launched a summer campaign around the Azores, making extensive use of signals intelligence to coordinate hunting groups of escort carriers. The main effort was the Bay of Biscay air offensive that had already begun in May, and by June involved twenty allied squadrons. The idea of such an offensive dated back to 1941 when RAF Coastal Command had been faced with the problem of how to best employ its short- and medium-range aircraft that made up the bulk of its frontline strength. Over the years these patrols had not achieved a great deal, but the arrival of better airborne radar, weapons and aircraft increased their impact. In addition, Support Groups from the Atlantic were sent into the Bay, protected by light cruisers and fleet destroyers, leading to a number of surface-air battles.

Dönitz's reaction to the air campaign was to rely on U-boats' defensive anti-aircraft fire and, in order to maximise its effect, he ordered boats to transit the Bay in groups. Anti-aircraft batteries were augmented and radar-warning devices fitted. Briefly, this had an impact, but allied aircrews adapted, and by concentrating his U-boats Dönitz was actually making it easier for the allies to destroy them. Next, he ordered them to transit the Bay submerged, and only surface to recharge their batteries. This improved their security, but greatly increased the time it took them to reach the open sea and did not stem the losses. In late July and early August, ten of seventeen U-boats making the crossing were sunk, and on average one boat had been sunk every four days since April. By the late summer U-boats were once again ordered to sail individually and keep close to the neutral Spanish coastline.

MERCHANT SHIPS AND U-BOATS LOST (ALL THEATRES AND CAUSES)			
	TONNAGE	SHIPS	U-BOATS
1940			
JUNE	123,825	28	17
JULY	365,398	61	37
AUGUST	119,801	25	27

OPERATION CARTWHEEL, NEW GUINEA AND THE SOLOMONS, 1943–44

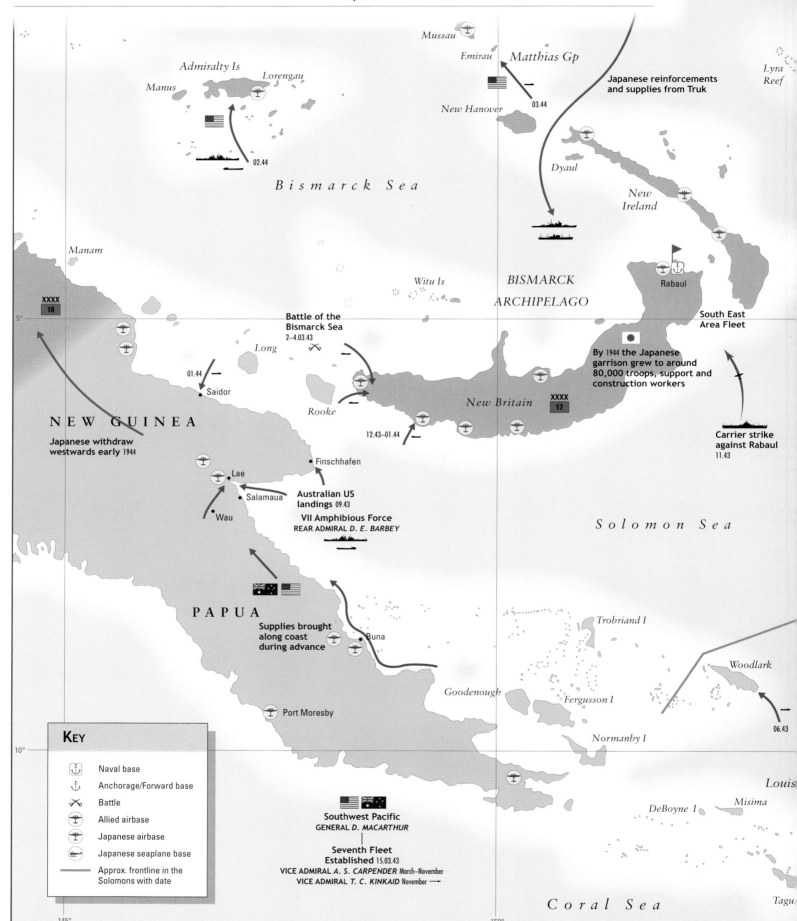

Mussau

Admiralty Is

Lorengau

Emirau   *Matthias Gp*

Manus

New Hanover

Lyra
Reef

03.44

**Japanese reinforcements
and supplies from Truk**

Bismarck   Sea

02.44

Dyaul

*New
Ireland*

Manam

Witu Is

**BISMARCK
ARCHIPELAGO**

Rabaul

XXXX
18

5°

**Battle of the
Bismarck Sea**
2–4.03.43

Long

**South East
Area Fleet**

**By 1944 the Japanese
garrison grew to around
80,000 troops, support and
construction workers**

01.44

Saidor

Rooke

New Britain   XXXX
17

NEW GUINEA

**Japanese withdraw
westwards early 1944**

12.43–01.44

**Carrier strike
against Rabaul**
11.43

Finschhafen

Lae

Solomon   Sea

Salamaua

Wau

**Australian US
landings** 09.43

VII Amphibious Force
REAR ADMIRAL *D. E. BARBEY*

PAPUA

**Supplies brought
along coast
during advance**

Buna

Trobriand I

Woodlark

Goodenough

Fergusson I

06.43

Port Moresby

Normanby I

10°

KEY

⚓ Naval base

⚓ Anchorage/Forward base

⚔ Battle

✈ Allied airbase

✈ Japanese airbase

✈ Japanese seaplane base

— Approx. frontline in the
Solomons with date

Southwest Pacific
GENERAL *D. MACARTHUR*

**Seventh Fleet
Established** 15.03.43
VICE ADMIRAL *A. S. CARPENDER* March–November
VICE ADMIRAL *T. C. KINKAID* November →

Louis

DeBoyne I   *Misima*

Coral   Sea

Tagu

145°

150°

AFTER THE JAPANESE defeat at Guadalcanal, General MacArthur proposed an immediate major allied offensive into New Guinea and New Britain with the aim of taking Rabaul by the end of the year. As such an operation would have required substantially more allied divisions, naval and air units than were available in the Southern Pacific it was turned down in favour of more modest and slower advance towards Rabaul. In the meantime, the Japanese also launched a counter attack to regain the initiative and lost heavily in the process. In March, a division being sent to New Guinea was destroyed in the Bismarck Sea while an aerial offensive in April, Operation *I*, incurred heavy losses. Shortly afterwards, Admiral Yamamoto was killed when the Americans shot down his aircraft in a targeted attack while he was visiting frontline troops. Thereafter, the Japanese went onto the defensive, but continued to pour troops and resources into the theatre in an attempt to fortify the perimeter. They initially had the advantage of an increasing network of airbases.

With Operation *Cartwheel* the allies planned a two-pronged assault to encircle Rabaul. Australian and American forces would clear New Guinea, while Americans and New Zealanders would come up through the Solomons. The original plan foresaw thirteen separate operations beginning with the landings on New Georgia in late June. Allied strategy was focused on taking key positions, airfields and anchorages, and over time Japanese resistance and limited allied resources led to defensive concentrations being bypassed. As long as allied naval forces controlled the sea, the Japanese could not resupply their outlying garrisons rendering them powerless. The objective of the Bougainville landings was to secure airbases from which to attack Rabaul, and once the bridgehead was secured the allies only slowly cleared the island with operations continuing into 1945. No direct allied assault on Rabaul was planned; instead, bases in western New Britain were secured along with the islands guarding the northern approaches. From these an air offensive against Rabaul was launched which effectively immobilised the Japanese on the island until the end of the war. Allied control of the sea allowed them to move forces around the theatre and successive amphibious operations along the northern coast of New Guinea cut off Japanese formations whose movement was greatly restricted by the hostile jungle terrain.

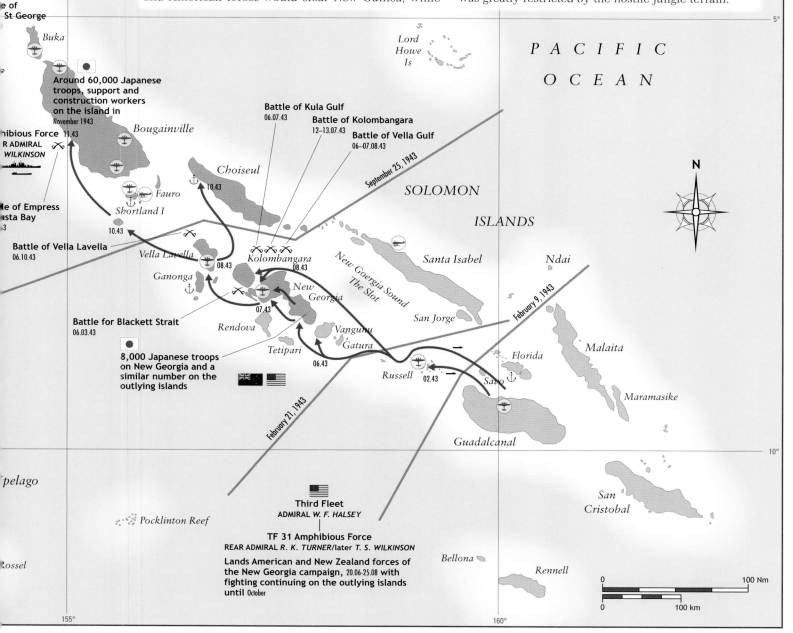

THE BATTLE OF KULA GULF, 6 JULY 1943

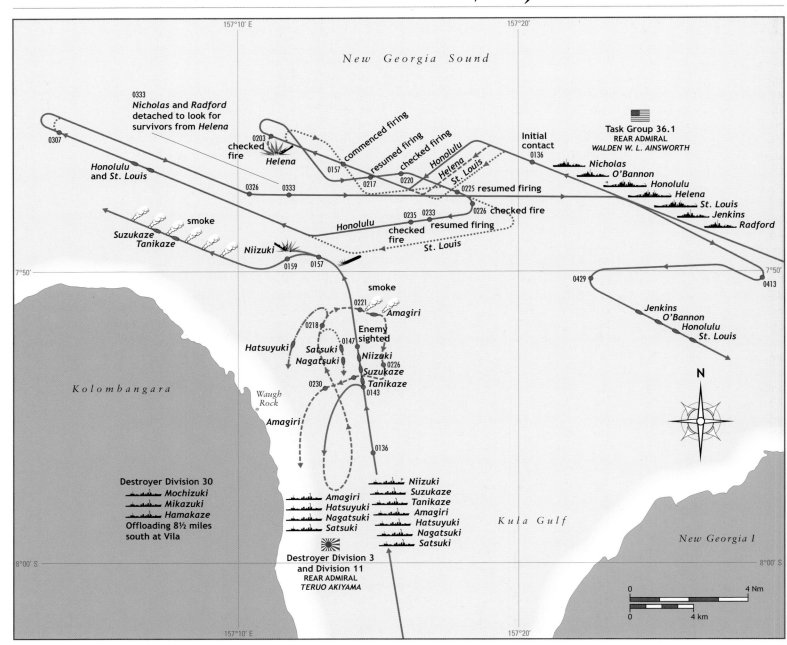

New Georgia Sound

0333
Nicholas and *Radford*
detached to look for
survivors from *Helena*

0307

0203
checked
fire
Helena

commenced firing
resumed firing
checked firing

Honolulu
Helena
St. Louis

Initial
contact
0136

Task Group 36.1
REAR ADMIRAL
WALDEN W. L. AINSWORTH

Nicholas
O'Bannon
Honolulu

Honolulu
and *St. Louis*

0326   0333

0157

0217   0220

0225 resumed firing

Helena
St. Louis

0226 checked fire

St. Louis
Jenkins
Radford

smoke

Suzukaze
Tanikaze

Niizuki

0235 0233
checked
fire

resumed firing
Honolulu

St. Louis

0159   0157

7°50'

0429

0413

7°50'

smoke

0221
Amagiri

0218

Enemy
sighted

0147

Jenkins
O'Bannon
Honolulu
St. Louis

Hatsuyuki

Satsuki
Nagatsuki

Niizuki
0226
Suzukaze

0230

Tanikaze
0143

N

Kolombangara

Waugh
Rock

Amagiri

0136

Destroyer Division 30
━━╾ *Mochizuki*
━━╾ *Mikazuki*
━━╾ *Hamakaze*
Offloading 8½ miles
south at Vila

Niizuki
Suzukaze
Tanikaze
Amagiri
Hatsuyuki
Nagatsuki
Satsuki

Amagiri
Hatsuyuki
Nagatsuki
Satsuki

Kula Gulf

New Georgia I.

Destroyer Division 3
and Division 11
REAR ADMIRAL
TERUO AKIYAMA

8°00' S

8°00' S

0   4 Nm

0   4 km

KEY

⟵━━ ⟍
⟵--- ⟩ US Navy TG 36.1
⟵····· ⟋ track

⟵━━ ⟍
⟵--- ⟩ Imperial Japanese
⟵····· ⟩ Navy
⟵·─·─ ⟋

JUST AFTER MIDNIGHT on 5 July an American force intercepted a Japanese destroyer squadron in the Kula Gulf attempting to land supplies at Vila on southern Kolombangara and forced it to retreat. In line with earlier such operations, Rear Admiral Ainsworth had also been undertaking a bombardment of Vila in an attempt to neutralise it prior to a planned American landing on northern New Georgia on 10 July. As Ainsworth withdrew to replenish, an allied coast watcher reported that further Japanese destroyers had departed from Shortland Island. Ainsworth was thus ordered back north to intercept and prevent this new resupply operation. Having been unable to get four destroyers to Vila on 5 July, the Japanese force under Rear Admiral Akiyama was increased by three destroyers and three destroyer-transports, and between the ten ships a force of 2,600 men was to be landed at Vila. The Americans were as yet unaware of the capabilities of the Japanese Type 93 torpedo so Ainsworth was not to know that his favoured tactic for night engagements – closing to between 8–10,000 yards –

placed his ships within Japanese torpedo range.

As Ainsworth had no specific information regarding the location of the Japanese ships, TG 36.1 was deployed in cruising order as it passed between New Georgia and Kolombangara. At 1.06am *Niizuki*'s radar picked up the American ships and Akiyama ordered his seven ships north. At 1.42am he ordered the four destroyer-transports with him to turn south only to order them back north five minutes later. This briefly confused the American radar operators and led Ainsworth to plan for two passes, one for each Japanese group. *Niizuki* was quickly overwhelmed by American gunfire, but the cruiser *Helena* illuminated herself by having to use smokeless powder and was hit by a torpedo. After the battle the destroyers *Nicholas* and *Radford* remained in the area to look for survivors from *Helena* and at around 5am they engaged and damaged *Amagiri*. *Nagatsuki* ran aground on a reef during the battle and after *Satsuki* failed to tow her off she was abandoned and then sunk by American aircraft later that day.

THE BATTLE OF KOLOMBANGARA, 12–13 JULY 1943

AFTER THE AMERICAN landings on New Georgia at Munda, and at Rice Anchorage on the Kula Gulf, Rear Admiral Ainsworth was tasked with preventing a Japanese naval attack on the Marines at the latter beachhead and if possible prevent Japanese reinforcements from reaching Vila. On 9 July the Japanese landed 1,200 troops at Vila and were preparing for another such operation for the 12 July. After a coast watcher reported the ten Japanese ships moving south, Ainsworth, then anchored at Purvis Bay, was given five additional destroyers and sailed north. Ahead of TF 18 a PBY Black Cat searched for the Japanese force. At 0.35am it made contact and seven minutes later Ainsworth ordered his destroyers into battle formation. As the force had not worked together there was some confusion. Rear Admiral Shunji had detached his four destroyer-transports and shortly before 1am also received a warning from a seaplane of the American presence. Just after 1am the battle started and followed in the established pattern of both sides rapidly firing torpedoes and shells. *Jintsu* was hit by 6in gunfire and sank. *Leander* was hit by a torpedo and heavily damaged. As the Japanese withdrew the Americans gave chase, but in the process they lost an overview of the battle. The Japanese destroyers turned back and prepared for a second torpedo attack. It was

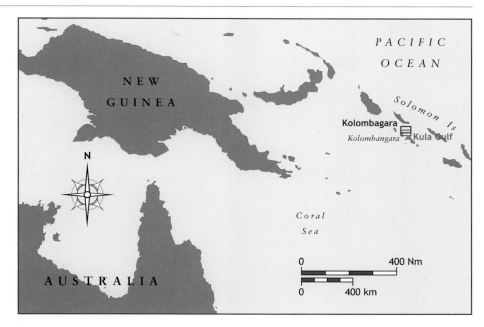

only when the Japanese torpedoes were in the water that the American cruisers fired illumination shells, but it was too late. The remaining two cruisers were heavily damaged and a destroyer sunk.

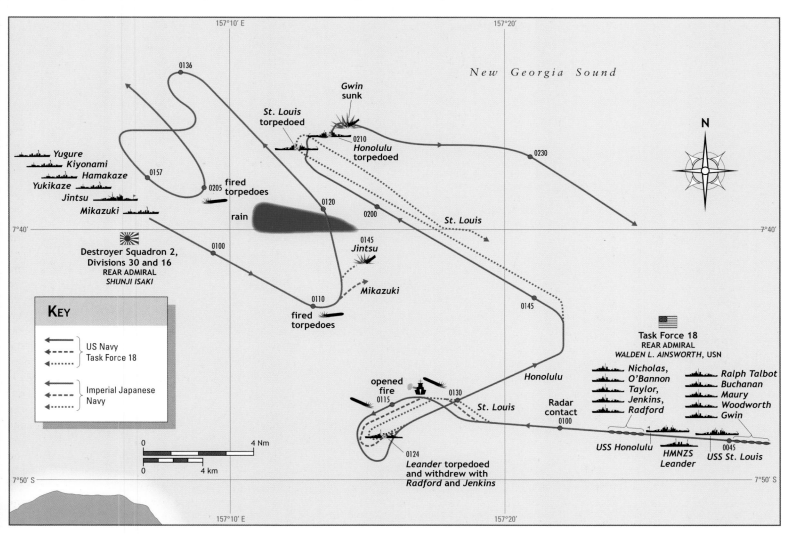

OPERATION HUSKY, 10 JULY 1943

THE DECISION TO land allied forces on Sicily was reached in January when Churchill, Roosevelt and their senior military staff met at Casablanca to decide the future of allied strategy after the axis forces in North Africa were defeated. Capturing the island was seen as vital to eventually opening up the Mediterranean for allied shipping. Initially, the plan foresaw widely dispersed landings across the island, but by late April these were moved to the south and southeastern coasts in order to concentrate the allied forces against the not insignificant axis defences, and facilitate the provision of air cover and build-up of supplies. Nonetheless, the landings were still conducted on a broad front split between a British and an American assault. The former would be conducted in five areas and the latter in three. As the threat of the Italian surface fleet remained, a large naval force, predominately furnished by the Royal Navy, was required to cover the assault. Two battle squadrons with together eight capital ships and carriers protected the flanks from possible intervention by the Italian fleet, while submarines were concentrated off all major Italian naval bases.

The amphibious assault was the largest in the war so far. The forces were assembled in North African ports from Oran to Alexandria in the first week of July. Some of the divisions came straight from America and Britain and had set sail from Norfolk, Virginia, and from the Clyde in mid June. The first wave landed comprised around 160,000 troops, 600 tanks, 1,800 guns and 14,000 vehicles. These were carried in seventeen convoys onboard more than 600 transports, major amphibious vessels and merchant ships. In total, 3,000 vessels of all types were involved. As some of the follow-up divisions were already at sea, more forces were afloat for *Husky* than during the Normandy landings.

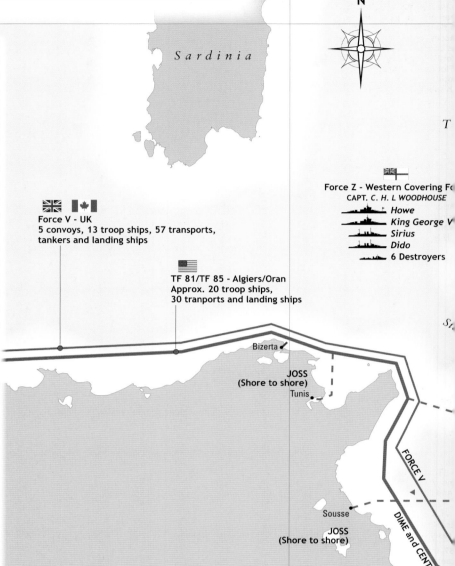

Force V - UK
5 convoys, 13 troop ships, 57 transports, tankers and landing ships

TF 81/TF 85 - Algiers/Oran
Approx. 20 troop ships, 30 tranports and landing ships

Force Z - Western Covering Fo
CAPT. C. H. L WOODHOUSE
Howe
King George V
Sirius
Dido
6 Destroyers

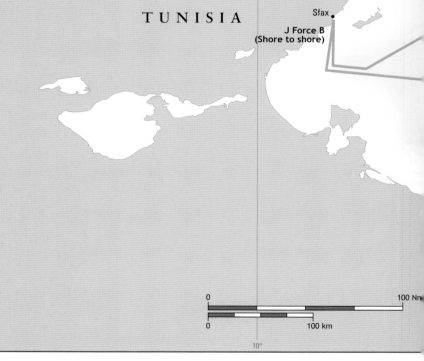

NAVAL FORCES FOR OPERATION HUSKY			
TYPE	BRITISH	AMERICAN	OTHER NATIONS
BATTLESHIPS	6	-	-
FLEET CARRIERS	2	-	-
CRUISERS	10	5	-
ANTI-AIRCRAFT SHIPS	4	-	-
FIGHTER DIRECTION SHIPS	2	-	-
MONITORS	3	-	-
GUNBOATS	3	-	2
MINELAYERS	1	3	-
H.Q. SHIPS	5	4	-
DESTROYERS	71	48	9
ESCORT VESSELS	35	-	1
MINSWEEPERS	34	8	-
LANDING SHIPS INFANTRY	8	-	-
MAJOR LANDING CRAFT	319	190	-
MINOR LANDING CRAFT	715	510	-
COASTAL CRAFT	160	83	-
SUBMARINES	23	-	3
MISCELLANEOUS VESSELS	58	23	-
MERCHANT SHIPS, TROOP TRANSPORTS AND M.T. SHIPS	155	66	16
TOTALS	1614	945	31

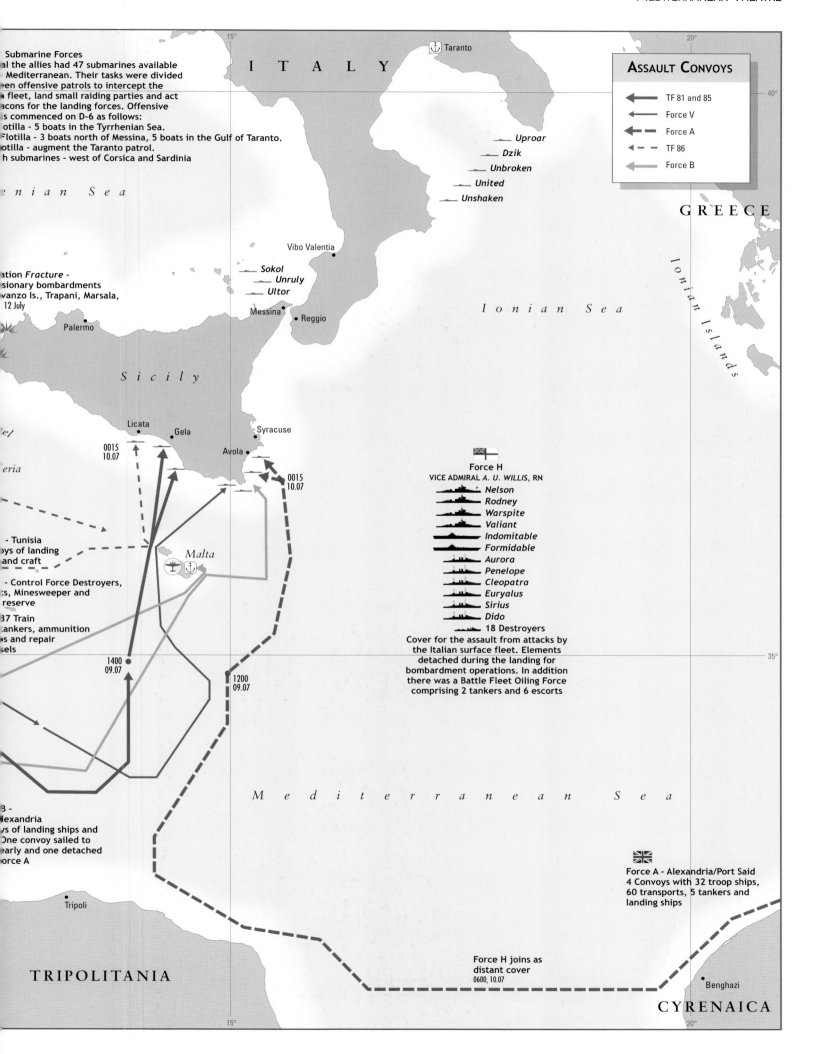

ITALY

⚓ Taranto

Assault Convoys

⬅	TF 81 and 85
←	Force V
⬅	Force A
←	TF 86
⬅	Force B

Submarine Forces
al the allies had 47 submarines available
Mediterranean. Their tasks were divided
en offensive patrols to intercept the
fleet, land small raiding parties and act
acons for the landing forces. Offensive
s commenced on D-6 as follows:
otilla - 5 boats in the Tyrrhenian Sea.
Flotilla - 3 boats north of Messina, 5 boats in the Gulf of Taranto.
otilla - augment the Taranto patrol.
h submarines - west of Corsica and Sardinia

Uproar

Dzik

Unbroken

United

Unshaken

nian Sea

GREECE

Vibo Valentia

ation *Fracture* -
sionary bombardments
vanzo Is., Trapani, Marsala,
12 July

Sokol

Unruly

Ultor

Ionian Sea

Ionian Islands

Palermo

Messina • Reggio

Sicily

Licata • Gela

Syracuse

0015
10.07

Avola

0015
10.07

— Tunisia
ys of landing
and craft

Malta

- Control Force Destroyers,
s, Minesweeper and
reserve

🇬🇧
Force H
VICE ADMIRAL *A. U. WILLIS*, RN
Nelson
Rodney
Warspite
Valiant
Indomitable
Formidable
Aurora
Penelope
Cleopatra
Euryalus
Sirius
Dido
18 Destroyers

37 Train
ankers, ammunition
s and repair
sels

1400
09.07

1200
09.07

Cover for the assault from attacks by
the Italian surface fleet. Elements
detached during the landing for
bombardment operations. In addition
there was a Battle Fleet Oiling Force
comprising 2 tankers and 6 escorts

3 -
lexandria
ys of landing ships and
One convoy sailed to
early and one detached
orce A

M e d i t e r r a n e a n   S e a

🇬🇧
Force A - Alexandria/Port Said
4 Convoys with 32 troop ships,
60 transports, 5 tankers and
landing ships

• Tripoli

Force H joins as
distant cover
0600, 10.07

TRIPOLITANIA

• Benghazi

CYRENAICA

OPERATION HUSKY, LANDING ZONES

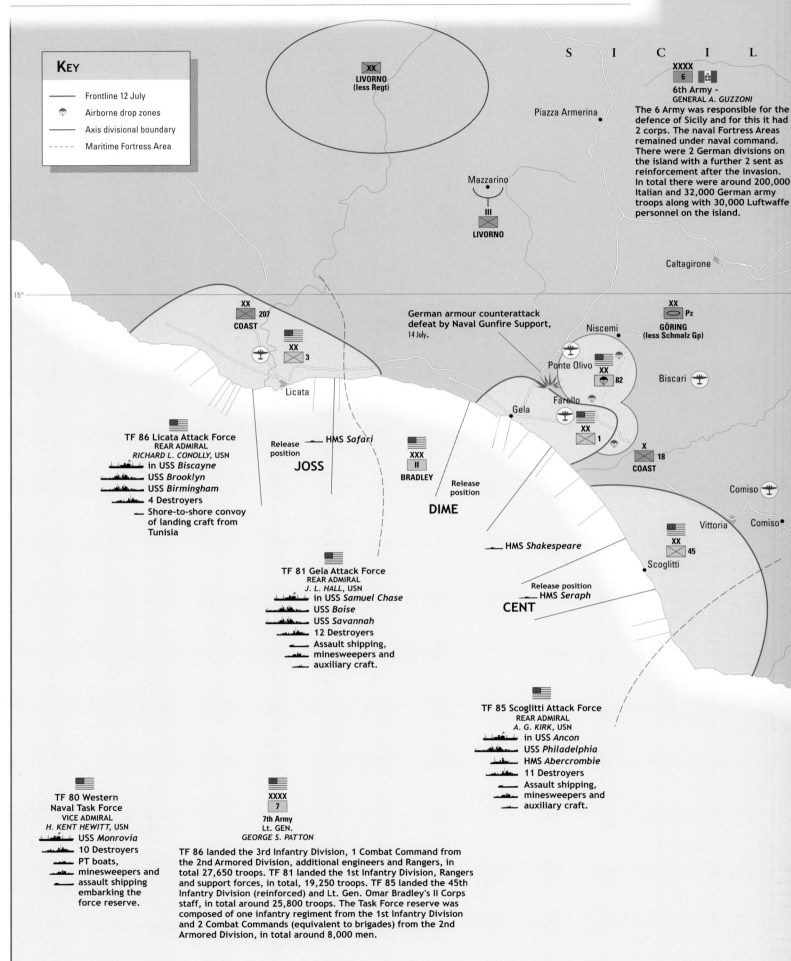

KEY

— Frontline 12 July

⊕ Airborne drop zones

— Axis divisional boundary

---- Maritime Fortress Area

SICIL

S I C I L

XXXX
6
6th Army -
GENERAL *A. GUZZONI*
The 6 Army was responsible for the defence of Sicily and for this it had 2 corps. The naval Fortress Areas remained under naval command. There were 2 German divisions on the island with a further 2 sent as reinforcement after the invasion. In total there were around 200,000 Italian and 32,000 German army troops along with 30,000 Luftwaffe personnel on the island.

XX
LIVORNO
(less Regt)

Piazza Armerina

Mazzarino

III
LIVORNO

Caltagirone

15°

XX 207
COAST

XX 3

Licata

German armour counterattack defeat by Naval Gunfire Support, 14 July.

Niscemi

Ponte Olivo

XX Pz
GÖRING
(less Schmalz Gp)

XX
82

Biscari

Farello

Gela

XX
1

X 18
COAST

Comiso

TF 86 Licata Attack Force
REAR ADMIRAL
RICHARD L. CONOLLY, USN
in USS *Biscayne*
USS *Brooklyn*
USS *Birmingham*
4 Destroyers
Shore-to-shore convoy of landing craft from Tunisia

Release position

— HMS *Safari*

JOSS

XXX
II
BRADLEY

Release position

DIME

— HMS *Shakespeare*

Release position
— HMS *Seraph*

CENT

Vittoria

Comiso

XX 45

Scoglitti

TF 81 Gela Attack Force
REAR ADMIRAL
J. L. HALL, USN
in USS *Samuel Chase*
USS *Boise*
USS *Savannah*
12 Destroyers
Assault shipping, minesweepers and auxiliary craft.

TF 85 Scoglitti Attack Force
REAR ADMIRAL
A. G. KIRK, USN
in USS *Ancon*
USS *Philadelphia*
HMS *Abercrombie*
11 Destroyers
Assault shipping, minesweepers and auxiliary craft.

TF 80 Western Naval Task Force
VICE ADMIRAL
H. KENT HEWITT, USN
USS *Monrovia*
10 Destroyers
PT boats, minesweepers and assault shipping embarking the force reserve.

XXXX
7
7th Army
Lt. GEN.
GEORGE S. PATTON

TF 86 landed the 3rd Infantry Division, 1 Combat Command from the 2nd Armored Division, additional engineers and Rangers, in total 27,650 troops. TF 81 landed the 1st Infantry Division, Rangers and support forces, in total, 19,250 troops. TF 85 landed the 45th Infantry Division (reinforced) and Lt. Gen. Omar Bradley's II Corps staff, in total around 25,800 troops. The Task Force reserve was composed of one infantry regiment from the 1st Infantry Division and 2 Combat Commands (equivalent to brigades) from the 2nd Armored Division, in total around 8,000 men.

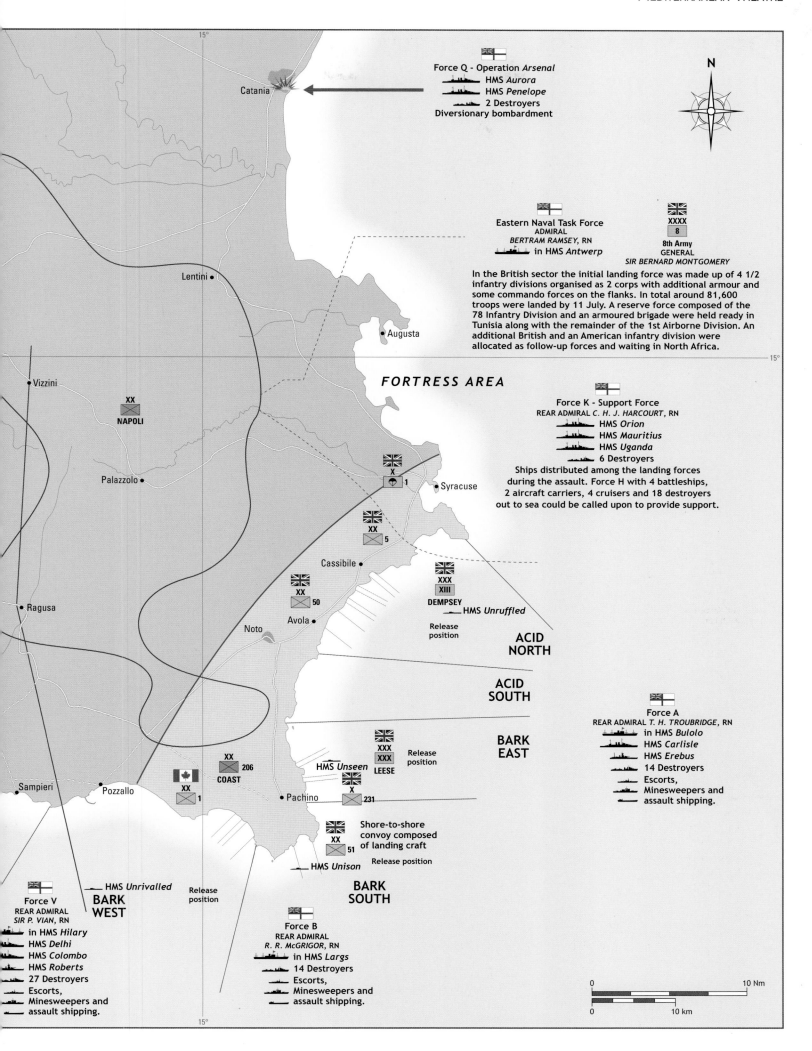

Force Q - Operation *Arsenal*
HMS *Aurora*
HMS *Penelope*
2 Destroyers
Diversionary bombardment

Catania

N

Eastern Naval Task Force
ADMIRAL
BERTRAM RAMSEY, RN
in HMS *Antwerp*

XXXX
8
8th Army
GENERAL
SIR BERNARD MONTGOMERY

In the British sector the initial landing force was made up of 4 1/2 infantry divisions organised as 2 corps with additional armour and some commando forces on the flanks. In total around 81,600 troops were landed by 11 July. A reserve force composed of the 78 Infantry Division and an armoured brigade were held ready in Tunisia along with the remainder of the 1st Airborne Division. An additional British and an American infantry division were allocated as follow-up forces and waiting in North Africa.

Lentini •

• Augusta

FORTRESS AREA

Force K - Support Force
REAR ADMIRAL *C. H. J. HARCOURT*, RN
HMS *Orion*
HMS *Mauritius*
HMS *Uganda*
6 Destroyers
Ships distributed among the landing forces during the assault. Force H with 4 battleships, 2 aircraft carriers, 4 cruisers and 18 destroyers out to sea could be called upon to provide support.

• Vizzini

XX
NAPOLI

Palazzolo •

X
1

• Syracuse

XX
5

Cassibile •

• Ragusa

XX
50

XXX
XIII
DEMPSEY
HMS *Unruffled*
Release position

ACID NORTH

Noto

Avola •

ACID SOUTH

Force A
REAR ADMIRAL *T. H. TROUBRIDGE*, RN
in HMS *Bulolo*
HMS *Carlisle*
HMS *Erebus*
14 Destroyers
Escorts,
Minesweepers and
assault shipping.

BARK EAST

XX
206
COAST

XX
1

HMS *Unseen*

XXX
XXX
LEESE
Release position

X
231

• Pachino

Sampieri •

Pozzallo •

XX
51

Shore-to-shore convoy composed of landing craft
Release position

HMS *Unison*

BARK SOUTH

HMS *Unrivalled*

BARK WEST

Force V
REAR ADMIRAL
SIR P. VIAN, RN
in HMS *Hilary*
HMS *Delhi*
HMS *Colombo*
HMS *Roberts*
27 Destroyers
Escorts,
Minesweepers and
assault shipping.

Release position

Force B
REAR ADMIRAL
R. R. McGRIGOR, RN
in HMS *Largs*
14 Destroyers
Escorts,
Minesweepers and
assault shipping.

0   10 Nm
0   10 km

183

ANTI-SUBMARINE OPERATIONS OFF THE AZORES, JULY – AUGUST 1943

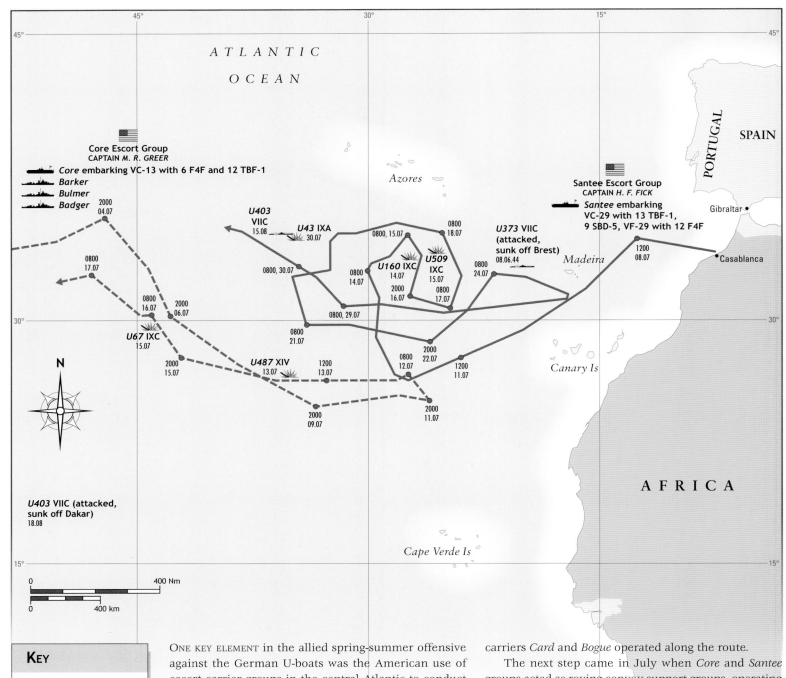

ONE KEY ELEMENT in the allied spring-summer offensive against the German U-boats was the American use of escort carrier groups in the central Atlantic to conduct offensive patrols in waters known to be used by submarines. The American focus on the region was the result of the build-up for Operation *Husky*, and further operations against Italy later in the summer, that meant that hundreds of troop transports, tankers, merchant and assault shipping were crossing central Atlantic. For some time the Americans had wanted to operate in the area, but until sufficient escort carriers became available, the ability to do so was restricted by the limited amount of air power that could be projected from Bermuda and, later, French North Africa.

Each hunting group had a carrier with a mixed air group and three to four destroyers. The first convoy to be escorted by such a group was UGS 8 from Chesapeake to Gibraltar, and by early June two groups around the carriers *Card* and *Bogue* operated along the route.

The next step came in July when *Core* and *Santee* groups acted as roving convoy support groups, operating only with convoys when they transited areas perceived as being particularly dangerous, or operating completely independently as hunter-killer groups. After being pushed from the North Atlantic, the U-boats had shifted to operating south of the Azores, and in early July there were around sixteen plus some Milchkuh supply U-boats in the area. The arrival of escort carrier groups took the Germans by surprise and the Americans focused on sinking the supply U-boats as without them the more numerous, but shorter ranged, Type VIIs could not operate so far from French bases. In total between the end of May and August American escort carrier groups alone sunk sixteen submarines, including eight supply boats in the Atlantic.

THE BATTLE OF VELLA GULF, 6–7 AUGUST 1943

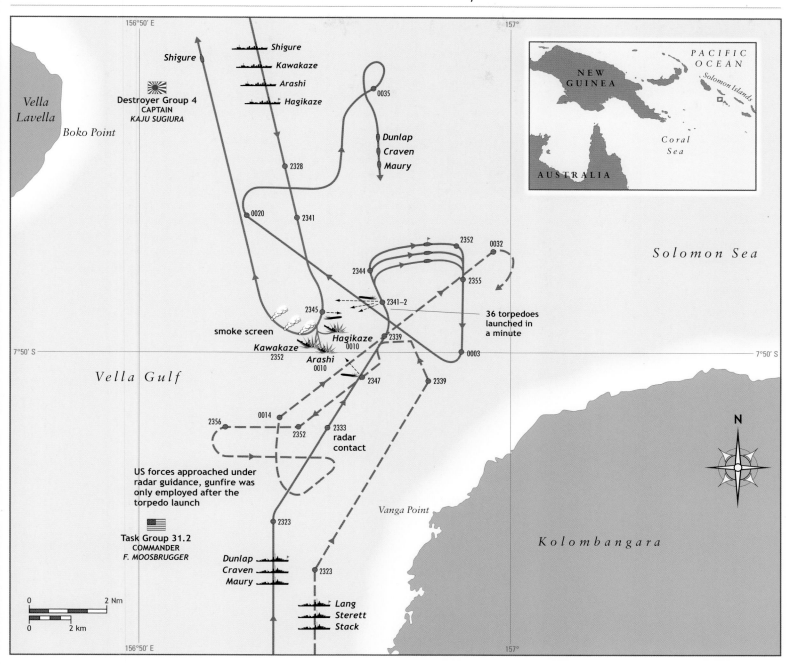

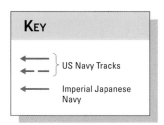

By EARLY AUGUST the Americans were on the verge of taking Munda airfield on New Georgia. Although the Japanese were able to keep Vila supplied by means of fast destroyer-transports, which became known as the 'Tokyo Express', after the battle of Kolombangara, sending supplies on to Munda became increasingly difficult. An attempt to force the allies into a naval engagement against a superior Japanese force on the night of the 19 July had no success and led to the loss of two destroyers and heavy damage to a cruiser as a result of allied air attacks. On 6 August, four Japanese destroyers embarked 950 troops to reinforce Vila, expected to be the next allied target. What became the battle of Vella Gulf was also the first engagement that the Americans fought as a destroyer action in the Solomons rather than relying on a cruiser-destroyer team. Although cruisers possessed considerably more firepower, previous battles showed they could also be vulnerable to massed Japanese torpedo attacks if not handled properly. In

this case, Rear Admiral Merrill's force was too far away and so the six destroyers under Commander Frederick Moosbrugger were the only option.

Moosbrugger's tactics for the battle were different to previous American approaches. He divided his force into two groups, rather than concentrating in a single formation, with a view to attacking from two directions with different weapons. Half his force had some torpedo tubes replaced by 40mm mounts that were better for attacking barges. Both the Japanese and Americans knew that each had a force in the area, but lacked specific information. The Americans made first radar contact at 11.33pm and eight minutes later fired a massive thirty-six torpedo attack into the Japanese flank while the 'gun' division of three destroyers opened up once the first torpedoes hit. In a short time three Japanese destroyers were sunk with around 1,200 sailors and soldiers killed. This was the first Japanese defeat in a night-time destroyer action.

The Invasion of Italy, 1943–44

Unternehmen Lehrgang - The Evacuation of Axis Forces from Sicily 3-17 August

——	German routes
M.F.P.	German naval ferry barges
S.F.	German Siebel ferries
88	Calibre in mm
(symbol)	German batteries
········	Italian routes
F.S.	Italian ferry steamers
M.Z.	Italian landing craft
90	Calibre in mm
A/A	Anti aircraft
D/P	Dual purpose
(symbol)	Italian batteries

After the *Husky* landings naval forces continued to support the allied armies on Sicily, albeit to slightly different degrees in the British and American sectors, by bringing in supplies and opening up ports. Further, the Sicilian geography, with its mountainous interior and concentration of communications along the coastline, provided ample opportunities for naval bombardments. The use of naval gunfire support had long been considered ineffective as a result of experiences in the First World War, but the Sicilian campaign marked a turning point in which land forces increasingly made use of bombardments to assist in assaults on heavily defended German positions and supply lines. General Patton's American Seventh Army employed direct naval support and conducted a number of smaller amphibious landings in an attempt to outflank retreating German forces. In the east, the British Eighth Army made less use of naval forces, although even battleships were on occasion employed to bombard German positions. Axis submarines had less of an impact on the campaign than expected and twelve were lost in the first three weeks of the operation while only eleven allied merchant and warships were sunk or damaged.

Towards the end of July it became clear to the Germans that Sicily was untenable in the face of allied materiel and numerical superiority, and thus was set in motion one of the most remarkable operations of the war. Despite allied naval and air superiority the Germans succeeded in evacuating an army from Sicily across the Strait of Messina secretly and almost without loss. The routes across the Strait were short and covered by substantial coastal, field and anti-aircraft artillery emplacements; nonetheless, the evacuation was a largely improvised affair. Confusion in the allied command and concerns about the strength of the German defences meant that in the end the evacuation went ahead unhindered.

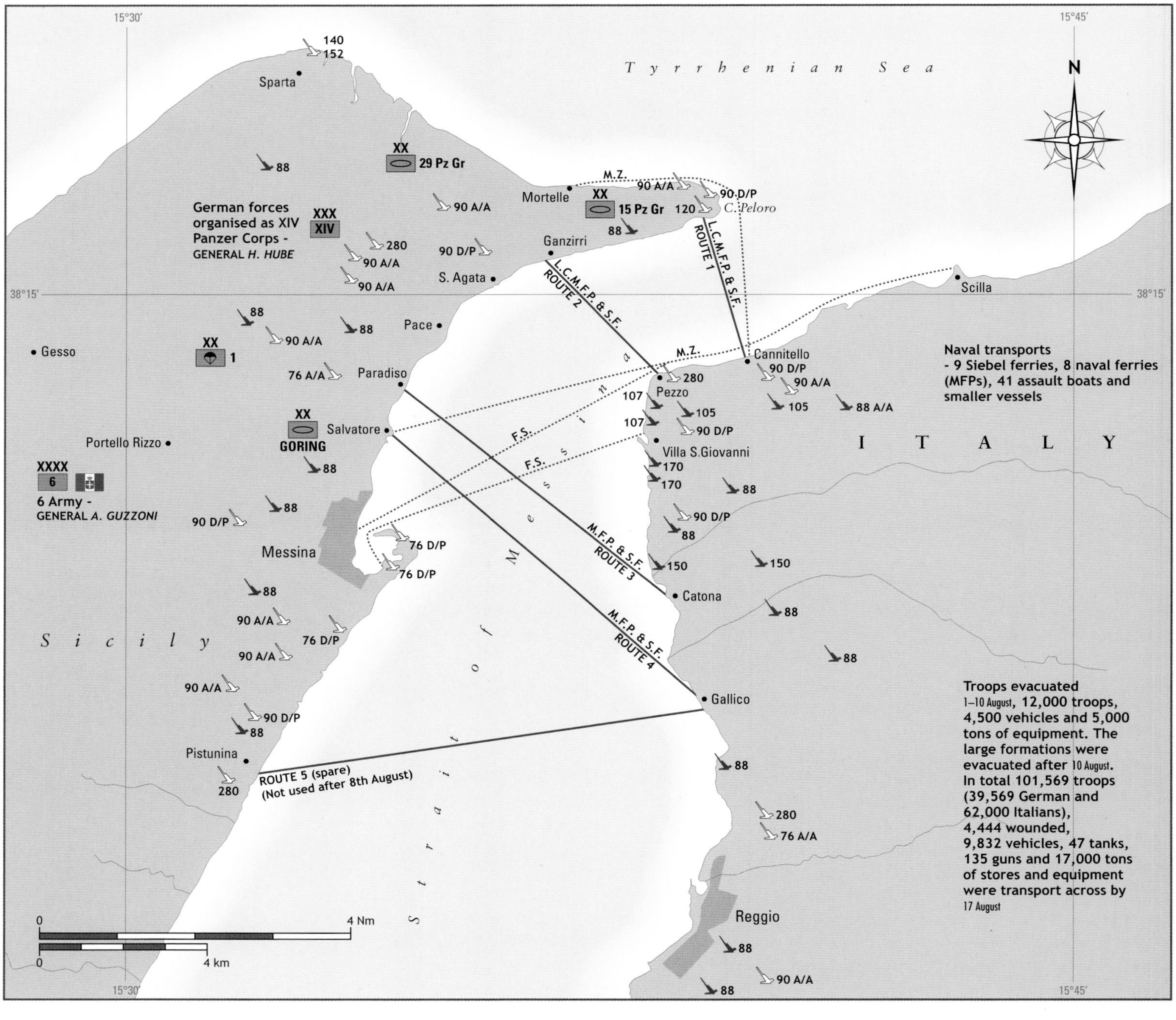

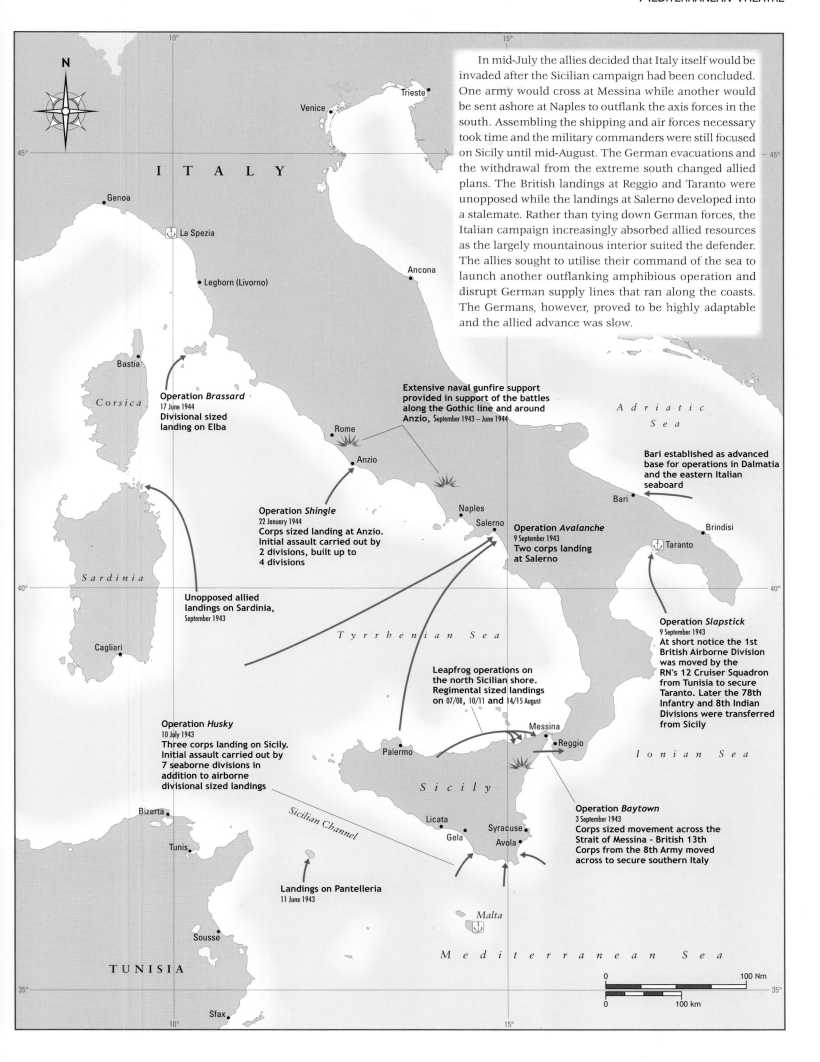

In mid-July the allies decided that Italy itself would be invaded after the Sicilian campaign had been concluded. One army would cross at Messina while another would be sent ashore at Naples to outflank the axis forces in the south. Assembling the shipping and air forces necessary took time and the military commanders were still focused on Sicily until mid-August. The German evacuations and the withdrawal from the extreme south changed allied plans. The British landings at Reggio and Taranto were unopposed while the landings at Salerno developed into a stalemate. Rather than tying down German forces, the Italian campaign increasingly absorbed allied resources as the largely mountainous interior suited the defender. The allies sought to utilise their command of the sea to launch another outflanking amphibious operation and disrupt German supply lines that ran along the coasts. The Germans, however, proved to be highly adaptable and the allied advance was slow.

Operation Brassard
17 June 1944
Divisional sized landing on Elba

Extensive naval gunfire support provided in support of the battles along the Gothic line and around Anzio, September 1943 – June 1944

Bari established as advanced base for operations in Dalmatia and the eastern Italian seaboard

Operation Shingle
22 January 1944
Corps sized landing at Anzio. Initial assault carried out by 2 divisions, built up to 4 divisions

Operation Avalanche
9 September 1943
Two corps landing at Salerno

Unopposed allied landings on Sardinia, September 1943

Operation Slapstick
9 September 1943
At short notice the 1st British Airborne Division was moved by the RN's 12 Cruiser Squadron from Tunisia to secure Taranto. Later the 78th Infantry and 8th Indian Divisions were transferred from Sicily

Leapfrog operations on the north Sicilian shore. Regimental sized landings on 07/08, 10/11 and 14/15 August

Operation Husky
10 July 1943
Three corps landing on Sicily. Initial assault carried out by 7 seaborne divisions in addition to airborne divisional sized landings

Operation Baytown
3 September 1943
Corps sized movement across the Strait of Messina - British 13th Corps from the 8th Army moved across to secure southern Italy

Landings on Pantelleria
11 June 1943

187

Operation Avalanche, 9 September 1943

THE PLAN FOR the Salerno landings was based on attaining surprise rather than subduing the German defences with firepower. The first wave of troops came ashore around 3.30am, an hour before sunrise; the Germans, however, had been expecting a landing and were prepared. The level of resistance varied; the commandos made good progress, while off some beaches in the British sectors destroyers had to engage German defences from point blank range. The American units chose to land without fire support and initially made little headway and suffered losses until cruiser fire subdued the beach defences. The use of carrier aircraft to provide combat air patrols over the beaches had mixed success. An average of twenty were aloft at any time on D-Day, amassing 265 sorties. However, more than forty were lost or damaged beyond repair, Seafires being unsuitable for operations off small escort carriers.

By the end of the day the beaches were secure, but in most areas the allies had not advanced as far inland as planned. Little armour was landed on the first day and throughout the night more heavy equipment was brought in. Over the next three days progress to expand the beachhead was hampered by German resistance and a considerable amount of congestion on the beaches. Luftwaffe strikes on shipping off Salerno, supplemented by night-time E-boat attacks, complicated the situation. On 13 September the Germans launched a counter attack that threatened to push the allied forces back into the sea and only extensive naval gunfire support and air strikes helped stabilise the situation. Late on 15 September the battleships *Warspite* and *Valiant* arrived, but only the former conducted a shoot as the immediate crisis had passed. The next day *Warspite* was hit by a wireless-controlled bomb and suffered serious damage. Lead elements of the 8th Army also arrived from the south.

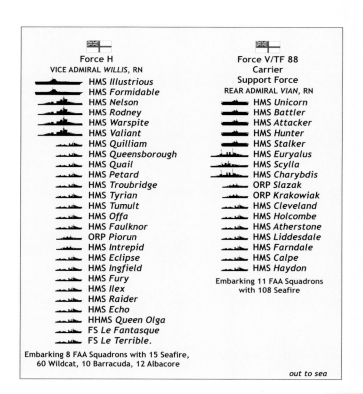

Force H
VICE ADMIRAL *WILLIS*, RN
- HMS *Illustrious*
- HMS *Formidable*
- HMS *Nelson*
- HMS *Rodney*
- HMS *Warspite*
- HMS *Valiant*
- HMS *Quilliam*
- HMS *Queensborough*
- HMS *Quail*
- HMS *Petard*
- HMS *Troubridge*
- HMS *Tyrian*
- HMS *Tumult*
- HMS *Offa*
- HMS *Faulknor*
- ORP *Piorun*
- HMS *Intrepid*
- HMS *Eclipse*
- HMS *Ingfield*
- HMS *Fury*
- HMS *Ilex*
- HMS *Raider*
- HMS *Echo*
- HHMS *Queen Olga*
- FS *Le Fantasque*
- FS *Le Terrible.*

Embarking 8 FAA Squadrons with 15 Seafire, 60 Wildcat, 10 Barracuda, 12 Albacore

Force V/TF 88
Carrier
Support Force
REAR ADMIRAL *VIAN*, RN
- HMS *Unicorn*
- HMS *Battler*
- HMS *Attacker*
- HMS *Hunter*
- HMS *Stalker*
- HMS *Euryalus*
- HMS *Scylla*
- HMS *Charybdis*
- ORP *Slazak*
- ORP *Krakowiak*
- HMS *Cleveland*
- HMS *Holcombe*
- HMS *Atherstone*
- HMS *Liddesdale*
- HMS *Farndale*
- HMS *Calpe*
- HMS *Haydon*

Embarking 11 FAA Squadrons with 108 Seafire

TF 80 Western Naval Task Force
VICE ADMIRAL
H. KENT HEWITT, USN
- USS *Ancon*
- HMS *Ulster Queen*
- HMS *Palomares*

XXXX
V
CLARK
LIEUTENANT GENERAL
MARK W. CLARK
UNITED STATES ARMY

out to sea

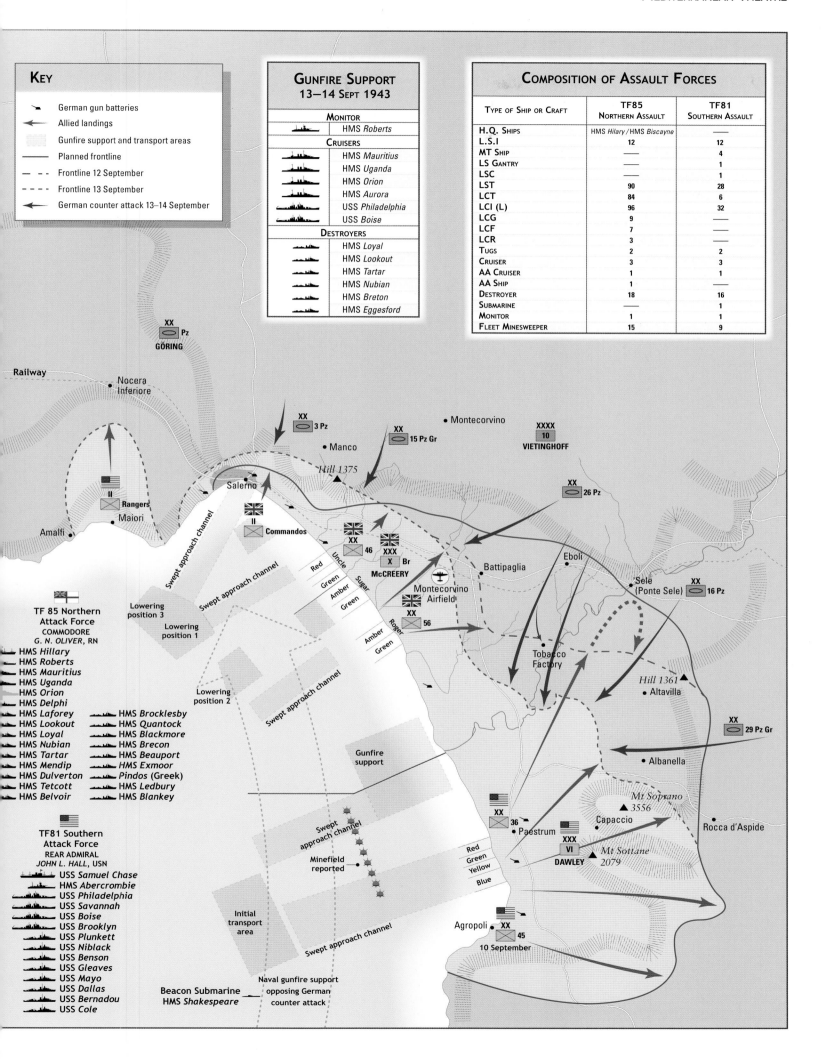

Key

- German gun batteries
- Allied landings
- Gunfire support and transport areas
- Planned frontline
- Frontline 12 September
- Frontline 13 September
- German counter attack 13–14 September

Gunfire Support 13–14 Sept 1943

Monitor
HMS *Roberts*

Cruisers
HMS *Mauritius*
HMS *Uganda*
HMS *Orion*
HMS *Aurora*
USS *Philadelphia*
USS *Boise*

Destroyers
HMS *Loyal*
HMS *Lookout*
HMS *Tartar*
HMS *Nubian*
HMS *Breton*
HMS *Eggesford*

Composition of Assault Forces

Type of Ship or Craft	TF85 Northern Assault	TF81 Southern Assault
H.Q. Ships	HMS *Hilary* / HMS *Biscayne*	—
L.S.I	12	12
MT Ship	—	4
LS Gantry	—	1
LSC	—	1
LST	90	28
LCT	84	6
LCI (L)	96	32
LCG	9	—
LCF	7	—
LCR	3	—
Tugs	2	2
Cruiser	3	3
AA Cruiser	1	1
AA Ship	1	—
Destroyer	18	16
Submarine	—	1
Monitor	1	1
Fleet Minesweeper	15	9

GÖRING XX Pz

Railway

Nocera Inferiore

XX 3 Pz

XX 15 Pz Gr

Montecorvino

XXXX 10 VIETINGHOFF

Manco

Hill 1375

Salerno

XX 26 Pz

II Rangers

Maiori

Amalfi

II Commandos

XX 46

XXX X Br McCREERY

Montecorvino Airfield

Battipaglia

Eboli

Sele (Ponte Sele) XX 16 Pz

TF 85 Northern Attack Force
COMMODORE
G. N. OLIVER, RN
HMS *Hillary*
HMS *Roberts*
HMS *Mauritius*
HMS *Uganda*
HMS *Orion*
HMS *Delphi*
HMS *Laforey*
HMS *Lookout*
HMS *Loyal*
HMS *Nubian*
HMS *Tartar*
HMS *Mendip*
HMS *Dulverton*
HMS *Tetcott*
HMS *Belvoir*

HMS *Brocklesby*
HMS *Quantock*
HMS *Blackmore*
HMS *Brecon*
HMS *Beauport*
HMS *Exmoor*
Pindos (Greek)
HMS *Ledbury*
HMS *Blankey*

Red
Uncle
Green
Amber
Sugar
Green

XX 56
Roger
Amber
Green

Lowering position 3
Lowering position 1

Lowering position 2

Swept approach channel

Tobacco Factory

Hill 1361
Altavilla

XX 29 Pz Gr

Albanella

Gunfire support

TF81 Southern Attack Force
REAR ADMIRAL
JOHN L. HALL, USN
USS *Samuel Chase*
HMS *Abercrombie*
USS *Philadelphia*
USS *Savannah*
USS *Boise*
USS *Brooklyn*
USS *Plunkett*
USS *Niblack*
USS *Benson*
USS *Gleaves*
USS *Mayo*
USS *Dallas*
USS *Bernadou*
USS *Cole*

Swept approach channel

Minefield reported

Swept approach channel

Initial transport area

Mt Soprano ▲ 3556

Capaccio

XX 36

Paestrum

XXX VI DAWLEY

Mt Sottane ▲ 2079

Rocca d'Aspide

Red
Green
Yellow
Blue

Agropoli XX 45

10 September

Beacon Submarine
HMS *Shakespeare*

Naval gunfire support opposing German counter attack

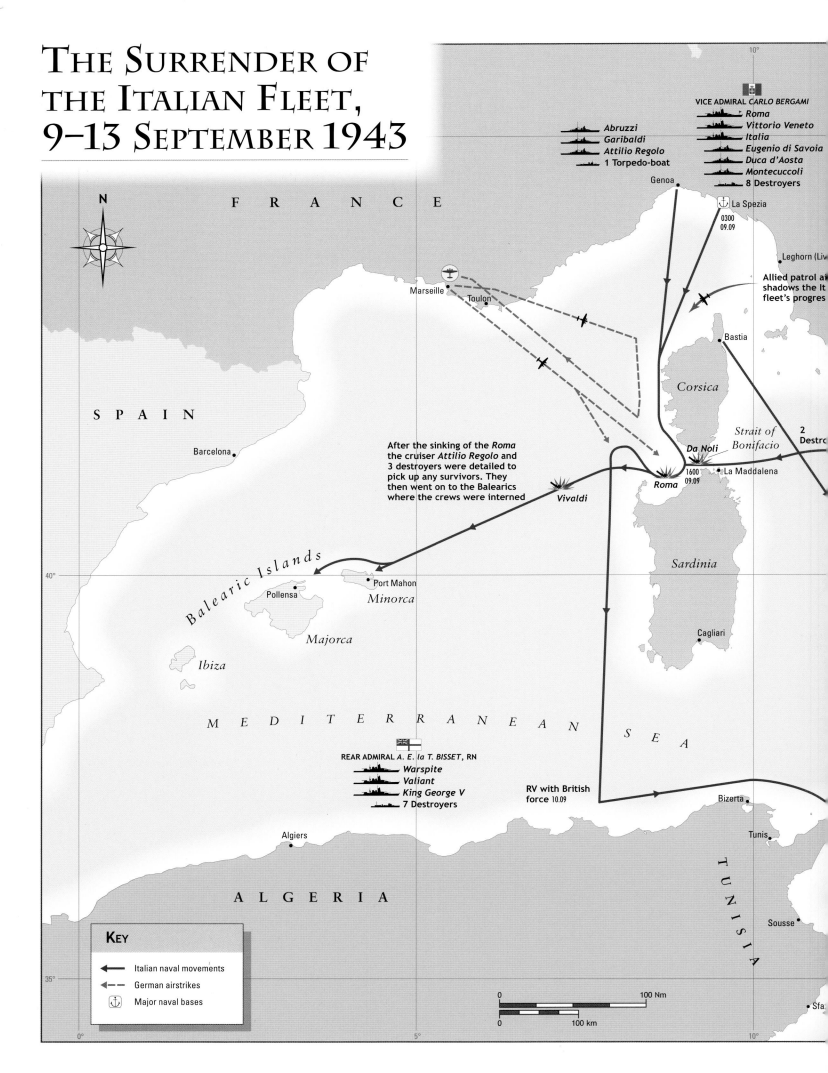

THE SURRENDER OF THE ITALIAN FLEET, 9–13 SEPTEMBER 1943

VICE ADMIRAL *CARLO BERGAMI*

Abruzzi
Garibaldi
Attilio Regolo
1 Torpedo-boat

Roma
Vittorio Veneto
Italia
Eugenio di Savoia
Duca d'Aosta
Montecuccoli
8 Destroyers

F R A N C E

Marseille
Toulon

Genoa

⚓ La Spezia

0300
09.09

Leghorn (Liv

Allied patrol ai
shadows the It
fleet's progres

Bastia

Corsica

*Strait of
Bonifacio*

2
Destro

S P A I N

Barcelona

After the sinking of the *Roma*
the cruiser *Attilio Regolo* and
3 destroyers were detailed to
pick up any survivors. They
then went on to the Balearics
where the crews were interned

Da Noli

La Maddalena

1600
09.09

Roma

Vivaldi

Balearic Islands

40°

Pollensa

Port Mahon

Minorca

Sardinia

Majorca

Ibiza

Cagliari

M E D I T E R R A N E A N   S E A

REAR ADMIRAL *A. E. la T. BISSET*, RN

Warspite
Valiant
King George V
7 Destroyers

RV with British
force 10.09

Bizerta

Algiers

Tunis

T U N I S I A

A L G E R I A

Sousse

35°

KEY

→ Italian naval movements

--▶ German airstrikes

⚓ Major naval bases

0   100 Nm

0   100 km

Sfa

0°   5°   10°

190

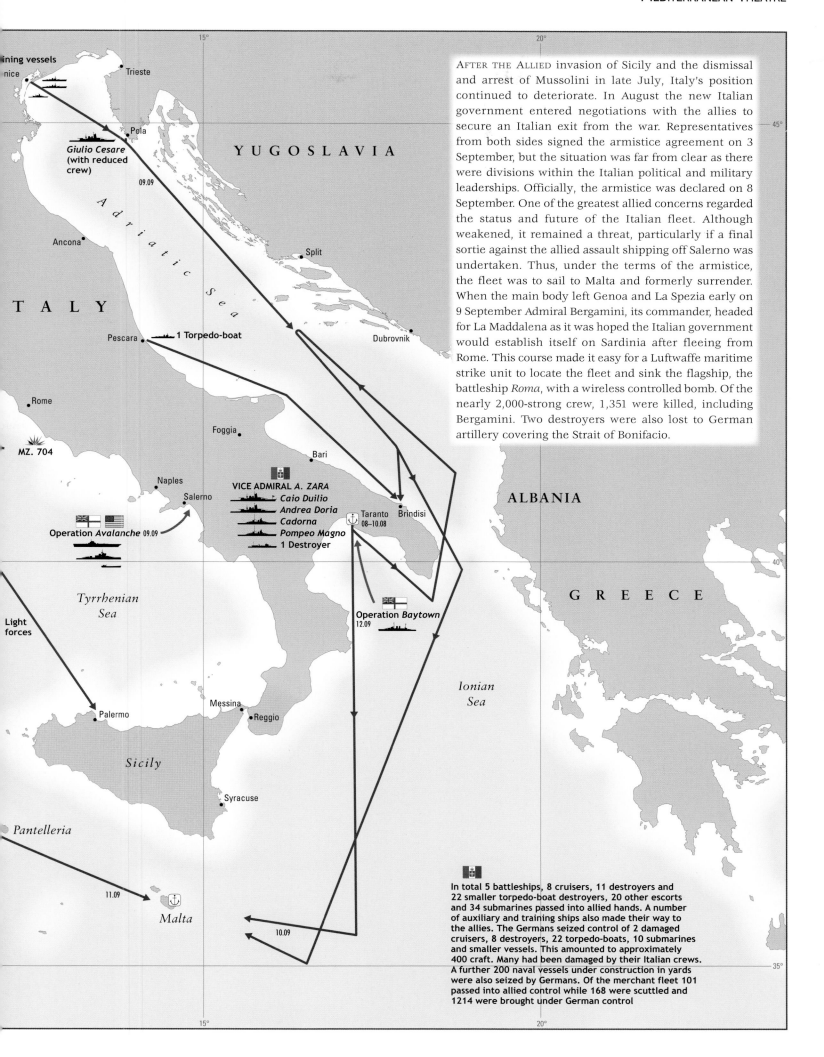

ining vessels
nice
Trieste

Giulio Cesare
(with reduced
crew)
09.09

Pola

Y U G O S L A V I A

45°

Ancona

A d r i a t i c   S e a

Split

I T A L Y

Pescara ▬ **1 Torpedo-boat**

Dubrovnik

Rome

Foggia

MZ. 704

Bari

Naples

VICE ADMIRAL *A. ZARA*
▬ *Caio Duilio*
▬ *Andrea Doria*
▬ *Cadorna*
▬ *Pompeo Magno*
▬ *1 Destroyer*

A L B A N I A

Salerno

Taranto
08–10.08

Brindisi

Operation *Avalanche* 09.09

*Tyrrhenian
Sea*

Operation *Baytown*
12.09

G R E E C E

40°

Light
forces

*Ionian
Sea*

Palermo

Messina
Reggio

Sicily

Syracuse

Pantelleria

11.09

Malta

10.09

35°

After the Allied invasion of Sicily and the dismissal and arrest of Mussolini in late July, Italy's position continued to deteriorate. In August the new Italian government entered negotiations with the allies to secure an Italian exit from the war. Representatives from both sides signed the armistice agreement on 3 September, but the situation was far from clear as there were divisions within the Italian political and military leaderships. Officially, the armistice was declared on 8 September. One of the greatest allied concerns regarded the status and future of the Italian fleet. Although weakened, it remained a threat, particularly if a final sortie against the allied assault shipping off Salerno was undertaken. Thus, under the terms of the armistice, the fleet was to sail to Malta and formerly surrender. When the main body left Genoa and La Spezia early on 9 September Admiral Bergamini, its commander, headed for La Maddalena as it was hoped the Italian government would establish itself on Sardinia after fleeing from Rome. This course made it easy for a Luftwaffe maritime strike unit to locate the fleet and sink the flagship, the battleship *Roma*, with a wireless controlled bomb. Of the nearly 2,000-strong crew, 1,351 were killed, including Bergamini. Two destroyers were also lost to German artillery covering the Strait of Bonifacio.

In total 5 battleships, 8 cruisers, 11 destroyers and 22 smaller torpedo-boat destroyers, 20 other escorts and 34 submarines passed into allied hands. A number of auxiliary and training ships also made their way to the allies. The Germans seized control of 2 damaged cruisers, 8 destroyers, 22 torpedo-boats, 10 submarines and smaller vessels. This amounted to approximately 400 craft. Many had been damaged by their Italian crews. A further 200 naval vessels under construction in yards were also seized by Germans. Of the merchant fleet 101 passed into allied control while 168 were scuttled and 1214 were brought under German control

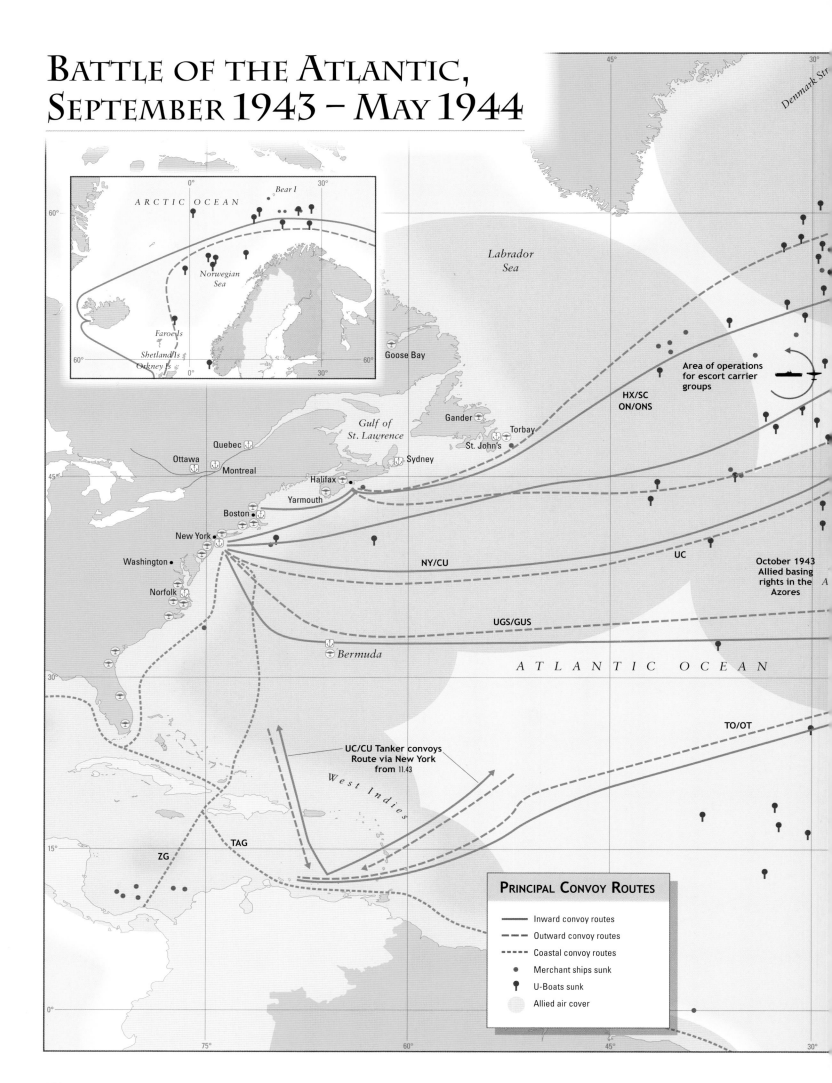

BATTLE OF THE ATLANTIC, SEPTEMBER 1943 – MAY 1944

ARCTIC OCEAN

Bear I

Norwegian Sea

Faroe Is

Shetland Is
Orkney Is

Denmark Str

Labrador Sea

Goose Bay

Area of operations for escort carrier groups

HX/SC
ON/ONS

Gander
Torbay
St. John's

Quebec
Ottawa
Montreal
Halifax
Yarmouth
Boston
New York
Washington
Norfolk

Gulf of St. Lawrence

Sydney

UC

October 1943
Allied basing
rights in the A
Azores

NY/CU

UGS/GUS

Bermuda

ATLANTIC OCEAN

TO/OT

UC/CU Tanker convoys
Route via New York
from 11.43

West Indies

ZG

TAG

PRINCIPAL CONVOY ROUTES

Inward convoy routes
Outward convoy routes
Coastal convoy routes
Merchant ships sunk
U-Boats sunk
Allied air cover

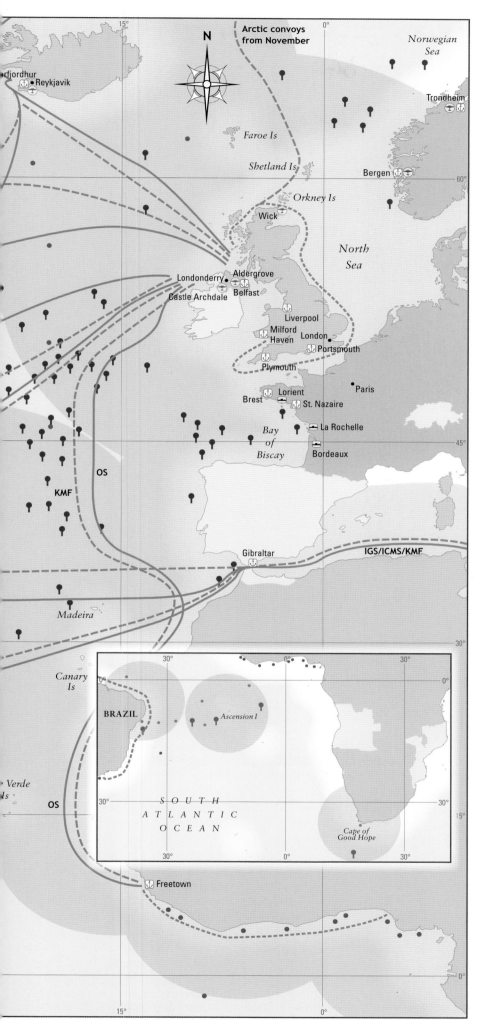

THE ALLIES WERE expecting the Germans to restart the U-boat campaign in the North Atlantic and with around two-hundred boats still available the threat was far from over. Admiral Dönitz believed that acoustic homing torpedoes, and improved anti-aircraft armament and radar warning receivers would enable the U-boats to recover some of the lost ground in the short-term. The new torpedoes were designed specifically to sink surface escorts prior to attacking merchant ships. The long-term solution lay in a new generation of faster, more capable submarines which were being designed and constructed.

On 20 September a group of nineteen U-boats attacked two outward-bound convoys that had merged, using the new torpedo for the first time operationally. Three escorts and six merchant ships were sunk, but it was far from a one-sided success as two U-boats were lost and another two severely damaged. Although the allies were surprised by the weapons, they quickly developed counter-measures and neither the acoustic homing nor the pattern running torpedoes had a decisive effect.

Eight ships were sunk from convoys in September, but this figure halved to four in October while at the same time twenty-three U-boats were sunk in the North Atlantic. The continuous presence of allied aircraft over convoys made attacks near impossible. Although more Very Long Range (VLR) aircraft were operating in the North Atlantic, it was the increased number of escort carriers available to protect convoys that had the greatest effect. These also embarked fighters that could shoot down German reconnaissance aircraft that briefly increased their activity in the eastern Atlantic. By the end of January an aircraft-carrying vessel escorted each convoy crossing the North Atlantic with more carriers deployed with the Support Groups. Escort forces could operate at sea for longer periods as oilers, from which they could replenish, were now accompanying them.

With the increase in allied aircraft, U-boats mainly operated submerged and this greatly limited their ability to function in the central Atlantic as it doubled, or tripled, the time it took them to reach their operational areas. The introduction of snorkel devices enabled U-boats to recharge their batteries while submerged, but it did little else to improve their chances of finding or sinking merchant ships. Refuelling from other U-boats also ceased, so apart from a few long-range boats the campaign was restricted to the eastern Atlantic and Arctic. Throughout 1944, in the North Atlantic more U-boats than merchant ships were being sunk, and by March the German offensive had effectively ended.

MERCHANT SHIPS AND U-BOATS LOST (ALL THEATRES AND CAUSES)			
	TONNAGE	SHIPS	U-BOATS
1943			
SEPTEMBER	156,419	29	12
OCTOBER	139,861	29	27
NOVEMBER	144,391	29	21
DECEMBER	168,524	31	8
1944			
JANUARY	130,635	26	15
FEBRUARY	116,855	23	20
MARCH	157,960	25	25
APRIL	82,372	13	21
MAY	27,297	5	22

Unternehmen Sizilien, 6–9 September 1943

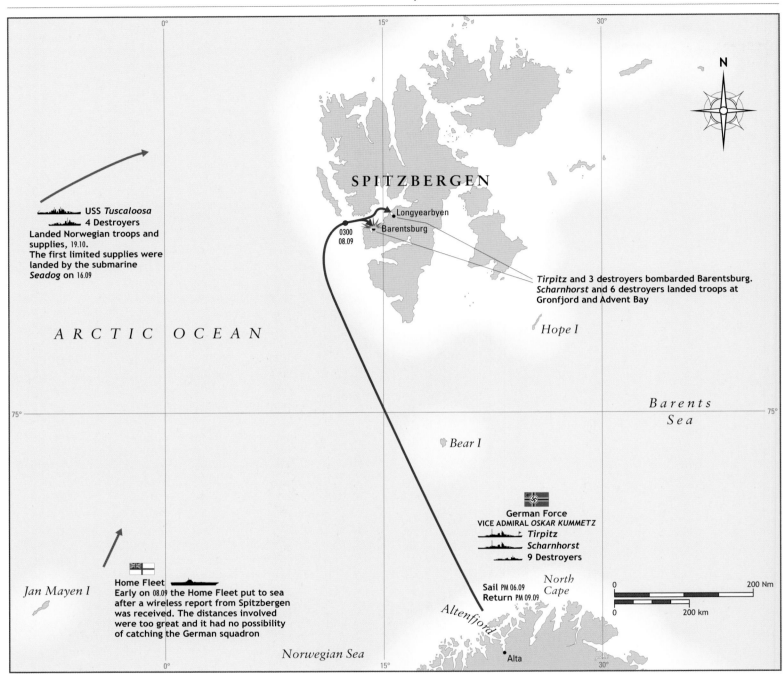

USS *Tuscaloosa*
4 Destroyers
Landed Norwegian troops and supplies, 19.10.
The first limited supplies were landed by the submarine *Seadog* on 16.09

Tirpitz and 3 destroyers bombarded Barentsburg. *Scharnhorst* and 6 destroyers landed troops at Gronfjord and Advent Bay

SPITZBERGEN

Longyearbyen

Barentsburg

0300
08.09

ARCTIC OCEAN

Hope I

*Barents
Sea*

Bear I

German Force
VICE ADMIRAL *OSKAR KUMMETZ*
Tirpitz
Scharnhorst
9 Destroyers

Home Fleet
Early on 08.09 the Home Fleet put to sea after a wireless report from Spitzbergen was received. The distances involved were too great and it had no possibility of catching the German squadron

Jan Mayen I

Sail PM 06.09
Return PM 09.09

*North
Cape*

Altenfjord

Alta

Norwegian Sea

0   200 Nm

0   200 km

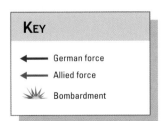

KEY

German force
Allied force
Bombardment

TIRPITZ NEVER ONCE engaged another warship, and the only occasion when the battleship fired its main armament in combat was during a raid on Spitzbergen in September 1943. Also known as Unternehmen *Zitronella*, the German operation involved the bombardment and the landing of troops to destroy shore facilities. Its strategic value was limited, and apart from giving the German warships the possibility of some time at sea, its main objective was to demonstrate to Hitler the continued utility of the surface fleet. On 6 September *Tirpitz*, *Scharnhorst* and nine destroyers, which together carried an infantry battalion, left for Spitsbergen. The major economic activity of mining coal had largely ceased with the allied evacuation in 1941, but there was still a small allied presence on the island with weather stations and communications facilities. The actual operation only lasted hours.

That *Tirpitz* was in commission was of real concern to the British and set in motion Operation *Source* that, along with *Chariot*, was one of the Royal Navy's most daring commando operations of the war. The north Norwegian fjords were perfect bases for the German warships to seek sanctuary as they were, as yet, out of range of allied air power. The British had insufficient carrier strength to mount a carrier strike, and the constrained waters of the fjords, combined with anti-submarine defences, made submarine attacks impossible. The only option was to employ midget submarines, and after the Italians and Japanese demonstrated their utility the British ordered some in 1942. Delivered in early 1943, and after a secret training programme, they were ready for action by the late summer. The losses incurred in the operation were considerable with nine men killed and six taken prisoner out of the total of eighteen who manned the six boats. *Tirpitz*, though not sunk, was severely damaged and required repairs that lasted until April 1944.

OPERATION SOURCE, SEPTEMBER 1943

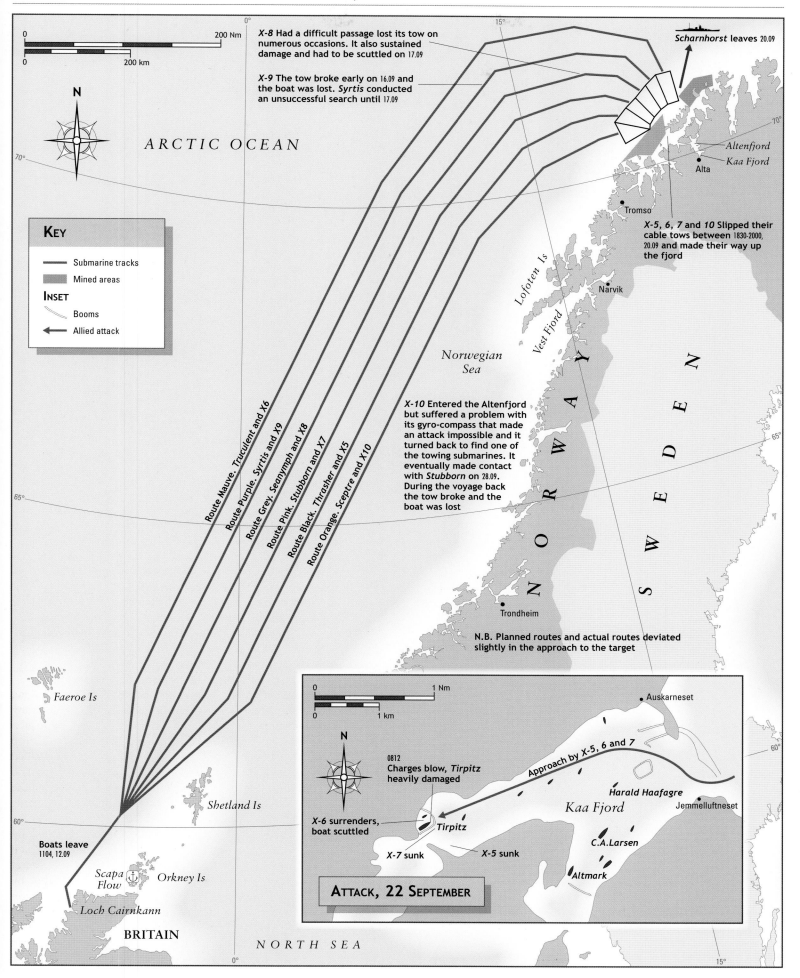

KEY

— Submarine tracks

▭ Mined areas

INSET

⋯ Booms

← Allied attack

X-8 Had a difficult passage lost its tow on numerous occasions. It also sustained damage and had to be scuttled on 17.09

X-9 The tow broke early on 16.09 and the boat was lost. *Syrtis* conducted an unsuccessful search until 17.09

Scharnhorst leaves 20.09

ARCTIC OCEAN

N

Altenfjord
Kaa Fjord
Alta

Tromso

X-5, 6, 7 and *10* Slipped their cable tows between 1830-2000, 20.09 and made their way up the fjord

Narvik

Lofoten Is

Vest Fjord

Norwegian Sea

X-10 Entered the Altenfjord but suffered a problem with its gyro-compass that made an attack impossible and it turned back to find one of the towing submarines. It eventually made contact with *Stubborn* on 28.09. During the voyage back the tow broke and the boat was lost

Route Mauve. Truculent and X6
Route Purple. Syrtis and X9
Route Grey. Seanymph and X8
Route Pink. Stubborn and X7
Route Black. Thrasher and X5
Route Orange. Sceptre and X10

N O R W A Y

S W E D E N

Trondheim

N.B. Planned routes and actual routes deviated slightly in the approach to the target

Faeroe Is

Shetland Is

Boats leave
1104, 12.09

Scapa Flow ⚓ Orkney Is

Loch Cairnkann

BRITAIN

NORTH SEA

INSET — ATTACK, 22 SEPTEMBER

0   1 Nm
0   1 km

N

0812
Charges blow, *Tirpitz* **heavily damaged**

X-6 surrenders, boat scuttled

Tirpitz

X-7 sunk

X-5 sunk

Approach by X-5, 6 and 7

Auskarneset

Harald Haafagre
Jemmelluftneset

Kaa Fjord

C.A.Larsen

Altmark

ATTACK, 22 SEPTEMBER

THE BAY OF BISCAY OFFENSIVE, SUMMER 1943

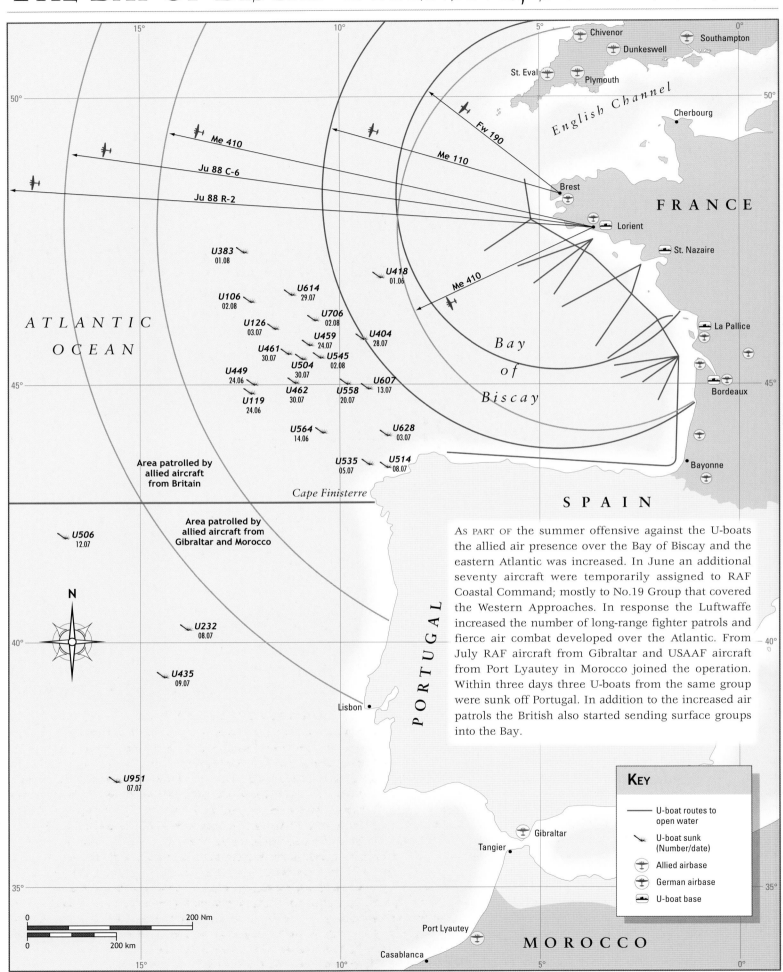

Chivenor
Southampton
Dunkeswell
St. Eval
Plymouth
English Channel
Cherbourg
Fw 190
Me 110
Me 410
Ju 88 C-6
Ju 88 R-2
Brest
FRANCE
Lorient
St. Nazaire
Me 410
U383
01.08
U614
29.07
U418
01.06
U106
02.08
U706
02.08
ATLANTIC
OCEAN
U126
03.07
U459
24.07
U404
28.07
La Pallice
U461
30.07
U545
02.08
Bay
U449
24.06
U504
30.07
of
Bordeaux
U462
30.07
U558
20.07
U607
13.07
Biscay
U119
24.06
U564
14.06
U628
03.07
Bayonne
Area patrolled by
allied aircraft
from Britain
U535
05.07
U514
08.07
Cape Finisterre
SPAIN

AS PART OF the summer offensive against the U-boats
the allied air presence over the Bay of Biscay and the
eastern Atlantic was increased. In June an additional
seventy aircraft were temporarily assigned to RAF
Coastal Command; mostly to No.19 Group that covered
the Western Approaches. In response the Luftwaffe
increased the number of long-range fighter patrols and
fierce air combat developed over the Atlantic. From
July RAF aircraft from Gibraltar and USAAF aircraft
from Port Lyautey in Morocco joined the operation.
Within three days three U-boats from the same group
were sunk off Portugal. In addition to the increased air
patrols the British also started sending surface groups
into the Bay.

Area patrolled by
allied aircraft
from
Gibraltar and Morocco

U506
12.07

N

U232
08.07

PORTUGAL

U435
09.07

Lisbon

U951
07.07

Gibraltar
Tangier

KEY

U-boat routes to
open water

U-boat sunk
(Number/date)

Allied airbase

German airbase

U-boat base

0   200 Nm
0   200 km

Port Lyautey
MOROCCO
Casablanca

SARDINIA AND CORSICA, SEPTEMBER 1943

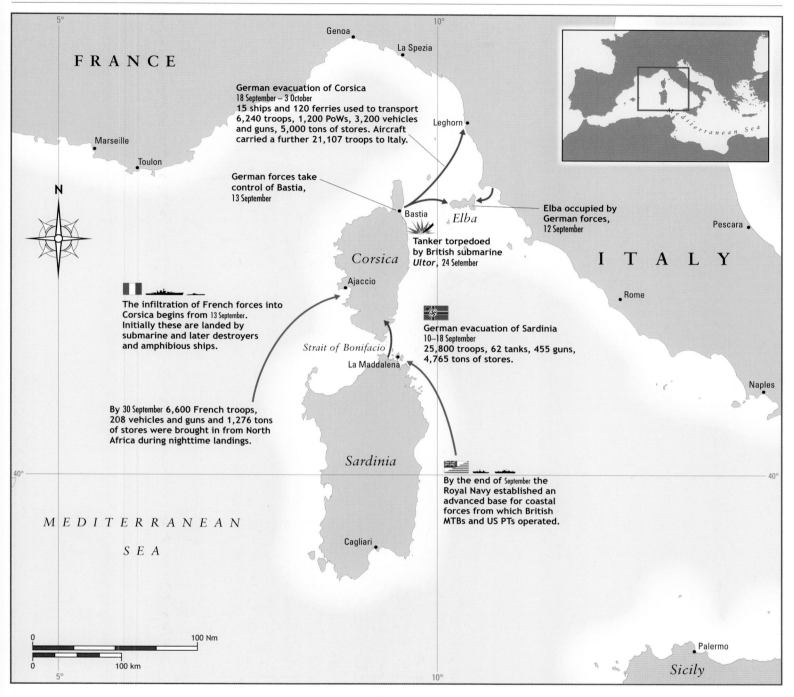

German evacuation of Corsica
18 September – 3 October
15 ships and 120 ferries used to transport 6,240 troops, 1,200 PoWs, 3,200 vehicles and guns, 5,000 tons of stores. Aircraft carried a further 21,107 troops to Italy.

German forces take control of Bastia, 13 September

Elba occupied by German forces, 12 September

Tanker torpedoed by British submarine *Ultor*, 24 Setember

The infiltration of French forces into Corsica begins from 13 September. **Initially these are landed by submarine and later destroyers and amphibious ships.**

German evacuation of Sardinia 10–18 September
25,800 troops, 62 tanks, 455 guns, 4,765 tons of stores.

By 30 September **6,600 French troops, 208 vehicles and guns and 1,276 tons of stores were brought in from North Africa during nighttime landings.**

By the end of September **the Royal Navy established an advanced base for coastal forces from which British MTBs and US PTs operated.**

FRANCE
Genoa
La Spezia
Marseille
Toulon
Leghorn
Bastia
Elba
ITALY
Pescara
Corsica
Ajaccio
Rome
Strait of Bonifacio
La Maddalena
Naples
Sardinia
MEDITERRANEAN SEA
Cagliari
Palermo
Sicily

Mediterranean Sea

0   100 Nm
0   100 km

FOLLOWING THE ALLIED landings at Salerno the Germans decided to evacuate their forces from Sardinia to Corsica: the 90th Panzer Grenadier Division, fortress troops and Luftwaffe units. It had been planned to hold Corsica, but on 12 September Hitler ordered that it too should be evacuated. The transfer from Sardinia, completed by 18 September, proceeded without allied interference. The first American forces parachuted into Sardinia on the night of 13/14 September and the first British vessels entered Cagliari on the day the German evacuation was completed.

Kapt.z.See Gustav von Liebenstein, the officer who had been responsible for the evacuation of Sicily, was placed in charge of the operation. The plan was to use the port of Bastia to extract the heavy equipment while the majority of the troops would be flown out. To this end the Germans took control of northeastern Corsica from

the Italians and occupied Elba. Meanwhile, the French resistance on the island began to take action against the retreating German forces. Fearing that this lightly-armed movement would be crushed by the Germans, the French authorities in North Africa sent forces and materiel across on French warships. This German evacuation also proceeded largely unhindered until 21 September when American and British bombers hit Bastia harbour sinking five ships. The Italian terminus ports and airfields were also bombed, but little effort was made to attack the routes with surface forces. In total only eighteen ships, all smaller vessels apart from a tanker being used as a transport that was torpedoed by a British submarine, were sunk. This was a greater achievement for the Germans than the earlier Messina evacuations as the distances involved were greater and they did not enjoy the protection of coastal defences.

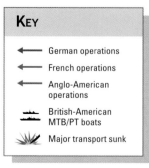

KEY

→ German operations
← French operations
← Anglo-American operations
⚓ British-American MTB/PT boats
✹ Major transport sunk

OPERATION LEANDER, 4 OCTOBER 1943

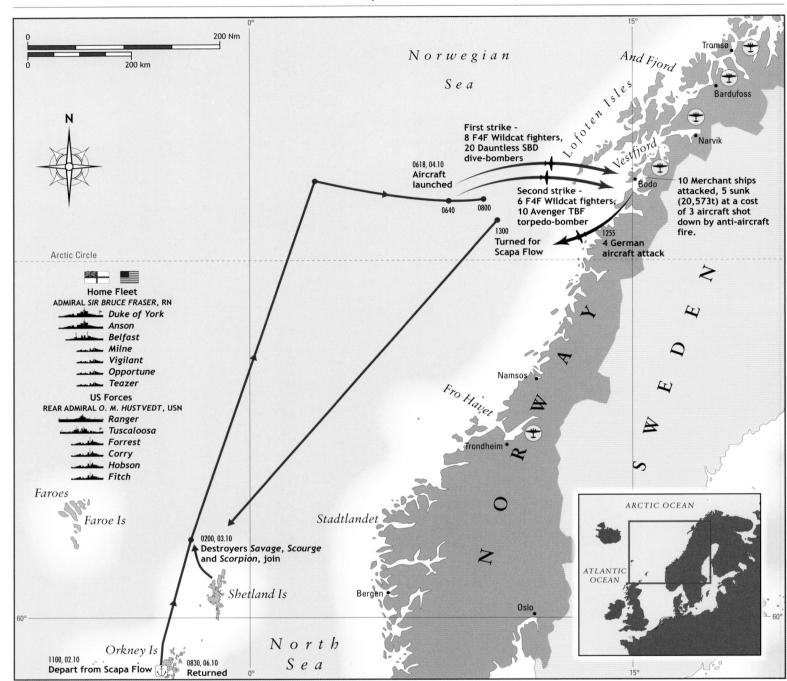

First strike -
8 F4F Wildcat fighters,
20 Dauntless SBD
dive-bombers

0618, 04.10
**Aircraft
launched**

Second strike -
6 F4F Wildcat fighters,
10 Avenger TBF
torpedo-bomber

1300
**Turned for
Scapa Flow**

1255
**4 German
aircraft attack**

10 Merchant ships
attacked, 5 sunk
(20,573t) at a cost
of 3 aircraft shot
down by anti-aircraft
fire.

Arctic Circle

Home Fleet
ADMIRAL *SIR BRUCE FRASER*, RN
Duke of York
Anson
Belfast
Milne
Vigilant
Opportune
Teazer
US Forces
REAR ADMIRAL *O. M. HUSTVEDT*, USN
Ranger
Tuscaloosa
Forrest
Corry
Hobson
Fitch

0200, 03.10
**Destroyers *Savage*, *Scourge*
and *Scorpion*, join**

1100, 02.10
Depart from Scapa Flow

0830, 06.10
Returned

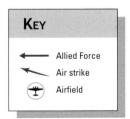
IN THE TWO years since the last British carrier strikes against northern Norway the capabilities of naval aviation had greatly increased. In August the American carrier *Ranger* joined the USN's task force operating with the Home Fleet, greatly augmenting the strike capability that Admiral Fraser had at his disposal. As the *Tirpitz* had been heavily damaged and immobilised during Operation *Source* he could also employ the Home Fleet more offensively against German positions in Norway. The first operation was a strike against German shipping around the port of Bodo. *Ranger*'s Air Group 4 comprised around sixty aircraft and for more than half the aircrews this was the first operational sortie.

Two strikes were launched between 6 and 7am on 4 October and owing to the good weather and visibility the aircraft approached the target area at very low level. A number of Luftwaffe airbases were located in the area,

but its strength in the Arctic had been greatly reduced and no fighters intercepted the strikes. As there was more shipping around Bodo than had been expected the attack inflicted a considerable amount of damage and was judged highly successful. In addition to the vessels sunk, a 10,000-ton tanker and troop transport were heavily damaged outside Bodo roadstead. By 9am the air group had returned to the carrier and only at 1pm did a small number of German aircraft locate the allied force. Two were shot down by the combat air patrol before Fraser decided to turn back for Scapa Flow. This was also the last major American operation in north European waters. The reduction of the German surface threat and growth of the Home Fleet's carrier capability, through the addition of escort carriers, prompted Admiral King to withdraw the USN from the theatre.

BATTLE OF VELLA LAVELLA, 6 OCTOBER 1943

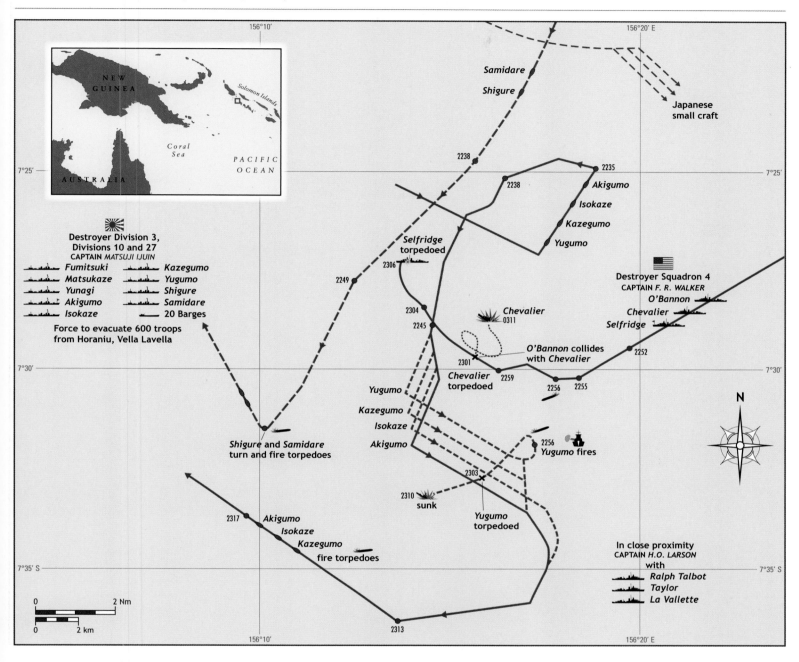

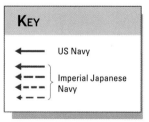

By October the Japanese had evacuated their positions in the central Solomons and all that remained was a small garrison of just under 600 troops on the northern tip of Vella Lavella that had been used as a staging post. Captain Ijuin was tasked with evacuating this force. He planned to use three destroyer-transports to escort around twenty barges into the area covered by a force of six destroyers. This force would distract the Americans from the movements of the actual evacuation force of around a dozen smaller vessels and might enable any American ships sent out to be ambushed. The Japanese left Rabaul in the morning and were northwest of Vella Lavella by 10pm. The only American force in the immediate area was Captain Walker's Destroyer Squadron 4, although another similar sized force was coming to reinforce it. Both sides knew of the presence

of the other. Ijuin had sent part of his force away to meet the barges.

At around 10.30pm Walker and Ijuin spotted each other and after some manoeuvring launched torpedoes, at 10.54pm and 10.56pm respectively, followed by gunfire. *Chevalier* was hit and accidentally rammed by *O'Bannon*. *Selfridge*, charging ahead, attacked alone but at 11.06pm was hit by a Japanese torpedo that blew off her bow. At 11.13pm Ijuin was informed by an air patrol that further American ships were within close proximity and, believing these to be cruisers, he withdrew. A final salvo of twenty-four torpedoes was launched at the three crippled American destroyers, but none hit. *Chevalier* was too badly damaged to be saved, and was sunk by a torpedo fired by the destroyer *La Vallette* at 3am. In the confusion of the battle the evacuation of the Japanese troops went unnoticed

OPERATION TUNNEL, 23 OCTOBER 1943

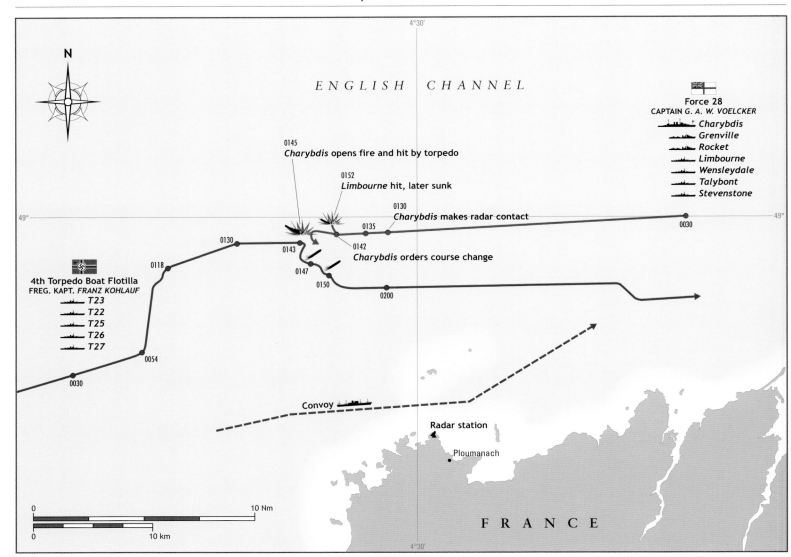

ENGLISH CHANNEL

Force 28
CAPTAIN G. A. W. VOELCKER
- Charybdis
- Grenville
- Rocket
- Limbourne
- Wensleydale
- Talybont
- Stevenstone

0145
Charybdis opens fire and hit by torpedo

0152
Limbourne hit, later sunk

0130
Charybdis makes radar contact

0135

0030

0142
Charybdis orders course change

0130

0118

4th Torpedo Boat Flotilla
FREG. KAPT. *FRANZ KOHLAUF*
- T23
- T22
- T25
- T26
- T27

0143

0147

0150

0200

0054

0030

Convoy

Radar station

Ploumanach

FRANCE

0   10 Nm

0   10 km

N

KEY

← Allied force
← German force
◀-- German convoy

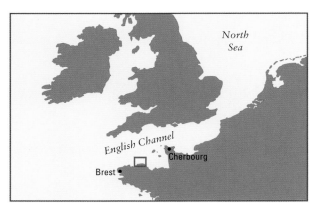

North Sea

English Channel

Cherbourg

Brest

AS THE ROYAL NAVY built up its force of destroyers, corvettes and coastal craft in the Channel during the year it was increasingly able to attack German coastal convoys. By 1943 these were irregularly run and involved the movement of merchant ships in stages from Atlantic ports to the North Sea. In the summer, action between opposing coastal forces frequently took place off the Dutch coast, and to a lesser degree between Cherbourg and Ushant. Here, in the western Channel, the Germans had a sizeable force of six large and six small destroyers and five large torpedo boats in addition to smaller auxiliary forces. In early October,

after a clash off Brittany between opposing destroyer forces resulted in a draw, the British decided to augment the striking power of such sweeps by attaching a light cruiser. Operation *Tunnel* was a contingency plan for a night raid on German shipping routes when intelligence suggested a German movement.

On 9 October the German blockade-runner *Münsterland* arrived in Brest and when she had still not arrived in Cherbourg by 20 October the British decided to conduct an offensive patrol on the night of 22–23 October to intercept her. However, the mixed force had never operated as a unit. In addition to the light cruiser *Charybdis*, there were two fleet destroyers and four smaller, and slower, Hunt-class destroyers normally employed in escorting convoys in the Western Approaches. *Münsterland* left Brest in the afternoon of 22 October as part of a convoy with eight smaller escort vessels. Five well-trained torpedo boats provided cover and the Germans also had advanced warning through shore-based radar. Thus they were able to track and set up a torpedo attack that hit the British when they were about to open fire at 1.45am. The latter were thrown into confusion and within minutes the action was over. *Charybdis* sank at 2.30am, and *Limbourne* followed at 6.40am as a result of multiple torpedo hits after the initial scuttling attempts failed.

THE AEGEAN, SEPTEMBER – NOVEMBER 1943

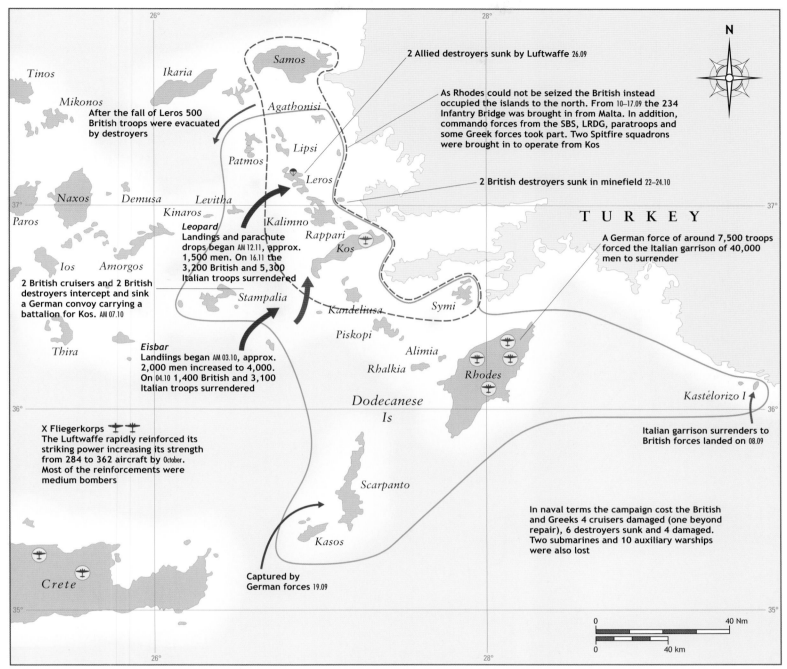

N

2 Allied destroyers sunk by Luftwaffe 26.09

As Rhodes could not be seized the British instead occupied the islands to the north. From 10–17.09 the 234 Infantry Bridge was brought in from Malta. In addition, commando forces from the SBS, LRDG, paratroops and some Greek forces took part. Two Spitfire squadrons were brought in to operate from Kos

2 British destroyers sunk in minefield 22–24.10

Tinos

Ikaria

Mikonos

After the fall of Leros 500 British troops were evacuated by destroyers

Samos

Agathonisi

Lipsi

Patmos

Leros

Naxos *Demusa* *Levitha*

Paros *Kinaros*

Leopard
Landings and parachute drops began AM 12.11, approx. 1,500 men. On 16.11 the 3,200 British and 5,300 Italian troops surrendered

Kalimno

Rappari

Kos

T U R K E Y

A German force of around 7,500 troops forced the Italian garrison of 40,000 men to surrender

Ios *Amorgos*

2 British cruisers and 2 British destroyers intercept and sink a German convoy carrying a battalion for Kos. AM 07.10

Stampalia

Kandeliusa

Symi

Piskopi

Thira

Eisbar
Landiings began AM 03.10, approx. 2,000 men increased to 4,000. On 04.10 1,400 British and 3,100 Italian troops surrendered

Alimia

Rhalkia

Rhodes

Kastélorizo I

Dodecanese Is

X Fliegerkorps
The Luftwaffe rapidly reinforced its striking power increasing its strength from 284 to 362 aircraft by October. Most of the reinforcements were medium bombers

Italian garrison surrenders to British forces landed on 08.09

In naval terms the campaign cost the British and Greeks 4 cruisers damaged (one beyond repair), 6 destroyers sunk and 4 damaged. Two submarines and 10 auxiliary warships were also lost

Scarpanto

Kasos

Captured by German forces 19.09

Crete

0   40 Nm
0   40 km

MAJOR OPERATIONS

	Area under Italian control
	Allied airbase
	German airbase
---	Perimeter occupied by allied forces
←	German operations
←	Allied operations

WHEN THE ARMISTICE with Italy came into effect on 8 September, the British sought to capitalise from the Italian possession of the Dodecanese and send a small force into the region. Strategically, the islands would provide bases from which coastal forces and submarines could attack German maritime communications in the Aegean, and the arrival of an allied presence in the area might induce Turkey to join the war against Germany. In fact, the three-month Aegean campaign ended in complete defeat due mainly to the lack of British resources for undertaking such an operation in parallel to the landings and opening stages of the Italian campaign. There were insufficient naval and air force units in the eastern Mediterranean and those available generally lacked the range and endurance to operate in the Aegean from bases on Cyprus, Egypt or Libya. Although the British had developed contingency plans to land on Crete and Rhodes, the necessary shipping and

troops were simply not available in September.

At the outset the Germans were able to secure the most important island, Rhodes, before any British forces arrived. Instead, the British gradually built up their strength on Kos, Leros and Samos. The Germans enjoyed air superiority and used this to maximum effect to compensate for their naval inferiority when the counter-offensive began at the end of September. The British found it difficult to continuously patrol all the approach routes and early on 3 October German troops succeeded in landing on Kos. While the Royal Navy brought in cruisers, which were instrumental in sinking a German follow-up convoy, the campaign increasingly became a contest between allied naval and German air power. The British lacked resources to substantially reinforce the Aegean and after the fall of Leros the remaining personnel, approximately 1,400 spread across the northern islands, were evacuated.

BATTLE OF EMPRESS AUGUSTA BAY, 1–2 NOVEMBER 1943

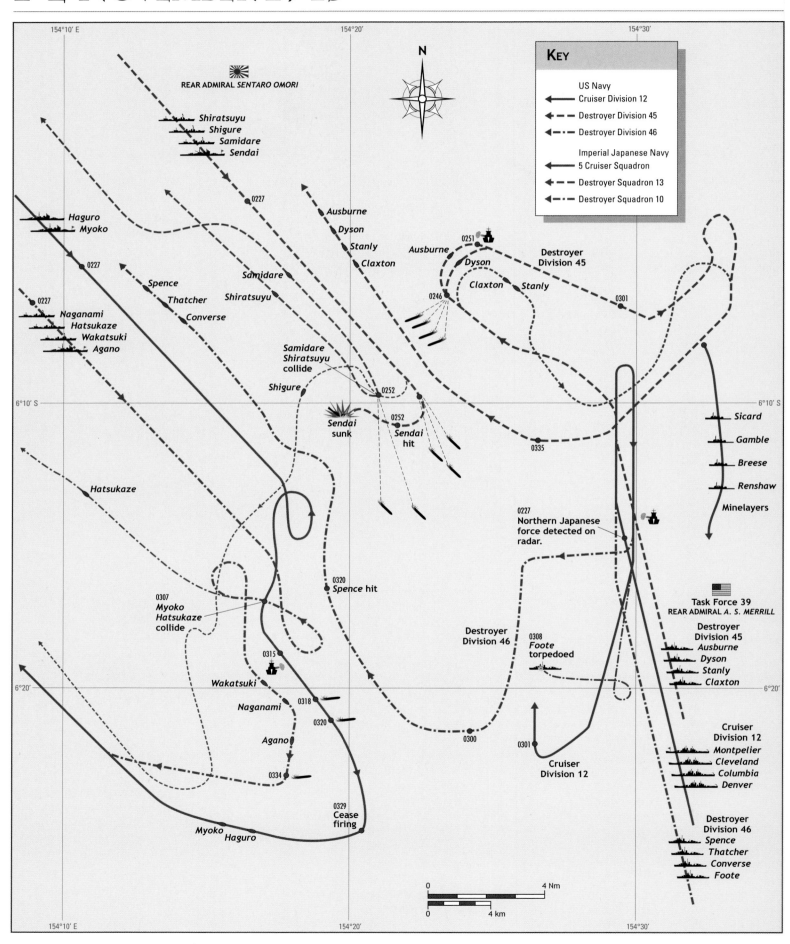

KEY

US Navy
- Cruiser Division 12
- Destroyer Division 45
- Destroyer Division 46

Imperial Japanese Navy
- 5 Cruiser Squadron
- Destroyer Squadron 13
- Destroyer Squadron 10

REAR ADMIRAL *SENTARO OMORI*

Shiratsuyu
Shigure
Samidare
Sendai

0227

Haguro
Myoko

0227

Spence
Thatcher
Converse

Samidare
Shiratsuyu

0227

Naganami
Hatsukaze
Wakatsuki
Agano

Ausburne
Dyson
Stanly
Claxton

Ausburne
Dyson
Claxton   Stanly

Destroyer
Division 45

0251

0246

0301

Samidare
Shiratsuyu
collide

Shigure

0252

Sendai
sunk

0252
Sendai
hit

0335

Sicard
Gamble
Breese
Renshaw
Minelayers

Hatsukaze

0227
Northern Japanese
force detected on
radar.

0320
Spence hit

0307
Myoko
Hatsukaze
collide

0315

Wakatsuki

Naganami

0318

0320

Agano

0334

0329
Cease
firing

Myoko
Haguro

Destroyer
Division 46

0308
Foote
torpedoed

0300

0301

Cruiser
Division 12

Task Force 39
REAR ADMIRAL A. S. MERRILL

Destroyer
Division 45
Ausburne
Dyson
Stanly
Claxton

Cruiser
Division 12
Montpelier
Cleveland
Columbia
Denver

Destroyer
Division 46
Spence
Thatcher
Converse
Foote

0   4 Nm

0   4 km

154°10' E   154°20'   154°30'

6°10' S

6°20'

BATTLE OF CAPE ST GEORGE, 25 NOVEMBER 1943

ON 1 NOVEMBER, the 3rd Marine Division was landed at Cape Torokina in Empress Augusta Bay, on Bougainville. Naval cover was provided by Rear Admiral Merrill's TF 39, which had also bombarded outlying Japanese positions the night before in support of the landing. Rear Admiral Omori, in command of the local Japanese naval forces, was ordered to use his warships to escort five destroyer-transports carrying around 900 troops to Empress Augusta Bay that night and, after disembarking them, attack the American transports. Unbeknown to him, the Marines had unloaded most of their equipment and the majority of transports departed the area by 6pm. American aircraft had also been tracking the Japanese force and attacked shortly after 9pm. Having lost the element of surprise, Omori sent the transports back and instead decided to conduct a sweep of the Bay. At 1.30am on 2 November a scout plane, launched from the *Haguro*, spotted American transports (actually a small force of minesweepers) and convinced Omori to continue. TF 39, coming from the southeast, detected

the Japanese on radar at 2.27pm. Merrill planned to engage with destroyer torpedo attacks from the flanks while initially keeping his cruisers back, out of Japanese torpedo range. This nearly worked, but at the last moment the Japanese cruiser *Sendai* spotted Captain Burke's destroyer division (DESDIV 45) and opened fire. The battle quickly developed into a confusing high-speed melee and, at around 3.30am, Omori decided to retire believing that he faced a numerically superior American force.

The battle of Cape St George was the last major surface action in the Solomon Islands campaign and the end of the Tokyo Express. After the Americans had landed on Bougainville, the Japanese army wanted to reinforce the garrison on Buka Island to the north. Around 900 troops were brought in on three destroyer-transports covered by two destroyers late on 24 November. On the return voyage to Rabaul, the force was ambushed by an American destroyer squadron, which used radar to launch a surprise torpedo attack.

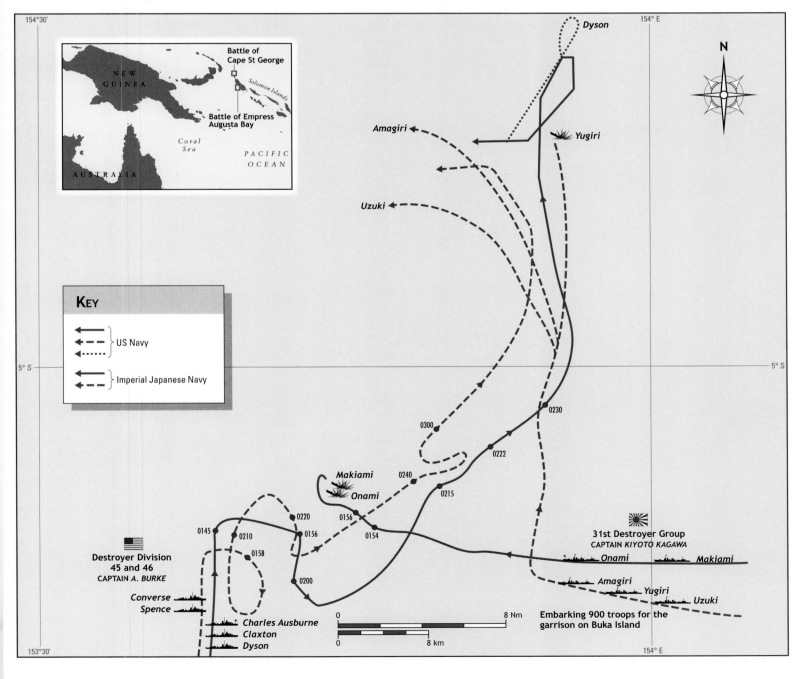

OPERATION GALVANIC, NOVEMBER 1943

**MAKIN ATOLL
20-23 NOVEMBER**

→ American landings

⬤ Pockets of Japanese resistance

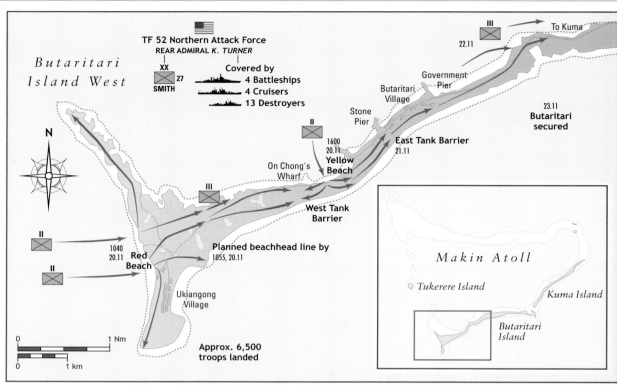

*Butaritari
Island West*

TF 52 Northern Attack Force
REAR ADMIRAL *K. TURNER*

XX 27
SMITH

Covered by
4 Battleships
4 Cruisers
13 Destroyers

To Kuma

III
22.11

Government
Pier

Butaritari
Village

Stone
Pier

East Tank Barrier
21.11

23.11
Butaritari
secured

II
1600
20.11
**Yellow
Beach**

On Chong's
Wharf

West Tank
Barrier

III

Planned beachhead line by
1855, 20.11

II
1040
20.11
**Red
Beach**

II

Ukiangong
Village

N

0   1 Nm
0   1 km

Approx. 6,500
troops landed

Makin Atoll

○ *Tukerere Island*

Kuma Island

*Butaritari
Island*

**TARAWA ATOLL,
20-23 NOVEMBER**

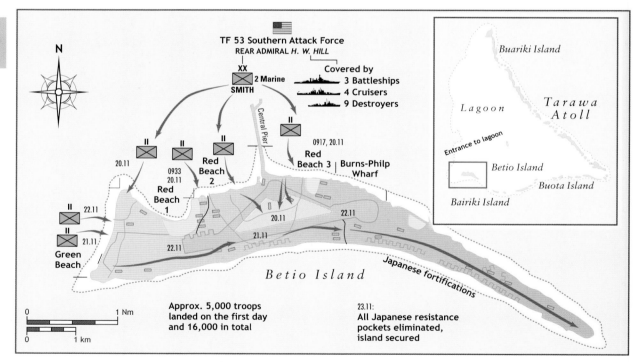

N

TF 53 Southern Attack Force
REAR ADMIRAL *H. W. HILL*

XX
SMITH
2 Marine

Covered by
3 Battleships
4 Cruisers
9 Destroyers

Buariki Island

Lagoon

*Tarawa
Atoll*

Entrance to lagoon

Betio Island

Buota Island

Bairiki Island

II
20.11

II
0933
20.11
**Red
Beach
1**

II
**Red
Beach
2**

Central Pier

II

II
0917, 20.11
**Red
Beach 3** | Burns-Philp
Wharf

II 22.11

II 21.11
**Green
Beach**

20.11

22.11

21.11

22.11

Japanese fortifications

Betio Island

0   1 Nm
0   1 km

Approx. 5,000 troops
landed on the first day
and 16,000 in total

23.11:
All Japanese resistance
pockets eliminated,
island secured

*PACIFIC
OCEAN*

Tarawa

Makin

AUSTRALIA

THE CENTRAL PACIFIC front remained quiet until the autumn of 1943. Except for submarine patrols and occasional raids by aircraft carriers or small Marine forces, the Americans undertook little against the Japanese perimeter in the Gilbert and Marshall Islands as the focus was on the southwest Pacific. The Marshalls had been under Japanese control before the war while the Gilberts were occupied in December 1941 and bases established there the following year. The island groups could not be ignored as the Japanese could use them to attack American supply lines and any advance into Micronesia. As the islands lay beyond land-based air cover their capture could only be undertaken once more carriers became available to the Pacific Fleet. In the summer it was decided to take the Gilberts first. Tarawa, with the only finished airfield, and lightly defended Makin, would be attacked, while Nauru, considered too well defended, was ignored. Two attack forces were deployed and they were supported by a large naval force. The landings provided many valuable lessons for future operations and casualties were heavy on both sides, with almost the entire Japanese garrison being killed. American naval losses amounted to one carrier damaged and an escort carrier sunk while the Japanese lost six of nine submarines involved in the campaign.

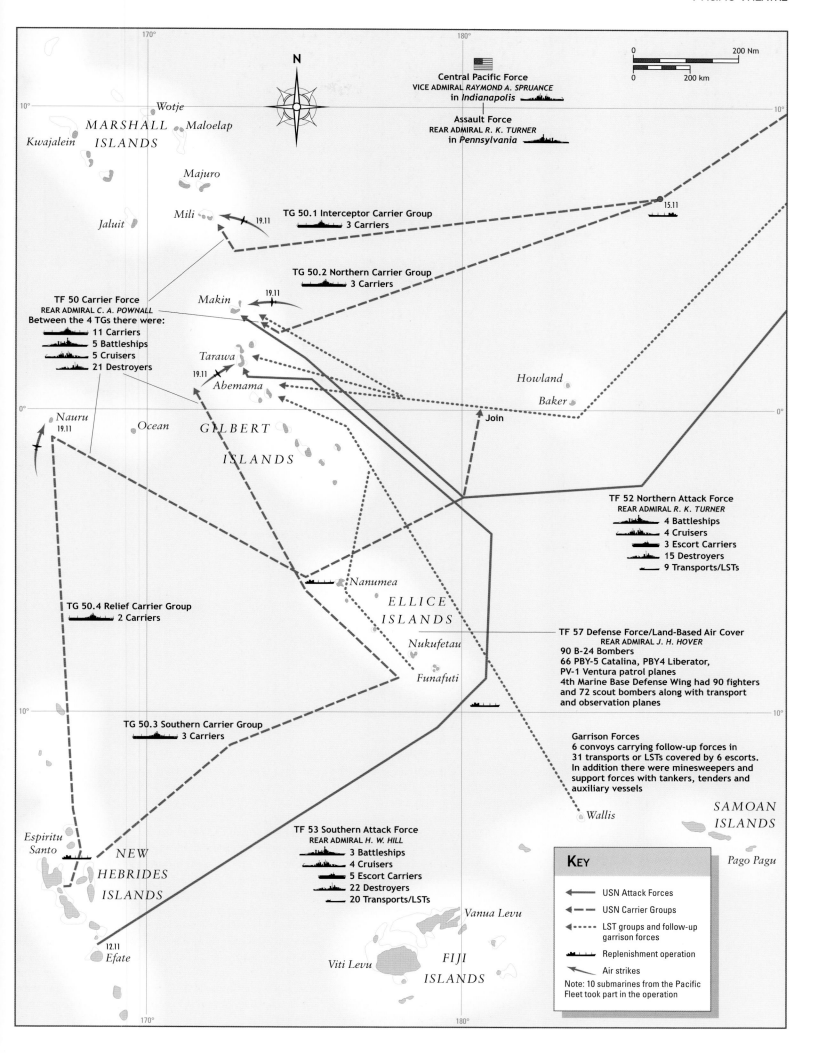

Central Pacific Force
VICE ADMIRAL *RAYMOND A. SPRUANCE*
in *Indianapolis*

Assault Force
REAR ADMIRAL *R. K. TURNER*
in *Pennsylvania*

TG 50.1 Interceptor Carrier Group
3 Carriers

TG 50.2 Northern Carrier Group
3 Carriers

TF 50 Carrier Force
REAR ADMIRAL *C. A. POWNALL*
Between the 4 TGs there were:
11 Carriers
5 Battleships
5 Cruisers
21 Destroyers

TF 52 Northern Attack Force
REAR ADMIRAL *R. K. TURNER*
4 Battleships
4 Cruisers
3 Escort Carriers
15 Destroyers
9 Transports/LSTs

TG 50.4 Relief Carrier Group
2 Carriers

TF 57 Defense Force/Land-Based Air Cover
REAR ADMIRAL *J. H. HOVER*
90 B-24 Bombers
66 PBY-5 Catalina, PBY4 Liberator,
PV-1 Ventura patrol planes
4th Marine Base Defense Wing had 90 fighters
and 72 scout bombers along with transport
and observation planes

TG 50.3 Southern Carrier Group
3 Carriers

Garrison Forces
6 convoys carrying follow-up forces in
31 transports or LSTs covered by 6 escorts.
In addition there were minesweepers and
support forces with tankers, tenders and
auxiliary vessels

TF 53 Southern Attack Force
REAR ADMIRAL *H. W. HILL*
3 Battleships
4 Cruisers
5 Escort Carriers
22 Destroyers
20 Transports/LSTs

KEY
→ USN Attack Forces
◄-- USN Carrier Groups
◄···· LST groups and follow-up
garrison forces
Replenishment operation
Air strikes
Note: 10 submarines from the Pacific
Fleet took part in the operation

Place names: Wotje, MARSHALL ISLANDS, Kwajalein, Maloelap, Jaluit, Majuro, Mili, Makin, Tarawa, Abemama, Nauru, Ocean, GILBERT ISLANDS, Howland, Baker, Join, Nanumea, ELLICE ISLANDS, Nukufetau, Funafuti, Wallis, SAMOAN ISLANDS, Espiritu Santo, NEW HEBRIDES ISLANDS, Efate, Vanua Levu, Viti Levu, FIJI ISLANDS, Pago Pagu

205

BATTLE OF THE NORTH CAPE, 26–27 DECEMBER 1943

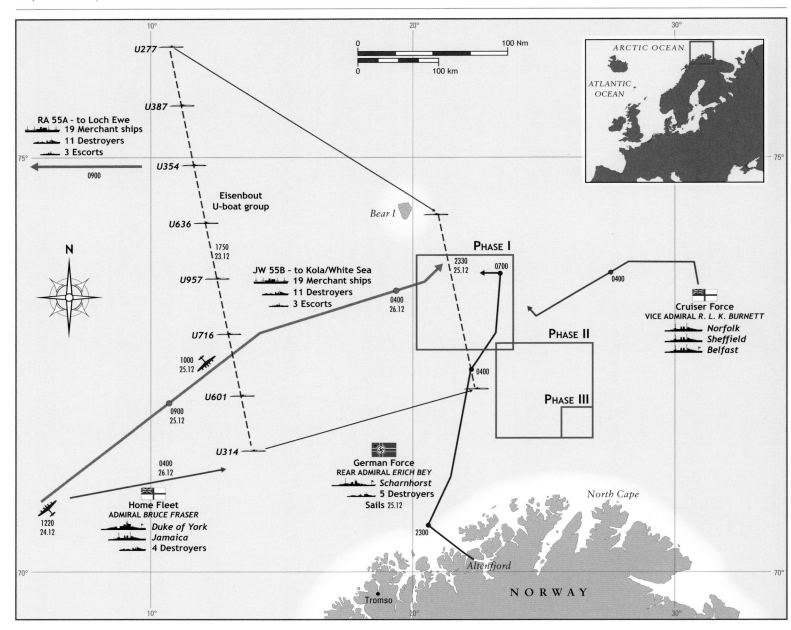

KEY

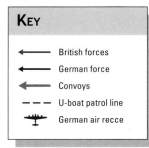

- ⟵ British forces
- ⟵ German force
- ⟵ Convoys
- --⟵ U-boat patrol line
- ✈ German air recce

AFTER A GAP of ten months the Arctic convoys were resumed in November and by this stage the overall conditions had changed and become more favourable for the allies. A reduction in German air and surface forces meant that the Home Fleet no longer had to deploy almost its entire strength to cover a convoy. Normally, one or two destroyer flotillas would escort a convoy, a cruiser squadron provide close cover, and a small force built around a battleship, provide distant cover. At the same time a similar sized force would be training or resting at Scapa Flow waiting for the next convoy group. The Germans had detected the resumption of the convoys, but with reduced strength, and concerns about the advantages of British radar in night fighting, combat was to be sought under only the most favourable circumstances. Set against this was the pressure that Admiral Dönitz was under to achieve a success after the collapse of the U-boat war in the Atlantic, and so he obtained Hitler's permission to employ *Scharnhorst*.

On 24 December the Germans located JW 55B and, as they had no indication that a heavy British force was at sea, U-boats were moved east and a surface force put to sea in anticipation of intercepting the convoy on the longitude of the North Cape. Rear Admiral Bey, commanding *Scharnhorst*, was not convinced of success though. Admiral Fraser had anticipated some operation, but owing to the earlier need to refuel, he was still too far away when intelligence informed him that *Scharnhorst* was at sea early on 26 December. Shortly before Bey met Burnett's cruisers he lost his destroyer escorts and a chance hit destroyed *Scharnhorst*'s radar around 9am. While the cruisers were evaded, later that day *Scharnhorst* ran into Fraser's force and was taken by complete surprise as the British had used radar to detect the approach and control their gunfire. Virtually blind in the poor weather and dark conditions, *Scharnhorst* was surrounded by superior British forces and sunk early in the evening.

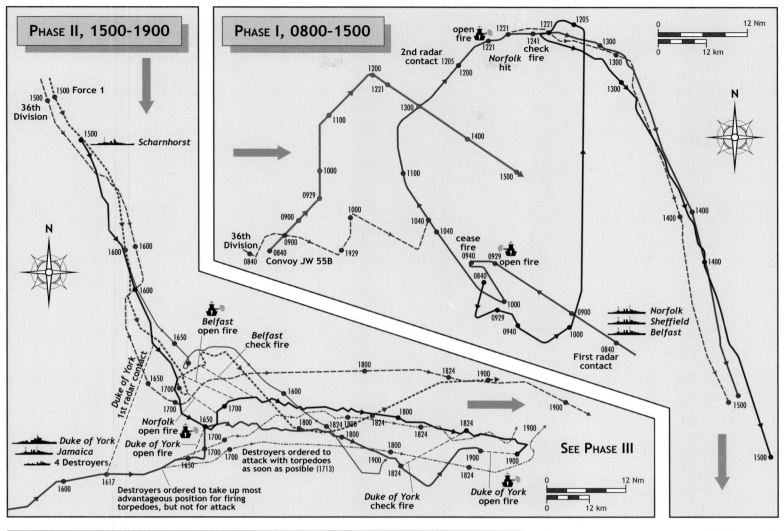

PHASE II, 1500-1900

1500 Force 1
1500 36th Division
1500
1500 _Scharnhorst_

N

1600 1600
1600
1650
1650
1700
1700
1650
1650
1617
1600

Belfast open fire
Belfast check fire

1600
1700
1700

1700
1700

Norfolk open fire
Duke of York open fire

1650 _Duke of York_ 1st radar contact

Duke of York
Jamaica
4 Destroyers

Destroyers ordered to take up most advantageous position for firing torpedoes, but not for attack

Destroyers ordered to attack with torpedoes as soon as posible (1713)

1800
1800
1800
1824 1800
1824
1800
1900
1824

1800 1824 1900
1824 1800 1824
1824

Duke of York check fire

1900
1900
1900
1900
1824

Duke of York open fire

SEE PHASE III

PHASE I, 0800-1500

open fire 1221
2nd radar contact 1205
1205 1221 1221 1205
1200 1200 1241 check fire
Norfolk hit
1300 1300
1300
1200
1221
1300
1100
1100
1400
1000
0929
0900
1000
1040
0900 1929
0900 1040
0840 1000
36th Division
0840 Convoy JW 55B
1500
cease fire
0940 0929 open fire
0840
0929
1000
0940
1000
First radar contact
0840

N

Norfolk
Sheffield
Belfast

1400
1400
1400
1500
1500

PHASE III, 1900-2000

1900
1850 1830 1840
1850
1910
1910
36th Division
1900
1920 _Belfast_ open fire
1930
1940
1820 1850
1830 1850
1840 1900
1840 1920
1910
1840 1930 1850 1850
1820
1940
1900 1934
1820
1900 1900
1850 1920 1840 1930
1840
1845 1910
1910 1920
1820
1950
1910

Duke of York open fire

Scharnhorst sunk 1945 approximately

Duke of York check fire

Jamaica closes for torpedo attack

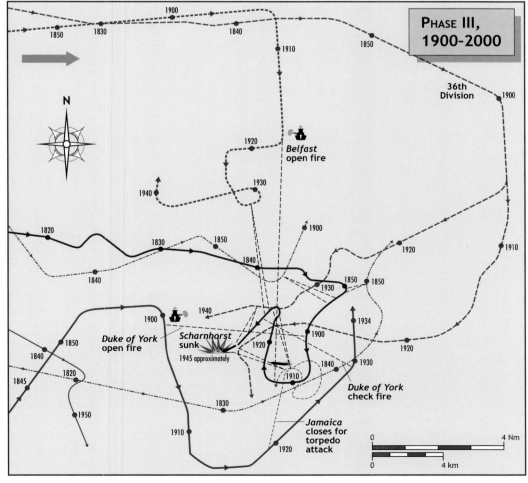
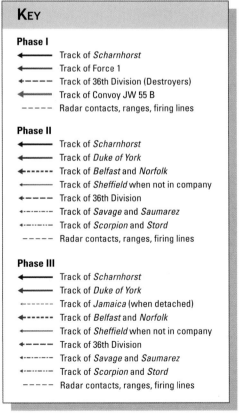

KEY

Phase I

Track of _Scharnhorst_
Track of Force 1
Track of 36th Division (Destroyers)
Track of Convoy JW 55 B
Radar contacts, ranges, firing lines

Phase II

Track of _Scharnhorst_
Track of _Duke of York_
Track of _Belfast_ and _Norfolk_
Track of _Sheffield_ when not in company
Track of 36th Division
Track of _Savage_ and _Saumarez_
Track of _Scorpion_ and _Stord_
Radar contacts, ranges, firing lines

Phase III

Track of _Scharnhorst_
Track of _Duke of York_
Track of _Jamaica_ (when detached)
Track of _Belfast_ and _Norfolk_
Track of _Sheffield_ when not in company
Track of 36th Division
Track of _Savage_ and _Saumarez_
Track of _Scorpion_ and _Stord_
Radar contacts, ranges, firing lines

THE WAR AT SEA, 1944

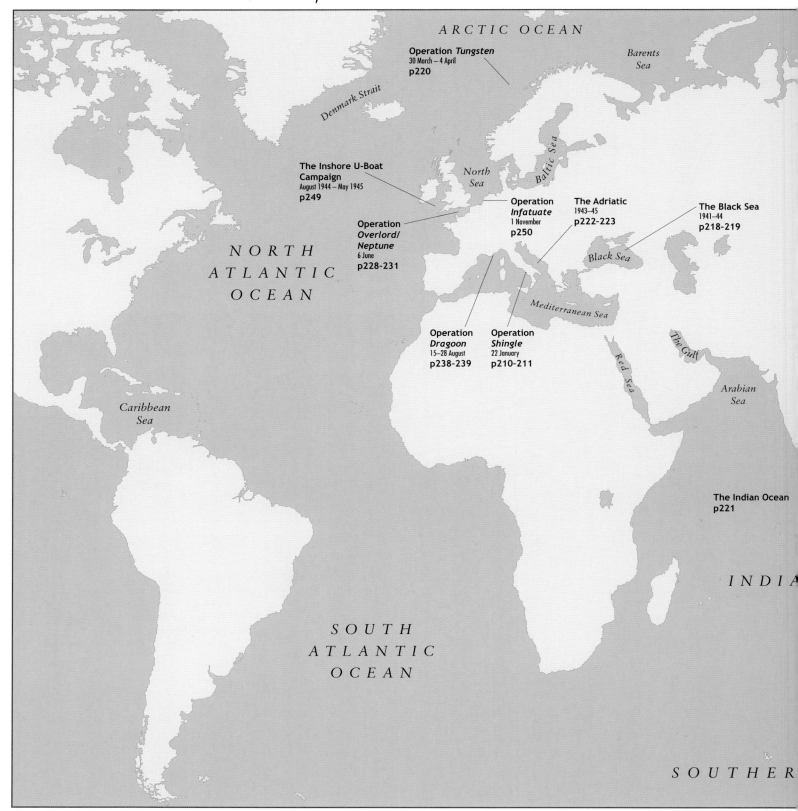

ARCTIC OCEAN

Barents
Sea

Operation *Tungsten*
30 March – 4 April
p220

Denmark Strait

Baltic Sea

**The Inshore U-Boat
Campaign**
August 1944 – May 1945
p249

North
Sea

**Operation
Infatuate**
1 November
p250

The Adriatic
1943–45
p222-223

The Black Sea
1941–44
p218-219

Black Sea

**Operation
Overlord/
Neptune**
6 June
p228-231

Mediterranean Sea

N O R T H
A T L A N T I C
O C E A N

**Operation
Dragoon**
15–28 August
p238-239

**Operation
Shingle**
22 January
p210-211

Red Sea

The Gulf

Arabian
Sea

Caribbean
Sea

**The Indian Ocean
p221**

I N D I A

S O U T H
A T L A N T I C
O C E A N

S O U T H E R

AFTER TWO YEARS of preparations the allies launched major amphibious offensives in both the European and Pacific theatres that, together with Soviet operations along the entire length of the eastern front, carried the war to the German and Japanese frontiers. Allied naval power had grown substantially, to the level that major operations could be conducted in two theatres; at the same time the axis threat to global maritime communications was reduced to negligible levels. The year began with mid-ranged amphibious operations in the Mediterranean and the Pacific. Although the former were well executed, the objective to outflank the strong defensive German positions in central Italy with the landings at Anzio

failed after the ground forces were unable to exploit the initial element of surprise. Instead, the campaign became bogged down and in the spring allied forces became dependent on naval support to maintain the bridgehead. Conversely, in the Pacific the Americans rapidly occupied key positions in the Marshall Islands and neutralised the main Japanese naval base at Truk in the Carolines, thus eliminating the outer perimeter of the Japanese empire.

The invasion of northwest Europe, Operation *Overlord*, as a precursor to the defeat of Germany, was the foremost allied priority. The scale of the landings and the need to rapidly expand the allied armies in France

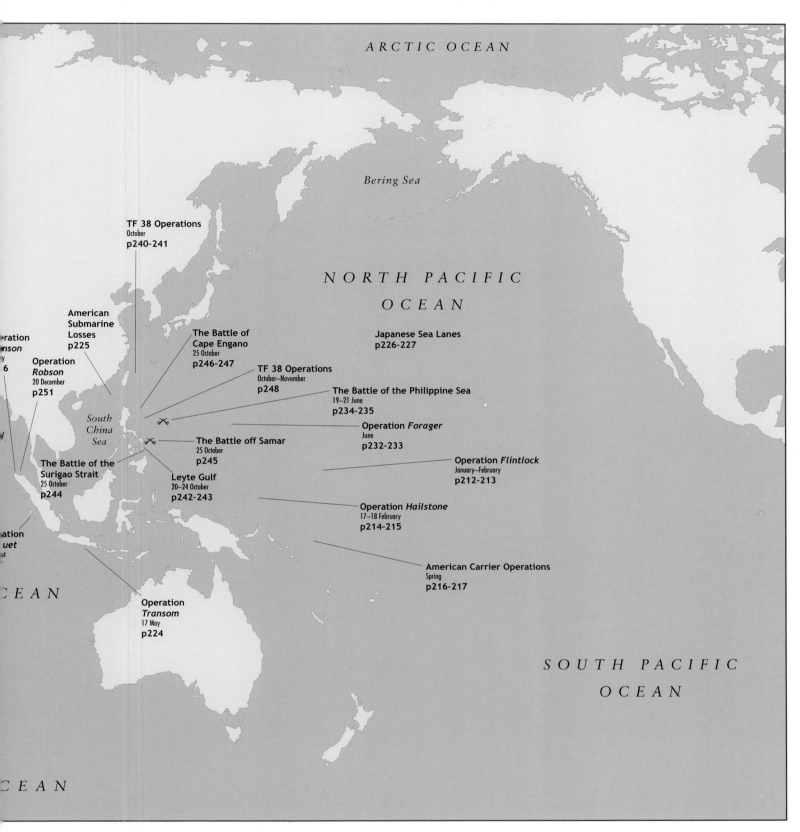

ARCTIC OCEAN

Bering Sea

TF 38 Operations
October
p240-241

American
Submarine
Losses
p225

•ration
nson
y
6

Operation
Robson
20 December
p251

*South
China
Sea*

The Battle of
Cape Engano
25 October
p246-247

TF 38 Operations
October–November
p248

NORTH PACIFIC

OCEAN

Japanese Sea Lanes
p226-227

The Battle of the Philippine Sea
19–21 June
p234-235

Operation *Forager*
June
p232-233

The Battle off Samar
25 October
p245

The Battle of the
Surigao Strait
25 October
p244

Leyte Gulf
20–24 October
p242-243

Operation *Flintlock*
January–February
p212-213

*ation
uet*
st

Operation *Hailstone*
17–18 February
p214-215

American Carrier Operations
Spring
p216-217

Operation
Transom
17 May
p224

CEAN

SOUTH PACIFIC

OCEAN

CEAN

required the services of an unprecedented amount of military and civilian shipping. During the spring and early summer the Arctic convoys were suspended and a second landing in southern France was delayed until August. Naval forces supported the allied armies in Normandy and in a number of operations along the coasts of France and the Low Countries.

A week after the D-Day landings, the Americans conducted another large-scale amphibious operation in the Pacific to take the Marianas. The landings on Saipan set in motion the first of two major naval engagements that would break the IJN by the close of the year. In the battle of the Philippines Sea, the strength of the

Japanese carrier force was exhausted. In October, the Americans landed in the Philippines and again the Japanese attempted to use their fleet to destroy the concentrations of assault shipping. In a complex three-day engagement in Leyte Gulf the remaining Japanese surface fleet was defeated, although it came close to inflicting heavy losses on the Americans. Throughout both campaigns most of the air support provided to the ground forces came from aircraft carriers, which demonstrated that naval aviation could take on and defeat land-based air power. Meanwhile, the American submarine campaign devastated the Japanese merchant fleet, leading to shortages throughout the empire.

OPERATION SHINGLE, 22 JANUARY 1944

BY THE AUTUMN of 1943 the allied advance through Italy had come to a halt along the German defensive positions that formed the Gustav line. This fortified line, which ran from the Tyrrhenian to the Adriatic coast, made excellent use of the mountainous terrain and effectively blocked the route to Rome. One option for overcoming the stalemate was to outflank the German position by means of an amphibious landing at Anzio, behind the frontline. However, the allies possessed only enough assault shipping in the Mediterranean to land one division, and this was considered too small a force to be able to withstand the inevitable German counter attacks while the main allied forces attempted to break through the Gustav line; nor did it represent so serious a threat that the Germans would need to deplete their frontline defences. Consequently, the idea was dropped, but as the lack of progress continued into December Winston Churchill revived the plan and increased its scale to a two-division assault. By withholding amphibious shipping allocated to the South East Asia Command, this new operation would be practicable and, although risky, the possibility of pushing on to Rome made it worthwhile.

The assault force was assembled in the Bay of Naples, and on 21 January sailed for Anzio. The Germans were taken by surprise and the landings, on 22 January, proceeded smoothly with few casualties; 36,604 troops and 3,069 vehicles were landed. However, the Germans recovered and quickly began to assemble forces around Anzio for a counter attack, while at the same time Major General John Lucas, the allied ground commander, made no attempt to break out. By the end of the first week four divisions comprising 68,886 men, 237 tanks, 508 guns and thousands of vehicles had been landed yet the bridgehead was no deeper than ten miles. Meanwhile, Luftwaffe attacks, particularly those employing glider-bombs, were having a serious impact on allied shipping off Anzio. Far from improving the allied position in Italy, by February *Shingle* had created another static front. The only means of keeping the bridgehead supplied was from the sea, yet as Operation *Overlord* drew closer naval forces and shipping were needed in northwest Europe. Only in late March did German resistance slowly diminish, but it was not until May that a breakout was finally achieved.

ALLIED STRATEGY IN ITALY JANUARY, 1944

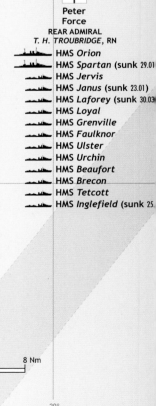

Peter Force
REAR ADMIRAL
T. H. TROUBRIDGE, RN

HMS *Orion*
HMS *Spartan* (sunk 29.01)
HMS *Jervis*
HMS *Janus* (sunk 23.01)
HMS *Laforey* (sunk 30.03)
HMS *Loyal*
HMS *Grenville*
HMS *Faulknor*
HMS *Ulster*
HMS *Urchin*
HMS *Beaufort*
HMS *Brecon*
HMS *Tetcott*
HMS *Inglefield* (sunk 25.)

Task Force 81
REAR ADMIRAL
FRANK J. LOWRY, USN
USS *Biscayne*

COMPOSITION OF ASSAULT FORCES		
	NORTHERN ASSAULT 'PETER FORCE'	SOUTHERN ASSAULT 'X-RAY FORCE'
H.Q. SHIPS	1 (British)	1 (British)
L.S.Is	3 (Polish)	5 (British)
CRUISERS	2 (British)	2 (1 U.S.)
A.A. SHIPS	1 (British)	1 (British)
DESTROYERS	11 (British)	13 (10 U.S., 2 Greek)
GUNBOATS	—	2 (Dutch)
MINESWEEPERS	16 (4 U.S.)	23 (U.S.)
LARGE L.S.Ts (BOXER CLASS)	3 (British)	—
L.S.Ts	30 (4 U.S.) (2 Greek) (24 British)	51 (10 U.S.) (41 British)
L.C.Gs AND L.C.Fs	4 (British)	4 (British)
L.C.Is	29 (British)	60 (54 U.S.) (6 British)
L.C.Ts	17 (British)	32 (7 U.S.) (25 British)
L.C.Ts (R)	1 (British)	2 (British)
SALVAGE & REPAIR CRAFT (L.C.Ts & L.C.Is)	5 (3 U.S.) (2 British)	6 (U.S.)
A/S-M/S TRAWLERS	4 (British)	—
BEACON SUBMARINES	1 (British)	1 (British)
TUGS	3 (2 U.S.) (1 British)	2 (1U.S.) (1 British)
M.Ls AND SCOUT CRAFT	17 (9 U.S.) (8 British)	23 (U.S.)
MISCELLANEOUS	1 (British)	2 (British)

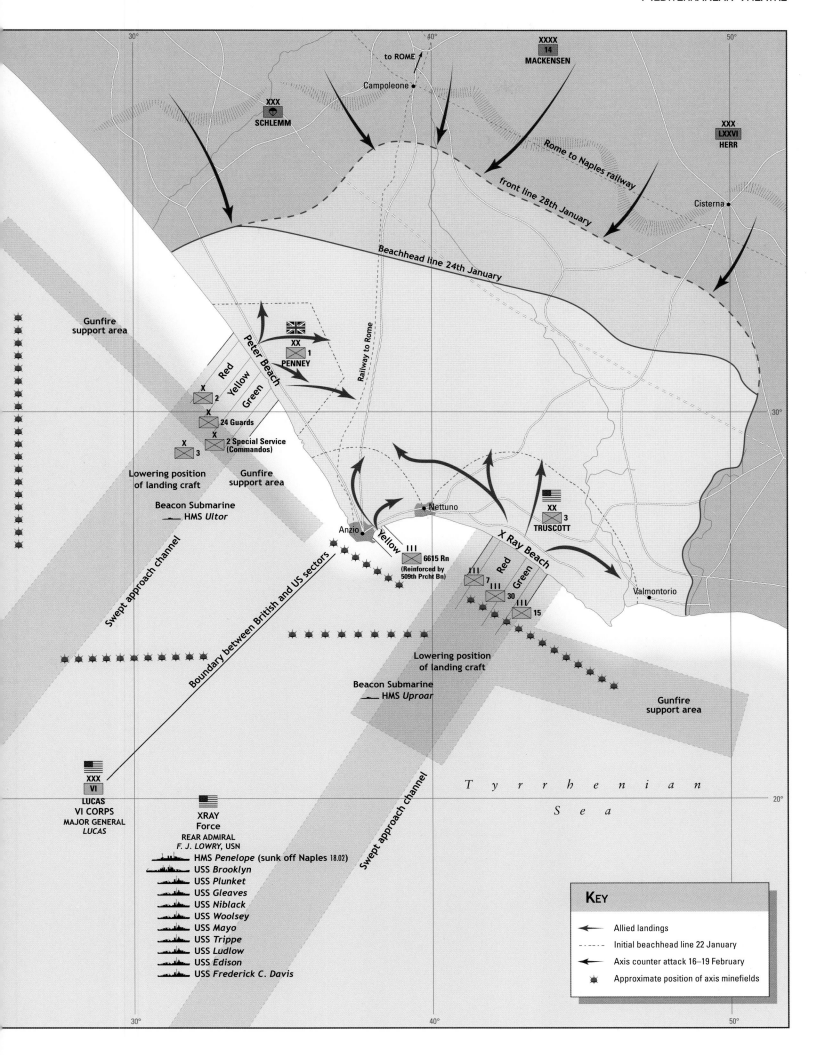

XXXX
14
MACKENSEN

XXX
SCHLEMM

to ROME

Campoleone

Rome to Naples railway

front line 28th January

XXX
LXXVI
HERR

Cisterna

Beachhead line 24th January

Gunfire
support area

Peter Beach

Red
Yellow
Green

XX
1
PENNEY

Railway to Rome

X
2

X
24 Guards

X
2 Special Service
(Commandos)

X
3

Lowering position
of landing craft

Gunfire
support area

Beacon Submarine
—— HMS *Ultor*

Swept approach channel

Boundary between British and US sectors

Anzio

Yellow

Nettuno

III
6615 Rn
(Reinforced by
509th Prcht Bn)

XX
3
TRUSCOTT

X Ray Beach

Red
Green

III
7

III
30

III
15

Valmontorio

Lowering position
of landing craft

Beacon Submarine
—— HMS *Uproar*

Gunfire
support area

XXX
VI

LUCAS
VI CORPS
MAJOR GENERAL
LUCAS

XRAY
Force
REAR ADMIRAL
F. J. LOWRY, USN
HMS *Penelope* (sunk off Naples 18.02)
USS *Brooklyn*
USS *Plunket*
USS *Gleaves*
USS *Niblack*
USS *Woolsey*
USS *Mayo*
USS *Trippe*
USS *Ludlow*
USS *Edison*
USS *Frederick C. Davis*

T y r r h e n i a n
S e a

Swept approach channel

KEY

← Allied landings

----- Initial beachhead line 22 January

◄ Axis counter attack 16–19 February

✦ Approximate position of axis minefields

OPERATION FLINTLOCK, JANUARY – FEBRUARY 1944

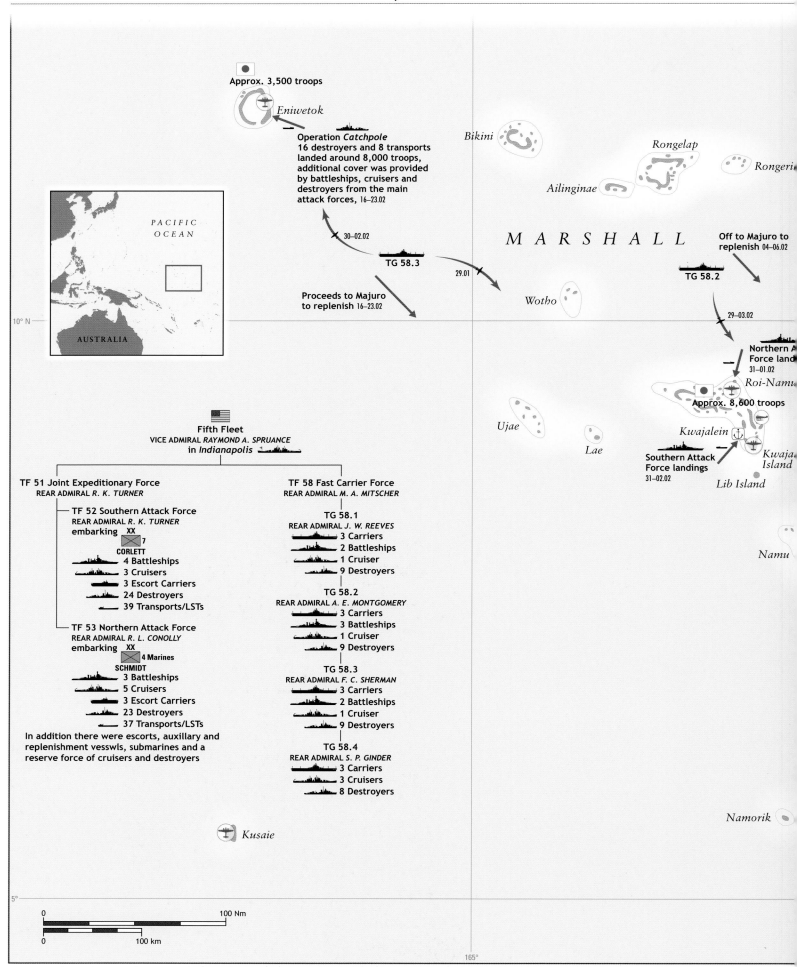

Approx. 3,500 troops

Eniwetok

Operation Catchpole
16 destroyers and 8 transports
landed around 8,000 troops,
additional cover was provided
by battleships, cruisers and
destroyers from the main
attack forces, 16–23.02

Bikini

Rongelap

Rongeri

Ailinginae

MARSHALL

Off to Majuro to
replenish 04–06.02

30–02.02

TG 58.3

29.01

TG 58.2

29–03.02

Proceeds to Majuro
to replenish 16–23.02

Wotho

10° N

Northern A
Force land
31–01.02

Roi-Namu

Approx. 8,600 troops

Ujae

Kwajalein

Lae

Southern Attack
Force landings
31–02.02

Kwaja
Island

Lib Island

PACIFIC
OCEAN

AUSTRALIA

🇺🇸
Fifth Fleet
VICE ADMIRAL *RAYMOND A. SPRUANCE*
in *Indianapolis*

TF 51 Joint Expeditionary Force
REAR ADMIRAL *R. K. TURNER*

TF 52 Southern Attack Force
REAR ADMIRAL *R. K. TURNER*
embarking ⊠ 7
CORLETT
4 Battleships
3 Cruisers
3 Escort Carriers
24 Destroyers
39 Transports/LSTs

TF 53 Northern Attack Force
REAR ADMIRAL *R. L. CONOLLY*
embarking ⊠ 4 Marines
SCHMIDT
3 Battleships
5 Cruisers
3 Escort Carriers
23 Destroyers
37 Transports/LSTs

In addition there were escorts, auxillary and
replenishment vesswls, submarines and a
reserve force of cruisers and destroyers

TF 58 Fast Carrier Force
REAR ADMIRAL *M. A. MITSCHER*

TG 58.1
REAR ADMIRAL *J. W. REEVES*
3 Carriers
2 Battleships
1 Cruiser
9 Destroyers

TG 58.2
REAR ADMIRAL *A. E. MONTGOMERY*
3 Carriers
3 Battleships
1 Cruiser
9 Destroyers

TG 58.3
REAR ADMIRAL *F. C. SHERMAN*
3 Carriers
2 Battleships
1 Cruiser
9 Destroyers

TG 58.4
REAR ADMIRAL *S. P. GINDER*
3 Carriers
3 Cruisers
8 Destroyers

Namu

Namorik

Kusaie

0   100 Nm
0   100 km

165°

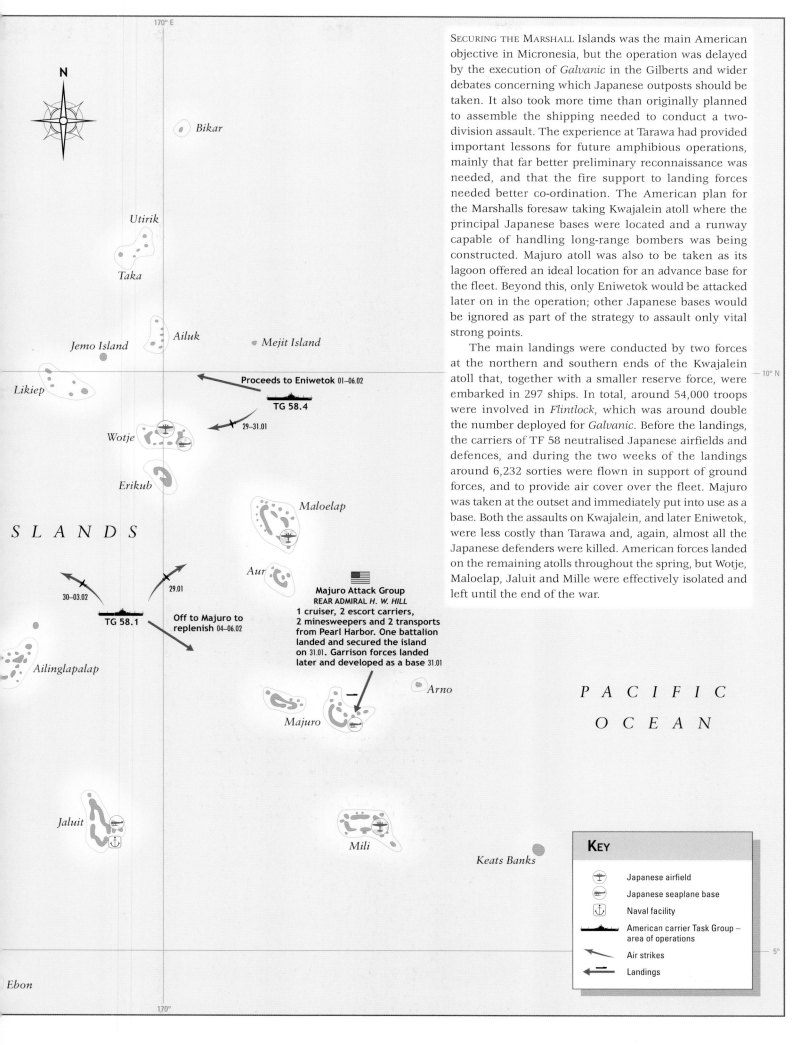

N

170° E

Bikar

Utirik

Taka

Ailuk

Mejit Island

Jemo Island

Likiep

Proceeds to Eniwetok 01–06.02

TG 58.4

29–31.01

Wotje

Erikub

Maloelap

S L A N D S

Aur

30–03.02

29.01

TG 58.1

Off to Majuro to
replenish 04–06.02

Majuro Attack Group
REAR ADMIRAL *H. W. HILL*
1 cruiser, 2 escort carriers,
2 minesweepers and 2 transports
from Pearl Harbor. One battalion
landed and secured the island
on 31.01. Garrison forces landed
later and developed as a base 31.01

Arno

P A C I F I C

O C E A N

Majuro

Ailinglapalap

Jaluit

Mili

Keats Banks

Ebon

170°

SECURING THE MARSHALL Islands was the main American objective in Micronesia, but the operation was delayed by the execution of *Galvanic* in the Gilberts and wider debates concerning which Japanese outposts should be taken. It also took more time than originally planned to assemble the shipping needed to conduct a two-division assault. The experience at Tarawa had provided important lessons for future amphibious operations, mainly that far better preliminary reconnaissance was needed, and that the fire support to landing forces needed better co-ordination. The American plan for the Marshalls foresaw taking Kwajalein atoll where the principal Japanese bases were located and a runway capable of handling long-range bombers was being constructed. Majuro atoll was also to be taken as its lagoon offered an ideal location for an advance base for the fleet. Beyond this, only Eniwetok would be attacked later on in the operation; other Japanese bases would be ignored as part of the strategy to assault only vital strong points.

The main landings were conducted by two forces at the northern and southern ends of the Kwajalein atoll that, together with a smaller reserve force, were embarked in 297 ships. In total, around 54,000 troops were involved in *Flintlock*, which was around double the number deployed for *Galvanic*. Before the landings, the carriers of TF 58 neutralised Japanese airfields and defences, and during the two weeks of the landings around 6,232 sorties were flown in support of ground forces, and to provide air cover over the fleet. Majuro was taken at the outset and immediately put into use as a base. Both the assaults on Kwajalein, and later Eniwetok, were less costly than Tarawa and, again, almost all the Japanese defenders were killed. American forces landed on the remaining atolls throughout the spring, but Wotje, Maloelap, Jaluit and Mille were effectively isolated and left until the end of the war.

10° N

5°

KEY

Japanese airfield

Japanese seaplane base

Naval facility

American carrier Task Group –
area of operations

Air strikes

Landings

OPERATION HAILSTONE, 17–18 FEBRUARY 1944

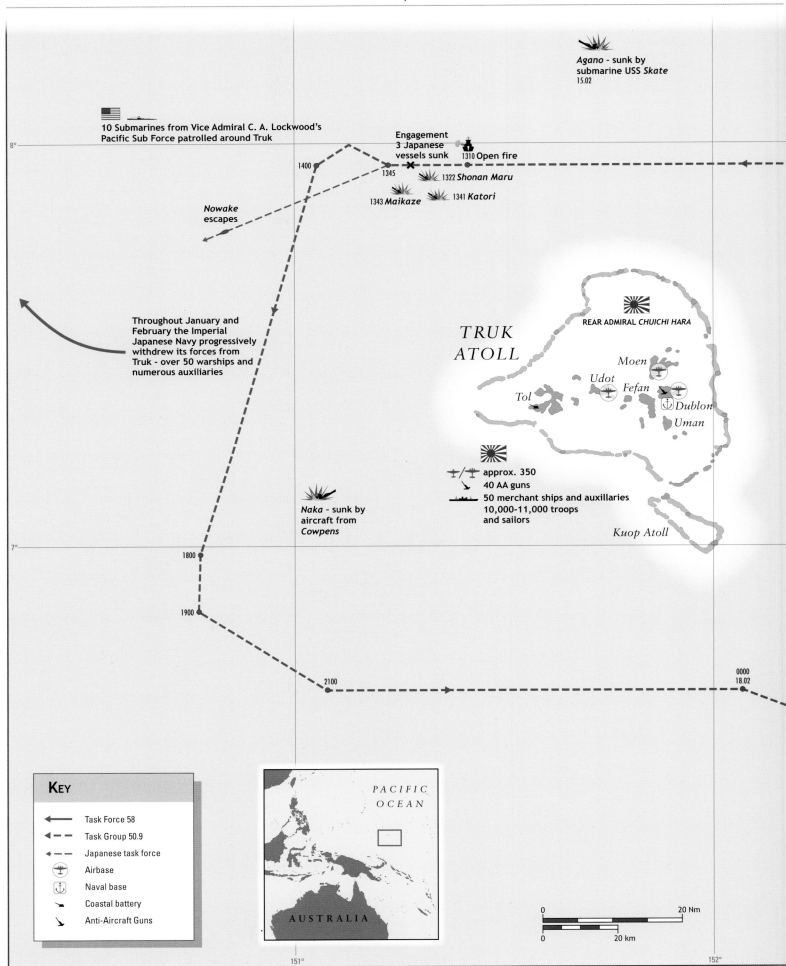

Agano - sunk by submarine USS *Skate*
15.02

10 Submarines from Vice Admiral C. A. Lockwood's Pacific Sub Force patrolled around Truk

Engagement 3 Japanese vessels sunk

1310 Open fire

1400

1345

1322 *Shonan Maru*

Nowake escapes

1343 *Maikaze*   1341 *Katori*

Throughout January and February the Imperial Japanese Navy progressively withdrew its forces from Truk - over 50 warships and numerous auxiliaries

TRUK ATOLL

REAR ADMIRAL *CHUICHI HARA*

Moen

Udot *Fefan*

Tol

⚓ *Dublon*

Uman

approx. 350
40 AA guns
50 merchant ships and auxillaries
10,000-11,000 troops and sailors

Naka - sunk by aircraft from *Cowpens*

Kuop Atoll

1800

1900

2100

0000
18.02

KEY

←	Task Force 58
◄- - -	Task Group 50.9
◄- - -	Japanese task force
⊕	Airbase
⚓	Naval base
➘	Coastal battery
➘	Anti-Aircraft Guns

PACIFIC OCEAN

AUSTRALIA

0 ————————— 20 Nm

0 ————————— 20 km

151°   152°

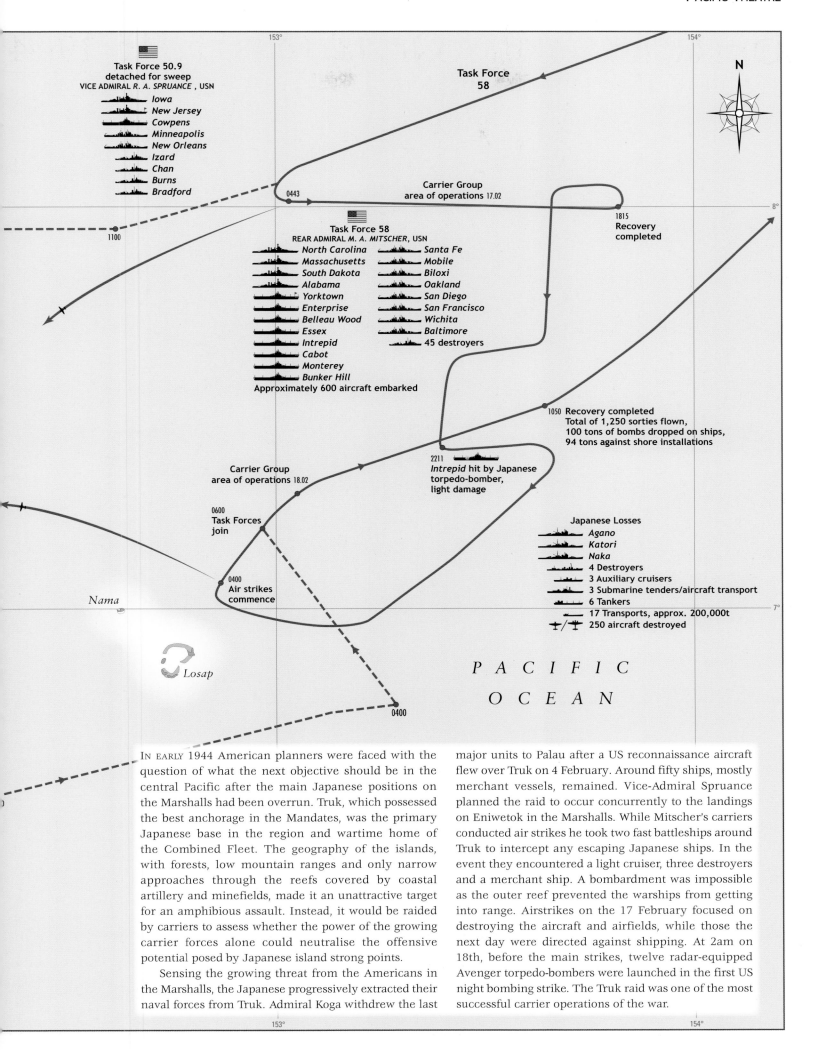

Task Force 50.9
detached for sweep
VICE ADMIRAL *R. A. SPRUANCE*, USN

- *Iowa*
- *New Jersey*
- *Cowpens*
- *Minneapolis*
- *New Orleans*
- *Izard*
- *Chan*
- *Burns*
- *Bradford*

Task Force 58

0443

Carrier Group
area of operations 17.02

1815
Recovery completed

8°

1100

Task Force 58
REAR ADMIRAL *M. A. MITSCHER*, USN

North Carolina	*Santa Fe*
Massachusetts	*Mobile*
South Dakota	*Biloxi*
Alabama	*Oakland*
Yorktown	*San Diego*
Enterprise	*San Francisco*
Belleau Wood	*Wichita*
Essex	*Baltimore*
Intrepid	45 destroyers
Cabot	
Monterey	
Bunker Hill	

Approximately 600 aircraft embarked

1050 Recovery completed
Total of 1,250 sorties flown,
100 tons of bombs dropped on ships,
94 tons against shore installations

Carrier Group
area of operations 18.02

2211
Intrepid hit by Japanese
torpedo-bomber,
light damage

0600
Task Forces join

0400
Air strikes commence

Japanese Losses
- *Agano*
- *Katori*
- *Naka*
- 4 Destroyers
- 3 Auxiliary cruisers
- 3 Submarine tenders/aircraft transport
- 6 Tankers
- 17 Transports, approx. 200,000t
- 250 aircraft destroyed

7°

Nama

Losap

P A C I F I C
O C E A N

0400

IN EARLY 1944 American planners were faced with the question of what the next objective should be in the central Pacific after the main Japanese positions on the Marshalls had been overrun. Truk, which possessed the best anchorage in the Mandates, was the primary Japanese base in the region and wartime home of the Combined Fleet. The geography of the islands, with forests, low mountain ranges and only narrow approaches through the reefs covered by coastal artillery and minefields, made it an unattractive target for an amphibious assault. Instead, it would be raided by carriers to assess whether the power of the growing carrier forces alone could neutralise the offensive potential posed by Japanese island strong points.

Sensing the growing threat from the Americans in the Marshalls, the Japanese progressively extracted their naval forces from Truk. Admiral Koga withdrew the last

major units to Palau after a US reconnaissance aircraft flew over Truk on 4 February. Around fifty ships, mostly merchant vessels, remained. Vice-Admiral Spruance planned the raid to occur concurrently to the landings on Eniwetok in the Marshalls. While Mitscher's carriers conducted air strikes he took two fast battleships around Truk to intercept any escaping Japanese ships. In the event they encountered a light cruiser, three destroyers and a merchant ship. A bombardment was impossible as the outer reef prevented the warships from getting into range. Airstrikes on the 17 February focused on destroying the aircraft and airfields, while those the next day were directed against shipping. At 2am on 18th, before the main strikes, twelve radar-equipped Avenger torpedo-bombers were launched in the first US night bombing strike. The Truk raid was one of the most successful carrier operations of the war.

AMERICAN CARRIER OPERATIONS IN THE PACIFIC, SPRING 1944

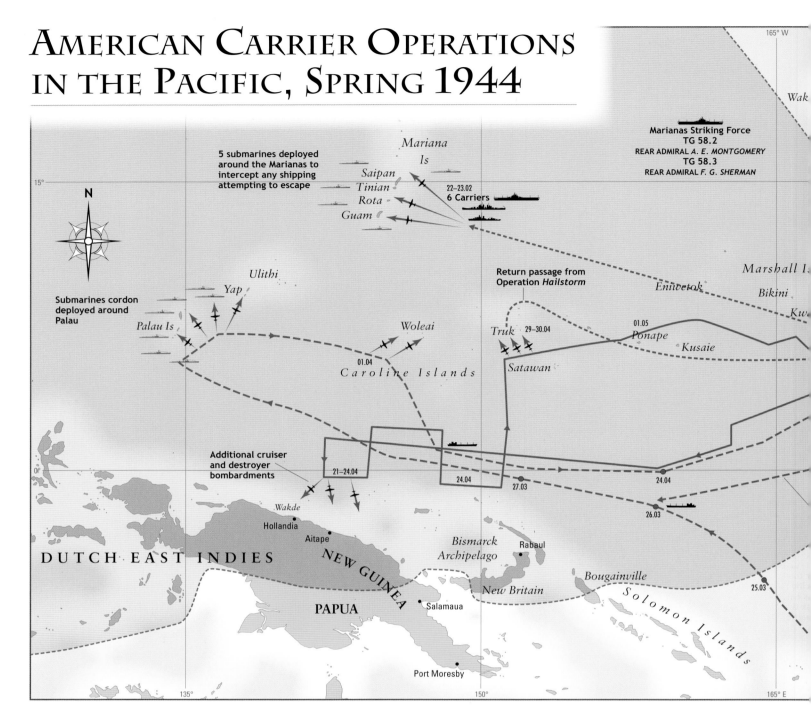

165° W

Wak

Marianas Striking Force
TG 58.2
REAR ADMIRAL *A. E. MONTGOMERY*
TG 58.3
REAR ADMIRAL *F. G. SHERMAN*

15°

N

Mariana
Is

5 submarines deployed
around the Marianas to
intercept any shipping
attempting to escape

Saipan
Tinian
Rota
Guam

22–23.02
6 Carriers

Ulithi

Return passage from
Operation *Hailstorm*

Marshall Is.

Eniwetok

Bikini

Submarines cordon
deployed around
Palau

Yap

Woleai

Truk 29–30.04

01.05
Ponape

Kw

Kusaie

Palau Is

01.04

Caroline Islands

Satawan

0°

Additional cruiser
and destroyer
bombardments

21–24.04

24.04

27.03

24.04

26.03

Wakde

Hollandia

Aitape

Bismarck
Archipelago

Rabaul

Bougainville

25.03

DUTCH EAST INDIES

NEW GUINEA

New Britain

Solomon Islands

PAPUA

Salamaua

Port Moresby

135°

150°

165° E

AFTER THE FIRST phase of the Central Pacific campaign was completed, the carriers of the Pacific Fleet were used to raid deep into Japanese-held territory and support General MacArthur's forces in New Guinea. Neutralising Japanese airbases on New Guinea and in the Carolines was vital for the next stage of the Pacific offensive against the Marianas. The operations in the Gilberts and Marshalls demonstrated the offensive potential of the new carrier task groups, and now the Americans sought to employ the strategic mobility that carriers possessed in raids that far exceeded those conducted in 1942. The first such operation took place against the Marianas in the immediate aftermath of the attack on the Japanese fleet anchorage and base on Truk. Vice Admiral Mitscher took two of his task groups within 100 miles of the islands and launched air strikes. Following a similar pattern, a submarine cordon was established around the islands to sink any Japanese vessels attempting to escape.

The next operation was in support of the Seventh Fleet to neutralise the Japanese air threat in advance of the Hollandia landings. While airbases in western Guinea could be hit with land-based aircraft, those on Palau were out of range. Nearly the entire Fifth Fleet was employed in the raid, and in addition to attacking airfields the carrier aircraft also laid mines in the main harbour, leading to the sinking or damaging of thirty-six ships. During the actual landings at Hollandia and on Wake, TF 58 again provided air cover. Throughout April nearly all Japanese aircraft on New Guinea were destroyed by land and naval aviation. On its return voyage TF 58 again hit Truk heavily, which the Japanese had reinforced with some hundred new aircraft since the February raid. Most of these were destroyed in air-to-air combat on 29 April, or on the ground. Henceforth, Truk no longer played any role in the conflict and on the return to Majura cruisers and battleships bombarded Satawan and Ponape Islands.

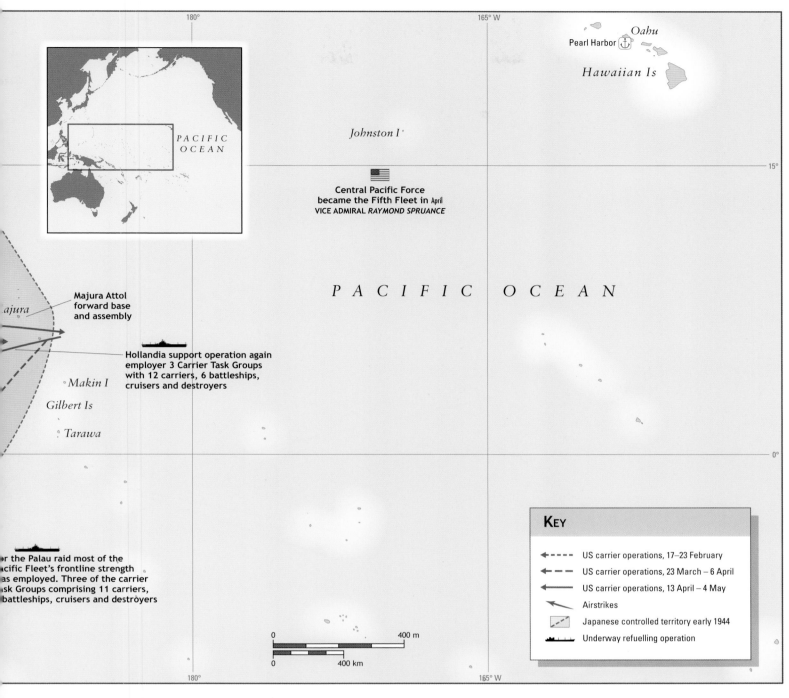

Central Pacific Force
became the Fifth Fleet in April
VICE ADMIRAL *RAYMOND SPRUANCE*

PACIFIC OCEAN

Oahu
Pearl Harbor
Hawaiian Is

Johnston I

Majura Attol
forward base
and assembly

ajura

Hollandia support operation again
employer 3 Carrier Task Groups
with 12 carriers, 6 battleships,
cruisers and destroyers

Makin I

Gilbert Is

Tarawa

r the Palau raid most of the
cific Fleet's frontline strength
as employed. Three of the carrier
sk Groups comprising 11 carriers,
battleships, cruisers and destroyers

KEY

◄------	US carrier operations, 17–23 February
◄- - -	US carrier operations, 23 March – 6 April
◄———	US carrier operations, 13 April – 4 May
◄—	Airstrikes
	Japanese controlled territory early 1944
	Underway refuelling operation

0 ——— 400 m

0 ——— 400 km

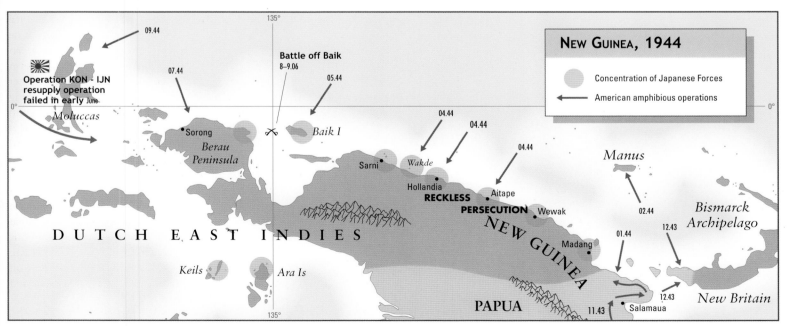

09.44

Operation KON - IJN
resupply operation
failed in early June

Moluccas

07.44

Battle off Baik
8–9.06

05.44

04.44

04.44

04.44

NEW GUINEA, 1944

Concentration of Japanese Forces

◄— American amphibious operations

Baik I

Manus

Sorong

*Berau
Peninsula*

Sarni

Wakde

Hollandia

RECKLESS

Aitape

02.44

*Bismarck
Archipelago*

PERSECUTION   Wewak

12.43

DUTCH EAST INDIES

NEW GUINEA

Madang

01.44

Keils

Ara Is

12.43

New Britain

PAPUA

11.43

Salamaua

12.43

THE BLACK SEA, 1941–44

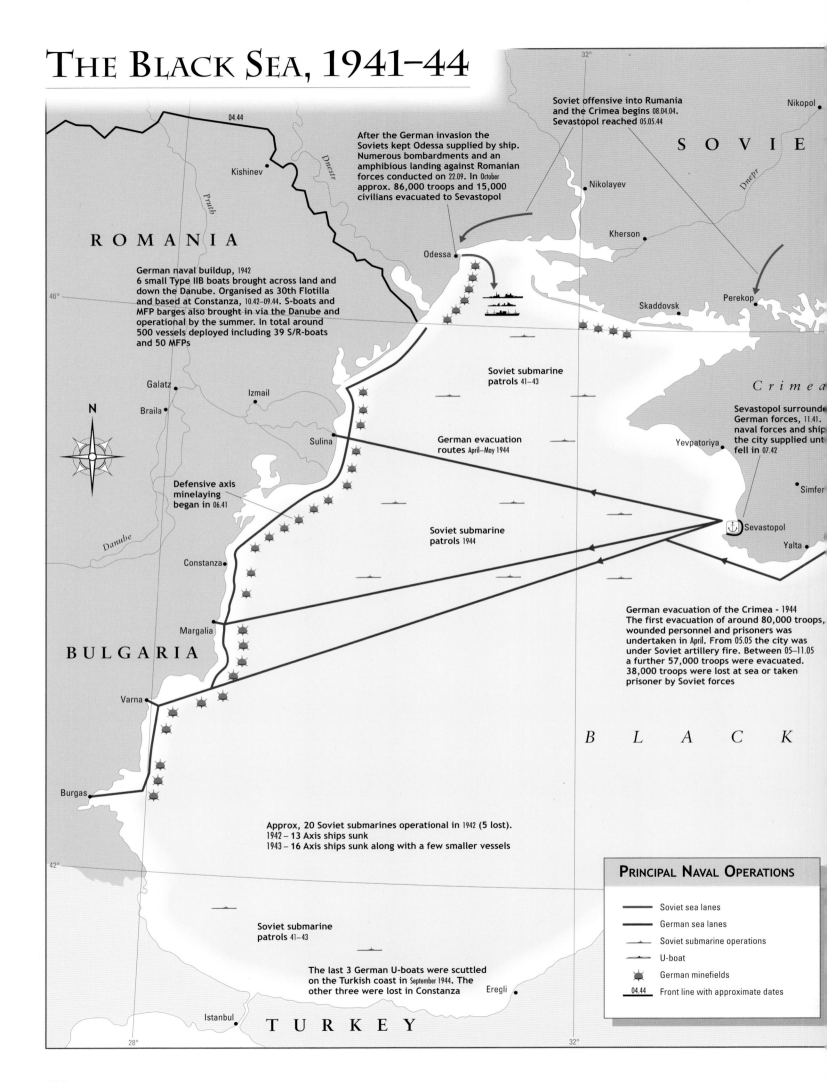

Soviet offensive into Rumania and the Crimea begins 08.04.04. **Sevastopol reached** 05.05.44

Nikopol

S O V I E

Nikolayev

Kishinev

Dnepr

After the German invasion the Soviets kept Odessa supplied by ship. Numerous bombardments and an amphibious landing against Romanian forces conducted on 22.09. **In** October **approx. 86,000 troops and 15,000 civilians evacuated to Sevastopol**

R O M A N I A

Kherson

Odessa

Perekop

Prut

German naval buildup, 1942
6 small Type IIB boats brought across land and down the Danube. Organised as 30th Flotilla and based at Constanza, 10.42–09.44. S-boats and MFP barges also brought in via the Danube and operational by the summer. In total around 500 vessels deployed including 39 S/R-boats and 50 MFPs

Skaddovsk

Galatz

Izmail

Soviet submarine patrols 41–43

C r i m e a

Braila

Sulina

German evacuation routes April–May 1944

Yevpatoriya

Sevastopol surrounde German forces, 11.41. naval forces and ship the city supplied unt fell in 07.42

Simfer

Defensive axis minelaying began in 06.41

Soviet submarine patrols 1944

Sevastopol

Danube

Yalta

Constanza

German evacuation of the Crimea - 1944
The first evacuation of around 80,000 troops, wounded personnel and prisoners was undertaken in April. From 05.05 the city was under Soviet artillery fire. Between 05–11.05 a further 57,000 troops were evacuated. 38,000 troops were lost at sea or taken prisoner by Soviet forces

Margalia

B U L G A R I A

Varna

B L A C K

Burgas

Approx, 20 Soviet submarines operational in 1942 (5 lost).
1942 – 13 Axis ships sunk
1943 – 16 Axis ships sunk along with a few smaller vessels

PRINCIPAL NAVAL OPERATIONS

————	Soviet sea lanes
————	German sea lanes
—⊥—	Soviet submarine operations
—⊤—	U-boat
✸	German minefields
04.44	Front line with approximate dates

Soviet submarine patrols 41–43

The last 3 German U-boats were scuttled on the Turkish coast in September 1944. **The other three were lost in Constanza**

Eregli

Istanbul

T U R K E Y

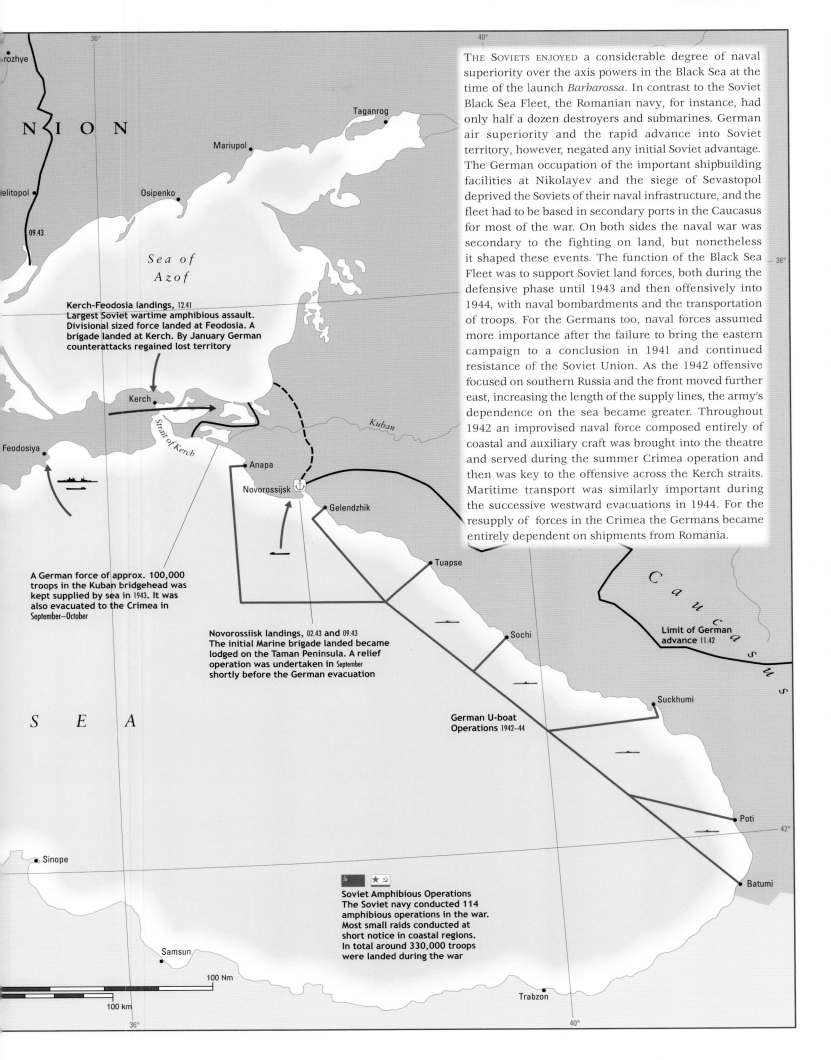

THE SOVIETS ENJOYED a considerable degree of naval superiority over the axis powers in the Black Sea at the time of the launch *Barbarossa*. In contrast to the Soviet Black Sea Fleet, the Romanian navy, for instance, had only half a dozen destroyers and submarines. German air superiority and the rapid advance into Soviet territory, however, negated any initial Soviet advantage. The German occupation of the important shipbuilding facilities at Nikolayev and the siege of Sevastopol deprived the Soviets of their naval infrastructure, and the fleet had to be based in secondary ports in the Caucasus for most of the war. On both sides the naval war was secondary to the fighting on land, but nonetheless it shaped these events. The function of the Black Sea Fleet was to support Soviet land forces, both during the defensive phase until 1943 and then offensively into 1944, with naval bombardments and the transportation of troops. For the Germans too, naval forces assumed more importance after the failure to bring the eastern campaign to a conclusion in 1941 and continued resistance of the Soviet Union. As the 1942 offensive focused on southern Russia and the front moved further east, increasing the length of the supply lines, the army's dependence on the sea became greater. Throughout 1942 an improvised naval force composed entirely of coastal and auxiliary craft was brought into the theatre and served during the summer Crimea operation and then was key to the offensive across the Kerch straits. Maritime transport was similarly important during the successive westward evacuations in 1944. For the resupply of forces in the Crimea the Germans became entirely dependent on shipments from Romania.

Kerch-Feodosia landings, 12.41
Largest Soviet wartime amphibious assault. Divisional sized force landed at Feodosia. A brigade landed at Kerch. By January German counterattacks regained lost territory

A German force of approx. 100,000 troops in the Kuban bridgehead was kept supplied by sea in 1943. It was also evacuated to the Crimea in September–October

Novorossiisk landings, 02.43 and 09.43
The initial Marine brigade landed became lodged on the Taman Peninsula. A relief operation was undertaken in September shortly before the German evacuation

German U-boat Operations 1942–44

Limit of German advance 11.42

Soviet Amphibious Operations
The Soviet navy conducted 114 amphibious operations in the war. Most small raids conducted at short notice in coastal regions. In total around 330,000 troops were landed during the war

Sea of Azof

Taganrog

Mariupol

Osipenko

Kerch

Feodosiya

Strait of Kerch

Kuban

Anapa

Novorossijsk

Gelendzhik

Tuapse

Sochi

Suckhumi

Poti

Batumi

Sinope

Samsun

Trabzon

C a u c a s u s

S E A

N I O N

rozhye

elitopol

09.43

100 Nm

100 km

36°   40°   36°

42°   40°

OPERATION TUNGSTEN, 30 MARCH – 4 APRIL 1944

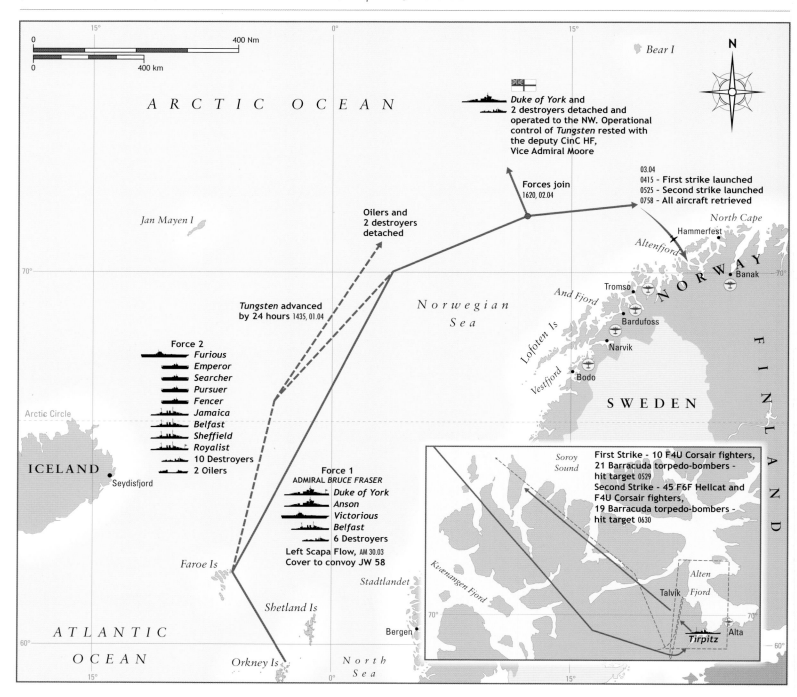

KEY

BY MARCH THE British received indications that the damage inflicted upon the *Tirpitz* during Operation *Source* had nearly been repaired and that once again there was a major surface threat to the Arctic convoys. In response, the Home Fleet planned a carrier strike on the *Tirpitz* while she was in her berth in Altenfjord. The operation would coincide with a convoy for Murmansk (JW 58) that would help to mask the carrier force, and German U-boats would be pulled back east of Bear Island in anticipation of the merchant vessels. In order to deal with the anticipated German fighters and air defences a squadron of escort carriers embarking fighters was attached. Many of the aircrews were relatively new and thus intensive training was undertaken throughout the month.

On 30 March the Home Fleet put to sea following behind JW 58, and it soon became clear that its escorts were experiencing little trouble and that the level of German activity was low. The strike was planned for 4 April, but when new intelligence suggested *Tirpitz* was about to sail it was brought forward by a day. In order to get into position, a new rendezvous point for the two forces was set and the accompanying oilers detached. The strike itself was divided into two waves and the first took the German defences by surprise. In total, sixteen hits or near misses were achieved and while none of the bombs penetrated the armoured deck the battleship was put out of action again. Two Barracudas were shot down and one crashed, as did a Hellcat fighter.

THE INDIAN OCEAN, 1944

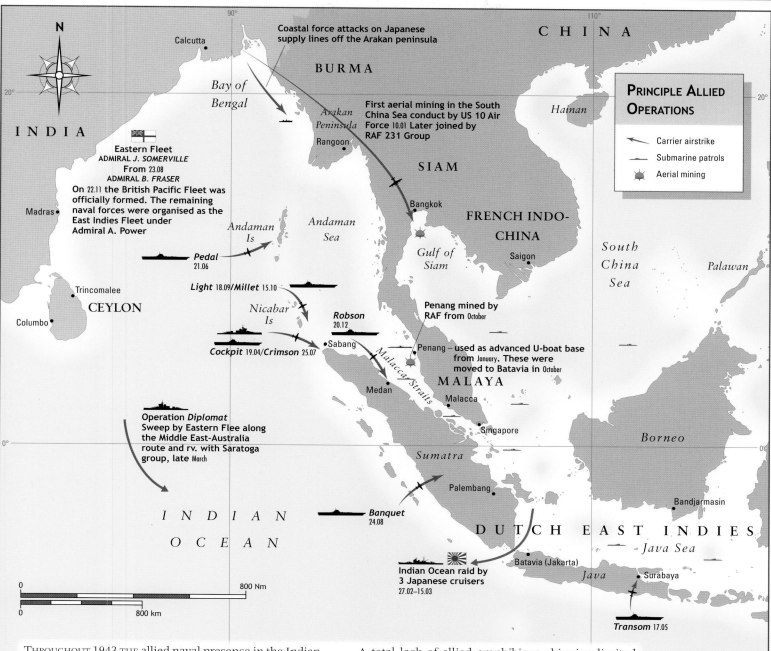

Coastal force attacks on Japanese supply lines off the Arakan peninsula

First aerial mining in the South China Sea conduct by US 10 Air Force 10.01 Later joined by RAF 231 Group

CHINA

BURMA

Bay of Bengal

Arakan Peninsula

Rangoon

SIAM

Bangkok

FRENCH INDO-CHINA

Saigon

Hainan

South China Sea

Palawan

PRINCIPLE ALLIED OPERATIONS

Carrier airstrike
Submarine patrols
Aerial mining

I N D I A

Calcutta

Madras

Eastern Fleet
ADMIRAL J. SOMERVILLE
From 23.08
ADMIRAL B. FRASER
On 22.11 the British Pacific Fleet was officially formed. The remaining naval forces were organised as the East Indies Fleet under Admiral A. Power

Andaman Is

Andaman Sea

Pedal 21.06

Light 18.09/Millet 15.10

Nicabar Is

Gulf of Siam

Penang mined by RAF from October

Robson 20.12

• Sabang

Cockpit 19.04/Crimson 25.07

Trincomalee

CEYLON

Columbo

Penang – used as advanced U-boat base from January**. These were moved to Batavia in** October

Penang *Malacca Straits*

Medan

MALAYA

Malacca

Singapore

Borneo

Operation *Diplomat*
Sweep by Eastern Flee along the Middle East-Australia route and rv. with Saratoga group, late March

I N D I A N

O C E A N

Sumatra

Palembang

Bandjarmasin

Banquet 24.08

Indian Ocean raid by 3 Japanese cruisers 27.02–15.03

DUTCH EAST INDIES
Java Sea

Batavia (Jakarta)

Java

Surabaya

Transom 17.05

0 _____ 800 Nm
0 _____ 800 km

In September the RN 8th Flotilla moved to Fremantle to operate with the boats attached to the US 7 Fleet

AUSTRALIA

THROUGHOUT 1943 THE allied naval presence in the Indian Ocean had been run down to an absolute minimum owing to the demands of other theatres. Having neutralised the Italian fleet in the Mediterranean and greatly reduced the German surface threat in the Arctic, the British began to reinforce Admiral Somerville's depleted and largely out of date forces. Three capital ships, two carriers, dozens of escorts and modern aircraft reached the theatre during the first six months of 1944. The arrival of more allied submarines allowed patrols to be pushed into the Malacca Straits and later the Java Sea. At the same time the IJN concentrated a large fleet at Singapore owing to the abundant supply of oil, and together with the Germans waged a renewed submarine campaign against allied shipping in the weakly defended Indian Ocean. The IJN, fully aware of British limitations, was content to remain on the defensive, but as the year progressed it was forced to redeploy most of its forces to the Pacific theatre.

A total lack of allied amphibious shipping limited the scope of offensive action that could be undertaken across the Bay of Bengal. Only a small coastal force operated on the Arakan front. As more long-range aircraft became available, the mining of Japanese-held ports and key choke points increased. By April, Somerville had gathered sufficient forces to begin raiding Japanese outposts in the East Indies. The purpose of these operations was to degrade the oil infrastructure upon which the Japanese depended, and to develop the necessary experience in sustained large carrier force operations across vast distances. This was needed for the fleet that the British intended to send into the Pacific in 1945. The appointment of Admiral Bruce Fraser, formerly in command of the Home Fleet, showed the shifting focus of British naval power from European to Asian waters.

THE ADRIATIC, 1943-45

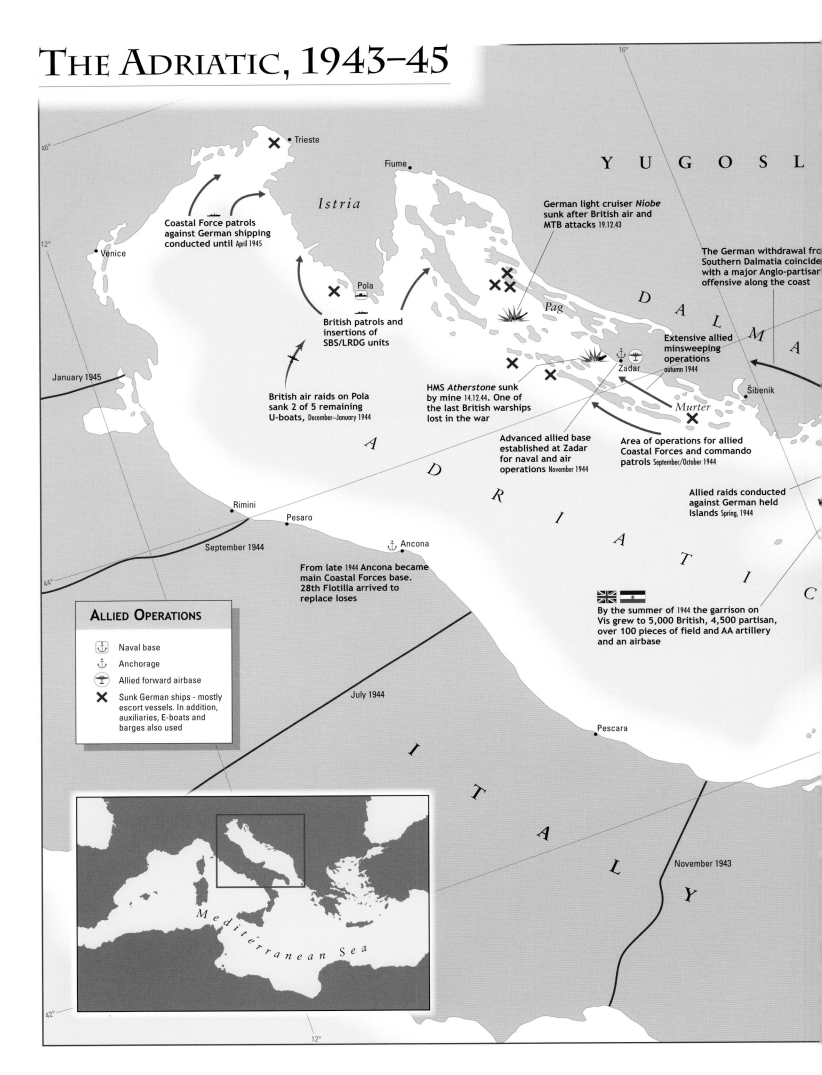

Trieste

Fiume

Istria

German light cruiser *Niobe* sunk after British air and MTB attacks 19.12.43

The German withdrawal fro Southern Dalmatia coincide with a major Anglo-partisar offensive along the coast

D A L M A

Coastal Force patrols against German shipping conducted until April 1945

Venice

Pola

British patrols and insertions of SBS/LRDG units

Pag

Extensive allied minsweeping operations autumn 1944

Zadar

Šibenik

January 1945

British air raids on Pola sank 2 of 5 remaining U-boats, December–January 1944

A

HMS *Atherstone* sunk by mine 14.12.44. **One of the last British warships lost in the war**

Murter

Area of operations for allied Coastal Forces and commando patrols September/October 1944

D

Advanced allied base established at Zadar for naval and air operations November 1944

Rimini

Allied raids conducted against German held Islands Spring, 1944

Pesaro

R

September 1944

Ancona

I

From late 1944 **Ancona became main Coastal Forces base. 28th Flotilla arrived to replace loses**

A

T

By the summer of 1944 **the garrison on Vis grew to 5,000 British, 4,500 partisan, over 100 pieces of field and AA artillery and an airbase**

C

ALLIED OPERATIONS

⚓ Naval base

⚓ Anchorage

⊕ Allied forward airbase

✕ Sunk German ships - mostly escort vessels. In addition, auxiliaries, E-boats and barges also used

I

July 1944

Pescara

T

A

November 1943

L

Y

Mediterranean Sea

THE BRITISH CONDUCTED only a small number of submarine patrols in the Adriatic between 1940 and 1943 owing to the distances involved and the unsuitability of the sea for submarine operations. After the allied landings in southern Italy in September 1943, British coastal forces began to move into the Adriatic to support the Eighth Army's northward advance. The straight and featureless Italian coastline, and lack of German shipping, prompted the British to start operating amongst the southern Dalmatian islands. Under the axis, Yugoslavia had been divided into German and Italian occupied sectors and with the latter's collapse a vacuum was created along the Yugoslav coast that the Germans could not immediately fill. The British were primarily concerned with destroying German shipping, but now an opportunity arose to supply the partisan movement. An advanced base to support coastal forces was established on Vis and supplies brought in from Italy.

It took the Germans until November to assemble the necessary forces to deal with the partisans in Dalmatia, but when the offensive began they rapidly took all the coast and inner islands, and by January only Vis, being somewhat further out to sea, remained under Anglo-partisan control. As a consequence, Royal Marines, followed by a large garrison force, were sent across the Adriatic and a major base was established on Vis under the protection of allied naval and air forces. The airbase on the island was crucial for the newly-established allied Balkan Air Force. Throughout the spring the marines, coastal and amphibious forces, along with the partisans, raided German positions on the southern islands. Although the latter could do little about the naval movements, on land they retained considerable strength and were able to inflict a defeat on allies during their raid on Brac. Slowly, however, the initiative passed to the allies, and in early September a major offensive against the Germans resulted in their withdrawal from southern Dalmatia. Allied naval forces moved northwards among the islands interfering with German traffic and opening up ports for military and civilian supplies. Zadar became the new forward base although little was achieved in the winter months. By this stage Anglo-partisan relations also began to deteriorate and thus most operations in 1945 were conducted from Italian bases. The British had considered undertaking a major amphibious operation in the northern Adriatic as a means of rapidly advancing on Vienna, but in reality the importance of the theatre was secondary to that of Italy itself, southern France or even the Aegean, and there were anyway insufficient resources for such an operation.

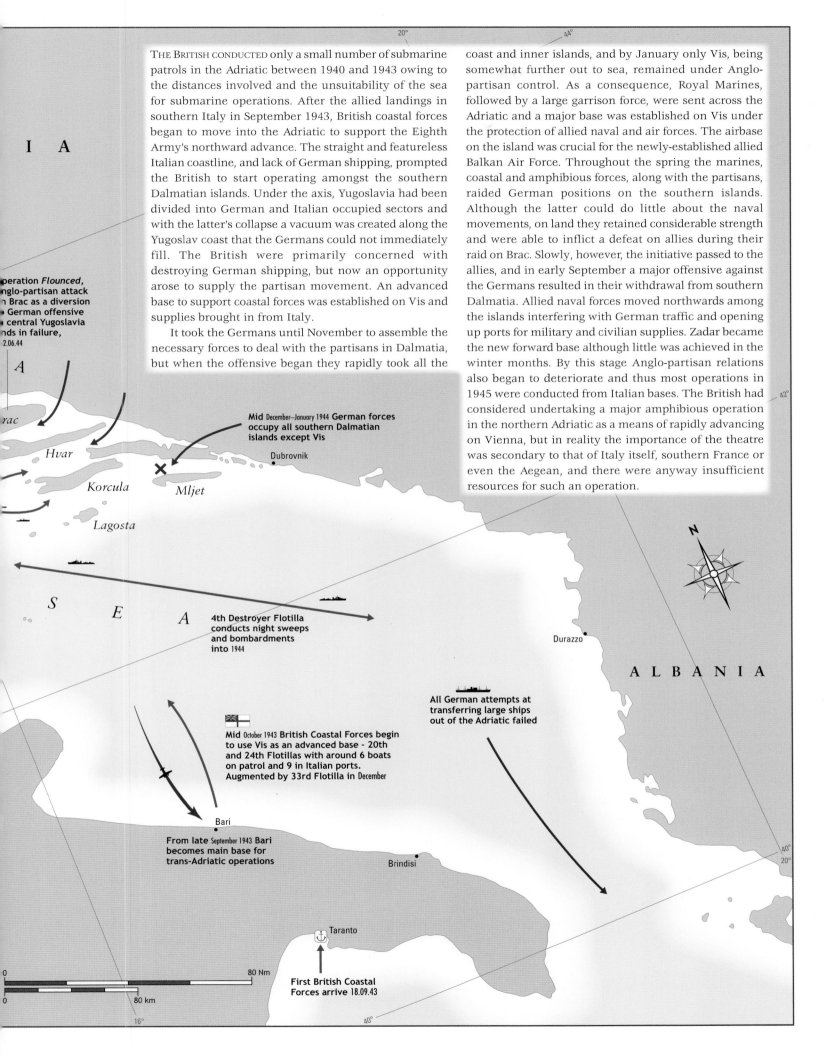

I A

operation *Flounced*,
nglo-partisan attack
n Brac as a diversion
German offensive
central Yugoslavia
nds in failure,
.2.06.44

A

rac

Hvar

Korcula   Mljet

Lagosta

Mid December–January 1944 **German forces occupy all southern Dalmatian islands except Vis**

Dubrovnik

×

S   E   A

4th Destroyer Flotilla conducts night sweeps and bombardments into 1944

Durazzo

A L B A N I A

All German attempts at transferring large ships out of the Adriatic failed

Mid October 1943 **British Coastal Forces begin to use Vis as an advanced base - 20th and 24th Flotillas with around 6 boats on patrol and 9 in Italian ports. Augmented by 33rd Flotilla in** December

Bari

From late September 1943 **Bari becomes main base for trans-Adriatic operations**

Brindisi

Taranto

First British Coastal Forces arrive 18.09.43

0   80 Nm

0   80 km

OPERATION TRANSOM, 17 MAY 1944

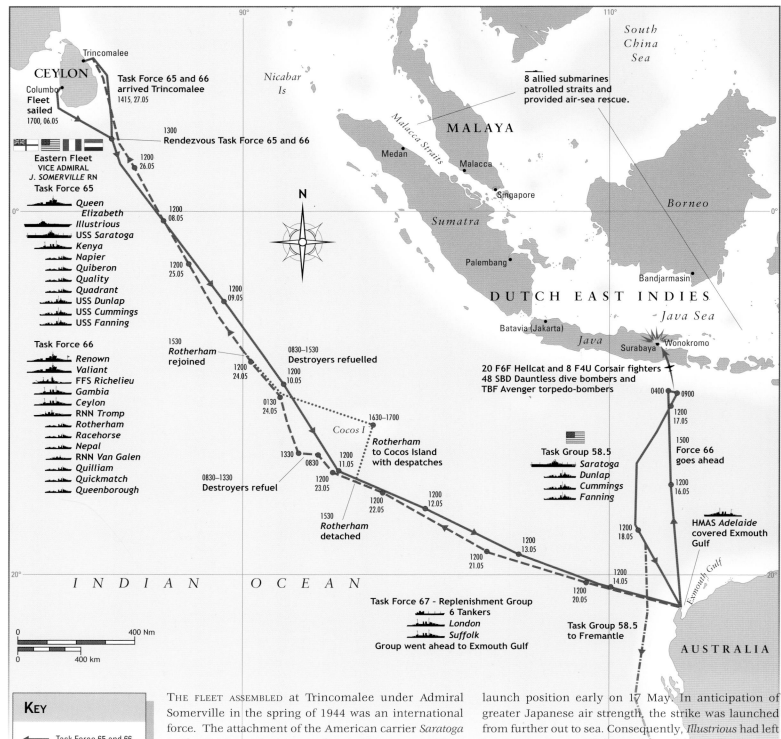

South
China
Sea

Trincomalee

CEYLON

Columbo
**Fleet
sailed**
1700, 06.05

Task Force 65 and 66
arrived Trincomalee
1415, 27.05

*Nicabar
Is*

8 allied submarines
patrolled straits and
provided air-sea rescue.

MALAYA

Medan

Malacca

Singapore

Borneo

1300
Rendezvous Task Force 65 and 66

1200
26.05

Eastern Fleet
VICE ADMIRAL
J. SOMERVILLE RN

Task Force 65

	Queen Elizabeth
	Illustrious
	USS *Saratoga*
	Kenya
	Napier
	Quiberon
	Quality
	Quadrant
	USS *Dunlap*
	USS *Cummings*
	USS *Fanning*

Task Force 66

	Renown
	Valiant
	FFS *Richelieu*
	Gambia
	Ceylon
	RNN *Tromp*
	Rotherham
	Racehorse
	Nepal
	RNN *Van Galen*
	Quilliam
	Quickmatch
	Queenborough

Sumatra

Palembang

Bandjarmasin

DUTCH EAST INDIES

Java Sea

Batavia (Jakarta)

Java

Surabaya   Wonokromo

20 F6F Hellcat and 8 F4U Corsair fighters
48 SBD Dauntless dive bombers and
TBF Avenger torpedo-bombers

1200
08.05

1200
25.05

1200
09.05

1530
Rotherham
rejoined

1200
24.05

0830–1530
Destroyers refuelled

1200
10.05

0130
24.05

Cocos I

1630–1700

Rotherham
to Cocos Island
with despatches

1330

0830

1200
11.05

0830–1330
Destroyers refuel

1200
23.05

1530
Rotherham
detached

1200
22.05

1200
12.05

0400   0900

1200
17.05

1500
Force 66
goes ahead

1200
16.05

Task Group 58.5

	Saratoga
	Dunlap
	Cummings
	Fanning

HMAS *Adelaide*
covered Exmouth
Gulf

1200
13.05

1200
18.05

1200
21.05

N

INDIAN   OCEAN

0   400 Nm

0   400 km

1200
14.05

1200
20.05

Task Force 67 - Replenishment Group

	6 Tankers
	London
	Suffolk

Group went ahead to Exmouth Gulf

Task Group 58.5
to Fremantle

Exmouth Gulf

AUSTRALIA

KEY

⬅ Task Force 65 and 66
outward journey

⬅-- Task Force 65 and 66
homeward journey

⬅-·- Task Force 58.5

Vessels without a
prefix are British

THE FLEET ASSEMBLED at Trincomalee under Admiral Somerville in the spring of 1944 was an international force. The attachment of the American carrier *Saratoga* to the Eastern Fleet not only greatly augmented its striking power, it also provided the opportunity for the British to practice operating multi-carrier task forces while the Royal Navy's other carriers were still working up for deployment to the Far East. After Operation *Cockpit* had been completed in late April, *Saratoga* was ordered back to the United States for a refit. As she would return via the Pacific it was decided to conduct a carrier strike against Surabaya with the Eastern Fleet. The distances involved were greater than in the Sabang strike of the previous month so the forces were to first refuel in the sheltered waters of Exmouth Gulf.

The fleet, organised into three task forces, left Ceylon on 6 May and had an uneventful voyage, reaching its

launch position early on 17 May. In anticipation of greater Japanese air strength, the strike was launched from further out to sea. Consequently, *Illustrious* had left her Barracuda aircraft in Ceylon and instead embarked Avengers, normally used in the fleet's escort carriers for anti-submarine duties. From 4.30am two strike groups were launched. The first against the Wonokromo oil refinery and the second against the harbour installations as Surabaya was an important base for Japanese anti-submarine forces operating against allied submarines in the East Indies. The strikes, although small by later standards, took the Japanese by surprise and inflicted considerable damage. *Saratoga* and her escorts detached themselves on 18 May while the fleet again refuelled in Exmouth Gulf. The operation provided many important lessons with regard to replenishment and the tactical handling of carriers.

AMERICAN SUBMARINE LOSSES IN THE PACIFIC

Submarine Force Pacific Fleet
The Pacific Fleet submarines initially were part of the Scouting Force Pacific Fleet. On 1 January 1942 they were assigned to Submarine Pacific Fleet which became Submarine Force Pacific Fleet on 10 September 1942. Based at Hawaii

REAR ADMIRAL *THOMAS WITHERS*, 7 December 1941 – 14 May 1942
REAR ADMIRAL *ROBERT H. ENGLISH*, 14 May 1942 – 21 January 1943 (killed in air accident)
REAR ADMIRAL *CHARLES A. LOCKWOOD*, 14 February 1943 – (promoted to Vice Admiral in October 1943)

Submarine Force South West Pacific
This force controlled all allied submarines in the southwest Pacific first under the Southwest Pacific Force and then the Seventh Fleet from February 1943 as TF 71. Split between Brisbane and Fremantle

REAR ADMIRAL *CHARLES A. LOCKWOOD*, May 1942 – February 1943
REAR ADMIRAL *RALF W. CHRISITE*, February 1943 – November 1944
REAR ADMIRAL *JAMES FIFE*, 30 December 1944 –

KEY

⚓	Known position
⚓	Estimated position

UPON THE OUTBREAK of war the majority of American frontline submarine strength was concentrated in the Asiatic Fleet. After the fall of the Philippines they moved to Australia and operated from Fremantle and Brisbane, but in time it was the boats of the Pacific Fleet that would come to dominate the submarine war. In December 1941 the Americans had 73 boats in the theatre out of a total force of 111 with a further 73 under construction. Between 1942 and 1945 201 boats were commissioned and the wartime strength of the submarine force grew to 288 boats, 263 of which undertook wartime patrols. In total 1,588 patrols were undertaken of which 1,474 were in the Pacific and they amounted to nearly 71,000 days at sea. The boat with the most patrols was the *Stingray* with sixteen.

Fifty-two American submarines were lost, about a fifth of the force, the vast majority in the Pacific. At least forty-one were due to enemy action and half of the losses came from the pre-war fleet. This translated into around one boat being lost for every six-and-a-half patrols undertaken. Around thirty-four Japanese ships were sunk for every American boat lost in action. The submarine force accounted for just under two per cent of the US Navy's personnel strength. Out of a total of around 30,000 submariners who went on operations or were trained 3,544 were killed. Although this was substantially less than the losses incurred by the German U-boat force, it still represented the highest casualty rate, in proportion to the size of the service, within the American military. By way of comparison 793 U-boats were sunk and around 28,000 German submariners killed which represented a seventy-five per cent casualty rate.

Japanese Sea Lanes

As an island nation, deficient in natural resources, and with a large population, Japan was heavily dependent on a merchant fleet and imports to keep its economy and the war effort going. This vulnerability was well understood by Britain and the United States, and both emphasised the role of an economic blockade in their pre-war planning. From the outset in December 1941, the United States Navy waged an unrestricted submarine campaign against Japanese merchant vessels, and during the course of the war American submarines accounted for more than half of all the merchant tonnage sunk. They also accounted for a third of all Japanese naval losses including eight carriers, a battleship and eleven cruisers.

After Pearl Harbor, the submarine force, alongside the aircraft carriers, became the first and ultimately most effective means of inflicting damage on the Japanese. Admiral Nimitz was also one of the navy's foremost submarine experts. Initially, in 1942 their yield was limited as a result of the need to reorganise the force after the Philippines campaign, and problems with torpedoes and boats. Nonetheless, even at this stage more ships were being sunk than Japan could replace. As more, and new, equipment reached the front in 1943 sinkings increased and from the end of the year this started to profoundly effect the Japanese economy.

The targeting of oil tankers – 338,000 tons being sunk in 1943 – in particular hit production and affected the military; aircrews no longer received as much training nor could ships put to sea as frequently. Similarly, the drop in bauxite imports reduced aluminium output and thus the quality of aircraft produced. Supplies to frontline troops progressively reduced, and one of the reasons the Americans could adopt an island hopping strategy was because these garrisons were effectively reduced to subsistence levels to survive. From 1944, aerial minelaying and carrier aircraft contributed to the economic blockade and by the summer of 1945 bulk imports into Japan had almost entirely ceased.

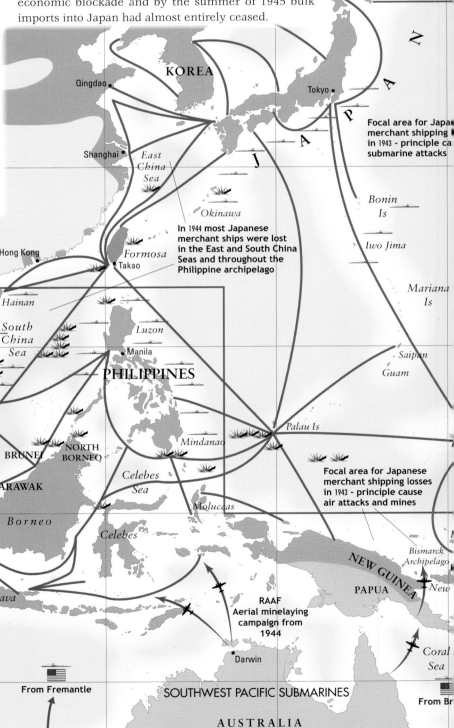

USAAF/RAF
Aerial minelaying
campaign from
1944

In 1944 most Japanese
merchant ships were lost
in the East and South China
Seas and throughout the
Philippine archipelago

Focal area for Japan
merchant shipping
in 1943 - principle ca
submarine attacks

Focal area for Japanese
merchant shipping losses
in 1943 - principle cause
air attacks and mines

RAAF
Aerial minelaying
campaign from
1944

EAST INDIES STATION

EASTERN FLEET SUBMARINES

From Fremantle

SOUTHWEST PACIFIC SUBMARINES

From Br

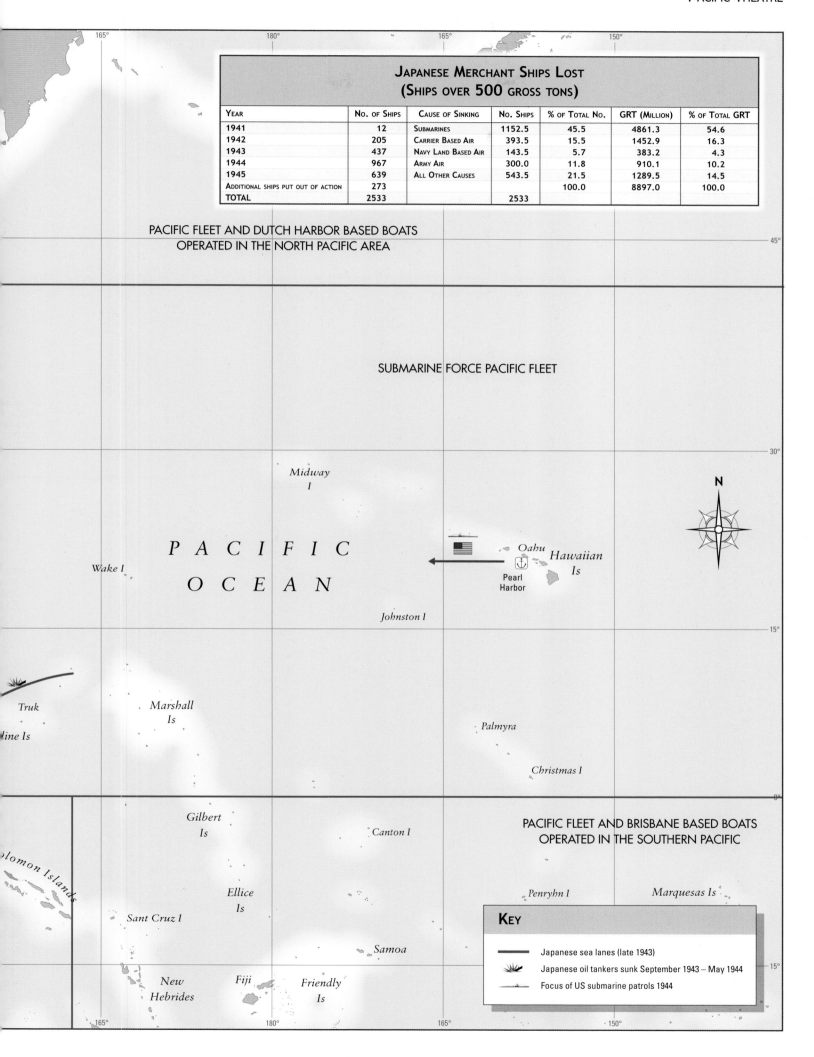

JAPANESE MERCHANT SHIPS LOST
(SHIPS OVER 500 GROSS TONS)

YEAR	NO. OF SHIPS	CAUSE OF SINKING	NO. SHIPS	% OF TOTAL NO.	GRT (MILLION)	% OF TOTAL GRT
1941	12	SUBMARINES	1152.5	45.5	4861.3	54.6
1942	205	CARRIER BASED AIR	393.5	15.5	1452.9	16.3
1943	437	NAVY LAND BASED AIR	143.5	5.7	383.2	4.3
1944	967	ARMY AIR	300.0	11.8	910.1	10.2
1945	639	ALL OTHER CAUSES	543.5	21.5	1289.5	14.5
ADDITIONAL SHIPS PUT OUT OF ACTION	273			100.0	8897.0	100.0
TOTAL	2533		2533			

PACIFIC FLEET AND DUTCH HARBOR BASED BOATS
OPERATED IN THE NORTH PACIFIC AREA

45°

SUBMARINE FORCE PACIFIC FLEET

N

30°

Midway I

PACIFIC
OCEAN

Wake I

Oahu
Hawaiian Is
Pearl
Harbor

15°

Johnston I

Truk

Marshall Is

Palmyra

...ine Is

Christmas I

0°

Gilbert Is

Canton I

PACIFIC FLEET AND BRISBANE BASED BOATS
OPERATED IN THE SOUTHERN PACIFIC

olomon Islands

Ellice Is

Penryhn I

Marquesas Is

Sant Cruz I

KEY

——	Japanese sea lanes (late 1943)
	Japanese oil tankers sunk September 1943 – May 1944
	Focus of US submarine patrols 1944

Samoa

15°

New Hebrides

Fiji

Friendly Is

165° 180° 165° 150°

OPERATION NEPTUNE, 5–6 JUNE 1944

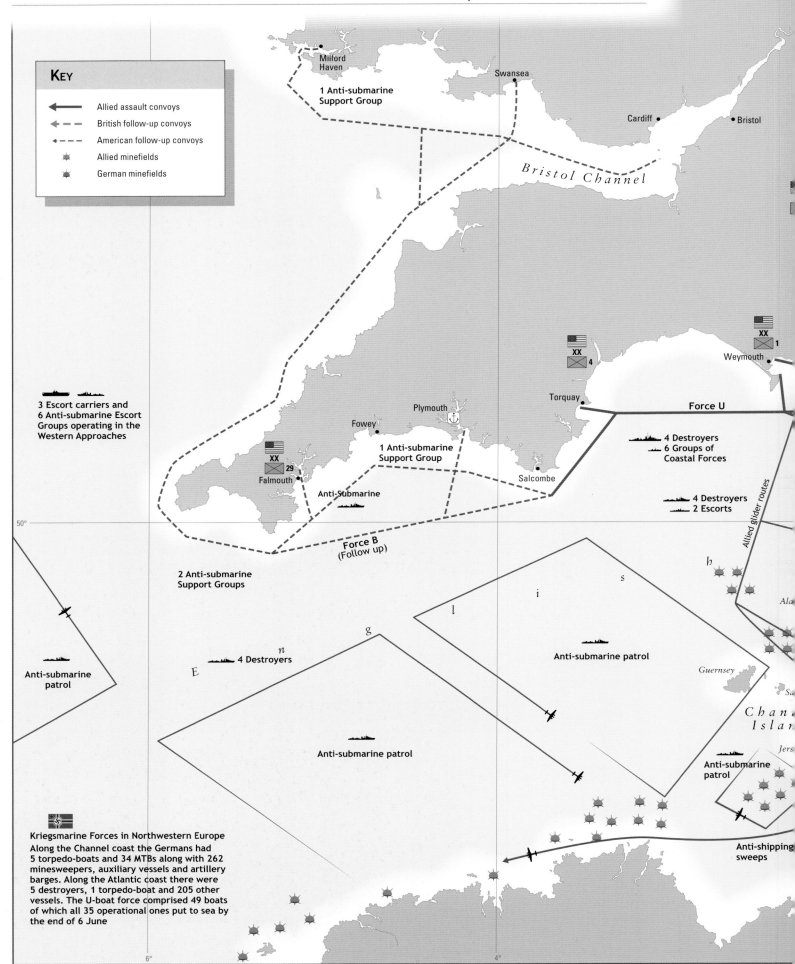

KEY

⬅ Allied assault convoys

⬅- - British follow-up convoys

◄- - American follow-up convoys

Allied minefields

German minefields

1 Anti-submarine
Support Group

Milford
Haven

Swansea

Cardiff

Bristol

Bristol Channel

3 Escort carriers and
6 Anti-submarine Escort
Groups operating in the
Western Approaches

XX 4

XX 1

Weymouth

Torquay

Force U

4 Destroyers
6 Groups of
Coastal Forces

Plymouth

Fowey

1 Anti-submarine
Support Group

4 Destroyers
2 Escorts

XX 29
Falmouth

Anti-Submarine

Salcombe

Allied glider routes

Anti-submarine patrol

b

s

i

l

Force B
(Follow up)

2 Anti-submarine
Support Groups

g

n

4 Destroyers

E

Anti-submarine patrol

Anti-submarine
patrol

Guernsey

Chan
Isla

Jers

Anti-submarine patrol

Anti-submarine
patrol

Kriegsmarine Forces in Northwestern Europe
Along the Channel coast the Germans had
5 torpedo-boats and 34 MTBs along with 262
minesweepers, auxiliary vessels and artillery
barges. Along the Atlantic coast there were
5 destroyers, 1 torpedo-boat and 205 other
vessels. The U-boat force comprised 49 boats
of which all 35 operational ones put to sea by
the end of 6 June

Anti-shipping
sweeps

6°

4°

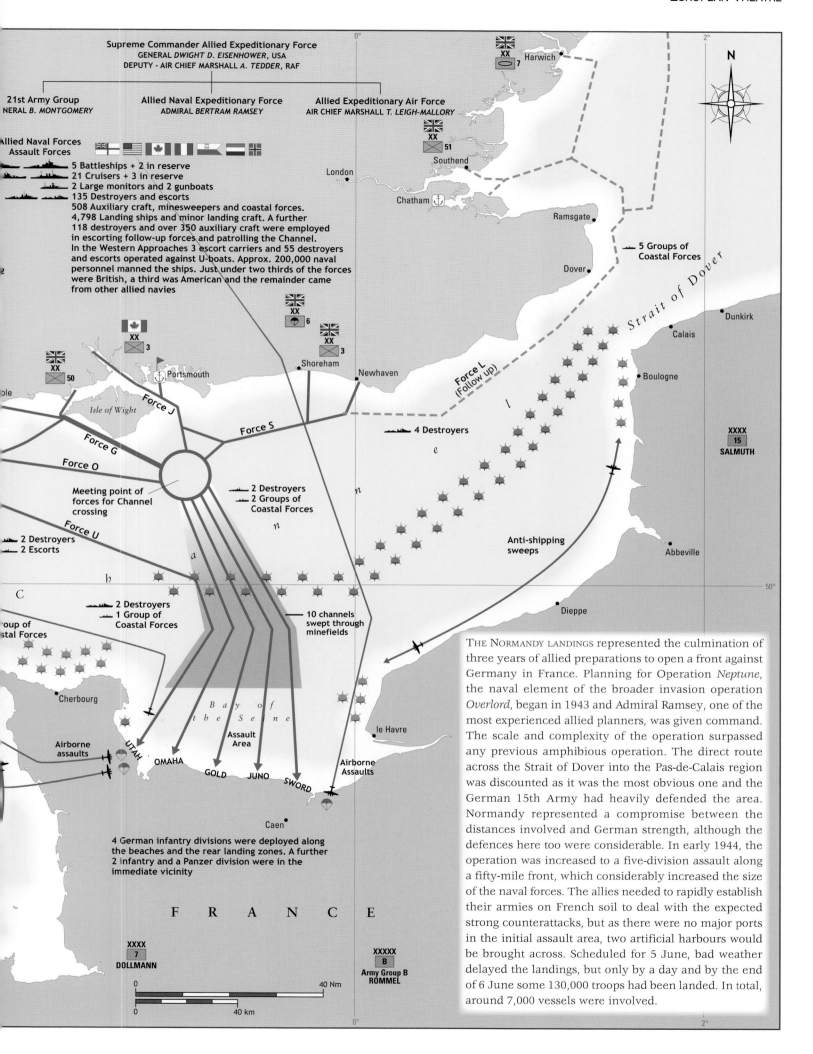

Supreme Commander Allied Expeditionary Force
GENERAL *DWIGHT D. EISENHOWER*, USA
DEPUTY - AIR CHIEF MARSHALL *A. TEDDER*, RAF

21st Army Group
NERAL *B. MONTGOMERY*

Allied Naval Expeditionary Force
ADMIRAL *BERTRAM RAMSEY*

Allied Expeditionary Air Force
AIR CHIEF MARSHALL *T. LEIGH-MALLORY*

Allied Naval Forces
Assault Forces

5 Battleships + 2 in reserve
21 Cruisers + 3 in reserve
2 Large monitors and 2 gunboats
135 Destroyers and escorts
508 Auxiliary craft, minesweepers and coastal forces.
4,798 Landing ships and minor landing craft. A further
118 destroyers and over 350 auxiliary craft were employed
in escorting follow-up forces and patrolling the Channel.
In the Western Approaches 3 escort carriers and 55 destroyers
and escorts operated against U-boats. Approx. 200,000 naval
personnel manned the ships. Just under two thirds of the forces
were British, a third was American and the remainder came
from other allied navies

Harwich 7

Southend 51

London

Chatham

Ramsgate

5 Groups of
Coastal Forces

Dover

Strait of Dover

Dunkirk

Calais

6

Shoreham 3

Portsmouth

Isle of Wight

Force J

Force S

Newhaven

Force L
(Follow up)

4 Destroyers

Boulogne

XXXX
15
SALMUTH

Force G

Force O

3

50

Meeting point of
forces for Channel
crossing

2 Destroyers
2 Groups of
Coastal Forces

Anti-shipping
sweeps

Abbeville

Force U

2 Destroyers
2 Escorts

10 channels
swept through
minefields

Dieppe

2 Destroyers
1 Group of
Coastal Forces

C

roup of
stal Forces

Cherbourg

*Bay of
the Seine*

Assault
Area

le Havre

Airborne
assaults

UTAH

OMAHA

GOLD   JUNO   SWORD

Airborne
Assaults

Caen

4 German infantry divisions were deployed along
the beaches and the rear landing zones. A further
2 infantry and a Panzer division were in the
immediate vicinity

F R A N C E

XXXX
7
DOLLMANN

XXXXX
B
**Army Group B
ROMMEL**

0   40 Nm

0   40 km

THE NORMANDY LANDINGS represented the culmination of
three years of allied preparations to open a front against
Germany in France. Planning for Operation *Neptune*,
the naval element of the broader invasion operation
Overlord, began in 1943 and Admiral Ramsey, one of the
most experienced allied planners, was given command.
The scale and complexity of the operation surpassed
any previous amphibious operation. The direct route
across the Strait of Dover into the Pas-de-Calais region
was discounted as it was the most obvious one and the
German 15th Army had heavily defended the area.
Normandy represented a compromise between the
distances involved and German strength, although the
defences here too were considerable. In early 1944, the
operation was increased to a five-division assault along
a fifty-mile front, which considerably increased the size
of the naval forces. The allies needed to rapidly establish
their armies on French soil to deal with the expected
strong counterattacks, but as there were no major ports
in the initial assault area, two artificial harbours would
be brought across. Scheduled for 5 June, bad weather
delayed the landings, but only by a day and by the end
of 6 June some 130,000 troops had been landed. In total,
around 7,000 vessels were involved.

OPERATION NEPTUNE, NAVAL BOMBARDMENTS

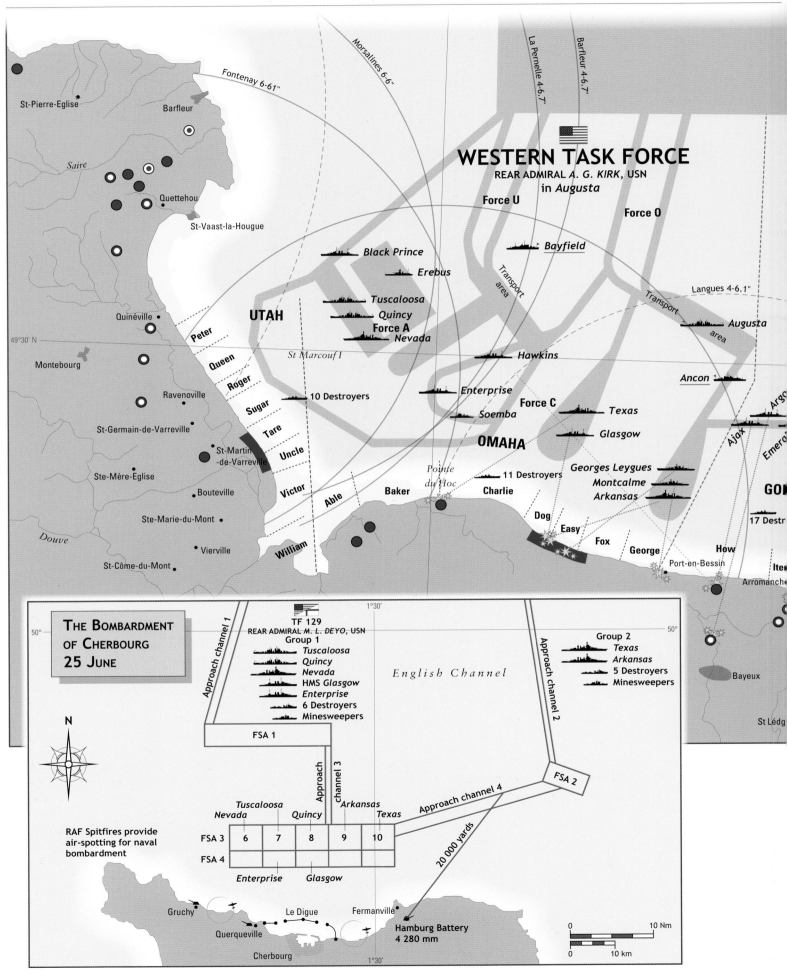

Fontenay 6-61"
Morsalines 6-6"
La Pernelle 4-6.7"
Barfleur 4-6.7"

St-Pierre-Eglise
Barfleur
Saire
Quettehou
St-Vaast-la-Hougue

WESTERN TASK FORCE
REAR ADMIRAL *A. G. KIRK*, USN
in *Augusta*

Force U
Force O

Bayfield

Black Prince
Erebus

Tuscaloosa
Quincy
Force A
Nevada

Quinéville
Peter
UTAH
St Marcouf I
49°30' N

Montebourg
Queen
Roger
Ravenoville
Sugar
St-Germain-de-Varreville
Tare
St-Martin-de-Varreville
Uncle
Ste-Mère-Eglise
Victor
Bouteville
Able
Ste-Marie-du-Mont
Douve
Vierville
William
St-Côme-du-Mont

Langues 4-6.1"

Transport area
Transport area

Augusta

Hawkins

Ancon

10 Destroyers
Enterprise
Force C
Soemba
Texas
Glasgow

Argo
Ajax
Emera

OMAHA
GO

Pointe du Hoc
Baker
Charlie
Dog
Easy
Fox
George
How
Iter

11 Destroyers
Georges Leygues
Montcalme
Arkansas

17 Destr

Port-en-Bessin
Arromanch

THE BOMBARDMENT OF CHERBOURG 25 JUNE

50°

Approach channel 1

1°30'

TF 129
REAR ADMIRAL *M. L. DEYO*, USN
Group 1
Tuscaloosa
Quincy
Nevada
HMS *Glasgow*
Enterprise
6 Destroyers
Minesweepers

English Channel

Approach channel 2

50°

Group 2
Texas
Arkansas
5 Destroyers
Minesweepers

St Lédg

FSA 1

N

Approach channel 3

Approach channel 4

FSA 2

Bayeux

RAF Spitfires provide air-spotting for naval bombardment

Tuscaloosa
Nevada
Quincy
Arkansas
Texas

FSA 3 | 6 | 7 | 8 | 9 | 10

FSA 4

Enterprise
Glasgow

20 000 yards

Gruchy
Le Digue
Fermanville
Querqueville
Hamburg Battery
4 280 mm
Cherbourg
1°30'

0 — 10 Nm
0 — 10 km

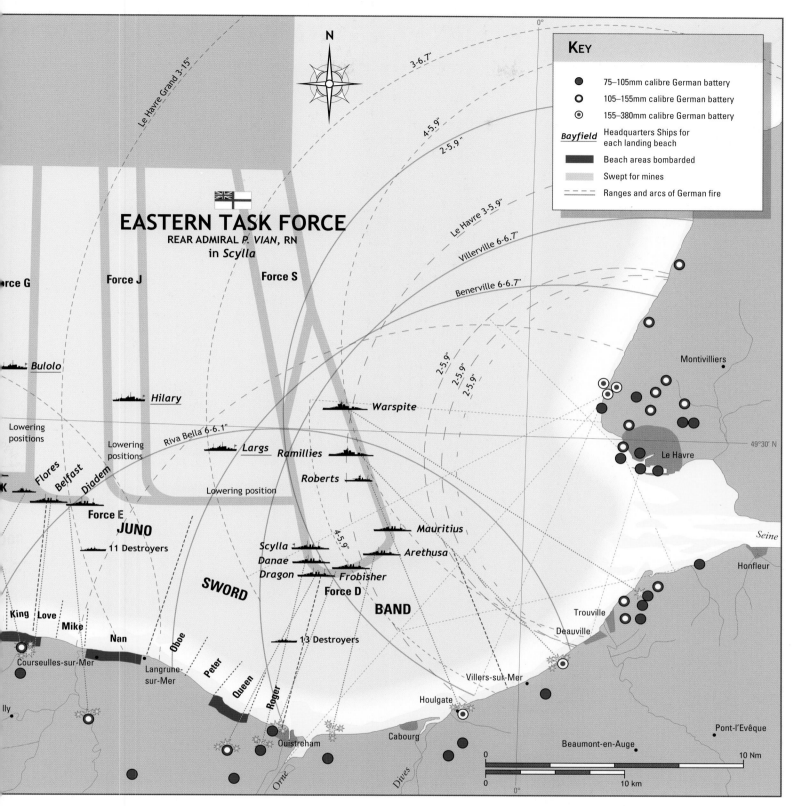

KEY

● 75–105mm calibre German battery

○ 105–155mm calibre German battery

◉ 155–380mm calibre German battery

Bayfield Headquarters Ships for each landing beach

Beach areas bombarded

Swept for mines

‐ ‐ ‐ Ranges and arcs of German fire

EASTERN TASK FORCE
REAR ADMIRAL P. VIAN, RN
in *Scylla*

Force G   Force J   Force S

Le Havre Grand 3-15"

Le Havre 3-5.9"

Villerville 6-6.7"

Benerville 6-6.7"

3-6.7"

4-5.9"

2-5.9"

Bulolo

Hilary

Montivilliers

2-5.9"

2-5.9"

2-5.9"

Warspite

Lowering positions

Lowering positions

Riva Bella 6-6.1"

49°30' N

Flores

Belfast

Diadem

Largs   *Ramillies*

Lowering position

Le Havre

Roberts

Force E

JUNO

Mauritius

Seine

11 Destroyers

Scylla

Danae   *Arethusa*

Honfleur

Dragon   *Frobisher*

SWORD

Force D

BAND

Trouville

King Love

Deauville

Mike

Nan

Oboe

Peter

Courseulles-sur-Mer

Langrune-
sur-Mer

Queen

Roger

Villers-sur-Mer

13 Destroyers

lly

Houlgate

Pont-l'Evêque

Ouistreham

Cabourg

Beaumont-en-Auge

10 Nm

Orne

Dives

0   10 km

THE VALUE OF naval gunfire support was demonstrated during the Mediterranean amphibious operations and overturned pre-war scepticism regarding the ability of warships to provide accurate fire for land forces. The nature of the German defences in Normandy and the scale of the D-Day assault presented a far more formidable challenge, and the former needed to be neutralised to enable the allied landings. A force of five battleships (with two more in immediate reserve), twenty-one cruisers, two 15in monitors and sixty-two destroyers covered the assault. While the battleships, cruisers and monitors bombarded German coastal artillery emplacements and inland artillery batteries, destroyers and specialised landing craft provided direct fire support to the troops landing on the beaches. More than 100 Spitfire and Mustang fighters provided aerial spotting until Forward Observation Officers, landed during D-Day, moved up to the front.

After D-Day, naval gunfire continued to support the allied armies for a number of weeks. In the east, daily naval bombardments were conducted to subdue German gunfire from the flanks against the heavily congested shipping off Sword beach. In the battle for Caen, British battleships shelled German troop concentrations until the fighting moved beyond the range of the 15in guns. In the west, a bombardment force, TF 129 under Rear Admiral Deyo, provided support in the final stages of the American VII Corps assault on Cherbourg on 25 June.

OPERATION FORAGER, THE MARIANAS, JUNE 1944

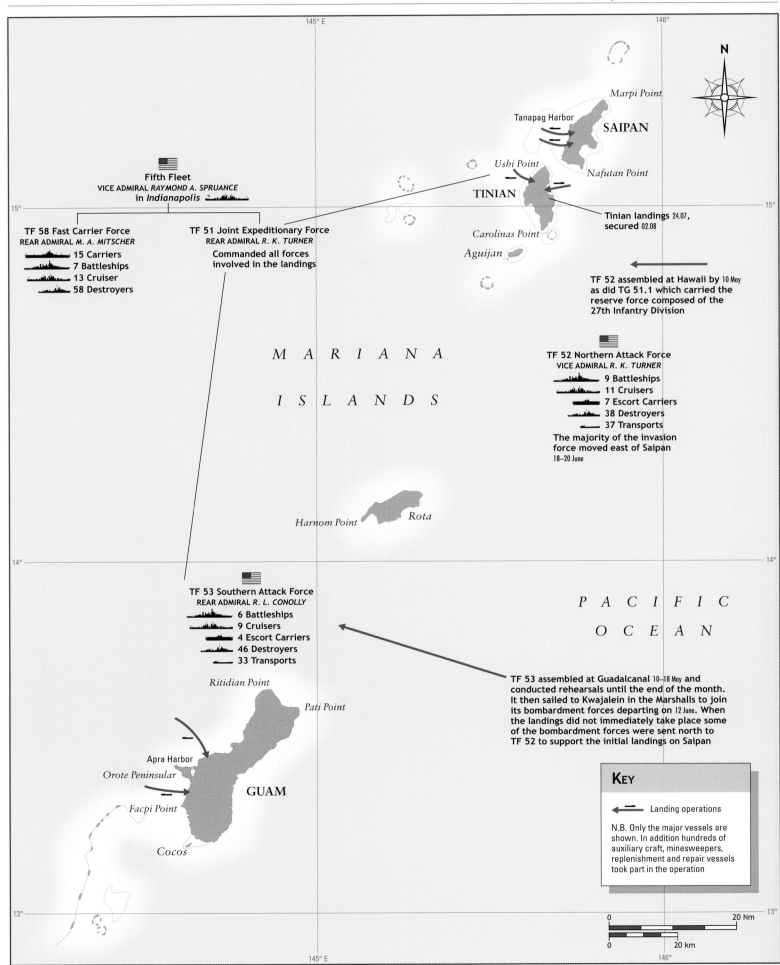

145° E

146°

N

Marpi Point

Tanapag Harbor

SAIPAN

Nafutan Point

Ushi Point

TINIAN

Carolinas Point

Aguijan

Fifth Fleet
VICE ADMIRAL *RAYMOND A. SPRUANCE*
in *Indianapolis*

15°

Tinian landings 24.07,
secured 02.08

TF 58 Fast Carrier Force
REAR ADMIRAL *M. A. MITSCHER*
15 Carriers
7 Battleships
13 Cruiser
58 Destroyers

TF 51 Joint Expeditionary Force
REAR ADMIRAL *R. K. TURNER*
**Commanded all forces
involved in the landings**

TF 52 assembled at Hawaii by 10 May
as did TG 51.1 which carried the
reserve force composed of the
27th Infantry Division

M A R I A N A

I S L A N D S

TF 52 Northern Attack Force
VICE ADMIRAL *R. K. TURNER*
9 Battleships
11 Cruisers
7 Escort Carriers
38 Destroyers
37 Transports
The majority of the invasion
force moved east of Saipan
18–20 June

Harnom Point *Rota*

14°

TF 53 Southern Attack Force
REAR ADMIRAL *R. L. CONOLLY*
6 Battleships
9 Cruisers
4 Escort Carriers
46 Destroyers
33 Transports

P A C I F I C

O C E A N

Ritidian Point

Pati Point

TF 53 assembled at Guadalcanal 10–18 May and
conducted rehearsals until the end of the month.
It then sailed to Kwajalein in the Marshalls to join
its bombardment forces departing on 12 June. When
the landings did not immediately take place some
of the bombardment forces were sent north to
TF 52 to support the initial landings on Saipan

Apra Harbor

Orote Peninsular

Facpi Point

GUAM

KEY

Landing operations

N.B. Only the major vessels are
shown. In addition hundreds of
auxiliary craft, minesweepers,
replenishment and repair vessels
took part in the operation

Cocos

13°

0   20 Nm

0   20 km

145° E

146°

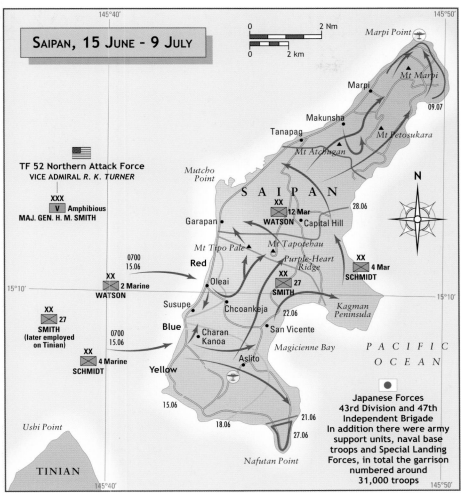

SAIPAN, 15 JUNE - 9 JULY

TF 52 Northern Attack Force
VICE ADMIRAL *R. K. TURNER*

XXX V Amphibious
MAJ. GEN. H. M. SMITH

XX 2 Marine WATSON
XX 27 SMITH (later employed on Tinian)
XX 4 Marine SCHMIDT
XX 12 Mar WATSON
XX 27 SMITH
XX 4 Mar SCHMIDT

Red
Blue
Yellow

Japanese Forces
43rd Division and 47th
Independent Brigade
In addition there were army
support units, naval base
troops and Special Landing
Forces, in total the garrison
numbered around
31,000 troops

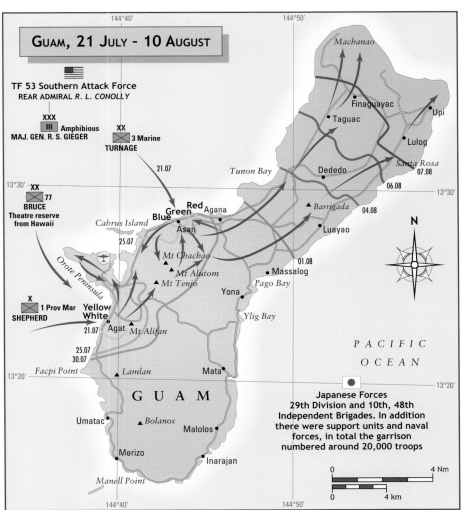

GUAM, 21 JULY - 10 AUGUST

TF 53 Southern Attack Force
REAR ADMIRAL *R. L. CONOLLY*

XXX III Amphibious
MAJ. GEN. R. S. GIEGER

XX 3 Marine TURNAGE
XX 77 BRUCE Theatre reserve from Hawaii
X 1 Prov Mar SHEPHERD

Red
Green
Blue
Yellow
White

Japanese Forces
29th Division and 10th, 48th
Independent Brigades. In addition
there were support units and naval
forces, in total the garrison
numbered around 20,000 troops

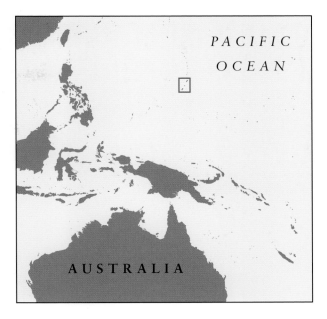

KEY
→ American attacks
→ Japanese attacks
— Front lines (with dates)
— Japanese positions
✈ Airfield

AFTER SECURING THE Marshall Islands, the Americans decided to bypass the rest of the Japanese strongholds in the Central Pacific and make straight for the Mariana Islands. This was a group of around fifteen islands of which the southernmost four hosted important air bases and secured the approaches both to the Japanese mainland and the oil rich East Indies; the largest island, Guam, had been under American control before the war. American carriers had already struck the Marianas in February, and in March the decision was taken to land on the islands in June. Saipan was the principle American target, as securing its airbases would allow long-range B-29 bombers to strike Japan. The IJN had also just moved the headquarters of its submarine force, the Sixth Fleet, onto the island. The operation presented a considerable challenge owing to the distances involved as the Marianas were around 1,000 miles from the nearest American bases.

In the two weeks before the landings on Saipan, the carriers of TF 58 struck at Japanese island airbases all around the Marianas before subjecting Saipan to intense air attacks. Two divisions came ashore under the cover of a large bombardment force, but it took two days to secure the beachhead. The Japanese had not expected Saipan as the target of an American landing, and they responded with a major fleet operation that culminated in the battle of the Philippine Sea. After this the Japanese naval response was limited to submarine operations that achieved little, and by the end of July thirteen out of twenty-one boats had been lost. On land Japanese resistance was fierce and it took 67,500 American troops over three weeks to secure Saipan. This delayed the landings on Guam by a month and the theatre-reserve division was brought out from Pearl Harbor to enable a three-division assault. Guam itself was subjected to two weeks of intense naval and air bombardments prior to the landings.

THE BATTLE OF THE PHILIPPINE SEA, 19–20 JUNE 1944

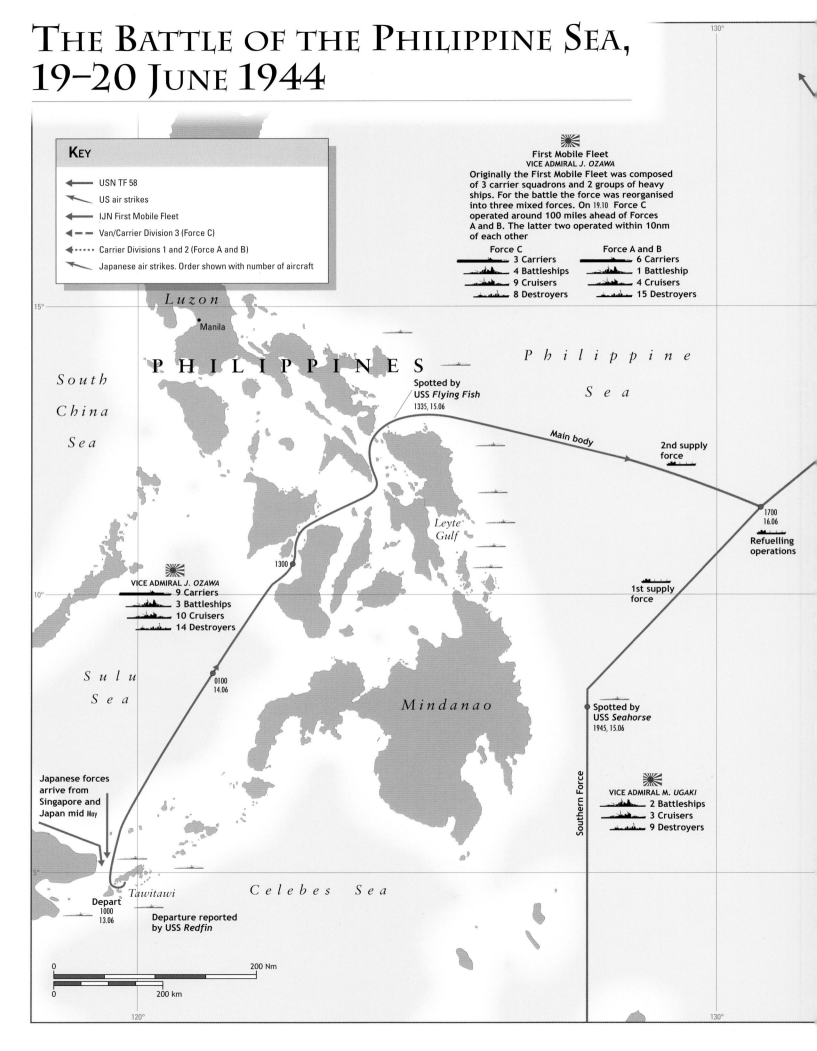

KEY

- USN TF 58
- US air strikes
- IJN First Mobile Fleet
- Van/Carrier Division 3 (Force C)
- Carrier Divisions 1 and 2 (Force A and B)
- Japanese air strikes. Order shown with number of aircraft

First Mobile Fleet
VICE ADMIRAL J. OZAWA
Originally the First Mobile Fleet was composed of 3 carrier squadrons and 2 groups of heavy ships. For the battle the force was reorganised into three mixed forces. On 19.10 Force C operated around 100 miles ahead of Forces A and B. The latter two operated within 10nm of each other

Force C	Force A and B
3 Carriers	6 Carriers
4 Battleships	1 Battleship
9 Cruisers	4 Cruisers
8 Destroyers	15 Destroyers

Luzon

• Manila

PHILIPPINES

South China Sea

Philippine Sea

Spotted by
USS *Flying Fish*
1335, 15.06

Main body

2nd supply force

1700
16.06

Refuelling operations

Leyte Gulf

1300

1st supply force

VICE ADMIRAL J. OZAWA
- 9 Carriers
- 3 Battleships
- 10 Cruisers
- 14 Destroyers

Sulu Sea

0100
14.06

Mindanao

Spotted by
USS *Seahorse*
1945, 15.06

Southern Force

VICE ADMIRAL M. UGAKI
- 2 Battleships
- 3 Cruisers
- 9 Destroyers

Japanese forces arrive from Singapore and Japan mid May

Depart
1000
13.06

Tawitawi

Celebes Sea

Departure reported by USS *Redfin*

0		200 Nm
0		200 km

120°   130°

234

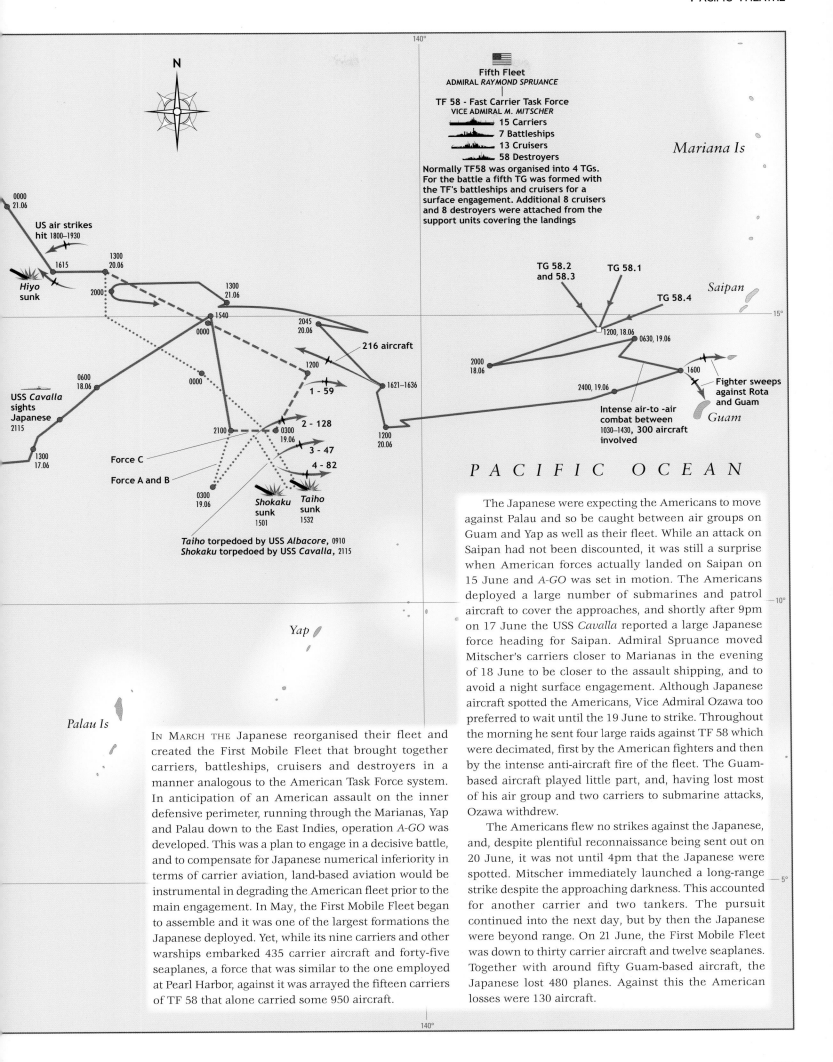

Fifth Fleet
ADMIRAL *RAYMOND SPRUANCE*

TF 58 - Fast Carrier Task Force
VICE ADMIRAL *M. MITSCHER*

15 Carriers
7 Battleships
13 Cruisers
58 Destroyers

Normally TF58 was organised into 4 TGs. For the battle a fifth TG was formed with the TF's battleships and cruisers for a surface engagement. Additional 8 cruisers and 8 destroyers were attached from the support units covering the landings

Mariana Is

Saipan

TG 58.2 and 58.3

TG 58.1

TG 58.4

1200, 18.06

0630, 19.06

2000 18.06

2400, 19.06

1600

Fighter sweeps against Rota and Guam

Intense air-to-air combat between 1030–1430, 300 aircraft involved

Guam

P A C I F I C   O C E A N

0000 21.06

US air strikes hit 1800–1930

1300 20.06

1615

2000

Hiyo sunk

1300 21.06

1540

0000

2045 20.06

216 aircraft

1200

1 - 59

1621–1636

0600 18.06

0000

USS *Cavalla* sights Japanese 2115

2100

0300 19.06

2 - 128

3 - 47

4 - 82

1200 20.06

1300 17.06

Force C

Force A and B

0300 19.06

Shokaku sunk 1501

Taiho sunk 1532

Taiho torpedoed by USS *Albacore*, 0910
Shokaku torpedoed by USS *Cavalla*, 2115

Yap

Palau Is

The Japanese were expecting the Americans to move against Palau and so be caught between air groups on Guam and Yap as well as their fleet. While an attack on Saipan had not been discounted, it was still a surprise when American forces actually landed on Saipan on 15 June and *A-GO* was set in motion. The Americans deployed a large number of submarines and patrol aircraft to cover the approaches, and shortly after 9pm on 17 June the USS *Cavalla* reported a large Japanese force heading for Saipan. Admiral Spruance moved Mitscher's carriers closer to Marianas in the evening of 18 June to be closer to the assault shipping, and to avoid a night surface engagement. Although Japanese aircraft spotted the Americans, Vice Admiral Ozawa too preferred to wait until the 19 June to strike. Throughout the morning he sent four large raids against TF 58 which were decimated, first by the American fighters and then by the intense anti-aircraft fire of the fleet. The Guam-based aircraft played little part, and, having lost most of his air group and two carriers to submarine attacks, Ozawa withdrew.

The Americans flew no strikes against the Japanese, and, despite plentiful reconnaissance being sent out on 20 June, it was not until 4pm that the Japanese were spotted. Mitscher immediately launched a long-range strike despite the approaching darkness. This accounted for another carrier and two tankers. The pursuit continued into the next day, but by then the Japanese were beyond range. On 21 June, the First Mobile Fleet was down to thirty carrier aircraft and twelve seaplanes. Together with around fifty Guam-based aircraft, the Japanese lost 480 planes. Against this the American losses were 130 aircraft.

IN MARCH THE Japanese reorganised their fleet and created the First Mobile Fleet that brought together carriers, battleships, cruisers and destroyers in a manner analogous to the American Task Force system. In anticipation of an American assault on the inner defensive perimeter, running through the Marianas, Yap and Palau down to the East Indies, operation *A-GO* was developed. This was a plan to engage in a decisive battle, and to compensate for Japanese numerical inferiority in terms of carrier aviation, land-based aviation would be instrumental in degrading the American fleet prior to the main engagement. In May, the First Mobile Fleet began to assemble and it was one of the largest formations the Japanese deployed. Yet, while its nine carriers and other warships embarked 435 carrier aircraft and forty-five seaplanes, a force that was similar to the one employed at Pearl Harbor, against it was arrayed the fifteen carriers of TF 58 that alone carried some 950 aircraft.

OPERATION CRIMSON, 25 JULY 1944

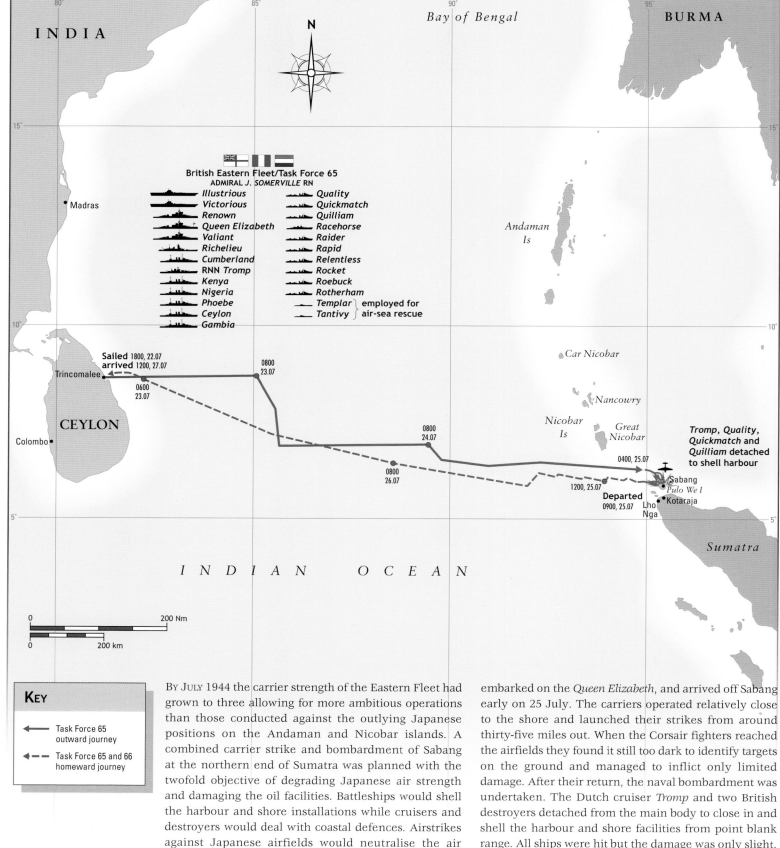

British Eastern Fleet/Task Force 65
ADMIRAL J. SOMERVILLE RN

Illustrious	Quality
Victorious	Quickmatch
Renown	Quilliam
Queen Elizabeth	Racehorse
Valiant	Raider
Richelieu	Rapid
Cumberland	Relentless
RNN Tromp	Rocket
Kenya	Roebuck
Nigeria	Rotherham
Phoebe	Templar ⎱ employed for
Ceylon	Tantivy ⎰ air-sea rescue
Gambia	

Sailed 1800, 22.07
arrived 1200, 27.07

0800 23.07

0600 23.07

0800 24.07

0800 26.07

0400, 25.07

1200, 25.07

Tromp, Quality, Quickmatch and *Quilliam* detached to shell harbour

Departed 0900, 25.07

Sabang
Pulo We I
Kotaraja
Lho Nga

KEY

Task Force 65 outward journey

Task Force 65 and 66 homeward journey

By July 1944 the carrier strength of the Eastern Fleet had grown to three allowing for more ambitious operations than those conducted against the outlying Japanese positions on the Andaman and Nicobar islands. A combined carrier strike and bombardment of Sabang at the northern end of Sumatra was planned with the twofold objective of degrading Japanese air strength and damaging the oil facilities. Battleships would shell the harbour and shore installations while cruisers and destroyers would deal with coastal defences. Airstrikes against Japanese airfields would neutralise the air threat and in addition some aircraft would fly photo-reconnaissance missions to gather intelligence. This was important for compared to other theatres the allies had only limited information on the Japanese positions in the Indian Ocean.

The fleet sailed on 22 July, with Admiral Somerville embarked on the *Queen Elizabeth*, and arrived off Sabang early on 25 July. The carriers operated relatively close to the shore and launched their strikes from around thirty-five miles out. When the Corsair fighters reached the airfields they found it still too dark to identify targets on the ground and managed to inflict only limited damage. After their return, the naval bombardment was undertaken. The Dutch cruiser *Tromp* and two British destroyers detached from the main body to close in and shell the harbour and shore facilities from point blank range. All ships were hit but the damage was only slight. In general, the Japanese response was limited and only in the afternoon did a force of around ten A6M Zero fighters attempt to attack the withdrawing fleet, but this was quickly broken up by the defending fighter screen. This was Somerville's last operation in command of the Eastern Fleet.

OPERATION BANQUET, 24 AUGUST 1944

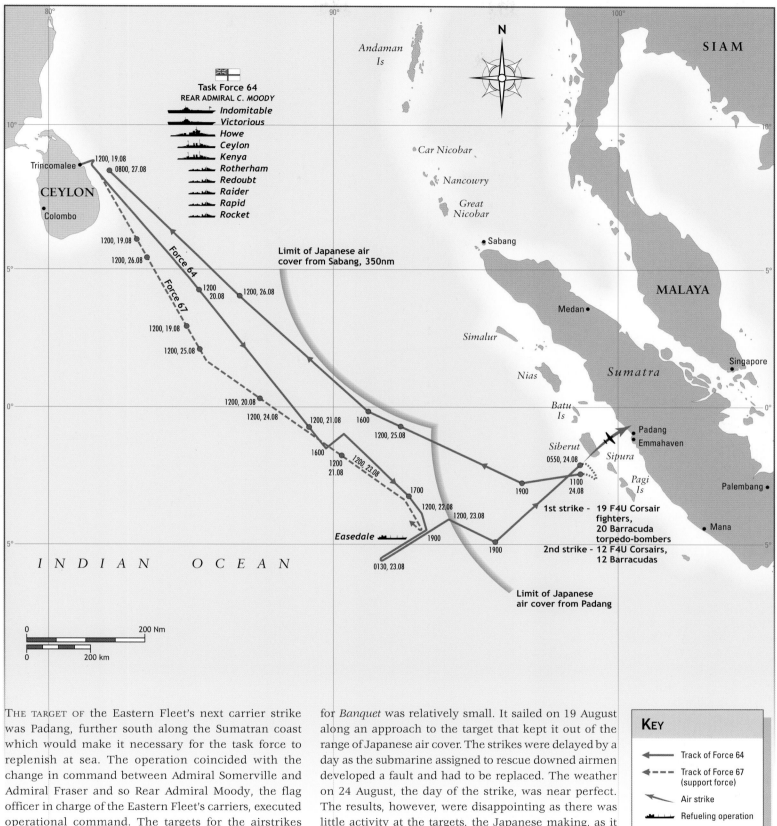

THE TARGET OF the Eastern Fleet's next carrier strike was Padang, further south along the Sumatran coast which would make it necessary for the task force to replenish at sea. The operation coincided with the change in command between Admiral Somerville and Admiral Fraser and so Rear Admiral Moody, the flag officer in charge of the Eastern Fleet's carriers, executed operational command. The targets for the airstrikes were the airfield at Padang, Emmahaven harbour and a cement works. It was also hoped that regular raids against Japanese positions in the Indian Ocean would divert attention and some resources away from other fronts in the southwest Pacific. In the event, these raids were too small to have an impact on the overall disposition of Japanese forces.

In comparison to most British operations, the force for *Banquet* was relatively small. It sailed on 19 August along an approach to the target that kept it out of the range of Japanese air cover. The strikes were delayed by a day as the submarine assigned to rescue downed airmen developed a fault and had to be replaced. The weather on 24 August, the day of the strike, was near perfect. The results, however, were disappointing as there was little activity at the targets, the Japanese making, as it turned out, little use of Padang as a base. With minimal opposition the aim of providing new aircrews with some combat experience was only partially achieved. The newly-arrived *Howe*, despite being one of the Royal Navy's most modern battleships, found it difficult to keep up with the carriers during air operations and consumed more fuel than anticipated forcing the task force to return at a slower speed than planned.

OPERATION DRAGOON, 15–28 AUGUST 1944

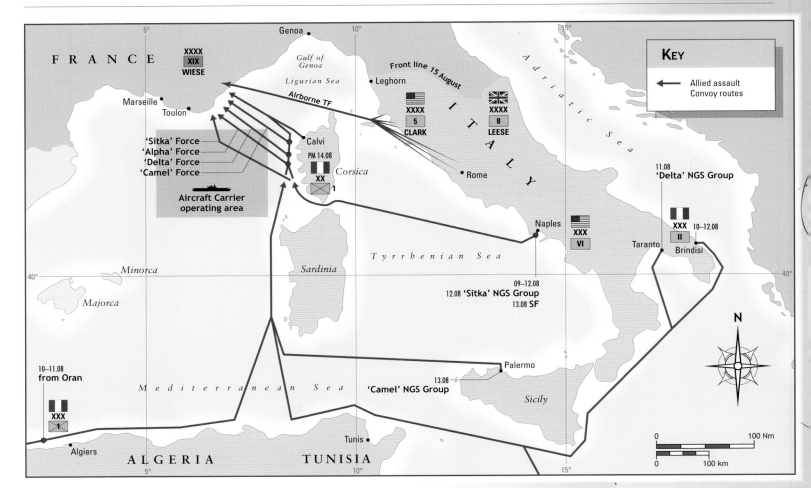

THE DEMANDS THAT operation *Overlord* made on amphibious assault shipping prevented a second landing in France from taking place until much later than had originally been hoped by the Americans and the French. It was not until 2 July that the planning for *Dragoon* (originally named *Anvil*) began. The operation involved an initial landing by three American divisions along a broad 65km front in southeast France, with seven French divisions and support troops in the following waves. This was the last major amphibious operation in the European theatre and its execution benefited greatly from the earlier experiences. In addition, German defences were weak and spread thinly. Anzio, however, had shown that even limited numbers of German aircraft and naval small battle units could inflict damage on vulnerable transports. Around sixty allied warships covered the operation and provided gunfire support, with additional escorts and the follow-up convoys bringing the second wave of French troops from North Africa along with supplies. The whole invasion force numbered 881 warships, large assault vessels and transports, and 1,370 smaller landing craft. As the beaches were out of range of most allied fighters, a force of British escort carriers provided close air cover. The landings, on 15 August, proceeded as planned and encountered only light German resistance. Deviating from the pattern of previous assaults, the main landings started comparatively late, at 8am, in order that lengthy naval bombardments could take place. By the end of the first day 86,575 men, 12,520 vehicles, and 46,140 tons of stores had been landed.

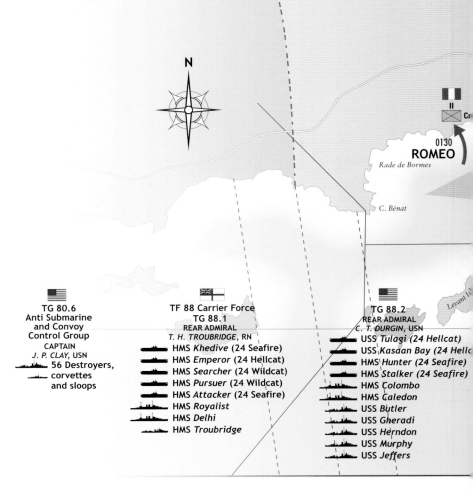

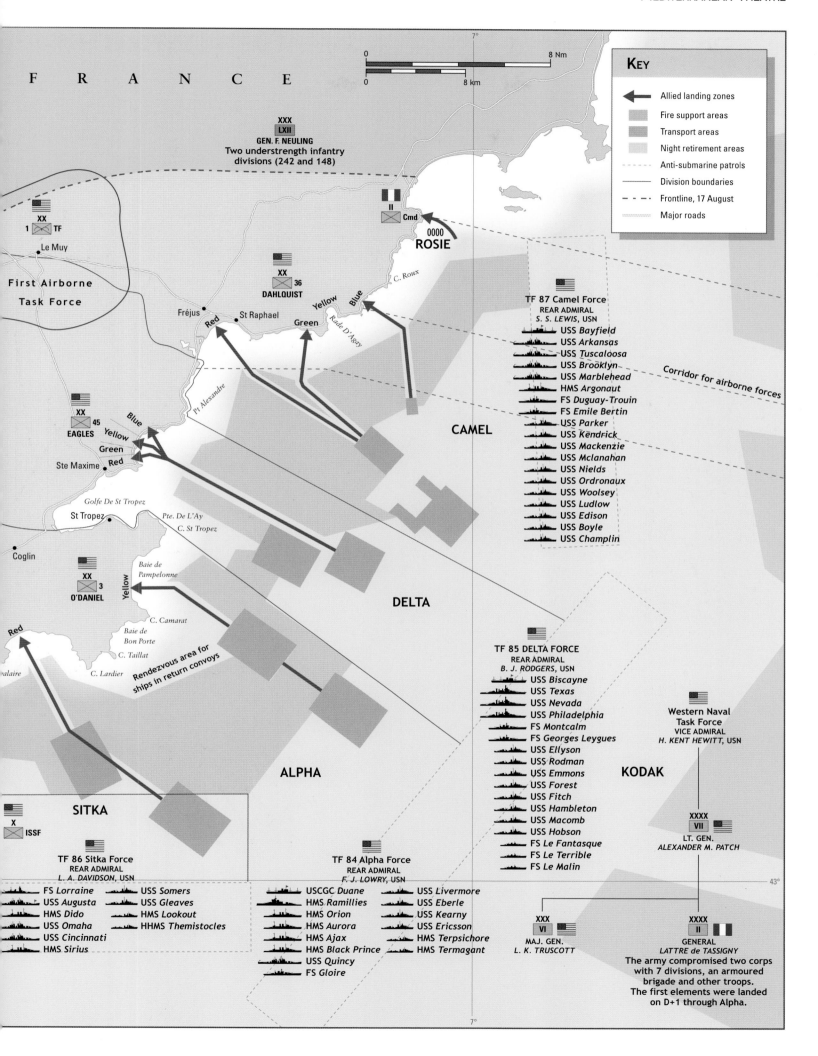

F R A N C E

0   8 Nm
0   8 km

KEY

→ Allied landing zones
Fire support areas
Transport areas
Night retirement areas
Anti-submarine patrols
Division boundaries
Frontline, 17 August
Major roads

XXX
LXII
GEN. F. NEULING
Two understrength infantry
divisions (242 and 148)

II
Cmd
0000
ROSIE

XX
1   TF
Le Muy

First Airborne
Task Force

XX   36
DAHLQUIST
Fréjus
St Raphael
Red   Green   Yellow   Blue
C. Roux
Rade D'Agay

Pt Alexandre

Corridor for airborne forces

TF 87 Camel Force
REAR ADMIRAL
S. S. LEWIS, USN
USS Bayfield
USS Arkansas
USS Tuscaloosa
USS Brooklyn
USS Marblehead
HMS Argonaut
FS Duguay-Trouin
FS Emile Bertin
USS Parker
USS Kendrick
USS Mackenzie
USS Mclanahan
USS Nields
USS Ordronaux
USS Woolsey
USS Ludlow
USS Edison
USS Boyle
USS Champlin

CAMEL

XX   45
EAGLES
Blue
Yellow
Green
Red
Ste Maxime

Golfe De St Tropez
St Tropez
Pte. De L'Ay
C. St Tropez

Coglin

XX   3
O'DANIEL
Yellow
Baie de
Pampelonne

DELTA

C. Camarat
Baie de
Bon Porte
C. Taillat
C. Lardier

Rendezvous area for
ships in return convoys

Western Naval
Task Force
VICE ADMIRAL
H. KENT HEWITT, USN

TF 85 DELTA FORCE
REAR ADMIRAL
B. J. RODGERS, USN
USS Biscayne
USS Texas
USS Nevada
USS Philadelphia
FS Montcalm
FS Georges Leygues
USS Ellyson
USS Rodman
USS Emmons
USS Forest
USS Fitch
USS Hambleton
USS Macomb
USS Hobson
FS Le Fantasque
FS Le Terrible
FS Le Malin

KODAK

XXXX
VII
LT. GEN.
ALEXANDER M. PATCH

Red

ALPHA

SITKA

X
ISSF

TF 86 Sitka Force
REAR ADMIRAL
L. A. DAVIDSON, USN

TF 84 Alpha Force
REAR ADMIRAL
F. J. LOWRY, USN

XXX
VI
MAJ. GEN.
L. K. TRUSCOTT

XXXX
II
GENERAL
LATTRE de TASSIGNY
The army comprimised two corps
with 7 divisions, an armoured
brigade and other troops.
The first elements were landed
on D+1 through Alpha.

FS Lorraine	USS Somers	USCGC Duane	USS Livermore
USS Augusta	USS Gleaves	HMS Ramillies	USS Eberle
HMS Dido	HMS Lookout	HMS Orion	USS Kearny
USS Omaha	HHMS Themistocles	HMS Aurora	USS Ericsson
USS Cincinnati		HMS Ajax	HMS Terpsichore
HMS Sirius		HMS Black Prince	HMS Termagant
		USS Quincy	
		FS Gloire	

TASK FORCE 38 OPERATIONS, OCTOBER 1944

THE ROLE OF Admiral William Halsey's Third Fleet during the invasion of the Philippines was to cover the Southwest Pacific Forces under General Douglas MacArthur, and to destroy Japanese naval and air forces in the area. If the opportunity to eliminate a major proportion of the IJN's remaining surface force presented itself this was to become the primary task. The most important component of the Third Fleet was Task Force 38, the fast carrier force, under Vice Admiral Marc Mitscher. It was augmented by the new fast battleships and supported by a large fleet train that continuously replenished it with fuel, ammunition and replacement aircraft. In preparation for the landings in the central Philippines, TF 38 would first attack Japanese airbases on Okinawa, Formosa and northern Leyte. Then it would focus on neutralising airfields in the central Philippines and continue to operate where needed after the actual landings on 20 October.

The weather in the western Pacific at the beginning of October was poor and this adversely affected underway replenishment; on the other hand, it also reduced Japanese aerial reconnaissance. A diversionary bombardment of Marcus Island, however, failed to distract Japanese attention, and the first prearranged US strikes against Okinawa came as no surprise. After hitting northern Luzon, TF 38 turned towards Formosa and engaged in a three-day operation (12–14 October) to destroy Japanese air power on the island. The Formosa air battle inflicted heavy damage on the Japanese, some 550 aircraft being destroyed. In total, the Japanese had around 1,200 aircraft from four Air Fleets stationed between the Ryukyu Islands and the Philippines. Two allied cruisers were badly damaged and incapacitated in the air attacks and so Halsey detached a small task force of cruisers, light carriers and destroyers to tow them back to Ulithi. Although not insignificant, American casualties were comparatively light in the face of what were some of the most intense air attacks of the war. The battle also demonstrated that carrier naval aviation could counter land-based air power, something that had not been thought possible before the war.

From 17 October, TF 38 operated off the Philippines in support of the forthcoming landings. As the main Japanese fleet had not yet made an appearance, Halsey also made plans for individual Task Groups to be sent to Ulithi for rest and replenishment. Naval aviation would target the airfields on the northern islands while land-based aircraft from the Southwest Pacific command hit the southern islands, and heavy B-29 bombers, based in China, pounded the west. Escort carrier groups of the Seventh Fleet provided direct air cover over the beaches at Leyte. The Japanese air response in the first days after the landings on 20 October was limited as they prepared for the forthcoming battle of Leyte Gulf. On 24 October, as the main part of Operation *Sho* commenced, the air attacks intensified and, mid-morning, a Japanese bomber managed to evade the American air defence and mortally damage the light carrier *Princeton*, forcing her to be abandoned and sunk.

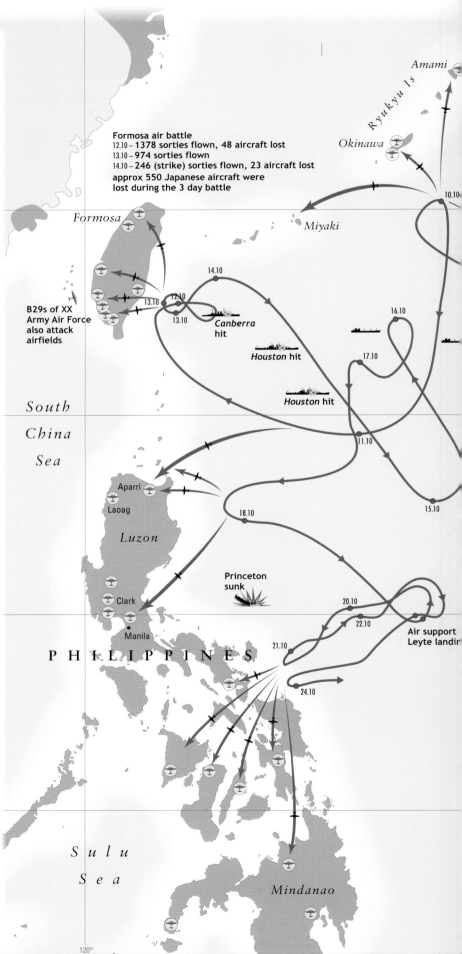

Formosa air battle
12.10 – 1378 sorties flown, 48 aircraft lost
13.10 – 974 sorties flown
14.10 – 246 (strike) sorties flown, 23 aircraft lost
approx 550 Japanese aircraft were lost during the 3 day battle

Amami

Ryukyu Is

Okinawa

Miyaki

Formosa

B29s of XX Army Air Force also attack airfields

Canberra hit

Houston hit

Houston hit

South China Sea

Aparri

Laoag

Luzon

Princeton sunk

Clark

Manila

P H I L I P P I N E S

Air support Leyte landin

Sulu Sea

Mindanao

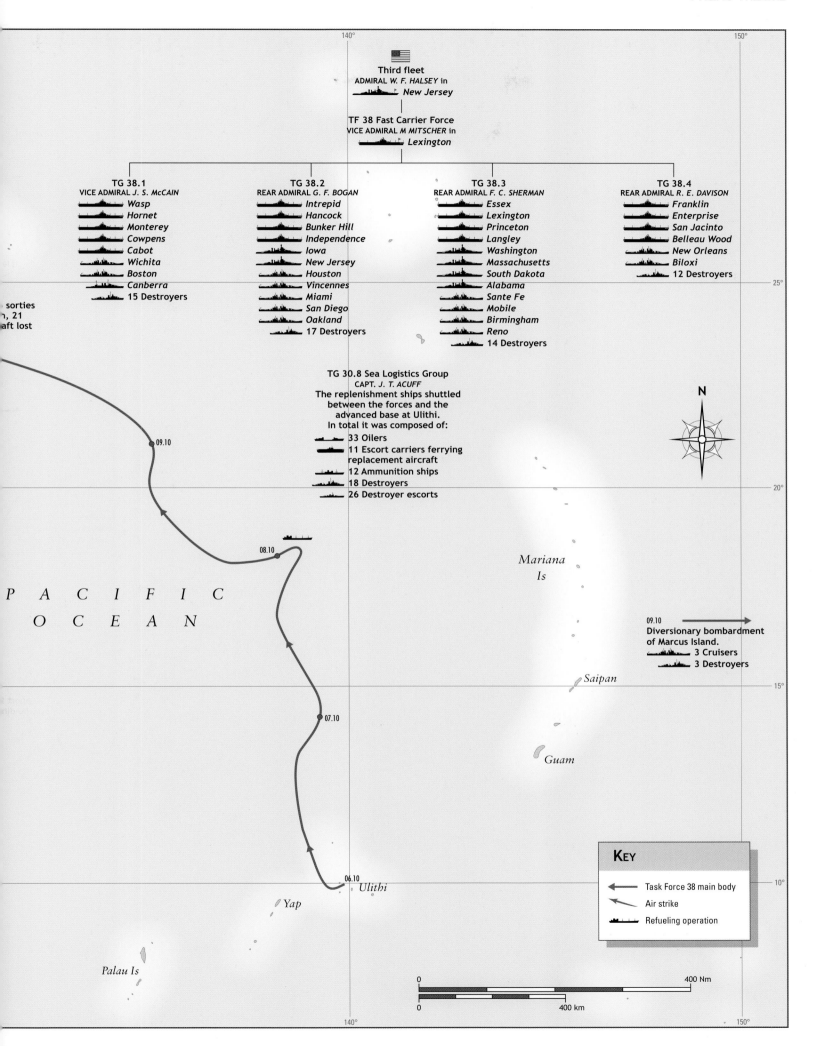

Third fleet
ADMIRAL *W. F. HALSEY* in
New Jersey

TF 38 Fast Carrier Force
VICE ADMIRAL *M MITSCHER* in
Lexington

TG 38.1
VICE ADMIRAL *J. S. McCAIN*
Wasp
Hornet
Monterey
Cowpens
Cabot
Wichita
Boston
Canberra
15 Destroyers

TG 38.2
REAR ADMIRAL *G. F. BOGAN*
Intrepid
Hancock
Bunker Hill
Independence
Iowa
New Jersey
Houston
Vincennes
Miami
San Diego
Oakland
17 Destroyers

TG 38.3
REAR ADMIRAL *F. C. SHERMAN*
Essex
Lexington
Princeton
Langley
Washington
Massachusetts
South Dakota
Alabama
Sante Fe
Mobile
Birmingham
Reno
14 Destroyers

TG 38.4
REAR ADMIRAL *R. E. DAVISON*
Franklin
Enterprise
San Jacinto
Belleau Wood
New Orleans
Biloxi
12 Destroyers

sorties
, 21
aft lost

TG 30.8 Sea Logistics Group
CAPT. *J. T. ACUFF*
The replenishment ships shuttled
between the forces and the
advanced base at Ulithi.
In total it was composed of:
33 Oilers
11 Escort carriers ferrying
replacement aircraft
12 Ammunition ships
18 Destroyers
26 Destroyer escorts

N

09.10

08.10

*P A C I F I C
O C E A N*

*Mariana
Is*

07.10

09.10 →
Diversionary bombardment
of Marcus Island.
3 Cruisers
3 Destroyers

Saipan

Guam

06.10 *Ulithi*

Yap

KEY	
←	Task Force 38 main body
←	Air strike
▬	Refueling operation

Palau Is

0   400 Nm

0   400 km

Leyte Gulf, 20–24 October 1944

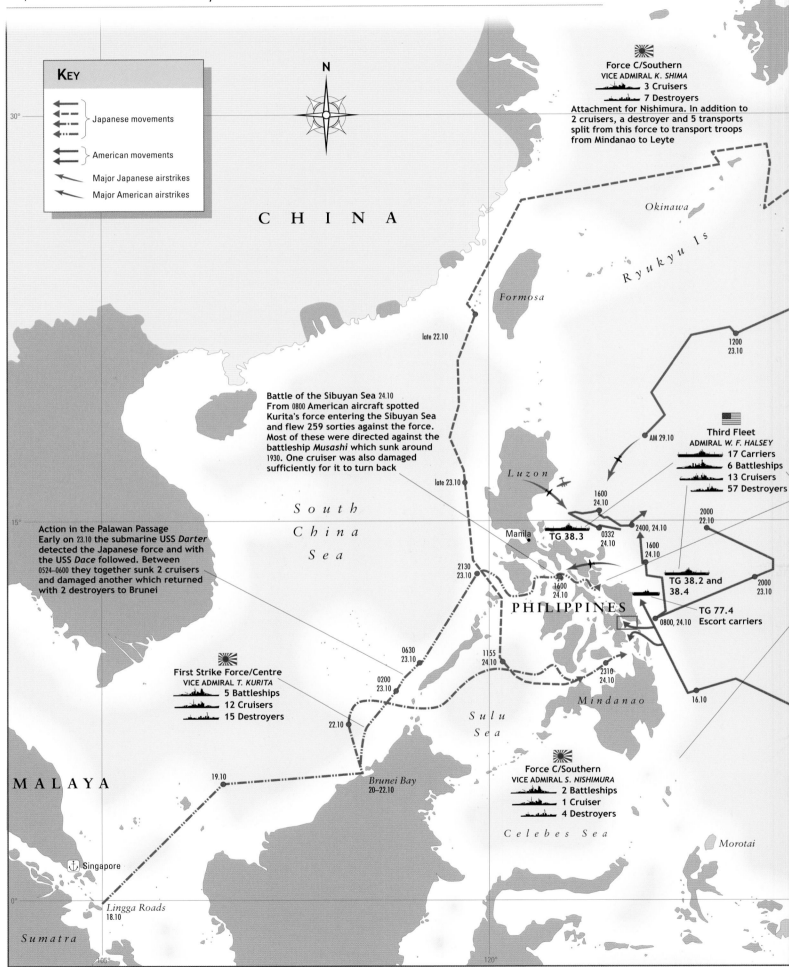

N

CHINA

Force C/Southern
VICE ADMIRAL *K. SHIMA*
3 Cruisers
7 Destroyers

Attachment for Nishimura. In addition to 2 cruisers, a destroyer and 5 transports split from this force to transport troops from Mindanao to Leyte

Okinawa

Ryukyu Is

Formosa

late 22.10

1200
23.10

Battle of the Sibuyan Sea 24.10
From 0800 American aircraft spotted Kurita's force entering the Sibuyan Sea and flew 259 sorties against the force. Most of these were directed against the battleship *Musashi* which sunk around 1930. One cruiser was also damaged sufficiently for it to turn back

AM 29.10

Third Fleet
ADMIRAL *W. F. HALSEY*
17 Carriers
6 Battleships
13 Cruisers
57 Destroyers

Luzon

late 23.10

1600
24.10

2000
22.10

Action in the Palawan Passage
Early on 23.10 the submarine USS *Darter* detected the Japanese force and with the USS *Dace* followed. Between 0524–0600 they together sunk 2 cruisers and damaged another which returned with 2 destroyers to Brunei

South China Sea

Manila ●

TG 38.3

0332
24.10

2400, 24.10

1600
24.10

2130
23.10

1600
24.10

TG 38.2 and 38.4

2000
23.10

PHILIPPINES

TG 77.4
0800, 24.10 Escort carriers

0630
23.10

1155
24.10

0200
23.10

First Strike Force/Centre
VICE ADMIRAL *T. KURITA*
5 Battleships
12 Cruisers
15 Destroyers

2310
24.10

Mindanao

16.10

22.10

Sulu Sea

Force C/Southern
VICE ADMIRAL *S. NISHIMURA*
2 Battleships
1 Cruiser
4 Destroyers

MALAYA

19.10

Brunei Bay
20–22.10

Celebes Sea

Morotai

⚓ Singapore

Lingga Roads
18.10

Sumatra

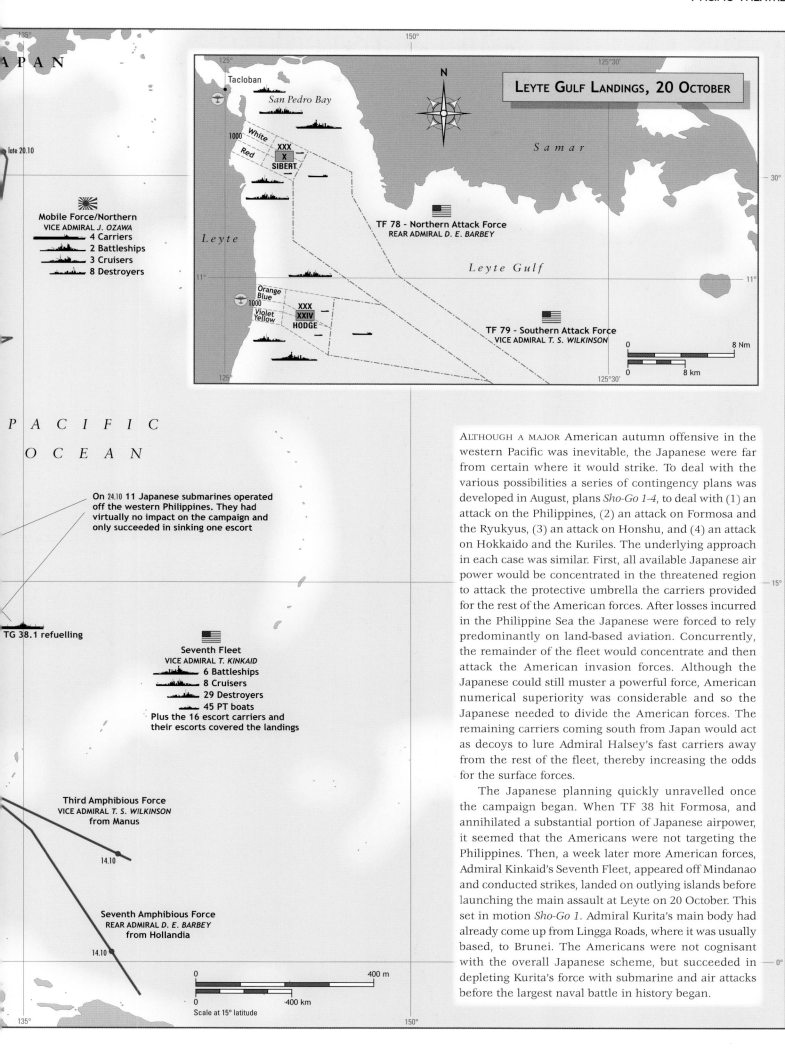

LEYTE GULF LANDINGS, 20 OCTOBER

Tacloban

San Pedro Bay

Samar

White
Red

XXX
X
SIBERT

TF 78 - Northern Attack Force
REAR ADMIRAL D. E. BARBEY

Leyte

Leyte Gulf

Orange
Blue
1000
Violet
Yellow

XXX
XXIV
HODGE

TF 79 - Southern Attack Force
VICE ADMIRAL T. S. WILKINSON

0   8 Nm
0   8 km

125°30'

Mobile Force/Northern
VICE ADMIRAL J. OZAWA
4 Carriers
2 Battleships
3 Cruisers
8 Destroyers

late 20.10

PACIFIC
OCEAN

On 24.10 11 Japanese submarines operated
off the western Philippines. They had
virtually no impact on the campaign and
only succeeded in sinking one escort

TG 38.1 refuelling

Seventh Fleet
VICE ADMIRAL T. KINKAID
6 Battleships
8 Cruisers
29 Destroyers
45 PT boats
Plus the 16 escort carriers and
their escorts covered the landings

Third Amphibious Force
VICE ADMIRAL T. S. WILKINSON
from Manus

14.10

Seventh Amphibious Force
REAR ADMIRAL D. E. BARBEY
from Hollandia

14.10

0   400 m
0   400 km
Scale at 15° latitude

ALTHOUGH A MAJOR American autumn offensive in the western Pacific was inevitable, the Japanese were far from certain where it would strike. To deal with the various possibilities a series of contingency plans was developed in August, plans *Sho-Go 1-4*, to deal with (1) an attack on the Philippines, (2) an attack on Formosa and the Ryukyus, (3) an attack on Honshu, and (4) an attack on Hokkaido and the Kuriles. The underlying approach in each case was similar. First, all available Japanese air power would be concentrated in the threatened region to attack the protective umbrella the carriers provided for the rest of the American forces. After losses incurred in the Philippine Sea the Japanese were forced to rely predominantly on land-based aviation. Concurrently, the remainder of the fleet would concentrate and then attack the American invasion forces. Although the Japanese could still muster a powerful force, American numerical superiority was considerable and so the Japanese needed to divide the American forces. The remaining carriers coming south from Japan would act as decoys to lure Admiral Halsey's fast carriers away from the rest of the fleet, thereby increasing the odds for the surface forces.

The Japanese planning quickly unravelled once the campaign began. When TF 38 hit Formosa, and annihilated a substantial portion of Japanese airpower, it seemed that the Americans were not targeting the Philippines. Then, a week later more American forces, Admiral Kinkaid's Seventh Fleet, appeared off Mindanao and conducted strikes, landed on outlying islands before launching the main assault at Leyte on 20 October. This set in motion *Sho-Go 1*. Admiral Kurita's main body had already come up from Lingga Roads, where it was usually based, to Brunei. The Americans were not cognisant with the overall Japanese scheme, but succeeded in depleting Kurita's force with submarine and air attacks before the largest naval battle in history began.

THE BATTLE OF SURIGAO STRAIT, 25 OCTOBER 1944

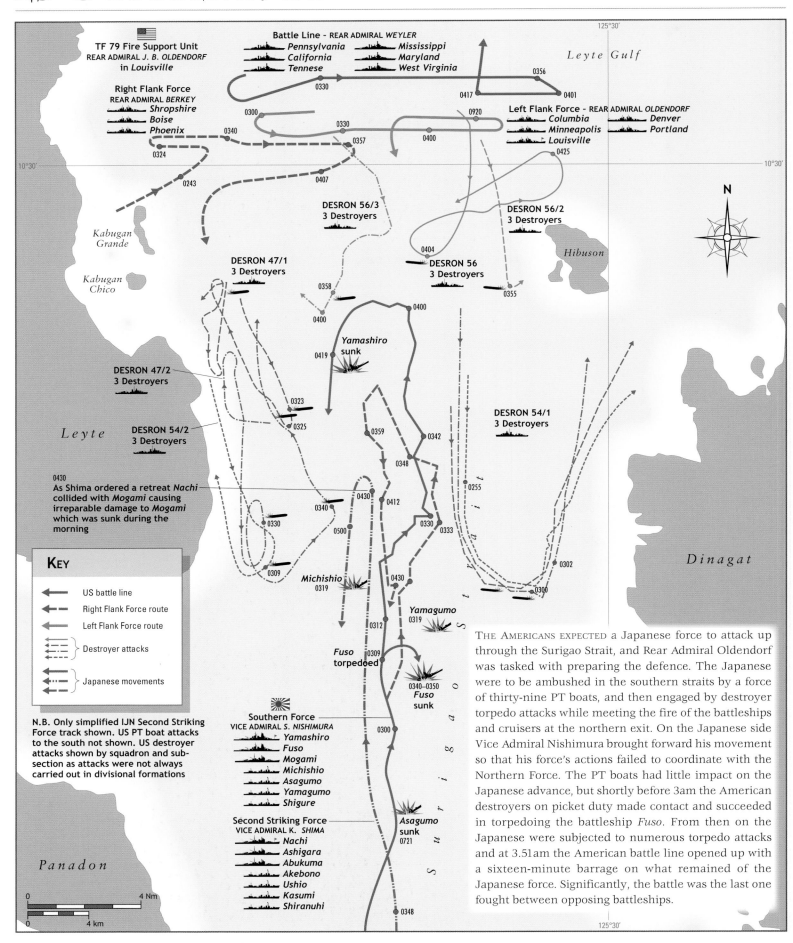

TF 79 Fire Support Unit
REAR ADMIRAL J. B. OLDENDORF
in *Louisville*

Battle Line – REAR ADMIRAL *WEYLER*

- *Pennsylvania*
- *California*
- *Tennese*
- *Mississippi*
- *Maryland*
- *West Virginia*

Leyte Gulf

0330 · 0356 · 0417 · 0401

Right Flank Force
REAR ADMIRAL *BERKEY*

- *Shropshire*
- *Boise*
- *Phoenix*

0300 · 0340 · 0330 · 0920 · 0357 · 0400

Left Flank Force – REAR ADMIRAL *OLDENDORF*

- *Columbia*
- *Minneapolis*
- *Louisville*
- *Denver*
- *Portland*

0324 · 0243 · 0407 · 0425

125°30′

10°30′

Kabugan Grande

Kabugan Chico

DESRON 56/3
3 Destroyers

DESRON 56/2
3 Destroyers

Hibuson

DESRON 47/1
3 Destroyers

0358 · 0400 · 0400

DESRON 56
3 Destroyers

0404 · 0355

N

DESRON 47/2
3 Destroyers

Yamashiro
sunk
0419

0323 · 0325

DESRON 54/1
3 Destroyers

Leyte

DESRON 54/2
3 Destroyers

0359 · 0342 · 0348 · 0255

0430
As Shima ordered a retreat *Nachi* collided with *Mogami* causing irreparable damage to *Mogami* which was sunk during the morning

0340 · 0430 · 0412 · 0330 · 0333

0309

0500

0302

0300

Dinagat

KEY

←	US battle line
←--	Right Flank Force route
←	Left Flank Force route
←⊨	Destroyer attacks
←·-	Japanese movements

0309

Michishio
0319

0430

Yamagumo
0319

N.B. Only simplified IJN Second Striking Force track shown. US PT boat attacks to the south not shown. US destroyer attacks shown by squadron and sub-section as attacks were not always carried out in divisional formations

0312

Fuso
torpedoed
0309

0340–0350
Fuso
sunk

Southern Force
VICE ADMIRAL S. NISHIMURA

- *Yamashiro*
- *Fuso*
- *Mogami*
- *Michishio*
- *Asagumo*
- *Yamagumo*
- *Shigure*

0300

Second Striking Force
VICE ADMIRAL K. SHIMA

- *Nachi*
- *Ashigara*
- *Abukuma*
- *Akebono*
- *Ushio*
- *Kasumi*
- *Shiranuhi*

Asagumo
sunk
0721

Panadon

0   4 Nm
0   4 km

0348

125°30′

THE AMERICANS EXPECTED a Japanese force to attack up through the Surigao Strait, and Rear Admiral Oldendorf was tasked with preparing the defence. The Japanese were to be ambushed in the southern straits by a force of thirty-nine PT boats, and then engaged by destroyer torpedo attacks while meeting the fire of the battleships and cruisers at the northern exit. On the Japanese side Vice Admiral Nishimura brought forward his movement so that his force's actions failed to coordinate with the Northern Force. The PT boats had little impact on the Japanese advance, but shortly before 3am the American destroyers on picket duty made contact and succeeded in torpedoing the battleship *Fuso*. From then on the Japanese were subjected to numerous torpedo attacks and at 3.51am the American battle line opened up with a sixteen-minute barrage on what remained of the Japanese force. Significantly, the battle was the last one fought between opposing battleships.

THE BATTLE OFF SAMAR, 25 OCTOBER 1944

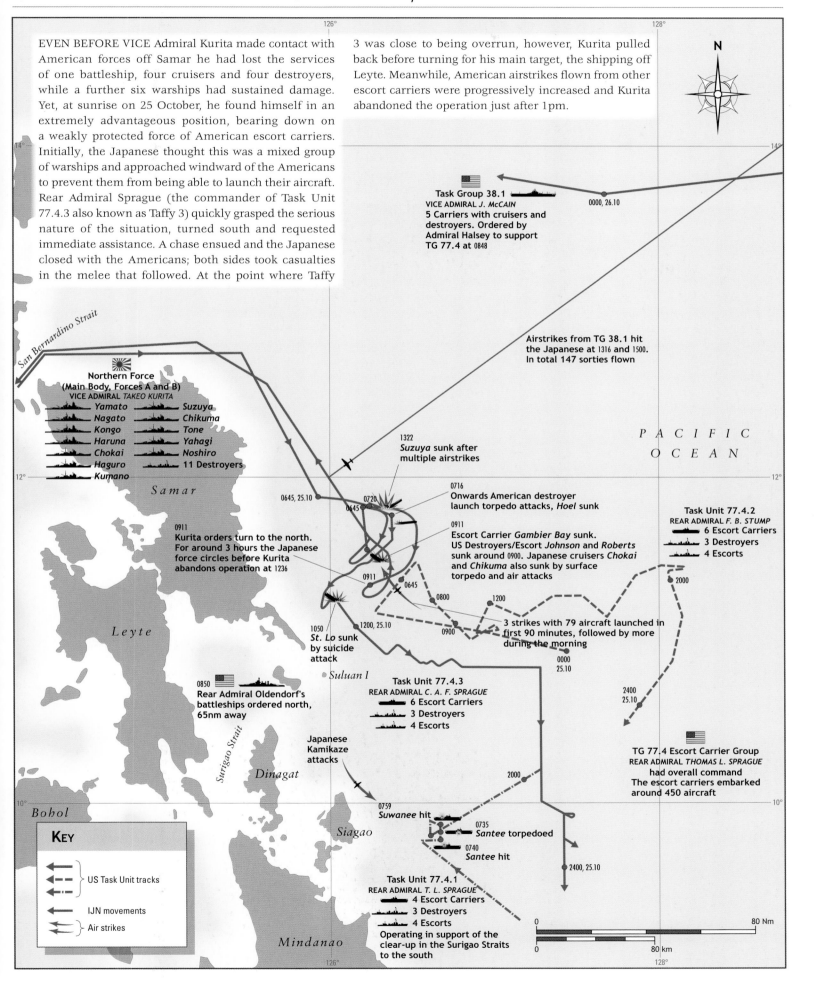

EVEN BEFORE VICE Admiral Kurita made contact with American forces off Samar he had lost the services of one battleship, four cruisers and four destroyers, while a further six warships had sustained damage. Yet, at sunrise on 25 October, he found himself in an extremely advantageous position, bearing down on a weakly protected force of American escort carriers. Initially, the Japanese thought this was a mixed group of warships and approached windward of the Americans to prevent them from being able to launch their aircraft. Rear Admiral Sprague (the commander of Task Unit 77.4.3 also known as Taffy 3) quickly grasped the serious nature of the situation, turned south and requested immediate assistance. A chase ensued and the Japanese closed with the Americans; both sides took casualties in the melee that followed. At the point where Taffy

3 was close to being overrun, however, Kurita pulled back before turning for his main target, the shipping off Leyte. Meanwhile, American airstrikes flown from other escort carriers were progressively increased and Kurita abandoned the operation just after 1pm.

Task Group 38.1
VICE ADMIRAL *J. McCAIN*
5 Carriers with cruisers and destroyers. Ordered by Admiral Halsey to support TG 77.4 at 0848

0000, 26.10

Airstrikes from TG 38.1 hit the Japanese at 1316 and 1500. In total 147 sorties flown

**Northern Force
(Main Body, Forces A and B)**
VICE ADMIRAL *TAKEO KURITA*

Yamato	Suzuya
Nagato	Chikuma
Kongo	Tone
Haruna	Yahagi
Chokai	Noshiro
Haguro	11 Destroyers
Kumano	

Samar

*PACIFIC
OCEAN*

1322
Suzuya sunk after multiple airstrikes

0645, 25.10

0720
0645

0716
Onwards American destroyer launch torpedo attacks, *Hoel* sunk

0911
Kurita orders turn to the north. For around 3 hours the Japanese force circles before Kurita abandons operation at 1236

0911
Escort Carrier *Gambier Bay* sunk. US Destroyers/Escort *Johnson* and *Roberts* sunk around 0900. Japanese cruisers *Chokai* and *Chikuma* also sunk by surface torpedo and air attacks

Task Unit 77.4.2
REAR ADMIRAL *F. B. STUMP*
6 Escort Carriers
3 Destroyers
4 Escorts

2000

0911
0645
0800
1200

Leyte

1050
St. Lo sunk by suicide attack

1200, 25.10
0900

3 strikes with 79 aircraft launched in first 90 minutes, followed by more during the morning

0000
25.10

2400
25.10

0850
Rear Admiral Oldendorf's battleships ordered north, 65nm away

Suluan I

Task Unit 77.4.3
REAR ADMIRAL *C. A. F. SPRAGUE*
6 Escort Carriers
3 Destroyers
4 Escorts

Japanese Kamikaze attacks

Dinagat

2000

TG 77.4 Escort Carrier Group
REAR ADMIRAL *THOMAS L. SPRAGUE*
had overall command
The escort carriers embarked around 450 aircraft

2400, 25.10

0759
Suwanee hit

Bohol

Siagao

0735
Santee torpedoed

0740
Santee hit

KEY

US Task Unit tracks

IJN movements

Air strikes

Task Unit 77.4.1
REAR ADMIRAL *T. L. SPRAGUE*
4 Escort Carriers
3 Destroyers
4 Escorts
Operating in support of the clear-up in the Surigao Straits to the south

Mindanao

0
80 Nm

0
80 km

The Battle of Cape Engano, 25 October 1944

After the strikes against Formosa and the northern Philippines, Admiral Halsey reorganised TF 38 and sent Vice Admiral McCain's TG 38.1 back to the advanced base at Ulithi to replenish. Halsey had wanted to push into the South China Sea or north against Japan, but was ordered to remain off the western Philippines during the landings to support Admiral Kinkaid's Seventh Fleet and General MacArthur's forces ashore. Taking in to account combat losses and McCain's temporary removal from the battlefield, TF 38's strength dropped from 19 carriers, embarking around 1,100 aircraft, to 10 with 600 on the eve of the battle.

Most of the attacks on Kurita's force in the Sibuyan Sea on 24 October were flown by aircraft from TG 38.3, with the other two groups operating further south. At around 2pm American aircraft observed Kurita's force moving westwards. He was, in fact, not retiring but merely loitering, and after sunset resumed the eastward approach through the San Bernardino Strait. This manoeuvring, coupled with an overestimation of the effects of the day's strikes and the sighting of two further Japanese forces to the north, shifted American attention away from the central force. In the north, where Ozawa's approach had remained undetected, Halsey now ordered his three task groups to move against the Japanese carrier force. Although he intended to form a surface strike force TF 34, under the most experienced American battleship commander Vice Admiral Lee, to deal with a Japanese surface fleet, this did not occur until the early hours of 25 October. Despite losses and detachments, Halsey still had a considerable force at his disposal, but he chose to concentrate this rather than split it into to groups. Thus the exit of the San Bernardino Strait remained unguarded and, owing to confusion in communications, this fact remained unknown to the Seventh Fleet and Admiral Nimitz in Pearl Harbor.

Meanwhile, Ozawa had detached a force to close with the Americans in an attempt to lure them north. He briefly thought the operation had been abandoned when Kurita turned back, but by the early morning it was clear that Halsey had taken the bait. Ozawa had few aircraft left to provide him with cover. Halsey detached TF 34, with which he sailed, to operate ahead of the carriers while Vice Admiral Mitscher had tactical command of the airstrikes. Air reconnaissance was sent out long before dawn and Mitscher launched the first strike waves before contact was made, with the aircraft circling the carriers, so as not to waste any time. Just as the second strike hit the Japanese force Halsey received news of

Kurita's force off Samar. Initially, he only ordered Vice Admiral McCain's task group to close in from the west, but after coming under pressure from Nimitz he turned south with his battleships and a carrier group. As many accompanying destroyers needed refuelling it was not until the late afternoon that full speed was made, by which time Kurita's force had withdrawn. A battleship-cruiser force was detached and sent through the San Bernardino Strait, but found nothing.

This left two carrier groups to pursue Ozawa and they conducted a further four airstrikes during the rest of the day. In total, over 500 strikes were flown. A smaller cruiser-destroyer force was also sent north to finish off any damaged Japanese ships. Ozawa briefly turned south again when it became clear how small this force was, and he hoped to engage it in a night action; but by then the Americans had withdrawn. Although they inflicted considerable losses on the Japanese this was only a partial victory; the majority of Japanese ships escaped, and the Americans came close to losing off Samar.

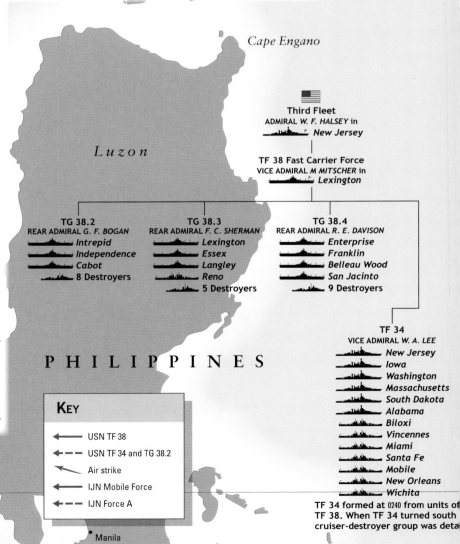

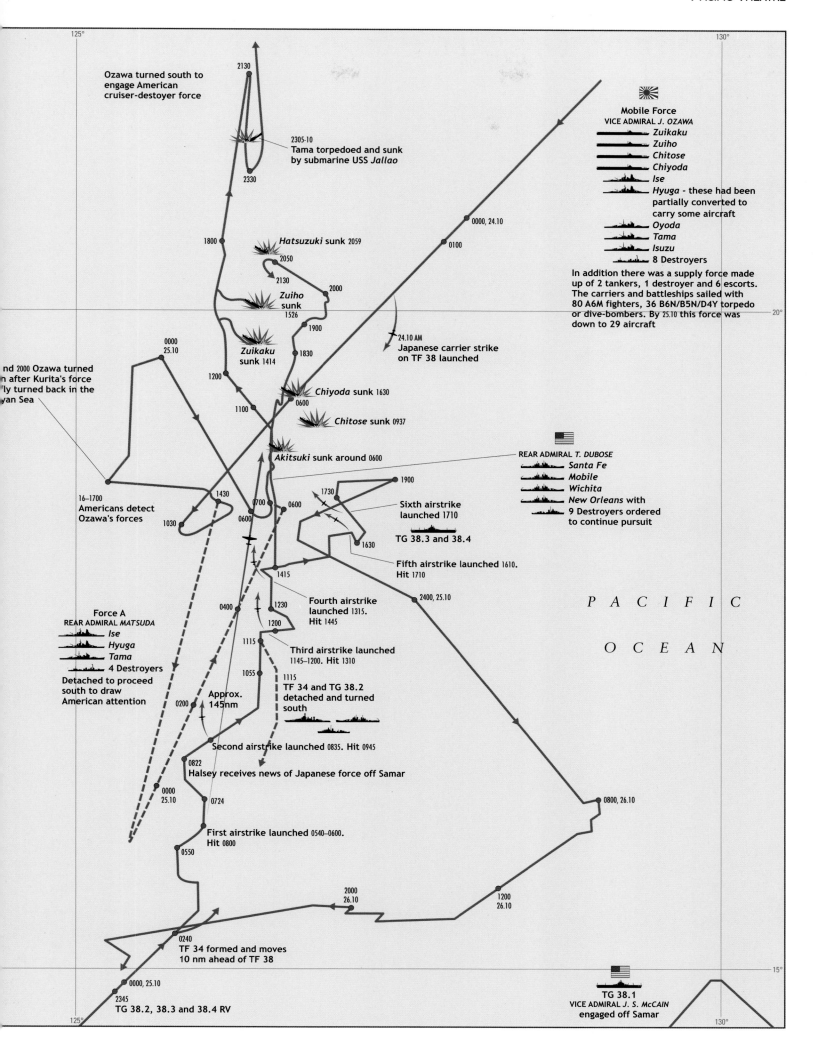

Ozawa turned south to engage American cruiser-destoyer force

2305-10
Tama torpedoed and sunk by submarine USS *Jallao*

Hatsuzuki sunk 2059

Zuiho sunk 1526

Zuikaku sunk 1414

Chiyoda sunk 1630

Chitose sunk 0937

Akitsuki sunk around 0600

and 2000 Ozawa turned in after Kurita's force ly turned back in the yan Sea

0000 25.10

16–1700
Americans detect Ozawa's forces

24.10 AM
Japanese carrier strike on TF 38 launched

Mobile Force
VICE ADMIRAL *J. OZAWA*
Zuikaku
Zuiho
Chitose
Chiyoda
Ise
Hyuga - these had been partially converted to carry some aircraft
Oyoda
Tama
Isuzu
8 Destroyers

In addition there was a supply force made up of 2 tankers, 1 destroyer and 6 escorts. The carriers and battleships sailed with 80 A6M fighters, 36 B6N/B5N/D4Y torpedo or dive-bombers. By 25.10 this force was down to 29 aircraft

REAR ADMIRAL *T. DUBOSE*
Santa Fe
Mobile
Wichita
New Orleans with
9 Destroyers ordered to continue pursuit

Sixth airstrike launched 1710
TG 38.3 and 38.4

Fifth airstrike launched 1610. Hit 1710

Fourth airstrike launched 1315. Hit 1445

2400, 25.10

Force A
REAR ADMIRAL *MATSUDA*
Ise
Hyuga
Tama
4 Destroyers
Detached to proceed south to draw American attention

Third airstrike launched 1145–1200. Hit 1310

TF 34 and TG 38.2 detached and turned south

Approx. 145nm

Second airstrike launched 0835. Hit 0945

Halsey receives news of Japanese force off Samar

P A C I F I C

O C E A N

0800, 26.10

First airstrike launched 0540–0600. Hit 0800

2000 26.10

1200 26.10

TF 34 formed and moves 10 nm ahead of TF 38

0000, 25.10

2345
TG 38.2, 38.3 and 38.4 RV

TG 38.1
VICE ADMIRAL *J. S. McCAIN*
engaged off Samar

247

TASK FORCE 38 OPERATIONS, NOVEMBER 1944

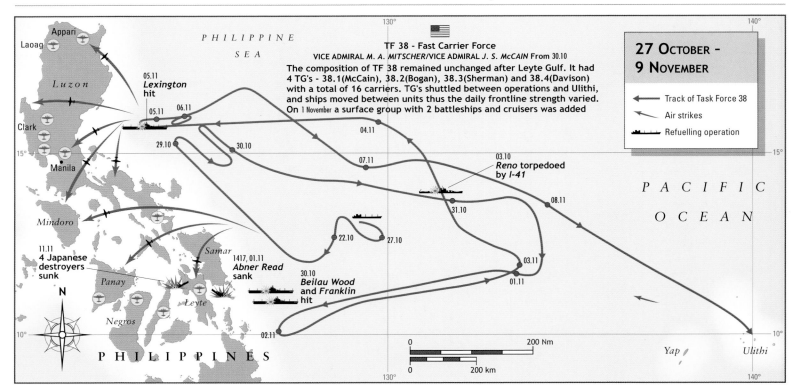

TF 38 - Fast Carrier Force
VICE ADMIRAL M. A. MITSCHER/VICE ADMIRAL J. S. McCAIN From 30.10
The composition of TF 38 remained unchanged after Leyte Gulf. It had
4 TG's - 38.1(McCain), 38.2(Bogan), 38.3(Sherman) and 38.4(Davison)
with a total of 16 carriers. TG's shuttled between operations and Ulithi,
and ships moved between units thus the daily frontline strength varied.
On 1 November a surface group with 2 battleships and cruisers was added

**27 OCTOBER -
9 NOVEMBER**

→ Track of Task Force 38
↘ Air strikes
▬ Refuelling operation

Lexington hit — 05.11
Reno torpedoed by *I-41* — 03.10
11.11 4 Japanese destroyers sunk
1417, 01.11 *Abner Read* sank
30.10 *Belau Wood* and *Franklin* hit

PHILIPPINE SEA
PACIFIC OCEAN
Luzon · Manila · Clark · Mindoro · Samar · Panay · Leyte · Negros
PHILIPPINES
Yap · Ulithi

0   200 Nm
0   200 km

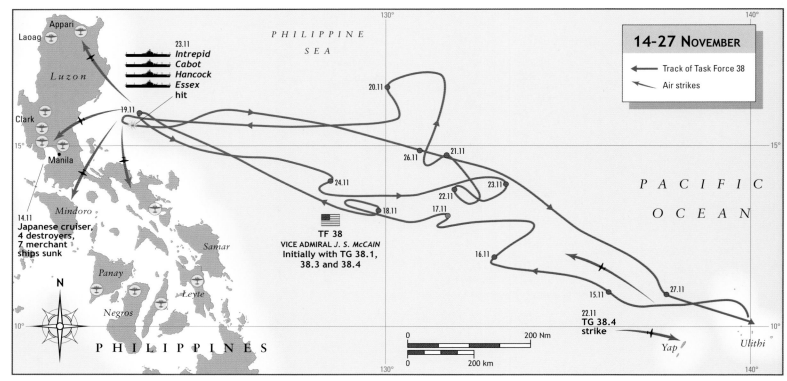

14-27 NOVEMBER

← Track of Task Force 38
↖ Air strikes

23.11 *Intrepid* *Cabot* *Hancock* *Essex* hit

14.11 Japanese cruiser, 4 destroyers, 7 merchant ships sunk

TF 38
VICE ADMIRAL J. S. McCAIN
Initially with TG 38.1,
38.3 and 38.4

22.11 TG 38.4 strike

PHILIPPINE SEA
PACIFIC OCEAN
Luzon · Manila · Clark · Mindoro · Samar · Panay · Leyte · Negros
PHILIPPINES
Yap · Ulithi

0   200 Nm
0   200 km

PACIFIC OCEAN
AUSTRALIA

IN THE IMMEDIATE aftermath of the Leyte Gulf battles
the fast carriers of TF 38 were required to provide air
cover for the troops ashore as it took some days for
land-based aircraft to arrive. Despite the naval defeat
the Japanese air threat still remained significant, with
attacks on the carriers occurring daily, so the carriers
struck at airfields throughout the northern Philippines.
At the end of October Japanese reinforcements began to
arrive and by early November they had regained control
of the air. As the US Third Fleet had been in continuous
action for over a month it needed a refit period. Ships
and aircraft shuttled between the front and the advanced

base on Ulithi, but by 1 November the strength of TF 38
was down to one TG. A fast battleship group was added,
as the possibility of a renewed Japanese surface attack
could not be discounted.

Originally, Admiral Halsey had been scheduled to
strike at Japan with TF 38 after the Leyte Gulf landings.
The level of Japanese resistance on the Philippines made
such a move unwise and until more American airbases
on Leyte could be built air support from the fast carriers
was crucial. Thus TF 38 sortied for another series of
strikes against the Japanese airfields on Luzon.

THE INSHORE U-BOAT CAMPAIGN, AUGUST 1944 – MAY 1945

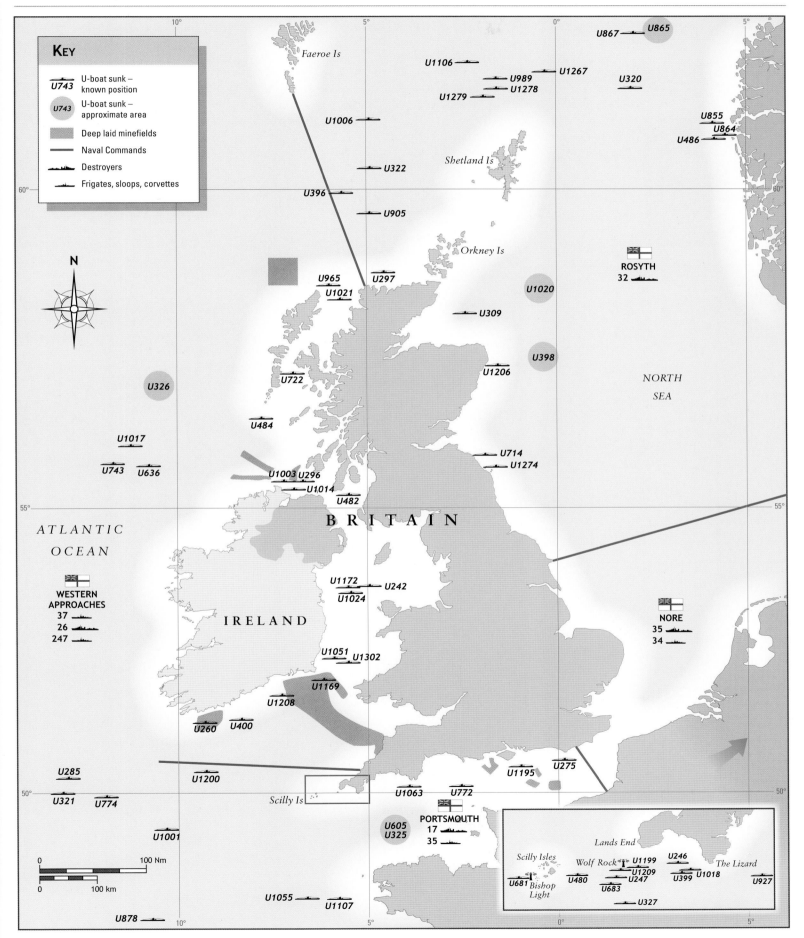

KEY

U743 ⎯ U-boat sunk – known position

U743 ⬤ U-boat sunk – approximate area

▨ Deep laid minefields

⎯ Naval Commands

Destroyers

Frigates, sloops, corvettes

Faeroe Is

U867 U865

U1106 U1267

U989 U320

U1278

U1279

U1006

U855

U864

U486

U322

Shetland Is

U396

U905

Orkney Is

ROSYTH
32

N

NORTH
SEA

U965 U297

U1021 U1020

U309

U398

U1206

U326

U722

U484

U714

U1274

U1017

U1003 U296

U743 U636 U1014

U482

BRITAIN

ATLANTIC

OCEAN

WESTERN
APPROACHES
37
26
247

U1172 U242

U1024

IRELAND

NORE
35
34

U1051 U1302

U1169

U1208

U260 U400

U275

U285 U1195

U1200

U321 U774 U1063 U772

Scilly Is

PORTSMOUTH
17
35

U605
U325

U1001

Lands End

Scilly Isles U246

Wolf Rock U1199

U1209 The Lizard

U681 U480 U247 U399 U1018

Bishop U683 U927

Light

U1055 U1107

U327

U878

0 100 Nm

0 100 km

Operation Infatuate, 1 November 1944

ONE OF THE largest problems the allied armies faced during the eastward advance across France in the late summer and autumn were the considerable delays and bottlenecks in the supply chain. Opening up more ports to keep the continuously expanding allied forces supplied was a priority. Of all the Franco-Belgian ports Antwerp was considered the most valuable, but it was also one of the most heavily defended, and the Germans had turned the island of Walcheren, which secured the approach via the Scheldt river, into a fortress. By mid-September the allied high command saw securing Antwerp and Rotterdam before the winter as a necessity. After the failure at Arnhem during Operation *Market Garden*, the focus of the Anglo-Canadian armies was to secure the area around Antwerp. Until a proper port could be opened, supplies could only be brought in by landing craft that were more limited in their transport capacity.

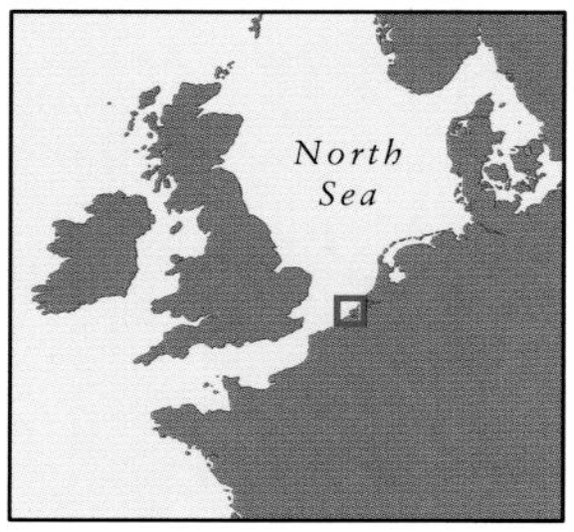

Capturing Walcheren was a formidable task as the only land connection from South Beveland was easily defended. Initially, the Canadian forces tasked with the operation wanted to attack from Beveland with the support of an airborne assault, but it soon became clear that some form of amphibious operation was necessary. The Royal Navy agreed to provide naval forces and also the service of the Royal Marines Commando brigade.

The plan foresaw two landings: one by army commandos at Flushing, and the second by the Royal Marines in the Westerkapelle area. The 15in guns of *Warspite*, *Erebus* and *Roberts* along with massed land artillery emplaced around Breskens provided heavy fire support. The rest of the naval force, assembled at Ostend, was composed of amphibious and coastal craft. The conditions on 1 November were poor. The southern assault achieved complete surprise but the main landings encountered serious problems. The weather initially prevented the spotting aircraft for the Bombardment Force from flying and also grounded the tactical air support. Not until 9am could German gun batteries be engaged and, without prior neutralisation, these responded with heavy and accurate fire against the assault craft from the outset. The marines began to land at around 9.45am and throughout the day fought their way through the German positions destroying the gun batteries. German resistance on the Scheldt continued for a number of days, but within three weeks supplies started flowing through Antwerp.

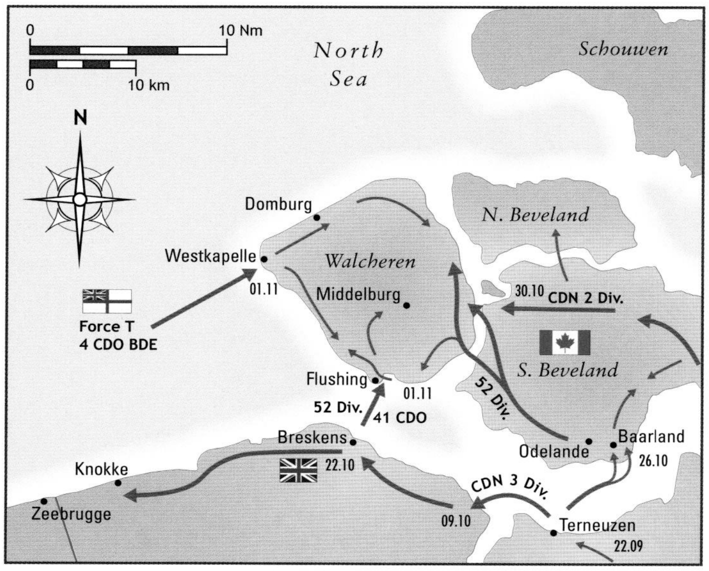

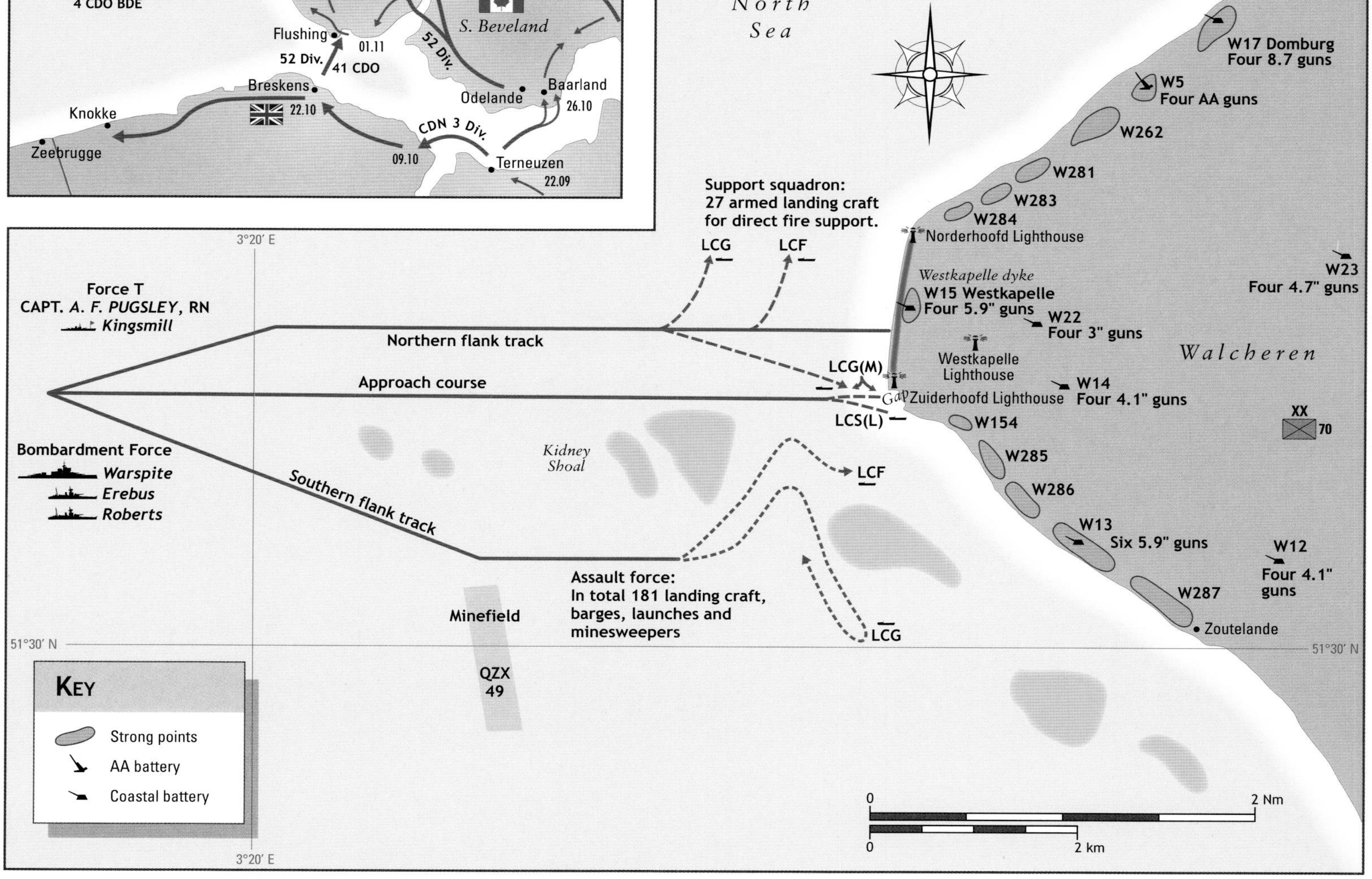

OPERATION ROBSON, 20 DECEMBER 1944

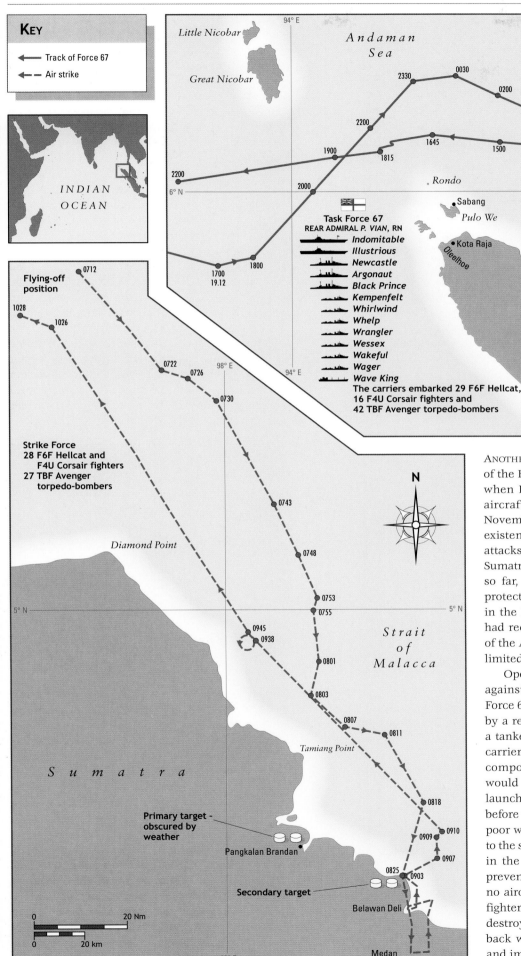

KEY

⟵ Track of Force 67

⟵--- Air strike

Little Nicobar

Great Nicobar

Andaman Sea

INDIAN OCEAN

Task Force 67
REAR ADMIRAL P. VIAN, RN
- *Indomitable*
- *Illustrious*
- *Newcastle*
- *Argonaut*
- *Black Prince*
- *Kempenfelt*
- *Whirlwind*
- *Whelp*
- *Wrangler*
- *Wessex*
- *Wakeful*
- *Wager*
- *Wave King*

The carriers embarked 29 F6F Hellcat, 16 F4U Corsair fighters and 42 TBF Avenger torpedo-bombers

Rondo

Sabang
Pulo We

Kota Raja

Oleelhoe

Sumatra

Diamond Point

Flying-off position

0615 Flying-off position

Flying-off position

Strike Force
28 F6F Hellcat and F4U Corsair fighters
27 TBF Avenger torpedo-bombers

Diamond Point

Strait of Malacca

Sumatra

Primary target – obscured by weather

Pangkalan Brandan

Secondary target

Belawan Deli

Tamiang Point

Medan

ANOTHER IMPORTANT CHANGE in the command structure of the British naval forces in the Indian Ocean occurred when Rear Admiral Vian took command of the fleet's aircraft carrier squadron in mid-November. On 22 November the British Pacific Fleet officially came into existence and the next phase of its work-up involved attacks on the strategically vital oil infrastructure on Sumatra, which was also more heavily defended. Targets so far, on the periphery, had been relatively lightly protected and were not comparable to the environment in the Pacific. In the meantime, the carrier air groups had received more capable strike aircraft in the shape of the Avenger torpedo-bombers that replaced the more limited Barracudas.

Operation *Robson*, the first such strike, was conducted against the oil refinery at Pangkalan Brandan. Task Force 67 left Ceylon on 17 December and was supported by a replenishment group, Task Force 69, consisting of a tanker and its destroyer escort. On this occasion the carriers, *Indomitable* and *Illustrious*, carried air groups composed entirely of American aircraft. The force would pass around the northern tip of Sumatra before launching the strike, which would fly south over the sea before turning inland to attack the target. Unfortunately, poor weather conditions forced the strike leader to shift to the secondary target, the harbour and railway facilities in the port of Belawan Deli. Low visibility here also prevented a proper assessment of the damage. However, no aircraft were lost. On the return some of the escort fighters attacked airfields in the vicinity of Sabang and destroyed some Japanese aircraft. Task Force 67 turned back westwards and reached Ceylon on 22 December and immediately prepared for the next strike.

THE WAR AT SEA, 1945

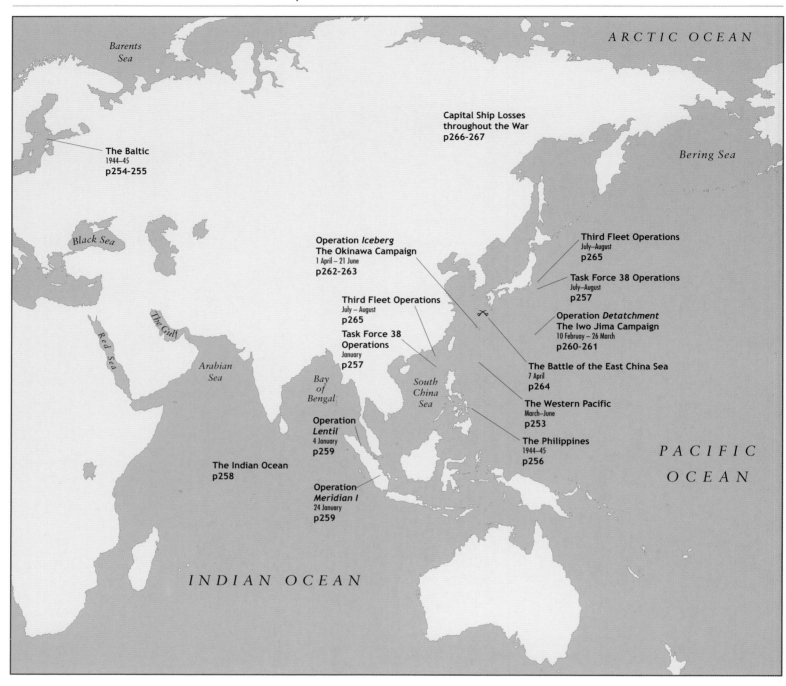

Barents
Sea

ARCTIC OCEAN

Bering Sea

**Capital Ship Losses
throughout the War
p266-267**

The Baltic
1944–45
p254-255

Black Sea

Third Fleet Operations
July–August
p265

**Operation *Iceberg*
The Okinawa Campaign**
1 April – 21 June
p262-263

Task Force 38 Operations
July–August
p257

The Gulf

Third Fleet Operations
July – August
p265

**Operation *Detachment*
The Iwo Jima Campaign**
10 February – 26 March
p260-261

Red Sea

**Task Force 38
Operations**
January
p257

The Battle of the East China Sea
7 April
p264

Arabian
Sea

Bay
of
Bengal

South
China
Sea

The Western Pacific
March–June
p253

**Operation
*Lentil***
4 January
p259

The Philippines
1944–45
p256

PACIFIC

**The Indian Ocean
p258**

OCEAN

**Operation
*Meridian I***
24 January
p259

INDIAN OCEAN

IN EUROPEAN WATERS the allied navies supported ground forces in the Low Countries, the north Italian shorelines, and Brittany where substantial German garrisons remained in isolated pockets. There was considerable concern that new German U-boats might result in an increase in merchant ship losses, so considerable effort was placed in laying new defensive minefields and increasing the number of aircraft and warships involved in anti-submarine warfare. The U-boat campaign returned to its origins in 1939 with boats operating individually close inshore around the British Isles. The war ended before the new boat types could have an impact on the campaign. The Kriegsmarine's most important role in the closing stages of the European war was to provide support to German forces in the Baltic states, East Prussia and Poland, and organise the evacuation of large numbers of troops and civilians from the advancing Soviet armies.

The focus of the naval war in 1945 was in the Pacific. The year began with major landings at Lingayen in the Philippines, and numerous further ones were conducted throughout the year to secure the archipelago. By this stage the allied naval-air campaign against Japanese maritime communications had sunk nearly the entire merchant fleet and brought about a collapse of the economy. However, the Japanese were unwilling to surrender and their fight to the death resulted in protracted and costly campaigns on Iwo Jima and Okinawa. The significant American materiel losses and casualties incurred during the latter raised concerns within the American military about the feasibility of the planned invasion of Japan in late 1945. By the summer, though allied naval forces operated off Japan with impunity, rather than launch an invasion the Americans relied on the atomic bomb to bring about the final Japanese surrender.

THE WESTERN PACIFIC, FEBRUARY–JUNE 1945

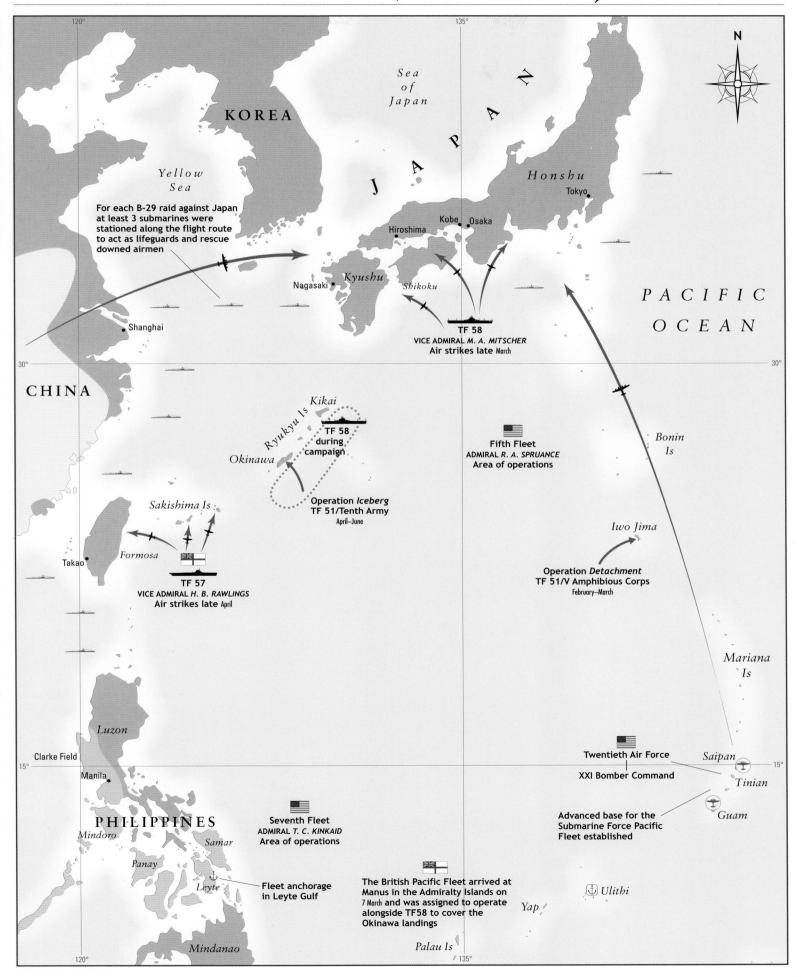

Sea of Japan

KOREA

Honshu

Tokyo

Yellow Sea

For each B-29 raid against Japan at least 3 submarines were stationed along the flight route to act as lifeguards and rescue downed airmen

Kobe
Osaka
Hiroshima

JAPAN

Nagasaki
Kyushu

Shikoku

Shanghai

TF 58
VICE ADMIRAL M. A. MITSCHER
Air strikes late March

PACIFIC
OCEAN

CHINA

Kikai

Ryukyu Is

TF 58 during campaign

Okinawa

Fifth Fleet
ADMIRAL R. A. SPRUANCE
Area of operations

Bonin Is

Operation Iceberg
TF 51/Tenth Army
April–June

Sakishima Is

Iwo Jima

Formosa

Takao

Operation Detachment
TF 51/V Amphibious Corps
February–March

TF 57
VICE ADMIRAL H. B. RAWLINGS
Air strikes late April

Mariana Is

Luzon

Twentieth Air Force

Saipan

Clarke Field

XXI Bomber Command

Manila

Tinian

Advanced base for the Submarine Force Pacific Fleet established

Guam

PHILIPPINES

Mindoro

Seventh Fleet
ADMIRAL T. C. KINKAID
Area of operations

Samar

Panay

Leyte

Fleet anchorage in Leyte Gulf

The British Pacific Fleet arrived at Manus in the Admiralty Islands on 7 March and was assigned to operate alongside TF58 to cover the Okinawa landings

Ulithi

Yap

Mindanao

Palau Is

THE BALTIC SEA, 1944–45

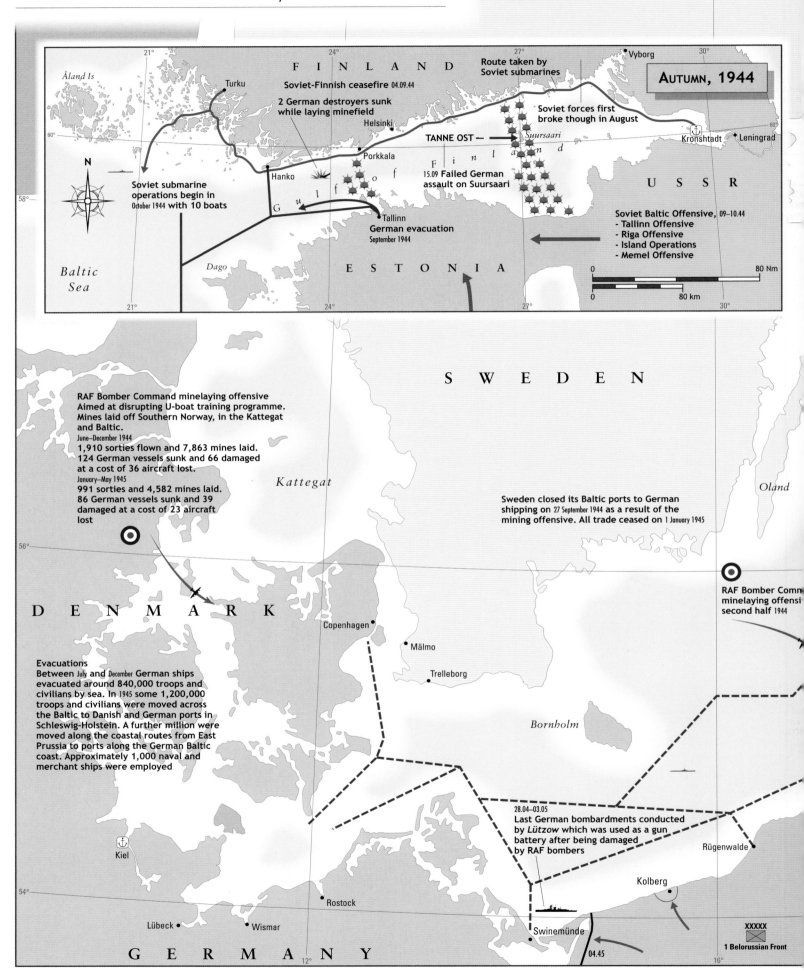

F I N L A N D

Soviet-Finnish ceasefire 04.09.44

Route taken by Soviet submarines

Vyborg

AUTUMN, 1944

2 German destroyers sunk while laying minefield

Helsinki

Soviet forces first broke though in August

TANNE OST —

Suursaari

Kronshtadt • Leningrad

Porkkala

N

Hanko

F i n l a n d

15.09 Failed German assault on Suursaari

U S S R

Soviet submarine operations begin in October 1944 with 10 boats

G u l f o f

Tallinn
German evacuation
September 1944

Baltic Sea

Dago

E S T O N I A

Soviet Baltic Offensive, 09–10.44
- Tallinn Offensive
- Riga Offensive
- Island Operations
- Memel Offensive

0   80 Nm

0   80 km

S W E D E N

RAF Bomber Command minelaying offensive
Aimed at disrupting U-boat training programme.
Mines laid off Southern Norway, in the Kattegat and Baltic.
June–December 1944
1,910 sorties flown and 7,863 mines laid.
124 German vessels sunk and 66 damaged at a cost of 36 aircraft lost.
January–May 1945
991 sorties and 4,582 mines laid.
86 German vessels sunk and 39 damaged at a cost of 23 aircraft lost

Kattegat

Oland

Sweden closed its Baltic ports to German shipping on 27 September 1944 as a result of the mining offensive. All trade ceased on 1 January 1945

RAF Bomber Comm
minelaying offensi
second half 1944

D E N M A R K

Copenhagen •

• Mälmo

• Trelleborg

Evacuations
Between July and December German ships evacuated around 840,000 troops and civilians by sea. In 1945 some 1,200,000 troops and civilians were moved across the Baltic to Danish and German ports in Schleswig-Holstein. A further million were moved along the coastal routes from East Prussia to ports along the German Baltic coast. Approximately 1,000 naval and merchant ships were employed

Bornholm

28.04–03.05
Last German bombardments conducted by *Lützow* which was used as a gun battery after being damaged by RAF bombers

Rügenwalde

Kolberg

Kiel

G E R M A N Y

Lübeck •

• Wismar

• Rostock

Swinemünde

04.45

XXXXX
1 Belorussian Front

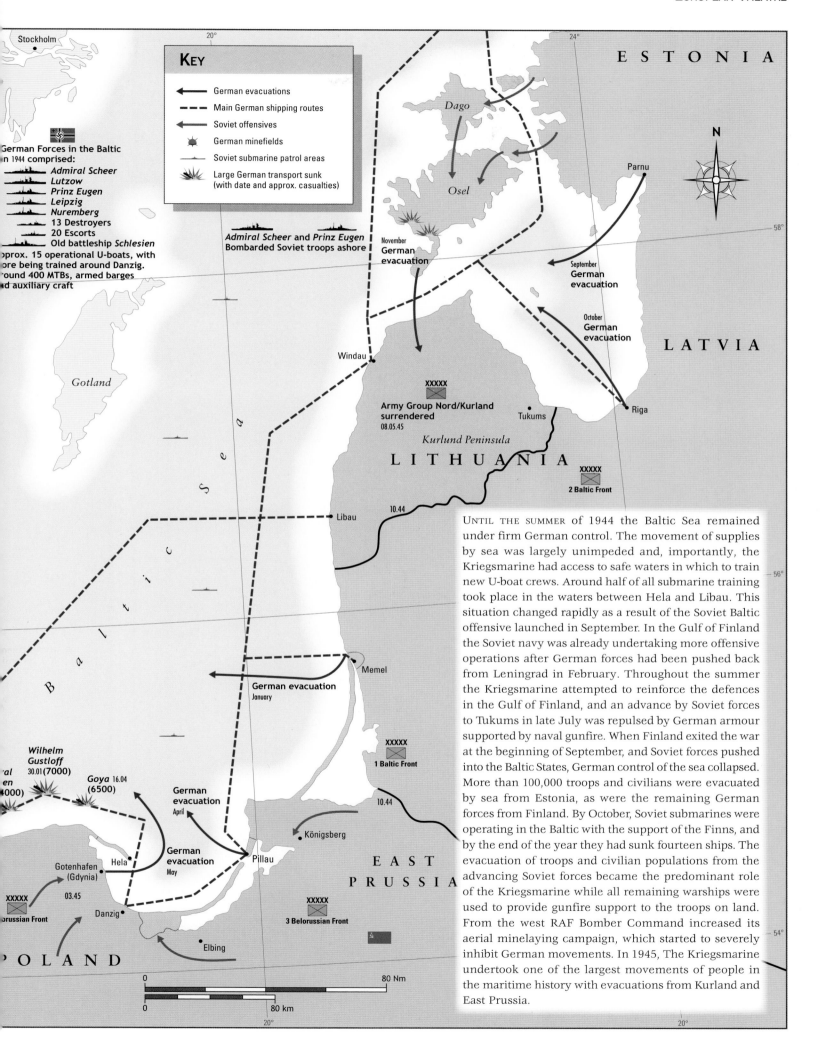

KEY

- → German evacuations
- --- Main German shipping routes
- → Soviet offensives
- ⚓ German minefields
- — Soviet submarine patrol areas
- 💥 Large German transport sunk (with date and approx. casualties)

German Forces in the Baltic in 1944 comprised:

- *Admiral Scheer*
- *Lutzow*
- *Prinz Eugen*
- *Leipzig*
- *Nuremberg*
- 13 Destroyers
- 20 Escorts
- Old battleship *Schlesien*

approx. 15 operational U-boats, with more being trained around Danzig. around 400 MTBs, armed barges and auxiliary craft

Stockholm

20°

24°

E S T O N I A

Dago

Osel

Parnu

Admiral Scheer and *Prinz Eugen* Bombarded Soviet troops ashore

November **German evacuation**

September **German evacuation**

October **German evacuation**

L A T V I A

Gotland

Windau

XXXXX
Army Group Nord/Kurland surrendered 08.05.45

Tukums

Riga

Kurlund Peninsula

L I T H U A N I A

XXXXX
2 Baltic Front

Libau

10.44

B a l t i c   S e a

58°

56°

Memel

German evacuation January

XXXXX
1 Baltic Front

10.44

Wilhelm Gustloff 30.01 (7000)

Goya 16.04 (6500)

German evacuation April

Königsberg

Pillau

German evacuation May

Gotenhafen (Gdynia)

Hela

03.45

XXXXX
Borussian Front

Danzig

E A S T
P R U S S I A

XXXXX
3 Belorussian Front

Elbing

P O L A N D

N

0   80 Nm

0   80 km

UNTIL THE SUMMER of 1944 the Baltic Sea remained under firm German control. The movement of supplies by sea was largely unimpeded and, importantly, the Kriegsmarine had access to safe waters in which to train new U-boat crews. Around half of all submarine training took place in the waters between Hela and Libau. This situation changed rapidly as a result of the Soviet Baltic offensive launched in September. In the Gulf of Finland the Soviet navy was already undertaking more offensive operations after German forces had been pushed back from Leningrad in February. Throughout the summer the Kriegsmarine attempted to reinforce the defences in the Gulf of Finland, and an advance by Soviet forces to Tukums in late July was repulsed by German armour supported by naval gunfire. When Finland exited the war at the beginning of September, and Soviet forces pushed into the Baltic States, German control of the sea collapsed. More than 100,000 troops and civilians were evacuated by sea from Estonia, as were the remaining German forces from Finland. By October, Soviet submarines were operating in the Baltic with the support of the Finns, and by the end of the year they had sunk fourteen ships. The evacuation of troops and civilian populations from the advancing Soviet forces became the predominant role of the Kriegsmarine while all remaining warships were used to provide gunfire support to the troops on land. From the west RAF Bomber Command increased its aerial minelaying campaign, which started to severely inhibit German movements. In 1945, The Kriegsmarine undertook one of the largest movements of people in the maritime history with evacuations from Kurland and East Prussia.

54°

20°

24°

20°

THE PHILIPPINES, 1944-45

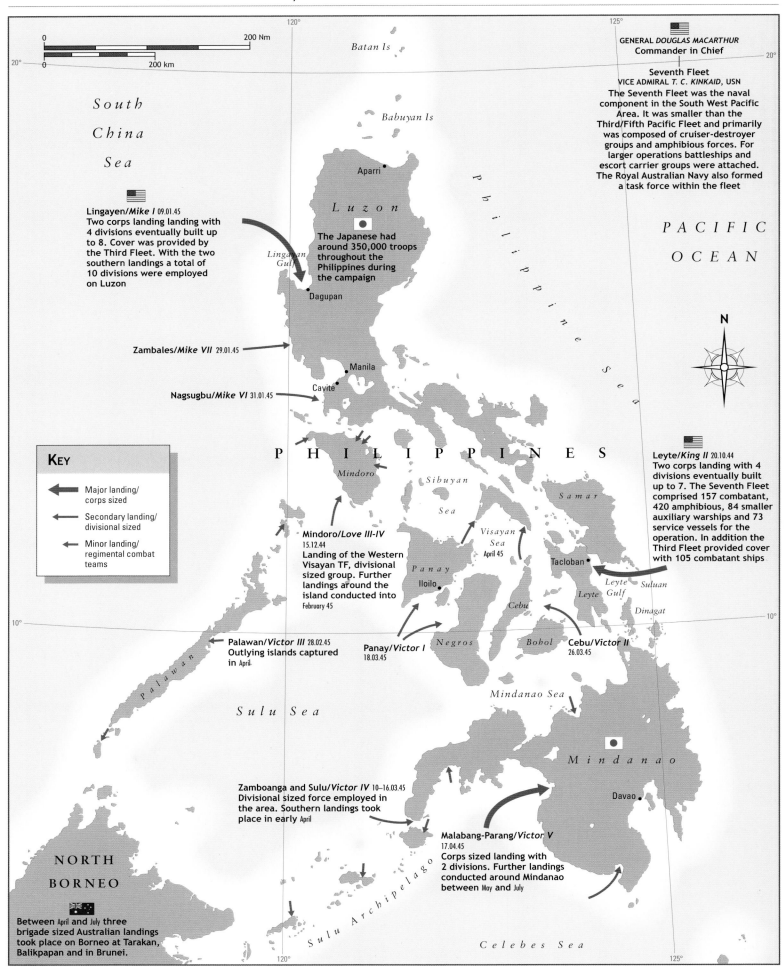

South China Sea

Batan Is

Babuyan Is

GENERAL *DOUGLAS MACARTHUR*
Commander in Chief

Seventh Fleet
VICE ADMIRAL *T. C. KINKAID*, USN
The Seventh Fleet was the naval component in the South West Pacific Area. It was smaller than the Third/Fifth Pacific Fleet and primarily was composed of cruiser-destroyer groups and amphibious forces. For larger operations battleships and escort carrier groups were attached. The Royal Australian Navy also formed a task force within the fleet

Aparri

Luzon

P A C I F I C
O C E A N

Lingayen/*Mike I* 09.01.45
Two corps landing landing with 4 divisions eventually built up to 8. Cover was provided by the Third Fleet. With the two southern landings a total of 10 divisions were employed on Luzon

The Japanese had around 350,000 troops throughout the Philippines during the campaign

Lingayen Gulf

Dagupan

P h i l i p p i n e S e a

Zambales/*Mike VII* 29.01.45

Manila

Nagsugbu/*Mike VI* 31.01.45
Cavite

N

KEY

⬅ Major landing/ corps sized

⬅ Secondary landing/ divisional sized

⬅ Minor landing/ regimental combat teams

P H I L I P P I N E S

Mindoro

Sibuyan Sea

Samar

Leyte/*King II* 20.10.44
Two corps landing with 4 divisions eventually built up to 7. The Seventh Fleet comprised 157 combatant, 420 amphibious, 84 smaller auxiliary warships and 73 service vessels for the operation. In addition the Third Fleet provided cover with 105 combatant ships

Visayan Sea
April 45

Tacloban

Panay
Iloilo

Leyte
Leyte Gulf *Suluan*

Mindoro/*Love III-IV*
15.12.44
Landing of the Western Visayan TF, divisional sized group. Further landings around the island conducted into *February 45*

Cebu

Dinagat

Palawan/*Victor III* 28.02.45
Outlying islands captured in *April*.

Panay/*Victor I*
18.03.45

Negros

Bohol

Cebu/*Victor II*
26.03.45

Palawan

Sulu Sea

Mindanao Sea

Mindanao

Davao

Zamboanga and Sulu/*Victor IV* 10-16.03.45
Divisional sized force employed in the area. Southern landings took place in early *April*

Malabang-Parang/*Victor V*
17.04.45
Corps sized landing with 2 divisions. Further landings conducted around Mindanao between *May* and *July*

NORTH BORNEO

Between *April* and *July* three brigade sized Australian landings took place on Borneo at Tarakan, Balikpapan and in Brunei.

Sulu Archipelago

Celebes Sea

TF 38 South China Sea Raid, January 1945

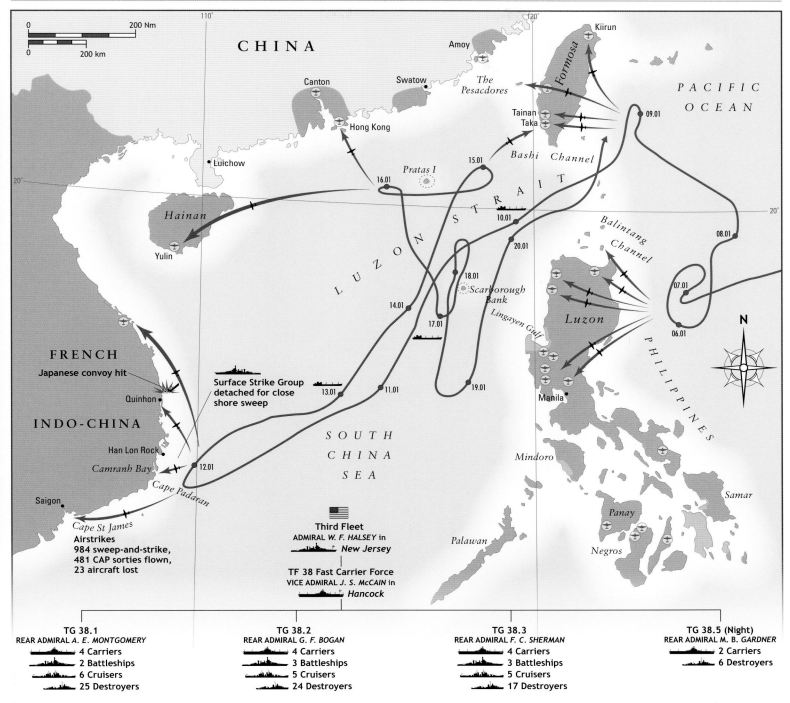

Third Fleet
ADMIRAL *W. F. HALSEY* in
New Jersey

TF 38 Fast Carrier Force
VICE ADMIRAL *J. S. McCAIN* in
Hancock

TG 38.1
REAR ADMIRAL *A. E. MONTGOMERY*
4 Carriers
2 Battleships
6 Cruisers
25 Destroyers

TG 38.2
REAR ADMIRAL *G. F. BOGAN*
4 Carriers
3 Battleships
5 Cruisers
24 Destroyers

TG 38.3
REAR ADMIRAL *F. C. SHERMAN*
4 Carriers
3 Battleships
5 Cruisers
17 Destroyers

TG 38.5 (Night)
REAR ADMIRAL *M. B. GARDNER*
2 Carriers
6 Destroyers

Cape St James
Airstrikes
984 sweep-and-strike,
481 CAP sorties flown,
23 aircraft lost

Japanese convoy hit

Surface Strike Group
detached for close
shore sweep

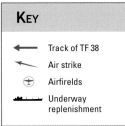

KEY

➤	Track of TF 38
→	Air strike
⊕	Airfields
⬛	Underway replenishment

In December 1944 Admiral Nimitz allowed Halsey to prepare for the latter's long-desired raid into the South China Sea with the fast carriers after they had provided cover during the initial stages of the Lingayen landings. The Third Fleet left Ulithi on 30 December and through out the first days of January attacked Japanese airfields on Luzon and Formosa to support General MacArthur's landings. In light of the Japanese adoption of kamikaze tactics during the Philippines campaign, the composition of the carrier air groups was modified to include more fighters. During the winter very heavy storms complicated the considerable American naval movements in the area. It had been expected that the remaining Japanese surface fleet would attempt to cut the long American supply lines to Lingayen Gulf. In the event no attempt was made, allowing Halsey to proceed with the operation.

During the night 9–10 January the Third Fleet entered the South China Sea while its supporting fast tankers came up from the south through the Philippines. The objective was to close onto Camranh Bay and sweep along the coast with airstrikes and surface forces in the hope of finding Japanese battleships *Ise* and *Hyūga*. They were not present, and the heavy strikes instead sank forty-four ships, mostly merchant vessels. Thereafter, Halsey moved north to search along the Chinese coast and again strike airfields on Formosa. Weather continued to cause problems, particularly for the destroyers that found it difficult to refuel in the poor conditions. The eleven-day raid was deemed a success despite the Japanese having moved their battleships beyond immediate striking distance.

THE INDIAN OCEAN, 1945

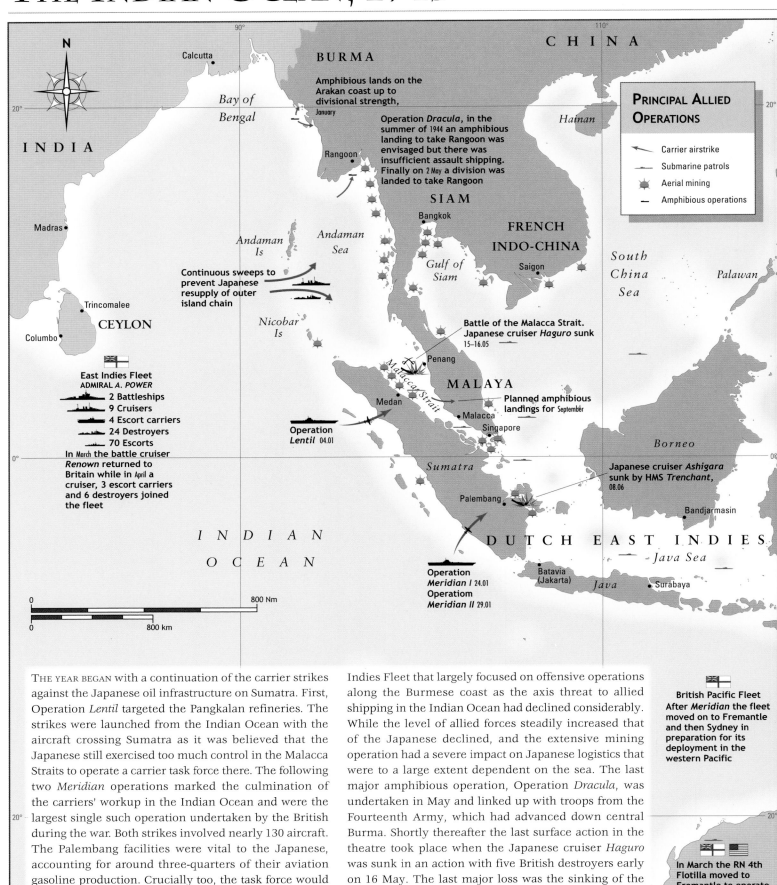

N

Calcutta

BURMA

Bay of Bengal

Amphibious lands on the Arakan coast up to divisional strength, January

Operation *Dracula*, in the summer of 1944 an amphibious landing to take Rangoon was envisaged but there was insufficient assault shipping. Finally on 2 May a division was landed to take Rangoon

Rangoon

SIAM

Bangkok

CHINA

Hainan

FRENCH INDO-CHINA

I N D I A

Madras

Trincomalee

CEYLON

Columbo

Andaman Is

Andaman Sea

Continuous sweeps to prevent Japanese resupply of outer island chain

Nicobar Is

Gulf of Siam

Saigon

South China Sea

Palawan

Battle of the Malacca Strait. Japanese cruiser *Haguro* sunk 15–16.05

Penang

MALAYA

East Indies Fleet
ADMIRAL A. POWER
- 2 Battleships
- 9 Cruisers
- 4 Escort carriers
- 24 Destroyers
- 70 Escorts

In March the battle cruiser *Renown* returned to Britain while in April a cruiser, 3 escort carriers and 6 destroyers joined the fleet

Medan

Malacca

Singapore

Planned amphibious landings for September

Operation *Lentil* 04.01

Sumatra

I N D I A N O C E A N

Palembang

Japanese cruiser *Ashigara* sunk by HMS *Trenchant*, 08.06

Borneo

D U T C H E A S T I N D I E S

Bandjarmasin

Java Sea

Operation *Meridian I* 24.01
Operatiom *Meridian II* 29.01

Batavia (Jakarta)

Java

Surabaya

0 ————— 800 Nm
0 ————— 800 km

PRINCIPAL ALLIED OPERATIONS

- ← Carrier airstrike
- ⟵ Submarine patrols
- ✹ Aerial mining
- — Amphibious operations

THE YEAR BEGAN with a continuation of the carrier strikes against the Japanese oil infrastructure on Sumatra. First, Operation *Lentil* targeted the Pangkalan refineries. The strikes were launched from the Indian Ocean with the aircraft crossing Sumatra as it was believed that the Japanese still exercised too much control in the Malacca Straits to operate a carrier task force there. The following two *Meridian* operations marked the culmination of the carriers' workup in the Indian Ocean and were the largest single such operation undertaken by the British during the war. Both strikes involved nearly 130 aircraft. The Palembang facilities were vital to the Japanese, accounting for around three-quarters of their aviation gasoline production. Crucially too, the task force would remain at sea, replenishing from a support group, and not retire to a base thus more realistically replicating the operating conditions in the Pacific.

After departure of the BPF the focus fell on the East Indies Fleet that largely focused on offensive operations along the Burmese coast as the axis threat to allied shipping in the Indian Ocean had declined considerably. While the level of allied forces steadily increased that of the Japanese declined, and the extensive mining operation had a severe impact on Japanese logistics that were to a large extent dependent on the sea. The last major amphibious operation, Operation *Dracula*, was undertaken in May and linked up with troops from the Fourteenth Army, which had advanced down central Burma. Shortly thereafter the last surface action in the theatre took place when the Japanese cruiser *Haguro* was sunk in an action with five British destroyers early on 16 May. The last major loss was the sinking of the *Ashigara* by the submarine *Trenchant* in the Banka Strait. Preparations for a major amphibious operation along the Malayan coast were underway when the war ended.

British Pacific Fleet
After *Meridian* the fleet moved on to Fremantle and then Sydney in preparation for its deployment in the western Pacific

In March the RN 4th Flotilla moved to Fremantle to operate with the Anglo-American submarine force based there

AUSTRALIA

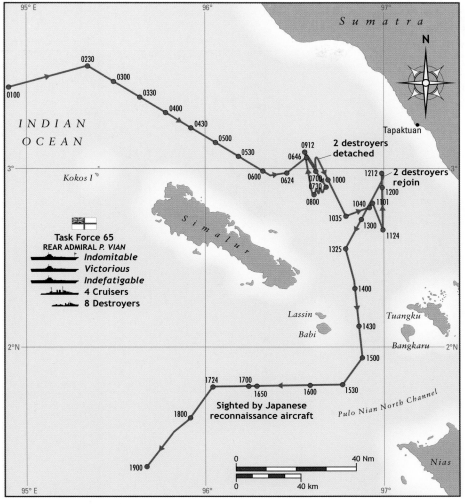

INDIAN OCEAN

0100
0230
0300
0330
0400
0430
0500
0530
0600
0624
0646
0912
0700
0730
0800
1000
1035
1040
1300
1325
1400
1430
1500
1530
1600
1650
1700
1724
1800
1900
1212
1200
1101
1124

Sumatra

Tapaktuan

2 destroyers detached

2 destroyers rejoin

Kokos I

Simalur

Task Force 65
REAR ADMIRAL P. VIAN
Indomitable
Victorious
Indefatigable
4 Cruisers
8 Destroyers

Lassin
Babi
Tuangku
Bangkaru

Pulo Nian North Channel

Sighted by Japanese reconnaissance aircraft

Nias

0   40 Nm
0   40 km

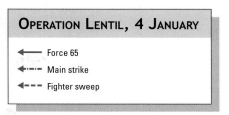

OPERATION LENTIL, 4 JANUARY

→ Force 65
—·—· Main strike
---- Fighter sweep

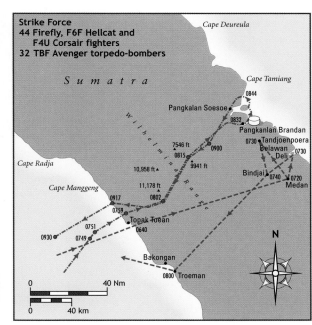

Strike Force
44 Firefly, F6F Hellcat and
F4U Corsair fighters
32 TBF Avenger torpedo-bombers

Sumatra

Cape Deureula
Cape Tamiang
Pangkalan Soesoe
0844
0832
Pangkanlan Brandan
7546 ft
0815
0900
0730
Tandjoenpoera
Belawan
Deli
0730
10,958 ft
9941 ft
Bindjai
0740
0720
11,178 ft
0802
Medan
Cape Radja
0917
Cape Manggeng
0759
Topak Toean
0751
0640
0930
0749
Bakongan
0800 Troeman

Wilhelmina Range

0   40 Nm
0   40 km

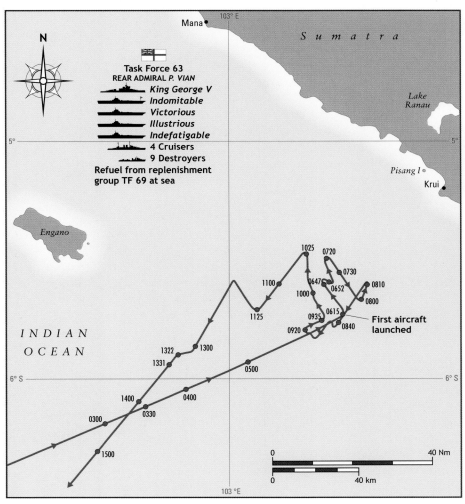

Mana
103° E
Sumatra

Task Force 63
REAR ADMIRAL P. VIAN
King George V
Indomitable
Victorious
Illustrious
Indefatigable
4 Cruisers
9 Destroyers
Refuel from replenishment group TF 69 at sea

Lake Ranau

Pisang I
Krui

Engano

INDIAN OCEAN

1025
0720
0647
0730
1100
0652
0810
1000
0800
1125
0935
0615
0920
0840

First aircraft launched

1322
1300
1331
0500
0400
0300
0330
1400
1500

0   40 Nm
0   40 km

OPERATION MERIDIAN I, 24 JANUARY

→ Track of Indomitable
—·—· Main strike
---- Secondary strike against Mana
✈ Airfields

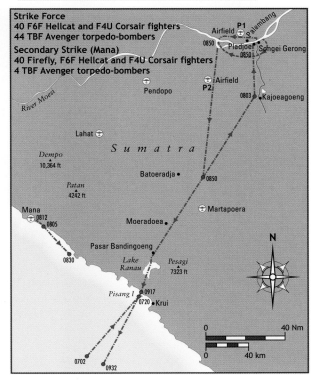

Strike Force
40 F6F Hellcat and F4U Corsair fighters
44 TBF Avenger torpedo-bombers
Secondary Strike (Mana)
40 Firefly, F6F Hellcat and F4U Corsair fighters
4 TBF Avenger torpedo-bombers

P1
Palembang
Airfield
0850
Pladjoe
Songei Gerong
0850

Airfield
P2
0803
Kajoeagoeng

River Moesi
Pendopo
Lahat
Sumatra
Dempo
10,364 ft
Batoeradja
Patan
4242 ft
0850

Mana
0812
0805
Moeradoea
Martapoera
Pasar Bandingoeng
0830
Lake Ranau
Pesagi
7323 ft
Pisang I 0917
0720 Krui
0702
0932

0   40 Nm
0   40 km

OPERATION DETACHMENT, 10 FEBRUARY – 26 MARCH 1945

THE AMERICAN DECICSION to take Iwo Jima was designed to provide emergency landing facilities for B-29 strategic bombers flying from Saipan against targets in Japan and a base for the fighters escorting them. Conversely, the island's capture would deny its use to the Japanese as a fighter base. More generally the island would provide for a secure base from which to launch the invasion of Japan itself. It was always considered that Iwo Jima and Okinawa in the Ryukyus chain would be captured as advance bases, but the former was tackled first because it was the easier of the two. Although different assault forces would be employed, the same naval forces were to land them so they could not be conducted concurrently. Since June 1944, the Japanese had been expecting an American assault and the island's garrison was reinforced and considerably dug in. This island proved to be one of the most fortified positions that the Americans assaulted in the war.

The aerial bombardment began as early as August 1944, but from 8 December daily American air raids were conducted and supplemented by the occasional naval bombardment. In view of the strong Japanese defences the Marines, who would be making the assault, wanted a ten-day preparatory naval bombardment. Admiral Spruance, however, wanted to strike at Japan with the fast carriers to neutralise the air threat before the landings, and as operations around the Philippines were on-going a shorter three-day bombardment was planned. TF 58 operated against Japan from 10–18 February while TF 51 arrived off Iwo Jima early on 16 February. First, minesweepers cleared the approaches and areas for the fire support vessels to work in. The island was divided into different areas, each being allocated to a battleship or cruiser. Aerial reconnaissance had identified around 700 targets and during the bombardment warships closed to within a mile or so of the beaches.

Early on 19 February, the day of the landings, TF 58 came into range from the north. Shortly before sunrise at 6.40am the heaviest pre-landing bombardment of the war began with carefully timed alternating phases of naval gunfire and air strikes. The first troops came ashore at 9am encountering almost no resistance. However, Japanese resistance soon increased and the battle for the island lasted over a month. Throughout this time warships and carriers continuously supported the Marines while the escort carriers provided the bulk of the air support. Japanese air attacks from the mainland increased throughout the battle and led to the loss of the escort carrier *Bismarck Sea* and heavy damage to numerous ships. At the end of February TF 58 conducted another raid against Japan before returning to Ulithi lagoon on 4 March to prepare for the assault on Okinawa.

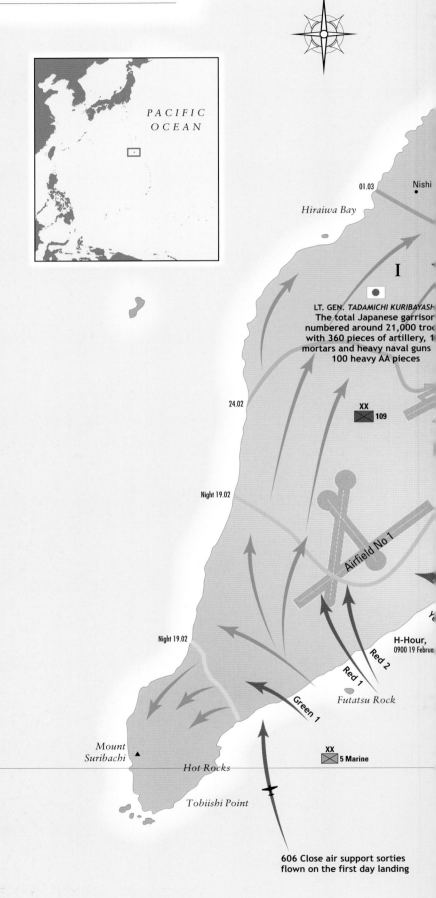

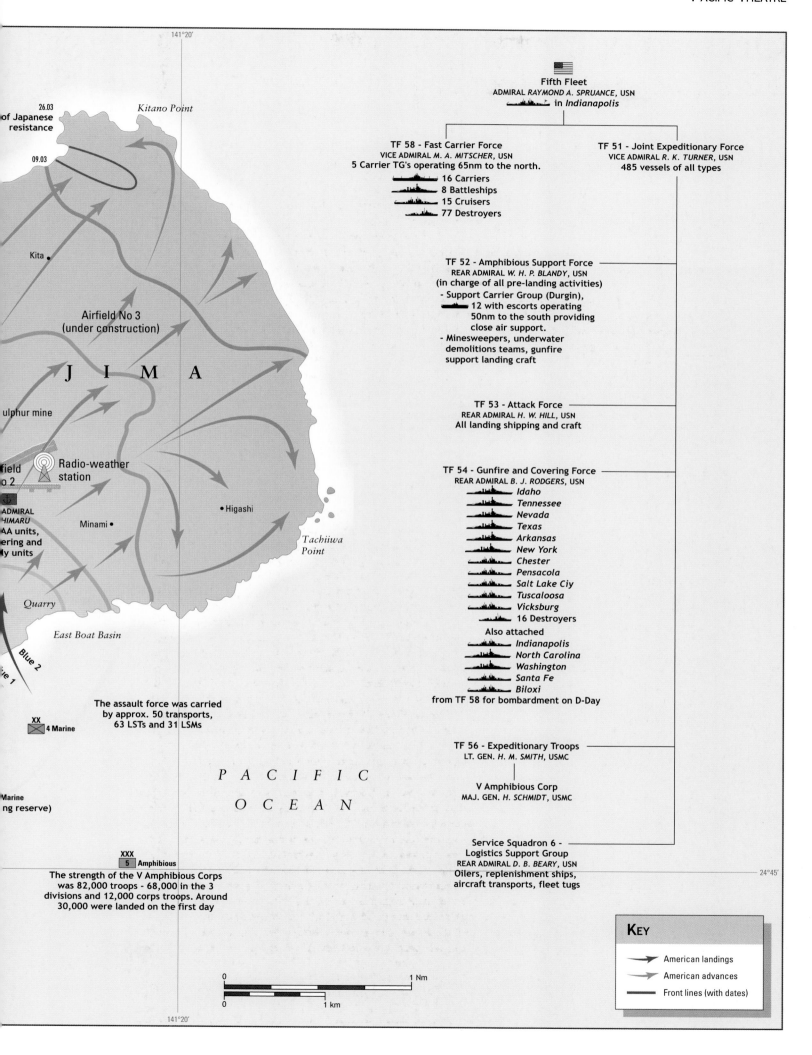

26.03
of Japanese
resistance

09.03

Kitano Point

Kita •

Airfield No 3
(under construction)

J I M A

ulphur mine

*ield
o 2*

Radio-weather
station

ADMIRAL
HIMARU
AA units,
ering and
ly units

Minami •

• *Higashi*

*Tachiiwa
Point*

Quarry

East Boat Basin

Blue 2

e 1

Fifth Fleet
ADMIRAL *RAYMOND A. SPRUANCE*, USN
in *Indianapolis*

TF 58 - Fast Carrier Force
VICE ADMIRAL *M. A. MITSCHER*, USN
5 Carrier TG's operating 65nm to the north.
16 Carriers
8 Battleships
15 Cruisers
77 Destroyers

TF 51 - Joint Expeditionary Force
VICE ADMIRAL *R. K. TURNER*, USN
485 vessels of all types

TF 52 - Amphibious Support Force
REAR ADMIRAL *W. H. P. BLANDY*, USN
(in charge of all pre-landing activities)
- Support Carrier Group (Durgin),
  12 with escorts operating
  50nm to the south providing
  close air support.
- Minesweepers, underwater
  demolitions teams, gunfire
  support landing craft

TF 53 - Attack Force
REAR ADMIRAL *H. W. HILL*, USN
All landing shipping and craft

TF 54 - Gunfire and Covering Force
REAR ADMIRAL *B. J. RODGERS*, USN
Idaho
Tennessee
Nevada
Texas
Arkansas
New York
Chester
Pensacola
Salt Lake Ciy
Tuscaloosa
Vicksburg
16 Destroyers
Also attached
Indianapolis
North Carolina
Washington
Santa Fe
Biloxi
from TF 58 for bombardment on D-Day

TF 56 - Expeditionary Troops
LT. GEN. *H. M. SMITH*, USMC

V Amphibious Corp
MAJ. GEN. *H. SCHMIDT*, USMC

Service Squadron 6 -
Logistics Support Group
REAR ADMIRAL *D. B. BEARY*, USN
Oilers, replenishment ships,
aircraft transports, fleet tugs

XX
4 Marine

The assault force was carried
by approx. 50 transports,
63 LSTs and 31 LSMs

P A C I F I C

O C E A N

*Marine
ng reserve)*

XXX
5 Amphibious

The strength of the V Amphibious Corps
was 82,000 troops - 68,000 in the 3
divisions and 12,000 corps troops. Around
30,000 were landed on the first day

24°45'

0   1 Nm

0   1 km

141°20'

KEY

American landings

American advances

Front lines (with dates)

Operation Iceberg, 1 April – 21 June 1945

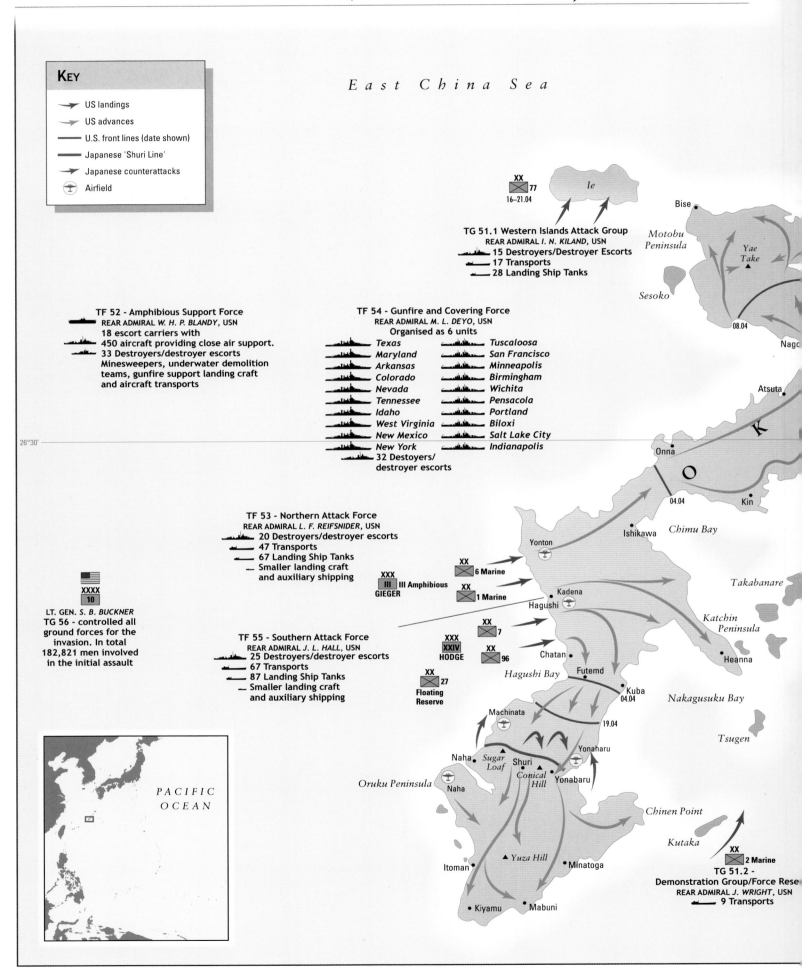

KEY

- → US landings
- → US advances
- — U.S. front lines (date shown)
- — Japanese 'Shuri Line'
- → Japanese counterattacks
- ✈ Airfield

East China Sea

XX 77
16–21.04

TG 51.1 Western Islands Attack Group
REAR ADMIRAL *I. N. KILAND*, USN
15 Destroyers/Destroyer Escorts
17 Transports
28 Landing Ship Tanks

Ie

Bise

Motobu Peninsula

Yae Take

Sesoko

08.04

Nago

TF 52 - Amphibious Support Force
REAR ADMIRAL *W. H. P. BLANDY*, USN
18 escort carriers with
450 aircraft providing close air support.
33 Destroyers/destroyer escorts
Minesweepers, underwater demolition
teams, gunfire support landing craft
and aircraft transports

TF 54 - Gunfire and Covering Force
REAR ADMIRAL *M. L. DEYO*, USN
Organised as 6 units

Texas	Tuscaloosa
Maryland	San Francisco
Arkansas	Minneapolis
Colorado	Birmingham
Nevada	Wichita
Tennessee	Pensacola
Idaho	Portland
West Virginia	Biloxi
New Mexico	Salt Lake City
New York	Indianapolis
32 Destoyers/ destroyer escorts	

Atsuta

26°30'

Onna

O

K

04.04

Kin

Ishikawa

Chimu Bay

TF 53 - Northern Attack Force
REAR ADMIRAL *L. F. REIFSNIDER*, USN
20 Destroyers/destroyer escorts
47 Transports
67 Landing Ship Tanks
Smaller landing craft
and auxiliary shipping

Yonton

Takabanare

XXX
III III Amphibious
GIEGER

XX 6 Marine

XX 1 Marine

Kadena

Hagushi

Katchin Peninsula

XXXX
10

LT. GEN. *S. B. BUCKNER*
TG 56 - controlled all
ground forces for the
invasion. In total
182,821 men involved
in the initial assault

TF 55 - Southern Attack Force
REAR ADMIRAL *J. L. HALL*, USN
25 Destroyers/destroyer escorts
67 Transports
87 Landing Ship Tanks
Smaller landing craft
and auxiliary shipping

XXX
XXIV
HODGE

XX 7

XX 96

Chatan

Futemd

Heanna

Hagushi Bay

Kuba
04.04

Nakagusuku Bay

XX 27
Floating
Reserve

Machinata

19.04

Tsugen

Yonaharu

Naha *Sugar Loaf* Shuri

Conical Hill Yonabaru

Oruku Peninsula Naha

Chinen Point

Kutaka

XX 2 Marine

TG 51.2 -
Demonstration Group/Force Rese
REAR ADMIRAL *J. WRIGHT*, USN
9 Transports

PACIFIC OCEAN

▲ *Yuza Hill*

Itoman

Minatoga

Kiyamu Mabuni

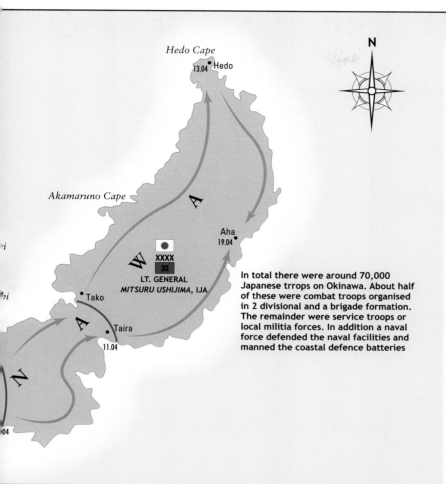

In total there were around 70,000 Japanese trrops on Okinawa. About half of these were combat troops organised in 2 divisional and a brigade formation. The remainder were service troops or local militia forces. In addition a naval force defended the naval facilities and manned the coastal defence batteries

PACIFIC

OCEAN

BEING SUBSTANTIALLY LARGER than Iwo Jima, Okinawa provided a better base and fleet anchorage from which to mount the invasion of Japan. Consequently, the Japanese force defending the island was larger, requiring Operation *Iceberg* to mount one of the largest amphibious operations in the war. Four divisions made the initial assault with two further afloat and a seventh follow-up making its way to Okinawa. As the island was well beyond the range of allied land-based aircraft, except for B-29 bombers, naval forces had to provide all the support for the landings. The operation began on 14 March when TF 58 left Ulithi for Japanese waters where the fast carriers would strike airfields on Kyushu and the remainder of the Japanese fleet in the Inland Sea. The first elements of TF 51, the amphibious force that had been assembled from across the Pacific, left Ulithi on 19 March. On 24 March minesweepers began to clear the approaches to Okinawa and the next day landings took place on the small islands of Kerma Retto, around fifteen miles to the south.

The bombardment force for *Iceberg* was the largest assembled during the war, and from 26 March it began to shell the Japanese defences in conjunction with the fast and escort carrier air groups. Against this array of firepower the Japanese stood little chance on the beaches. Instead, the American forces were to be drawn inland against heavily fortified positions while air attacks whittled down American naval forces. As there were no other major operations on-going, the Japanese were able to concentrate virtually all their remaining airpower, some 3,000 aircraft. The landings on 1 April proceeded smoothly, but quickly the campaign became bogged down in heavy fighting on land and over the task forces at sea. Between April and June there were ten mass air raids involving between fifty and three hundred Japanese aircraft. Around ninety allied warships were heavily damaged or sunk; casualties were particularly high among the destroyers fanned out around the island as radar pickets to provide early warning for incoming air raids.

26°30'

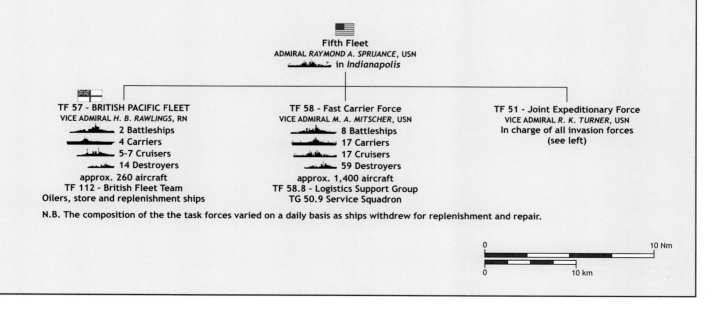

Fifth Fleet
ADMIRAL *RAYMOND A. SPRUANCE*, USN
in *Indianapolis*

TF 57 - BRITISH PACIFIC FLEET
VICE ADMIRAL *H. B. RAWLINGS*, RN
2 Battleships
4 Carriers
5-7 Cruisers
14 Destroyers
approx. 260 aircraft
TF 112 - British Fleet Team
Oilers, store and replenishment ships

TF 58 - Fast Carrier Force
VICE ADMIRAL *M. A. MITSCHER*, USN
8 Battleships
17 Carriers
17 Cruisers
59 Destroyers
approx. 1,400 aircraft
TF 58.8 - Logistics Support Group
TG 50.9 Service Squadron

TF 51 - Joint Expeditionary Force
VICE ADMIRAL *R. K. TURNER*, USN
In charge of all invasion forces
(see left)

N.B. The composition of the the task forces varied on a daily basis as ships withdrew for replenishment and repair.

0   10 Nm

0   10 km

THE BATTLE OF THE EAST CHINA SEA, 7 APRIL 1945

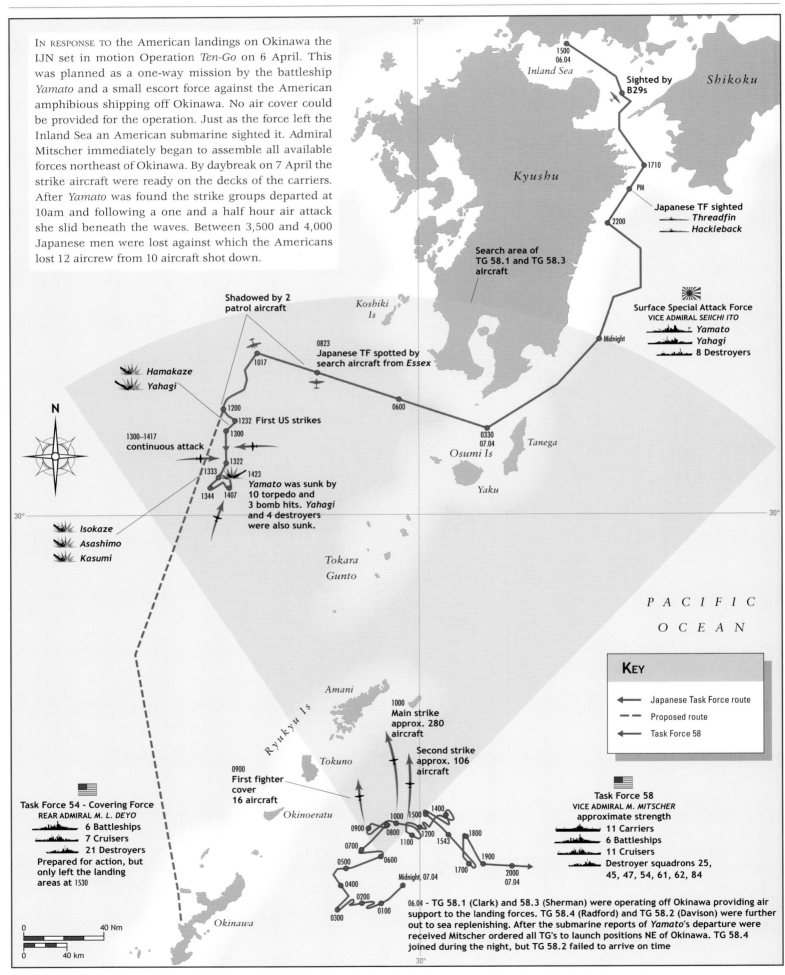

IN RESPONSE TO the American landings on Okinawa the IJN set in motion Operation *Ten-Go* on 6 April. This was planned as a one-way mission by the battleship *Yamato* and a small escort force against the American amphibious shipping off Okinawa. No air cover could be provided for the operation. Just as the force left the Inland Sea an American submarine sighted it. Admiral Mitscher immediately began to assemble all available forces northeast of Okinawa. By daybreak on 7 April the strike aircraft were ready on the decks of the carriers. After *Yamato* was found the strike groups departed at 10am and following a one and a half hour air attack she slid beneath the waves. Between 3,500 and 4,000 Japanese men were lost against which the Americans lost 12 aircrew from 10 aircraft shot down.

1500
06.04
Inland Sea

Shikoku

Sighted by
B29s

1710

PM

Japanese TF sighted
Threadfin
Hackleback

2200

Kyushu

Search area of
TG 58.1 and TG 58.3
aircraft

Surface Special Attack Force
VICE ADMIRAL *SEIICHI ITO*
Yamato
Yahagi
8 Destroyers

Shadowed by 2
patrol aircraft

Koshiki Is

0823
Japanese TF spotted by
search aircraft from *Essex*

Midnight

1017

Hamakaze
Yahagi

1200

0600

N

1232 First US strikes

1300

1300–1417
continuous attack

0330
07.04

Tanega

Osumi Is

1322

1333

1423
Yamato was sunk by
10 torpedo and
3 bomb hits. *Yahagi*
and 4 destroyers
were also sunk.

1344 1407

Yaku

30°

30°

Isokaze
Asashimo
Kasumi

*Tokara
Gunto*

PACIFIC

OCEAN

Amani

1000
Main strike
approx. 280
aircraft

KEY

Japanese Task Force route

Proposed route

Task Force 58

Second strike
approx. 106
aircraft

Ryukyu Is

Tokuno

0900
First fighter
cover
16 aircraft

0900
0700

1000 1500 1400

0800
1100 1200

1800

1543

Task Force 54 - Covering Force
REAR ADMIRAL *M. L. DEYO*
6 Battleships
7 Cruisers
21 Destroyers
Prepared for action, but
only left the landing
areas at 1530

Okinoeratu

0500 0600
0400
0200
0300 0100

Midnight, 07.04

1700

1900

2000
07.04

Task Force 58
VICE ADMIRAL *M. MITSCHER*
approximate strength
11 Carriers
6 Battleships
11 Cruisers
Destroyer squadrons 25,
45, 47, 54, 61, 62, 84

0 40 Nm

0 40 km

Okinawa

06.04 - TG 58.1 (Clark) and 58.3 (Sherman) were operating off Okinawa providing air
support to the landing forces. TG 58.4 (Radford) and TG 58.2 (Davison) were further
out to sea replenishing. After the submarine reports of *Yamato's* departure were
received Mitscher ordered all TG's to launch positions NE of Okinawa. TG 58.4
joined during the night, but TG 58.2 failed to arrive on time

THIRD FLEET OPERATIONS, JULY – AUGUST 1945

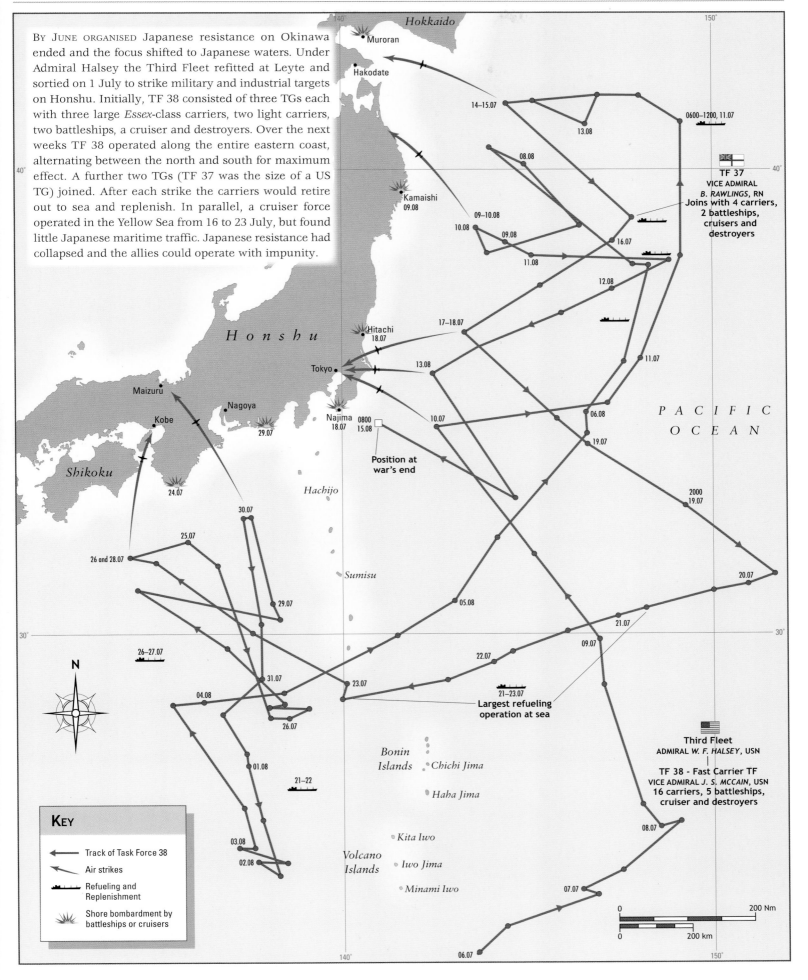

BY JUNE ORGANISED Japanese resistance on Okinawa ended and the focus shifted to Japanese waters. Under Admiral Halsey the Third Fleet refitted at Leyte and sortied on 1 July to strike military and industrial targets on Honshu. Initially, TF 38 consisted of three TGs each with three large *Essex*-class carriers, two light carriers, two battleships, a cruiser and destroyers. Over the next weeks TF 38 operated along the entire eastern coast, alternating between the north and south for maximum effect. A further two TGs (TF 37 was the size of a US TG) joined. After each strike the carriers would retire out to sea and replenish. In parallel, a cruiser force operated in the Yellow Sea from 16 to 23 July, but found little Japanese maritime traffic. Japanese resistance had collapsed and the allies could operate with impunity.

Hokkaido

Muroran

Hakodate

14–15.07

0600–1200, 11.07

13.08

08.08

TF 37
VICE ADMIRAL
B. RAWLINGS, RN
Joins with 4 carriers,
2 battleships,
cruisers and
destroyers

Kamaishi
09.08

09–10.08

10.08

09.08

16.07

11.08

12.08

11.07

Honshu

Hitachi
18.07

17–18.07

13.08

Tokyo

10.07

06.08

19.07

PACIFIC
OCEAN

Maizuru

Nagoya

Najima
18.07

0800
15.08

2000
19.07

Kobe

**Position at
war's end**

Shikoku

Hachijo

24.07

30.07

25.07

Sumisu

05.08

20.07

26 and 28.07

29.07

21.07

26–27.07

09.07

22.07

31.07

23.07

21–23.07
**Largest refueling
operation at sea**

04.08

26.07

01.08

21–22

*Bonin
Islands* *Chichi Jima*

Third Fleet
ADMIRAL *W. F. HALSEY, USN*

TF 38 - Fast Carrier TF
VICE ADMIRAL *J. S. McCAIN, USN*
16 carriers, 5 battleships,
cruiser and destroyers

Haha Jima

03.08

02.08

Kita Iwo

*Volcano
Islands* *Iwo Jima*

08.07

Minami Iwo

07.07

06.07

KEY

→ Track of Task Force 38

→ Air strikes

⊢⊣ Refueling and
Replenishment

✴ Shore bombardment by
battleships or cruisers

0   200 Nm

0   200 km

CAPITAL SHIP LOSSES, 1939–45

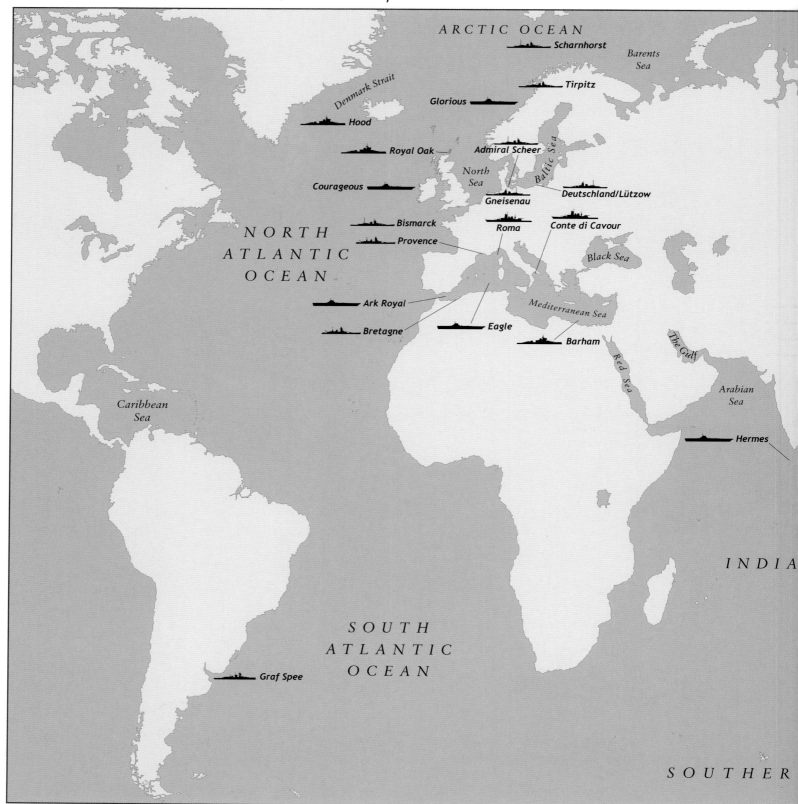

ARCTIC OCEAN

Scharnhorst

Barents Sea

Denmark Strait

Tirpitz

Glorious

Hood

Royal Oak

Admiral Scheer

North Sea

Baltic Sea

Courageous

Deutschland/Lützow

NORTH ATLANTIC OCEAN

Bismarck

Gneisenau

Roma

Conte di Cavour

Provence

Black Sea

Mediterranean Sea

Ark Royal

Bretagne

Eagle

Barham

Red Sea

The Gulf

Caribbean Sea

Arabian Sea

Hermes

INDIA

SOUTH ATLANTIC OCEAN

Graf Spee

SOUTHER

Date and Cause of Loss

British
Courageous, 17.09.39, submarine attack.
Royal Oak, 14.10.39, submarine attack
Glorious, 08.06.40, surface action.
Hood, 24.05.41, surface action.
Ark Royal, 13.11.41, submarine.
Barham, 25.11.41 submarine.
Prince of Wales, 10.12.41, air strike.
Repulse, 10.12.41, air strike.
Hermes, 09.04.42, air strike.
Eagle, 11.08.42. submarine.

France
Bretagne, 03.07.40, surface action/
shelled in port.
Provence, 27.11.42, scuttled.

Italian
Conte di Cavour, 11.11.40, air strike.
Roma, 09.09.43, air strike.

American
Arizona, 07.12.41, air strike.

Oklahoma, 07.12.41, air strike.
Lexington, 08.05.42, air strike/scuttled.
Yorktown, 07.06.42, air strike/submarine.
Hornet, 26.10.42, air strike/surface action.
Wasp, 15.09.42, submarine.
Princeton, 24.10.44, air strike.

German
Graf Spee, 17.12.39, scuttled.
Bismarck, 27.05.41, air and surface action.
Gneisenau, 26-27.02.42, bombed in port.

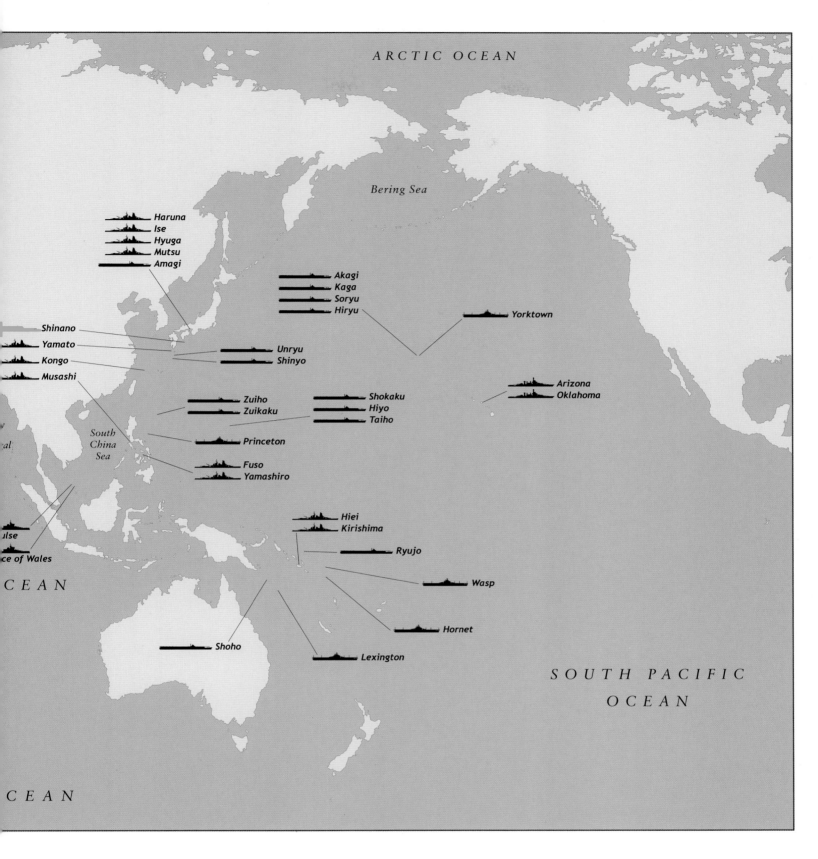

ARCTIC OCEAN

Bering Sea

Haruna
Ise
Hyuga
Mutsu
Amagi

Akagi
Kaga
Soryu
Hiryu

Yorktown

Shinano
Yamato
Kongo
Musashi

Unryu
Shinyo

Arizona
Oklahoma

South
China
Sea

Zuiho
Zuikaku

Shokaku
Hiyo
Taiho

Princeton

Fuso
Yamashiro

ulse
ce of Wales

Hiei
Kirishima

Ryujo

Wasp

CEAN

Hornet

Shoho

Lexington

SOUTH PACIFIC

OCEAN

CEAN

Scharnhorst, 26.12.43, surface action.
Tirpitz, 12.11.44, air strike.
Admiral Scheer, 09.04.45, air strike.
Deutschland, 04.05.45, scuttled.

Japanese
Shoho, 06.05.42, air strike.
Kaga, 04.06.42, air strike/scuttled.
Soryu, 04.06.42, air strike.
Akagi, 05.06.42, air strike/scuttled.
Hiryu, 05.06.42, air strike/scuttled.

Ryujo, 24.08.42, air strike.
Hiei, 13/14.11.42, surface action/air strike.
Kirishima, 15.11.42, surface action.
Mutsu, 08.06.44, internal explosion.
Shokaku, 19.06.44, submarine.
Taiho, 19.06.44, submarine.
Hiyo, 20.06.44, air strike.
Musashi, air strike, 24.10.44.
Yamashiro, 25.10.44, surface action.
Fuso, 25.10.44, surface action.
Zuikaku, 25.10.44, air strike.

Zuiho, 25.10.44, air strike.
Shinyo, 17.11.44, submarine.
Kongo, 21.11.44, submarine.
Shinano, 29.11.44, submarine.
Unryu, 20.02.45, submarine.
Yamato, 07.04.45, air strike.
Hyuga, 27.07.45, run aground.
Amagi, 28.07.45, bombed in port.
Haruna, 28.07.45, bombed in port.
Ise, 28.07.45, bombed in port.
Amagi, 28.07.45, bombed in port.

BIBLIOGRAPHY

Primary Sources

The National Archives, Kew, Surrey, United Kingdom

Naval Staff History – Second World War – Battle Summaries & Naval Staff Histories

ADM 234/317 No. 13 Actions with Enemy Disguised Raiders 1940-1941

ADM 234/327 Selected Operations Mediterranean, 1940: Nos. 2,8,9 & 10

ADM 234/331 No. 15 Naval Operations off Ceylon 29th March to 10th Arpil 1942 & No. 16 Naval Operations at the Capture of Diego Suarez, May 1942

ADM 234/334 No. 52 The Tobruk Run: June 1940 to January 1943

ADM 234/340 No. 22 Russian Convoys 1944

ADM 234/341 No. 23 Naval Operations of the Campaign for Guadalcanal, August 1942 – February 1943

ADM 234/344 No. 25 Naval Strategy in the Pacific, December 1941 – February 1945

ADM 234/345 No. 27 Naval Aircraft Attack on the Tirpitz: Operation Tungsten, 3rd April 1944

ADM 234/346 No. 28 Battle of the Java Sea, 27th February 1942

ADM 234/348 No. 29 The Attack on the Tirpitz by Midget Submarines: Operation Source 22nd September 1943

ADM 234/352 No. 31 Cruiser and Destroyer Actions in English Channel 1943-1944

ADM 234/351 No. 30 Naval Operations English Channel and Southern North Sea, September 1939 – April 1940

ADM 234/353 No. 32 Malta Convoys 1942

ADM 234/356 No. 35 The Invasion of Sicily: Operation Husky

ADM 234/357 Naval Strategy in the Pacific: February 1943 to August 1945

ADM 234/358 No. 37 The Invasion of Italy Landing at Salerno, 9th September 1943

ADM 234/359 No. 38 Operation Torch: Invasion of North Africa November 1942 to February 1943

ADM 234/360 No. 41 The Evacuation from Dunkirk: Operation Dynamo, 26th May – 4th June 1940

ADM 234/362 No. 12 The Attack on St. Nazaire

ADM 234/363 No. 49 The Campaign in North-West Europe June 1944-May 1945

ADM 234/364 No. 38 Aegean Operations 1943

ADM 234/365 No. 40 Battle for Leyte Gulf 23rd-26th October 1944

ADM 234/368 No. 37 Naval Operations Okinawa, Operation Iceberg March-June 1945

ADM 234/372 Home Waters and the Atlantic Volume II: 9th April 1940-6th December 1941

ADM 234/380 Submarines Volume 1: Operations in Home, Northern and Atlantic Waters

ADM 234/381 Submarines Volume II: Operations in the Mediterranean

ADM 234/382 Submarines Volume III: Operations in Far Eastern Waters

ADM 234/436 The Navy and the Threat of Invasion 1940

ADM 234/578 Defeat of the Enemy Attack on Shipping 1939 – 1945 A Study of Policy and Operations Volume 1A

ADM 234/579 Defeat of the Enemy Attack on Shipping 1939 – 1945 A Study of Policy and Operations Volume 1B (Plans and Tables)

Air Historical Branch: Narrative and Monographs

AIR 41/45 The RAF in the Maritime War: Vol I The Atlantic and Home Waters: The Prelude 1918 – Sept 1939

AIR 41/48 The RAF in Maritime War: The Atlantic and Home Waters: Vol IV The Offensive Phase Feb 1943 – May 1944

AIR 41/54 The RAF in Maritime War: Vol VII Part I Mediterranean Reconquest and the Submarine War May 1943 – May 1944

Official Histories

Collier, B., *The Defence of the United Kingdom* (London: HMSO, 1957)

Douglas, W.A.B., R. Sarty & M. Whitby, *No Higher Purpose: The Official Operational History of the Royal Canadian Navy in the Second World War, 1943–1945, Vol. II Part 1* (Ontario: Vanwell, 2002)

———, *A Blue Water Navy: The Official Operational History of the Royal Canadian Navy in the Second World War, 1943–1945, Vol. II Part 2* (Ontario: Vanwell, 2007)

Gill, G.H., *Royal Australian Navy 1939–45* 2 Volumes (Australia in the War of 1939–1945) (Canberra, 1957-8)

Ministry of Defence, *War With Japan (Naval Staff History)* 6 Volumes (London: HMSO, 1995)

Morison, S.E., *History of the United States Naval Operations in World War II* 25 Volumes (1947–1960, numerous editions used)

Playfair, I.S.O., W Jackson *et al.*, *The Mediterranean and Middle East* 6 Volumes (London: HMSO, 1954–1988)

Roskill, S.W., *The War at Sea 1939-1945*, 3 Volumes. (London: HMSO, 1954-1961)

Waters, S.D., *The Royal New Zealand Navy* (1956)

Woodburn-Kirby, S., *The War Against Japan*, 5 Volumes (London: HMSO 1957–1969)

Secondary Sources

Abbazia, P., *Mr. Roosevelt's Navy: The Private War of the U.S. Atlantic Fleet, 1939-1942* (Annapolis, MD: Naval Institute Press, 1975)

Agawa, H. *The Reluctant Admiral: Yamamoto and the Imperial Navy* (Tokyo: Kodansha, 1980)

Aselius, G., *The Rise and Fall of the Soviet Navy in the Baltic, 1921-1941* (London: Frank Cass, 2005)

Ball, S., *The Bitter Sea: The Brutal World War II Fight for the Mediterranean* (London: HarperCollins, 2009)

Barbey, D.E., *MacArthur's Amphibious Navy: Seventh Amphibious Force Operations, 1943–1945* (Annapolis, MD:

Naval Institute Press, 1969)

Barnett, C., *Engage The Enemy More Closely: The Royal Navy in the Second World War* (London: Penguin, 2000)

Bartlett, M.L., *Assault from the Sea: Essays of the History of Amphibious Warfare* (Annapolis, MD: Naval Institute Press, 1983)

Bergerud, E., *Touched With Fire: The Land War in the South Pacific* (London: Penguin, 1996)

———, *Fire in the Sky: The Air War in the South Pacific* (Boulder, CO: Westview Press, 2000)

Bidlingmaier, G., *Einsatz der schweren Kriegsmarineeinheiten im ozeanischen Zufuhrkrieg: Strategische Konzeption und Führungsweise der Seekriegsleitung September 1939 – February 1942* (Neckargemünd: Kurt Vowinckel Verlag, 1963)

Bird, K., *Erich Raeder: Admiral of the Third Reich* (Annapolis, MD: Naval Institute Press, 2006)

Blair, C., *Hitler's U-Boat War: The Hunters, 1939–1945* (London: W&N, 1997)

———, *Hitler's U-Boat War: The Hunted 1942–45* (London: Cassell, 2000)

———, *Silent Victory: The U.S. Submarine Victory Against Japan* (Annapolis, MD: Naval Institute Press, 2001)

Bonatz, H., *Seekrieg im Äther: Die Leistungen der Marine-Funkaufkläung 1939-1945* (Herford: Mittler & Sohn, 1981)

Boyd, C. & A. Yoshida, *The Japanese Submarine Force and World War II* (Shrewsbury: Airlife, 1996)

Brown, D., *Warship Losses of World War Two* (London: Arms and Armour, 1995)

———, *Carrier Operations in World War II* (Barnsley: Seaforth Publishing, 2009

Buell, T.B., *The Quiet Warrior: A Biography of Raymond A. Spruance* (New York: Little, Brown and Company, 1974)

———, *Master of Sea Power: A Biography of Fleet Admiral Ernest J. King* (New York: Little, Brown and Company, 1980)

Calvocoressi, P., G. Wint & J. Pritchard, *The Second World War* (London: Penguin, 1999)

Adam Classen, *Hitler's Northern War: The Luftwaffe's Ill-Fated Campaign, 1940-1945* (Lawrence, KS: University of Kansas Press, 2001

Crenshaw, R.S., *The Battle of Tassafaronga* (Annapolis, MD: Naval Institute Press, 1995)

———, *South Pacific Destroyer: The Battle for the Solomons from Savo to Vella Gulf* (Annapolis, MD: Naval Institute Press, 1998)

Creswell, J., *Sea Warfare 1939-1945: A Short History* (London: Longmans, Green & Co., 1950)

Costello, J., *The Pacific War* (London: Pan, 1985)

Cumming, A.J., *The Royal Navy and the Battle of Britain* (Annapolis, MD: Naval Institute Press, 2010)

Dull, P.S., *A Battle History of the Imperial Japanese Navy (1941–1945)* (Annapolis, MD: Naval Institute Press, 2007)

Evans, D.C. and M.R. Peattie, *Kaigun: Strategy, Tactics and Technology in the Imperial Japanese Navy 1887-1941* (Annapolis, MD: Naval Institute Press, 1997)

Ford, D., *The Pacific War: Clash of Empire in World War II* (London: Continuum, 2012)

Frank, R.B., *Guadalcanal: The Definitive Account of the Landmark Battle* (New York: Penguin, 1992)

Friedman, N., *Carrier Air Power* (Greenwich: Conway Maritime Press, 1981)

Gannon, M., *Operation Drumbeat: The Dramatic True Story of Germany's First U-boat Attacks Along the American Coast in World War II* (New York: HarperCollins, 1991)

———, *Black May: The Epic Story of the Allies' Defeat of the German U-boats in May 1943* (London: HarperCollins, 1998)

Gardner, W.J.R. *Decoding History: The Battle of the Atlantic and Ultra* (Basingstoke: Macmillan, 1999)

Greene, J. & A. Massignani, *The Naval War in the Mediterranean 1940–1943* (London: Frontline Books, 2011)

Grinnell-Milne, D., *The Silent Victory: September 1940* (London: The Bodely Head, 1958)

Grove, E., *Price of Disobedience* (Annapolis, MD: Naval Institute Press, 2001)

Hague, A., *The Allied Convoy System 1939-1945: Its Organization, Defence and Operation* (London: Chatham Publishing, 2000)

Hammel, E., *Carrier Clash: The Invasion of Guadalcanal & The Battle of the Eastern Solomons August 1942* (St. Paul, MN: Zenith Press, 2004)

———, *Carrier Strike: The Battle of the Santa Cruz Islands October 1942* (St. Paul, MN: Zenith Press, 2004)

Haarr, G.H., *The German Invasion of Norway: April 1940* (Barnsley: Seaforth Publishing, 2009)

———, *The German Invasion of Norway: April – June 1940* (Barnsley: Seaforth Publishing, 2010)

Hinsley, F.H., *Command of the Sea: The Naval Side of British History from 1918 to the end of the Second World War* (London: Christophers, 1950)

Hobbs, D., *The British Pacific Fleet: The Royal Navy's Most Powerful Striking Force* (Barnsley: Seaforth Publishing, 2011)

Hone, T.C. & T. Hone, *Battle Line: The United States Navy 1919–1939* (Annapolis, MD: Naval Institute Press, 2006)

Howarth, S. & D. Law, *The Battle of the Atlantic 1939–1945* (London: Greenhill, 1994)

Hubatsch, W.H., *"Weserübung" Die deutsche Besetzung von Dänemark und Norwegen 1940* (Gotingen: Musterschmidt Verlag, 1960)

Humble, R., *Fraser of North Cape: The Life of Admiral of the Fleet Lord Fraser (1888–1981)* (London: Routledge Kegan Paul, 1983)

Isely, J.I. & P A. Crowl, *The U.S. Marines and Amphibious War: Its Theory, and Its Practice in the Pacific* (Princeton, NJ: Princeton University Press, 1951)

Johnson, W.B., *The Pacific Campaign in World War II: From Pearl Harbor to Guadalcanal* (London: Routledge, 2010)

Jordan, G. (ed.), *Naval warfare in the twentieth century* (London: Croom Helm, 1977)

Levy, J.P., *The Royal Navy's Home Fleet in World War II* (Basingstoke: Palgrave Macmillan, 2003)

Kahn, D., *Seizing the Enigma, The race to break the German U-boat codes, 1939-1943* (Boston, MA: Houghton Mifflin, 1991)

Kemp, P., *U-Boats Destroyed: German Submarine Losses in the World Wars* (London: Arms & Armour Press, 1997)

Klee, K., *Das Untermehmen "Seelöwe" Die geplante deutsche Landung in England 1940*, 2 Volumes (Gottingen: Musterschmidt-Verlag, 1958)

Lorelli, J.A., *To Foreign Shores: U.S. Amphibious Operations in World War II* (Annapolis, MD: Naval Institute Press, 1995)

Lovering, T., *Amphibious Assault: Manoeuvre from the Sea* (Seafarer Books, 2007)

Lundstrom, J.B., *The First Team: Pacific Naval Air Combat from Pearl Harbor to Midway* (Annapolis, MD: Naval Institute Press, 1990)

——, *The First Team and the Guadalcanal Campaign: Naval Fighter Combat from August to November 1942* (Annapolis, MD: Naval Institute Press, 1994)

——, *Black Shoe Carrier Admiral: Frank Jack Fletcher at Coral Sea, Midway and Guadalcanal* (Annapolis, MD: Naval Institute Press, 2006)

Marder, A., *Operation Menace: The Dakar Expedition and the Dudley North Affair* (London: Oxford University Press, 1976)

Mars, A., *British Submarines at War 1939–1945* (London: William Kimber, 1971)

McGee, W.L. *The Amphibians Are Coming! Emergence of the 'Gator Navy and its Revolutionary Landing Craft* (Santa Barbara, CA: BMC Publications, 2000)

——, *The Solomons Campaigns 1942–1943: From Guadalcanal to Bougainville* (Santa Barbara, CA: BMC Publications, 2002)

McLean, D.M (ed.), *Fighting At Sea: Naval Battles from the Ages of Sail and Steam* (Robin Brass Studio, 2008)

Middlebrook, M., *Convoy* (London: Penguin, 1990)

Millett, A.R., *Semper Fidelis: The History of the United States Marine Corps* (New York: The Free Press, 1991)

Milner, M., *Battle of the Atlantic* (Tempus Publishing, 2003)

Murfett, M., *Naval Warfare 1919–1945: An operational history of the volatile war at sea* (Abingdon: Routledge, 2009)

Neitzel, S., *Der Einsatz der deutschen Luftwaffe über dem Atlantik und der Nordsee 1939–1945* (Bonn: Bernard & Graefe Verlag, 1995)

Padfield, P., *War Beneath the Sea: Submarine, 1939–45* (London: John Murrary, 1995)

Parshall, J. & A. Tully, *Shattered Sword: The Japanese Story of the Battle of Midway* (Potomac Books, 2005)

Peattie, M.R., *Sunburst: The Rise of Japanese Naval Air Power, 1909–1941* (Annapolis, MD: Naval Institute Press, 2001)

Plowman, P., *Across the Sea to War: Australia and New Zealand Troop Convoys from 1856 through two World Wars to Korea and Vietnam* (NSW, Australia: Rosenberg, 2003)

Polmar, N., *Aircraft Carriers: A History of Carrier Aviation and its Influence on World Events, Vol. I 1909–1945* (Dulles, VA: Potomac Books, 2006)

Pope, D., *Flag 4; The Battle of Coastal Forces in the Mediterranean 1939–1945* (London: Chatham, 2006)

Potter, E.B., *Admiral Arleigh Burke: A Biography* (New York: Random House, 1990), *Nimitz* (Annapolis, MD: Naval Institute Press, 1995)

O'Hara, V.P., *The U.S. Navy Against the Axis: Surface Combat 1941–1945* (Annapolis, MD: Naval Institute Press, 2007)

O'Hara, V.P., W.D. Dickson & R. Worth, *On Seas Contested: The Seven Great Navies of the Second World War* (Annapolis, MD: Naval Institute Press, 2010)

Reynolds, C.G., *The Fast Carriers: Forging of an Air Navy* (Annapolis, MD: Naval Institute Press, 2003)

——, *On The Warpath in the Pacific: Admiral Jocko Clark and the Fast Carriers* (Annapolis, MD: Naval Institute Press, 2005)

Rohwer, J., *Chronology of the War At Sea 1939: The Naval History of World War Two, 3rd Edition* (London: Chatham Publishing, 2005)

Santoni, A., *Ultra siegt im Mittlelmeer* (Koblenz: Bernard & Graefe, 1985)

Saunders, M.G. (ed.), *The Soviet Navy* (London: Weidenfeld and Nicolson, 1958)

Schmalenbach, P., German Raiders: *A History of Auxiliary Cruisers of the German Navy 1895–1945* (Cambridge: P Stephens, 1980)

Schofield, B., *The Arctic Convoys* (London: Macdonald & Jane's, 1977)

Simpson, M., *A Life of Admiral of the Fleet Andrew Cunningham: A Twentieth-Century Naval Leader* (London: Frank Cass, 2004)

Spector, R.D., *Eagle Against the Sun: The American War with Japan* (London: Cassell, 2001)

Syrett, D., *The Defeat of German U-Boats: The Battle of the Atlantic* (Columbia, SC: University of South Carolina Press, 1994)

Taylor, T., *The Magnificent Mitscher* (Annapolis, MD: Naval institute Press, 2006)

Terraine, J., *Business in Great Waters* (London: Wordsworth, 1999)

Thomas, C.S., *The German Navy in the Nazi era* (London: Unwin Hyman, 1990)

Tully, A.P., *Battle of Surigao Strait* (Bloomington, IN: Indiana University Press, 2009)

Vego, M., *Operational Warfare at Sea: Theory and Practice* (London Routledge, 2009)

——, 'Major Convoy Operation to Malta 10-15 August 1942 (Operation Pedestal)', *Naval War College Review* 63/1 (2010), pp. 108–53

White, J.F., *U-Boot Tanker 1941–1945* (Hamburg: Koehler, 1998)

Whitley, M.J., *German Capital Ships of World War Two* (London: Cassell, 2000)

Williford, G., *Racing the Sunrise: Reinforcing America's Pacific Outposts, 1941–1942* (Annapolis, MD: Naval Institute Press, 2010)

Willmott, H.P., *Empires in the Balance: Japanese and Allied Pacific Strategies to April 1942* (Annapolis, MD: Naval Institute Press, 2008)

——, *The Barrier and the Javelin: Japanese and Allied Pacific Strategies, February to June 1942* (Annapolis, MD: Naval Institute Press, 2008)

——, *The Battle of Leyte Gulf: The Last Fleet Action* (Bloomington, IN: Indiana University Press, 2005)

Winton, J., *Convoy: The Defence of Sea Trade 1890–1990* (London: Michael Joseph, 1983)

Wheatley, R., *Operation Sea Lion: German Plan for the Invasion of England 1939-1942* (London: Oxford University Press 1958)

Yung, C.D., *Gators of Neptune: Naval Amphibious Planning for the Normandy Invasion* (Annapolis, MD: Naval Institute Press, 2006)

INDEX